This is the first comprehensive study of the theatre of nineteenth-century Spain, a most important genre consisting of more than 10,000 plays that were written, staged, reviewed, and published during the course of the century. David Gies assesses this mass of material – much of it hitherto unknown – as text, spectacle, and social phenomenon. He shows how theatrical productions reveal the deep concerns of a society which moved from war and dictatorship, through rebellion, reaction, and the growth of a small but powerful middle class. His book sheds light on political drama during Napoleonic times, the theatre of dictatorship (1820s), Romanticism, women dramatists, socialist drama, neo-Romantic drama, the relationship between parody and the dominant literary currents of the day, and the challenging work of Galdós. A chapter on the battle to create a National Theatre reveals the deep conflicts generated by the various interested factions in the middle of the century. This readable account will at last allow students and scholars properly to re-evaluate the canon of texts.

The theatre in nineteenth-century Spain

The theatre in nineteenth-century Spain

David Thatcher Gies

Commonwealth Professor of Spanish and Chairman of the Department of Spanish, Italian and Portuguese at the University of Virginia

CAMBRIDGE
UNIVERSITY PRESS

Published by the Press Syndicate of the University of Cambridge
The Pitt Building, Trumpington Street, Cambridge CB2 1RP
40 West 20th Street, New York, NY 10011-4211, USA
10 Stamford Road, Oakleigh, Melbourne 3166, Australia

First published 1994

Printed in Great Britain at the University Press, Cambridge

A catalogue record for this book is available from the British Library

Library of Congress cataloguing in publication data

Gies, David Thatcher.
The theatre in nineteenth-century Spain/David Thatcher Gies.
  p.   cm.
Includes bibliographical references and index.
ISBN 0 521 38046 4
1. Theatre – Spain – History – 19th century.
2. Spanish drama – 19th century – History and criticism.
I. Title.
PN2783.G54 1994
792'.0946'09034 – dc20   93-31543 CIP

ISBN 0 521 38046 4 hardback

The publisher gratefully acknowledges the generous financial support given to this
publication by the Program for Cultural Cooperation between Spain's Ministry of
Culture and United States' Universities and the National Endowment for the
Humanities.

CE

In memoriam MJ

So I wish you first a
Sense of theatre; only
Those who love illusion
   And know it will go far:
Otherwise we spend our
Lives in a confusion
Of what we say and do with
   Who we really are.
W. H. Auden

Contents

Preface

I have many people to thank for what has been a project I have spent many years researching and writing. First, I am grateful for the released time and financial support provided by the University of Virginia, the National Endowment for the Humanities, and Spain's Ministry of Culture (Ángeles Gutiérrez Fraile, Director of "Cooperación Internacional," and the at-the-time Subdirector, Javier López Facal), whose assistance enabled me to travel to many libraries and archives in search of materials. I am also grateful for information, materials, and answers to queries provided by Pedro Álvarez de Miranda, Noël M. Valis, Ana Vázquez, John C. Dowling, Russell P. Sebold, Michael Schinasi, Margaret Ballantyne, and my research assistants Jeffrey T. Bersett, Elizabeth Franklin Lewis, Alvin Sherman, and Karen Rauch. My colleague Donald Shaw provided invaluable insights following the reading of various drafts. Additional materials were secured by the impressive Interlibrary Loan Department of the University of Virginia's Alderman Library as well as the librarians at the Biblioteca Nacional de Madrid, the Hemeroteca Municipal de Madrid, the Biblioteca Municipal de Madrid, New York Public Library, the Library of Congress, the University of Pennsylvania Library, the Oberlin Library, and the Harry Ransom Humanities Research Center at the University of Texas. I also owe a deep debt of gratitude to my students at the University of Virginia who have been willing to read non-canonical texts with me and to think about them in fresh ways. Two entities have provided generous financial support for the publication of this book: the Program for Cultural Cooperation Between Spain's Ministry of Culture and U.S. Universities, and the National Endowment for the Humanities. Finally, Katharina Brett has displayed impressive patience and expert guidance during the editorial process at Cambridge University Press. To all, my most sincere thanks.

A note on the English translations: all translations from the Spanish are mine, unless otherwise indicated. I have attempted to render the often-convoluted prose of the Spanish nineteenth century in a readable and accessible modern English, abandoning stylistic quirks when not relevant to the quotation. The reader will often find paraphrases rather than direct translations, but in all cases I have closely followed the spirit and content of the Spanish quote. Citations in verse will appear in prose. Unless otherwise indicated, references to the plays under discussion will be given by Act and Scene (II, 3, for example).

A version of Chapter 1 originally appeared as "Glorious Invalid: Spanish Theater in the Nineteenth Century," in *Hispanic Review* 61 (1993), 37–60. I am grateful to the Editor for permission to use it here.

Introduction: literary history and canon formation

In 1978 Hayden White wrote, "Every representation of the past has specifiable ideological implications,"[1] a statement which rings particularly true for nineteenth-century Spanish theatre. The history of the theatre in nineteenth-century Spain is usually told through the study of certain selected masterworks, plays which have been read and studied in university classrooms and which have been said to have had a major impact on the direction of theatrical activity in the last century. Students are all familiar with the shocking rebellion of the Duque de Rivas's *Don Alvaro o la fuerza del sino* (Don Alvaro or the Force of Destiny), the poetic beauty of Zorrilla's *Don Juan Tenorio*, Tamayo's neatly structured *Un drama nuevo* (A New Drama), Galdós's dramatic renderings of his concerns for the Spanish middle-class, or Echegaray's delicious excesses of honor and betrayal. Yet these works do not necessarily reflect what really happened in the theatre in nineteenth-century Spain nor do they reveal much about what changes took place in the mind-set of the public going to see them. They certainly do not tell the whole story. In fact, they frequently provide false clues as to the development of the theatre by leading modern readers to assume that they represented the dominant trends, the most popular theatre of their time, or an organic "progress" throughout the century. In many cases, nothing could be further from the truth. As Jesús Rubio Jiménez has quite correctly stated, the history of nineteenth-century Spanish theatre is "mucho más compleja y variada que la que presentan los manuales de literatura"[2] ("much more complex and varied than the one presented in manuals of literature").

What follows is an investigation into the theatre of nineteenth-century Spain in its many aspects – its performance frequency and problems, the battles for control waged in the offices of theatre administrations, the personality conflicts initiated and maintained by the dominant impresarios and actors, the public reception of certain key plays, the economic

[1] Hayden White, *The Tropics of Discourse* (Baltimore: Johns Hopkins, 1978): 69.
[2] Jesús Rubio Jiménez, "La censura teatral en la época moderada: 1840–1868. Ensayo de aproximación," *Segismundo* 18 (1984): 231.

1

problems faced by the theatres, the constant skirmishes with the censors, the struggle to capture in "art" the predominant themes of the day, and all of this against the background of the political and ideological reality of Spain during the last century. The nineteenth century in Spain was a time which witnessed the most dramatic transformation of social, literary and political realities ever seen in that country. Spain began the century oppressed by the corrupt monarchy of Carlos IV, the harsh dictates of the Napoleonic occupation, and finally the reaction of one of the worst rulers ever to sit upon its throne (Fernando VII). Soon it was decimated by civil wars, troubled by the instability of government leaders, confused by the fall of the monarchy of Isabel II, chastened by the failure of an attempt at Republican government, and finally humiliated by the loss of its last colonies in 1898.

Readers will discover that this book is determinedly non-deconstructionist, because I believe that there *is* an author behind the text, and to study dramatic literature in nineteenth-century Spain totally removed from its personal, ideological, economic, and social context would be interesting, perhaps, but pointless, at least until we have begun to establish a clear idea of which authors and texts constitute theatrical activity during that time. In order to deconstruct texts we need to construct a context for them, something which has not been done for nineteenth-century Spanish theatre. In the words of Juan Antonio Ríos Carratalá:

Es preciso seguir profundizando en las grandes figuras y tenerlas siempre presentes como nervios centrales en la vida literaria, pero al mismo tiempo – y desde la perspectiva de una historia de literatura tal y como fue, sin criterios selectivos que acaben siendo simplemente excluyentes – resulta necesario fijarnos en la multitud de autores que a lo largo del siglo XIX se lanzaron a la palestra literaria con un entusiasmo insospechado.[3]

(It is important to continue acquiring more profound knowledge of the great figures and to keep them in mind as central nerves of literary life, but at the same time – and from the perspective of a history of literature as it really was, without selection criteria which end up being merely exclusivist – it is necessary to pay attention to the multitude of authors who over the course of the nineteenth century joined the literary fray with unsuspected enthusiasm.)

The theatre, as the most immediate of literary forms, reflected the rapid and, for many, unnerving changes taking place in society. It became a battle ground on which were waged a series of skirmishes – and at times, wars – for the control of the public's mind. Theatre is both a reflection and an agent of social/cultural shifts in the nineteenth century. For this reason, the importance of nineteenth-century theatre cannot be over-

[3] Juan Antonio Ríos Carratalá, *Románticos y provincianos (La literatura en Alicante, 1839–1866)* (Universidad de Alicante, 1986): 21.

emphasized – not only was it the traditional "mirror on society." What was in life chaotic and frequently threatening was, when transformed into word and movement, comprehensible and thereby controllable. The creation of theatre suggested the creation of a new society (we will see this most clearly in Zorrilla and Galdós), and the tension between art and life played itself out in compelling and lively ways.

The present study will be predominantly chronological, better allowing us to chart the changes in theatrical activity and to assess its impact on future productions and public attitudes. We will look not only at those plays best remembered today, but also at many works which were important in their time but which have since been forgotten. Produced, published, commented upon and debated, these little-known plays and playwrights often more clearly reveal the contours of the debate which raged in theatrical circles throughout the century. It is my hope to bring some balance back to our understanding of Spanish theatre, to demonstrate how Grimaldi's *La pata de cabra* (The Goat's Hoof) was more "popular" for many years than Rivas's *Don Alvaro*, or how Eusebio Asquerino's *Españoles sobre todo* created a much deeper polemic in the year it was written (1844) than Zorrilla's celebrated *Don Juan Tenorio*, or how Narciso Serra was considered to be one of the "jewels" of Spanish dramaturgy during his time, to cite just three examples. A generation of women writers, unknown and unmentioned in most literary histories, makes an attempt to be "recanonized" in these pages. Of course, even this study is a selection, a series of choices, perhaps even an ideological act. Yet as Jonathan Brown has written about the painters of Golden Age Spain:

This approach, and the desire to keep the book at a manageable length, has also compelled me to make choices, often painful ones, about what to include and what to leave out. Students of the period and admirers of the many fine secondary artists will certainly note the absence of particular favorites. Besides offering apologies to those who are thus disappointed, I can say only that, short of doubling the length of the book, or, indeed, writing another kind of book entirely, I could see no way to make the coverage complete. The same process of selection has required me to omit important works even by the artists discussed in these pages.[4]

Throughout the nineteenth century it became almost *de rigueur* to begin a piece on the theatre by bemoaning the terrible state to which theatre had sunk in the previous few years. From Juan de Grimaldi's early negotiations with the Madrid city government, to Agustín Durán's influential *Discurso sobre el influjo que ha tenido la crítica moderna en la decadencia*

---

[4] Jonathan Brown, *The Golden Age of Painting in Spain* (New Haven: Yale University Press, 1991): vii.

del teatro antiguo español (Discourse on the Influence that Modern Criticism Has Had on the Decline of Old Spanish Theatre, 1828), to Juan Lombía's "Causa principal de la decadencia del teatro en España" ("Principal Cause of the Decline of Theatre in Spain," 1845), and right up to M. Martínez Espada's "Decadencia del Teatro Español" ("Decline of the Spanish Theatre," 1900), critics lamented – and predicted – the demise of Spanish theatre. For some, each new year, each new decade seemed to mark a nadir in the health (both literary and economic) of the theatre, and yet we will discover that this lament was (and is) based purely on opinion, rarely backed up by the facts. In reality, during the nineteenth century Spain produced and published not a few dozen or even a few hundred plays, as we have previously thought, but literally *thousands* of one- to four-act works destined to be performed, published, read, and discussed in high and low circles. The richness of theatrical activity is both astonishing and significant, and in the present study it is hoped that what we have traditionally thought of as the "history" of nineteenth-century Spanish theatre will be seen as merely an outline of what really transpired. Rivas, in a letter to Manuel Cañete, spoke of the immense riches of Spanish theatre in his day, referring to "la monstruosa e inmensa *Galería dramática*"[5] ("the monstrous and immense *Dramatic Gallery*"). I have tried to address this "monstrous" body of work, but also to avoid creating a mere list of names, dates and titles of plays written and performed in Spain in the nineteenth century. This book is not inclusive, that is, it is not a compendium or full analysis of every play, major and minor, from the Spanish repertory. Such a task would not only be impossible, it would be foolhardy and doomed to boring failure. Instead, I have tried to capture the ebb and flow of theatrical activity focusing not only on those playwrights remembered today (and "canonized" in schoolroom classes) but also those who during their time exercised significant impact on the direction and development of the theatre. This book, directly and indirectly, is about canon formation and the writing of literary history: *praxis* in the nineteenth century.

Wherever possible I have used first editions of the plays under consideration since they provide more immediate access to the reaction of the public and critics in the times in which they were performed and read and can allow us more accurately to track the public reaction to their meaning. I urge the readers of the following pages to allow for ambiguities, even inconsistencies and contradictions. The fabric of nineteenth-century Spanish drama is tightly woven from many threads and colors into various patterns and textures, but there are tears in the fabric and

---

[5] Cited by Peers, "Some Observations on *El desengaño en un sueño*," *Homenaje ofrecido a Menéndez Pidal* (Madrid: Hernando, 1925), 583–587.

loose ends not yet accounted for. Perhaps future scholars will weave those loose ends into a fabric of their own.

"Yes, but is it any good?" is the question which inevitably arises when one discusses the repositioning of plays within the "canon," and one I have attempted studiously to avoid in the following pages. "Good" as a descriptor phrase of literary quality has little value when one is attempting to chart the ebb and flow of theatrical activity; instead, I have tried to bring to the discussion notice of plays which were not only "good" (or perhaps not even good) but also polemical, revolutionary, significant in their time, popular, or important as socio-historical artifacts. As Arnold Krupat has suggested, "In our own time, the canon is established primarily by the professoriat, by teacher-critics who variously – passively or actively but for the most part – support the existing order."[6] That is, we teach what is available; we make available what we teach. It is a closed circle. Where are the modern editions of many of these plays? While publishers and editors produce several, sometimes dozens of modern editions of certain texts, others – literally thousands of them – languish in difficult (or impossible) to find collections, gathering dust and decaying daily. I hope the present study will help to break that closed circle and open up new paths of study for students of nineteenth-century Spanish literature.

[6] Arnold Krupat, "Native American Literature and the Canon." In *Canons*, ed. Robert von Hallberg (University of Chicago Press, 1983): 310.

1   Spanish theatre in the nineteenth century. (An overview)

The century seemed to open auspiciously enough. The wars over theatrical reform waged in the eighteenth century seemed to have been won by those who demanded less censorship, more involvement by the acting companies, and better working conditions. The 1799 *Idea de una reforma de los teatros de Madrid* (Idea for an Improvement of the Theatres of Madrid) had been approved in November of that year and was to be put into effect for the theatrical season 1800–1801.[1] Madrid's finest actor, Isidoro Máiquez, had gone off to Paris to study the techniques of that city's dazzling François Joseph Talma, much acclaimed for his natural acting style.[2] Even the terrible fire that in 1802 destroyed one of the capital's main theatres, the Príncipe, held the possibility that with the new edifice would come a new (and enlightened) administration. Meanwhile, the enormous – and unprecedented – success of Leandro Fernández de Moratín's neoclassical comedy, *El sí de las niñas* (The Maidens' Consent) in 1806, seemed to confirm that the curtain was going up on a new and exciting period of stability and quality for the Spanish theatre.[3] Alas, such was not the case. The reforms of 1800 were dashed by a series of conflicting interests, Moratín's triumph produced no immediate heirs of merit, and the new Príncipe (opened in 1807) was placed back under the control of the *Ayuntamiento* (City Hall). As a final blow, when Napoleon's army entered Madrid in May, 1808, all hopes for a glorious uplift in theatrical life came to a crushing end when the theatres were shut down. The real drama moved into the streets.

The question of who owned and who controlled the theatres had been a key one since the very beginnings of "official" theatre in Spain, and it took on particular intensity during the eighteenth century, when religious

[1] René Andioc, *Teatro y sociedad en el Madrid del siglo XVIII* (Madrid: Castalia, 1976): 547.
[2] Alberto Colao, *Máiquez, discípulo de Talma* (Cartagena: F. Gómez, 1980).
[3] John C. Dowling has called the play's première a "social event." "The Madrid Theatre Public in the Eighteenth Century: Transition from the Popular Audience to the Bourgeois," *Transactions of the Seventh International Congress on the Enlightenment: Studies on Voltaire and the Eighteenth Century* (Oxford: The Voltaire Foundation, 1989): 1361. See also Moratín, *El sí de las niñas*, ed. René Andioc (Madrid: Castalia, 1969).

and moral crusaders equated the theatre, and the actors, naturally, with iniquity and moral laxity.[4] The concept of free enterprise was a problematic one, since it was – from as far back as the early seventeenth century – frequently a money-losing proposition. Ironically, though, a constant tug-of-war for ownership was often played out between private and public owners, since the theatre was viewed as a mechanism through which the government could control, or at least influence, the behavior of the public. The government frequently refused to take full ownership and financial responsibility for theatrical activity, yet it published a bewildering array of rules and decrees aimed at curtailing what it viewed as the excesses of theatre people. Hence, the spirited hostilities and lively debates over the direction, content, and control of the theatre became the dominant discourse in the previous century and set the stage, so to speak, for what would happen in the nineteenth century.[5]

The Napoleonic invasion produced a series of conflicting events relating to the theatre in Madrid. Depending on which political group was in the ascendency during the War of Independence (the *afrancesados* who supported the "enlightened" policies of Joseph Bonaparte or the "liberales" who defended the claims of Fernando VII and who fought heroically against the foreign invaders), the theatre became just as much of a battleground as did the fields around Bailén or Zaragoza. Words poured out instead of blood. Joseph was not uninterested in the theatre, nor unaware of its value as propaganda, and he struggled to have plays staged which underscored the "enlightened" nature of his reign and which attempted to link him with the Spanish national past. Francisco Comella, a dramatist excoriated by Moratín (in *La comedia nueva o el café*, 1792 [The New Comedy, or the Café]), and Gaspar Zavala y Zamora became two of the most represented Spanish playwrights during the 1808–1813 occupation for their appeal to the "glorious" history of Spain.[6] When the French government officials were forced to abandon

---

[4] For information concerning the ownership and development of Spanish theatre in the late sixteenth- through early eighteenth-century, see J. E. Varey, N. D. Shergold, and Charles Davis (eds.), *Los arriendos de los corrales de comedias de Madrid: 1587–1719* (London: Tamesis Books, Ltd., 1987).

[5] See, for example, the details provided by Andioc, *Teatro y sociedad*, Emilio Cotarelo y Mori, *Bibliografía de las controversias sobre la licitud del teatro en España* (Madrid: Archivos, Bibliotecas y Museos, 1904), I. L. McClelland, *Spanish Drama of Pathos, 1750–1808* (University of Toronto Press, 1970), and Francisco Aguilar Piñal, *Sevilla y el teatro en el siglo XVIII* (Oviedo: Cátedra Feijoo, 1974). See also Jovellanos's *Memoria para el arreglo de la policía de los espectáculos y diversiones públicas y sobre su origen en España* (Madrid: Sancha, 1812).

[6] This period has been studied by Emilio Cotarelo y Mori, *Isidoro Máiquez y el teatro de su tiempo* (Madrid: José Perales, 1902), and more recently by Emmanuel Larraz, *Théâtre et politique pendant la Guerre d'Indépendance espagnole: 1808–1814* (Aix-en-Provence:

Madrid temporarily in August 1808, a resurgence of plays dealing with the Spanish monarchy or celebrating the Spanish victories over the French at Bailén, Zaragoza or Arapiles were played in the two main theatres, the Príncipe and the Cruz.[7] Theatre became a major tool in the war of propaganda waged by both sides. Interesting examples of the "literary" response to the political situation include strident diatribes against Napoleon, Murat, and Joseph Bonaparte, performed whenever possible in Madrid. Dozens of subversive plays satirized Joseph's alleged drinking problem or Napoleon's well-known megalomania, as we will see in the next chapter.

When the war finally came to a close in 1814 and Fernando VII returned to the throne, the theatre suffered from the same fierce censorship which stifled the free exchange of ideas in every part of Spanish society. Many young intellectuals were forced to flee the country – even, sadly, many of those who had fought in defense of the legitimate monarch – and would initiate their writing careers in exile. Ángel de Saavedra and Francisco Martínez de la Rosa, both of whom would later distinguish themselves as playwrights and politicians, began to write in the years during and immediately following this divisive war. In the theatres themselves, a cycle began to develop which would dominate theatre ownership for decades: the city government, frustrated by the efforts to organize and regulate the theatres, would appoint entrepreneurs and charge them with putting the theatres on a sound financial footing. These attempts frequently resulted in the actors complaining (often with total justification) that the impresarios cared little for their wellbeing and were not even living up to the modest contractual responsibilities they had vis à vis the actors and the actors' families. The impresarios, unable to gain full control of the repertory (the city administration's censors held those reins) and feeling unfairly burdened by the pension and charitable costs demanded by the actors, often lost money and went bankrupt. The actors would then demand more control over their destinies and the theatres would be turned over to them in an attempt to quiet their complaints and to improve the administration of the enterprise. This is precisely what happened in 1815, for example, when Máiquez was named *autor* of the Príncipe while his chief rival for that post, Bernardo Gil, took over the

Université de Provence, 1988). I have placed certain words in quotes to indicate that these were the actual terms bandied about during the period in question.

7 John J. Allen provides an interesting history of the Príncipe Theatre in *The Reconstruction of a Spanish Golden Age Playhouse. El Corral del Príncipe, 1583–1744* (Gainesville: University of Florida Press, 1983). A history of the Cruz Theatre can be found in Phillip Brian Thomason's doctoral dissertation, "The *Coliseo de la Cruz:* Madrid's First Enclosed Municipal Playhouse (1737–1859)," University of Kentucky, 1987.

reins of the Cruz.[8] However, these "reforms" failed, and the city government found itself, yet again, in charge of the theatres. It was a boom-and-bust cycle, only with very little boom.

Similar problems reoccurred at a time when the ostensible hope for a real liberal reform seemed possible, the so-called Liberal Triennium ushered in by Rafael de Riego's uprising against Fernando VII in 1820. Many of the young exiles were able to return to Spain, and interest in theatrical activity grew accordingly. It was Bernardo Gil who once again demanded control over the theatres he acted in, and in a strident and acrimonious paper published and circulated in Madrid, he complained of the "despotic," "whimsical" and "demeaning" decrees traditionally issued by the city fathers regarding the theatre.[9] Such outbursts would not have been tolerated during the reign of Fernando VII, but even these complaints came to nothing. By 1821 the theatres were back in the hands of a private businessman, and by the time of the collapse of the liberal experiment in May 1823 (hastened by the invasion of the "One Hundred Thousand Sons of St. Louis," an army backed by the Holy Alliance whose purpose was to reinstate Fernando VII to his throne) the theatres were once again bankrupt.[10]

The first real revolution in theatre ownership and literary taste was to take place after 1823 and at the hands of a transplanted Frenchman, a soldier who came to Madrid that year with the invading forces, but who stayed to change significantly the way theatre was looked upon, performed, and organized. The story of Juan de Grimaldi's battles with the city government during his first year in Madrid (1823–1824) is instructive for what it reveals about ownership, censorship, finances, and power struggles among the three main forces (the administration, the actors, and the impresario) vying for control.[11]

After convincing the reluctant city authorities to turn the two main theatres over to him, Grimaldi set about hiring new actors, playwrights, and translators, redecorating the theatres (or at least repairing the myriad cracks and leaks that made the theatres both uncomfortable and frequently downright dangerous places to be), and attempting to bring the

---

8 Cotarelo, *Máiquez*, p. 380.
9 Bernardo Gil and Antonio González, *Manifiesto que dan los autores de los teatros de la Cruz y Príncipe* (Madrid: Repullés, 1820).
10 I have given some details of this crisis in *Theatre and Politics in Nineteenth-Century Spain: Juan de Grimaldi as Impresario and Government Agent* (Cambridge University Press, 1988): 10–13.
11 I have told this story in detail in "Juan de Grimaldi y el año teatral madrileño, 1823–1824," *Actas del VIII Congreso Internacional de Hispanistas* (Madrid: ISTMO, 1986): 607–613. What follows is a brief synopsis of that recounting. Full details about Grimaldi's activity in Madrid's theatres in the first years of the nineteenth century are to be found in my *Theatre and Politics*.

repertory more in line with innovations in Europe (primarily in his home country, France). His initial experiment was not entirely successful, but he did inaugurate a period of optimism and growth for Spanish theatre, and as he grew in confidence and power a real transformation began to be felt in Madrid. With Grimaldi, the role of the impresario changed from what it had been previously. No longer was the impresario merely a financial manager, mediating between the artistic director, the actors, and the government officials who oversaw the acceptability of the repertory. Now he was more involved in artistic decisions, concerned with the aesthetic achievement of his theatre, and charged with the overall wellbeing of the theatrical enterprise. As Romero Tobar notes:

El empresario, para obtener el lucro congruente, debe realizar una doble operación económico-artística: en primer lugar, el arrendamiento del teatro – el empresario no suele ser el propietario del teatro, especialmente si éste es un edificio y no un tenderete veraniego – tiene que conseguirlo en las mejores condiciones posibles; en segundo lugar, ha de acertar con las exigencias del público en el momento de confeccionar el elenco de actores y las piezas que se han de representar durante la temporada. Si ambos objetivos son atendidos satisfactoriamente, puede aventurarse que el negocio de la *empresa* tendrá resultados *positivos*.[12]

(The impresario, in order to obtain suitable profits, should carry out a double economic-artistic operation: in the first place, the renting of the theatre – the impresario is not normally the owner of the theatre, especially if it is a building and not merely a summer set-up – he must acquire it under the most favorable conditions possible; in the second place, he must take the public's demands into account when he begins to make up the list of actors and the pieces that will be performed during the season. If both objectives are satisfactorily attended to, he can bet that the business of the *business* will have *positive* results.)

The 1820s witnessed the expansion of the repertory into several areas which produced applause in some quarters and bitter complaints in others. Grimaldi encouraged the public's taste for opera (Bretón de los Herreros thought it was more than interest; in fact, he recalled that it increased to a veritable "furor")[13] as well as the continued production of rewrites, called "refundiciones," of Spanish Golden Age plays and translations of new melodramas recently played in Paris. He has been credited with improving acting technique during the 1820s and putting the theatre on a sounder intellectual footing, that is, making it a more "respectable" enterprise than it had been in the first years of the century. Grimaldi

---

[12] Leonardo Romero Tobar, "Noticias sobre empresas teatrales en periódicos del siglo XIX," *Segismundo* 8 (1972): 235. I have drawn on this article for some of the details that follow.
[13] See David T. Gies, "Entre drama y ópera: la lucha por el público teatral en la época de Fernando VII," *Bulletin Hispanique* 91 (1989): 37–60.

himself, while controversial and combative, was an elegant and highly intelligent man who made theatre fashionable again not only among the upper crust of Madrid but also among the lower classes. His appeal to the uneducated masses was confirmed by his production of a magical comedy called *Todo lo vence amor o La pata de cabra* (known simply as *La pata de cabra*) in 1829, a play that became so wildly popular that thousands of people from the provinces flocked to Madrid to see performances of it, much to the distress of local police authorities.[14] Spin-offs and imitations of this trifling play were performed in Madrid as late as the 1870s (Enrique Zumel's *El anillo del diablo* [The Devil's Ring], 1871, owes much to Grimaldi's work).

Even though production quality, acting technique,[15] repertory offerings, and general respectability of the theatre improved, Grimaldi and the companies were frustrated by the restrictive atmosphere of suspicion, censorship, and excessive bureaucracy imposed by the government of Fernando VII. Censorship was ubiquitous and explicit, not only aimed at new plays being written for the stage, but also at plays from the classical repertory which might allude to contemporary circumstances and reflect negatively on the king or any of his ministers. It even extended to a prohibition on naming names, an absurdity which seriously curtailed theatre discourse since critics were unable to comment on the faults of specific actors and playwrights. The government, in turn, was not entirely happy with Grimaldi's performance, and it periodically put the theatres up for public auction. In 1831, to cite just one example, the following notice appeared in the *Gaceta de Madrid* (24 November):

Habiendo transcurrido el tiempo señalado sin que se haya hecho proposición alguna a la empresa de los teatros de esta Corte, y debiendo encargarse de ellos el Ayuntamiento, se anuncia de nuevo al público para que los que gusten tomar a su cargo la empresa de los referidos teatros, presenten sus proposiciones en la secretaría del Ayuntamiento.

(Since the allotted time has passed and no one has made a bid to take over the theatres of this capital, and since City Hall will have to take charge of them, we make this announcement to the public yet again so that anyone who may wish to

---

[14] The full tale of the startling success of *La pata de cabra* is told in David T. Gies, " 'Inocente estupidez': *La pata de cabra* (1829), Grimaldi and the Regeneration of the Spanish Stage," *Hispanic Review* 54 (1986): 375–396.

[15] An instructive anecdote from 1835 reveals, however, that actors never became completely professionalized. It seems that Concepción Rodríguez, Grimaldi's wife, was accused and convicted of overselling tickets to a performance for which she was to receive the receipts (a benefit performance). Threatened with jail and a substantial fine, she fled Madrid and only returned after her husband, Martínez de la Rosa, and the Queen Regent herself intervened on her behalf. The 50 *ducado* fine was forgiven, but she was forced to pay a 20 *ducado* fine for failing to appear at the jail as ordered. Archivo de la Villa: Corregimiento 1–186–55.

take over the direction of said theatres should present his proposals to the secretary's office at City Hall.)

Only after 1834, following the death of the King and the advent of his moderate and enlightened wife, María Cristina, did theatrical production and critical discourse achieve any sort of plurality.

While it can hardly be said that María Cristina's governments had a laissez-faire policy regarding the theatre – quite the contrary – they did at least tolerate more public comment and criticism in the newspapers, a continued expansion of the repertory, some restrictions of the role of the theatre censor, and the opening of additional theatres. Her accession to the throne ushered in a period of real excitement for the Spanish theatre. It is after 1834 that Madrid audiences saw plays such as Martínez de la Rosa's *La conjuración de Venecia* (The Venice Conspiracy), Larra's *Macías*, Saavedra's (now Duke of Rivas) *Don Alvaro o la fuerza del sino*, Antonio García Gutiérrez's *El trovador* (The Troubador), and dozens of other provocative and thrilling dramas. 1834 was recognized immediately by observers of the literary scene as a key year in the history of Spanish theatre, one which ushered in a "revolution": "El año 34 cambió del todo este aspecto y se efectuó una gran revolución en el teatro" ("1834 changed this aspect completely and ushered in a great revolution in the theatre") (*El Entreacto*, 5 May 1839). The expansion of the repertory, to include these often shocking Romantic plays, initiated a lively debate among the defenders and detractors of the new literary movement,[16] and what startled some critics as excessive freedom (moral and political laxity) eventually led to the return of the theatre censor in 1836.

Not everyone opposed the concept of censorship for plays (in fact, it was a generally agreed-upon premise that some censorship was essential since the theatre was viewed as a school for morals, a pulpit from which to preach and teach ethics as well as politics, and a mirror in which society viewed its achievements and aspirations), but most intellectuals rigorously protested the often arbitrary nature of theatre censorship. Ecclesiastical censorship was abandoned in 1835, although naturally the Church never relinquished its self-defined right to guard the morality of society by trying to regulate its spectacles, putting constant pressure on the civil

---

[16] The debate on Romanticism has been recounted numerous times in recent years. Different perspectives are developed by Guillermo Carnero, *Los orígenes del romanticismo reaccionario español* (Universidad de Valencia, 1978); Vicente Llorens Castillo, *El romanticismo español* (Madrid: Castalia, 1979); Juan Luis Alborg, *Historia de la literatura española, IV, El romanticismo* (Madrid: Gredos, 1980); Ricardo Navas Ruiz, *El romanticismo español* (Madrid: Cátedra, 1990); Iris M. Zavala, "La literatura: romanticismo y costumbrismo," *Historia de España, XXXV, 2. La época del romanticismo*, ed. José María Jover Zamora (Madrid: Espasa Calpe, 1988): 5–183; and Derek Flitter, *Spanish Romantic Literary Theory and Criticism* (Cambridge University Press, 1992).

authorities to ban works which were disrespectful of the Church or its teachings. However, the civil government was more concerned with ideological irregularities, and spent much effort trying to stamp out any ideas which would undermine its authority. Such concerns were codified in the Royal Order of 1836, which addressed the theatre's obligation not to "exaltar las pasiones políticas de los espectadores"[17] ("excite the political passions of the spectators"). Censorship haunted the theatre, in varying degrees of intensity, throughout the century and, as Jesús Rubio Jiménez states, "Por debajo de la moralidad social y religiosa, existió siempre una inmoralidad política y financiera"[18] ("Beneath social and religious morality, there always existed a political and financial immorality").

Don Alvaro o la fuerza del sino, El trovador, Carlos II el Hechizado (Charles II the Bewitched), Anthony, Los amantes de Teruel (The Lovers of Teruel), Españoles sobre todo, Bandera negra (Black Flag), and other plays sparked heated controversies in the 1830s and 1840s that went well beyond the borders of literature. In the eyes of many observers they threatened the status quo and forced critics and public to consider alternatives to the traditional, conservative social structure which dominated Spanish life. The new dramas also had to compete with the still popular translations of French plays and the ever-present "refundiciones" of Golden Age dramas and they did so, at least in part, successfully.[19] One of the points of contention between the playwrights and those who paid for their services (usually the impresarios) was the fact, voiced eloquently by Larra among others, that translations paid as well, or better, than original comedies and therefore economic reality forced men of talent to squander their time producing translations instead of writing original plays. Real attempts were made to correct this injustice. There gradually developed not only a balance in payments to writers of

---

[17] Cited by Jean Louis Picoche, Los amantes de Teruel. Introduction, edition critique et synoptique precedées d'une étude sur le monde du théâtre à Madrid entre 1833 et 1850 (Paris, Centre de Recherche Hispanique, 1970): 35.

[18] Jesús Rubio Jiménez, "La censura teatral en la época moderada: 1840–1868. Ensayo de aproximación," Segismundo 18 (1984): 200.

[19] The following studies provide valuable information about translations and "refundiciones" in Madrid theatres during the period in question. N. B. Adams, "French Influence on the Madrid Theatre in 1837," Estudios dedicados a D. Ramón Menéndez Pidal VII (Madrid: Consejo Superior de Investigaciones Científicas, 1950–1962): 135–151; "Notes on Spanish Plays at the Beginning of the Romantic Period," Romanic Review 27 (1926): 128–142; "Sidelights on the Spanish Theaters of the Eighteen-Thirties," Hispania 9 (1926): 1–12; "Siglo de Oro Plays in Madrid," Hispanic Review 4 (1936): 342–357; and Sterling A. Stoudemire, "Dionisio Solís's 'refundiciones' of Plays (1800–1834)," Hispanic Review 8 (1940): 305–310. Also Piero Menarini, "La statistica commentata. Vent'anni di teatro in Spagna (1830–1850)," Quaderni di Filologia Romanza 4 (1984): 65–89, and Piero Menarini, Patricia Garelli, Félix San Vicente, eds., El teatro romántico español (1830–1850). Autores, obras, bibliografía (Bologna: Atesa, 1982).

translations and of original plays, but also a system to pay royalties to playwrights. Such measures had less to do with a perceived injustice to playwrights than with a declared need to enrich the repertory with "national" plays, as the following notice makes clear:

Parece que uno de los medios que piensa adoptar la empresa de los teatros de esta corte para alentar a los ingenios españoles es la de igualar sus producciones originales a las francesas traducidas, pagándoles al mismo precio que suelen pagarse estas últimas. (*Eco del Comercio*, 9 March 1837)

(It seems as though one of the means which the management of the theatres of this capital plans to adopt in order to encourage Spanish talent is to equate their original productions with French translations, paying them the same for original plays that they usually pay for translations.)

By the 1840s the fragmentation of Spanish theatrical structure grew more acute. Grimaldi was gone, and his absence was lamented.

Grandes adelantos ha tenido la escena, especialmente desde que estuvo al frente de la dirección de los teatros de Madrid el inteligente señor Grimaldi: mucho ha ganado el público en la parte tan descuidada antes de decoraciones, trajes, y costumbres, pero aun le falta mucho que adelantar si ha de estarse al nivel de lo que el público exige y de lo que reclama el decoro mismo de la escena. Desde que el citado Grimaldi dejó de dirigirla, nada se ha adelantado. (*El Entreacto*, 2 February 1840)

(The stage has made great advances, especially since the intelligent Mr. Grimaldi was in charge of the theatres of Madrid: the public has gained much in the previously abandoned areas of decorations, costumes, and customs, but it still has a long way to go if it is to reach the level of what the public should have and what scenic decency demands. Since the above-mentioned Grimaldi quit directing it, nothing has moved forward.)

Impresarios and city agents were still dissatisfied with the chaos and constant deficits created by the theatres, and the belief that theatre could not only reflect but also mold public opinion intensified. The strife-ridden 1830s had produced what was close to panic among some of the country's intellectuals and top bureaucrats who viewed the theatre not as an idle pastime, but, as was the case during the Aranda reforms in the eighteenth century and during the reign of Joseph Bonaparte, as another weapon in the battle for control of the reins of power. Actors, who several times in the past two dozen years had taken over as impresarios of the theatres, formed, as in the case of the Cruz Theatre, a "sociedad de artistas" ("society of artists") to take charge of the administration of that theatre in 1839. Plays which commented, directly or indirectly, on the Carlist Wars, the international intrigues over the Spanish succession and the role of Isabel II, the divisions among conservatives, moderates, and liberals, and the nature of political legitimacy aired these issues on the stage in the same way that similar ones were aired in the newspapers and in the Cortes. Additionally, these plays began to reflect the slow consolidation of the growing middle classes, whose concerns over money, social status, and hierarchy were revealed and satirized in numerous dramas. Many of the pieces written, performed, and published in the 1840s, far from being the rather mindless pulp they have heretofore been considered to be, in fact become important documents for our understanding of the ideological and social struggles of that decade. Important changes ocurred in playwriting in the 1840s, changes which are reflected in Zorrilla's *Don Juan Tenorio*, the plays of Rodríguez Rubí, and, especially, *Españoles sobre todo*, by Eusebio Asquerino.

The 1840s also witnessed the growth of local, private theatres that offered some competition to the city-owned and -sponsored main theatres. Clubs – called "sociedades dramáticas" ("dramatic societies") – formed around these theatres. One of the first was the old Liceo Artístico y Literario, followed by societies at the Teatro del Museo, Teatro de la Unión, Teatro del Genio, Teatro La Venus, Teatro La Talía, Teatro El Numen, Teatro Parnaso and others (according to a newspaper report, there existed twenty-six in Madrid alone by 1847). People paid a weekly or monthly quota which permitted them to attend a "meeting" at which a play was performed. These meetings became as much a social experience as a theatrical one, and often the plays were penned by members or were more experimental in nature than the main theatres would permit. These associations naturally engendered the hostility of the main theatres, which viewed them as unhealthy competition and accused them of lowering standards, although, in one of the many contradictions of theatrical activity of the times, members were often recognized playwrights. Ventura de la Vega, for example, belonged to the Liceo, wrote plays for it, and sometimes acted in the plays being staged there (he played the lead in a revival of Moratín's *El barón* [The Baron] in April, 1842). As early as 1842 *El Pasatiempo* noted that

¡Hay actualmente en Madrid entre Liceos, Academias, Museos, Circos, y teatros caseros, más de cuarenta diversiones particulares! Ahora bien, ¿cómo es posible que una población de doscientas mil almas sea suficiente a llenarlas todas? De ningún modo, pues no es mayor el número de las que hay en París, cuando la población es allí cuádruple que la nuestra. Se pretende culpar a las empresas de teatros de la poca concurrencia, cuando la culpa es solo de los mismos que las acriminan. (14 April 1842)

(Today in Madrid between Lyceums, Academies, Museums, Circuses, and private home theatres, there are more than forty different places for entertainment! Now, how is it possible that a population of two hundred thousand souls is enough to fill them all up? It is not; there aren't more people here than in Paris, where the population is four times ours. They try to blame the theatre managements for the lack of attendance, when the blame is only to be put on those very people who make the accusations.)

La Luneta (20 December 1846) labeled these competing theatres nothing less than a "rémora fatal y perniciosa al desenvolvimiento de verdadero teatro" ("fatal and pernicious hindrance to the development of true theatre"). The complaints were not entirely unjustified, since from the impresario's point of view the dramatic societies did compete unfairly given that they were exempt from paying the pension and unemployment benefits which had for so long been one of the major points of contention between the actors and the businessmen who ran the theatres. *El Pasatiempo*'s recommendation in 1842 was to spread the charges around among all the theatres. The society theatres were also exempted from paying full royalties to authors, another way for them to save money and provide theatrical spectacles at a cheaper price than the legitimate theatres. *La Luneta* begrudgingly admitted one benefit of the societies: "Sus secciones de declamación han sido hasta ahora el plantel artístico de donde han salido los actores de profesión" ("Their acting sections have been until now the artistic training-school from which the professional actors have come"). However, in a later article (24 December 1846), the newspaper issued the standard lament on "el estado de decadencia en que por desgracia se halla la literatura dramática nacional" ("the state of decadence in which our national dramatic literature unfortunately finds itself"), a lament which would be heard over and over throughout the century.

By the mid-1840s regular performances of plays were held in the Teatro del Circo, the Teatro de Buenavista, the Teatro del Genio, and the Teatro Variedades.[20] The Teatro de la Cruz was reconstituted as the Teatro del Drama, and the Teatro del Instituto grew in importance and took on the name Teatro de la Comedia. New theatres were built to accommodate the growing demand for this type of entertainment, a phenomenon labeled by Angel Luis Fernández Muñoz as "el singular desarrollo de la arquitectura teatral madrileña durante el siglo XIX ... el nuevo lugar que la burguesía diseña para la celebración del espectáculo"[21] ("the extraordinary development of theatrical architecture in Madrid during the nineteenth century ... the new place designed by the bourgeois for the celebration of spectacle"). Some observers viewed the growth with scepticism and questioned

---

[20] See María del Carmen Simón Palmer, "Construcción y apertura de teatros madrileños en el siglo XIX," *Segismundo* 11 (1975): 85–137.

[21] Angel Luis Fernández Muñoz, *Arquitectura teatral en Madrid* (Madrid: Editorial El Avapiés, 1988): 83.

whether it had a positive or negative impact on the industry. Juan Lombía, for one, believed the expansion of theatres had a clearly deleterious effect on public taste, while admitting the growing popularity of stage productions:

La revolución ha aumentado el círculo de concurrentes y ha disminuído la afición al teatro ... Quien recuerde que hace quince años no había más teatros en Madrid que los de la Cruz y el Príncipe, que apenas estaban concurridos; y que ahora por haberse aumentado considerablemente con diferentes obras el número de sus localidades y existir el del Circo, que es mucho más grande, resulta un doble espacio para el público, y que sin embargo, en el invierno hay días en que se llenan dos veces cada uno de estos teatros, que igualmente se llenan algunos subalternos que antes no había, y además un sin número de teatros caseros o de sociedades particulares, convendrá en que o Madrid ha triplicado su población, lo cual no es así, o en que son muchos más las personas que en el día asisten a estos espectáculos.[22]

(The revolution has increased the number of spectators and has decreased true interest in the theatre ... Anyone who remembers that just fifteen years ago there were no theatres other than the Cruz and the Príncipe, which were seldom full; and now because the number of seats has been considerably increased by the presentation of different works, and that the Circo Theatre exists, which is much larger, twice the size as before, and yet, during the winter there are days on which each of these theatres is filled twice, and that some secondary theatres that did not even exist before are also full, as well as an endless number of home or private club theatres, would believe that either Madrid has tripled its population – which is not the case – or that many more people today attend these shows.)

As we will see in more detail, the 1840s also institutionalized copyright and author's rights for plays, giving dramatists more security against being forced to sell their plays for small fees to impresarios who later, if the play was a hit, reaped the benefits. Abuses had been legion, notwithstanding the half-hearted attempts at reform as seen in the laws of 1813, 1834, and 1837. Writing laws was one thing; enforcing them quite another. As P. P. Rogers states:

A dramatist might put the finishing touches (such as they were) on his piece, have it accepted by the producer, and stand proudly to receive the plaudits of an enthusiastic public, only to fail to recognize his play on the boards, to see it played elsewhere without his consent, to find it coming from the press without his name or knowledge, to have it corrected, copied, changed, mutilated, added to and taken from, while he stood helplessly by and pondered none too cheerfully the irony of the laurels which sat upon his brow.[23]

---

[22] Juan Lombía, *El teatro: origen, índole e importancia de esta institución* (Madrid: Sánchez, 1845): 130–131.

[23] P. P. Rogers, "Dramatic Copyright in Spain Before 1850," *Romanic Review* 25 (1934): 35–36.

The well-known case of Zorrilla's sale of *Don Juan Tenorio* would not, to the immense relief of the dramatists, be repeated with any frequency after the 1840s.[24] After 1847, extracts from the *Reglamentos orgánicos de Teatros, sobre la propiedad de los autores* (Organic Rules on Theatres and Authors' Rights) were reprinted in many of the plays published in Spain. This *Reglamento* stipulated the kind of compensation due an author whose plays were being performed, and warned that "ninguna composición dramática podrá representarse en los teatros públicos sin el previo consentimiento del autor" ("no dramatic composition can be performed in public theatres without the prior consent of the author") a right that "durará toda su vida" ("will last for life") plus twenty-five years. Only after 1849, however, with the creation of the Teatro Español, did the government seriously attempt to enforce the code.

As impresarios became used to paying these charges, the costs of running a theatre naturally increased. Reports indicate that in 1862, for example, the owner of the Teatro de Variedades had paid out 57,501 *reales* to acquire the rights to new plays, and an additional 28,302 *reales* in royalties for plays already in the repertory (*La Epoca*, 26 May 1862). These were not huge sums (the newspaper *La España* reported in 1863 during the squabbles over the ownership of the Teatro Real that its annual revenues were close to five million *reales*) but they were costs which owners and impresarios had to take into account when planning the theatre calendar. The institution of the regulations clearly did not mean that all problems were solved concerning royalties and copyright. Quite the contrary. As late as 1861 Antonio García Gutiérrez, one of the country's most famous playwrights, was forced to sue the owners of the Teatro Real over the matter of his plays *El trovador* and *Simón Bocanegra*, which had been converted to librettos for operas by Verdi. After much squabbling, he received 8,000 *reales* compensation (*El Contemporáneo*, 6 January 1861). Still, the business side of the theatre never seemed to improve much. In 1848 when the government offered the Cruz and Príncipe theatres up for public bid, no one came forth. In the same year the Teatro del Instituto went bankrupt, the actors were all left unemployed, and the theatre was put up for rent. Shortly thereafter, in February of 1850, announcements appeared in *El Heraldo* that the Teatro

---

[24] Zorrilla sold the rights to the play to his editor Manual Delgado for 4,200 *reales*. The contract, as reproduced by Narciso Alonso Cortés, *Zorrilla. Su vida y sus obras* (Valladolid: Santarén, 1943), 329, goes as follows: "Creo en favor de don Manuel Delgado la propiedad absoluta, y para siempre, del drama original en siete actos y en verso, titulado *Don Juan Tenorio*, por la cantidad de 4.200 reales vellón, que recibo en este acto, a fin de que, como cosa suya privativa, pueda disponer de dicho drama libremente para su impresión y representación en todos los teatros, eceptuándose únicamente los de esta corte. – Madrid, 18 de marzo de 1844."

de la Comedia had also gone under and that even the venerable Cruz "está en peligro de quiebra" ("is in danger of going bankrupt").

It seemed as though many years of hoping and carping about government subsidies of theatres were going to pay off in 1849 with the creation of the Teatro Español. Time and again critics, actors, impresarios, and playwrights had bemoaned the lack in Spain of a national theatre, and the chorus of complaints reached fever pitch in the late 1840s. *La Luneta* summed it up with typical hyperbole: "Cuando el teatro nacional se halla en un estado lastimoso de postración y decaimiento; cuando arrastra una existencia oscura y precaria; cuando yacen tristemente postergadas y casi reunidas en el olvido las glorias dramáticas del país ..." (24 December 1846) ("When the national theatre finds itself in a woeful state of prostration and decline: when it leads a dark and precarious existence; when the dramatic glories of the country lie sadly abandoned and nearly forgotten ..."). This same paper published a satirical engraving which summed up the audience's apparent participation in this "decaimiento" ("decline") – the scene depicts the inside of a theatre in which the audience is talking and looking anywhere but the stage; one man is even reading a book (27 December 1846). A truly national theatre – something akin to the impressive Comédie Française – was, it was hoped, about to be born. It would rekindle high-quality theatre and spark more interest among the spectators. At last there existed a fully subsidized theatre directed by one of the top dramatists of the period, Ventura de la Vega, and backed by the government. Its ostensible mission was the creation and recreation of a national theatre tradition, a theatre administration charged with developing and performing plays by Spanish authors and which would be more in tune with the middle class idea of itself at mid-century and, presumably, free Spanish authors from having to compete with the translations of French dramas, still one of the staples of the repertory. It was a time of great expectations. Apart from the numerous small theatres which were now operating in Madrid, seven official and permanent theatres were in operation at mid-century. Led by the Teatro Español, they also included the Teatro del Drama (the old Cruz), the Teatro de Variedades, the Teatro de la Comedia (old Instituto), the Teatro Lope de Vega, the Teatro Real, and the Teatro del Circo. As a symbol of the national scope of the Teatro Español, the Spanish flag – for the first time ever in the history of the Spanish stage – was raised over the theatre when it opened in April, 1849.

Alas, the experiment was short-lived: mismanagement, jealousy, petty arguments, and the hostility expressed in several newspapers (primarily, *La Luneta*, and a new newspaper, *La Ortiga*, directed by Vega's ex-ally, Tomás Rodríguez Rubí) forced the Teatro Español to close its doors as *the* official theatre in less than two years. Attempts were made in subsequent years to reactivate the concept of a fully government-supported theatre (most notably by Manuel de la Revilla in 1876), but nothing concrete came of the proposals.[25]

As Romantic plays and political dramas gave way to what has been called the "alta comedia" (high comedy) in the 1850s, more theatres opened and more public debate on their nature, goals, failures and accomplishments took place in the pages of the newspapers. Not everyone agreed that the increasing number of theatres was a good thing. Eugenio de Ochoa, writing in 1853, clearly stated that the eight theatres operating in the capital (Príncipe, Cruz, Teatro Real, Lope de Vega, Circo, Instituto, Genio, Variedades) were the major cause of the lack of quality and stability since Madrid's population was not sufficiently high to support so much theatrical activity; he thought four theatres would be more than enough.[26] The repertory still contained plays by Golden Age authors and by the men who had dominated the Spanish stage for the past decade (Zorrilla, Hartzenbusch, García Gutiérrez, Bretón, Rodríguez Rubí), but new works by Gómez de Avellaneda, Adelardo López de Ayala, Ventura de la Vega, and others, were actively encouraged and received with enthusiasm. Censorship remained in place, but constantly adjusted to meet both the perceived needs of the government that imposed it and the demand for more artistic freedom voiced by playwrights and actors. The two years of the *Bienio Liberal* (Liberal Biennium) (1854–1856) were years of more openness for the stage, but the appearance of Fernando Garrido's anti-monarchical *Un día de revolución* (A Day of Revolution), whose highly charged political message was clearly anathema to a government struggling for legitimacy, initiated the reinstitution of a harsher censorship. Cándido Nocedal stated the problem clearly in December, 1856, referring to both the "perturbaciones políticas" ("political disturbances") and the "perversas tendencias sociales y funesta enseñanza moral" ("perverse social tendencies and dismal moral teachings") he detected in the theatre.[27] The Junta de Censura, a committee which for years had been charged with maintaining the orthodoxy of the theatres gave way in early 1857 to a single individual charged with overseeing the moral and ideological purity of the stage. In some cases well-known intellectuals and playwrights were appointed to the post (Antonio Ferrer del Río held it from 1857 to 1864, Narciso Serra from 1864 to 1867, and Luiz Eguílaz

---

25 Section III of his article "La decadencia de la escena española y el deber del gobierno," *El Globo* (January 1876), reprinted in *Obras de D. Manuel de la Revilla* (Madrid: Imprenta de Víctor Saiz, 1883), 457–479, details his ideas for a national theatre.

26 Eugenio de Ochoa, "Sobre el estado actual de los teatros en España," *Revista Española de Ambos Mundos* , vol. 1 (1853): 62.

27 Cited by Rubio Jiménez, "La censura," p. 203.

held it in its last year of existence, 1868), but they were unsuccessful in imparting any significant degree of freedom to the stage. Some theatres closed, too: both the Variedades and the Circo went temporarily bankrupt in late 1850, and fear was expressed in early 1852 that Temístocles Solera, the impresario of the Teatro Real, would be forced to close his theatre after having suffered a loss of nearly 367,000 *reales*. That fear was realized. As the newspaper *La España* reported in March, "Ya no hay esperanzas. El teatro Real ha fallecido. Los artistas que formaban parte de su compañía lírica empiezan a dispersarse" ("There is no hope left. The Royal Theatre has failed. The artists who made up the lyric company have begun to disperse").

Hundreds of plays were produced, published, and written about in the 1850s which underscored both the social instability of the times and the public's growing discomfort with political realities. New theatres were built but the plays that appeared in them failed to break daring new ground (as had the Romantic plays) or stray from a self-congratulatory bourgeois smugness. As Jesús Rubio Jiménez perceptively writes, "la burguesía, ya no agitadora y revolucionaria, sino instalada en el poder, fue el grupo social que controló en aquellos años la sociedad española. Utilizó el teatro para su lucimiento y para imponer su ideología"[28] ("the middle class, no longer agitated and revolutionary, but rather now installed in power, was the social group which controlled Spanish society during those years. It used the theatre for its own lustre and to impose its ideology").

The fifties were years of transition rather than innovation in Spanish theatre although several playwrights (Tamayo y Baús, Gómez de Avellaneda, Núñez de Arce, and López de Ayala, to name the best-known examples) broke through the morass of conventionality. Theatre was very much alive and would remain so, despite the continuing stream of laments over its imminent demise. Playwrights, critics, impresarios, actors, administrators, and the public in general disagreed, often radically, on what constituted good theatre, but they remained committed to the idea of a viable, active theatrical life in Madrid, and, increasingly, in the provinces.[29] Rodríguez Rubí, Díaz, the Asquerino brothers, Luis Equílaz,

---

[28] Jesús Rubio Jiménez, "El teatro en el siglo XIX (1845–1900)," in *Historia del teatro en España* II, ed. José María Díez Borque (Madrid: Taurus, 1988): 627.

[29] For information on theatrical activity in the provinces, see Francisco Aguilar Piñal, *Cartelera prerromántica sevillana, 1800–1836* (Madrid: CSIC, 1968); Juan Barceló Jiménez, *Historia del teatro en Murcia*, 2nd. edn. (Murcia: Academia de Alfonso X el Sabio, 1980); Rosa Julia Cañada Solaz, "El col.loqui valenciano en los siglos XVIII y XIX," in *Actas de las jornadas sobre teatro popular en España* , eds. Joaquín Alvarez Barrientos and Antonio Cea Gutiérrez (Madrid: CSIC, 1987): 85–107; Francisco Curet, *El arte dramático en el resurgir de Cataluña* (Barcelona: Editorial Minerva, 1917); Xavier Fábregas, *Aproximació a la historia del teatre català* (Barcelona: Curial, 1972); *Historia*

Bretón, and others continued to produce their works, and new voices such as Pérez Escrich (later to be renowned for his steady stream of "novelas folletinescas" ["serialized novels"]), Juan de Ariza, and Narciso Serra were heard ringing out from the playhouses. Many of the plays were written purely for purposes of political propaganda, as happened following O'Donnell's declaration of war against Morocco in 1859, but in others, a growing social consciousness, very different from the conservative complacency of the mass of spectators, was evident. Sixto Cámara and Pablo Avecilla demonstrated a concern for the lower classes, the problems of working conditions, job security, and the division between rich and poor, a concern which would intensify as the years went on, and spill out into the streets by the end of the century. All the same, the Teatro del Circo went bankrupt again in 1858, and shut its doors temporarily.

The decade of the 1850s was "la de mayor producción teatral de todo el siglo XIX"[30] ("the decade of the greatest number of theatrical productions in the entire nineteenth century") and subsequently brought with it significant improvements in theatrical space and comfort. Grimaldi had already made strides towards improving the sight lines, comfort of the seating, and general safety of the theatres in the 1820s and 1830s, but much work remained to be done to bring Madrid's theatres up to the standards held in other European capitals. With the installation of gas lighting many new theatrical effects could be intregrated into plays and the theatres themselves became more pleasant places to spend an evening. Women in particular voiced approval of the new lighting system, not having to duck drippings from the candles nor wipe oil stains from their dresses. Theatres began to acquire gas lighting (the Teatro el Circo, purchased and reconstructed at mid-century by the famously rich banker,

del teatre català (Barcelona: Millà, 1978); Lucio Izquierdo, "El teatro en Valencia (1800–1832)," *Boletín de la Real Academia Española* 69 (1989): 257–305; Joan Mas i Vives, *El teatre a Mallorca a l'època romàntic* (Barcelona: Ediciones Catalanes, 1986); Gabriel Núñez Ruiz, "El teatro en la Almería de Fernando VII," *Cuadernos Hispanoamericanos* 407 (1984): 102–107; Enrique del Pino, *Historia del teatro en Málaga durante el siglo XIX*, 2 vols. (Málaga: Arguval, 1985); *Tres siglos de teatro malagüeño (xvi – xviii)* (Málaga: Sección de Publicaciones, 1974); Mercedes de los Reyes Peña, "El Teatro de Vista Alegre: Un coliseo de segundo orden en la Sevilla de la primera mitad del siglo XIX," *Archivo Hispalense* 70 (1987): 93–114; Emilio Salcedo, *Teatro y sociedad en el Valladolid del siglo XIX* (Valladolid: Ayuntamiento, 1978); Manuel Sanchis Guarner, *Els inicis del teatre valencià modern, 1845–1874* (Università de Valencia, 1980); Antoni Serrà Campins, *El teatre burlesc mallorquí, 1701–1850* (Barcelona: Curiel, 1987); Josep Lluís Sirera, *El teatre Principal de Valencia* (Valencia: Institució Alfons el Magnànim, 1986); María Teresa Suero Roca, *El teatre representat a Barcelona de 1800 a 1830*, 2 vols. (Barcelona: Institut del Teatre, 1987); and Concha María Ventura Crespo, *Historia del teatro en Zamora* (Zamora: n.p., 1988).

30 José Yxart, cited by César Oliva, "Espacio y espectáculo en la comedia de magia de mediados del siglo XIX," in *La comedia de magia y de santos*, eds. F. J. Blasco, E. Caldera, J. Alvarez Barrientos and R. de la Fuente (Madrid: Júcar, 1992): 421.

the Marqués de Salamanca, was among the first to install gas lighting in Madrid; even earlier, the Teatro Principal was outfitted with gas lighting in 1845[31]), and the actual installation of the new lights frequently became a public event. María del Carmen Simón Palmer writes of the opening of the Teatro de la Comedia in 1875:

Siguiendo la costumbre, una semana antes de su inauguración oficial, el 11 de septiembre de 1875, se realizó la prueba del alumbrado, acontecimiento al que acudió numeroso público y muchos periodistas, que elogiaron la decoración del teatro y el tapiz hecho por el señor Vallejo para el telón de la embocadura. El resplandor de los mecheros de gas, que salía por las velas de porcelana blancas, colocadas en candelabros de bronce dorado, distribuidos alrededor de los palcos, resaltaba el aspecto brillante de la sala. Un regulador de todas las luces, ideado por el señor Picoli, permitía rebajar a la mitad la intensidad del gas y podía apagar simultáneamente el alumbrado.[32]

(Following the custom, a week before the official inauguration of the theatre, on 11 September 1875, a test run of the lighting was made, an event attended by a large audience and many journalists, who praised the theatre's decor and the tapestry made by Mr. Vallejo for the front curtain. The brightness of the gas burners, which came out from white porcelain candles located in gilded bronze candelabras, and distributed around the theatre-boxes, underscored the brilliance of the room. A switch for all the lights, conceived by Mr. Picoli, made it possible to turn down the intensity of the gas to half strength and to turn off all the lights simultaneously.)

The following decade saw the consolidation of the "alta comedia" and the continued presence on the boards of old-time melodramas, some remaining vestiges of the "comedia de magia" ("magical comedy") and the final examples of old-time historical drama. Critics kept up their stream of complaints. Rodríguez Rubí joined the chorus of those who lamented the decline of the theatre, but insisted that the theatre would – could, must – revive. "El teatro español se halla enfermo," he declared to his colleagues in the Real Academia Española in 1860, "se encuentra en una de esas crisis que en otras ocasiones ha soportado y vencido heroicamente; pero el teatro español no ha muerto, ¡porque no puede morir!"[33] ("The Spanish theatre is sick; it finds itself in one of those crises which it

---

[31] ... la obra notable, la envidiable mejora que ha recibido este teatro, que lo hace muy superior a todos los de su clase en España, es el brillante alumbramiento de gas; es sorprendente el efecto que produce la elegante, a la par que sencilla lucerna, los hermosos candelabros colocados en los intercolumnios de la embocadura, y la acertada distribución de las luces que iluminan hasta lo más remoto del edificio. *Revista de Teatros*, 11 September 1845.

[32] María del Carmen Simón Palmer, *El gas y los madrileños* (Gas Madrid y Espasa Calpe, 1989): 236.

[33] Tomás Rodríguez Rubí, "Excelencia, importancia y estado presente del teatro," *Discursos leídos ante la Real Academia Española* (Madrid: Matute, 1860): 23.

has suffered before and which it has heroically overcome; but Spanish theatre has not died, because it cannot die!'') García Gutiérrez came back into favor with the production of *Venganza catalana* (Catalan Vengeance) in 1864 (which was instantly parodied by Juan de Alba as *La venganza de Catana* [The Vengeance of Catana] and performed in September of that year, just months after the debut of García Gutiérrez's work) but his next play, *Juan Lorenzo* (1865), ran into trouble with the chief censor Narciso Serra, who saw in it too much "tendencia política" ("political tendency") and sought its prohibition. The ensuing uproar in the press managed to save the play, which was put on as scheduled. Other dramatists who today have been completely relegated to oblivion, such as Enrique Zumel, began careers which in their time brought them considerable attention and acclaim. One of the most interesting innovations of these years was the increased popularity of shorter, satirical and comical pieces played not only during the intermissions of longer, three-act comedies, but also served up themselves as the evening's entertainment. These one-act plays developed into one of the richest, most lucrative (and most ignored) theatrical enterprises of the second half of the century.[34] The theatres themselves changed hands frequently, as they always had, from private entrepreneurs to the city government and back again. When the Teatro Español was put up for rent yet again in March 1865 only one individual came forth to take it over, and the government reluctantly agreed to rent it to a Sr. Roca.

A further step toward the protection of dramatists' rights to share in the profits from their plays occurred in 1867 when the government ruled that any author who had a play run more than twenty-five consecutive nights, and which had covered its costs, would be granted a benefit performance, meaning that the intake from one performance of the play would be given to the author. These benefits were a frequent phenomenon for actors, but now playwrights were to be included (*La Correspondencia de España*, 13 August 1867).[35] Two of the most interesting plays produced in that year were Tamayo's *Un drama nuevo* and *Lances de honor* (Disputes of Honor). The infamous "Noche de San Daniel" (10 April 1865), the Revolution of 1868 and the subsequent exile of Queen Isabel II,

---

[34] The only complete study to date of this interesting phenomenon is the recent doctoral dissertation by Nancy Membrez, "The 'teatro por horas': History, Dynamics and Comprehensive Bibliography of a Madrid Industry, 1867–1922 ('género chico,' 'género ínfimo' and Early Cinema)," University of California at Santa Barbara, 1987. See her article, "The Mass Production of Theater in Nineteenth-Century Spain," *Hispanic Issues* 3 (1988): 309–356. See also Patricia Bentivegna, "Parody in the Género Chico," dissertation, University of Pittsburgh, 1974.

[35] Apparently, the rule was taken seriously. *La Iberia* reported on 14 November 1875 that Echegaray was given a benefit for the success of his drama, *En el puño de la espada*.

brought with them trouble for the theatres along with the by-now expected plays which commented on or otherwise reflected the political storms being weathered in Madrid. The Teatro Español was put up for sale (not for rent) in November. Enrique Zumel summed up the situation most cogently in *Oprimir no es gobernar* (To Oppress is Not to Govern), performed during the same month. The play eschews any pretense at historical cover; it takes place in "Madrid: en nuestros días" ("Madrid: in our times"). In a brief prologue, Zumel writes:

Aunque ningún pueblo necesita vindicarse al conquistar sus sagrados derechos, pues la historia nos enseña que en todo tiempo, cuando una nación ha derrocado a un tirano, ha sido cuando se ha llenado la medida del sufrimiento; y aún cuando la misma historia y la publicidad de los escandalosos hechos que con tanta resignación ha sufrido este noble pueblo español, bastan para que el mundo y las generaciones futuras proclamen la justicia de nuestra santa revolución, he credído oportuno hacer en una escena de familia una caricatura de los ridículos alardes absolutistas que hicieron rebosar el cáliz de amargura que veníamos apurando, proponiéndome dos fines: primero, hacer más públicos aún nuestra razón y nuestro derecho: y segundo, para que vistos de relieve en la escena, nos confirmen en el propósito de que no se vuelvan a repetir jamás.

(Although no nation needs to vindicate itself on winning its sacred rights, history teaches us that in all times, when a nation has brought down a tyrant, it has been when suffering has become too much; and even when history itself and the publicity of scandalous occurrences which this noble Spanish people has suffered with such resignation are sufficient for the world and future generations to proclaim the justice of our sainted revolution, I have thought it opportune to paint in a familiar scene a caricature of the ridiculous absolutist vanity which we were forced to take in, putting forth two goals: first, to publicize once again our reasoning and our rights; and second, once seen clearly on stage, that they strengthen our conviction that such things will never again be repeated.)

They were not repeated, of course (at least not for many years), but the theatre was entering a period characterized by both the difficulty of confronting squarely the social and political realities of Spain and by the fragmentation of dramatic styles. The uncertain political times produced reluctance on the part of public and impresarios alike to stand fully behind the theatre; many lost considerable sums of money in the 1868–1869 season,[36] but most nonetheless reacted directly and quickly to the turmoil of the Revolution of 1868 by staging dramas in keeping with the political times. As Chicote writes:

El 29 de septiembre de 1868 corrió por Madrid la noticia del triunfo de los liberales en la batalla de Alcolea. Fue recibida la buena noticia con vivas a la Revolución, a los personajes triunfadores; por todas las calles manifestaciones de

[36] According to José Subirá, the impresario Teodoro Robles lost 1,645,000 *reales* in one year alone. As usual, the government bailed him out (partially). *Historia y anecdotario del Teatro Real* (Madrid: Plus Ultra, 1949): 202.

alegría ... En los teatros no era menos el regocijo. Arderíus [the main impresario of the day] resucitó la zarzuela titulada *Pan y toros*, de Picón y Barbieri, que había sido prohibida por el Gobierno de Isabel II. D. Pedro Delgado exhumó *Carlos II el hechizado*, de Gil y Zárate. En Novedades estrenaron los apropósitos *La soberanía nacional, El olimpo pronunciado o Esta casa se alquila, y La aurora de la libertad*. En Variedades, *La rendición de la patria*. En la Zarzuela, *El sol de la libertad*, y en el Circo, *España libre* y *El puente de Alcolea*.[37]

(On 29 September 1868, news of the triumph of the liberals in the Battle of Alcolea ran through Madrid. The good news was received with shouts of "long live the Revolution" for the winners; the streets were filled with manifestations of joy ... In the theatres there was no less rejoicing. Arderíus revived the operetta called *Bread and Bulls*, by Picón and Barbieri, which had been banned by the government of Isabel II. D. Pedro Delgado exhumed Gil y Zárate's *Carlos II the Bewitched*. At the Teatro Novedades several short pieces were performed, *National Sovereignty, Olympus in Insurrection, or This House for Rent*, and *The Dawn of Liberty*. At the Teatro Variedades, *The Surrender of the Country*. At the Zarzuela Theatre, *The Sun of Freedom*, and at the Circo, *Free Spain* and *The Bridge at Alcolea*.)

The censors still kept playwrights guessing about what would be permitted and what would be challenged or cut. Censorship was more than arbitrary; it was chaotic. Even José Echegaray, who would dominate playwriting in the final years of the century, complained that "lo difícil es escribir dramas que gusten en época de transición, cuando todo anda revuelto, cuando una sociedad entera vacila y no sabe lo que quiere ni dónde va"[38] ("the difficult thing is to write plays which please the public during times of transition, when everything is all topsy-turvy, when an entire society is wavering and does not know what it wants nor where it is going").

The number of new theatres that were built after 1867 (too many, according to Manuel de la Revilla) underlines the great public interest in theatre in the second half of the century and the public's refusal to abandon one of its most cherished pastimes.[39] Not everyone agreed, naturally, that high activity was equal to high quality. The "decline" of the theatre was still a major topic of conversation. Reacting against what Eduardo de Cortázar characterized as the excessive generosity of newspapers and newspaper critics ("A juzgar por la lectura de ciertos periódi-

---

37 Enrique Chicote, *Cuando Fernando VII gastaba paletó ... Recuerdos y anécdotas del año de la nanita* (Madrid: Instituto Editorial Reus, 1852): 130.
38 Luis Antón del Olmet and Arturo García Carraffa, *Echegaray* (Madrid: Impr. "Alrededor del Mundo", 1912).
39 Teatro de la Esmerelda (1867), Teatro Martín (1870), Teatro Alhambra (1870), Teatro Eslava (1871), Teatro del Circo (1872), Teatro Apolo (1873), and Teatro Romea (1873). See Fernández Muñoz, *Arquitectura teatral*. Revilla's opinion is given in "La decadencia de la escena española y el deber del gobierno," p. 461.

cos, pudiera creerse que cuantas obras se estrenan en los coliseos de Madrid son muy aplaudidas"[40] "to judge from the reading of certain newspapers, one might believe that every work put on in Madrid's theatres is enthusiastically applauded"), he challenged his readers to deny the "decaimiento de nuestro teatro" ("decline of our theatre"). As proof, he published a long series of titles and types of works being performed in the capital's theatres. He was attempting to demonstrate the poor quality of playwriting in his day. What his list unwittingly reveals, however, is the impressive fecundity of playwrights of the period, and the dazzling plethora of new productions on view in Madrid (two or three openings per night). These included twenty-four new productions at the Teatro Español, thirteen at the Teatro del Circo, thirteen at the Teatro de la Zarzuela, fifteen at the Circo de Paul, thirty-three at the Teatro Variedades, thirty-five at the Teatro Martín, thirty-seven at the Teatro Eslava, and eighty-six others, sprinkled around town in various places. The catch was, he complained, that of the total of 267 productions, only 6 were of four-act plays, 39 of three-act plays, 15 of two-act plays, and the rest (207) of one-act plays. "Qué laboriosidad," he writes, "tan infructuosa" ("what a waste of effort"). He clearly equates decline with length, and laments the fact that even famous and talented playwrights waste their time on one-act trivialities. This is one critic's opinion, but not his final word, since in the next year's installment of his overview report of the theatres, he categorizes the 1872–1873 dramatic year as being "fecundísima en cantidad y bien fecunda en calidad"[41] ("very fertile in quantity and quite fertile in quality"), even though a similar range of length versus number of productions was evident.

The laments over the "decadencia" and "rápido decaimiento de nuestro teatro" ("rapid decline of our theatre") continued apace. A lively debate at the Ateneo de Madrid centered on the topics, "Ventajas e inconvenientes del realismo en el arte dramático" ("Advantages and disadvantages of realism in dramatic art") and "¿Se halla decadencia en el teatro español?" ("Is There Decline in Spanish Theatre?") and were followed by many articles in the press.[42] In the newspaper El Globo

---

40 Eduardo de Cortázar, "Crítica estadística-teatral (La temporada de 1871–1872)," *Revista de España* 26 (28 June 1872): 624.

41 Eduardo de Cortázar, "Crítica estadística-teatral (La temporada de 1872–1873)," *Revista de España* 33 (25 July 1873): 282.

42 Among the titles are two by Clarín ("Contrapunto" [*El Solfeo*, 7 March 1875] and "La decadencia del teatro y la protección del gobierno" [*El Solfeo*, 11 April 1876]), and one each by J. Alcalá Galiano ("¿Se halla en decadencia el teatro español?" [*Revista Contemporánea* II, 1876]), Aureliano J. Pereira ("La decadencia del Teatro Español" [*Revista Europea* 1 April 1877]), Demetrio Araujo ("El teatro español y su decadencia," [*Revista Contemporánea* IX, 1877]), and C. Peñaranda ("Algunas observaciones sobre la decadencia del teatro español contemporáneo," [*Revista Contemporánea* XIII, 1878]).

(January, 1876) Manuel de la Revilla printed a polemical article entitled "La decadencia de la escena española y el deber del gobierno" ("The Decline of the Spanish Theatre and the Government's Duty to Remedy It"), which argued that something needed to be done immediately to save the theatre from "una próxima e inevitable ruina" ("an immediate and inevitable ruin"). His opening words could have been written (and, indeed, similar ones frequently were written) in any decade during the nineteenth century.

No hace muchos días que entre las personas que ven con dolor el rápido decaimiento de nuestro teatro corrió la noticia de que a la iniciativa de algunos hombres de elevada posición se debería muy en breve un esfuerzo poderoso en pro de la escena española, esfuerzo a que contribuiría en no pequeña parte S.M.

(Just a few days ago there circulated among people who look with sadness upon the rapid decline of our theatre the news that several highly-placed men will soon initiate a strong effort on behalf of the Spanish stage, an effort to which His Majesty will contribute in no small way.)

Revilla places much of the blame on the poor quality of plays being written by Spanish authors, singling out for special condemnation those who – like José Echegaray, although he remained unnamed here – insisted on "una absurda e insensata restauración romántica que a nada bueno puede conducir" ("an absurd and senseless Romantic revival which can lead to no good end").[43] He also pointed the finger at the "deplorable" organization of the acting companies, which fought openly with one another and became bogged down in petty rivalries, ego battles, and hostilities which affected their work. He correctly underlined the problem of allowing actors to serve both as directors of the companies and, at times, as impresarios, perpetuating a system that lacked checks and balances, and enabled actors to pick roles which favored their talents, or which were just plain easier to perform than some of the more demanding pieces in the repertory. "Judges without appeal," he called them, who behaved like indisciplined autocrats.

The misconduct of the actors had serious repercussions on the playwrights themselves, who wrote their plays wondering whether there would be enough actors in the company to play in them, or when the numbers were sufficient, if the actors would deign to act the part of someone old, ugly, unsympathetic to the audience, or against type. This creates, according to Revilla, a curious and dangerous reversal: "de esta manera el drama se hace para los actores, y no los actores para el drama"

43 Manuel de la Revilla, "La decadencia de la escena española y el deber del gobierno," in *Obras de Manuel de la Revilla* (Madrid: Víctor Saiz, 1883), p. 458. Clayton Baker has studied the relationship between Revilla and Echegaray in "Echegaray and His Critics," unpublished doctoral dissertation, Indiana University, 1969.

("this way the play is made for the actors, and not the actors for the play") (459). Shockingly, the power of the actors was such that playwrights were often forced to write not only specifically delimited parts but also within certain genres, since some actors favored one genre over another and refused to act in (or to act *properly* in) plays not to their generic liking. By the mid-seventies, the old system of passing a new play through various censors, then through a Reading Committee which determined the suitability of the play for performance in the theatre in question, gave way to a system in which the main actor/director had absolute control over what was performed in his theatre, becoming what Revilla called a "comité unipersonal de lectura" ("a single-member reading committee") (459). These are not the complaints of a hysterical critic; time and again throughout the nineteenth century similar accusations are leveled at the poor preparation of the actors, their disdain for roles which they deemed unappealing, and their general lack of professional behavior. It was one of the most contentious points facing Grimaldi in the early 1820s when he attempted to reform the acting guild. Part of his success can be credited to his foresight in marrying the principal company's leading actress and working with her to improve her skills.[44] Larra, too, was consistently articulate on these points.

Echegaray's plays dominate the repertory of the 1870s and 1880s,[45] but many old voices continued to attract the public and several new ones to distinguish themselves. Narciso Serra, Enrique Zumel, Leopoldo Cano, and Enrique Gaspar continued their successful careers while Eugenio Sellés, Eduardo Navarro Gonzalvo and others produced plays worthy of note, plays which often reflected theatrically the same artistic concerns being expressed in the novel, that is, what has come to be called realism,[46] naturalism, and neo-Romanticism. The question of the popular "teatros por horas" ("theatres by hours") ("teatrillos" ["mini-theatres"] as they were often dismissively called) became central in the debate over theatre during this decade. Many serious playwrights and critics loathed them, accusing them of perverting public taste and pandering to the lowest common denominator of "entertainment," to the detriment, naturally, of the serious theatre. In Revilla's words:

[44] See David T. Gies, "Larra, Grimaldi and the Actors of Madrid," *Studies in Eighteenth-Century Literature and Romanticism in Honor of John C. Dowling*, ed. Douglass and Linda Barnette (Newark, Delaware: Juan de la Cuesta Press, 1985): 113–122.

[45] "Don José Echegaray es, a pesar de lo que se haya dicho sobre él, el dramaturgo más representativo y casi único entre 1875 y 1888." Carmen Menéndez Onrubia, "Las 'despedidas' de Antonio Vico y la crisis teatral de 1888–1892," *Segismundo* 19 (1985): 220.

[46] Jesús Rubio Jiménez rightly laments that "El teatro realista español del siglo XIX parece haber caído prácticamente en el olvido." "El realismo escénico a la luz de los tratados de declamación de la época," *Realismo y naturalismo en España en la segunda mitad del siglo XIX*, ed. Yvan Lissorgues (Barcelona, Anthropos, 1988): 257.

No nos asustaría la terrible competencia que hacen a los teatros de primer orden, si en ellos se diera culto al arte; pero sí nos indigna que en su mayor parte se consagren a depravar el gusto artístico y el sentido moral del público que a ellos acude. Cierto que hay algunos en que se cultiva con buen éxito el género cómico, ofreciendo al espectador grato solaz, sin mengua del arte y del público decoro; pero en otros sólo se representan farsas absurdas o inmorales, bufonadas grotescas, piezas políticas de malísimo carácter y otras lindezas análogas, acompañadas no pocas veces de impúdico can-can. (467)

(We would not fear the terrible competition that they give to first-class theatres if there really existed a respect for art; but we are indignant that for the most part these theatres are determined to pervert the artistic taste and the moral senses of the public that attends them. Clearly there are some theatres in which the comic genre is cultivated successfully, offering the spectator a pleasant moment without threat to art or public decorum; but in others only absurd and immoral farces are performed, grotesque buffooneries, political pieces of the most evil nature, and other analogous insults, accompanied not infrequently by the lewd can-can.)

The most interesting innovation of the 1870s is the appearance of several women dramatists, whose plays were not only produced and published, but who achieved a degree of respectability in a profession dominated by men. Women were not an entirely unknown quantity in the theatre. Since the 1840s women dramatists like Manuela Cambronero, Carolina Coronado and Joaquina Vera were staging plays in Madrid and in the provinces, and in the early 1850s, Gertrudis Gómez de Avellaneda competed successfully with her male counterparts to have her plays staged and published, but there did not exist either a tradition of women writing for the stage or a core group of female dramatists. After 1876, however, several women playwrights followed in Gómez de Avellaneda's footsteps to produce works of lasting worth and public acceptance. Rosario de Acuña y Villanueva's *Rienzi el tribuno* (Rienzi the Political Orator, 1876)[47] and *Amor a la patria* (Love of the Fatherland, 1877) and Elisa de Luxán de García Dana's *Ethelgiva* (1877) initiated a small but important flowering of works written by women. The final year of this decade also brought with it a reinforcement of the copyright regulations of 1849, putting playwrights on firmer financial ground.

Not surprisingly, the 1880s opened with the oft-heard laments over the crisis of the theatre, its decline and possible death, but some voices remained optimistic that solutions could be found to the many problems plaguing Spanish theatre. Julio Nombela showed himself to be critical, yet hopeful.

---

[47] An excellent modern edition of this play has just been published by María del Carmen Simón Palmer, *Rienzi el tribuno. El padre Juan* (Madrid: Castalia, 1990) (Biblioteca de Escritoras 14).

En los momentos en que emprendemos tan difícil tarea sigue siendo el Teatro, porque esa es su misión fatal, reflejo del estado intelectual, afectivo y social de la época en que vivimos. Como la sociedad actual, atraviesa una crisis profunda ... Pero esos períodos de crisis, de vacilación, de locura, por largos que parezcan pasan, y el enfermo se cura o muere. Cuando una institución social tiene las raíces que el Teatro tiene en Europa y particularmente en España, por quebrantada que parezca, por enferma que esté, puede salvarse y robustecerse.[48] (*El Teatro*, 25 April 1880)

(In the moments when we begin such a difficult task the Theatre continues to be, because this is its fatal mission, a reflection of the intellectual, emotional, and social state of the period in which we live. Like contemporary society, it is going through a profound crisis ... But those periods of crisis, of vacilation, of craziness pass, no matter how long they may seem to last, and the patient either gets better or dies. When a social institution has the deep roots that Theatre has in Europe and, particularly, in Spain, no matter how broken it may seem to be, no matter how sick it is, it can save itself and become stronger.)

He categorically denied the reports on the theatre's demise: "¿Pero es cierto que el Teatro español se halla tan achacoso, tan enfermo, tan moribundo como le pintan los que viven de su calor o siquiera de sus reflejos? Yo me atrevo a negarlo" ("But is it true that Spanish Theatre is as unhealthy, as ill, as moribund as it is being painted by those who live off its warmth or even off its reflection? I would dare to deny it") (*El Teatro*, 25 May 1880).

By the 1880s the influence of foreign theatre was again notable in Spain, just as it had been in the first half of the century. Zola and naturalistic theatre became fashionable, and realism, which had been the dominant narrative mode for nearly a decade, made its appearance on the stage as well.[49] However, it is difficult to point to any one style which monopolized theatrical activity in these years; even the "neo-Romantic" Echegaray tried his hand at several different styles. Rather, a rich mixture of interests, themes, forms, and styles characterizes the playwriting of the period. Realism, naturalism, neo-Romanticism, socialism, incipient symbolism and other "-isms" jostled with parodies, religious plays, political satires, and musicals for the attention of critics and the public. The first play ever to achieve three hundred (!) consecutive performances was a political satire with music by Navarro Gonzalvo entitled *Los bandos de Villa-frita* (The Edicts of Villa-frita, 1884) which reached three published editions in the *five months* following its première in August of that year.

[48] Nombela recapped the general view of the decline of theatre in the next issue of *El Teatro* (25 May 1880): "Autores, actores, críticos, aficionados, hasta el público mismo que tanto afecto profesa en nuestro país al arte teatral, viene desde hace algunos años repitiendo que el Teatro español se halla en lastimoso período de decadencia."

[49] See Jesús Rubio Jiménez, "La recepción crítica del naturalismo teatral en España," *Boletín de la Biblioteca Menéndez Pelayo* 62 (1986): 345–357, and "El realismo escénico."

As was to be expected, though, success for one theatre did not necessarily mean success for all theatres; when the administrators of the Teatro Apolo declared bankruptcy in mid-1883, the recently-formed Sociedad de Autores (a society of intellectuals whose plan was to "regenerar el arte lírico-dramático nacional" ["regenerate national lyrical and dramatic art"]) took over the theatre and tried to make a go of it. The price of acquisition of a theatre was not small. In 1889 the impresario of the Teatro Maravillas, Joaquín de la Concha Alcalde, paid three million *reales* for the Teatro Príncipe Alfonso, a sum difficult to recoup but which nonetheless did not inhibit investment in the theatres (*El Imparcial*, 6 January 1889). It was during this decade that the government decreed that electric lighting should replace the gas lights used in the theatres since the mid-fifties, although between the decree and the actual implementation of it there remained a gap of many years, in part due to public resistance to the noise of electric steam generators: "Se instala entonces la luz eléctrica, pero un año más tarde los vecinos de las casas colindantes solicitan del Ayuntamiento que prohíba el funcionamiento de la nueva máquina de vapor que la produce. El ruido del artefacto era, al parecer, insoportable y les impedía dedicarse a sus ocupaciones y reposo, además de ocasionar con su trepidación oscilaciones en las fincas 'como de terremoto' "[50] ("Electric light is installed then, but one year later the neighbors of the surrounding houses asked City Hall to ban the new steam machine that produced it. The contraption's noise, it seemed, was unbearable, and it interrupted their work and sleep, in addition to causing 'earth-quake like' vibrations on their property"). Gas and electricity competed with each other in the theatres for several decades to come.

In some regards, the final decade of the century brought with it an upsurge in theatrical activity, both in quantity and in quality, although it started out displaying few signs of health. Luis Alfonso pointed out in the pages of *El Imparcial* (9 December 1889) that of Madrid's eleven theatres only two gave themselves over regularly to serious or original plays, the others being crammed with operas sung in foreign languages and "funciones por horas," the short, burlesque-like pieces which had become so popular in the past fifteen years. This was a crisis, indeed, since once-noble theatres – the Apolo, Lara, Alhambra, Price, Martín, Eslava – were forced to put on superficial spectacles ("fútiles y livianos espectáculos" ["useless and libidinous spectacles"] in the words of Alfonso) in order to survive financially. The theatres had settled into a kind of routine: opera was generally restricted to the Teatro Real; musical comedies and short pieces appeared at the Apolo, Eslava and Zarzuela; "juguetes cómicos"

[50] Simón Palmer, *El gas*, p. 237.

(comic one-act pieces) were put on at the Lara; melodramas at the Novedades; translated French comedies at the Princesa; Spanish classics at the Español; and at the Teatro de la Comedia, under the enlightened leadership of Emilio Mario, contemporary Spanish plays and plays of a more experimental nature.[51]

The years from 1888 to 1892 were fraught with tension and difficulty. Still, the great novelist Galdós had tried his hand at playwriting, and the results turned out to be as exciting as they were controversial: *Realidad* marked a new moment in Spanish theatrical history. Other progressive authors such as Clarín and Pardo Bazán wrote plays, and the best of the lot, Enrique Gaspar, Angel Guimerà, Eugenio Sellés, and Narciso Oller attempted to infuse their works with the social ideals they defended as much in front of the footlights as behind them. Progressive actors such as Antonio Vico struggled to create a serious theatre which could compete with the zarzuelas,[52] "teatro por horas" and sentimental comedies which seemed to dominate the stage. María Guerrero, one of the brightest and most energetic actress/impresarios ever to work in Madrid, became a powerful voice in the capital's theatrical circles. Maeterlinck and Ibsen influenced Spanish playwrights (Echegaray's *El hijo de don Juan* [Don Juan's Son], 1891, is a notable example), Jacinto Benavente began to produce his subtle dissections of the Spanish middle class, and workers' theatre came into vogue, particularly in Barcelona. In fact, sometime after the 1880s the theatrical balance of power began slowly to shift from Madrid to Barcelona, or at least it began to tilt. Previously, a nearly direct line of influence radiated out from Madrid to the provinces. Plays were performed first in the capital, followed later by performances in the provinces, either by actors from the Madrid companies on tour (mostly during the summer months) or by homegrown, local companies. Such activity created a pattern like the spokes of a wheel with Madrid as the hub. However, artistic vitality in Barcelona was such that it began to welcome new types of theatre and to develop new models before Madrid. What have come to be called "teatro anárquico" ("Anarchist theatre") and "teatro obrero" ("worker's theatre") were welcomed much more warmly in Barcelona than in Madrid, and Barcelona gradually developed the reputation of being a more cosmopolitan – European – city than the capital. Theatre in Spanish and in Catalán flourished in Barcelona, and playwrights such as Víctor Balaguer and Angel Guimerà consistently

---

[51] See Gonzalo Sobejano, "Efectos de *Realidad*," *Estudios Escénicos* 8 (1974): 55.

[52] The passion for zarzuela became a type of national obsession in the 1890s similar to the "furor filarmónico" protested by serious dramatists in the 1820s and 1830s. Fernando Porset remembered that many of the biggest stars of the day were "tiples" (sopranos) who sang in the zarzuelas (Antonia Arrieta, Rosario Soler, and Luisa Campos, for example). *De telón adentro* (Madrid: R. Álvarez, 1912): 35.

created new models aimed at the audience in Cataluña rather than that in Madrid.[53]

It is curious and disconcerting to follow the ebb and flow of theatrical activity during the nineteenth century since the attentive reader experiences an odd mixture of *déjà vu* when reading of the unending struggles undergone by impresarios, actors, and playwrights, combined with bursts of confidence in the strides taken. Bankruptcy, war, political conflict, economic stagnation, illness, epidemic and death, excessive heat, and strikes, were just some of the many calamities which forced theatres to close for short periods of time. Actors and their families lived in constant fear of national catastrophes because one of the first institutions to suffer was the theatre, which closed for periods of national mourning such as that which followed the death of Fernando VII in 1833. When the theatres closed, the actors lost all income, since pensions and unemployment insurance were tied to gate receipts and were not yet institutionalized for them. "Thousands" of families (according to the *Semanario Teatral*) suffered real hardships between October 1833 when the King died and December of that year when the Queen Regent finally allowed the theatres to reopen. During that time the actors had begged for help and had been granted half-salaries by the Queen Regent, but even that was not enough to stave off misery. Sometimes it was a public epidemic, such as the one in 1865 as reported by *El Contemporáneo* ("La empresa del teatro Variedades decide suspender las representaciones dramáticas sólo por el tiempo que duren las circunstancias por que está atravesando el vecindario de Madrid a causa de la enfermedad reinante" ["The owners of the Teatro Variedades decide to suspend performances only as long as the situation caused by the current sickness in Madrid lasts"], 22 October) or the one reported by *La Iberia* in 1889 ("Se han reunido los empresarios de teatro con el fin de acordar el cierre de sus puertas, solicitando del gobierno una Real Orden que declare epidémica la enfermedad reinante" ["Theatre owners have met to reach agreement about closing their doors, asking the government for a Royal Decree that declares the current illness a full-fledged epidemic"], 31 December) which closed the theatres. Other times, closures were caused by illnesses suffered by the actors themselves, such as those which forced the Teatro Real to shut its doors in February 1896. The country-wide War of Independence and the Carlist Wars naturally had had an adverse effect on the stability of theatres, but even smaller disturbances could force them to suspend performances, as happened in 1873 when the growing pains of the First Republic caused "inestabilidad política" ("political instability") which reverberated over

---

[53] Xavier Fábregas details the history of theatre in Cataluña in *Història del teatre català* .

the Teatro Madrid (*La Iberia*, 3 July 1873). Even a natural phenomenon threatened the livelihood of the actors: an unseasonable heat wave at the end of May, 1873, forced the impresario of the Teatro Eslava to cancel all performances for several days (*La Iberia*, 30 May 1873). By the end of the century strikes and work stoppages caused most of the disturbances in the theatres. Early in January, 1896, for example, the musicians threatened to close the Teatro Real over a dispute created when the previous year's impresario left his post without paying their full wages; the new impresario refused to take over old debts, and the entire orchestra threatened to stop work (*La Iberia*, 9 January 1896). Shortly thereafter, actors refused to perform at the Teatro Eslava when the owners were delinquent with their salary payments (*La Epoca*, 26 January 1896).

Throughout the century attempts had been made to improve acting technique. Juan de Grimaldi had proposed in the mid-twenties a drama school where actors could learn the details of their craft, a suggestion finally realized when Queen María Cristina established the Real Conservatorio de Música y Declamación in 1831. The Conservatorio functioned efficiently but with little real success. Although many great actors ended up teaching there (among them, Carlos Latorre, Julián Romea, Antonio Vico, Fernando Díaz de Mendoza, Matilde Díez and Teodora Lamadrid), it never produced the desired core of skilled actors which had been the hope of its founders. Dozens of manuals for actors had been written and published since the beginning of the century, with a notable acceleration following Fernando VII's death.[54] These manuals addressed acting technique, gesture, oratory, voice projection, facial expression, costumes, education, and other matters associated with the acting profession, and many were written by the century's most respected practitioners of the art, such as Latorre, Romea (who assigned his text to his students at the Conservatorio, accounting perhaps for the numerous reprints published during his lifetime), Manuel Catalina, and Vico.[55] At intervals calls were repeated for centers of acting, government support for actors in the process of learning and improving their craft, and government-funded

[54] An excellent bibliography is provided by Rubio Jiménez, "El realismo escénico," pp. 279–282.

[55] Carlos Latorre, *Noticias sobre el arte de la declamación* (Madrid: Yenes, 1839); Julián Romea, *Manual de declamación para uso de los alumnos del Real Conservatorio de Madrid)* (Madrid: F. Abienzo, 1858; reprinted and augmented in 1859, 1865, and 1879); Manuel Catalina, *Los actores* (Madrid: Víctor Sáiz, 1877); and Antonio Vico, "Isidoro Máiquez, Carlos Latorre y Julián Romea. La escena española desde comienzos de siglo. La declamación en la tragedia, en el drama y en la comedia de costumbres," in his *La España del siglo XIX* (Madrid: Ateneo, 1886). Other manuals were written by Juan Lombía, *El teatro*, and Ramón de Valladares y Saavedra, *Nociones acerca de la historia del teatro, desde su nacimiento hasta nuestros días* (Madrid: Imprenta de la Publicidad, 1848).

Chairs in Acting Theory and Practice. Larra's famous spoof of actors, "Yo quiero ser cómico" ("I Want to be an Actor" 1833) voiced publicly what many had been concerned with for years. What we read in *La Iberia* in late 1876 could have been written in any decade of the century:

La empresa del teatro de Novedades, que está formando una excelente compañía de declamación en la que ya figuran primeros actores de los teatros de esta corte, ha solicitado del ministro de Fomento una autorización para establecer en aquel coliseo una cátedra teórico-práctica de declamación que deberá abrirse cuando comience a funcionar dicho teatro. (13 September 1876)

(The owner of the Novedades Theatre, which is forming an excellent acting company in which the principal actors of the theatres of the capital are already included, has asked the Minister of Public Works for permission to establish in his theatre a special theoretical and practical Chair of Acting which would open as soon as said theatre becomes operational.)

In part, the crisis of the 1888–1892 period was caused by the death of one great actor, Rafael Calvo (1888), and the decision of another, Antonio Vico, to tour America. Until the appearance of María Guerrero, the other actors were not competent enough to carry the full weight of serious theatre, although in increasing numbers they insisted on being called "primeros actores" ("principal actors"), an absurd designation since any one company could hardly have more than one or two truly leading roles.[56] Vico, who worked primarily at the Teatro Español where he also served as impresario, was accused of accelerating the "death" of that theatre, but he and his defenders claimed that his decision to leave was hastened by the already notable decline in serious theatre in Madrid. He viewed his travails as a "lucha titánica" ("Titanic struggle"), one he was no longer capable of waging.[57] Embittered, Vico left Madrid and did not return until 1895.

Vico's case is symptomatic of the troubles which plagued Madrid's theatres in the 1890s. He was an inspired actor, but an exceedingly unreliable one; reports on his performances frequently complained that he saved his voice, coasted through scenes, "muttered" speeches, and really acted only when he felt like it . As an impresario, he lost money due in part to his lack of concern for the financial aspects of the enterprise. José Deleito y Piñuela, a friend and observer of Vico's, confessed that he did not bother to select the works to be performed with any care nor did

---

[56] Fernando Porset complained of this inflation where every actor is a "first." *De telón adentro*, p. 65.

[57] His letter to *El Imparcial* (28 December 1889) is reproduced by Carmen Menéndez Onrubia, "Las 'despedidas' de Antonio Vico," pp. 227–229. Vico's troubles were aggravated by an injury he suffered during a performance of Zorrilla's *El zapatero y el rey*, when a bridge he was on collapsed, causing him to fall "desde una altura muy elevada."

he give enough thought to their staging and rehearsals.[58] The consequence of this carelessness, of course, was that the audience voted with its feet and went to the Teatro de la Comedia or the Teatro Real for diversion. Ironically, however, Vico's abandonment of Madrid did not bring about "la muerte del Teatro Español" ("the death of the Teatro Español"), as Ortega Munilla forecast in *El Imparcial* (30 December 1889); on the contrary, it seemed to bring new life to it when Rafael Calvo's brother Ricardo took over the reins. In 1895 Joaquín Dicenta's *Juan José* created a tidal wave of criticism by glorifying a proletarian hero, a man very different from the comfortable bourgeois gentilshommes typically seen on Spanish stages. This play, following quickly on the heels of other social dramas such as Felíu y Codina's *La Dolores* (1892), L. Cano's *La pasionaria* (The Passionaria, 1893), Guimerà's *María Rosa* (1894), and Clarín's *Teresa* (1895), marks, in Jaime Mas's words, a moment which "nos conduce a lo que hoy entendemos por drama contemporáneo"[59] ("leads us towards what we understand today as contemporary drama").

Other aspects of the theatre, such as the teaching and study of scenery painting and stage design, never got beyond theory, although there were brilliant and highly acclaimed set designers working in Madrid since the mid-twenties, when Grimaldi imported Juan Blanchard from Paris to design the sets and curtains for the Cruz and Príncipe theatres.[60]

Throughout the nineteenth century much ink was spilled in an attempt to identify the problems of the theatre (this was easy) and to correct them (this was more difficult). The seriousness of the enterprise was never in question, since the existence of a "glorious" national theatre tradition became inextricably linked with a national sense of self-worth. Honorable theatre was, in many minds, one of the last vestiges of national glory. As Spain gradually sank into a political stupor, wracked with wars at home and abroad, and struggling to maintain a dignity that was strongly identified with the Golden Age, the theatre became emblematic not only of the troubles facing the country, but also of its hope for recovery. Renewed attacks against the "plague" of foreign translations were heard in words which echoed similar words written in the first half of the century. Spanish national theatre came to be seen as the last line of defense against a general decay. Revilla stated the equation with typical candor in 1876:

---

[58] José Deleito y Piñuela, *Estampas del Madrid teatral fin de siglo* (Madrid: Saturnino Calleja, [1946]): 82.
[59] Joaquín Dicenta, *Juan José*, ed. Jaime Mas (Madrid: Cátedra, 1982): 47.
[60] Attempts to codify set design came late in the century. Julio Nombela, *Proyecto de bases para la fundación de una escuela especial del arte teatral* (Madrid: Imprenta del Hospicio,

fácil es comprender que urge poner un remedio fuerte a la aflictiva situación de nuestra escena, si no se quiere que se hunda en el abismo el teatro español, *único resto de nuestras gloriosas tradiciones y de nuestra pasada grandeza.* (461–462; emphasis added)

(it is easy to understand the urgent need to find a strong cure for the distressing situation of our theatre, if one does not want Spanish theatre, *the last remnant of our glorious traditions and of our past greatness,* to sink into the abyss.)

The theatre in Spain changed in significant ways during the nineteenth century. What never changed was the precariousness of the enterprise and the constant calls for reform. As a new century dawned, new critics took up the lament, among them M. Martínez Espada, who decried "la ruina de la dramática española, que agoniza con espantosa rapidez"[61] ("the ruin of Spanish playwriting, which is dying with frightening swiftness"), and Fernando Porset, who stated categorically, "En los tiempos infaustos que corremos, el arte de Talía camina dando tumbos por diversos y tortuosos caminos, sin rumbo fijo y, lo que es más deplorable todavía, sin lucimiento alguno"[62] ("In these accursed times in which we live, the art of Thalia stumbles along diverging and tortuous paths, without a fixed course and, more deplorable yet, without any splendour whatsoever"). José Yxart, the most distinguished theatre critic of his time, nonetheless discerned a ray of hope which countered the avalanche of negative opinion heaped on the theatre:

a despecho del eterno grito pesimista de que el teatro se muere, lo positivo es que en todas las naciones europeas vemos enardecerse el anhelo de reformas teatrales. Las nuevas generaciones literarias vuelven a soñar con el teatro ... Hay todavía quien toma el teatro como el instrumento más hábil para satisfacer sus nuevos deseos de creación artística.[63]

(in spite of the eternal pessimistic chorus that the theatre is dying, the positive note is that in all European nations we can detect an impulse toward theatrical renovation. New literary generations are beginning to dream again about the theatre ... There still are those who view the theatre as the best means to satisfy their new desires for artistic creation.)

The nineteenth century had been one which witnessed the staging and publication of thousands of plays, written by men and women of talent and conviction. It is a century which produced important and enter-

---

1886) and Sebastián Carner, *Tratado de arte escénico* (Barcelona: La Hormiga de Oro, 1890) are two examples recorded by Rubio Jiménez, "El realismo escénico," p. 282.

61 M. Martínez Espada, *Teatro contemporáneo. Apuntes para un libro de crítica* (Madrid: Ducazcal, 1900): 28.

62 Porset, *De telón adentro*, p. 160.

63 José Yxart, *El arte escénico en España*, 2 vols. (Barcelona: La Vanguardia, 1894–1896); repr. Barcelona: Alta Fulla, 1987). Cited here from I: 242.

taining plays by Larra, Martínez de la Rosa, Grimaldi, Bretón de los Herreros, Rivas, García Gutiérrez, Hartzenbusch, Rodríguez Rubí, Vega, Gil y Zárate, Zorrilla, Asquerino, Gómez de Avellaneda, Tamayo y Baús, López de Ayala, Eguílaz, Núñez de Arce, Zumel, Acuña, Serra, Echegaray, Guimerà, Sellés, Cano, Dicenta, Burgos, Navarro Gonzalvo, Gaspar, Galdós, and dozens of other authors. The richness of the activity belies the constant stream of death notices: the theatre lumbered on.

2   Theatre and dictatorship: from Napoleon to Fernando VII

The Revolution and the *comedia*

Logically, theatrical activity in the capital should have come to a halt with the invasion of Napoleon's troops in May, 1808. The city was in chaos, its inhabitants fighting heroically in the streets for their freedom, shedding blood to defend the right of the legitimate rulers of the country, the Bourbon monarchs, to remain on the throne. The theatres did close for four days during the most intense period of fighting, then opened briefly in June only to be forced again to shut their doors due to an inability to sell tickets to their performances.[1] However, Joseph Bonaparte, Napoleon's brother, who had been installed as King of Spain, quickly perceived the value of the theatre as a useful tool in his battle to win over the hearts of his new subjects. Clearly considering the theatres to be an "instrument de propagande,"[2] he ordered them to reopen in December, 1808 and set about trying to calm and "educate" the masses in Madrid. He subsidized the theatres directly in an effort to control them. What was forthcoming, as the power balance shifted from the French occupation force to the Spanish nationalists throughout the course of the war, was a surprising growth of theatrical activity. Perhaps one of the reasons for this seemingly contradictory phenomenon (that is, during intense war one would expect to see less activity in the theatre rather than more) is summed up by the author of an article in the *Semanario Patriótico* of Cádiz in 1812, who wrote: "Pero el teatro no sólo es un ramo tan interesante de literatura, es también una de las atenciones más delicadas de la policía de las capitales, y suele ser un instrumento muy poderoso en manos de la política"[3] ("But the theatre is not just an interesting branch of literature, it is also one of the most delicate affairs for the policing of capital cities, and it tends to be a very powerful instrument in the hands of political leaders").

[1] This difficult period is documented by Cotarelo, *Máiquez*, chapter 12.
[2] Larraz, *Théâtre et politique*, p. 2.
[3] Cited by Larraz, *ibid.* p. 1.

40

Hence, theatre was clearly viewed as much as a political and social activity as it was a literary one, a view which will be maintained throughout the nineteenth century. Theatre was naturally not the only tool in the war of propaganda (newspapers, pamphlets, fliers, brochures and other easy-to-move and -hide printed media were especially useful), but the theatre seemed to lend itself especially well to political needs. It was instantaneous and stirring. These are the years when Spain experienced what Jorge Campos has called "el nacimiento del teatro patriótico"[4] ("the birth of patriotic theatre").

The nature of that "birth" took two forms. One was the scouring of the classical repertory for plays which would solidify the political aspirations of the ruling party, thereby confirming the legitimacy of, in turns, the Bourbon kings or the French government. The other was the production of new plays which either reflected political realities (battles won or lost on both sides), attempted to create a new mind-set in the audience, or disparaged the "tyranny" and "oppression" of the enemy. Attendance at one play or another, therefore, became a kind of political statement by the audience and, as Larraz has demonstrated, the majority of the inhabitants of Madrid simply voted with their feet: the anti-French plays put on by the Spanish nationalists in September drew good crowds, but when the French regained control of the theatres in December, and began to stage dramas designed to convince the city's inhabitants of the enlightened nature of the French occupation, the people simply stayed away. Larraz guesses that the December performances attracted less than fifty people per day.[5]

The plays written by the Spanish nationalists during the brief respite from French rule (August–December, 1808) and from exile during the course of the war were clearly designed to stir up the emotions of the populace against the invading forces, to reconfirm the "glorious" nature of the Spanish state, to mock the French government, and to prepare the people for the struggle which lay ahead. Many were written quickly for the occasion, others were dredged up from the repertory and retooled for the current purposes. Allegory became particularly useful, and numerous plays appeared in which "Spain," "Freedom," "Joy," "Abundance," "Virtue," and other figures underscored the importance of the resistance against the French and the heroic nature of the Spanish people. Three of the most popular writers of these anti-French tirades were Gaspar Zavala y Zamora, Félix Enciso Castrillón, and Luciano Francisco Comella.

Zavala y Zamora (1762–?), contemporaneous with the younger

---

[4] Jorge Campos, *Teatro y sociedad en España (1780–1820)* (Madrid: Moneda y Crédito, 1969): 143.
[5] Larraz, *Théâtre et politique*, p. 35.

Moratín (b. 1760), was one of the best-known playwrights of the period. He had written a steady stream of hit plays in the last years of the eighteenth century and the first years of the nineteenth, and had gained the enmity of the Neoclassicists for his refusal to write according to the "rules of art" as they defined them. The "Plan de Reforma" ("Plan for Reform") published by the Neoclassicists in 1799 went so far as to ban several of his plays for their disdain of such elements as verisimilitude, decorum, and the three unities.[6] His plays tended to reach for spectacular effects rather than for ideas or reasoned emotion, and he consequently became known as a creator of a type of "national heroic drama."[7] Of particular interest for our purposes are three plays written and published in Madrid in 1808 in response to the French invasion: *Los patriotas de Aragón* (The Patriots of Aragón), *La alianza española con la nación inglesa. Alegoría cómica en un solo acto* (The Spanish Allegiance with the English Nation. Comic Allegory in One Act), and *La sombra de Pelayo, o El día feliz de España. Drama alegórico en un acto* (Pelayo's Shadow, or The Happy Day of Spain. Allegorical Drama in One Act).

  The first of these plays, *Los patriotas de Aragón*, was performed on 24 September and dealt with the defense of Zaragoza by General José de Palafox against the French siege. As we might expect, it was bombastic, biased, and uplifting, ending with the people of Zaragoza singing, "Zagales del Ebro / laureles cojed / y a nuestros guerreros / ciñamos la sien" ("Fine youth of the Ebro River, pick up your laurels and let us place them on the brows of our warriors"). Zavala enjoyed so much success with the play that he produced a second part two months later,[8] although neither play can be said to contain much literary merit. The same can be said for *La alianza española*. Its allegory left no room for subtleties and even the most uneducated audience would be expected to comprehend the visual messages being presented by the author. As the play opens, "El Orgullo Francés" (French Pride) is seen surrounded by Commerce, Navigation, Industry, Agriculture and "demás artes" ("other arts") all of whom are asleep at his feet.

---

[6] Guillermo Carnero, "Recursos y efectos escénicos en el teatro de Gaspar Zavala y Zamora," *Bulletin Hispanique* 91 (1989): 22. See also his "Temas políticos contemporáneos en el teatro de Gaspar Zavala y Zamora,"*Teatro politico spagnolo del primo ottocento*, ed. Ermanno Caldera (Roma: Bulzoni, 1991): 19–41, and two studies by Rosalía Fernández Cabezón, "Pervivencia de Calderón de la Barca en los albores del siglo XIX: *El soldado exorcista* de Gaspar Zavala y Zamora," *El teatro español a fines del siglo XVII*, ed. Javier Huerta Calvo (Rodopi: Amsterdam, 1989): 623–635, and "Los sainetes de Gaspar Zavala y Zamora," *Castilla* 12 (1987): 59–72.

[7] See I. L. McClelland, *The Origins of the Romantic Movement in Spain* (Liverpool University Press, 1937): 242–258.

[8] Cotarelo discusses *Los patriotas de Aragón. Segunda parte* in *Máiquez*, p. 292. It was performed in Madrid on 22 November 1808.

Obra fue mía, y me complazco en ella,
indómita Nación: el día vino
en que abatiese tu altanera frente
la francesa política. Hartos siglos
burlaste su poder: mas ya por siempre
huelle mi pie tus glorias y tu brillo.[9]

(It was my work, and I take pride in it, ungoverned nation: the day came in which French politics brought down your haughty brow. For centuries you mocked its power: but now forever let my foot trample on your glories and your lustre.)

When España enters, "con diadema real, y manto sembrado de Castillos y Leones" ("with a royal diadem, and a cloak covered with castles and lions") she addresses the sleeping arts:

¿Por qué me abandonasteis, si sabíais
que erais delicia, apoyo y dulce asilo
de vuestra madre tierna? Sin vosotras,
¿cómo arrostrar a tantos enemigos
que con tesón ansiaban mi ruina?
Cedí al fin a su fuerza, y de sus tiros
fui víctima infeliz. Gemí hasta [a]hora
el estrangero yugo, y mis dominios
de la calamidad y la miseria
sufrieron el rigor.   (p. 86)

(Why did you abandon me, if you knew you were the delight, support and sweet refuge of your tender mother? Without you, how could I shake off so many enemies who tenaciously longed for my ruin? I finally gave myself over to their force, and I became the unhappy victim of their fire. I bemoaned their foreign yoke until now, and my domains suffered the harshness of calamity and misery.)

She confronts "El Orgullo Francés" by reminding him that Spain's real King is "Fernando / el desgraciado, el fuerte, el perseguido, / centro de la virtud y la constancia" ("Fernando the disgraced, the strong, the persecuted, center of virtue and constancy") (90) whom they are fighting to rescue from the "lazos" ("snares") that bind him. Fernando's portrait is unveiled in a scene whose visual imagery the audience at the Teatro Príncipe could readily understand: "Corren las Virtudes el pavellón, y se descubre un rico cuadro, que representa a Fernando VII, y a sus pies cubiertos de un mismo manto, y coronados de un mismo laurel, los escudos de España, e Inglaterra, enlazados con la banda ... saliendo de su boca este lema: *Mientras la fe os una sereis irresistibles*" ("The Virtues open the curtain and uncover a rich painting of Fernando VII, and at his feet, covered by a mantle and crowned with laurel, the coats-of-arms of

---

[9] Gaspar Zavala y Zamora, *La alianza española con la nación inglesa*, in *La guerre d'indépendance espagnole au théâtre: 1808–1814. Antologie*, ed. Emmanuel Larraz (Aix-en-Provence: Université de Provence, 1987): 82. All quotations are from this edition.

Spain and England, linked together with a sash on which one reads this motto: *As long as faith unites you, you will be unbeatable"*) (96). "El Orgullo Francés" confesses defeat ("Ya acabó la esperanza que tenía / de extinguir su valor y patriotismo" ["Thus ends the hope I had of extinguishing her valor and patriotism"] [96]) and the allegory closes with a series of choruses expressing the joy and happiness of a free Spain.

The third piece drew upon the audience's knowledge of one of the most highly praised Spanish historical figures, Pelayo, the hero of the Christian Reconquest who had recently (1805) been brought to their attention by Quintana's tragedy. *La sombra de Pelayo*, performed on 14 October 1808 (in celebration of Fernando VII's birthday), contains much ranting about Spanish valor, freedom, and loyalty, and harshly criticizes the by-now despised Godoy. It draws upon a deeply rooted dichotomy of Spanish history, that of the "infidel" Moors against the embattled Christians, which had traditionally been resurrected during times of political stress. The myth of the Crusade turned the War of Independence into another Holy War against Islam, a myth reflected on the stages of Madrid. In *La sombra*, Pelayo appears to Spain in a dream and encourages her to rise up in rebellion against her oppressors. The play has little literary merit (Cotarelo judges it "largo y malo"[10] ["long and bad"]), but visually it is interesting because Zavala includes here, as he had done before, settings and costumes which serve as emblems for the action. The audience witnesses characters in costumes which symbolize their status in the play; it opens, for example, with "España sentada, y apoyado el rostro sobre una mano, y con cadenas"[11] ("Spain seated, in chains, supporting her head on her hand") and maintains a clear visual notion of good versus evil, Spain versus France, nobility versus deceit, etc. The audiences, exposed as they had been for years to the *autos sacramentales* (allegorical one-act plays), had no difficulty understanding the allegory and no doubt cheered loudly, as Spain – with the help of the ghost of Pelayo – succeeded in awakening the sleeping Bravery and Loyalty in order to defeat Despotism and his "dulces pasiones" ("sweet passions"), Adulation, Ambition, Greed, Pride, Lust, Selfishness, and Cruelty. Pelayo's last words unite Spain's past glories with her desired future in a condensed civics lesson for the audience.

> Ya respiraste, España, ya por siempre
> acabó tu tirano Despotismo,

10 Cotarelo, *Máiquez*, p. 291.
11 Gaspar Zavala y Zamora, *La sombra de Pelayo o el día feliz de España*, in Larraz, *Antologie*, p. 51. A survey of the drawings and cartoons published during the War of Independence is found in Claudette Dérozier's *La Guerre d'Independance espagnole à travers l'estampe (1808–1814)*, 2 vols. (Université de Lille III, 1976).

debiendo a la memoria de Pelayo
tu gran restauración. Alza al Olimpo
esa abatida frente: reconoce
en tu adorado Príncipe el alivio
de tus amargas penas; pues el cielo
desde su caos destinarle quiso
para delicia y ornamento tuyo:
mandará sobre tí, y un día unido
a la grande Nación de los Britanos
serán llamados tus valientes hijos
domadores del mundo: el orgulloso
y pérfido Francés será abatido
y tirará el carro de tu gloria
que así grabado queda ya en el libro
de los hados.   (p. 72)

(You may now breathe free, Spain, now for forever your tyrannical despotism has ended, your great restoration owing to the memory of Pelayo. Raise up to Olympus that disheartened forehead: see in your adored Prince the alleviation of your bitter afflictions. Out of Heaven's chaos he has been sent for your comfort and embellishment. He will rule over you, and one day, together with the great Britannic nation, your valiant sons will be called rulers of the world. The haughty and treacherous French leader will be brought down, and will pull the carriage of your glory, as is already written in the Book of Destiny.)

Zavala's own loyalty to his purse evidently overrode his political convictions, however, since within two years he was writing plays praising Joseph Bonaparte.[12] In the one-act allegory, *El templo de la gloria* (The Temple of Glory) and the three-act play, *La clemencia de Tito* (Tito's Clemency, most likely a version of Metastasio's work, on which Mozart based his opera), both performed in Madrid in March, 1810, Zavala develops themes which praise the enlightened leadership of Joseph. In *El templo de la gloria* Spain still first appears on stage dressed in chains, but now she has been oppressed by a Despotism more clearly associated with the *bête noire* of Spanish politics, Carlos IV's Prime Minister, Manuel Godoy. Her salvation comes at the hands of Joseph:

Aparece una vistosa decoración de templo, que están edificando con el mayor ahinco varios obreros, y en el centro se eleva una ara todavía informe, y en su base se lee una inscripción que dice: "A España, el Amor de José 1°." Al descubrirse la decoración se ve España magníficamente ataviada y sin cadenas, y el Despotismo y el Error a sus pies con ellas.[13]

---

[12] It is possible, of course, as Larraz suggests, that Zavala was genuinely grateful to the King for his interest in theatre. "Peut-être crut-il tout simplement à la sincérité d'un roi 'philosophe et protecteur des arts', qui ne dédaignait pas d'assister aux représentations théâtrales, et avait rendu leur dignité aux dramaturges et au comédiens." *Théâtre et politique*, p. 104.

[13] Cited by Larraz, *ibid.* p. 108.

(There appears a fine scene with a temple which several workmen are building with great earnestness, and in the center they are raising up a still incomplete altar, and at its foot one reads the following inscription: "To Spain, with the Love of José I." When the curtain is drawn back one sees Spain, magnificently attired without chains, with Despotism and Error at her feet enchained.)

La clemencia de Tito is a three-act effort to convey similar ideas and contains, in Larraz's words, "quelques belles scènes pathétiques"[14] ("some beautiful scenes of pathos").

Félix Enciso Castrillón wrote poetry and dramas from the last decade of the eighteenth century.[15] He wrote seventy-nine plays, some original, some translated from the French, and others "refundiciones" of Golden Age works. Of his eight political propaganda plays, two interest us here: *El sermón sin fruto* (The Fruitless Sermon, 1808) and *Las cuatro columnas del trono español* (The Four Columns of the Spanish Throne, 1809), both written to mock the French invaders and inspire the Spaniards to resist them. *El sermón* , a one-act satire, enjoyed enormous popularity when it played at the Cruz Theatre in November, 1808. Copies of it circulated, it was played in theatres across Spain (in Seville and Palma de Mallorca, among other places), and it was even reprinted several times.[16]

Joseph Bonaparte had the (unfair) reputation in Spain of being a heavy drinker (he was popularly referred to as "Pepe Botellas"), and he was frequently portrayed in verse, prose and cartoons as a confused lush. Enciso's play has the King in Rioja, the center of Spain's wine country, delivering a calming speech to the inhabitants of the region. He arrives slightly inebriated ("Un tanto quanto / borracho, mas no del todo" ["A little bit drunk, but not completely"]), becomes progressively more so as he samples the local product, and loses the thread of his talk. His speech is a disaster, and he ends up making a spectacle of himself. This "Son of Bacchus" does not even speak proper Spanish, and Enciso puts in his mouth a bizarre discourse of predominantly Italian expressions, further reducing him to an object of scorn. He even has an aide who interprets for him.

14 *Ibid.* p. 109.
15 His first known publication is a sonnet which appeared in the *Diario Curioso* on 4 April 1789. Joaquín Álvarez Barrientos, "Acercamiento a Félix Enciso Castrillón," *II Seminario de Historia de la Real Sociedad Bascongada de los Amigos del País* (San Sebastián: n.p., 1989): 61. A complete listing of his works can be found in Francisco Aguilar Piñal, *Bibliografía de autores españoles del siglo XVIII*, III (Madrid: CSIC, 1984): 154–167.
16 Hans-Joachim Lope looks at this play and Antero Benítez Núñez's *Calzones en Alcolea* (1811) in "La imagen de los franceses en el teatro español de propaganda durante la Guerra de la Independencia (1808–1813)," *Bulletin of Hispanic Studies* 68 (1991): 219–229.

JOSEPH.	Seguiamo.
	Pensateci bene mei subditi in la potencia dell mio germano é in vostra felicita.
BENITO.	Pensad bien vasallos míos en el poder de mi hermano, y en vuestra felicidad.
JOSEPH.	Si voi restate tranquilli tuto sara opulenza.
BENITO.	Si permanecéis sosegados, todo será opulencia.
JOSEPH.	Tutto richeza.
BENITO.	Todo riqueza.
JOSEPH.	Tutto amore.
BENITO.	Todo amor.
JOSEPH.	Tutto denaro.
BENITO.	Todo dinero.
JOSEPH.	Tutto...tu...tu...tu...tu...tu (*Se va cayendo sobre la silla*)
(JOSEPH.	Let's a-go.
	Think-a well mi subjectos about mi broter's potency, and in-a you happ'ness.
BENITO.	Think well my vassals about my brother's power, and in your happiness.
JOSEPH.	If you keep-a calm, all-a will be opulenza.
BENITO.	If you stay quite, all will be opulence.
JOSEPH.	All-a richness.
BENITO.	All riches.
JOSEPH.	All-a loving.
BENITO.	All love.
JOSEPH.	All-a moola.
BENITO.	All money.
JOSEPH.	All-a...a...a...a...a... [He gradually falls into his chair.])

"Damn wine," curses Benito.

The hostility to Joseph and his brother is outright and strong. In one scene, the King's aide-de-camp tries to praise the locals for their acceptance of enlightened French ideas, but their response states clearly their position.

EDECÁN.	Oh gui, la gente de Logroño ha penetrado las ideas del francés.
DOCTOR.	Así hubiera penetrado (aparte) un cuchillo en tus entrañas, en las de Pepe y su hermano.
AIDE-DE-CAMP.	Oh, oui, the people of Logroño have penetrated the Frenchman's ideas.
DOCTOR.	A knife should have (aside) penetrated your guts, and those of Pepe and his brother.)

Castrillón's allegorical musical piece, *Las cuatro columnas del trono español,* called for unity among the provinces against the invaders. It played in Cádiz on 30 May 1809, and was, according to Larraz, heavily indebted to Zavala's *La sombra de Pelayo.* The spectre here was Hernán Cortés instead of Pelayo, but he shared the goal of the latter hero to inspire his countrymen to rise up in defense of their past national glory.

Perhaps the most popular playwright of them all was Luciano Francisco Comella (1751–1812) whose lively battle scenes, military parades, appeals to patriotic sentiment, and stylistic spontaneity caused near apoplexy among the Neoclassicists. Moratín in particular registered disgust at his unregulated plays, and called don Eleuterio, the playwright in his satirical *La comedia nueva o el café* (The New Comedy, or the Café, 1792), a character he based, it is said, on Comella, "el compendio de todos los malos poetas dramáticos que escribían en aquella época"[17] ("the compendium of all the bad dramatic poets who wrote during that time"). He was certainly the most prolific of the three authors we have mentioned, but hardly as bad as Moratín would have us believe.[18] As Mario Di Pinto has justifiably written, "Comella no era el autorcillo inculto y ramplón que pretendía Moratín, sino un literato completo, conocedor de su oficio"[19] ("Comella was not the uneducated and vulgar little author that Moratín painted him to be, but a fully literate man who knew his profession well"). He was not directly enmeshed in the propaganda campaign against the French as were Zavala and Enciso, but his plays were the most frequently performed in Madrid during the years from 1808 to 1813, and many of them drew upon foreign heroes and themes to give his viewers a vicarious boost. Even plays written in the 1780s and 1790s, well before the French invasion, were seen as inspirational when they were staged during the War.[20] *Federico II, rey de Prusia* (Frederick II, King of Prussia, 1789), for example, presented a king noted for his justice and nobility, and the audience could read into that personage their own feelings for either Joseph or Fernando VII when it played in Madrid in 1809, 1810, and 1812. The French authorities clearly read into it a reflection of Joseph: in the *Gaceta de Madrid* in January, 1809, readers

17 Leandro Fernández de Moratín, *Obras de D. Leandro Fernández de Moratín,* II (Madrid: Real Academia de la Historia, 1830): 183.
18 See Francisco Aguilar Piñal, *Bibliografía de autores españoles del siglo XVIII,* II (Madrid: CSIC, 1983): 460–513.
19 Mario Di Pinto, "En defensa de Comella," *Insula* 504 (1988): 16.
20 Alba Ebersole provides a list and summary of fifty-three plays by Comella in *La obra teatral de Luciano Francisco Comella* (Valencia: Ediciones Albatros, 1985). A more complete listing of Comella's plays is found in McClelland, *Spanish Drama of Pathos,* II: pp. 585–588. Comella deserves more serious study. The last studies of him are Carlos Cambronero, "Comella," *Revista Contemporánea* CII, CIII, CIV (1896) and José Subirá, *Un vate filarmónico: Don Luciano Comella* (Madrid: Real Academia Española, 1932).

learned of Joseph's visits to a hospital and his concern for the poor and suffering, a trait of Frederick II notably highlighted in Comella's play.[21]

Dozens of other plays were written and performed which excoriated or praised Joseph and Napoleon. Antonio Valladares de Sotomayor, who penned more than one hundred and thirteen works between 1765 and 1814, wrote a harsh condemnation of "el tirano destructor de los / derechos más sagrados" ("the tyrant who destroyed the holiest rights") of Spain in *La gran victoria de España en los campos de Vitoria* in 1814 (Spain's Great Victory on the Fields of Vitoria).[22] In this play, Napoleon's subjects praise him of course as "el Gran Napoleón, de / quien tiembla el Universo" ("Great Napoleon, who makes the Universe tremble") (p. 113), but Don Lucas, a "spy" for the Spaniards, sees the Emperor as a monster who

> ha tratado a la Iglesia
> Católica, dexándola sin cabeza, sin
> miembros, y a sus ministros sin liber-
> tad, ni un dinero. Esto no tiene ejem-
> plar aun entre los Atilas y Nerones.			(p. 135)

(he has dealt with the Catholic Church leaving it without a head, without arms and legs, and leaving its ministers without freedom or funds. Not even the Attilas or the Neros of the world did anything like this.)

The object of reverence of the "true" Spaniards in these plays is Fernando VII, the legitimate monarch, who is correctly seen as suffering a "cautiverio" ("captivity") at the hands of Napoleon. A mythology springs up around Fernando, who is not only a captive of the enemy, but "El Deseado" ("The Desired One") destined to save Spain from the tyranny of the Emperor.[23] Since the King cannot be represented on stage, many of these works end with the populace bowing to a portrait of him, as is done in *La gran victoria* ("venero a vuestro retrato / como al mismo original" ["I venerate your portrait as if it were the original"] 166).

The most enduring myth propagated in the theatre of this time, however, is not of Fernando as a "desired" monarch (although this was consistent), but rather of Napoleon as a monstrous, deranged tyrant. Dozens of plays contain portraits of the Emperor as unbalanced, stupid, mentally defective, and suicidal. They contain no philosophical reflection or aesthetic merit, and little sophistication of structure or theme, but the

---

[21] See Larraz, *Théâtre et politique*, pp. 99–103.

[22] Antonio Valladares de Sotomayor, *La gran victoria de España en los campos de Victoria* (Madrid: Vega, 1814), in Larraz, *Antologie*, pp. 105–168.

[23] Rogers registers a dozen pro-Fernando pieces in "The Peninsular War as a Source of Inspiration in the Spanish Drama of 1808–1814," *Philological Quarterly* 8 (1929): 264–269; there were many others. See also Guillermo Carnero, "Un ejemplo de teatro revolucionario en la España revolucionaria," *España Contemporánea* 1 (1988): 49–66.

force and immediacy of their words had an important galvanizing effect on the public who saw or read them. They strike us as pure, raw emotion put on stage. The titles of the plays provide a wish-list for the defenders of the Spanish crown, that is, they forecast Napoleon's downfall and death. For example: *La muerte de Bonaparte* (The Death of Bonaparte, 1808), *Napoleón rabiando* (Napoleon Enraged, 1808), *Napoleón desesperado* (Desperate Napoleon, 1808), *El fin de Napoladrón por sus mismos sequaces* (The Killing of Napoladron[24] by his Own Troops, 1808), *Napoleón y sus satélites residenciados por el rey del abismo* (Napoleon and His Henchmen Ministered to by the King of the Abyss, 1809), and *El fin de Napoleón* (The Death of Napoleon, n.d.). In them, Napoleon is called (often by himself) "cruel," "fiero" ("fierce"), "despreciable" ("contemptible"), "alevoso" ("treacherous"), and a host of other negative epithets. He is compared, as we have seen, with Attila and Nero, and with the Devil himself. He is ridiculed, diminished, and transformed into a "perro" ("dog"), a "niño" ("child"), an "embustero" ("liar"), a "gran bellaco" ("great villain"), a "muñeco" ("puppet"), a "trapacero" ("swindler"), and so on and on. In several of the plays, he commits suicide after realizing the futility of his attempt to conquer Spain. These plays are not historical since they hardly reflect what happened, but they are optimistic projections of what the defenders of the Spanish nation hoped would occur in a short time. In *Napoleón rabiando*, the Emperor kills himself, but his "supporters" add a grotesque touch which clearly satisfied the audience's thirst for French blood:

NAPOLEÓN.	Ayudadme a morir, hombres infames.
LEBRAC.	Tírale de las patas, porque sepa
	que hasta para morir le hemos servido.
DUROC.	Obra de caridad sin duda es esta:
(*tirándole*)	una muerte ha tenido como un ángel:
	¡Qué actos de contrición y penitencia
	ha hecho el maldito! Bien que en los infiernos
	le tienen preparada buena cena.
(NAPOLEON.	Help me to die, you vile men.
LEBRAC.	Throw him out feet first so that he knows we have
	even served him in death.
DUROC.	This is certainly an act of mercy:
(*throwing him*)	he has died like an angel. What acts of contrition
	and penitence this damned man has done! In Hell
	they will have prepared a fine meal for him.)

---

[24] "Napoladrón" is a play on words which combines the emperor's name with the word "thief" in Spanish; it was commonly used during the period by his enemies; notice the wonderful pun in the title.

The hatred for him reached fever pitch in the theatres, just as it did in the streets.[25] As Paul Rogers has reminded us, "the Spanish theatre of the period of the War of Independence served as a medium for the expression of public sentiment on matters that touched the heart, and as a means of executing propaganda against the French."[26]

The post-war years

The French troops abandoned Madrid on 27 May 1813, and the capital reacted with a year-long explosion of patriotic enthusiasm, dampened only, ironically, with the return of "El Deseado." The years following the War of Independence and the return of Fernando VII to the Spanish throne were difficult ones for the Spanish theatre. Continuing economic struggles, rivalries among actors and acting companies, a strengthened censorship, and general lethargy led the theatres down a precarious road. Leandro Fernández de Moratín's five Neoclassical comedies had created the paradigm for comedy in the years to follow.

There had been inspiring and hopeful moments before the war ended, particularly in Cádiz, where the liberals, exiled from Madrid, had assembled to set up their government. Intellectual, political, and literary activity was intense in Cádiz following the convocation of the Cortes and the promulgation of the radical Constitution of 1812. Many of the names which would dominate Spanish letters in the next few decades were first heard in that provincial capital, among them Martínez de la Rosa, Angel de Saavedra (the future Duque de Rivas), and Antonio Alcalá Galiano. Francisco Martínez de la Rosa (1787–1862) wrote his satirical two-act ¡Lo que puede un empleo! (What a Job Can Do!) in August 1812, just months after the creation of the Constitution in March of that year. This play mocked the repressive "serviles" ("partisans of absolutist monarchy"), those ultra-conservatives who considered the theatres to be repositories of pornography and evil and who had tried, often successfully, to close them down.

Structurally, the comedy shows the influence of Moratín: it has only six characters and takes place in one room, coincidentally the same type of

---

[25] For more information on these anti-Napoleon plays, see Larraz, *Théâtre et Politique*; also, "La satire de Napoleon Bonaparte et de Joseph dans le théâtre espagnol: 1808–1814," in *Hommage à André Joucla-Ruau* (Aix-en-Provence: Université de Provence, 1974): 125–137; David T. Gies, "Hacia un mito anti-napoleónico en el teatro español de los primeros años del siglo XIX," *Teatro politico spagnolo del primo ottocento*, ed. Ermanno Caldera (Rome: Bulzoni Editore, 1991): 43–62; and Lluis Roura i Aulinas, "Napoleón: ¿Un punto de acuerdo entre la reacción y el liberalismo en España?," in *Les espagnoles et Napoleon*, ed. Gerard Dufour (Aix-en-Provence: Université de Provence, 1984): 35–50.

[26] Rogers, "Peninsular War," p. 264.

room used by Moratín in *El sí de las niñas* (Martínez moves it to Alicante from Alcalá de Henares). The political note is evident from the first scene when Carlota complains that Teodoro does not love her because of what her father has referred to as "esas malditas ideas liberales, que os han trastornado la cabeza"[27] ("those damned liberal ideas which have messed up your head") (I, 1). Around this, Martínez spins a tale of love and parental opposition. Carlota's father Fabián staunchly opposes the marriage because Teodoro is not the young man he thought him to be.

Hija . . . todo se acabó; no hay que pensar más en boda con Teodoro, si no quieres quitarme la vida; yo le creía un joven juicioso y moderado, capaz de hacerte feliz; pero ya has visto: sus ideas son las peores del mundo; el trato con esos locos de liberales le ha quitado el juicio y se ha vuelto un revolucionario . . . , un jacobino. (I, 1)

(Daughter . . . it's over. Do not think any more about your marriage to Teodoro, if you do not want to end my life; I thought he was a judicious and moderate young man, capable of making you happy. But you have seen what happened: his ideas are the worst in the world. His contact with those crazed liberals has affected his judgment and has turned him into a revolutionary . . ., a Jacobin.)

Soon thereafter, Fabián points to Teodoro's "malditos libros modernos" ("damned modern books") (I, 3) as the source of his vicious liberal ideas. Teodoro, far from being a wild-eyed revolutionary, displays truly heroic tolerance when he counsels Carlota to obey her father, who is "naturalmente bondadoso, y sus defectos nunca nacen de su corazón, sino de los errores de su educación, de las malas ideas que le han imbuído" ("good by nature, and his defects are not born in his heart, but are the errors of his education, of the bad ideas that have been instilled in him") (I, 2). Who is behind the father's poor education and ignorance? Don Melitón is the hypocritical and superstitious priest who believes that liberal ideas are intended to bring "revuelta a España y van a arruinar nuestra religión santa" ("revolt to Spain and are going to ruin our sacred religion") (I, 2). The intellectual battle lines drawn after 1812 included not only the differences between Spanish and French nationals, but also now between "liberal" and "servil" (ultra-reactionary, absolutist) Spaniards, and the theatre became even more politicized to reflect those differences. Martínez de la Rosa's explicit goal was to ridicule "una cierta clase de hipócritas políticos, que so color de religión se oponen entre nosotros a las benéficas reformas" ("a certain type of political hypocrite who, under the guise of religion, opposes beneficial reforms") and expose "los enemi-

---

[27] Francisco Martínez de la Rosa, *¡Lo que puede un empleo!*, in *Obras de D. Francisco Martínez de la Rosa*, ed. Carlos Seco Serrano (Madrid: Atlas, 1962) (Biblioteca de Autores Españoles 148): 9–26.

gos de nuestra libertad"[28] ("the enemies of our freedom"). Even Fabián has to confess that as bad as Teodoro is, he is not as bad as the French.

FABIÁN.	¡Esos liberales son gentes tan levantiscas y mal sufridas!
MELITÓN.	Estoy para decir que son peores que los franceses ...
FABIÁN.	No, amigo, eso no. ¡Como los franceses! Eso no: nada malo es capaz de igualarlos. (I, 7)
(FABIÁN.	Those liberals are troublesome and rude characters!
MELITON.	I even think they are worse than the French...
FABIÁN.	No, my friend, not that. Worse than the French! No, nothing can be as bad as them.)

The play betrayed its author's youth and lack of literary experience so that it reads more like a debate than a drama, but it articulated accurately his ideological stance and revealed a playwright of promise and commitment. It enjoyed a successful run and was replayed in theatres all over the country.

Martínez de la Rosa's next play, *La viuda de Padilla* (Padilla's Widow), is a tragedy patterned after Alfieri, an author much in vogue in Spain in the first decades of the nineteenth century. Written and performed in Cádiz in 1812, it confronts similar concerns to those developed in *¡Lo que puede un empleo!* but from a radically different perspective. In this play, Martínez attempts to capture "la catástrofe de un pueblo" ("the catastrophe of a nation") by developing a tragic tale of heroic sacrifice set in Castilla during the reign of Carlos I. It clearly has contemporary resonances and parallels to the current Spanish revolt against the French, and it garnered an enthusiastic reception when it was performed in 1812 and printed in 1814. This penchant to mine history for contemporary purposes would have its most successful repercussions in *La conjuración de Venecia*, written and performed nearly twenty years later. Modern criticism has salvaged *La viuda* which had for many years been considered mere political propaganda and "drama de circunstancia" ("circumstantial drama"). Juan Luis Alborg praises its "caracteres ... cuidadosamente estudiados, con gradaciones y matices humanísimos"[29] ("characters, which have been carefully studied, with gradations and very human shadings").

Another play which attacked the "serviles" was Francisco de Paula Martí's (1762–1827) *La constitución vindicada* (The Constitution Vindicated),[30] performed in Madrid at the Cruz Theatre in 1813. The first

[28] Martínez de la Rosa, "Advertencia," in *Obras*, p. 9.
[29] Juan Luis Alborg, *Historia de la literatura española, vol. IV. El romanticismo* (Madrid: Gredos, 1980): 435.
[30] Francisco de Paula Martí, *La constitución vindicada* (Madrid: Benito García y Compañía, 1813), reprinted in Larraz, *Antologie*, pp. 215–266.

words shouted by the residents of the Spanish town where *La constitución vindicada* is set are "Viva la Constitución" ("Long live the Constitution") (I, 2). Don Ruperto, the "servil," complains that "se han acabado / los antiguos privilegios" ("the old privileges have been done away with") (I, 5) in the new Constitution, and plans to combat the "papeluchos / de los liberales" ("nonsensical tracts of the liberals") (I, 7). Martí mocks the vision of the liberals held by the conservatives; doña Eufrosia's comment, "Juzgué que los liberales / eran unos chuchumecos / petimetres" ("I thought that liberals were contemptible little dandys") (I, 8) is designed not only to make the audience laugh, but to reflect rather accurately the disdain with which the liberals were looked upon by the defenders of the Ancien Régime. Even don Juan, the liberal in question, warns a friend that around doña Eufrosia and don Ruperto he must "guardar silencio / en quanto a ideas modernas, / o condenarte a un eterno / disputar" ("keep quiet about modern ideas or you will condemn yourself to eternal battles") (I, 9). Don Ruperto's main concern is to discredit the Constitution and, according to Juan,

> los pinta que todo esto
> de Constitución es sólo
> una apariencia, y siguiendo
> por el estilo común
> de esta gente, pinta en riesgo
> la religión y la Patria,
> desacredita al Gobierno ...
>
> (I,9)

(he tells everyone that this business about a constitution is only an appearance, and following up on these people's commonly held ideas, he tells them that it jeopardizes religion and the nation, that it discredits the government ...)

An interesting and subtle distinction is established by Juan's friend when he inquires as to whether don Ruperto is a "servil por ignorancia / o por malicia" ("reactionary due to ignorance or malice") (I, 9). Ruperto soon thereafter warns the people that "Dentro de poco veremos, / así como pasó en Francia, / hecho república el reyno" ("We'll soon see the kingdom turned into a republic, just like what happened in France") (I, 14), a thought immediately denied by the patriots. The clever dénouement comes when a trick is played on Ruperto and his only means of salvation is to appeal to the articles of the Constitution which he has previously so vociferously rejected: "Tengo / la Constitución que es / mi defensa" ("I have the constitution to defend me") (I, 17). Only then does he see the value of that document, and the play ends on a conciliatory note.

Martí wrote several patriotic plays which were seen in Madrid in 1813 and 1814, including *La caída de Godoy* (The Fall of Godoy), *La batalla de*

Pamplona y derrota del mariscal Soult (The Battle of Pamplona and the Defeat of Marshall Soult), *El mayor chasco de los afrancesados* (The Greatest Sham of the Supporters of the French). One of the best was *El día Dos de Mayo de 1808 en Madrid y muerte heroica de Daoíz y Velarde* (The Second of May 1808 in Madrid and the Heroic Death of Daoíz and Velarde) (Madrid, 1813) which, according to Cotarelo, "logró éxito enorme"[31] ("achieved enormous success") when it was performed in July of 1813, and went on to be reprinted numerous times. The immediacy of its theme, combined with the careful production it was given (new sets were painted to represent the four main points of defense against the invading French troops), lent the play "interés y grandeza trágica"[32] ("interest and tragic grandeur"). The return of Fernando VII to the throne silenced Martí's constitutional fervor, and it was not until after the Riego uprising of 1820 that his real beliefs – defense of constitutional values and freedom, opposition to absolutism – were again seen on stage.

The political plays reached their peak in 1813 and tapered off when Fernando VII recovered the throne. The repertory returned to its usual diet of bland comedies, translations of French and Italian pieces, and "refundiciones," many of them written, it must be noted, with skill and care.[33] Máiquez – referred to by Bretón de los Herreros as the Hernán Cortés of Spanish theatre because of his need to "conquistar su nuevo mundo"[34] ("conquer his new world") – struggled to maintain a healthy theatrical life in Madrid, but was in constant conflict with the administration and with rival acting companies. Bernardo Gil set up a competing company at the Cruz Theatre in early 1814, taking with him several of the best actors from Máiquez's company, including Gil's wife Antera Baus who, because there was little for her to do in the new company, managed to return to the Príncipe by the end of the summer. The Príncipe company under Máiquez's direction concentrated on comedies and tragedies while Gil's company at the Cruz mixed its offerings with operas, zarzuelas and other musical pieces, and dance recitals, although it did not eschew political satire (*El sermón sin fruto* was played at the Cruz). Máiquez was unable to escape the wrath of the returning monarch. Even as he rehearsed his role in Racine's *Atalía*, which he had decided to perform in honor of the return of Fernando VII in May, 1814, he was caught up in a police sweep of suspected liberals and jailed along with several important writers, including Manuel José Quintana, Juan Nicasio Gallego, Bernardo Gil, and Dionisio Solís. The Príncipe Theatre was shut down

---

[31] Cotarelo, *Máiquez*, p. 347. [32] *Ibid.*
[33] Cotarelo provides a detailed schedule of plays performed in Madrid from 1793 to 1819 in *Ibid.* pp. 574–837.
[34] Enrique Funes, *La declamación española* (Seville: Díaz y Carballo, 1894): 102.

temporarily and the political tragedies which had become a staple there – "ni nada que oliese a liberal" ("nothing that smelled even faintly of liberalism") in the words of Cotarelo (*Máiquez*, p. 371) – were seen no more. Máiquez's release from jail in June enabled the Príncipe to begin its functions again, but the repertory had changed inalterably by that time. Weary of politics or perhaps merely liberated from having to think too much, the public filled the theatres to see *refundiciones* of Golden Age plays such as Moreto's *El desdén con el desdén* (Treat Disdain Disdainfully), Lope's *El perro del hortelano* (The Dog in the Manger), Calderón's *A secreto agravio secreto venganza* (For a Secret Offense, a Secret Vengeance), and Tirso's *El vergonzoso en palacio* (The Shy Man at Court) and *Don Gil de las calzas verdes* (Don Gil of the Green Breeches), interspersed with periodic performances of *sainetes* or Moratín's *El viejo y la niña* (The Old Man and the Young Girl) or *La comedia nueva, o el café*.

The situation in Madrid during the years of the first Fernandine repression (1814–1820) was less innovative than some playwrights and critics would have hoped, but outside the capital signs of creativity were detected on several fronts. One of the most momentous developments for the history of the Spanish theatre was the appearance in 1816 in Seville of a new tragedy written by a young man who had already distinguished himself as an able soldier and politician for the liberal cause. Ángel de Saavedra's first two plays, *Ataúlfo* and *Doña Blanca*, tragedies which followed many of the neoclassical guidelines, were never staged (the former was rejected by the censors),[35] but the appearance of *Aliatar* revealed the existence of a new playwright blessed with conviction, poetic grace, and dramatic force.

Even though it was never staged, *Ataúlfo* is an important drama for what it reveals not only of the artistry of Rivas, but also for the ideological posture of its young author at the moment of its conception. The theme, which had been drawn upon by the Neoclassicists (Montiano's play of the same title and García de la Huerta's *Raquel* were the most immediate examples), was hardly new, but the manner of its presentation has lead critics to link it with the past rather than with the future. That is, in *Ataúlfo* Rivas leaves few indications that twenty years later he would be the author of the "watershed" *Don Alvaro o la fuerza del sino*.[36] D. L. Shaw has rightly criticized him for failing to portray a truly tragic hero in the play (the main character "undergoes no tragic evolution of character

---

35 *Ataúlfo* has recently been discovered and published by Juan Manuel Cacho Blecua in *El Crotalón* 1 (1984): 393–465. *Doña Blanca* is presumed lost. Gabriel Boussagol suggests that the example of regicide in *Ataúlfo* was the principal reason for its prohibition. *Angel de Saavedra, duc de Rivas. Sa vie, son oeuvre poétique* (Toulouse: Privat, 1926): 164.
36 Donald L. Shaw, "*Ataúlfo*: Rivas' First Drama," *Hispanic Review* 56 (1988): 231.

and fails to convince us of his tragic stature," p. 233) and for failing to link the main love story with the power of unleashed emotion. In this play, Ataúlfo's love for Placidia is seen not as a purifying force but as a dangerous emotion which carries with it the potential destabilization of the state. Rivas, even as a liberal crusader in the fight against the French invaders, shows himself to be true to his class – not yet fully ready to subvert the status quo – although the regicide which closes the play could be interpreted in terms of political allegory.[37] The king, seen by his subjects as betraying his royal duties and as arbitrarily wielding his royal power (he arrests Vinamaro for criticizing him), becomes then not a failed tragic hero but a vague stand-in for Fernando VII. The play, written, it must be remembered, in 1814, and banned by the censors, may not "question the existential confidence of the audience" (Shaw, 242) but it does confirm the audience's tragic experience of the past six years. Why was it banned when offered for performance in Seville in 1815? In line with the recently established laws restricting freedom of the press and the subsequent curtailing of public spectacles (2 May 1815), the play was considered to be "revolucionaria":

Atento a la conjura que se nos ha dado sobre esta tragedia titulada *Ataúlfo*, en que se la trata de revolucionaria i contraria a las buenas costumbres, negamos por lo que toca a esta jurisdicción la licencia de representarla en este teatro de Sevilla. Noviembre 3. de 815. Miranda.[38]

(Sensitive to the machinations that have swirled around this tragedy entitled *Ataúlfo*, which is considered to be revolutionary and contrary to good manners, we deny permission for it to be put on in this theatre in Seville. 3 November 1815. Miranda.)

Even though it was finally passed by censors in Madrid in mid-1815, certain political statements are underlined in the manuscript, and the play was never performed.

Aliatar is seen by Caldera as "un dechado casi completo de sensibilidad neoclásica" ("a nearly perfect example of neoclassical sensibility") because of the rhetorical devices employed by Rivas,[39] but Shaw notes that it reflects concerns similar to those expressed in *Ataúlfo* and is developed with greater dramatic force.[40] Once again Rivas confronts the issue of love versus power but here he manages to give tragic dimension to the struggling Aliatar. He also moves closer to the romanticism of *Don*

[37] See Rosalía Fernández Cabezón, "Ataúlfo visto por dos trágicos: D. Agustín de Montiano y el duque de Rivas," *Castilla* 8 (1984): 95–100.
[38] Cacho, "*Ataúlfo*," 396.
[39] Ermanno Caldera, "De *Aliatar* a *Don Alvaro*: Sobre el aprendizaje clasicista del duque de Rivas," *Romanticismo* 1 (1982): 109.
[40] D. L. Shaw, "Acerca de *Aliatar* del Duque de Rivas," *Entre Siglos*, 2 (1993): 237–245.

Alvaro by highlighting the role of adverse fortune in the play, a role which Shaw defines as a conflict between fatality and divine providence. No fewer than thirty-five times do characters refer to their cruel fate or unjust destiny, in terms often very reminiscent of what will later be expressed so powerfully in *Don Alvaro*. Destiny wins out over divine protection, just as it will in the full-blown Romantic dramas of Rivas and others, and it is precisely this element which underscores the importance of *Aliatar* as a significant drama of its time. It is more than "potentially Romantic"[41]: Rivas was willing to challenge the inherited tropes and themes of his day by signalling a radical shift away from the God-centered universe of the Neoclassicists to the man-centered universe of the Romantics, a shift which would be clearly seen (and fought against) in Spain in the 1830s. *Aliatar* played in Seville in July, September and November of 1816 and in February of 1817, but not in Madrid where, presumably, acting companies and playwrights were kept under closer vigil by the authorities.[42]

In Madrid, the theatre lurched along as always, suffering from a lack of exciting new plays, unfocused competition between the two main companies, conflicts between the actors and the musicians (the latter wanted to be dealt with separately from the actors, whom they considered to be inferior and often notorious), and much meddling but little guidance by the authorities. By 1815 Máiquez had recruited the not untalented Agustina Torres for his company, soon to be joined by Antonio Guzmán, who would become the leading comic actor of the first half of the century. The Príncipe company, with Máiquez at its head, became the leading company of the capital and Máiquez now began to be celebrated for his talent and durability. Goya painted his portrait, which was engraved and sold throughout Madrid, and Dionisio Solís, one of the most admired poets and dramatists of the day, sang his praises in verse.[43] Still, Lope, Moreto, Calderón, Ramón de la Cruz, and other representatives of the seventeenth- and eighteenth-century repertories, dominated the offerings, and the audience showed up in record numbers, inured by now to the restrictions of censorship, poor translations and frequently unskilled acting.[44] The theatre was one of the only pastimes available to the public and, notwithstanding the uninspired offerings, people went to see Máiquez with such frequency that tickets to some performances were difficult to come by. Scalpers appeared in the streets, prompting protests in some

---

[41] Gabriel Lovett, *The Duke of Rivas* (Boston: Twayne, 1977): 40.

[42] Aguilar Piñal, *Cartelera prerromántica sevillana (1800–1836)*, p. 10.

[43] See David T. Gies, "Hacia un catálogo de los dramas de Dionisio Solís (1774–1834)," *Bulletin of Hispanic Studies* 68 (1991): 197–210 and "Dionisio Solís, entre dos/tres siglos," *Entre Siglos*, 2 (1993): 163–170.

[44] Cotarelo, *Máiquez*, gives much detailed information and commentary on the plays offered during these years.

quarters (such crowds formed when tickets to certain functions were
made available that pickpockets had a field day, according to Cotarelo
[*Máiquez*, p. 401]). Not everyone was satisfied with the status quo, as an
article in the *Diario de Madrid* (11 January 1816) reveals: addressing
himself to the "Lost and Found" section, the author complained of the
"loss" of Spanish "dramatic poetry" – it was nowhere to be found among
the plague of translations and ridiculous ("disparatado") pieces performed nightly. But fashion ruled. The King himself was a regular
theatre-goer who took delight precisely in the most "ridiculous" pieces,
the *comedias de magia* which had never disappeared from the repertories.
Marta la Romarantina, El anillo de Giges (Giges's Ring) and *El mágico de
Eriván* (The Magician from Eriván) were particular favorites. All of this
was happening at exactly the same time that other plays, for example
Moratín's already-classic *El sí de las niñas*, were being prohibited by the
inconsistent censors.[45] Meanwhile other plays, which some would say
were clearly more subversive than *El sí*, were allowed to be printed and
circulated in the capital. Martínez de la Rosa's *La viuda de Padilla*,
composed in 1812 and published in 1814, is a case in point.

Martínez de la Rosa's neoclassical tragedy conformed to the precepts
established as early as 1737 by Luzán and the 1750s by Montiano, who
had penned *Virginia* (1750) and *Ataúlpho* (1753) as examples of classical
writing. Following the lead of Nicolás Fernández de Moratín, who wrote
Lucrecia (1763) and then drew upon Spanish national themes for his
tragedies *Hormesinda* (1770) and *Guzmán el Bueno* (1777), Martínez de la
Rosa chose to present "a single action with no side episodes, no confi-
dants, few monologues, and few characters,"[46] but with contemporary
political resonance. In 1827, reflecting back on the play, he remembered
the circumstances of its composition:

Al haber de elegir el argumento, el deseo de que fuese original y tomado de la
historia de mi nación, y quizá más bien las extraordinarias circunstancias en que
se hallaba por aquella época la ciudad de Cádiz, en que a la sazón residía,
asediada estrechamente por un ejército extranjero y ocupada en plantear reformas
domésticas, llamaron naturalmente mi atención e inclinaron mi ánimo a preferir
entre varios asuntos el fin de las Comunidades de Castilla.[47]

(When I was about to choose the plot, the desire that it be original and taken from
my country's history, and perhaps because of the rather extraordinary circumstances that the city of Cadiz found itself in during that time – which was at the
moment closely surrounded by a foreign army and busy with domestic reforms –

45 John C. Dowling, "The Inquisition Appraises *El sí de las niñas*, 1815–1819," *Hispania* 44
    (1961): 237–244.
46 Nancy and Robert Mayberry, *Francisco Martínez de la Rosa* (Boston: Twayne, 1988): 39.
47 Martínez de la Rosa, "Advertencia," *La viuda de Padilla*, in *Obras* I, p. 27.

naturally I found myself inclined, among various topics, toward the end of the Comunidades de Castilla.)

Even though he knew the play was a failure as tragedy (he confessed so in the above-cited preface), he likewise knew that its political content would capture the audience's full attention. The heroic widow encourages her dead husband's father to defend their freedom.

> Juramos
> ser libres o morir; y el cielo mismo,
> que dio el injusto triunfo a los tiranos,
> nuestro voto aceptó; pues que nos veda
> el ser libres, nos manda que muramos.
> ...
> ... Por ocho siglos
> decís que nuestros padres batallaron
> por rescatar la patria; ¿y ahora, esclava,
> entregada a merced de los tiranos,
> la dejarán sus vergonzosos nietos?
>
> (II, 3)

(We swore to be free or die; and Heaven itself, which favored the unjust victory of the tyrants, accepted our vow. If it prohibits us from being free, it orders us to die ... You say that for eight centuries our fathers fought to reclaim the nation. And now, enslaved and at the mercy of tyrants, will her shameful grandchildren abandon her?)

The parallels to the situations both in 1812 and the early 1820s could not have been more clear. Still, this play and others like it had little real impact on the development of theatre history within the country. No truly new playwrights were developing. The repertory stagnated with the same fare as usual, but with the addition of more and more horror-laden melodramas imported from France, whose orphans, tyrants, and natural catastrophes paved the way, in part, for elements of the Romantic stage. Such plays might have been popular, but they were not to everyone's liking. Moratín, writing from Barcelona in 1815 to his friend, the playwright, translator, and *refundidor*, Dionisio Solís, mockingly carped,

Y ¿qué hay de teatros? ¿Qué nuevos ingenios pululan por ahí? No duda que en la Corte de tanto imperio nazcan a docenas cada día, y hagan sonar la escena con tragedias que no hagan dormir ni exciten el vómito, y con comedias que instruyan y alegren. En este emporio cataláunico asoman la cabeza, bastante amenudo, tres o cuatro ropavejeros, muy amigos de sepulcros, paletillas, cráneos rotos y tierra húmeda ... y pobrecita mujer embovedada que llora y gime, hasta que en el quinto acto bajan con hachas y estrépito, y el crudo marido la abraza tierna y cariño-samente, y la consuela diciéndola que todo aquello no ha sido más que una equivocación. El auditorio queda contento, los impresarios ni más ni menos, los autores dicho se está.[48]

(And what's the situation with the theatres? What new geniuses are budding in it? Don't doubt that in such an imperious Court dozens are born each day, and that they are producing tragedies that neither make the audience fall asleep nor throw up, and comedies that instruct and cause joy. In this Catalaunique marketplace three or four ragsellers frequently stick out their heads – much taken as they are by sepulcres, shoulder-blades, broken skulls, and humid earth – ... and a poor little hunched-over wife who cries and whimpers, until the fifth act when they come out with axes and noise, and the crude husband embraces her tenderly and lovingly, and consoles her by saying that it was all merely a misunderstanding. The audience goes away happy, the impresarios the same, and of course the authors.)

One playwright from this time who has been nearly forgotten by the critics is Fernando Joseph Cagigal, Marqués de Casa-Cagigal (1756–1824), soldier, translator, poet, and author of several original comedies.[49] *El matrimonio tratado* (The Negotiated Marriage, 1817), written under the pseudonym Arístipo Megarco, dealt with the same who-will-marry-whom? theme treated so cleverly years before by Moratín. It had little success when performed in Madrid by Andrés Prieto, who had taken over from Máiquez at the Príncipe Theatre, or in Barcelona. Casa-Cagigal, a fervent monarchist, produced three other comedies: *La sociedad sin máscara* (Society Unmasked, 1818), *La educación* (Education, 1818) and *Los perezosos* (The Lazy Ones, 1819), which dealt with themes popularized years earlier by Leandro Fernández de Moratín such as educational reform, the relations between parents and their children, or a woman's right to choose her mate (this latter theme will be picked up by Bretón in his famous *Marcela*).[50] Stifling tradition versus enlightened progress form the major conflict in these comedies – the rich, noble, well-educated members of the upper class inevitably lead the others to accommodation and harmony by the end of the plays. García Castañeda sums up his literary perspective:

Don Fernando Cagigal fue de aquellos militares y marinos ilustrados como Cadalso, el conde de Noroña, Císcar o Jorge Juan, que tuvieron una educación moderna y algunos, un genuino deseo de reformas. Como tantos ilustrados,

[48] Leandro Fernández de Moratín, *Epistolario*, ed. René Andioc (Madrid: Castalia, 1973): 316.
[49] See Salvador García Castañeda, "El marqués de Casa-Cagigal (1756–1824), escritor militar," *La Guerra de la Independencia (1808–1814) y su momento histórico* II (Santander: Centro de Estudios Montañeses, 1979): 743–756, and "Moralidad y reformismo en las comedias del marqués de Casa-Cagigal," *Romanticismo* 1 (1982): 25–34. Casa-Cagigal's plays were published by Agustín Roca in Barcelona.
[50] Ermanno Caldera, *La commedia romantica in Spagna* (Pisa: Giardini Editori, 1978): 59–60.

habría querido transformar la vieja España inmóvil en sus tradiciones y en su fe en otra razonable y abierta a los adelantos de Europa. Fue absolutista y enemigo de revolucionarios, valga decir constitucionales, aunque éstos pidiesen muchas de las innovaciones que él esperaba de un depotismo ilustrado. ("Moralidad," p. 33)

(Don Fernando Cagigal was one of those enlightened military and navy men like Cadalso, the Count of Noroña, Císcar or Jorge Juan, who had a modern education and, at least in some cases, a genuine desire to reform things. Like so many enlightened individuals, he would have preferred to transform the old Spain, set in her ways and in her faith, into a different country, more reasonable and open to European advances. He was an absolutist and enemy of revolutionaries, that is of the defenders of the constitution, even though these individuals were demanding many of the same innovations that he hoped would come from enlightened despotism.)

Men of talent were writing for the Madrid stage, but were channelling their energies mostly into the production of *refundiciones* and translations. Félix Enciso Castrillón[51] and Dionisio Solís[52] were the best examples of *refundidores* working during this period; both men received much praise for their efforts, but the absence of truly original plays kept the theatres from developing their full, if limited, potential.[53] Only *Indulgencia para todos* (Indulgence for Everyone) by Manuel Eduardo de Gorostiza (1789–1851),[54] which opened on 14 September 1818, offered some glimmer of hope for that year's season. It is a surprisingly mature play, written with a rich command of vocabulary, superb dramatic control, and interesting characters. The parts were played by the Príncipe's best actors (Máiquez, Agustina Torres, Gertrudis Torre, Joaquín Caprara, Antonio Guzmán) and the author emphasized the theme of a brilliant but rigid suitor whose severe (he is named "don Severo") criticism of others comes back to haunt him, forcing him to learn tolerance

51 See Joaquín Álvarez Barrientos, "Acercamiento a Félix Enciso Castrillón," *II Seminario de Historia de la Real Sociedad Bascongada de los Amigos del País* (San Sebastián: n.p., 1989): 59–84.

52 On Solís, see Juan Eugenio Hartzenbusch, "Noticias sobre la vida y escritos de D. Dionisio Solís. 1839," *Ensayos poéticos y artículos en prosa, literarios y de costumbres* (Madrid: Yenes, 1843), pp. 173–214; Sterling A. Stoudemire, "Dionisio Solís's 'refundiciones' of Plays (1800–1834)," *Hispanic Review* 8 (1940): 305–310; H. L. Ballew, "The Life and Work of Dionisio Solís," doctoral dissertation, University of North Carolina, 1957; Gies, "Hacia un catálogo," and "Dionisio Solís, entre dos/tres siglos."

53 More work needs to be done on the important issue of *refundiciones* during this period. See Edward V. Coughlin, "Neoclassical *refundiciones* of Golden Age *comedias* (1772–1831)," doctoral dissertation, University of Michigan, 1965. Some information on staging is available in A. M. Coe, *Catálogo bibliográfico y crítico de las comedias anunciadas en los periódicos de Madrid desde 1661 hasta 1819* (Baltimore: Johns Hopkins University Press, 1935), and Charlotte M. Lorenz, "Seventeenth Century Plays in Madrid From 1801–1818," *Hispanic Review* 6 (1938): 324–331.

54 See Armando de María y Campos, *Manuel Eduardo de Gorostiza y su tiempo* (Mexico: La Nación, 1959).

and "indulgence," two characteristics which he normally rejected: "La indulgencia es flojedad, / la tolerancia simpleza" ("Indulgence is a weakness; toleration a foolishness") (II, iv). The play attracted enough of an audience to keep it on the boards for a few days. Don Carlos provides the moral early on:

> Que quien no conoce el mundo
> sino por libros; quien trata
> de encontrar en cada hombre
> un Catón, mucho se engaña
> a sí mismo, y mil pesares
> para los demás prepara.
> La perfección está lejos
> de nosotros por desgracia;
> y el que se juzga perfecto,
> mal podrá sufrir las trabas
> que el lazo social impone ...
>
>   (I, 3)

(Whoever knows the world only through books; whoever tries to find a Cato in every man, deceives himself and creates a thousand sorrows for everyone else. Unfortunately, we are far from perfect: whoever judges himself to be perfect will not be able to deal with the bonds that the social contract imposes ...)

It is a play in the tradition of Moratín, and Gorostiza is often viewed as a transitional figure between Moratín's neoclassical comedies and Bretón's more modern renditions. Caldera has rightly called Gorostiza "el príncipe de la escena cómica madrileña hasta el advenimiento de Bretón de los Herreros"[55] ("the prince of the Madrid comic theatre until the arrival of Bretón de los Herreros") for this play, along with two others which would gain him lasting attention: *Don Dieguito* (Little Don Diego, 1821) and, on the eve of Romanticism, *Contigo pan y cebolla* (Bread and Onion and Thou, 1833).[56]

The actors enriched their ranks with new, but raw, talent (Concepción Rodríguez, future leading lady of the Romantic stage, performed her first roles in Madrid in March 1818), so true reform would not come from that quarter either. Fernando VII disliked Máiquez, and rarely attended performances at the Príncipe (he assiduously attended performances at the Cruz). Perhaps it was because Máiquez was among the intellectuals and writers jailed briefly in 1814; perhaps it was jealousy of Máiquez's enormous public appeal. As Cotarelo writes, "Verdaderamente parece increíble que cuando todo Madrid corría presuroso a oír a este actor

---

55 Ermanno Caldera and Antonietta Calderone, "El teatro en el siglo XIX (1808–1844)," in *Historia del teatro en España* II, ed. José María Díez Borque (Madrid: Taurus, 1988), p. 407.
56 See the recent edition of this play by John Dowling (Valencia: Albatros Ediciones, 1992).

célebre tragedias y comedias que no había ejecutado hacía bastante tiempo, no acudiese el Rey, que tampoco se las había oído, a unir su aplauso con el de todo un pueblo"[57] ("It truly seems incredible that when all of Madrid ran anxiously to hear this celebrated actor perform tragedies and comedies he had not performed in some time, that the King, who had also not heard them, did not join his applause to the people's"). Whatever the reason, Máiquez was *persona non grata* in royal circles. The theatre limped along, even under Máiquez's energetic command, until three events occurred which would threaten it with complete extinction: Máiquez's second banishment ("retirement") from the Príncipe company in 1819, his subsequent death in Granada a year later, and the political crisis brought on by the Revolución de Riego in 1820.

Spanish theatre in the 1820s

Once again, Spanish theatre was deeply immersed in a crisis, only partly of its making. The political and economic circumstances of the country were such that little enthusiasm could be engendered for theatrical reform and even the arrival in Madrid in 1820 of many of the exiled intellectuals was not enough to reinvigorate the theatre. The companies themselves, battered and diminished by Máiquez's mistreatment and, now, absence, suffered a lack of leadership. When Máiquez disappeared, so did the audience, and the theatres struggled in vain to remain financially solvent (receipts fell to half their previous levels following Máiquez's first dismissal from the Príncipe in 1818).

The years of the Trienio Constitucional (1820–1823) inspired some minor theatrical *piezas de circunstancia* on the themes of the Constitution, tyranny, and political opportunism, and the like, similar to what had been seen on stage during the 1808–1812 period. In these plays the liberal progressives are pitted against the reactionary "serviles," with the former usually emerging victorious. Gorostiza wrote and staged *Virtud y patriotismo, o El 1 de enero de 1820* (Virtue and Patriotism, or 1 January 1820) to commemorate the Riego revolt (the author dedicated the play to "Ciudadano Riego" ["Citizen Riego"]) and, similarly, *Una noche de alarma en Madrid* (A Night of Alarm in Madrid, 1821).[58]

At least two important dramatists had plays staged during the turbulent years of the Trienio. Gorostiza's *Don Dieguito* was performed in the capital on 7 January 1820, and dealt with – among other things – the

[57] Cotarelo, *Máiquez*, p. 446.
[58] Little is known of the theatre during the Trienio. Much valuable information about repertory and performances is available in A. K. Shields, "The Madrid Stage, 1820–1833," unpublished doctoral dissertation, University of North Carolina, 1933.

pompous ways of a silly *petimetre*, the Frenchified fop which had been a popular object of satire since the mid-eighteenth century (the elder Moratín's *La petimetra*, 1762, is a good example). What does Don Dieguito know? "¡Sabe francés!" ("He knows French!"), which apparently is all he thinks he needs to know in order to win the hand (and the estates) of Adela.

More important than Gorostiza's play was that staged by one of the most significant political and literary figures of the first half of the nineteenth century in Spain. Francisco Martínez de la Rosa (1787–1862), released from prison in 1820, wrote *La niña en casa y la madre en la máscara* (The Girl at Home and the Mother at the Masked Ball) in order to address an issue of major concern during these times, one with which Moratín had grappled earlier on: the education of young women. It premièred on 6 December 1821, and ran eleven times at the Príncipe that season, as well as three times at the Cruz. As has been seen, his plays were not unknown in Spain (aside from *La viuda de Padilla*, he had also written a minor comedy, *¡Lo que puede un empleo!* in 1812), but during the Trienio he briefly consolidated his literary and political power. In *La niña en casa* Teodoro pursues two women at one time, the innocent but foolish Inés and her mother, the greedy social climber Leoncia. The play has conscious echoes of *El sí de las niñas* in it, but Martínez manages to shift the focus of attention from the old man–young woman axis to one of rivalry between a mother and her daughter, which leads, naturally, to disharmony and conflict.[59] Tragedy is averted when both women realize that real love consists in a warm mother–daughter friendship and a true man–woman relationship (Inés marries the real object of her love, Luis). When *La niña en casa* reappeared in Madrid in April, 1834 (just days before the première of *La conjuración de Venecia*), Larra, while remaining critical of several failed scenes and characters, compared its comic censure of customs with those of Molière, Kotzebue, Regnard, Ducange, and, of course, Moratín.[60] Such comparisons are entirely justified: *La niña en casa* is a Moratinian comedy, anxious to maintain the concepts and structures of neoclassical theatre (*utile dulce*, three classical unities, didacticism). As the author himself noted in the "Advertencia" to the version published in his *Obras literarias* in 1827,

Como el mejor de nuestros poetas cómicos modernos [Moratín] ya había presentado en varios cuadros las resultas de la educación apocada y monjil que solía darse a las hijas en España, me propuse por argumento de esta composición

---

59 See John Dowling's "Moratín's Creation of the Comic Role for the Older Actress," *Theatre Survey* 24 (1983): 55–63.
60 "Representación de *La niña en casa y la madre en la máscara*," *La Revista Española* (14 April 1834), in BAE 127, 370–374.

censurar un vicio diferente, más común en el estado actual de nuestras costumbres, cual es el que se origina, en el teatro del mundo, del mal ejemplo y del descuido de las madres.[61]

(Since the best of our modern dramatic poets had already presented in various works the results of the limited, nun-like education that Spain's daughters tend to receive, I decided in this play to censure a different vice, one more common today, which is the result of the poor example and negligence of mothers.) ·

The rest of the repertory during these turbulent times drew from the same *refundiciones* and translated comedies, tragedies, and melodramas which appeared consistently on Madrid stages, some of which would, however, gain new life during the decade. Plays such as *El huérfano y el asesino* (The Orphan and the Assassin), Solís's *refundición* of Tirso's *Por el sótano y el torno* (Through the Basement and the Dumbwaiter), *El abate L'Epée* (The Abbot from Epée), and the silly *comedia de magia* entitled *Lo necesario y lo superfluo* (What's Needed and What's Not) (which would enjoy enormous popularity in 1830 when transformed into *El diablo verde* [The Green Devil]) were the staple offerings of the times. Some interest in opera, interest which would soon develop into a veritable "frenzy," is also evident during the Trienio in the stagings of Rossini's *La cenerentola, Elisabetta, Tancredo, El barbero de Sevilla*, and *Otelo*. (Rossini, who turned thirty in 1822 was, of course, the rage in all of Europe.) Martínez de la Rosa's *¡Lo que puede un empleo!* and *La viuda de Padilla* appeared with some frequency (increasingly in 1822 after he was named Prime Minister) and Moratín's *El barón* (The Baron), *La comedia nueva, El sí de las niñas* and *La mojigata* (The Pious Deceiver), which had never disappeared from the repertory, were also seen during these years.[62] During moments of the most intense political uncertainty, the theatre became a reflection of the public's concerns, but such moments were short-lived. One typical period is September, 1821, following Riego's series of defeats (he was dismissed from his post in Aragón, for example, on 4 September) when there appeared in the theatres those dramas calculated to underscore not only the rightness of resistance to "tyranny" but also support for the liberal cause. Quintana's *Pelayo*, Martínez de la Rosa's *La viuda de Padilla*, and the anonymous *Juan de Padilla o los comuneros* (Juan de Padilla or the Landowners) showed up briefly on stages in the capital to assure their audiences of the worthiness of their ideas.

The most significant change in the structure, ownership, and place of the theatre in Madrid society during this decade came in mid-1823 with the French invasion. Among the foreigners arriving in the capital with the

---

[61] Martínez, *Obras*, BAE 148, p. 67.
[62] Shields, "The Madrid Stage," gives specific information about performances.

Cien Mil Hijos de San Luis was a soldier named Jean Marie Grimaldi, soon to be known in intellectual circles as Juan de Grimaldi. I have provided the details of his astonishing renovation of the Spanish stage elsewhere,[63] but it is important here to note his deep commitment to his adoptive country and his belief in the ability of theatre to affect social change. Grimaldi was a supreme opportunist with an uncanny ability to convince those around him to do his bidding, but his passion for literature and his respect for writers and actors won him the admiration of a budding group of important literary people. His elegance, wit and, later, immense wealth, also earned him a following among the aristocracy, and thereby, access to important circles of "political movers and shakers." His relations with the theatre hierarchy (mostly, the City Council which owned the theatres and contracted them out on an annual basis) were never smooth, but he usually managed to have his way in matters dealing with the repertory, the training of actors, and the staging of selected plays.

When Grimaldi arrived in Madrid the theatres had been closed due to bankruptcy and the disruptions caused by the political situation. After long and contentious negotiations with the City Council he took charge of the Cruz and the Príncipe and opened his first theatrical season on 21 September 1823. No immediate surprises were noted in the schedule, which contained such stock items as *Don Gil de las calzas verdes*, *El viejo y la niña*, *Misantropía y arrepentimiento* (Misanthropy and Repentance), *El vergonzoso en palacio*, *El tutor celoso y la lugareña astuta* (The Jealous Tutor and the Astute Village Lass), *A falta de hechiceros* (When There are no Wizards Available), *Del rey abajo, ninguno* (None Below the King), *El perro de Montargis* (The Dog from Montargis) and *El mejor alcalde, el rey* (No Greater Judge than the King Himself). Several facts merit attention. First is the appearance of José María de Carnerero as a playwright. Carnerero, whose important career as a journalist would develop fully during this "Ominous Decade" (1823–1833), has properly not been remembered as a dramatist, but he worked closely with Grimaldi during the 1820s and was counted among the lively group attempting to bring high-quality literary life into the capital. Second is the appearance of two actors who would develop into major stars in the coming years, José García Luna (1798–1865) and Carlos Latorre (1799–1851). In 1825 Grimaldi married the soon-to-be leading lady of the Spanish stage, Concepción Rodríguez (1802–1859), and transformed her from a second-rate ingénue into a woman whose performances in the great Romantic plays were often memorable events.

Few plays from the 1820s have received re-readings, or even mention,

---

[63] See Gies, *Theatre and Politics*.

by modern students of Spanish theatre. Most "histories" of Spanish theatre gloss over this time period, preferring instead, with some natural justification, to focus all attention on the Romantic stage. However, full comprehension of Spanish Romantic theatre is impossible without a solid knowledge of the type of plays which informed the new playwrights and which prepared the audiences to understand what they were seeing. The intellectual world of the 1820s was lively and contentious, if clipped and hedged in by the rigors of censorship, fear of ecclesiastical and political authorities, and lack of access to the best of the modern European stage. Still, under Grimaldi's guidance interesting developments were taking place in Spain which need to be studied if we are to get a full picture of what was going on.

Grimaldi's commitment to the professionalization of the theatre made its mark in several ways. He managed to challenge the city stranglehold on theatre management, if not with complete success, at least enough to bring into question the long-standing tradition of public ownership (and hence control). While he never managed to wrest the theatres away from the government entirely, he did open the way for the mixture of public and private ownership which developed in the late 1830s and which would become the dominant *modus operandi* of the theatres in Spain from that time on. As a businessman, he was of course interested in maximizing his potential gain while minimizing his risk, but he must be credited with investing sizeable amounts of time and thought into improving the theatres in the 1820s and 1830s. Those improvements included the training of actors, the call for a nationally subsidized School of Acting (which came into being when the Real Conservatorio de María Cristina was founded in 1831), the enrichment of the repertory, the physical rehabilitation of the two theatres in which he worked, the nourishing of a group of intellectuals who wrote or translated plays, the development of an intelligent, appreciative audience, and the insistence on proper dress, props and scenery for the performances he directed. His overarching goal, as he explained many times, was to bring Spanish theatre up to the level of theatre in the rest of Europe. The individuals recruited by Grimaldi for his enterprise included two men who would dominate the literary scene for the next dozen years.

Manuel Bretón de los Herreros (1796–1873) and Ventura de la Vega (1807–1865) entered Grimaldi's sphere early, in the 1824–1825 season, and stayed with him through the triumphant and chaotic years of the 1830s, until Grimaldi was forced to flee, under mysterious circumstances, back to France in 1836. Bretón wrote his first comedy, *A la vejez viruelas* (A Pox on Old Age), in 1818 but was forced by circumstances to await its production until October, 1824, when it was shown at the Príncipe.

Bretón's adherence to Moratín's style can be seen in the comical characters and confusions which dominate the play. The decrepit don Braulio[64] wishes to marry the young and lovely Joaquina; the old lady doña Francisca wants to marry young Enrique, who naturally is in love himself with Joaquina. No mystery could exist about how the play would end – foolish old-age vanity is frustrated and young love triumphs – but Bretón's adroit manipulation of language and sharp observations on the foibles of humanity kept the audience laughing. Bretón diverted the audiences away from the harsh political realities of the day. As Larra would later remember,

Negar a este autor el mérito de una laboriosidad infinita, fuera grave parcialidad: desde el año 1825 [*sic*, although Larra was not entirely wrong since *A la vejez* was first published in 1825], en que, si mal no nos acordamos, dio por primera vez a luz sus producciones, hasta el día, no sólo se ha presentado infatigable sectario de la musa cómica, sino que ha sido el único perseverante, el único que ha conservado constantemente encendido el fuego sacro; el único que poco o ningún homenaje ha tributado al genio político que nos traquetea; conoció su verdadera misión y, no habiendo abandonado nunca el puesto que su vocación y la gratitud le designaron, ha sido una columna de nuestro teatro nacional. Por nuestra mala dicha, éste ha degenerado en gran manera de su antigua gloria; pero, al menos, débese al señor Bretón la consideración de haber contribuído por su parte con todas sus fuerzas a que no acabara de extinguirse.[65]

(It would be unjust to deny this author credit for his amazing industriousness: since 1825 when, if we remember correctly, he presented his first production, until now, not only has he shown himself to be an indefatigable supporter of the comic muse, but he has also been the only one who has persevered, the only one who has constantly kept alight the sacred fire, the only one who has paid little or no homage to the political genius that agitates us. He knew what his true mission was, and never abandoning the post that his vocation and our gratitude assigned him, he has been a buttress of our national theatre. Unfortunately, our theatre has degenerated from what was its ancient glory, but at least we can credit Mr. Bretón with having contributed with all his might to the fact that it has not been extinguished completely.)

Bretón was the first great heir to the Moratinian tradition. Other dramatists had patterned their works on the master of neoclassical comedy (most successfully, Gorostiza and Casa Cagigal) but none had the wit, fluidity, and satirical bent of Bretón. Moratín was the undisputed "authority" of the moment,[66] but we shall see that his influence over the

---

[64] Flynn notes that the *senex* figure is a staple in Bretón's theatre. Gerard Flynn, *Manuel Bretón de los Herreros* (Boston: G. K. Hall, 1978): 23.

[65] "*La redacción de un periódico*, comedia original en cinco actos y en verso, por don Manuel Bretón de los Herreros," *El Español* (8 July 1836).

[66] Patrizia Garelli, *Bretón de los Herreros e la sua 'formula comica'* (Imola: Galeati, 1983), 15. Garelli posits that Bretón considered Moratín more of a "compagno ed amico" than "maestro" (18).

younger dramatist was neither total nor, certainly, oppressive. Bretón claimed solidarity with Moratín's style of comedy not only because Inarco's plays were so rich and suggestive, but also because it was expedient for him to identify himself with the revered playwright in the early stages of his career. The younger dramatist needed to chart a course between imitation of Inarco and the creation of an original brand of comic production. The plays from the 1820s were marked heavily by the style of the master, but by the early 1830s (with *Marcela o ¿a cuál de los tres?* [Marcela, or Which of the Three Suitors to Choose?], 1831) he was beginning to develop a recognizably Bretonian style. In 1850, looking back upon the beginnings of his career, he distanced himself from Moratín by pointing out that the times in which the two men wrote were clearly different, leaving the suggestion that different responses to those times were needed. His posture, he claimed, was to "admirar al inmortal Inarco, y rara vez de proponérselo por modelo hasta donde la índole particular de su pobre ingenio y la diferencia de tiempos y circunstancias se lo han permitido"[67] ("admire the immortal Inarco, and rarely to set him up as a model except to the degree that his poor genius and the different times and circumstances permitted"). What is clear is that Bretón is not to be considered a mere imitator of Moratín.

During the 1820s Bretón wrote several amusing plays which received enthusiastic applause in the capital. Among these were *Los dos sobrinos* (The Two Nephews, 1825), whose young independent widow Catalina and terrible rhymester Joaquín prefigure Marcela and Agapito of *Marcela*, and *A Madrid me vuelvo* (I'm Going Back to Madrid, 1828), which develops the city/country conflict Bretón mined so successfully in *El pelo de la dehesa* (The Country Bumpkin at Court, 1840). Ermanno Caldera perceptively detects in *Los dos sobrinos* Bretón's embryonic confrontation of contemporary middle class life with the life and values of the *Ancien Régime*,[68] a posture suggesting that the change from the old world view to the new was already, if subtly, being seen in the capital. *Los dos sobrinos* played in 1825, 1827, 1829 and 1831; *A Madrid* in 1828, 1829, 1830, and 1832.

The *comedia de magia*

Madrid audiences respectfully attended the comedies, tragedies, translations, and *refundiciones* presented to them during the Fernandine era. They made high demands on the impresarios and actors, not of quality

---

67 Manuel Bretón de los Herreros, "Prólogo a la edición de 1850," in *Obras* I (Madrid: Miguel Ginesta, 1883): 1.
68 Caldera, "El hecho literario," in *Historia del teatro en España* II, ed. Díez Borque, p. 416.

but of quantity. That is, while they were often indifferent to the way a play was presented, what was essential for them was a rapidly changing repertory of diversions which would keep them coming back to the theatre every evening. The dizzying array of performances explains why much of the acting was so abysmal,[69] but the audience's hunger for diversion was such that impresarios and stage directors – mostly Grimaldi in the 1820s – created a veritable cottage industry of writers, translators, and *refundidores* to meet the demand. What truly excited these audiences, though, were the spectacular magical comedies which had had such a checkered history since their first appearance in the court of Felipe IV in the seventeenth century.

What Andioc writes for the eighteenth century is equally valid for the first half of the nineteenth:

sin contradicción posible, es una variedad de comedia de teatro, la comedia de magia, la que, como hemos visto, supera con regularidad todas las marchas de asistencia y duración, al menos hasta los últimos años del setecientos.[70]

(Speaking without contradiction, it is a kind of theatrical comedy, the magical comedy, which, as we have seen, regularly beat out other plays in attendance and duration, at least until the end of the 1700s.)

Plays such as José Cañizares's *Don Juan de Espina en Milán* (Don Juan de Espina in Milan, 1713), *Marta la Romarantina* (1716), and *El anillo de Giges* (1740), Juan Salvo y Vela's multiple-part *El mágico de Salerno* (The Magician from Salerno, 1718–1720), *El asombro de Jerez, Juana la Rabicortona* (The Terror of Jerez, Juana the Tailcutter, 1741), Ramón de la Cruz's *Marta abandonada y carnaval de París* (Martha Abandoned, and Carnaval in Paris, 1762), the anonymous *Brancanelo el herrero* (Brancanelo the Blacksmith) and numerous others were staged frequently during the eighteenth century[71] in spite of the bitter opposition to them mounted by the Neoclassicists and the government censors. Their performances were banned by decree in 1788 and 1799, but neither ban was honored by impresarios, actors, or public; frequently, *comedias de magia*

---

[69] See Gies, "Larra, Grimaldi and the Actors of Madrid," pp. 120–122.

[70] Andioc, *Teatro y sociedad*, p. 49. As Joaquín Álvarez Barrientos points out, the *comedia de magia* as "género definido" is a product of the eighteenth century. "Problemas del género en la comedia de magia," in *El teatro español a fines del siglo XVII. Historia, cultura y teatro en la España de Carlos II*, eds. Javier Huerta Calvo, et al., II (Amsterdam: Rodopi, 1989): 301–310.

[71] See Antonietta Calderone, "Catalogo delle commedie di magia rappresentate a Madrid nel Secolo XVIII," in *Teatro di magia*, ed. Ermanno Caldera (Rome: Bulzoni, 1983): 236–268. On the history of the *comedia de magia* in Spain, see Julio Caro Baroja, *Teatro popular y de magia* (Madrid: Revista de Occidente, 1974) and Joaquín Álvarez Barrientos, "La comedia de magia. Estudio de su estructura y recepción popular," Ph.D. dissertation, Madrid, Universidad Complutense, 1987.

were staged, but with altered titles which ostensibly masked their true nature.[72] Yet Fernando VII was enchanted by the spectacular effects of these silly but entertaining comedies, and they recaptured their fashionable status by the second decade of the nineteenth century. Cotarelo documents that "El Rey asistió muchas veces a los dos teatros en este año [1815–1816], sin desdeñar las funciones más populares, pues volvieron las comedias de magia, como *Marta la Romarantina, El anillo de Giges* y *El mágico de Eriván* [by Valladares]"[73] (The King frequently attended the two theatres this year, without looking down on more popular plays, and as a result magical comedies like *Marta la Romarantina, El anillo de Giges* and *El mágico de Eriván* returned to the theatres"). The *comedias de magia* appealed to a wide public precisely because they offered something for everyone: they were often visually impressive, funny, suspenseful, witty, and colorful: "De este modo, la comedia de magia se convierte en algo amable para muchos, pues tiene algo que ofrecer a casi todos. Tiene diversión verbal, visual, humor, espectáculo, moral, sentencias, baile, música, incluso sentido común"[74] ("This way, the magical comedy becomes something beloved by many people, since it has something for almost everyone. It has verbal and visual wit, humor, spectacle, a moral lesson, dogma, dance, music, and even common sense").

While the *comedias de magia* had long been a staple in the Spanish repertory, it was the appearance of Grimaldi's astonishingly successful *La pata de cabra* in 1829 that provided both the final major impetus for the genre in the nineteenth century and an important transition into the Romantic theatre. Its unprecedented popularity has been documented elsewhere,[75] but it is well to remember that Zorrilla's claim that his father signed 72,000 regional passports so their holders could "pasa[r] a Madrid a ver *La pata de cabra*" ("come to Madrid to see *The Goat's Hoof*") was not an exaggeration, as had previously been thought. Grimaldi's strength was to draw upon the improved acting and staging techniques he had been developing since 1823, graft them onto his play (adapted from a French original)[76] and pitch it at the correct level for an audience somewhat more sophisticated than those who went to the *comedias de magia* decades before.

en las comedias de magia decimonónicas, dirigidas a un público más culto que asiste también a otras manifestaciones teatrales, se intenta divertir, pero incorpo-

[72] Joaquín Álvarez Barrientos, "Aproximación a la incidencia de los cambios estéticos y sociales de finales del siglo XVIII y comienzos del XIX en el teatro de la época: comedias de magia y dramas románticos," *Castilla* 13 (1988): 18.
[73] Cotarelo, *Máiquez*, p. 397.   [74] Álvarez Barrientos, "Aproximación," p. 21.
[75] See Gies, " 'Inocente estupidez'," and *Theatre and Politics*, pp. 63–80.
[76] Ermanno Caldera, "*La pata de cabra* y *Le pied du mouton*," *Studia Historica et Philologica in honorem M. Batllori* (Rome: Instituto Español de Cultura, 1984): 567–575.

rando al mismo tiempo aquello que es del gusto de ese público. Es decir, los nuevos elementos estéticos identificadores de la naciente burguesía. El teatro tiene que exponer al hombre en su individualidad, o como representante de una clase. No se propone al hombre abstracto ... sino al concreto, determinado por la historia y por las leyes, por la sociedad, por lo público y lo privado.[77]

(in nineteenth-century magical comedies, aimed at a more sophisticated public that was also attending other theatrical performances, there was an attempt to entertain, but at the same time to incorporate something that this public liked. That is to say, the new aesthetic elements which identified the nascent middle classes. The theatre must depict man as an individual or as a representative of a class. It does not depict an abstract man ... but rather a concrete one, determined by history and the law, by society, by public and by private considerations.)

In his *Discurso* (1828) Agustín Durán had perceived a similar shift from the abstract to the concrete in the theatre, and he defended Spain's new concept of drama against those who blindly attacked it for being too "Spanish."[78]

La pata de cabra was a marvellously entertaining creation, full not only of spectacular visual effects (there are thirty-five magical effects, some quite difficult to execute) but also topical references, humorous plays on words, visual gags, and strong, interesting characters. Don Simplicio is the prototypical buffoon whose combination of arrogance and cowardice gave Antonio Guzmán one of the most famous roles of his career. Its simple, moralistic love tale ("love conquers all") plays itself out against a background of farce and magic. The importance of Grimaldi's enterprise cannot be exaggerated for the history of the Spanish stage in the first half of the nineteenth century: it brought enormous sums of money into the theatre (and into his own pockets) and helped to create an audience prepared for the extravagances it would soon witness when the Romantic plays – most of them staged by Grimaldi – burst upon Madrid. *La pata de cabra* brought audiences back into the theatre and helped, as José Yxart has claimed, to "levantar al teatro de su postración"[79] ("raise the theatre from its prostration").

Grimaldi's success with *La pata de cabra* stimulated new interest in the *comedias de magia*. Following close on the debut of *La pata de cabra* was the première on 14 January 1830, of the anonymous *El diablo verde*, written with the sole intent of competing with Grimaldi's runaway hit. As *El Correo Literario y Mercantil* reported on 19 October 1829, the play was being prepared to "usurpar su puesto y rivalizar con [*La pata de cabra*]" ("usurp the place of and rival *La pata de cabra*"). Juan Blanchard, the

[77] Álvarez Barrientos, "Aproximación," p. 23.
[78] See Gies, *Agustín Durán: A Biography and Literary Appreciation* (London: Tamesis, 1975): 69–91.
[79] Yxart, *El arte escénico en España* I, p. 19.

talented French set decorator who had come to Madrid at Grimaldi's invitation and who had done the decorations for *La pata de cabra*, set about designing the sets for *El diablo verde* as well.[80] The emphasis on the sets often masked the lack of real literary quality of these *comedias de magia*, but the audience did not seem to mind. What we know about the poor quality of Spanish theatres – the uncomfortable seating, bad lighting, non-existent temperature control, decrepit backdrops – allows us to understand why the public would be impressed with set designs which were professionally done and frequently quite remarkable.[81] Dozens of new scenes and backdrops were painted for *El diablo verde*'s arrival at the Cruz Theatre, whose "escenario se ha hecho famoso ya por su mezquindad" ("scenery has become famous for its cheapness") (*Correo Literario y Mercantil*, 19 October 1829). The play itself, a *refundición* of an adaptation of a translation of a short story (!)[82] betrays its close association with *La pata de cabra* (in fact, murmurs of plagiarism were heard in the press at the time). Several scenes certainly were directly "inspired" by Grimaldi's hit, such as Grimaldi's famous Forges of Vulcan scene (III, 2),[83] which resonates in *El diablo verde*'s scene with Alí and the savages (III, p. 229), or don Simplicio's frustrated attempt to catch his food (II, 8) which is repeated by Cadige (II, p. 166) in *El diablo verde*. One wonders whether the comic reference to a "pata" ("hoof") is not an inside joke for the audience, which was well aware of the attempted rivalry between the two plays:

MAHOMET:	Pobre vieja	
	roed siquiera una pata	
	de pollo.	(*Le da un hueso*)
CADIGE:	Anda al demonio	
	tú y la pata.	(II, p. 171)
MOHAMMED:	Poor old thing, chew at least on a chicken foot [pata	
	= hoof].	(*He gives her a bone*)
CADIGE:	You and the hoof can go to Hell.)	

---

[80] On Blanchard and other related matters, see Joaquín Muñoz Morillejo, *Escenografía española* (Madrid: Real Academia de Bellas Artes de San Fernando, 1923).

[81] Foreign and national observers of the theatre scene wrote harsh evaluations of Spanish theatres in the 1820s. See especially Théodore Anne, *Madrid ou Observations sur les moeurs et usages des espagnols au commencement du XIX siècle* (Paris: Pillet Aîné, 1825); Adolphe Custine, *L'Espagne sous Ferdinand VII* II (Paris: Ladvocat, 1838); Fernando Fernández de Córdoba, *Mis memorias íntimas* I (Madrid: Atlas, 1966); and Dionisio Chaulié, *Cosas de Madrid* II (Madrid: Correspondencia de España, 1886).

[82] *Le necessaire et le superflu*, written in 1813 by Dumersan and Dartois based on an oriental story, was translated and staged in Madrid in 1820 as *Lo necesario y lo superfluo, o El mágico y el cestero*. See *El diablo verde*, ed. Pilar Quel Barastegui (Rome: Bulzoni, 1989). Quel Barastegui inexplicably does not divide the acts into scenes.

[83] See Juan de Grimaldi, *La pata de cabra*, ed. David T. Gies (Rome: Bulzoni, 1986).

Even the protagonist's name called to mind Grimaldi's hilariously exaggerated hero, don Simplicio Bobadilla de Majaderano y Cabeza de Buey; in *El diablo verde* the name is "Alí Aben Zulema Benjajil Ben-Jumejín, el borriquí de la excelsa familia de los Ben-burros," which contains an obviously similar play on words based on reference to the animal kingdom. This use of exotic animals to produce laughter became popular after the appearance of a monkey in *La pata de cabra*; in *El diablo verde* it is a bear which arrives to frighten the comic characters. Bretón's successful translation of *Jocó o el orangután* (Joco or the Orangutan, 1831) added to the trend. The simplistic moral of *El diablo verde* is repeated with such frequency that the audience could not fail to draw some contemporary lesson from the need to distinguish between "lo necesario y lo superfluo" ("what's needed and what's not"). As the Caliph declaims at the play's conclusion:

> el hombre no se contenta
> jamás con lo necesario
> ...
> Mientras que vivido hubieras,
> este bien disfrutarías
> si con cordura y modestia
> lo supieras conservar
> ...
> Tus riquezas
> pasarán al pescador
> que envuelto entre su miseria
> vive sin quejarse.
> ...
> Termínase, pues, la audiencia
> y tened siempre presente
> que el hombre a quien no contenta
> disfrutar lo necesario,
> y lo superfluo desea,
> es un loco criminal
> digno de la mayor pena.

(Man is never content with what he needs ... As long as you live you will enjoy this wealth if you know how to manage it with sense and modesty ... Your riches will be passed on to the fisherman who lives wrapped up in his poverty and does not complain ... End your visit with him and always keep in mind that whoever is not content with enjoying what he needs, and who desires what he does not need, is an insane criminal worthy of the greatest punishment.)

The message could not have been more explicit for Spain in 1830: the magnanimous Caliph insists that his subjects learn to live with their poverty and misery, not questioning his wisdom and guidance, nor demanding what they cannot have ("lo superfluo"). The wife Zaida must sacrifice herself to learn how to care for "esas criaturas tiernas / y del pobre pescador" ("those tender creatures and the poor fisherman"). By learning how to "disfrutar lo necesario" they will avoid being considered "loco criminal" by the wise and kind Caliph. Everything remains in order, in control based on obedience to the rules of society as defined by the Caliph/King.

The play was immensely popular during the 1830–1831 season. It was performed nineteen consecutive days in Madrid at the Cruz Theatre, as well as other performances during the season, although it could not really compete with *La pata de cabra*, which was still going strong at the Príncipe. Still, it was seen on stage fifty-seven times during the first three years of its run. While the public enjoyed the spectacle, serious critics continued their carping about the superficiality of such plays. Early in 1829, as the theatres prepared for *La pata de cabra* and *El diablo verde*, an anonymous voice in *El Correo Literario y Mercantil* (27 January 1829) complained:

Dicen algunos que de algún tiempo a esta parte el Correo apenas habla de teatro. ¿Qué ha de hablar cuando las patas y los diablos reinan exclusivamente en ellos, y apenas hay entrada para un espectáculo regular y tolerable? Las empresas teatrales no se forman con el objeto de perfeccionar el arte, ni de cuidar de dar estímulos a los autores, ni de cultivar el decoro de la escena: se forman para ganar dinero; y si la parte mercantil se llena, poca o ninguna cuenta tendrá el impresario con que se prostituyan las musas.

(Some say that the *Correo* has not talked about the theatre for some time now. What is there to talk about when hoofs and devils predominate exclusively in them, and no regular and tolerable plays are to be found? Theatrical companies are not formed in order to perfect art, nor to stimulate authors, nor to cultivate theatrical decorum: they are formed to make money, and if coffers get filled up, the impresario will not worry too much about the prostitution of the muses.)

"The prostitution of the muses" aside, the author did have a legitimate complaint, but even he realized that the public's tolerance for neoclassical comedies and what he called "comedias arregladas" ("rule-bound plays") was understandably low: "¡Comedias arregladas! ¡Lindo empeño! Para comedias arregladas estamos. Las gentes de los barrios no van a las comedias arregladas, y el círculo de los abonados es demasiado estrecho para llenar el teatro todos los días" ("Rule-bound plays! That's great! We all are in favor of rule-bound comedies. People from the poorer neighborhoods do not go to rule-bound comedies, and the number of people who buy season tickets is not large enough to fill the theatre every day"). This critic pointed to an important truth about theatre in the 1820s: the real patrons for the spectacle-driven and diverting *comedias de magia* (and other similar types of entertainment) were the "gentes de los barrios," and the more educated segment of society patronized (although not exclusively, as *La pata de cabra*'s receipts prove) more serious fare. However, these lines blurred during the 1820s – again, in some respect due to Grimaldi's presence and influence – and theatre audiences melded into a more democratic mixture as the Romantic plays of the mid-1830s appeared on stage. These plays contained serious thought (presumably for the educated theatre-goers) along with flash and spectacle.

As we shall see below, the only real competitors for the attention of the audiences were the operas, which during the late 1820s threatened (in the minds of some critics) to suffocate serious theatre completely, but even they could not keep people, high society and low, away from the *comedias de magia*.[84] As one critic noted, "hasta la ópera *palidece*, y los gorgoritos más finos pierden el pleito en esta lucha. Gallí no puede con don Simplicio Majaderano; y la Albini y la Lorenzani tienen que ceder el paso al corpanchón de la ballena"[85] ("even the opera is losing strength, and the finest vocal trills get defeated in this struggle. Gallí can't compete with don Simplicio Majaderano and Albini and Lorenzani are forced to yield way to the huge body of the whale"). Some critics were prepared to judge the *comedias de magia* more leniently than serious dramas. The noted *refundidor* Féliz Enciso Castrillón allowed in 1832 that

En estas se pintan los prodigios que se supone obra un encantador o mágico; y como en estas piezas apenas cabe el fin moral, se exige del poeta que dé al mágico un buen carácter, y que emplee su fingido poder en auxiliar la virtud y castigar el crimen. Como piezas dedicadas únicamente a la diversión, no se limitan al tiempo y lugar que piden las reglas, y su lenguaje puede ser más artificioso que el de las piezas regulares, pues al poeta que escribe dramas de magia le es permitido violar la verosimilitud con tal que divierta, conservando el decoro que exige el teatro.[86]

(In these plays the marvels supposedly perpetrated by an enchanter or a magician are painted; and since moral concerns rarely figure in these pieces the author needs to make the magician a man of good character who uses his supposed power to enhance virtue and chastise crime. Since they are written merely to entertain they do not limit themselves to the time and place constraints that the rules of theatre require, and their language can be phonier than plays which follow the rules since the author of magical comedies is allowed to avoid verisimilitude as long as he entertains, while maintaining, of course, the decorum that the theatre demands.)

---

[84] This issue is discussed at some length in Gies, "Entre drama y ópera."

[85] *Correo Literario y Mercantil* (27 January 1830). Gallí, Albini and Lorenzani were famous opera stars; the "corpanchón de la ballena" is a reference to *El diablo verde*, in which Alí is swallowed by a whale (Quel Barastegui, *El diablo verde*, p. 236).

[86] Félix Enciso Castrillón, *Principios de literatura, acomodados a la declamación, estractados de varios autores españoles y estrangeros para el uso de los alumnos del Real Conservatorio de Música de María Cristina* (Madrid: Repullés, 1832): 42.

Heightened interest in the *comedias de magia* meant not only that they would be constantly included in the repertories of the 1830s and 1840s, but that new ones would be written by the same authors who were penning the best Romantic dramas and neoclassical comedies of the period. Men who had gained fame with plays such as *Marcela* (1831), *Elena* (1834), and *El pelo de la dehesa* (1840; all by Bretón) and *Los amantes de Teruel* (1837; Hartzenbusch) also wrote and staged pure *comedias de magia*; other plays revealed unmistakable *comedia de magia* influences, for example, *El desengaño en un sueño* (Disillusioned by a Dream, 1842; Rivas) and *Don Juan Tenorio* (1844; Zorrilla).[87] Beyond the Romantic period the *comedias de magia* still enjoyed a lively existence, as *La almoneda del diablo* (The Devil's Auction, 1864), *La espada de Satanás* (Satan's Sword, 1867), and *La gata de oro* (The Golden Cat, 1891; all by Rafael María de Liern), or the six magical plays staged by Enrique Zumel will attest.

Juan Eugenio Hartzenbusch, who had earned fame with his Romantic recreation of a well-known story of tragic young love in *Los amantes de Teruel* (1837), turned in 1839, during the most intense years of the Romantic debate, to the *comedia de magia* for dramatic inspiration. None of his three magical plays has been remembered with much favor today, but all of them were popular in their time and all added to the climate of "spectacular" theatre which characterized the Romantic period. *La redoma encantada* (The Enchanted Flask), which premièred at the Príncipe on 26 October 1839, was hailed somewhat hyperbolically as an "obra maestra" ("masterwork") in *El Entreacto* (31 October 1839), at least for a play "entre las de su género" ("of its type"). Hartzenbusch perhaps entertained the thought of bridging "serious" theatre with his *comedia de magia*; at least *El Entreacto* thought that "en ella encuentra el literato que admirar y el público menos inteligente que aplaudir" ("the intelligent man will find in it things to admire and the less intelligent public things to applaud"). This legitimization of the *comedia de magia* post-Grimaldi was underscored by the same reviewer:

Hemos dicho que el literato encuentra que admirar en *La redoma encantada*, porque su autor ha hecho interesante la fábula y por consiguiente a los personajes, siendo así que luchaba con el peligroso escollo de que intervenía en ella un poder sobrenatural; porque los constrastes están bien entendidos; porque los caracteres están bien marcados y con inteligencia sostenidos; porque el lenguaje es fluido y castizo y en fin porque la versificación es seductora y bella, y en particular sorprendente la que está escrita en castellano antiguo.

---

[87] See Ermanno Caldera, "La magia nel teatro romantico," in *Teatro di magia*, ed. Caldera (Rome: Bulzoni, 1983): 185–205, and Álvarez Barrientos, "Problemas del género," pp. 308–309.

(We have said that the intelligent man will find things to admire in *La redoma encantada* because its author has made the plot and characters interesting, especially since he was flirting with the danger of having a supernatural power intervene in the plot, because the language is fluid and correct, and finally because the versification is seductive and beautiful, in particular the parts he wrote in old Spanish.)

Hartzenbusch demonstrated clear literary talent in the dialogue and development of characters, avoiding easy laughs ("gracias chocarreras") and maintaining "buen gusto" ("good taste"), a neoclassical term which had not yet fallen out of favor among critics. As we will see with *Don Juan Tenorio*, it is significant that this play – and Hartzenbusch's other *comedias de magia* – was performed (by Bárbara Lamadrid, José García Luna, and Juan Lombía) and favorably reviewed during the years preceding the production of Zorrilla's masterpiece. It never really disappeared from the repertory: it played more than thirty times in 1839 alone, and thirty times in the 1840s; a playbill from the Teatro Principal in Barcelona announced that as of 1876 this play "desde su estreno lleva ya más de 160 representaciones" ("since its debut it has had more than 160 performances") (Corbière claims that it had received 292 performances by 1875[88]). Zorrilla himself, along with Ventura de la Vega and Patricio de la Escosura, was one of the backers of *El Entreacto*, so he too, knew and approved of the *comedias de magia*.

La redoma encantada not only lifted elements from *La pata de cabra* (the candles which automatically relight, the echo heard by the protagonist, the comic character's inability to satisfy his hunger), but it anticipated in several important ways Zorrilla's *Don Juan Tenorio* by the inclusion of references to one character as a "don Juan de nuestro tiempo" ("a don Juan for our times") and the arrival of two statues who come to dine with Garibato, "¡dos convidados de piedra!" ("two stone guests!"). These are drawn from Tirso, naturally, but they brought the Tenorio theme back to popular literature through the *comedia de magia*, something which Zorrilla would capitalize upon five years later.

Los polvos de la madre Celestina (Mother Celestina's Powders) (Príncipe, 11 January 1841) followed a similar pattern of "literate" magical effect, and enjoyed a similar popularity (fifty performances during the 1840s and nearly three hundred by the author's death in 1880).[89] It fulfilled the prediction of the critic for *El Panorama*, who wrote, "Ya han dicho sus milagros *Los polvos de la madre Celestina*. El público ha

---

[88] Anthony S. Corbière, *Juan Eugenio Hartzenbusch and the French Theater* (Philadelphia: University of Pennsylvania Press 1927): 78.

[89] Carmen Iranzo inexplicably writes that this play, "filled with inanities, magic tricks, forced humor, allusions to historic and fictional figures, [was] probably impossible to perform." *Juan Eugenio Hartzenbusch* (Boston: G. K. Hall, 1978): 46.

aplaudido este brillante espectáculo, que promete larga vida y con ella abundantes entradas" ("*Los polvos de la madre Celestina* has already displayed its wonders. The public has applauded this brilliant spectacle, which promises to have a long life and sell a lot of tickets") (13 January 1841). Hartzenbusch drew not only on the *comedia de magia* tradition and French plays,[90] but also, as he had done with *Los amantes de Teruel*, on Spain's own literary tradition. His Celestina had little to do with Rojas's (his play takes place near the end of the seventeenth century), but the verbal connection was not lost on an audience by now used to being taken back to the middle ages and Golden Age in the theatre. Álvarez Barrientos points out that "las comedias de Hartzenbusch tuvieron éxito porque traslucían, recordaban muchos pasos de aquellas comedias dieciochescas, aparte de que podían evocar momentos de *La pata de cabra*, como la semejanza entre Don Simplicio y Don Junípero Mastranzos, protagonista de *Los polvos de la madre Celestina*"[91] ("Hartzenbusch's comedies were successful because they reflected, remembered many moments from those eighteenth-century comedies, besides the fact that they could evoke moments from *La pata de cabra*, such as the similarity between don Simplicio and don Junípero Mastranzos, the protagonist of *Los polvos de la madre Celestina*"). The same critic suggests that these comedies attempt to reconcile the past with the present, something which had been one of the major characteristics (the attempt at reconciliation, that is) of the Romantic movement, but which had created rupture and discord instead of synthesis. Perhaps unity through laughter was a more achievable goal. Hartzenbusch had exhausted his interest in, or talent for, *comedias de magia* by the time he wrote *Las Batuecas*, which failed when it appeared in October, 1843 (it received only seven performances during the 1843–1844 season, and disappeared from the repertory completely). The author drew upon the public's knowledge of the backward region (which had been satirized by Larra in the mid-1830s) and, perhaps, their memory of the witch-who-steals-a-young-child theme popularized by García Gutiérrez in *El trovador* in 1836; he combined both items with his main source, Lope's comedy, *Las Batuecas del duque de Alba* (The Duke of Alba's Rural Lands).[92] One critic prematurely announced the death of the *comedia de magia* genre, while at the same time criticizing Hartzenbusch's seemingly declining interest in it.

90 Hartzenbusch's main source was *Les pilules du diable*, written in 1839 by Ferdinand Laloue.
91 Álvarez Barrientos, "Aproximación," p. 27.
92 The play had been rewritten by Matos Fragoso and Hoz y Mota, although it hadn't been seen in Madrid for years. As Corbière has demonstrated, Hartzenbusch also drew upon two French sources. *Juan Eugenio Hartzenbusch*, p. 88.

No cabe duda: las comedias de magia van caducando: para escribirlas se requiere más paciencia y mecanismo que inspiración y talento: por eso desearíamos que el señor Hartzenbusch no malgastase sus brillantes cualidades dramáticas en obras de este género, en que de la *Redoma encantada* descendió a los *Polvos de la madre Celestina* y de allí a *Las Batuecas*, cuyo éxito ha sido poco lisonjero. (*Revista de Teatros*, 29 October 1843)

(There is no doubt about it: magical comedies are dying, since to write them one needs more patience and technical skill than inspiration and talent. That is why we wish Mr. Hartzenbusch would not waste his brilliant dramatic skills on works of this nature. His *Redoma encantada* declined into *Los polvos de la madre Celestina*, and this declined further into *Las Batuecas*, whose success has been less than flattering.)

Hartzenbusch did not include his *comedias de magia* in the edition of his *Obras escogidas* he approved for publication in 1850,[93] but he did revise *La redoma encantada* for restaging in 1862 and 1875.

Bretón, the most fertile comic genius of his day, did not have quite as much success with his *comedias de magia* as did Hartzenbusch. *La pluma prodigiosa* (The Prodigious Pen) (Príncipe, 3 November 1841) was performed a respectable number of times after its debut (18 times), but it never became part of the standard repertory of offerings. It draws on several recently popularized motifs – the gypsy, the three wishes, the magic talisman – to present a simple tale of love and adventure. In fact, it cannibalized several earlier productions by lifting ideas and figures from productions with which the audience had some familiarity. There are scenes of a gypsy reading the hero's fortune (seen previously in *Don Alvaro*), complaints by the heroine who was "en hora infausta nacida" ("born at an accursed hour") (also reminiscent of *Don Alvaro*), the comic hero's sudden elongation (seen in *La pata de cabra*), the appearance of comic animals (here, an elephant and a dromedary, which crudely explodes "truenos por la boca y por el estremo opuesto" ["thunder from his mouth and from his other end"] [I, 19]), and so on. Bretón, so deeply immersed in the theatrical world which he in part helped to create, drew upon it to cobble together this innocuous and self-conscious (Buitrago, the comic figure, proclaims early, "yo nací para gracioso / de una comedia de magia" ["I was born to be the jokester in a magical comedy"] [I, 1]) entertainment. Antonio Ferrer, writing in the pages of the *Revista de Teatros* (16 November 1841), declared it the weakest of the *comedias de magia* he has seen, suggesting rather nastily that the decorations were more interesting than the text itself.

Asistimos pues al Príncipe y entre bailes y música vocal e instrumental pasamos tres buenas horas, que nos condujeron naturalmente a recordar todas las

---

[93] *Obras escogidas de don J. E. Hartzenbusch* (Paris: Baudry, 1850).

comedias de magia que conocemos, para concluir que tenemos por la más excelente a la *Redoma encantada*, y por la peor a la *Pluma prodigiosa* ... A no saber de antemano que la comedia era del señor Bretón de los Herreros, difícilmente lo hubiéramos conocido por la versificación harto débil para ser suya, si se esceptúan algunos romances en agudos. Las diez y nueve decoraciones nuevas solo merecen elogios y aplausos, y creemos sinceramente que con irlas desarrollando sucesivamente a la vista del público y con las danzas y los coros de música, podía haberse suprimido todo lo demás, sin que por eso hubieran salido los espectadores menos satisfechos de la fiesta.

(We went to the Principe Theatre and between dances and vocal and instrumental music we spent three pleasant hours, which naturally got us thinking about all the magical comedies we know, concluding that *La redoma encantada* is the best and that *La pluma prodigiosa* is the worst ... If one did not know beforehand that it was by Mr. Bretón de los Herreros, it would have been difficult for us to figure that out because the versification was too weak to be his [excluding a few romances]. The nineteen new set decorations only deserve praise and applause, and we sincerely believe that had the sets and dances and musical choruses kept coming, everything else could have been left out, and the audience would have gone home no less satisfied.)

Ferrer captures the weaknesses of the play, but he overlooks one of its most interesting elements – the use of the "pluma prodigiosa" as a metaphor for writing, and for Bretón's profession, in the early 1840s. The quill is used symbolically in the play. It is a magic talisman with which Gonzalo, the hero, will help humanity, and it provides the author with several opportunities to comment on the fate of the artist in Romantic Spain. For one thing, the gypsy tells Gonzalo that "debereis a la pluma / lo que pedís a la espada" ("you owe to the pen what you demand of the sword") (I, 2), privileging the written word over arms, suggesting perhaps a writer's response to the militaristic turmoil assaulting Spain in the early 1840s. The pen will save the hero and put things right: "Si quieres ver cumplido tu deseo, / en el aire o escribes y laus deo" ("If you want to see your dream come true, write and praise God"). When he loses the magic pen, the world becomes ominous and unfeeling. Finally, when Gonzalo admits that he really wants to be a poet ("Musas divinas, ¡inspiradme!" ["Divine muses, inspire me!"] [II, 4]), a serpent appears to steal the quill and Gonzalo is given a stern lecture by the magician Abenjabul.

> Verás cumplida
> tu vocación. ¿Pero ignoras
> la suerte que predestinan
> inexorables los hados
> al que las musas cultiva?
> Perseguidos donde quiera
> por la ignorancia y la envidia,
> visten mal, comen peor,

duermen en una guardilla,
mueren en un hospital
...
Esa es la que a tí te aguarda.
Pero acaso a tus cenizas
tributarán los laureles
que te negarán en vida.   (II, 5)

(You will be what you wish to be. But don't you know the future that the fates have decreed for those who cultivate the muses? They are persecuted wherever they go by ignorance and envy, they dress poorly and eat worse, sleep in attics and die in public hospitals ... That is the future that awaits you. But maybe your ashes will recieve the laurels that you are denied in life.)

Ultimately, however, Ferrer is right. The play is too busy (there are ninety-one scenes in three acts!) and unfocused to hold our interest for long. Bretón, chastened by the poor reception of his only foray into this genre, decided that his talents lay elsewhere, and returned to what he wrote best: the comedy of social customs.

Comedias de magia have been criticized as escapist fare, a genre which avoided confronting the realities, often harsh, of their times. This is not an entirely fair judgment. Caldera, for example, points to the satire of daily life in *La redoma encantada*,[94] and others have detected criticism, however attenuated, of contemporary society in *La pata de cabra*. Further evidence of the recognition of a "real" life context for the *comedias de magia* is found in the plays of Enrique Zumel, the last gasp of the *comedia de magia* in nineteenth-century Spain.

Enrique Zumel (1822–1897), author of no fewer than 122 plays, has been forgotten by modern criticism,[95] but his work is emblematic of much of the theatre of nineteenth-century Spain: popular, topical, frequently interesting, well-received, and now completely out of fashion. His works were performed in theatres in Madrid and in the provinces, where they received continuous press attention, and were published, often in multiple editions, throughout the second half of the century. Between 1849 and 1893 he produced a steady stream of comedies, historical dramas, religious plays, satirical one-acters, and other diversions, including seven

---

[94] Caldera and Calderone, "El teatro en el siglo XIX," p. 524.
[95] Zumel is not mentioned by Caldera or Jesús Rubio Jiménez in Díez Borque, *Historia del teatro en España* II, nor by Francisco Ruiz Ramón in *Historia del teatro español (Desde sus orígenes hasta 1900)*, 5th. edn. (Madrid: Cátedra, 1983). Even Enrique del Pino, in his two-volume history of the theatre in Zumel's home town, mentions only a dozen of the "50 or 60" (*sic*) titles supposedly written by Zumel. (*Historia del teatro en Málaga durante el siglo XIX* I, p. 195). See David T. Gies, "*In re magica veritas*: Enrique Zumel y la comedia de magia en la segunda mitad del siglo XIX," in *La comedia de magia y de santos*, eds. F. J. Blasco, J. Álvarez Barrientos, E. Caldera and R. de la Fuente (Madrid: Júcar, 1992): 433–461.

comedias de magia. Zumel, a member of the generation which includes Rubí, the Asquerino brothers, and Vega, is hardly a lost treasure ripe for rediscovery and rehabilitation, but it is important for us to keep in mind such individuals if we are to attempt to understand the full contours of nineteenth-century Spanish theatre. Francos Rodríguez remembered him as "el encanto de la muchachería en la segunda mitad del siglo pasado [whose plays] agradaban de modo extraordinario, repitíendose las representaciones de tales obras durante muchos años"[96] ("the delight of young people in the second half of the past century [whose plays] produced extraordinary pleasure, being repeated for many years"). His *comedias de magia* are what interest us here.

When Zumel began writing his *comedias de magia* in the late 1840s, the genre was still in high vogue. New magical plays appeared regularly in Madrid's theatres and the newspapers reflect steady interest in them. It is not certain whether Zumel's first magical comedy ever appeared on the stage, but *El himeneo en la tumba o la hechicera* (Marriage in the Tomb, or the Enchantress) was written in 1849 "para representarse en Madrid" ("to be performed in Madrid") and was printed in the capital.[97] In his foreword he grapples with the issue of "playability," that is, what differences an author might encounter between a text to be read and one to be performed. In his case, since the comedy was based on a French novel, he needed to solve certain technical matters in bringing a narrative to life as a theatrical dialogue. He unwittingly reveals one of the weaknesses of the *comedia de magia* genre – that plot and character are subservient to stage effects. He writes:

Alguna parte del plan de este drama está tomada de la obra del vizconde de Arlincourt que se titula *La hechicera*: obra enteramente fantástica como lo es el drama. Los bellos pensamientos de aquella no todos podían ponerse en escena, por ser imposibles de realizar sus transformaciones. He tenido que introducir dos personajes que son Resbalón y Quirica, con el objeto de que den tiempo a los tramoyistas para disponer los trastos necesarios. Y últimamente he arreglado el argumento y situaciones de la escena, apartándome a veces del todo de la novela, pues como pueden conocer los lectores, todo lo que puede leerse no puede ejecutarse.

(Part of the plan for this play is taken from the work of the Viscount of Arlincourt entitled *The Enchantress*, a completely fantastic work as is my drama. It was not possible to put all of the beautiful passages of that work on stage, since many of the transformations were impossible to visualize. I have had to introduce two new

96 José Francos Rodríguez, *Contar vejeces. De las memorias de un gacetillero (1893–1897)* (Madrid: Compañía Ibero-Americana de Publicaciones, 1928): 336.
97 Madrid: Lalama, 1849. No performances of it are recorded in Félix Herrero Salgado's *Cartelera teatral madrileña (1840–1849)* (Madrid: CSIC, 1963) nor in José Simón Díaz's *Veinticuatro diarios. Madrid 1830–1900*, 4 vols. (Madrid: CSIC, 1968–1975). It was approved for performance by the Junta de Censura de los Teatros on 24 September 1849.

characters, Resbalón and Quirica, in order to give the stagehands time to set up the necessary equipment. And finally I have rewritten the plot and some scenes, moving away at times from the novel since as the reader knows, everything that is read cannot necessarily be performed on stage.)

El himeneo is a curious mix of Romantic tropes and magical effects, a mixture which had become standard in these types of plays by the mid-1840s. Zumel drew on Romantic drama for the intense passion that propels Oscar and the beautiful Elvira into doomed situations, for the Gothic scenery (castles and cemeteries), for the *chiaroscuro* use of lighting, for the lightning and thunder that indicate terror and evil, and for the everpresent "¡Ay de mí!" ("Woe is me!") and timely fainting spells so characteristic of Romantic heroines. The sad and vengeful witch Marta evokes the memory of *El trovador*'s Azucena. Yet *El himeneo* is hardly a Romantic drama. Although it drew upon the popularized elements of that genre, it also drew heavily on the French melodramas staged with such frequency in Madrid in the 1820s (one thinks of *La huérfana de Bruselas*, for example, staged by Grimaldi in 1825 and played so memorably by his wife, Concepción Rodríguez). The difference between the hyperbolic melodramas and the Romantic drama was that the former inevitably ended, not with tragedy or death, but with a restored cosmic order brought about by the intercession of a Divine power or a natural force. This is the hallmark of *Don Juan Tenorio*, of course, and Zumel even ends his play with a nod to Zorrilla's masterpiece. It will be remembered that the souls of don Juan and doña Inés float Heavenward "al compás de la música" ("to the sound of music"); in Zumel, "Sube una elevación con Oscar, Elvira y el ángel pausadamente, música angélica mientras baja el telón" ("A panel slowly rises up with Oscar, Elvira and the angel, and one hears angelic music as the curtain descends"). Whatever horror had remained in the Romantic cosmos is gone. To all of this Zumel adds magic (transformations, shadows which pass through walls, aparitions, flights), a vocabulary learned from other magical plays, and a strong moral lesson.[98] His other *comedias de magia* followed similar patterns.

In the mid-1860s, Zumel's *Batalla de diablos* (Battle of Devils, 1865) was competing with Rafael María Liern y Cerach's popular *La almoneda del diablo* and *La paloma azul* (The Blue Dove), and into the 1870s he continued to grind out *comedias de magia* along with his other plays. *El anillo del diablo* (The Devil's Ring) appeared in 1871, following difficult moments for the Spanish monarchy, a fact which Zumel did not fail to integrate, however subtly, into his work. In a scene in which three heroes, Alvaro de Luna, Catalina Howard, and Juan de Padilla appear in dreams

---

[98] For details of the connections to previous *comedias de magia*, especially *La pata de cabra*, see Gies, "*In re magica veritas*," pp. 439–443.

to Mandoble, Zumel first makes a trite political joke (Luna confesses that he was killed "por ser mal ministro" ["because he was a bad minister"], prompting Mandoble to retort, "Pues si por esos motivos / aquí degollaran ... / a muchos conozco / que ya no estuvieran vivos" ["Well if that's the case I know a lot more who would not be alive right now"]) then continues with a direct reference to the very touchy subject of the Queen's exile in France:

MAND:	¡Pues ahora con arrogancia
	los que explotan la nación,
	con oro y sin aprensión
	se van a gozar a Francia,
	mientras aquí nos quedamos
	poniendo en el cielo el grito,
	sin que les importe un pito
	la sangre que derramamos!
LUNA:	También me debí escapar
	y no hubiera muerto así:
	en el tiempo en que viví
	no era moda el emigrar. (III, 8)
(MAND:	Well those who exploit the nation arrogantly are now going with our gold and without hesitation to enjoy life in France, while we stay here screaming to Heaven, and they could not care less about all the blood we are spilling!
LUNA:	I too should have escaped. Had I done so I would not have died, but when I lived there was no way to emigrate.)

This post-Zorrilla play underscores the author's orthodoxy. The Romantic "I love you" is not the operative phrase here, nor are the magic talismans (the goats' hooves, special rings, or other baubles) what extricate the hero from improbable situations, but rather a forceful "¡Creo en ti [Dios]! *La fe* nos valga, / que es talismán del cristiano!" ("I believe in God! Faith is our protection, it is the Christian's talisman!"). Christian faith is Zumel's new magic amulet, and his message was as comforting to audiences in the 1860s and 1870s as Zorrilla's was in the 1840s. Also like Zorrilla, Zumel has his antagonist repent at the last moment and win eternal salvation: "El bondadoso y clemente / por tu fe te perdonó, / y del poder del demonio / te salva el poder de Dios" ("The good and merciful one pardoned you because of your faith, and God's power saves you from the power of the devil") (III, 13).

Similar ideas and effects are developed in Zumel's other *comedias de magia* – *La leyenda del diablo* (The Legend of the Devil, 1872), *Quimeras de un sueño* (A Dream's Fantasies, 1874; the title is taken from Don Juan

Tenorio's soliloquy in the panteón, II, I, 5), *El talismán de Sagras* (The Sagras Amulet, 1878), and *El torrente milagroso* (The Miraculous Avalanche, 1883). He draws upon his rich vocabulary, intimate knowledge of stagecraft, showy control of scenic color and action, facility with verse and linguistic games, and the long, but by now rather shopworn, tradition of the *comedias de magia*. His comforting message for the 1870s and 1880s was the triumph of good over evil through Christian means, and the restoration of peace, harmony, and love. Magical comedies tended to appear and gain popularity during times of political and social instability, when their simple messages could divert the audiences from more serious concerns (Zorrilla noted that Grimaldi's *La pata de cabra* "distrajo de la política al público de Madrid por algunos meses"[99] ["distracted Madrid's audience from the political situation for a few months"]). As did others, Zumel's comedies confirmed the needs and desires of a nascent middle class, unsure of their futures and hungry to see Christian values triumph over evil in the theatre. A careful reading of these plays reveals much about the moral pulse of the times. Underneath the facile transformations and superficial tricks lay some important truths about Spanish society in the second half of the nineteenth century. Zumel, as a representative of the final stage of the *comedias de magia* in Spain, captured many of those truths. *Comedias de magia* were spectacle more than "art" and were conceptualized and written as such. They were a theatrical experience for the audience because it was not merely, if at all, the text that was important, but the entire theatrical support system of stage machinery, decorations, dance interludes, flights and transformations, jokes, puns, and some topical humor.[100] As Melveena McKendrick reminds us, the same could be said for most Golden Age plays.[101] The magical comedies died a slow but sweet death in the nineteenth century.

Rewrites, translations, operas, and other diversions

The need to draw upon foreign theatre and rewritten plays from Spain's Golden Age authors reached an almost frenzied height in the first decades of the nineteenth century. Censorship, war, and exile had depleted the ranks of playwrights, leaving impresarios and acting companies at the mercy of two competing needs: one was the reformers' desire to present

---

[99] José Zorrilla, *Obras completas*, ed. Narciso Alonso Cortés, II (Valladolid: Santarén, 1943): 2004.
[100] See Ermanno Caldera, "Sulla 'spettacolarità' delle commedie di magia," *Teatro di magia* (Rome: Bulzoni, 1983): 11–32. Also César Oliva, "Espacio y espectáculo," p. 428.
[101] Melveena McKendrick, *Theatre in Spain, 1490–1700* (Cambridge University Press, 1989).

"proper" plays to the audiences in Madrid and the other was the impresarios' need to have enough plays to present each day (sometimes, as on holidays and Sundays, twice a day). The reformers looked to what they considered to be "good" theatre, that is, the melodramas and boulevard comedies being written and produced in Paris, or to the masters of the seventeenth century, but only after they had been corrected, purged of the – to their mind – absurd lack of verisimilitude, ignorance of the classical unities, mixture of tragic and comic modes, and questionable political content.

The act of recasting previous plays to conform to the aesthetic and political realities of the times was not new in the nineteenth century, of course. Calderón and Moreto had themselves based many of their plays on works of their predecessors. In the eighteenth century Ignacio de Luzán had legitimized the practice in his *Poética* (1737) and it was taken up in earnest after the 1770s when Tomás Sebastián y Latre (d. 1792), Cándido María Trigueros (1736–1798), and others turned their attention to the *refundiciones*. As the nineteenth century developed, several other *refundidores* contributed their efforts to the enrichment of the repertory, first Dionisio Solís, Vicente Rodríguez de Arellano, and Félix Enciso Castrillón, then followed by Bretón, Vega, Mesonero Romanos, Gorostiza, and even Larra.

Dionisio Solís (1774–1834) was the acknowledged master of the *refundición* in the first thirty years of the nineteenth century. His activity as a *refundidor*, translator and writer of original plays places him at the center of playwriting in the crucial if turbulent years which opened the century. It is not an exaggeration to say that without him the history of the Spanish stage would be very different. His refined artistic sensibility – Leandro Fernández de Moratín praised his "talento, instrucción y práctica de los efectos del teatro"[102] ("talent, knowledge, and practice of theatrical effects") – endowed him with the ability to transform the plays upon which he focused his attention into playable and interesting dramas, rather than merely ransacking and squeezing the dramatic juices from them as did less talented *refundidores*. He rewrote twenty-five plays by Lope, Tirso, Rojas Zorrilla, Moreto, Calderón, and others for performances in the theatres run by Máiquez and his followers, plays such as *El alcalde de Zalamea* (The Mayor of Zalamea), *La celosa de sí misma* (Jealous of Herself), *Marta la piadosa* (Pious Martha), *La dama duende* (The Phantom Lady), and *Del rey abajo, ninguno*.[103] Some of these plays had been seen in other versions previously[104]; some were newly discovered

102 Moratín, *Epistolario*, ed. René Andioc (Madrid: Castalia, 1973): 401.
103 See Gies, "Hacia un catálogo," pp. 199–208.
104 See Coe, *Catálogo bibliográfico*, for complete listings.

by the audiences in Solís's version. His *refundiciones* restimulated, and even "preserved," according to Stoudemire,[105] interest in Golden Age plays during the years he was writing; between 1820 and 1850 his plays achieved nearly 600 performances in the theatres in Madrid, more than all of the *refundiciones* of his major competitors combined.[106] One instructive example is Lope's *El mejor alcalde, el rey*, which had been seen an average of once per year throughout the eighteenth century; Solís's *refundición* was played more than three times per year for nearly forty years after its appearance in 1810, reaching between five and seven performances in 1814, 1817, 1823, 1828, and 1850.

Most critics complained about the plethora of *refundiciones* seen on Spanish stages, considering them, along with translations, an ignoble activity which demeaned real dramatists and impoverished the repertory. Nevertheless, they recognized the economic realities which forced playwrights to cannibalize the works of others in order to make a living in an atmosphere which did not foster original creation. Indeed, *refundiciones* and translations served a useful purpose, albeit one which many critics were loathe to acknowledge: they brought to public view not only the classics of Spain's national theatre (however refocused to fit new aesthetic or political demands) but also the most current plays from Europe's stages, giving the Madrid public at least the illusion of "keeping up" with trends abroad. Gorostiza recast Calderón's *Bien vengas, mal si vienes solo* (You're Welcome But Not if You Come Alone) as *También hay secreto en la mujer* (Women Also Keep Secrets), which played in 1821. Grimaldi's band of authors was quite proficient at *refundiciones* and translations, which held their place in the repertory fully into the second half of the century. Bretón adapted Lope's *Los Tellos de Meneses* (The Tello Family from Meneses) for performance in 1826, as well as his *Si no vieran las mujeres* (If Women Did Not See) in 1828, Calderón's *La carcelera de sí misma* (Her Own Jailer) in 1826, *No hay cosa como callar* (There is Nothing Like Silence) in 1827, and *Con quien vengo vengo* (I Come With Whom I Want) in 1831, Moreto's *El príncipe y el villano* (The Prince and the Commoner) in 1827, and Alarcón's *Las paredes oyen* (The Walls Have Ears) in 1829. Hartzenbusch rewrote plays by Lope, Rojas Zorrilla, Tirso and Calderón, attesting to the "close connection existing between the Siglo de Oro and the Romantic period in Spain."[107] Mesonero Romanos recast Diego Hurtado y Mendoza's *El marido hace mujer* (The Husband Makes His Wife) in 1826, although it does not seem to have been

---

[105] Stoudemire, "Dionisio Solís's 'refundiciones' of Plays," p. 310.
[106] See David T. Gies, "Notas sobre Grimaldi y el 'furor de refundir' en Madrid (1820–1833)," *Cuadernos de Teatro Clásico* 5 (1990): 111–124.
[107] Adams, "Notes on Spanish Plays," pp. 128–142.

performed. As Coughlin observes, "The adaptations of the Golden Age plays reflect a general agreement among the recasters in favor of a structural cohesiveness with an emphasis on the unity of action rather than a strict observance of the unities of time and place. In conclusion it must be stated that the *refundidores* were essentially dramatists who strove to entertain their audiences with interesting theatre."[108]

Not all Golden Age plays seen and read in Madrid were in adapted versions. Agustín Durán, one of the first nineteenth-century critics to recognize the value of Spain's national theatre and to defend it against the attacks of the Neoclassicists, published, along with Manuel García Suelto and Eduardo de Gorostiza, an important collection of Golden Age plays between 1826 and 1834, whose main objective was to "erigir un monumento a la gloria de nuestra patria"[109] ("erect a monument to our country's glory"). His *Colección general de comedias* (General Play Collection) comprised an impressive 118 plays by authors such as Calderón, Lope, Morteo, Tirso, Ruiz de Alarcón, Pérez de Montalbán, Rojas Zorrilla, Cubillo de Aragón, Antonio Solís, Matos Fragoso, and others, precisely those authors being rewritten by the *refundidores*. Such plays naturally helped to create what Romero Tobar has called "una nueva generación literaria que modificó sensiblemente los usos literarios establecidos" ("a new literary generation that modified sensibly established literary practices") by establishing "un horizonte de referencias teatrales entre los jóvenes de los años treinta"[110] ("a horizon of theatrical references among young people in the 1830s"). Subscribers to the series included García Luna, Bretón, Hartzenbusch, Vega, Javier de Burgos, and several hundred other writers, bookdealers, politicians, aristocrats, and military leaders.[111] These plays are also precisely the plays designated "Romantic" by Durán, thereby intensifying the debate between the new, developing aesthetic and the Baroque theatre. It was around 1827 when theatres began to distinguish between "clásico" and "romántico" as descriptive theatrical terms. In 1828, Larra applied the term Romantic (meaning melodramatic) to Ducange's *Treinta años o la vida de un jugador* (Thirty Years or the Life of a Gambler).[112]

---

108 Coughlin, "Neoclassical *refundiciones*," p. 53.

109 In Durán's analysis of Calderón's *El mayor monstruo los celos* (1828).

110 Leonardo Romero Tobar, "La *Colección general de comedias* de Ortega (Madrid, 1826–1834)," in *Varia Bibliographica. Homenaje a José Simón Díaz* (Kassel: Editions Reichenberger, 1988), 599, 609.

111 Romero Tobar, "La *Colección general*," p. 609.

112 "Esta pieza melodramática pertenece a un nuevo género de poesía que no fue del tiempo de Horacio, ni de Terencio, ni de Plauto, ni mucho menos de Menandro, y todos aquellos *clásicos* antiguallas, que no sabían hacer más que piezas muy arregladas a razón, con muchas reglas, como si fueran precias para hacer comedias, siendo así que éstas hacen solas y sin gana, que no tenían genio para emanciparse de su esclavitud; ésta

Translations posed a similar problem. Translated plays formed one of the mainstays of the repertory (not surprising, given that the most important impresario of the times was a transplanted Frenchman) and translating became a small industry during the 1820s and 1830s. Lafarga's catalogue of *Las traducciones españolas del teatro francés (1700–1835)* documents the rich availability of translated French plays, both in manuscript and printed form.[113] Larra, as usual, is eloquent and bitter about the situation in which impresarios and book sellers in Madrid offered paltry sums for original works because translations were easier and cheaper to produce; in the provinces, works performed on stage rarely, if ever, produced royalties for their authors. In 1832 he writes:

También suelo traducir para el teatro la primera *piececilla* buena o mala que se me presenta, que lo mismo pagan y cuesta menos: no pongo mi nombre, y ya se puede hundir el teatro a silbidos la noche de la representación. ¿Qué quiere usted? En este país no hay afición a esas cosas. (p. 81)[114]

(I also tend to translate the first playlet that is given to me, because it pays the same and costs much less work: I don't put my name on it, and don't care if the audience brings down the house booing it on opening night. What do you want? In this country there is no fondness for such things [that is, for good theatre].)

This is not an exaggeration. Larra, highly paid as a newspaper columnist (he received 20,000 *reales* for his work on *El Español* and Adams reports that he signed a contract for 40,000 in early 1837[115]), was as poorly compensated as other playwrights for his theatre work. For example, his translation of *Julia* in 1833 (original by Scribe) netted him a paltry 600 *reales* while his *Partir a tiempo* (Leaving on Time) brought him only 240 *reales*, less than half of what Lope de Vega had received for his play *La hermosa Alfreda* (Pretty Alfreda) more than 200 years earlier! As Larra wrote, original theatre work was hardly worth the effort. Mesonero was even more caustic in his complaint: "La manía de las traducciones ha llegado a su colmo. Nuestra nación, en otros tiempos tan *original*, no es otra cosa en el día que una nación *traducida*"[116] ("The mania for trans-

es la poesía *romántica*, objeto de una gran disputa que hay en el día en el Parnaso sobre si han de entrar en él o han de quedarse a la puerta estas señoras piezas desarregladas dichas del *romanticismo*." "Una comedia moderna: *Treinta años o la vida de un jugador*," *El Duende Satírico del Día* (31 March 1828) in BAE 127: 16.

113 Francisco Lafarga, *Las traducciones españolas del teatro francés (1700–1835)*. 2 vols. (Universidad de Barcelona, 1983–1988).

114 Mariano José de Larra, "Carta a Andrés escrita desde las Batuecas por el Pobrecito Hablador." *El Pobrecito Hablador* (11 September 1832). *Obras de Mariano José de Larra* I, ed. Carlos Seco Serrano. (Madrid: Atlas, 1960) (BAE 127): 80–85. See Adams, "Sidelights," pp. 3–7.

115 Adams, "Sidelights," p. 3.

116 *Correo Literario y Mercantil*, cited by John K. Leslie, *Ventura de la Vega and the Spanish Theatre, 1820–1865* (Princeton University Press, 1940): p. 25.

lations has reached a peak. Our country, during other times so *original*, today is nothing more than a *translated* country").

Such realities did not stop Bretón from translating Lebrun, Racine and Alfieri, Hartzenbusch from translating Voltaire, Larra from translating Ducange, or everyone from translating Scribe. Larra began his review of a new translation of Scribe's *La Neige* by Bretón: "¿Comedia nueva? ¿Traducida? Claro está. ¿Autor? Scribe: eso ya no se pregunta; cosa es sabida"[117] ("A new comedy? Translated? Of course. Its author? Scribe: that goes without saying, it's so well known"). Dozens of French authors, as Larra stated, "vienen como un torrente a inundar nuestra escena"[118] ("come like an avalanche to inundate our theatre") in the 1820s and 1830s, most of them for performance on the stage. Bretón enjoyed great success – the "estreno más importante" ("most important première") of the 1831–1832 season, in Andioc's words[119] – with the translation of a French melodrama called *Jocó o el orangután*.[120] Ventura de la Vega's translation of *La expiación* (The Atonement) by St. Aulaire played at the Príncipe twenty times in 1831 and eleven more in 1832. Grimaldi's rendition of the melodramatic *La huérfana de Bruselas*, starring Concepción Rodríguez, had been a steady income producer since 1825 (it was still pulling in an average of 7,100 *reales* per performance in 1831[121]). Shields catalogues hundreds of performances of plays during the 1820–1833 period written originally in French, and Adams further chronicles the popularity of French theatre in Madrid during the Romantic period.[122] Increasingly, works by Hugo, Dumas, and others settled into Madrid for respectable runs; Gassin estimates that between 1830 and 1850 nearly 60 percent of the works seen on the two main stages were foreign, mostly French, in origin.[123] Larra complained that such focus on translation "contribuye a pervertir el gusto"[124] ("contributes to the perversion of taste") but it also enriched the repertory and brought new currents of thought into the capital.

The rich array of theatrical activity in Fernandine Spain was in many

---

117 Larra, "Primera representación de *La nieve*, drama en cuatro actos," *La Revista Española* (24 May 1833), in BAE 127: 227.
118 "Donde las dan las toman," *El Duende Satírico del Día* (31 December 1828), in BAE 127: 58.
119 Andioc, "Sobre el estreno de *Don Alvaro*," p. 69.
120 Alvin F. Sherman, Jr., "*Jocó o El orangután*: Another Step Toward the Understanding of the Romantic Hero," *Ojáncano* 5 (1991): 24–38.
121 Andioc, "Sobre el estreno de *Don Alvaro*," p. 69.
122 Shields, "The Madrid Stage"; Adams, "French Influence."
123 Roberto Dengler Gassin, "El drama romántico francés en Madrid (1830–1850)," in *Imágenes de Francia en las letras hispánicas*, ed. Francisco Lafarga (Barcelona: PPU, 1989), 307.
124 Cited by Adams, "Notes on Spanish Plays," p. 138.

ways the despair of serious playwrights, impresarios and critics. The public's attention and disposable income were constantly diverted from what many hoped would be "serious" theatre to all of the other spectacles which were put on, often by the very impresarios and playwrights who decried their existence, in the two main theatres. Competing for space with the few serious plays being penned were not only the above-mentioned *refundiciones*, translations, magical comedies, and melo-dramas, but also performances of what would come to be the most enthusiastically followed entertainment in the 1820s and early 1830s, the Italian opera. The opera came to be for the upper classes what the magical comedies had become for the lower classes – escapist, colorful enter-tainment which diverted their attention from the harsh realities of the day.

The full story of the symbiotic relationship between opera and Roman-tic drama in Spain is still to be told, but some details, gleaned from archives and newspapers of the period, are available to us. Put most plainly, the vogue for Italian opera reached "manic" (the word was used frequently in newspaper accounts of opera performances and the public response to them) proportions in the years immediately preceding the explosion of Romantic drama in Madrid. What Mesonero Romanos labled "el furor filarmónico"[125] ("philharmonic furor") reached a cre-scendo when the well-heeled ladies of the capital imitated the dress and hairstyles of their favorite opera singers, sung selections of operas at their nightly tertulias, and jostled for preferential treatment when the king of opera, Rossini, made a visit to Madrid in 1831.

Luis Carmena y Millán states categorically that "La absoluta concur-rencia a la ópera engendraba el absoluto abandono del teatro de verso" ("The unconditional attendance at the opera engendered the uncon-ditional abandonment of verse theatre") in Madrid.[126] This slight exag-geration nevertheless underscores the fact that performances of opera consistently pulled in more spectators, and consequently more money, than any other theatrical performances save certain *comedias de magia* (*La pata de cabra*, mostly). Statistics published elsewhere[127] reveal how, in one typical year (1832–1833), gate receipts for Rossini's operas ranged between 8,628 and 9,732 *reales*, while the *comedias* brought in between 4,930 and 8,232 *reales* (*La pata de cabra*, now in its third year on the boards, brought in a respectable 7,258 during one afternoon perform-

---

[125] Ramón de Mesonero Romanos, "La filarmonía," in *Obras completas de D. Ramón de Mesonero Romanos*, ed. Carlos Seco Serrano. (Madrid: Atlas, 1967). 5 vols. I: 176.
[126] Luis Carmena y Millán, *Crónica de la ópera italiana en Madrid* (Madrid: Manuel Minuesa de los Ríos, 1878): 52.
[127] Gies, "Entre drama y ópera," pp. 58–59.

ance). In 1826 the disparity was even greater: average receipts for dramas was 2,868 *reales*, while for operas it was 5,278.[128] The impresario Grimaldi's ambiguous approach to opera – on the one hand he complained that it was ruining the production of serious plays and on the other he was encouraging their performances since they made money – typifies the ambiguity discernible in the entire period.

Operas had been a staple in Madrid since the early eighteenth century, when Felipe V imported an Italian company to sing in the capital. Periodic waves of xenophobia prohibited the performance of non-Spanish operas (one such ban from 1799, for example, legislated against "representar, cantar ni bailar las piezas que no sean en idioma castellano y actuadas por actores y actrices nacionales o naturalizados en estos reinos"[129] ["performing, singing or dancing pieces which are not written in the Spanish language and put on by national actors and actresses or ones naturalized in these lands"]) but public demand kept them reappearing. A major upsurge took place in the mid-1820s when Saverio Mercadante's company arrived in Madrid at Grimaldi's bidding, and built a loyal – to some observers, fanatic ("un delirio, una fiebre, un fanatismo" ["a delirium, a fever, a fanatism"] according to Carmena[130]) – following in the last years of the reign of Fernando VII. The king himself, whose tastes in theatre ran more to the silly magical spectacles than to serious plays, issued a decree in 1827 commanding the permanent presence of an Italian opera company in the capital.[131] Soldiers were pressed into service to maintain order at the box office when tickets were released for new operas.[132] These were the years characterized by Peña as the time when "el delirio filarmónico ... avasalló por completo a los pacíficos habitantes de la villa y corte. Después de la revolución política, la revolución musical"[133] ("philharmonic delirium ... completely enslaved the normally tranquil inhabitants of the capital. The musical revolution followed on the heels of the political one"). That "revolution" included performances of Rossini's *La pietra del paragone*, *Il Barbiere di Siviglia*, and *Zelmira* (in fact, between 1822 and 1836 no fewer than twenty Rossini operas were performed in Madrid[134]), Mercadante's *Il posto abbandonato*, Donizetti's *La Fausta*, *L'Esule di Roma*, and *La travesura*, Bellini's *I*

129 See Antonio Peña y Goñi, *España, desde la ópera a la zarzuela* (Madrid: Alianza, 1967), 38.
130 Carmena, *Crónica*, p. 51.   131 Madrid, Archivo de Protocolos, 23799.
132 Dionisio Chaulié wrote to Peña: "Desde un principio se agolpó al despacho del teatro de la Cruz, escogido para las óperas por la mayor expansión de su escenario, gran multitud de gente solicitando comprar billetes, y la confusión creció a tal punto que se hizo necesario establecer un turno riguroso, mantenido por dos filas de soldados, entre los cuales había que pasar para acercarse al ventanillo." Peña, *España, desde la ópera*, p. 42.
133 *Ibid.* p. 41.   134 Gies, "Entre drama y ópera," p. 56.

Capuleti ed i Montecchi, *Norma*, and *La Straniera*, Rossi's *Chiara di Rosemberg*, and dozens of others. The "Golden Age of Opera" lasted until the mid-thirties, when the performances became slipshod and the best talents moved on to other capitals. The public remained enthusiastic, but by then opera was merely another offering in the diverse repertory of the Spanish theatres.

All of these strands of theatre – *refundiciones*, comedies, magical spectacles, translations, opera, melodrama – would fuse together into what has been remembered as the most significant contribution to Spanish theatre in the middle third of the nineteenth century, the Romantic drama.

3 Romanticism and beyond (1834–1849)

This is not the place to rehearse the arguments over the origins of the Romantic movement in Spain. Instead, we shall turn immediately to the theatre of the years following the death of Fernando VII in 1833, years generally agreed to encompass the core of Spanish Romanticism. Theatrical activity can be described alternatively or simultaneously as rich and active, or chaotic and fragmented. Performance repertories included translations (some 60 percent as we remember, according to Gassin), *comedias de magia*, operas, *refundiciones*, historical dramas, melodramas, neoclassical comedies, comedies of manners, classical tragedies, old-time comedies (cloak and dagger, intrigue, character), and, soon, Romantic dramas. However, Romantic drama cannot be completely understood if separated from what we have been discussing, that is, the complex mix of theatrical performance and spectacle which had been developing since the War of Independence. Romantic drama in Spain did not emerge from a void, nor was it imported from France or England, but rather it grew out of the rich brew of disparate elements which made up the theatre in the first thirty years of the century. As Caldera perceptively notes,

No debe, pues, extrañar que, al lado de las obras de Martínez de la Rosa o del Duque de Rivas, salgan en seguida a la escena madrileña, en algún caso precediéndolas, las de Bretón, Larra, Ochoa, Pacheco, que habían conocido directamente todas las etapas del reinado fernandino. Lo que prueba que el romanticismo no fue para España una verdadera inyección de motivos extranjeros: o, por decirlo mejor, esos motivos no fueron más que el elemento catalizador que favoreció la conclusión de un proceso iniciado hacía tiempo.[1]

(It should not surprise us that along with works by Martínez de la Rosa or the Duke of Rivas, there appear immediately on Madrid stages, and sometimes even preceding them, works by Bretón, Larra, Ochoa, Pacheco, who had personal experience of every stage during the reign of Fernando VII, which means that Romanticism was not for Spain a mere injection of foreign themes; better said, it means that those themes were nothing more than a catalyst that brought to an end a process initiated some time previously.)

[1] Caldera and Calderone, "El teatro en el siglo XIX," p. 450.

Historical events certainly changed the atmosphere, and the return of the exiled liberals had an energizing effect on the intellectual world of the capital. As we shall see, Romantic drama in Spain remains incomprehensible if we ignore its immediate indigenous history.

Literary beginnings: the majors

The reviewer of Rivas's *Don Alvaro o la fuerza del sino* in *El Correo de las Damas* (22 March 1835) found the play to be "románticamente romántico." Our focus in the first section of this chapter will be the key "Romantically Romantic" plays of the 1834–1844 period: *La conjuración de Venecia, Don Alvaro, Alfredo, El trovador, Carlos II el hechizado, Los amantes de Teruel,* and *Don Juan Tenorio.* Later we will move into the spaces between these plays in order to see what was happening in and around the non-Romantic theatre.

Martínez de la Rosa, La conjuración de Venecia

Interest in opera and magical comedies had led Madrid audiences to demand, and receive, spectacle and variety. When Martínez de la Rosa's *La conjuración de Venecia* was first performed on 23 April 1834, audiences got perhaps more than they bargained for, since he brought to the theatre not only the *chiaroscuro* scenic effects and lugubrious ambience so prevalent in melodramas, the multiple scene changes and visually interesting backdrops popular in the magical comedies, and the high emotion which characterized operatic performances, but something new: a radical existential reorientation which questioned the fairness of existence. *La conjuración* was the first play written by a respected Spaniard and performed in Madrid that captured "intencionalmente"[2] the new Romantic aesthetic of gloom and frustration, and which contained, in Eugenio de Ochoa's words, a "desenlace ... en extremo dramático y terrible"[3] ("an extremely dramatic and frightening dénouement"). It was, as Caldera notes, "una sagaz mezcla de lo viejo y de lo nuevo, que debía responder, seguramente, a la expectativa del gran público"[4] ("a wise mix of the old and the new that certainly corresponded to the public's expectations"). It ran for thirteen straight performances.

[2] *Ibid.* p. 451.
[3] *El Artista* I, p. 158. The censors had attempted to get Martínez de la Rosa to attenuate the shocking ending of the play. On 18 January 1833 it was recommended that he "disminuya una afección tan dolorosa" at the end and "retirar de la vista del público el patíbulo, suponiéndole existente detrás del foro." Madrid, Archivo de la Villa: Corregimiento 1–78–25.
[4] Caldera and Calderone, "El teatro en el siglo XIX," p. 451.

Martínez de la Rosa's drama combined an old tale of love thwarted by political tyranny with a revealing look at the consequences of that tyranny. He had long been attracted to such themes, although none of his previous plays developed them to the extreme we see in *La conjuración*. *La viuda de Padilla* (1812), *Morayma* (1818), his adaptation of *Edipo* (1828), and *Aben-Humeya o la rebelión de los moriscos* (Aben-Humeya or the Rebellion of the Moors, 1830), contain indications of his interest in oppression, rebellion, and the role of fate in man's existence.[5] In *La conjuración*, Rugiero's dual aspirations – to live openly with the lovely Laura (they are secretly wed) and to topple the oppressive rule of the Tribunal de los Diez in Venice in 1310 – fuse into one as it is discovered that not only is Laura the niece of Pedro Morosini, the president of the Tribunal, but that Rugiero himself is Morosini's long-lost son. Many of the elements which are soon to be recognized as characteristic of Spanish Romantic drama are present in this work. Such elements include the historical time frame, fearful and mysterious settings, the use of masks, the orphaned hero whose origins are discovered through surprise revelations, intense expressions of love, the belief that love transcends life itself, the rebellion against perceived injustice and oppression, and the bloody joining of love and death at the play's conclusion. The play is clearly a modern allegory, and Madrid's audiences had no difficulty identifying with the atmosphere of secrecy, political intrigue, governmental excess, and conspiracy depicted on the stage. Rugiero's desire to live in a "free" Venice had resonance in Madrid in 1834. As Javier Herrero has perceived, Martínez captured perfectly the fusion of political and cosmic terror which fascinated Romantic authors and which would be played out in the capital during the next decade.[6] In fact, the whole attraction to gothic terror, developing since the mid-eighteenth century, "expresa la angustia de una sociedad que se siente caminar hacia el abismo; de un mundo que, incapaz de resolver las contradicciones entre la Ilustración, la crítica de sus instituciones, y las abismales distancias existentes en las clases y grupos que lo componen, se refugia en las fantasías de conspiraciones satánicas y de clubes infernales"[7] ("expresses the anguish of a society that feels itself marching toward the abyss; of a world which, incapable of

---

[5] Nancy and Robert Mayberry correctly observe, "The tendency to violent, opposing passions, melancholy forebodings, and sentimental heroes had been evident in every play written by Martínez to that date." *Martínez de la Rosa*, p. 58.

[6] Beginning in the late eighteenth century, "un sentimiento colectivo de terror se traducirá artísticamente en un mundo de imágenes que reflejará esa profunda emoción." Javier Herrero, "Terror y literatura: Ilustración, revolución y los orígenes del movimiento romántico," in *La literatura española de la Ilustración: Homenaje a Carlos III*, ed. José Luis Varela (Madrid: Universidad Complutense, 1988): 131.

[7] *Ibid.* p. 141.

resolving the contradictions inherent in the Enlightenment, the criticism of its institutions, and the abysmal distances which existed in the classes and groups which made it up, takes refuge in fantasies of satanic conspiracies and infernal clubs").

Martínez claimed that his historical drama was original and that he got his information mostly from Ludovici Moratori's *Rerum italicarum scriptores*, but Sarrailh suggests that Daru's *Histoire de la République de Venise* (also mentioned by Martínez) provided the important historical source material.[8] Javier Herrero has recently demonstrated, however, that the real and most immediate sources for Martínez's play were works of gothic literature popular in the late eighteenth and early nineteenth centuries. He cites Abate Saint Real's *Conjuration des espagnoles contre la République de Venice* (1674) and J. H. D. Zschohke's *Aböllino, der Grosse Bandit*, brought to the French stage by the prolific René Charles Guilbert de Pixérécourt in 1801 and seen frequently on European stages, including those in Madrid (Shields documents nine performances of a Spanish translation in the 1820s and early 1830s), and M. G. Lewis's translation of the Zschohke play as *Rugantino, the Bravo of Venice* (1806). We might also profitably take a look at another play, overlooked by critics: Antoine Vincent Arnault's tragedy *Blanche et Moncasin, ou les vénitiens*, written in 1798 in Paris, translated into Spanish in 1802 and again in 1814, and performed frequently in Madrid not only during the reign of José I[9] but also in the 1820s and early 1830s. Shields documents no fewer than thirty-six performances of this play between 1820 and 1832. Martínez was in Paris during most of this time, of course (save his years in Madrid during the Trienio Liberal, when the play was performed nearly fifteen times), but its popularity in Spain indicates not only that the theme was attractive to playwrights and audiences alike, but also that it was known in literary circles. Favorable reviews of the translation appeared in the *Correo Literario y Mercantil* in 1828, 1829, and 1831. The similarities of plot between Arnault's play and Martínez's are suggestive. In Arnault, Montcassin arrives in Venice to save the city from the tyranny of the "perfides Allemands." Like Rugiero, he is a stranger to the town, and falls in love with young Blanche, daughter of one of the state Inquisitors, Contarini, who is also a member of the ruling Council of Ten. The circumstances conspire to find Blanche, at the play's finale, overcome with grief as she arrives too late to save her lover, whose cadaver is

---

[8] See Robert Avrett, "A Brief Examination into the Historical Background of Martínez de la Rosa's *La conjuración de Venecia*," *Romanic Review* 21 (1930): 132–137, and Jean Sarrailh, ed., *Francisco Martínez de la Rosa. Obras dramáticas* (Madrid: Espasa-Calpe, 1933, 1972): 234.

[9] Larraz, *Théâtre et politique*, p. 131.

revealed tied to the garrotte on which he was executed. (This *coup de théâtre* is repeated in *La conjuración*.) Blanche, as does Laura, faints before the final curtain. These similarities do not prove that Martínez took his plot directly from Arnault, but they do suggest the importance of the interplay of plot, character and stage effects seen in Madrid's theatres in the first half of the century.

Larra, who several months later would himself enjoy a modest success with another play dealing with the theme of conspiracy against tyranny – *El arte de conspirar* (The Art of Conspiracy), his translation of Scribe's *Bertrand et Raton* – was impressed with the play and the performances given by Concepción Rodríguez (Grimaldi's wife) and Carlos Latorre, praising not only their interpretative skills but also the play's moving emotional impact. After seeing the play he wrote:

La señora Rodríguez ha interpretado con perfección su papel: esa es la Laura sensible amante, que ha puntado el poeta. ¡Qué calor y qué verdad en aquellas palabras!: "Es mi esposo a los ojos de Dios y yo debo salvarle a costa de mi vida ... ¿Qué me importa lo que digan los hombres?" Es difícil imaginar mejor la escena con Rugiero y con el padre; imposible confundir y mezclar mejor en uno los sentimientos de amor y de pavor de su salida en el panteón."[10]

(Miss Rodríguez has played her role perfectly: she is the sensitive lover Laura written by the author. What warmth and what truth in those words, "He is my husband in God's eyes and I must save him even if it costs me my life ... What do I care what people might say?" It is difficult to imagine the scene between Rugiero and his father done better; impossible to mix and bind better into one sentiment the feelings of love and terror of his departure from the family crypt.)

Larra was moved by the combination of "amor y pavor," as was the audience: "el terror hace enmudecer; las manos no pueden reunirse y golpear cuando han de acudir a los ojos"[11] ("terror makes one quiet; one's hands cannot clap when they must be used to cover one's eyes"). As I have written elsewhere:

El gusto por la fantasía macabra y por lo gótico en los años inmediatamente anteriores al pleno florecimiento del romanticismo marca toda la época y deja profundas huellas en el período siguiente. Este interés, claro está, no apareció de repente en los albores del romanticismo, pero es evidente que la creciente división entre el control racional ilustrado y la libertad emocional romántica llega a ser una de las características más notables de esta coyuntura histórico-estética. Cada época desarrolla su propio lenguaje, un código literario que corresponde a su *Weltanschaung*; y para expresar la nueva experiencia romántica en forma literaria, los autores de aquel período formularon una complicada red de imágenes con la

---

[10] Larra, "Representación de *La conjuración de Venecia*," *La Revista Española* (25 April 1834), in BAE 127: 386. For more on Concepción Rodríguez and acting, see Gies, "Larra, Grimaldi, and the Actors of Madrid."

[11] Larra, "Representación de *La conjuración de Venecia*," p. 385.

que comunicar la profunda desilusión que sentían ante la triste realidad circundante. El mundo romántico, necesitado de nuevas formas de expresión, desarrolló una nueva iconografía y un nuevo vocabulario para presentar en forma concreta las ideas que llegarían a dominar la primera mitad del siglo XIX.[12]

(Taste for macabre fantasy and for the gothic during the years immediately preceding the full flowering of Romanticism marks the entire period and leaves deep tracks on the following period. This interest, of course, did not suddenly appear at the beginning of the Romantic movement, but it is evident that the growing division between rational, enlightened control and emotional, Romantic freedom becomes one of the most notable characteristics of this historical-aesthetic juncture. Each period develops its own language, its own literary code which corresponds to its *Weltanschaung*; and in order to express the new Romantic experience in literary form, authors formulated a complex network of images which they used to express the profound disillusionment they felt when faced with their sad everyday reality. The Romantic world, in need of new forms of expression, developed a new iconography and a new vocabulary in order to present in concrete form the ideas that would dominate literary discourse in the first half of the nineteenth century.)

Larra recognized *La conjuración* as a turning point for contemporary Spanish theatre: "No hemos visto nada mejor en Madrid"[13] ("We have seen nothing better in Madrid").

Martínez de la Rosa had been a leading voice in the recuperation of history as appropriate source material for contemporary drama and had expressed his views in both his theoretical work and in his dramatic practice. This focus on history as a vehicle for the expression of modern ideas was nothing new, as he readily admitted, but it was to acquire a special intensity during the Romantic period when playwrights writing in the Romantic mode chose the medium of historical drama almost exclusively to express their views. In "Apuntes sobre el drama histórico" (Notes on the Historical Drama, 1830) he confessed his allegiance to Madame de Staël's (and Durán's) conviction that, in his words, "la literatura de una nación es el reflejo de la sociedad"[14] ("a nation's literature is a reflection of society"), and it was in its history that key characteristics of that society could be found and dramatized for effect. This idea would be played out with startling results during the next fifteen or twenty years. Martínez thought of himself more as a moderate, classical Aristotelian in his literary aesthetic than as a wild-eyed Romantic[15], but he opted for the

---

[12] David T. Gies, "Larra, *La galería fúnebre* y el gusto por lo gótico," *Romanticismo* 3–4 (1988): 60.

[13] Larra, "Representación de *La conjuración de Venecia*," p. 387.

[14] Martínez de la Rosa, "Apuntes sobre el drama histórico," in *Obras dramáticas*, p. 339.

[15] Michael McGaha provides an interesting comparison of the "Romantic" characteristics of *La conjuración* and Jovellanos's earlier *El delincuente honrado* in "The 'Romanticism' of *La conjuración de Venecia*," *Kentucky Romance Quarterly* 20 (1973): 235–242. McGaha

presentation of "sentimientos naturales y lucha de pasiones" ("natural feelings and a battle of passions") in order to "ganar *por fuerza* el ánimo de los espectadores"[16] ("win over *forcibly* the minds of the viewers"). Martínez is frequently credited with being an author of the "justo medio" ("perfect balance") (words he uses in the "Apuntes"), but a closer reading of this work combined with the plays he was writing at the time might lead us to accuse him of waffling, or at least of searching for an interim solution between his respect for the neoclassical rules – he frequently cited directly or indirectly Luzán and Moratín – and the "lucha de pasiones" he deemed important by the end of the 1820s to move audiences. The "Apuntes" were written after the majority of his Moratinian comedies, and after his two "Romantic" plays, *Aben Humeya* and *La conjuración de Venecia*. They appeared in the same volume as these two last dramas, in 1830, when he had searched for and found an alternative solution to his dramatic needs, since neither play remains rigidly boxed in by the "rules" of drama as dictated by the classical and neoclassical theorists. Is this "justo medio" or *ex post facto* defense of his dramatic practice, which Robert and Nancy Mayberry have recognized as "a new dramatic form"?[17] Whatever it is, the impact of *La conjuración* on the charged world of post-Fernandine Spain was decisive.

Larra, Macías

Not long after the staging of *La conjuración de Venecia*, Larra, who had translated French dramas and reviewed countless plays for the various newspapers with which he was associated, gave his own original drama to Grimaldi to be performed at the Príncipe Theatre. *Macías*, a "drama histórico" ("historical drama") much in the vein of *La conjuración*, finally opened on 24 September 1834 (it had been prohibited when Larra first proposed its staging in late 1833[18]), and took Romantic theatre one step closer toward authenticity. Once again, the leads were played by Carlos Latorre and Concepción Rodríguez. Larra drew on historical drama and the Spanish national theatre in such a way as to confirm his belief that theatre and politics were one and the same thing. Theatre was, he wrote,

concludes that "the few formal elements of Romanticism which appear in *La conjuración de Venecia* do not make of it a truly Romantic play" (242). On the other hand, María José Alonso Seoane views the play as fully Romantic, in the Schlegelian sense of Romanticism. "Introducción," *La conjuración de Venecia* (Madrid: Cátedra, 1993), pp. 85–86, 92–93.

16 Martínez de la Rosa, "Apuntes," p. 342. Emphasis added.
17 Mayberry and Mayberry, *Martínez de la Rosa*, p. 36.
18 See comments in *El Correo de las Damas* (27 November 1833). Bretón's *Elena* was also banned.

"una diversión que dirige la opinión pública de las masas que la frecuen-
tan; un instrumento del mismo gobernante, cuando quiere hacerle servir a
sus fines"[19] ("a diversion that shapes the opinions of the masses who go;
an instrument of the ruling class when it wants it to serve its ends"), which
is why historical drama would be for him – and for his Romantic
compatriots – such an instructive genre. Caldera speculates that the
audiences perhaps believed they were seeing yet another *refundición* of a
Golden Age play,[20] because of its roots in a previously treated subject
matter, its thematic concentration, use of reason, adherence to several of
the classical unities, and interest in dramatic verisimilitude. Yet they got
something quite different: the accomplished blending of love, fate, and
adverse political circumstances makes *Macías* a "pieza capital del teatro
romántico español"[21] ("a major work in Spanish romantic theatre").

Larra goes beyond Martínez's model by mixing misinterpretations and
conflict with a terrifying tragic dénouement. Elvira, in love with the
troubadour Macías but convinced by her fiancé Don Tello that Macías
has married someone else, plunges a dagger into herself, swearing, "La
tumba será el ara donde pronto / la muerte nos despose" ("The tomb will
be the altar on which we will soon be married") (IV, 4). Unlike Laura,
who merely faints into oblivion ("descubre Laura el patíbulo, cae hacia
atrás exánime, y Matilde la recibe en sus brazos"[22] ["Laura sees the
gallows, and faints into Matilde's arms"]), Elvira takes an active role in
her rejection of life without Macías and ends her own life in an act which
prefigures Don Alvaro's shocking leap into the void. "Dichosa / muero
contigo" ("I am happy to die with you") (IV, 4), she exclaims. Not only
the linking of love and death, but also the recognition that death will
become both the mechanism through which and the place where the
unhappy lovers can finally be united, is central to the Spanish conception
of Romanticism and Larra exploits it skilfully. The tomb and the marriage bed become one and the same. Critics who do not see the importance of Larra's defense of passion and rebellion – beginning with Alberto
Lista, who judged it "una composición dramática muy débil y sus versos
son generalmente malos"[23] ("a very weak play and its verse is in general
bad") – failed to interpret the drama's symbolic value and hence wrote it
off as a failed autobiography, an unrealistic ("inverosimil") story, or a

[19] "Reflexiones acerca del modo de hacer resucitar el teatro español," *El Pobrecito Hablador* (20 December 1832) in BAE 127: 123.
[20] Caldera and Calderone, "El teatro en el siglo XIX," p. 453.
[21] Alborg, *Historia* IV, p. 276.
[22] Martínez de la Rosa, *Obras dramáticas*, p. 336.
[23] Alberto Lista, "Informe sobre la Elegía del poeta Verneuil dedicada a la muerte de
Larra," 30 June 1837.

poorly conceived hybrid of neoclassical rules and pseudo-Romantic ardor.

Macías is a complex drama which is only beginning to receive the critical attention it deserves. Yet as Alborg pointed out in 1980, it was surprising to discover that nearly 150 years after his death only two articles on Larra bothered to concentrate on *Macías* (and even then one of them shared billing with Zorrilla).[24] Casalduero efficiently cast aside the decades of repetition of the same clichés about the work in order to focus on Larra's own confession that "Macías es un hombre que ama, y nada más"[25] ("Macías is a man who loves, and nothing else"). Still, he criticizes Larra's execution of the drama as too "intelectual." Sánchez put to rest the erroneous linking of Macías and Larra.

Curiously (rather, perhaps not so curiously once we look at the entire theatrical picture of the times), the ghost of Moratín hovers close to Larra in *Macías*. While the themes of the play are those which become central to the Romantic ethic – murder, vengeance, unbridled passion, tyranny, the quest for freedom – the structure remains faithful to the reasoned aesthetic of Neoclassicism. *Macías* contains just five main characters, the action takes place in don Enrique's castle, and it all unfolds in a matter of hours. The joining of the past and the future is not uncommon in Larra[26] and it serves as an important juncture in the development of nineteenth-century drama. Larra's search was for that which was, as he later expressed, "Nuevo, original ... En una palabra, la naturaleza en las tablas, la luz, la verdad, la libertad en literatura, el derecho del hombre reconocido, la ley sin ley"[27] ("New, original ... In a word, nature on the boards, light, truth, freedom in literature, the rights of man recognized, law without restrictions"). Alborg rightly confirms that

Macías expresa en forma dramática, dentro del vehículo literario que le es propio, idénticas ideas de libertad, de afirmación del individuo frente a convenciones y trabas sociales, de rebeldía y de inconformismo, de exaltación del yo, que en los más audaces artículos; no idénticas, sino mucho más atrevidas y radicales, porque lo que en aquéllos no le dejaban decir y tampoco venía al caso por tratarse de materias más prácticas y concretas, podía ponerlo en boca del apasionado trova-

24 Alborg, *Historia* IV, p. 272; he is referring to Joaquín Casalduero's "La sensualidad en el romanticismo: sobre el *Macías*," in *Estudios sobre el teatro español* 2nd. edn. (Madrid: Gredos, 1967): 219–231, and Roberto Sánchez's "Between Macías and Don Juan," *Hispanic Review* 44 (1976): 27–44. See also Ermita Peñas Varela, *Macías y Larra* (Universidad de Santiago de Compostela: 1992).

25 "Dos palabras," reprinted in *Macías*, eds. Lorenzo-Rivero and Mansour (Madrid: Espasa-Calpe, 1990): 70.

26 See in particular José Escobar, *Los orígenes de la obra de Larra* (Madrid: Editorial Prensa Española, 1973) and Susan Kirkpatrick, *Larra: el laberinto inextricable de un romántico liberal* (Madrid: Gredos, 1977).

27 Larra, "Una primera representación," *Revista Mensajero* (3 April 1835), BAE 128: 69.

dor, con toda la proyección de un símbolo, protegido por la circunstancia de que lo hacía hablar entre los muros de un castillo del siglo XV. Estamos persuadidos de que en todo el romanticismo español no existe otra proclama más enérgica de la libertad individual que los parlamentos de Macías.[28]

(Macías expresses in dramatic form, within a literary vehicle which is appropriate to him, the same ideas of freedom, affirmation of the individual faced with conventions and social obstacles, rebellion and lack of conformity, and the exaltation of the "I" that are expressed in the boldest articles; they are not exactly the same, but in fact much more daring and radical because the things that either he was not able to say in his articles or which were not particularly relevant because they dealt with more concrete and practical matters, he could put in the mouth of his passionate troubadour who, with all the force of a symbol, could say things protected by what could be said within the walls of a fifteenth-century castle. We are convinced that there does not exist a more energetic declaration of individual freedom than that found in the speeches of Macías.)

Those speeches included confirmations of the Romantic ideology such as "si en la tierra / asilo no encontramos, juntos ambos / moriremos de amor. ¿Quién más dichoso / que aquel que amando vive y muere amando?" ("if we cannot find sanctuary on earth we will find it together in death. Who could be luckier than he who lives and dies loving?") (III, 4) and "¿Qué es la vida? / Un tormento insufrible, si a tu lado / no he de pasarla ya. ¡Muerte! ¡Venganza!" ("What is life? An insufferable torment if I cannot live it by your side. Death! Vengeance!") (III, 4). Larra scrutinized his society and his soul through the prism of Macías, and did so with complete seriousness: "el drama titulado *Macías*, al que yo daba toda la importancia que un autor da a sus obras"[29] ("the play called *Macías*, to which I gave all the importance an author gives his works"). Susan Kirkpatrick has noted, "*Macías* helped establish the vogue of Romantic theatre in Madrid through its portrayal of a fiery young hero prepared to follow the dictates of his own heart against the opposition of any authority, but Macías is more a political emblem than a Romantic hero of any subjective depth,"[30] although it must be recognized that he cleverly linked politics and subjectivity creating, in Kirkpatrick's view, an emblem of "bourgeois man."[31]

The intensification of heightened dramatic expression as a proper conduit for personal emotion is a hallmark of Romantic theatre in Spain. Unbound by the rules of proper, dignified (and frequently repressed)

---

[28] Alborg, *Historia* IV, p. 274.
[29] Letter sent to *El Castellano*; reproduced in Carmen de Burgos, *Fígaro. Revelaciones.* (Madrid: Impr. Alrededor del Mundo, 1919): 191.
[30] Susan Kirkpatrick, '*Las románticas*': *Women Writers and Subjectivity in Spain, 1835–1850* (Berkeley: University of California Press, 1989): 98.
[31] Susan Kirkpatrick, "Liberal Romanticism and the Female Protagonist in *Macías*," *Romance Quarterly* 35 (1988): 52.

behavior, Romantic heroes let loose a maelstrom of pain, anger, frustration, and confusion upon unsuspecting audiences. Those audiences were precisely the "bourgeois men" who were struggling to understand their place in the new society and anxious to see themselves reflected, and resolved, on the stage. The images they saw were often not to their liking, but, being presented by two highly regarded figures (Martínez de la Rosa was President of the Counsel of Ministers and Larra was the capital's most respected journalist and theatre critic), they were impossible to ignore. *Macías*, which received ten performances during its first season, was not as immediately popular as *La conjuración*, but it was published in three successive editions within six years (1834, 1838, 1840) and was lampooned in 1863 in a two-act satire called *Matías o el jarambel de Lucena* (Matias or the Ragpicker from Lucena) (*La Epoca*, 24 September 1850). It was not until 1844, when Zorrilla gave them his comforting, reformed don Juan that spectators could relax and fully embrace the Romantic hero. Until that time, however, they would be subjected to more troubadours, suicidal mestizos, mad monks, crazed kings, and evil sorcerers who would force them to confront both their external and internal realities, as well as satires of these very types.

Larra's journalism has clearly overshadowed his work in the theatre, and perhaps rightly so. Still, it surprises us to realize that in his short career he wrote not only dozens of theatre reviews and observations on the state of the theatre, but also twenty plays, among which are included *Macías*, along with translations from French originals, scores for operas, and several original pieces. Long before the appearance of *Macías* he had written *El conde Fernán González y la exención de Castilla* (Count Fernan Gonzalez and the Privilege of Castile), which failed to pass the censor's review in 1831, and his rendition of Scribe's *Les adieux au comptoir*, which was performed at the Cruz as *No más mostrador* (No Longer an Office-worker) on 29 April 1831. Several months later, *La madrina* (The Godmother), another translation/adaptation of a Scribe original, played at the Cruz (9 November 1831). The recent edition of *Textos teatrales inéditos* of Larra by Leonardo Romero Tobar provides up-to-date information on this theatrical activity and reproduces three interesting and previously overlooked pieces: *Julia*, "comedia en dos actos del célebre Scribe arreglada a nuestra escena" ("a two-act comedy by the celebrated Scribe, arranged for our theatre") in 1833, *Los inseparables* (The Inseparable Pair) a one-act comedy also by Scribe, and the 1832 libretto for *El rapto* (The Abduction), a short opera with music by Spain's most highly regarded composer of the period, Tomás Genovés.[32] Hence, as Romero

---

[32] Leonardo Romero Tobar, *Mariano José de Larra. Textos teatrales inéditos* (Madrid: CSIC, 1991). See also Herman Hespelt, "The Translated Dramas of Mariano José de

Tobar points out, Larra's initiation into the world of theatre included historical drama, satire, boulevard comedy, and opera, that is, the genres which dominated the theatrical scene (with the exception of magical comedy) at the end of the *ominosa década*. It simply will not do to remove Larra's theatrical activity from the trajectory of his intellectual development; they are integrally related. He dedicated much time and energy to the theatre and, in spite of his constant complaints about the plague of translations and *refundiciones*, his reasons for translating plays were more than mere financial. He might have found it difficult to resist the encouragement of Grimaldi, whose theatres needed a constant supply of "product." As Romero Tobar reminds us, "Larra, entre otros, se lucró de esta amistad que, sin lugar a dudas, tuvo proyección sobre sus primeras experiencias en la escritura de textos teatrales"[33] ("Larra, among others, profited from this friendship which, without a doubt, influenced his first experiences with writing theatrical texts"). Larra also viewed in his northern neighbor, France, much of what was good and modern in contemporary society and his collaboration in the project of bringing current European thinking into Spain is not to be underestimated. He himself captured what was the dominant thinking about original plays in relation to translations when he wrote:

Varias cosas se necesitan para traducir del francés al castellano una comedia. Primera, saber lo que son comedias; segunda, conocer el teatro y el público francés; tercera, conocer el teatro y el público español; cuarta, saber leer el francés, y quinta, saber escribir el castellano. Todo eso se necesita, y algo más, para traducir una comedia, se entiende, bien, porque para traducirla mal, no se necesita más que atrevimiento y diccionario ... Traducir bien una comedia es adoptar una idea y un plan ajenos que estén en relación con las costumbres del país a que se traduce, y expresarlos y dialogarlos como si se escribiera originalmente; de donde se infiere que por lo regular no puede traducir bien comedias quien no es capaz de escribirlas originales.[34]

(One needs several things in order to translate a French comedy into Spanish. First, one must know what comedies are; second, one must know French theatre and the French theatre public; third, one must know Spanish theatre and the Spanish theatre public; fourth, one must know how to read French; and fifth, one must know how to write Spanish. One needs to know all of this and more in order to translate a comedy, and, of course, to translate it well, because in order to translate poorly one need not have more than some courage and a dictionary ...

Larra and their French Originals," *Hispania* 15 (1932): 117–134, and Albert Brent, "Larra's Dramatic Works," *Romance Notes* 8 (1967): 207–212. More recently, James Durnerin has evaluated Larra's work as a translator: "Larra, traducteur de Scribe et de Ducange," in AA.VV., *Ecriture des marges et mutations historiques* (Université de Besançon, 1983): 41–52.

[33] Romero Tobar, *Textos teatrales*, p. 13.
[34] "De las traducciones," *El Español* (11 March 1836) in BAE 127: 180.

To translate a comedy well is to adopt an idea and an argument which are foreign to the customs of the country to which it is being transplanted, and express them and make dialogue out of them as if one were writing something original; from which one infers that in general one who is not capable of writing original comedies cannot translate them very well.)

Rivas, Don Alvaro o la fuerza del sino

The Romantic rediscovery of historical drama made its presence felt in Rivas's best-known play, *Don Alvaro o la fuerza del sino*, written during his exile in France but not performed until its Madrid première at the Príncipe Theatre on 22 March 1835. Rivas had been a proponent of the use of history from his first plays (*Ataúlfo, Aliatar, Duque de Aquitania, Malek-Adhel, Lanuza, Arias Gonzalo*) and had gradually been developing a view of life, particularly post-*Aliatar*, which coincided with the anguished, fateful desperation of the Romantic hero. Caldera stresses the evolutive nature of Rivas's dramatic development:

La 'conversión' del Duque de Rivas no fue, pues, sino el último acto de un proceso evolutivo (constante, a pesar de algunos altibajos) que indujo al autor – a un momento dado y en circunstancias bien conocidas – a coordenar y sistematizar las experiencias anteriores en el marco de una perspectiva existencial y una concepción estética renovadas.[35]

(The "conversion" of the Duke of Rivas was nothing more than the final act in an evolutionary process [a steady one, in spite of some ups and downs] that persuaded the author – at a given moment and in well-known circumstances – to coordinate and systematize his previous experiences within the model of a renewed existential perspective and aesthetic idea.)

Rivas not only agreed, in 1835 at least, with an interpretation of society and the cosmos which underscored its absurdity, but the central character of his most famous play became the prototype of the frustrated, and in many ways tragic, Romantic Man. Rivas successfully privileges passion over power, and even though the latter seems to "win," the clash of passion, power, and fate creates the full typography for Romantic drama. Love, complicated and threatened by the forces of blind fate, discovers that its only salvation is physical death with the vague hope of fulfillment in an undefined, un-Christian afterlife. What distinguishes Rivas's conception of tragedy from that of the classical authors is his refusal to provide his main characters with recognizable flaws which could therefore be blamed for their downfall. The "tragic flaw" in Rivas's dramas is not a personality quirk or a human weakness of the hero, but rather a much wider, social/cosmic flaw which is neither the fault of the hero nor

[35] Caldera, "De *Aliatar* a *Don Alvaro*," p. 119.

anything that could have been avoided by judicious behavior or the application of reason. The chaotic nature of adverse fate makes it all the more compellingly tragic for the audiences of the 1830s who were struggling to make sense of their fragmented world. It was difficult, if not impossible, to feel ennobled after witnessing two passionate lovers being crushed by the absurd turns of the Wheel of Fortune. As Shaw has stated, "En vez de verse llevado hacia la aceptación de la necesidad o hacia la reconciliación con el sufrimiento, el espectador sólo contempla el dolor y la desesperación; la emoción trágica se convierte en indignación o en pasividad resignada"[36] ("Instead of seeing himself carried toward the acceptance of the need for or towards a reconciliation with suffering, the spectator merely sees pain and desperation: tragic emotion is converted into indignation or into passive resignation").

This is best exemplified, of course, in two moments in *Don Alvaro*. The first comes early, when don Alvaro, resigned to accept the dictates of Leonor's father, suppresses his passion and kneels before the Marqués de Calavatrava in an act of resignation (I, 8). When he tosses his gun aside it goes off and mortally wounds the Marqués, setting in motion the chain of events which will lead to his final act of cosmic defiance. The second is his reconciliation with Leonor. Don Alvaro has spent five years suppressing the pain of her death (as he thinks) and submerging his ego in other identities (soldier, monk) in order to come to some resolution in his own life. When by chance he discovers that she has been living as a hermit in the craggy mountains near his own monastery and reaches out to her in a final embrace, he finds that she has been mortally wounded, in an ironic reversal of his first confrontation with the Marqués, by her very brother. "¡Te hallé, por fin ... sí, te hallé ... muerta!" ("Finally I found you! ... Yes, I found you...dead!") (V, 10) His spiritual death occurs at that precise moment ("Queda inmóvil" ["He remains motionless"]), but Rivas pushes him further than we expect him to go with his crazed, diabolical ("Desde un risco, con sonrisa diabólica, todo convulso" ["From a peak, with a diabolical smile, all convulsed"]), and apocalyptic ("Húndase el cielo, perezca la raza humana; exterminio, destrucción" ["Let the Heavens fall, let humanity perish; extermination, destruction"]) leap into the void of nonexistence.

Don Alvaro's central place in the Romantic canon was not immediately recognized, however. The play's revolutionary message of man's desperation in a chaotic and unjust cosmos hardly sat well with audiences in the capital, although they were evidently pleased with the fifteen or sixteen newly painted decorations for the play (as compared to only five for *La*

---

[36] Shaw, "Acerca de *Aliatar*" p. 242.

conjuración de Venecia, which in their time produced enthusiastic praise from Larra: "¡Cinco decoraciones nuevas en un día, y qué decoraciones!" ("Five new painted sets in one day, and what sets!").[37] *El Eco del Comercio* implied its similarity to magical spectacle by comparing it to "una linterna mágica donde se ve de todo" ("a magic light show where we see everything") (24 March 1835); in 1844 *El Laberinto* used almost the same language to describe Zorrilla's *Don Juan Tenorio*.[38] René Andioc has studied the visual appeal of this drama, in which Rivas "explota sistemáticamente, con la variedad y riqueza de las decoraciones, un medio eficaz de atraer a la multitud"[39] ("systematically exploits, in the variety and richness of the sets, an efficient way to bring people into the theatre"), as well as that audience's initial confusion at witnessing don Alvaro's final, wild-eyed suicide. Modern criticism, particularly following Richard Cardwell's groundbreaking study,[40] has been able to see the play within an historical context and place it properly as a pivotal work in the development of drama from the reasoned, comprehensible, classical and neoclassical tragedy to the random, disorienting message of the modern Theatre of the Absurd. Viewed as a symbolic drama, rather than as a realistic one, *Don Alvaro* becomes the first play in Spain to capture fully the step into the modern world's conception of life as less than ordered, less than reasonable, and less than subject to rules of proper behavior. It told its audience that there was not necessarily a connection between misdeed and punishment, good behavior and reward; in fact, it crossed the equation by insisting that good behavior could, for no comprehensible reason, be punished. Susan Kirkpatrick rightly sees don Alvaro as "fragmented and confused," but seems more ready to blame him for his condition than appears justified: "It is this inevitable failure of desire to affect existence that don Alvaro calls fate...While society's resistance plays a part in this fatality, the subject's own weakness, its internal incoherence, is a major factor."[41] This reading follows Pattison's belief that don Alvaro suffered from a psychological weakness (his mestizo background).[42] I prefer Cardwell's archetypal/symbolic reading, which places don Alvaro's actions within a wider philosophical context and enables us to see more clearly the play's role in capturing the "metaphysical crisis"[43] of nineteenth-century Spain. Ochoa perceived clearly

---

[37] Review of *La conjuración*, BAE 127: 387.
[38] "No podemos dar iguales alabanzas al desenlace y final del drama, convertido en un juego de linterna mágica con la aparición de tanto difunto ... "
[39] Andioc, "Sobre el estreno de *Don Alvaro*," p. 80.
[40] Richard Cardwell, "*Don Alvaro* or the Force of Cosmic Injustice," *Studies in Romanticism* 12 (1973): 559–579.
[41] Kirkpatrick, *Las románticas*, p. 113.
[42] Walter T. Pattison, "The Secret of Don Alvaro," *Symposium* 21 (1967): 67–81.
[43] D. L. Shaw, "Towards the Understanding of Spanish Romanticism," *Modern Language Review* 58 (1963): 191.

the play's newness and value as a representative expression of the modern condition: it was for him a "tipo exacto del drama moderno, obra de estudio y de conciencia, llena de grandes bellezas y de grandes defectos, sublime, trivial, religiosa, impía, *terrible personificación del siglo XIX*"[44] ("an exact model of modern drama, the result of study and conscience, full of great beautiful moments and great defects, sublime, trivial, religious, impious; it is a *fearful personification of the nineteenth century*"). Audiences may have been dispirited and confused, but they were nonetheless attracted to the power of the message: *Don Alvaro o la fuerza del sino* was performed more frequently than any other drama in 1835.

The unnerving views expressed by Rivas and lived by don Alvaro apparently unsettled the author, too, since his post-*Don Alvaro* work draws on more stable, more traditional touchstones. He quickly retreated from the extremist position he staked out in *Don Alvaro*, joined the Spanish establishment, and even came close to repenting his youthful indiscretions in the 1854 edition of his *Leyendas*: "Son, pues, estas leyendas la verdadera expresión, o en otros términos la medida exacta, de lo que representa y vale hoy su autor"[45] ("These legends are the true expression, or put in other terms, the exact measure, of what their author stands for and values today"). Still, the work remains, and it must be understood in the context of its times rather than in the author's later view of it. A very similar trajectory of birth followed by disownment will be seen in Zorrilla's orientation to his *Don Juan Tenorio*, but *Don Alvaro* remains "la obra de ruptura, el primer drama romántico plenamente logrado ... la obra maestra que llevaba a cabo el arraigo firme y definitivo del romanticismo en el teatro dramático español"[46] ("the work which breaks the mold, the first fully successful Romantic drama ... the masterwork that carried off the complete and definitive rooting of Romanticism in Spanish dramatic theatre").

Pacheco, Alfredo

"Seguro es que nos hallamos en una época de transición en política, en literatura y en todo; sentimos que nos hace falta algo, pero no sabemos qué: sólo estamos seguros de que esto que nos hace falta no es lo que hemos tenido hasta aquí" ("It is certain that we find ourselves in a period of transition in politics, literature, and everything; we feel as though we

---

44 Ochoa, *El Artista* I, p. 177.
45 Rivas, *Obras completas* (Madrid: Real Academia Española, 1854). 5 vols. III.
46 Caldera and Calderone, "El teatro en el siglo XIX," p. 458. Two recent editions of the play contain thorough analyses of its plot, structure, images, and critical reception: see *Don Alvaro*, ed. D. L. Shaw (Madrid: Castalia, 1986), and *Don Alvaro*, ed. Ermanno Caldera (Madrid: Taurus, 1986).

are missing something, but we don't know what; we only know that what we need is not what we have had up until now") wrote Eugenio de Ochoa in a telling attempt to define the disquiet of the Romantic period in Spain.[47] Where Rivas's play surprised the public with its revolutionary message ("estamos en revolución" ["we are in revolution"] according to *La Revista Española*, 25 March 1835), Joaquín Francisco Pacheco's vibrant if overwritten *Alfredo*, performed two months after *Don Alvaro* (23–25 May 1835; it was written and published in 1834), was received with hostility and indifference, in spite of the high hopes it generated among certain critics.[48] Pacheco draws on melodrama and gothic horror in his tale of implied incest, demonic happenings, and "infernal" passion. By doing so, he captures the hesitancy of the times in ways surprisingly similar to Rivas. From the outset, Alfredo, in an echo of Hamlet, feels himself pursued by a "fantasma" ("ghost"), "una potencia misteriosa" ("a mysterious power"). He, like the other Romantic heroes, is fatherless (or thinks he is) and feels compelled to encounter his progenitor. (Is this search for the father a metaphor for the Spanish intelligentsia in the immediate post-Fernandine era?) Alfredo (played by Carlos Latorre) must follow his "destino" ("destiny") (I, 1), wherever it may lead him, and he wonders, as did don Alvaro, "¿Será por ventura la fatalidad la única ley del mundo? ¿No seremos todos sino débiles instrumentos de su poder; vanos juguetes de sus arcanos misteriosos?" ("Can it be that destiny is the world's only law? That we are nothing but weak instruments of its power, vain playthings for its strange mysteries?") (II, 4). Curiously, unlike Rugiero or Alvaro, Alfredo, at least at the beginning of his play, is not in love or consumed with passion for a woman; rather, a vague suspicion of "una pasión incestuosa" ("an incestuous passion") (II, 3) begins to trouble his friend Rugero until Alfredo confesses that "un amor frenético, infernal" ("a frenetic, infernal love") (II, 4) has taken possession of him. That passion is for Berta (played by Concepción Rodríguez), the "widow" of his absent father.

The play never rises above its obvious weaknesses. The characters substitute energy for conviction, change emotion precipitously and without dramatic motivation, suffer too many imagined slights and worries, and act irrationally. The writing is ripe with lugubrious images and meaningful symbols. Yet it is these very characteristics which underscore the Romantic tone and once again, if viewed symbolically instead

47 Review of Bretón's *Mérope*, *El Artista* (1835), p. 216.
48 "Bien se conoce que estamos en una época santa y privilegiada. Solo así puede explicarse la inaudita prodigalidad de piezas españolas que se observa en nuestros teatros ... se habla con grandes elogios de otra titulada *Alfredo* que no tardará en ponerse en escena." *El Artista* I, p. 144.

of realistically, this play reveals key elements of the Romantic mindset. Alfredo sums up the Romantic hero's frustration with his unjust circumstances by asking, "Y ¿es acaso culpa mía, si el mundo está dominado por un principio maléfico?" ("And is it my fault if the world is governed by a malevolent principle?") (V, 8). Pacheco is intent on pushing the break with orthodoxy even further than Rivas. Incest, seemingly the last taboo, hovers close to the two protagonists, ready to draw them into a vortex of passion and tragedy. Alfredo and Berta, his supposedly widowed stepmother, fall inexorably into what they prematurely define as an illicit love brought about by adverse fate:

¡Yo no sé cuál va a ser nuestra suerte ... rodeados sin cesar de esa sombra que no nos deja un sólo instante, que nos persigue más en los momentos de más ventura! ... ¡Fatalidad de maldición! ... Nuestra vida está dominada por el mal ... enhorabuena. (III, 7)

(I do not know what our fate will be ... we are surrounded by that shadow which will not leave us alone for a moment, which pursues us even more in our happiest moments! ... The ill luck of damnation! ... Our life is governed by evil ... Congratulations.)

Yet they too prefer the doubts, anguish, and fear of "esos fantasmas que te persiguen" ("these ghosts which pursue you") to living apart from one another, confirming once again the defiance of Romantic love in the face of insuperable cosmic odds. "¿Llevaré por ventura como Caín la marca de la maldición divina?" ("Will I by chance carry with me Cain's mark of divine damnation?") (III, 10) wails Alfredo. Rugero, Alfredo's longtime friend, quotes his belief that "La fatalidad es la única ley del mundo ... " ("Fate is the world's only law ... ") (IV, 2) and asks himself, as did Don Alvaro, "¿Estará por ventura determinada nuestra suerte por un destino inexorable, imposible de doblegar, sean los que fueren nuestros esfuerzos?" ("Is our fate somehow determined by an inexorable destiny, one impossible to change no matter how much we try?") (IV, 2). The answer, once again, is a resounding yes, and Alfredo pulls out a dagger and, with a scream of "¡Maldición sobre mí!" ("Damnation upon me!") (V, 10) plunges it into his breast. The cosmic connection is made patently clear in the final stage direction, where Pacheco writes of "customary horror": "Al herirse Alfredo, aparece el Griego en el fondo. Vese en sus labios una sonrisa infernal, y se desvanece. Horror general." ("As Alfredo wounds himself, the Greek appears at the back of the stage. One sees on his lips an infernal smirk, and he disappears. Customary horror") (V, 10).

Alfredo's dramatic development paralleled that of the new man, the anguished Romantic hero pushed to the limits of his existence. As

Espronceda noted in his review of the play in *El Artista*, Alfredo was "primero inocente y puro, pero indeciso, melancólico y ansioso de algo que llenara el vacío de su alma, después apasionado, delirante, tratando de fortalecerse contra su conciencia y arrastrado y despeñado por su pasión"[49] ("at first innocent and pure, but indecisive, melancholic, and wishing for something to fill his soul's void; later he is passionate, delirious, trying to strengthen himself against his own conscience and dragged along and finally pushed over the edge by his passion"). Not everyone agreed. Donoso Cortés, who defended the Romanticism-as-Catholicism thinking originally brought into Spain by Böhl de Faber and Durán, penned an indignant review of Pacheco's play in which he voiced the concerns of those who viewed this type of Romantic excess as socially and morally destructive. He complained about their attachment to a muse who "lleva escrito en su frente *incesto, profanación*"[50] ("carries the words *incest* and *desecration* on her forehead"). However, it was Donoso and his followers who ultimately failed to understand Romanticism in Spain. He seemed to think that it was merely a matter of self-control, of will power to dominate one's passions.[51] What Donoso did not comprehend fully was that Pacheco and the other Romantic dramatists did not necessarily seek "la gloria y la posteridad" ("glory and posterity") but rather a way of understanding, of dealing with, the "confusión de sistemas y de doctrinas que arrastran a la Europa en encontradas direcciones" ("confusion of systems and doctrines that is dragging Europe in opposite directions") (659). Even Donoso had to admit that *Alfredo* was a modern play, "inspirado por el siglo XIX" ("inspired by the nineteenth century") (665). After Martínez de la Rosa, Rivas, and Pacheco, were there any other ways to grapple with the problem? Were there any taboos left to be broken by the authors who sought not only scandal but a real reflection of their existential predicament? García Gutiérrez would answer that question in the affirmative.

García Gutiérrez, El trovador

García Gutiérrez pressed the limits of respectability about as far as they could go during the 1830s with his beautifully crafted, intensely dramatic

---

[49] *El Artista* I, p. 263.

[50] "*Alfredo* de Pacheco," *La Abeja* (25 May 1835); reproduced in *Obras de don Juan Donoso Cortés* IV, ed. Manuel Donoso Cortés (Madrid: San Francisco de Sales, 1904): 651–666; quote here from 658.

[51] "Alfredo es el cristiano que sucumbe, no ante la fatalidad de los antiguos, fatalidad exterior, fría, irresistible, sino ante la fatalidad de sus pasiones, *fatalidad moderna*, borrascosa; fatalidad que es un combate, combate que se verifica en lo más íntimo del

El trovador. Its debut on 1 March 1836, at the Príncipe theatre received such a clamorous ovation that the audience's shouts of "Author!, Author!" are now the stuff of theatre lore; it reached eight editions in the fifteen years following its first performance. Even the play's stars, Carlos Latorre and Concepción Rodríguez ("la primera actriz de estos teatros" ["the first lady of these theatres"]), both of whom Larra criticized as miscast, garnered acclaim (*El Español*, 4 March 1836). García Gutiérrez staked out a gutsy position for a 23–year-old novice by transforming his bleak, rebellious vision of life into a moving theatrical spectacle, replete with witches, bonfires, poison, gypsies, and the thirst for vengeance. His most revolutionary step was to allow his Romantic hero, Manrique, the eponymous troubadour, to break into the convent where Leonor is just moments from taking her holy vows, sweep her into his arms, and escape with her. This shocking and unconventional penetration of sacred space aptly symbolizes the Romantic disdain for restraints (chains, cells, prisons, caves) and served notice on the Madrid public that a new world order had been, if not yet triumphant, at least conceptualized. They apparently got the message: reviewers consistently praised the author's arrival into "la más deslumbradora claridad" ("the most astonishing celebrity") and the "enérgicas sensaciones" ("enthusiastic emotions") inspired in the play's viewers.[52] As Peers recognized, García Gutiérrez's contemporaries were perfectly aware of the revolutionary nature of the play. Hartzenbusch confirmed it, as did Mesonero Romanos.[53] It was *El trovador*, not *Don Alvaro*, that took Romantic rebellion to its apogee during the years in question. The play contains resonances of Larra's troubadour and of Martínez de la Rosa's last-minute discovery of close parentage between the antagonists (Manrique turns out to be Nuño's brother), but the headlong spin into the modern world had been so vertiginous that where Larra's hero was still constrained in 1834 by forces beyond his control, García Gutiérrez's declared that not even God would stand between him and his love. *El trovador* drew together many of the strands of Romantic theatre,[54] both thematically and structurally, and

corazón humano, adonde no penetraron nunca los ojos de la antigüedad . . . ." (*ibid.*, p. 659) Emphasis added.

[52] *El Artista* III, p. 120.

[53] E. A. Peers, *Historia del movimiento romántico español* I (Madrid: Gredos, 1967), 344–3 45.

[54] Piero Menarini has written that "*El trovador* representa una especie de compendio de *todas* las experiencias realizadas en los dramas originales (o no), precedentemente escritos y representados, que cubren el espacio de tiempo que va de 1830 a 1836." "Hacia *El trovador*," *Romanticismo* 1 (1982): 95. See also Nicholson B. Adams, *The Romantic Dramas of Antonio García Gutiérrez* (New York: Instituto de las Españas, 1922) and Carlos Ruiz Silva, "El teatro de Antonio García Gutiérrez," *Segismundo* 19 (1985): 151–216.

created one of the most deeply disturbing (yet somehow satisfying) plays of the nineteenth-century canon. Caldera is right to focus attention on this play by stating, "La importancia de *El trovador* en la historia del teatro romántico quizá no sea inferior a la del *Don Alvaro*"[55] ("The importance of *El trovador* in the history of Romantic theatre is perhaps not inferior to that of *Don Alvaro*").

Another revolutionary step taken by García Gutiérrez is the definitive defeat of his lovers, a crushing blow to those who held out any hope for redemption in the Romantic world. Although it seemed as though the other Romantic heroes had been defeated in death by their antagonists (Rugiero is executed by his father, Macías dies after Elvira has taken poison, don Alvaro kills himself after discovering Leonor dead by the hand of her brother), in fact these deaths contained a somewhat twisted, but logical, optimism. Morosini must live with the reality of his terrible deed ("la supresión del protagonista no corresponde al triunfo del antagonista" ["the elimination of the protagonist does not correspond to the triumph of the antagonist"], Menarini reminds us[56]); Macías and Elvira triumph morally since their love will redeem them after death (Macías confirms this: "Es mía / para siempre ..., sí ..., arráncamela ahora, / tirano" ["She is mine forever ..., yes ..., tear her away from me now, tyrant"] [IV, 5]); don Alvaro's suicide can be interpreted as a final confirmation of his existential freedom. Yet *El trovador* offers no such redemptive vision. The protagonists are crushed, even their love is not strong enough to enable them to triumph over political, ecclesiastical, social, and biological reality. Even the tragic Azucena, whose confusing of love and vengeance leaves her abandoned and, finally, dead, cannot put right the evil world she has helped to create.[57]

García Gutiérrez privileges vengeance above all other human motivations in *El trovador*. The opening story, which lays out the details of the burning of Azucena's mother by the Artal family, sets in motion a series of actions which revolve around Azucena's quest for vengeance. At the play's conclusion, after the revelation that Manrique is Nuño's brother, after the death of Leonor, after the execution of the troubadour, there remains one sentence, a sentence which ties in with the opening scene and places Azucena at the very center of the story: "¡Ya estás vengada!" ("So now you're avenged!") (V, 9) she screams to the spirit of her mother before collapsing. Her obsessive bitterness has brought not only the

55 Caldera and Calderone, "El teatro en el siglo XIX," p. 466.
56 Menarini, "Hacia *El trovador*," p. 104.
57 Azucena has been the focus of several interesting critical articles. See in particular Jerry Johnson, "Azucena, Sinister or Pathetic?," *Romance Notes* 12 (1970): 114–118, and Ernest A. Siciliano, "La verdadera Azucena de *El trovador*," *Nueva Revista de Filología Hispánica* 20 (1970): 107–114.

desired vengeance but also tragedy and death to everyone, even to her own son (whom she mistakenly threw into the fire in a rage years before). She consumes them all and is consumed herself, and nothing, not even love, can save any of them. The devastating pessimism of the play goes even beyond that expressed in *Don Alvaro*. "En *El trovador* García Gutiérrez suma y modifica todo"[58] ("In *El trovador* García Gutiérrez sums up and alters everything"). It is a wonder that the Madrid audience clapped for García Gutiérrez rather than hissing him or slinking out of the theatre thoroughly demoralized; instead, it sat there "fascinado"[59] ("bewitched") before breaking into clamorous applause. Larra, too, joined the chorus of praise for this play in which vengeance overshadows love, and hoped that many more like it would pour from the pen of its young author ("síganle muchas como ella"[60] ["let's hope that many more plays like this one follow"]). Performances were immediately sold out, everyone went to see it, and *El trovador* became the most talked-about play of the season. It was being played in provincial theatres within two months of its debut in Madrid and, according to Mesonero, in some small towns *El trovador* became the first ever play to be seen by the uneducated provincials. "Se representó en pueblos donde no se conocían antes las representaciones escénicas, sirviendo de teatro un desván destinado a pajar ..."[61] ("It was performed in towns which had never before had a theatrical performance; the 'theatres' were haylofts ..."). One can only speculate on the audiences' reaction. It ultimately captured the tenor of the times, "épocas de revueltas intestinas como la presente, en que las pasiones son todo" ("periods of domestic upheavals like the present one in which passions become everything"), as confirmed by *El Artista* (III, p. 121).

Curiously, one observer in Madrid also compared its success to that of the *comedias de magia*, underscoring once again our belief that a permeable membrane existed between theatrical genres during the first half of the nineteenth century:

Al día siguiente no se hablaba en Madrid de otra cosa que del *drama caballeresco*: desde muy temprano asediaban el despacho de billetes ayudas de cámara y revendedores: los padres de familia más metódicos prometían a sus hijos llevarles al teatro, *como si se tratara de una comedia de magia*: la primera edición del *Trovador* se vendía en dos semanas; se oían de boca en boca sus fáciles versos; se repetía su representación muchas noches.[62]

58 Menarini, "Hacia *El trovador*," p. 106.
59 Mesonero Romanos, *Memorias de un setentón, Obras completas* II: 147.
60 "*El trovador*, drama caballeresco, en cinco jornadas, en prosa y verso. Su autor, don Antonio García Gutiérrez," *El Español* (4 March 1836) BAE 128: 168.
61 Mesonero Romanos, *Memorias de un setentón*, p. 254.
62 A. Ferrer del Río, *Galería de la literatura española* (Madrid: Mellado, 1846): 257–258. Emphasis added. The play received more than three dozen performances before the decade of the 1830s was over.

(The next day the whole of Madrid was talking about the *chivalresque drama*: from early in the morning the ticket booth was beseiged by chambermaids and scalpers. The most formal parents promised to take their children to the theatre, *as if they were taking them to a magical comedy.* The first edition of the *Trovador* sold out in two weeks; its wonderful verses were heard on everyone's lips; the performance was repeated for many nights.)

Two key years

The turning point: 1837

García Gutiérrez is the Spanish dramatist who most consistently remained faithful to the Romantic creed. Unlike Martínez de la Rosa or Rivas, who immediately turned their literary attentions to more moderate enterprises, this author, in four other plays written between 1837 and 1864, presented the Romantic interpretation of an unjust world controlled by forces of chaos or evil. He immediately returned to his Romantic world in 1837 with two plays which elaborated his vision of chaos: *El paje* (The Page) and *El rey monje* (The Monk King).

The first, performed on 22 May 1837, at the Príncipe, opens with a scene that underscores metaphorically one of the key elements in Spanish Romantic theatre: the role of fate. Ferrando, the young page of the title, is playing dominoes with Bermudo; he is, significantly, losing. Right from the start he reveals himself to be intemperate, daring, passionate, and ambitious. The other key players are Blanca, now married to the Conde de Niebla, and Rodrigo, her ex-lover who has just returned to Córdoba unable to forget her in spite of the years which have passed since they have last seen one another. Blanca, as was Leonor in *El trovador*, is presumably unavailable (she is married), but García Gutiérrez does not hesitate to eliminate conjugal bonds as a barrier. What is more, Rodrigo and Blanca have a son whom she has not seen in years and she is both moved and motivated by her desire to take him into her arms. Like Azucena, she is first a desperate, loving mother. The opening scenes are packed with a dizzying amount of information, mystery, secrets to be revealed, and tension, which culminate later on with the breaking of yet another taboo: the restriction against incest. Ferrando confesses that he loves Blanca, who in turn has rediscovered her intense passion for don Rodrigo de Vargas. As the play unfolds, it becomes clear that Ferrando is Blanca's son (although he does not know this) and that his rival for Blanca is his own father. This pre-Freudian Oedipal conflict is handled with abrupt juxtapositions of emotion which are difficult to sustain dramatically and impossible to accept as realistic or probable. However, once again we must remember that Spanish Romantic drama takes its meaning from a symbolic interpretation of man's struggle for existence, and it is in symbol and metaphor where we can best understand García Gutiérrez's aims and achievements. The *Gaceta de Madrid* criticized the play for the "idealization" of its characters ("no son posibles" ["they are not realistic"] [26 May 1837]), thereby missing the point. Still, by mid-1837, much of the novelty of the Romantic theatre had already worn out (as we shall see below) and the astute reader/spectator could pick up early on the encoded signals and figure out what would be officially revealed in the last act – that the page is Blanca and Rodrigo's long-lost son. While in one regard this dilutes much of the dramatic impact of the play since the surprise is gone, the audience's knowledge that Ferrando is about to kill his own mother significantly intensifies its emotional impact. The author has held yet another surprise in the wings: Ferrando suddenly pulls out a vial of poison and drinks it before forcing Blanca at knifepoint to pray for her life. He refuses to kill her and as he expires, he tells her in passing that Rodrigo is his father which informs her, of course, of the true identity of her page. Like don Alvaro, Ferrando discovers at the last possible moment, and too late, that he could have had what he most desired – the love, in his case, of his mother. "Y ¿es verdad? / ¡Dicha es, madre, el conocerte, / cuando me espera la muerte / y una horrible eternidad!" ("And, is it true? I am lucky, mother, to have met you, just when death and a horrible eternity await me!") (IV, 9). Withal, the author's vision remained consistent: "¿Qué me importa el porvenir, / si es hoy mi destino adverso?" ("What do I care about the future if today my fate is so adverse?") (II, 1) asks Rodrigo, a thought seconded by Ferrando's realization that "Hijo soy de la desgracia" ("I am the son of misfortune") (IV, 5). These ideas remain consistent through the entire genealogy of Romantic heroes, from Rugiero, Macías, and don Alvaro to the Trovador and beyond.

García Gutiérrez also draws on the Romantic love/death dichotomy in clearly symbolic ways. Where previous dramatists had established the connection between love and death, García Gutiérrez literally transforms the marriage bed in *El paje* into a tomb. Ferrando makes the connection when he sees the nuptial bed of Blanca and Rodrigo and proclaims, "Y está su lecho desierto, / desierto como una tumba ... Ven, allí está tu ataud" ("And their bed is deserted, deserted like a tomb ... Come, there is your coffin") (V, 7). Later, after poisoning himself, he dies in her arms. Was his love for her as a mother or as a woman? His confused emotions never allow him to answer that question satisfactorily; neither does the author.

El rey monje is more along the lines of a historical drama, also popular in Spain since the mid-1820s, but it draws on similar Romantic tropes. All of the gothic language and imagery popularized in the past few years appear in *El rey monje*. García Gutiérrez gives us several *verdugos*, an unfulfilled passion, rebellion against tyranny, a mysterious and noble hero, a crowded plaza scene, a coffin, a last-minute tragic dénouement, talk of prisons, chains, angels, broken illusions, dreams, Hell, shadows, masked characters, and pessimism which had come to characterize – almost to the point of becoming clichés – Spanish Romantic drama[63]. A sampling of García Gutiérrez's internalization of these Romantic tropes comes in Act V, scenes 4–6, where Ramiro, echoing Espronceda and don Alvaro, laments:

> La vida es bella
> para el que goza y rie sin dolores,
> sin este padecer negro y eterno ...
> Para el que sufre como yo, la vida
> es un preludio horrible del infierno
> ...
> Y otros felices al nacer al mundo
> huellan tal vez entapizada senda
> de jardines, de risas y de amores ...
> Y yo, desde la cuna moribundo,
> hallé una senda triste, oscura, estrecha,
> y espinas y dolor en vez de flores.
> Allá muy lejos, como luz del cielo,
> una hermosa ilusión encantadora
> soñando vislumbré, y esa luz bella
> me reveló que el mundo era apacible ...
> ¡Un mundo de placer! ... para mí entonces
> era un caos tenebroso, incomprensible.
> ...
> Si esa vida es un sueño, si es un sueño
> ese mundano amor que al alma inspira,
> ¡Qué bello es el soñar, aunque es mentira![64]

(Life is beautiful for whoever enjoys it and laughs without sorrow, without this black and eternal suffering. But for whoever suffers as I do, life is a horrible prelude to Hell ... And some other happy souls who are born can follow the adorned path through gardens, laughter and loves: I, who have been dying since I was born, found a sad, dark, narrow path full of thorns and sorrow instead of flowers. There in the distance, like light from Heaven, I dreamingly discerned an enchanting and beautiful vision, and that beautiful light revealed to me that the

---

[63] See David T. Gies, "Imágenes y la imaginación románticas," *Romanticismo* 1 (1982): 49–59, and "Larra, *La galería fúnebre.*"

[64] Ramiro continues in a vein worthy of Espronceda: "'¡Así pasan por la vida / una tras otra ilusión, / que con belleza mentida / despiertan del corazón / la esperanza adormecida! / Y palpitando y ardiente / se arrastra el afán del hombre / tras de un fantasma luciente, / tras de una cosa sin nombre, / sueño tal vez de su mente." See David T. Gies, "Visión, ilusión y el sueño romántico en la poesía de Espronceda," *Cuadernos de Filología* 3 (1983): 61–84.

world was a peaceful place . . . A world of pleasure! . . . up to that point the world
for me was a dark and incomprehensible chaos . . . If that life is a dream, if that
worldly love that inspires the soul is a dream, how beautiful it is to dream, even if
the dream is a lie!)

El rey monje appeared at the Príncipe Theatre on 18 December 1837,
just following the crescendo of intensely Romantic – and frequently
shocking – dramas. But what was left to shock the public? García
Gutiérrez had already shown them a mother's tragic vengeance, several
suicides, and the suggestion of incest. Reaching even deeper into the
world of the illicit and morally reprehensible shadows of man's psyche, he
serves up in this play the love of a monk for a young girl. Turning to
novelistic titles (as many Romantic playwrights had done, including
García Gutiérrez himself) for the acts of this interestingly structured play
("La cita" ["The Appointment"], "La escala" ["The Stopping Place"],
"Muerta para el mundo" ["Dead to the World"], "El obispo de Roda"
["The Bishop of Roda"], "Una orgía" ["An Orgy"], "La campana de
Huesca" ["The Huesca Bell"], and "La confesión" ["The Confession"])
the author played on the personal and political conflict of Ramiro,
brother to King Alfonso. Ramiro was raised "encarcelado"
("imprisoned") by monks and has just been ordered by his brother to
assume the directorship of the monastery at Sahagún, but he finds himself
in love with Isabel, the beautiful young daughter of the noble and
tyrannical don Ferriz Maza de Lizana. Ramiro must suppress his true
identity in order to see Isabel (at first he presents himself as a simple
nobleman, later he adopts the guise – as did don Alvaro – of a monk, Fray
Pedro). García Gutiérrez draws heavily on Golden Age drama, and
sprinkles elements from *La Celestina* into his work, but he remains most
faithful to the new conception of drama which allowed, even demanded,
melodrama, rebellion, and a shocking climax (even one perhaps too
reminiscent of *Don Alvaro*).

The year of 1837 – *annus mirabilis*, according to Peers – also witnessed
the appearance of Juan Eugenio Hartzenbusch's (1806–1880) now classic
Los amantes de Teruel, often hailed as one of the mainstream Romantic
works. Hartzenbusch staged the play at the Príncipe on 19 January 1837,
but he had begun writing it in 1834, making it one of the first of the new
wave of dramas to be developed in Spain, along with Martínez de la
Rosa's *La conjuración de Venecia* and Larra's *Macías*.[65] He was one of the
most prolific dramatists of his time, and his total production includes
some twenty-nine original plays in a mixture of genres (*comedia de magia*,

---

[65] See the excellent introduction and edition of *Los amantes de Teruel* by Jean Louis Picoche
(Madrid: Alhambra, 1980). Much of this edition is based on the even more thorough one
by the same author (Paris: Centre de Recherches Hispaniques, 1970).

comedy, zarzuela, drama, historical drama) plus thirty-one translations and *refundiciones*. His penchant for *refundición*, even of his own works, makes the work of the modern editor relatively complex, and the constant rewriting frequently produced eloquent scenes although much of his work is workmanlike and merely competent rather than soaring or profound.[66] *Los amantes*, *Doña Mencía* (1839), and *Alfonso el Casto* (1841) rise above mediocrity, and the *comedias de magia* – particularly *La redoma encantada* (1839), and *Los polvos de la madre Celestina* (1840) – contain frequent moments of humor and clarity. However, his reputation rests mainly on *Los amantes de Teruel*, his first important play (a youthful *refundición* of a Rojas Zorrilla play, *El amo criado*, was performed at the Cruz Theatre in April, 1829, and then with some frequency through the 1830s).

The varied sources of *Los amantes de Teruel* – indirectly, some 119, according to Salvador García Castañeda[67] – do not interest us here; suffice it to note that the author drew upon a long tradition of Spanish and European works to forge a drama which has given definitive shape to the legend. As Picoche notes, it is not really a historical drama in the sense given to that genre by the likes of Martínez de la Rosa.[68] Still, it blended together some historical incidents, a believable historical ambience (it takes place betwen 1211 and 1217, during the reign of Jaime I) and authentic family names to create the impression of historicity.

Los amantes de Teruel is not a drama of rebellion or cosmic angst, but it is nevertheless a profoundly Romantic drama because of its deep pessimism. It is a love story played out against the forces of secular and, at times, divine intervention. It shares with its Romantic brethren a belief in the transcendence of love and a conviction that true love is as important to man's happiness as it is impossible to achieve in an imperfect world. Diego Marsilla is ready to do anything to quench his passion for Isabel. "Para la pasión no hay obstáculo, no hay mundo, no hay hombres, no hay más Dios ... las penas y las pasiones han llenado más cementerios que los médicos y los necios" ("Passion recognizes no obstacle, no external world, no other men, no other God ... pain and passion have filled more cemeteries than doctors and fools") as Larra reminds us just days before his own suicide.[69] Marsilla and Isabel, lovers separated by the unfortunate twists of fate, are reunited at the end only – as in the cases of other

---

66 Picoche rightly laments the fact that *La jura en Santa Gadea* (1844), a dull retelling of Guillén de Castro's *Las mocedades del Cid*, is among Hartzenbusch's best-known dramas because of a fortuitous modern edition. Picoche, *Los amantes* (1970), p. 14.

67 *Los amantes de Teruel*, ed. Salvador García Castañeda (Madrid: Castalia, 1971): 11.

68 Picoche, *Los amantes*, p. 23. Picoche provides a cogent discussion of the historical and literary sources used by Hartzenbusch.

69 Larra, "*Los amantes de Teruel*, drama en cinco actos, en prosa y verso, por don Juan Ignacio [*sic*] Hartzenbusch," *El Español* (22 January 1837) BAE 128.

Romantic lovers – when it is too late: Isabel collapses lifeless on the body of Marsilla (when Hartzenbusch rewrote the drama in its definitive version in 1849 he had her fall, rather more chastely, *near* Marsilla's body rather than on top of it) and the desired union in life is permanently denied.[70] This is the way it had to be. Isabel, after all, was forcibly married to Marsilla's rival don Rodrigo after hearing of Marsilla's death from Zulima, the jealous moorish queen who also loves Marsilla, and in an effort to save her mother from Rodrigo's blackmail. The complicated love triangles created by Hartzenbusch fuel the play's tension and plot twists, and the inclusion of multiple surprises, intensely emotional scenes of hate, vengeance, and envy, and a careful blending of the sacred and the profane maintained the audience's interest to the last passionate words uttered by the unfortunate lovers. The audience responded warmly to it, and it became a frequent offering in the repertory, playing thirteen times in 1837 alone, and a couple of dozen more times through the end of the next decade. Clearly, though, it was not a smash hit, and it was not even Hartzenbusch's most widely performed play – *La redoma encantada* had more performances than *Los amantes de Teruel* through the end of the decade of the 1840s – although it is certainly his best-remembered today. Larra praised Hartzenbusch's talent: "El drama que motiva estas líneas tiene en nuestro pobre juicio bellezas que ponen a su autor no ya fuera de la línea del vulgo, pero que lo distinguen también entre escritores de nota ... *Los amantes de Teruel* están escritos en general con pasión, con fuego, con verdad"[71] ("The drama that inspires these lines has, in our humble judgment, beauties that put its author not entirely out of the reach of the masses, but which distinguish him also among writers of note ... *Los amantes de Teruel* is written for the most part with passion, with fire, with truth"). Part of its success, aside from the evident interest of the story and Hartzenbusch's superb craftsmanship, was the quality performances given the play by the leading actors of the capital, principally Carlos Latorre, Bárbara Lamadrid, and Teresa Baus (Larra criticized Julián Romea and Catalina Bravo for underplaying their roles).

The success of *Los amantes* encouraged Hartzenbusch to try his hand at other plays. *Doña Mencía*, staged on 9 November 1838, follows in the line of Gil y Zárate and García Gutiérrez (the Inquisition, incest, surprise revelations, lugubrious settings, tales of people being burned at the stake) and is referred to by Ruiz Ramón, with his usual low tolerance for

---

[70] There exists an interesting debate concerning which of the versions is the more "Romantic." See, for example, Richard A. Curry, "Dramatic Tension and Emotional Control in *Los amantes de Teruel*," *West Virginia University Philological Papers* 21 (1974): 36–47, and Kay Engler, "Amor, muerte y destino: la psicología de Eros en *Los amantes de Teruel*," *Hispanófila* 70 (1980): 1–15.

[71] Larra, "*Los amantes de Teruel*," p. 295.

Romantic emotion, as a "tremebundo dramón"[72] ("frightful melodrama"). Still, it is well structured and its modern sensibility (in spite of its historical setting) attracted critics and public alike. As Gil y Carrasco noted in his review in *El Correo Nacional* (14–16 November 1838), contemporary drama was "la expresión literaria más completa de la época presente, la que más influjo está llamada a ejercer sobre la actual sociedad" ("the most complete literary expression of the present day, which will have the greatest impact on contemporary society"), and Hartzenbusch's new play – "cumplida y preciosa" ("accomplished and witty") – reflected the heightened sensibilities of the times. The complicated plot weaves together strands of honor, vengeance, mistaken identity, jealousy, frustrated love, danger, betrayal, incest (don Gonzalo marries doña Mencía by proxy, only to discover that she is not only his wife, but also his daughter!), a lover disguised as a priest, women on the verge of professing as nuns, a suicide (like don Alvaro, doña Inés pleads, "Abreme aquí, a tus pies, la sepultura" ["Let my tomb open here at your feet"] [II, 13]), and other by-now standard elements of Romantic dramaturgy. Yet its rejection of the oppressive Office of the Inquisition ("esa especie de pesadilla que por tanto tiempo ha comprimido el corazón de España" ["that nightmare which for so long has troubled Spain's heart"], according to Gil[73]) and its willingness to allow its characters to abandon watertight logic and cool reasoning for emotional outburst places it squarely within the theatrical mentality of the mid-1830s, much to the disgust of those who viewed in such flighty emotionalism a sign of the decline of Spanish civilization. Much of the modern audience wanted tension, an emotional and tragic denouement, and spectacle on stage, rather than dry reasoning or philosophical treatises on correct behavior. "Tales resultados hablan más alto al corazón del pueblo que todos los recursos de la lógica más acerada" ["Such effects speak louder to the public's heart than all of the tricks of the most steely logic"], as Gil reminded his readers.[74] In spite of such emotional intensity, Manuel de la Revilla, one of the most respected literary critics of the second half of the century, praised in Hartzenbusch "el buen gusto sin intransigencia, la inspiración sin extravío"[75] ("his good taste without intransigence, his inspiration without disorder"). Once again, the period's best-known and best-loved actors performed the main roles: Bárbara Lamadrid, Matilde Díez, Carlos Latorre, and Antonio Guzmán all took part in *Doña Mencía.*

---

[72] Francisco Ruiz Ramón, *Historia del teatro español* (Madrid: Alianza, 1967): 433.
[73] See his review of *Doña Mencía*, reprinted in *Obras completas de D. Enrique Gil y Carrasco*, ed. Jorge Campos (Madrid: Atlas, 1964) (BAE 74): 407–415. Quote here from p. 410.
[74] *Ibid.* p. 410.   [75] Revilla, "D. Juan Eugenio Hartzenbusch," *Obras*, p. 31.

This "hyper-Romanticism" was also evident in several dramas presented by Antonio Gil y Zárate (1793–1862), one of which, *Carlos II el hechizado*, played on 2 November 1837 at the Príncipe, "dejando pasmado al público por el atrevimiento"[76] ("leaving the public aghast at its daring"). Gil, one of the century's most interesting – and most forgotten – dramatists, is, as Alborg has perceptively noted, a representative figure of his period.[77] He was highly regarded in his lifetime and given several important positions in the government and in literary societies (he was one of the founding members of the Liceo Artístico, for example). However, he had been chastened by the criticism of his 1835 play, *Blanca de Borbón*, which the critics interpreted as a statement against the new Romantic movement so in response, Gil wrote a play which would contain all of the established tropes of Romanticism. In don Froilán, he created one of the most deliciously evil characters in all of Spanish Romantic drama. His satanic lust for Inés, who later is revealed to be the illegitimate daughter of Carlos II, turns him, in Gil's exaggerated vision, into the embodiment of blind obsession. Froilán manipulates both the King and the officials of the Inquisition to try to win over Inés, who sensibly resists his advances not only because he is an evil individual but also because of her real love for don Florencio. Froilán, a monk who serves as the King's confessor, abandons his religious vows when confronted with his irrepressible physical passion for the lovely young girl. Gil skilfully presents a psychologically complex character, motivated by illicit passion yet conscious both of its impossibility and the pleasure of its torments. Caldera has pointed to Froilán's sadomasochistic underpinnings by citing the monk's speech from the first act:

> En el odio también delicias hallo;
> en él también encontraré consuelos:
> si no puedo gozarme en tus caricias,
> en tu llanto podré gozarme al menos.   (I, 7)[78]

(I also find satisfaction in hatred; in it I shall take comfort. If I cannot have your caresses, then in your sobs I shall at least be able to find pleasure.)

Froilán is an authentically revolutionary character bent on undermining both the government and his religious vocation for immediate self-

[76] Valladares y Saavedra, *Nociones acerca de la historia del teatro*, p. 135.
[77] Alborg, *Historia* IV, p. 627. The bibliography on Gil is slim. It includes comments in various manuals of literature, plus an unpublished dissertation by Sterling A. Stoudemire, "The Dramatic Works of Gil y Zárate" (University of North Carolina: 1930), and several articles by the same author: "Don Antonio Gil y Zárate's Birth Date," *Modern Language Notes* 46 (1931): 171–172; "A Spanish Play on the Fair Rosamond Legend," *Studies in Philology* 28 (1931): 325–329 (on his play, *Rosamunda*); and "Gil y Zárate's Translations of French Plays," *Modern Language Notes* 48 (1933): 321–325.
[78] Caldera and Calderone, "El teatro en el siglo XIX," p. 486.

gratification. Still, he is not a one-dimensional cartoon character in his evil ways. Gil makes it clear that he has struggled against his lustful inclinations, but has failed to dominate them. Like Iago or the evil friar Claude Frollo in Hugo's *Notre Dame de Paris*, Froilán battles within himself his conflicting demons. In typical Romantic fashion he views his fight as larger than life, divine, "sin igual, tremenda" ("without equal, tremendous"):

> Oyeme ... Un año
> luché con este amor para vencerlo;
> lucha penosa, sin igual, tremenda,
> cual la lucha de Dios con el infierno.
> Huí del mundo, y mi fervor piadoso
> buscó en un claustro el sepulcral silencio.
> Al pie del ara me postré rogando,
> y su mármol bañé con llanto acerbo.
> Mi cabeza cubrí con vil ceniza;
> cruel cilicio atormentó mi cuerpo;
> mi mano armada de nudosas cuerdas;
> regó con sangre mis rasgados miembros;
> ...
> Pensé que Dios tan penitente vida
> al fin premiara sofocando el fuego
> de mi funesto amor ... ¡Vana esperanza!   (I, 7)

(Hear me out ... For a year I fought against this love in order to overcome it. It was a painful battle, without equal, tremendous, like God's fight against Hell. I fled the world, and my pious zeal sought a silent tomb in the cloister. I prostrated myself, pleading at the foot of the altar, and I bathed its marble in bitter tears. I covered my head with vile ashes; a cruel hair shirt tortured my body; I armed myself with knotted ropes that washed my shredded limbs with blood; ... I thought that God would reward this penitent life by putting out the fire of my mournful love ... Vain hope!)

Froilán expresses his torment in typical Romantic fashion – vengeance, "destino injusto" ("unjust fate"), "hado ciego" ("blind destiny"), passion, "mi infausta estrella" ("my unlucky star") – in a brief soliloquy in Act II, but ultimately he is so self-centered that he uses his power and knowledge solely for personal ends. Froilán manipulates both Carlos and Inés in order to save himself. Gil sets up an interesting dichotomy between Carlos and Froilán, whose actions reflect each other's mental state at various points in the drama. When Carlos becomes crazed ("con risa sardónica, delirando" ["with a sardonic grin, ranting"] [V, 2]) we see Froilán agonizing and confused (V, 3); the latter becomes a type of twisted alter ego of the former. Yet in the end, when the power of the monarchy is pitted against the psychological-religious power of Froilán, it is the evil confessor who triumphs. Carlos's tragedy lies in the fact that in spite of his supposed power as monarch, and following the last-minute discovery of the real identity of Inés, he is still incapable of saving her or of finding happiness. Just as in *Don Alvaro*, peace and a possible happy ending – in this case in which the King would have a daughter, an heir and a family – are thwarted at the last possible moment by the cosmic forces of chaos.

Carlos II himself is yet another in the series of twisted monarchs that Romantic authors were fond of portraying. By the end of 1837 the *Eco del Comercio* noted with some slight exasperation that "Todos los reyes que hayan sido despóticos y perversos hallan favorable acogida por los autores románticos, que sin escrúpulo ninguno los reproducen en el teatro aún más perversos y despóticos que fueron" ("All of our despotic and perverse kings are favorably received by our Romantic authors, who without any scruples at all reproduce them in the theatre even more perverse and despotic than they actually were") (3 December 1837). This was certainly the case with Gil's depiction of Carlos II, but historical authenticity held little interest for Romantic dramatists who were more concerned with emotional effect, intensity of feeling, and scandal than they were with history. Carlos is much less a seventeenth-century monarch than an anguished Romantic struggling to understand his place in the universe.

> Nacido en día fatal,
> todo a mí contrario veo:
> el bien conozco y deseo,
> y sólo consigo el mal.
> Al solio niño subí,
> y entre encontradas facciones,
> juguete de sus pasiones,
> sólo rey en nombre fui:
> Su infame ambición tal vez
> mi juventud marchitaba,
> y a degradarme aspiraba
> en perdurable niñez.
> Mi humillación conocí;
> romper logré mis cadenas;
> mas libre el yugo apenas,
> en otro yugo caí ...   (I, 3)

(Born on an ominous day I see that everything is against me: I want to do the right thing, and know what that is, but all I do is wrong. I sat on the throne as a child and became the plaything of various factions; I was king in name only. Their despicable ambition deprived me of a vigorous youth and tried to keep me in perpetual infancy. I recognized my humiliation and managed to break my chains, but once free of that yoke I found another around my neck ...)

As were other Romantic characters, he is compared with the Devil
("parece, Dios me perdone, / un endemoniado" ["he seems to be, God
forgive me, demonic"] [I, 1], "¡Y que en un cuerpo tan santo / esté metido
el demonio!" ["That the devil is in such a saintly body!"] [II, 4], etc.) and
made to suffer the unjust twists of fate. We even begin to suffer with this
crazed, confused figure, all the more so near the end of the play when he
finally discovers his long-lost daughter, only to lose her to the stronger
forces of the Inquisition. Like don Alvaro, his only recourse is delirium
and, ultimately, death.

Such exaggerated monarchs also served to allow the audience to draw
easy parallels to Spain's recent history without risking censorship or overt
reaction by government officials. The court itself is depicted as a place full
of conspiracies, lies, vested interests, competing factions, superstitions,
and betrayal, all of which were also unfortunately recognizable weaknesses of the current government and of which the audience, given the
more lively and open nature of the periodical press, was fully aware.
There were those, in fact, who viewed this play as an allegory of the
contemporary situation in which the seven-year-old Queen Isabel II was
dominated by her moderate, almost liberal mother (Carlos II inherited his
throne when he was four years old and his mother also served as his regent
until he came of age). Such parallels were not difficult to believe, when we
read not-so-subtle allusions to the problem of Isabel's succession to the
throne:

OROPESA.	Los derechos de la infanta su esposa ¿no renunció? Pues, bien, ¿por qué los reclama?
SAN ESTEBAN.	No los pudo renunciar. ¿Por ventura así se cambian las leyes de un reino? Sólo se quiso evitar que entrambas coronas se reuniesen: Si este obstáculo se allana, al legítimo heredero ¿quién la sucesión arranca?
OROPESA.	La unión y la independencia de monarquía tan vasta sólo puede conservar la dinastía austriaca. (I, 5)
(OROPESA.	Didn't his wife give up the princess's rights? Why is she reclaiming them?
SAN ESTEBAN.	She couldn't renounce them. Do you think that a kingdom's laws are changed so freely? They only

wanted to insure that the two crowns were not united:
if this obstacle is removed, who could ever keep the
legitimate heir from inheriting the throne?

OROPESA.   The unity and independence of such a vast kingdom
can only be preserved by the Austrian dynasty.)

The play was polemical, defended by some for its intense passion and
criticized by others as an "aborto" ("abortion") pertaining to "la escuela
satánica [read Romantic], que debía ser enteramente abandonada en este
siglo, en el que sabemos muy bien cómo destruir y muy poco cómo
edificar"[79] ("the satanic school, which should be abandoned completely
during this century, which knows too much about how to destroy but too
little about how to build up"). This critic thought this immensely popular
play to be a masterpiece and therefore much more dangerous than a
mediocre and consequently easily forgotten piece. Mesonero judged it to
have been written by Gil in "un momento de satánica tentación"[80]
("during a moment of satanic temptation"). Even Gil himself seemed to
repent this youthful indiscretion (as did Zorrilla with his don Juan) –
following his death in 1861, the newspaper *La Esperanza* claimed that Gil
asked forgiveness for having published such a "monstrosity." However,
the deed was done and the play became a standard in the repertory. It
even enjoyed a small surge in popularity in small theatres following the
Revolution of 1868 which ejected the unpopular Isabel II from the throne.
A curious anecdote from 1883 reveals the power of Gil's final *coup de
théâtre*, when Florencio, whom everyone thought to be dead, tears off his
disguise as one of the Inquisition's officials and plunges a dagger into
Froilán shouting, as did Azucena in *El trovador*, "¡venganza!" ("vengeance!"):

La prensa de Almería refiere el siguiente incidente ocurrido en el teatro Apolo de
aquella ciudad al terminarse la representación del drama popular, *Carlos II el
hechizado*. Al concluir el drama, el público llamaba a grandes voces a los actores.
Estos se presentaban, pero aquel tumulto no se calmaba, aun después de salir
cuarto o cinco veces. El señor Méndez, todavía vestido de las hopalandas,
preguntó valiéndose de la mímica, qué querían los espectadores, y uno de las
primeras filas contestó: "Que le maten a Vd. otra vez." Volvió a presentarse el
señor Cachet y sepultó el puñal en el pecho del fraile. El público se retiró
tranquilamente. (*El Imparcial*, 6 January 1883)

(The newspapers in Almería recount the following incident which happened at the
Apolo Theatre there following a performance of the popular drama *Carlos II el
hechizado*. Just as the play ended, the public shouted for the actors to come out on

---

[79] Salas y Quiroga, *No me olvides*, 28 (1838), p. 6.
[80] Mesonero Romanos, *Memorias de un setentón*, p. 165.

stage. They came out, but the clamor did not subside, even after four or five curtain calls. Mr. Méndez, still wearing his costume, asked the audience what it wanted, when someone in the first row said, "We want them to kill you again." Mr. Cachet came back out on stage and sank the dagger in the friar's heart. The audience dispersed calmly.)

Even playing the part of Froilán could be hazardous to an actor's health, so despised could he be by an audience engrossed in the play's plot.[81]

Less than four weeks after the appearance of *Carlos II el hechizado*, Bretón de los Herreros staged his own version of the Romantic conflict in *Don Fernando el emplazado* (Príncipe Theatre, 30 November 1837). He had already mined some Romantic tropes in *Elena* (1837) and *Muérete ¡y verás!* (Die and You'll See!, 1837), but now he capitalized fully on the year's intense attention to this type of theatre spectacle. The historical action, set in Martos and Jaén in 1312, opens with a conflict similar to that of *El trovador*. Benavides demands that Pedro Carvajal forget the idea of marrying his sister Sancha, whom he wishes to betroth to someone else. Nevertheless, Carvajal, insisting that "Amor, que es ya frenesí, / la rinde mi corazón" ("Love, already a frenzy, has conquered my heart") (I, 1), tells Benavides that "A entrambos guía una estrella ... / que no queremos la vida / ella sin mí, y yo sin ella" ("A star guides us both ... we cannot live one without the other") (I, 1). Benavides swears vengeance against his sister's rebellion. This personal conflict is set against the background of factional war in Andalucía, the king's refusal to grant clemency to his exiled mother, and additional calls for vengeance against what is seen by her supporters to be a breach of justice. As it happens, of course, Carvajal turns out to be the brother of the leader of the rebellious faction and thus faces a seemingly unresolvable conflict between his family loyalty and his love for Sancha. To complicate matters, the king also reveals that he is in love with Sancha and soon a situation arises in which Sancha must choose between saving Carvajal (by marrying Fernando) or remaining true to her honor and love. The lovers declare "La tumba nos unirá / ya que los altares no" ("The tomb will unite us since the altar has not") (II, 15) as forces seem inexorably to move them toward

---

[81] Como en algunos teatros llegase la hostilidad del público hasta el extremo de pasar a *vías de hecho* con el tal fraile, arrojándole patatas y otros comestibles *contundentes*, el actor encargado de dicho antipático papel, en un momento determinado, cuando más imponentes eran las agresiones, se abría o se remangaba los hábitos y enseñaba debajo de los mismos su traje de miliciano nacional, exclamando: 'Señores: que soy Fulano de Tal y pertenezco, además de pertenecer a esta compañía, a la cuarta del primer batallón de ligeros ... ¡Viva la libertad!' El público respondía con otra ¡viva! al susodicho, la orquesta tocaba unos compases del himno de Riego ... y continuaba la representación, ya sin peligro para el mencionado *traidor* ...
Francisco Flores García, *Memorias íntimas del teatro* (Valencia: F. Sempere, 1909): 47.

tragedy. Sancha, in a beautifully written soliloquy (IV, 9), which reminds us of don Alvaro's similar lament (III, 4), cries in typically Romantic fashion, "¡Ay de mí, / que en hora amarga nací!" ("Woe is me! Born at such a bitter hour!"). Bretón drags his characters through prisons, disguises them, surrounds them at important moments with a typically Romantic natural landscape (threatening clouds, lightening bolts, thunder, an "áspero y desnudo risco" ["rugged and naked mountain peak"] à la *Don Alvaro*, pitch blackness), confronts them with spectres, and provides his audience with a disquieting mixture of familiar and horrifying elements.

Bretón writes multiple climaxes into the drama. One comes in Act III: the King, refusing to pardon Carvajal from being thrown off a cliff, declares, in the presence of Sancha (who has just fainted) and an increasingly unruly mob who defends Carvajal, "No perdono" ("I do not forgive him"). The stage directions read:

Las nubes se condensan por instantes; los truenos, ya muy cercanos, se multiplican; parte del pueblo se va retirando a la villa huyendo de la tormenta que amenaza ... El teatro queda enteramente oscuro; sólo algún relámpago deja ver los objetos por intervalos; arrecia la lluvia; pocos del pueblo permanecen en la escena; los demás huyen consternados; el Rey queda solo en el mirador haciendo vanos esfuerzos para retirarse ... Los Carvajales se dan las manos vueltos hacia el bastidor de la derecha, y en el momento de ser precipitados por el verdugo óyese un trueno espantoso, y un grito universal; el Rey cae en tierra sin sentido, y baja el telón. (III, 8–9)

(The clouds thicken; thunder, closer now, increases; some of the people begin to move away toward town in order to get away from the threatened storm ... The theatre remains completely dark. Only a periodic flash of lightning allows one to see the stage. The rain increases. Few townspeople are left on stage, the rest flee terrified. The king remains alone in the tower, trying in vain to get away ... The Carvajals join hands to the right of the stage and at the moment they are thrown over the edge by the executioner, a terrifying thunderbolt is heard, along with a cry of horror from the remaining crowd. The king falls to the ground in a faint, and the curtain comes down.)

Another climax, in the brief fifth act, reveals that the priest who comes to give Fernando extreme unction (he is dying of a mysterious cause) is really Gonzalo Carvajal, determined to avenge his brother's death; but the King dies and Carvajal, who pardons him in a surprise move, can switch his allegiance to the new king, Alfonso XI.

Notwithstanding the intense Romanticism and popularity of these plays by Hartzenbusch, García Gutiérrez, Gil y Zárate, and Bretón, by 1837 the tide was turning against the exaggerated, hyperbolic emotionalism of such dramas. The public's head and emotions were spinning. In just one year it had witnessed the premières of

Hartzenbusch, *Los amantes de Teruel*	19 January 1837
García Gutiérrez, *El paje*	22 May 1837
Gil y Zárate, *Carlos II el hechizado*	2 November 1837
Bretón, *Don Fernando el emplazado*	30 November 1837
García Gutiérrez, *El rey monje*	18 December 1837

Still, in newspaper criticism, satires, and even some plays, one can detect a movement toward a more conservative stance which integrated many of the themes of liberal Romanticism, but which shied away from its more revolutionary aspects. The public, for example, wasn't buying Bretón's intrusion into the Romantic world; embarrassingly for him, they laughed aloud during the performances of *Don Fernando el emplazado* at what they thought to be his "mal dibujados" ("poorly drawn") characters (*El Eco de Comercio*, 3 December 1837), although the play's skilled verses and above-average performances by the actors kept it on the boards for eleven performances.

An ending and a new beginning: 1844

The other year of greatest importance to the time period in question is 1844, when two plays – one remembered today as perhaps the most popular play in the entire Spanish repertory and the other completely forgotten – dominated theatrical discourse. Both in their own ways signaled a shift away from the Romantic movement.

José Zorrilla (1817–1893) was already one of the dominating figures of the Spanish theatre scene when he wrote *Don Juan Tenorio* (in six weeks, according to his own testimony).[82] Zorrilla was well known in Madrid not only for his poetry and newspaper work (he was one of the founders of *El Entreacto* in 1839), but mostly as the author of *Juan Dándolo* (written in collaboration with García Gutiérrez in 1839), the very successful *El zapatero y el rey* (The Shoemaker and the King, in two parts, 1840 and 1842), *El puñal del godo* (The Goth's Dagger, 1843), and numerous other plays. His genius in *Don Juan Tenorio* was to draw from historical and theatrical tradition (Golden Age, *comedias de magia*, Romanticism[83]) in order to create a *successful* hero, that is, an individual who achieves,

---

[82] Biographical and bibliographical information on Zorrilla can be found in Alonso Cortés, *Zorrilla. Su vida y sus obras*; Alborg, *Historia*, IV: pp. 553–617; and Navas Ruiz, *El romanticismo español*, pp. 294–319.

[83] The *Revista de Teatros* (17 March 1844) reported that "Nosotros asistimos en su día a la lectura de *Don Juan Tenorio* y aunque pertenece a un género que hoy día no encuentra muchas simpatías [the magical comedy], estamos casi seguros que aparte de esto el drama gustará por lo bien versificado." I have studied Zorrilla's uses of Spanish theatrical

unlike his Romantic contemporaries, happiness and salvation through love.

Don Juan is significantly different from the other Romantic heroes developed by Martínez de la Rosa, Rivas, García Gutiérrez, Hartzenbusch, Gil y Zárate and others, and therefore must be studied from outside the Romantic canon rather than from inside it. If we look for characteristics in him or in his behavior similar to those of previous Romantic heroes, it becomes clear that in many ways he stands apart from them. In the first part of the play he does indeed display the rebelliousness which defines many of the other Romantic heroes, but one notes immediately that rather than being a noble, generous, and loyal individual pushed by circumstances beyond his control to behave rebelliously, he glories in his small rebellions and in fact takes joy and pride in his evil deeds. His famous claim:

> Llamé al cielo y no me oyó
> y pues sus puertas me cierra,
> de mis pasos en la tierra
> responda el cielo, y no yo.   (I, iv, 8)

(I called out to Heaven but was not heard, and since it closed its doors to me, let Heaven answer for my time on earth, not I.)

would have been a fitting ending for many Romantic plays; here, Zorrilla uses it as a turning point to close the first part in order to allow don Juan to move away from his life of crime to one of profound repentance. He is considered by the other characters, including his own father, to be an evil individual set on a path of seduction and murder for the pure fun of it (how different this behavior is from that of Rugiero, don Alvaro or Manrique *el trovador!*). "Es la más mala cabeza / del orbe" ("he is the most evil person on earth") says his friend Centellas about him (I, i, 10). Zorrilla, with one eye on the public taste and the other on the political circumstances in which he was living, created a hero who could mollify both the need for shock and spectacle (hence, the magical elements in *Don Juan Tenorio*) and his – and his audience's – longing for a calming, conservative message which neatly paralleled society's return to the policies of Ramón de Narváez. Don Juan, in spite of his past misdeeds, is saved because he repents his evil ways and accepts God's grace through the intercession of the one woman he finally realizes he loves, Inés. Whereas Rugiero went to his death proudly, don Alvaro jumped into the

tradition elsewhere: see "José Zorrilla and the Betrayal of Spanish Romanticism," *Romanistiches Jahrbuch* 31 (1980): 339–346; "Don Juan contra don Juan: apoteosis del romanticismo español," *Actas del VII Congreso Internacional de Hispanistas* II, ed. G. Bellini (Rome: Editore Bulzoni, 1982): 545–551; and "*Don Juan Tenorio* y la tradición de la comedia de magia," *Hispanic Review* 58 (1990): 1–17.

void in a stunning rejection of any calming message of redemption or forgiveness, and many other characters encountered death and unrequited love in this world (the body count of Romantic drama is impressively high), Zorrilla's "Romantic" hero begs for forgiveness, accepts God's grace, and floats Heavenward on a bed of flowers to the sound of soothing celestial music. Romantic theatre disappears into the clouds with don Juan – the burning flame of pessimistic rebellion had been irrevocably extinguished. This is not to say that there would not be "Romantic" plays written after 1844 (Zorrilla's *Traidor, inconfeso y mártir*, 1849, and García Gutiérrez's *Venganza catalana*, 1864, and *Juan Lorenzo*, 1865 share much Romantic imagery and language), but the impulse for Romantic rebellion had, by the mid-1840s, been superseded by a middle-class need to see itself and its interests more accurately reflected on the stage. Even though the play was to become the best-loved play in the Spanish repertory, and certainly the most frequently performed, it was not an immediate hit: "gustó más la primera parte que la segunda: esta se roza más con *El convidado de piedra* y el público está ya muy familiarizado con la cena del comendador en casa de don Juan Tenorio; si bien Zorrilla ha tenido la habilidad de prepararla con más naturalidad y maestría … Su éxito ha sido satisfactorio, no brillante" ("the audience liked the first part more than the second: this part had more to do with *El convidado de piedra* and the public already knows quite well the scene of the Commendador's dinner at don Juan's house. Zorrilla had the talent to write it with greater naturalness and skill … The play's success has been satisfactory, but not brilliant") (*Revista de Teatros*, 30 March 1844).

As the popularity of *Don Juan Tenorio* grew, so too did the penchant of other playwrights to parody it and there developed an odd cottage industry in nineteenth-century Spain dedicated to making fun, at times lovingly, at times corrosively, of Zorrilla's eponymous hero. These parodies will be discussed below.

What is even more significant is the fact that we have clear evidence of the public's desire to return to a more tranquil, safer, calmer world, something that *Don Juan Tenorio* would offer them. With reference to Zorrilla's *La copa de marfil* (The Ivory Cup), which was poorly received at its debut, the *Revista de Teatros* (12 May 1844) observed:

Refiérese a la época de la dominación de los Lombardos en Italia: figura como principal personaje el rey Alboino, que tenía por copa el cráneo del padre de su esposa Rosamunda. Ya esta circunstancia es suficiente para que repugne en el teatro y especialmente *en país y en época en que lo que se necesita es calma y consuelos en vez de aflicciones y exterminios.*[84]

---

[84] Emphasis added. This last word reminds us of don Alvaro's final, cataclysmic scream, not, I would suggest, unintentionally.

(It deals with the period when the Lombards dominated Italy. Its main character is King Alboino, who used the skull of his wife Rosamunda's father as a drinking cup. This circumstance alone is enough to repel people, and particularly in *a country and a time when what we most need is calm and consolation instead of anguish and destruction.*)

However, not everyone agreed with Zorrilla's conservative answer to the tumult of the times. Just one month after the debut of *Don Juan Tenorio*, Eusebio Asquerino (1822–1892), a contemporary of Zorrilla and Tomás Rodríguez Rubí (1817–1890) wrote a play which provoked much more of a reaction than Zorrilla's work, and proved to be much more commented upon and polemical (hence, "popular") than *Don Juan Tenorio*, at least through the decade of the 1840s. *Españoles sobre todo*, which premièred at the Cruz theatre on 22 May 1844, was an unabashedly political potboiler set on commenting on contemporary political events. The play ostensibly dealt with the machinations surrounding the Spanish War of Succession in the early eighteenth century, when French interests battled Austrian and English ones for the control of the Spanish crown. In reality it was a rabble-rousing modern political tract in dramatic form.

The contemporary political situation was, by all standards, confused and difficult. Since Fernando VII's death in 1833, the country had experienced the crisis of competing ideologies, tensions which had exploded into the bloody Carlist War, so trenchantly commented upon by Larra. Popular protests, government instability, periods of repression, political assassinations, and a host of other problems moved the country between conservative and moderate ("liberal") forces. Partisans of a republican government vied with defenders of the old monarchy for influence at the highest levels. María Cristina, the Queen Regent, was first humiliated at her palace at La Granja in 1837 when forced to sign a new constitution by a group of dissatisfied military leaders, then forced into exile in 1840 when General Espartero (who was eventually supported by the English) rose against her. When María Cristina's daughter, Isabel, was declared of legal age in 1843, diplomatic jockeying began in earnest to find her a suitable husband among the various international factions interested in making a claim on the Spanish crown. Battle lines were redrawn, with conservative and "moderate" forces aligned on one side against progressive and radical interests on the other. By the time Espartero was forced to flee the country (September 1843) and Ramón de Narváez named Prime Minister and War Minister (May 1844) the Moderates had won the day, but their hold on power was tenuous at best. As Carr has stated, when the maneuvering intensified in 1846 (after Narváez's dismissal by the Queen) the ministers of France and Britain "backed different ministries and acted at times as if Spanish politicians had ceased to count as governors of an independent nation."[85]

Asquerino, a newspaperman and dramatist of outspokenly republican leanings, wrote plays which García Castañeda has accurately called "dramas históricos de inclinación política."[86] Sometimes in collaboration with his brother Eduardo, he penned several "historical" dramas which addressed the current political situation, including *Doña Urraca* (1838), *Gustavo Wasa* (1841), *Españoles sobre todo* (Part 1, 1844; Part 2 [with Eduardo], 1847), *Las guerras civiles* (The Civil Wars, 1849), and *Las dos reinas* (The Two Queens, 1853). The brothers became known for their outspoken political plays. *Felipe el Hermoso* (Philip the Handsome, 1845), written by Eusebio in collaboration with Gregorio Romero Larrañaga, was censored (its most interesting scenes "mutilated" according to the *Revista de Teatros* [9 March 1845]) for its political content. The polemic over political content in the theatre remained lively during these years, and politics as an apt subject matter for drama was seen as a form of "enlightenment": "[How are we to thrive] en nuestra carrera de ilustración, si no puede hoy desarrollarse en la escena un pensamiento político, un pensamiento social ... Y que nuestra época es política, que nuestras costumbres son políticas, que todo es política entre nosotros es una verdad aunque verdad desgraciada" ("[How are we to thrive] on the road to enlightenment, if political thought, social thought, cannot be expressed in the theatre ...] And that our era is political, that our customs are political, that everything is politics among us is a truism, even if it is an unfortunate truism") (*Revista de Teatros,* 3 March 1845). As *La Luneta* wrote in 1846, Eduardo was writing "una obra de política cuyo objeto es publicar con las galas de la imaginación la historia del partido a que pertenece" ("a political work the objective of which is to publicize with imaginative flourish the history of the party to which he belongs") (27 December 1846). Political and/or historical drama was nothing new on the Spanish scene, of course, and the Romantic experiments with historical drama – beginning with *La conjuración de Venecia* – underscored the attractiveness of the linking of historical atmosphere with contemporary reality for Spanish audiences in the thirties and forties. For the past dozen years the theatre had also (as it had during the Napoleonic invasion) served as a forum for political activism, becoming the focal point for political causes, exhortations to the audience to support this side or that, and bully pulpits to raise money and spirits. Many of the most active intellectuals of the day were involved in such activities in one way

85 Raymond Carr, *Spain 1808–1975* (Oxford: Clarendon Press, 1982): 241.
86 Salvador García Castañeda, "Los hermanos Asquerino o el uso y mal uso del drama histórico," *Quaderni di Filologia Romanza* 4 (1984): 25.

or another (Espronceda, Grimaldi, García Gutiérrez, Ventura de la Vega, Gregorio Romero Larrañaga, Tomás Rodríguez Rubí, Hartzenbusch, etc.). This move toward the politicization of the theatre was decried with some frequency in the pages of the newspapers, but it continued unabated. In a clear allusion to *Españoles sobre todo*, the *Revista de Teatros* wrote:

Tendríamos por la mayor de las calamidades para la literatura el que se posesionara del teatro la política militante, cual si no tuviera ancho campo donde esparcirse en los artículos de fondo de los periódicos, en los discursos de la tribuna y en las conversaciones de los corrillos. Todavía nos parece más impropio atribuir a personajes de principios del siglo XVIII las mismas ideas que fermentan en las cabezas de los demagogos del día, revistiéndolos con sus propias pasiones y tendencias. (8 June 1845)

(We would think that the worst calamity that could happen to the theatre would be for it to be taken over by militant politics, as if such politics did not already have ample grounds for expression in articles in the newspapers, in speeches from the rostrum, and in conversations in little cliques. It seems even more inappropriate to attribute to characters from the beginning of the eighteenth century the same ideas that ferment in the heads of modern-day demagogues, investing the former with the passions and political inclinations of the latter.)

In *Españoles sobre todo* the ambitious Princesa de los Ursinos is actively manipulating both María, her niece, and the Count of Montellano, her rival for influence at court, in order to solidify the interests of her secret backers, the French cabinet. María is threatened with marriage to Montellano, but she loves instead Ricardo, a leader of the faction which supports Austrian interests (the Archduke Carlos) in the war. The scene becomes a constant power struggle, both secretly and publicly, between these two contending sides, and it neatly parallels one of the crises facing the country in the mid-1840s. The prize is Spain, and the question of whether France or Austria would dominate her forms the core of the play's argument. However, Asquerino refuses to accept the possibility that foreign interests will hold sway over Spanish politics, and as the title clearly states, believes that Spaniards should defend their independence against those who would either take it away or sell it to the highest foreign bidder.

The play contains many Romantic elements, but it cannot be considered a Romantic play. Talk of a "fatal estrella" ("fatal star"), a "delirio loco" ("crazy delirium"), a "fatal destino" ("fatal destiny"), dominate the play's language, and the love affair between Ricardo and María strongly recalls the dangerous liaisons depicted so vividly in Romantic theatre. However, two things move this play out of the Romantic cosmos. The first is that the love affair, Romantic in many ways, does not occupy the play's emotional center. Asquerino clearly reserves this space for his political argument, and the love affair becomes a tangential, if interesting and moving, subplot. Prohibited and conflictive love, and the hero's transformation into an anguished rebel, all serve in Asquerino to underscore the characters' various roles in determining the political future of Spain. The second is something that the true Romantics never allowed themselves to present: a happy ending. Here, the warring political parties join together to create a new order, and the lovers are permitted to marry. Asquerino's focus on the political situation enables him to create a look at that situation not from without (as in *La conjuración de Venecia* or *El trovador*), but rather from within, that is, the audience is privy right from the start to the thoughts and actions of the competing factions in the halls of power. We witness the treason of the Princesa de los Ursinos,[87] the conflicts between the various ministers and foreign ambassadors, and the maneuvering of all parties to control the King, whose presence is strongly felt although he never makes an appearance on stage. The Princesa confesses at the beginning:

> ¡Qué necios! A mi ambición
> cortar las alas pretenden.
> . . .
> Hoy domino a mi placer
> la monarquía española,
> y el mundo rigiendo sola
> quisiera a mis plantas ver.
> No más que amor al poder
> siente el alma en su desvelo;
> pero con tan loco anhelo,
> que me agita sin cesar
> no poder yo dominar
> cuanto abarca tierra y cielo.   (I, 7)

(What fools they are! They try to clip the wings of my ambition ... Today I dominate the Spanish monarchy as I wish, and I want to see the world bowing at my feet. My anxious soul feels love only for power, but with such crazed desire that I am constantly disturbed because I cannot rule all of heaven and earth.)

Asquerino cynically depicts Spanish politicians as corrupt and easily sold to the highest bidder.

> En el siglo que vivimos
> no hay fenómeno que asombre
> tanto como una persona

---

[87] When this interesting figure reappeared in Rodríguez Rubí's play *Alberoni* (1846) she was once again compared with contemporary royal figures (María Cristina) and the play provoked a similarly heated polemic. Unlike *Españoles sobre todo*, however, *Alberoni* was banned after just a few performances.

que el poder no la soborne;
como que se ha hecho de moda
el comercio de opiniones,
unos las venden por más,
otros por menos, conforme
lo profundas y arraigadas
que tienen sus convicciones,
y si algunos no las venden
es ... porque no hay quien las compre.   (II, 1)

(In today's world the greatest surprise is a person who cannot be bribed by power; since opinion-making has become so fashionable, some people sell information for a lot of money, some for much less, depending on how deeply felt their convictions are. And if some do not sell it at all it's only because they don't have anyone who will buy it.)

At first, the defense of an independent Spain comes from Montellano, whom Asquerino first paints as the possible hero of the play:

Me afano por conservar
de España la independencia
para que extraña influencia
no la llegue a dominar.
Y no imagino otro modo ...
quien piense otra cosa yerra;
que somos en esta tierra
españoles sobre todo.   (I, 10)

(I really want to preserve Spain's independence, so a foreign influence does not come to dominate her. And I can't imagine another way of doing it ... Anyone who thinks differently is making a mistake, because we are on this land Spaniards over all.)

Soon we learn, however, that he too is subject to the same corruptions as the Princesa. The play's real hero turns out to be Diego Mendoza, a dignified peasant in the manner of Calderón's Pedro Crespo, who has come to Madrid to argue the case for Aragón's *fueros*. He warns that "Las rebeliones provoca / del poder la tiranía. / Que los pueblos bien regidos / no se sublevan jamás; / esto lo hacen nada más / los que se ven oprimidos" ("The tyranny of power provokes rebellions. A well-governed populace never rises up. Only those who consider themselves to be oppressed do so") (II, 8) and supports an independent nation. Yet the most interesting character is the Princesa de los Ursinos, who is depicted as ambitious, smart, vindictive, quick to act and, in fact, better than a man: as the French ambassador tells her, "Os admiro / más cada día, princesa: / hombres de Estado aun no he visto / que a vos puedan igualarse" ("I admire you more every day, Princesa. I have never seen a statesman who could match you") (IV, 6).

The anti-foreign message of *Españoles sobre todo* becomes tendentious and xenophobic at times, accurately reflecting the author's stated opinions on foreign intervention. Asquerino liberally sprinkles throughout the play statements against foreign meddling in Spanish affairs. Some examples:

> Deciden en este instante
> de los destinos de España
> dos extranjeros.   (III, 2)

(Two foreigners are deciding the fate of Spain at this moment.)

> ¡Los extranjeros ... ! ¡Jamás!
> Porque el libre aragonés
> no es austriaco ni francés;
> sino español, nada más.   (III, 3)

(Foreigners! Never! Because the free Aragonese man is neither Austrian nor French, but Spanish, nothing more.)

> ¡Ah! ¡Franceses!
> A la España pretendeis
> dominar a vuestro antojo.   (IV, 1)

(Ah, Frenchmen! You attempt to rule Spain at your whim.)

In the play's most overtly political speech, Diego himself puts forth the view that:

> Pues yo entiendo que la España
> no necesita andadores,
> y puede pasar, señores,
> sin la Francia y la Bretaña.
> ¡Qué debemos a las dos?
> Con máscara de aliados
> sus odios inveterados
> quieren vengar, ¡vive Dios!
> Ambas sumisión exigen,
> y por campo de batalla
> cuando su rencor estalla
> nuestro fértil suelo eligen.
> Nuestros campos y sol bellos
> envidian, y en su furor
> quieren que anuble el vapor
> de la sangre sus destellos.
> Hoy mismo de horrible guerra
> están el foco atizando,
> Francia a Felipe apoyando,
> y al austriaco la Inglaterra.
> ¿Y qué hace la gran Bretaña?
> quitarnos a Gibraltar.
> ¿Y la Francia? bombadear
> nuestras ciudades de España.   (III, 3)

(I understand that Spain does not need inferior ministers to rule it, and it can get along nicely, gentlemen, without France and Britain. What do we owe them? They merely want to avenge their old hatreds masquerading as allies of ours, by God! They both want our submission, and when their grudges explode they choose our soil as their battleground. They envy our beautiful fields and sun, and in their fury want that brilliance to be clouded over by the steam of blood. Just today they are stirring up the fire of horrible war, France supporting Philip and England supporting the Austrian. And what does Great Britain do? It takes Gibraltar away from us. And France? Bomb our Spanish cities.)

Mendoza glosses the Constitution of 1812 in his defenses of the sovereignty of the people, the equality of all men, the importance of national independence, and the need to eliminate unnecessary hierarchies. However, Asquerino does not spill all his venom on foreigners. He also criticizes his own countrymen who have "prostituted" themselves to foreign interests:

> ¿Qué español a no ser él
> se hubiera prostituido
> hasta el punto de vender
> a la Francia sus servicios
> en daño y mengua de España?   (IV, 6)

(What Spaniard except him would have prostituted himself to the point of selling his services to France, to Spain's detriment and disgrace?)

These examples lead us inexorably to the play's final message, stated without guile or subtlety:

> A extraños una nación
> su independencia no debe,
> sino a su valor y unión.
> Y es el mal de los mayores
> llamar a los extranjeros
> a ser sus libertadores,
> pues si vencen, altaneros
> se convierten en señores.
>
> . . .
>
> Y si otra vez gente extraña
> intenta de cualquier modo
> dominar la pobre España,
> seamos sin mutua saña
> ESPANOLES SOBRE TODO.   (IV, 18)

(A nation does not owe its independence to foreigners, but rather to its own courage and unity. It is a big mistake to call in foreigners to be one's liberators because if they are successful, they immediately become arrogant rulers. And if any foreign people try in any way to take over poor Spain, let us be without mutual anger SPANIARDS ABOVE ALL.)

This reductive message nonetheless lit a firestorm of controversy for the simple reason that Asquerino, in a skillfully crafted drama populated by interesting – if overtly Manichean – characters and good scenic tension, had hit upon a raw nerve in the Spanish politic.[88] With growing nationalistic sentiment sweeping Europe, the Spaniards felt demoralized by their own current political stagnation and looked toward the past to find either reasons for or solutions to their predicament.

Huelga decir que estos casos recuerdan al público la situación de inestabilidad política por la que atravesaba España desde principios de siglo, invadida por los franceses, desgarrada por la guerra carlista, y convertida en fértil campo para los manejos de Inglaterra y Francia en asuntos matrimoniales y de alianzas.[89]

(It must be said that these cases remind the public of the unstable political situation in which Spain has been living since the beginning of the century, invaded by the French, torn apart by the Carlist War, and converted into a fertile ground for the manipulations of England and France in matters dealing with marriages and alliances.)

Asquerino offered no sensible solution; rather, he inflamed passions which frequently spilled off the stages and into the streets, but he always viewed his goal – Spain's destiny to be decided by Spaniards – to be patriotic, noble, and urgent.

Public response to *Españoles sobre todo* was immediate. Following its debut, *El Eco del Comercio* claimed that Madrid's "pueblo ilustrado y liberal" ("enlightened and liberal populace") (29 May 1844) received the play with generous acclaim, and the *Revista de Teatros* (30 May 1844) reported that more than thirty curtain calls were demanded of the author: "Sigue representándose con extraordinario aplauso en el teatro de la Cruz el drama del señor Asquerino titulado *Españoles sobre todo*; produce entradas llenas y todas las noches llueven sobre su joven autor flores y coronas: no recordamos producción alguna que se haya representado al compás de más de treinta aplausos nutridos ... " (*"Españoles sobre todo* continues to be performed to extraordinary applause in the Cruz Theatre; it is producing sell-out crowds, and every evening flowers and laurel wreaths rain down on its young author. We cannot remember any production that has received more than thirty enthusiastic ovations in a row ... ") Similar notices recorded the "estrepitosos aplausos" ("clamorous applause") of other performances (*Revista de Teatros*, 3 June 1844) and the newspaper kept a running tally of the number of times it appeared. By 16 June it had reached seventeen performances. Interestingly, however, the *Revista de Teatros* expressed serious reservations about the play's

[88] See David T. Gies, "Rebeldía y drama en 1844: *Españoles sobre todo*, de Eusebio Asquerino," *Homenaje a Ermanno Caldera* (Rome: Bulzoni, in press).

[89] García Castañeda, "Los hermanos Asquerino," p. 28.

ideological content, because it feared (correctly, as it turned out) that the play's political content would merely "pervertir el gusto, *fomentar el espíritu de división* ... " ("pervert taste, *foment the spirit of division* ... ") (16 June 1844; emphasis added) in the country. For this reviewer, the play was too much a reflection of a "política militante" ("militant politics"), a "*rendez-vous politique* para el teatro de la Cruz" ("a political meeting at the Cruz Theatre"), more in keeping with a political rally than a theatrical production. However, the play's reception was such that the reviewer was reduced to complaining of the anachronisms he detected in it.

Ha prestado un servicio eminente a su partido, no a la literatura dramática, cuya absoluta decadencia sería inevitable si muchos imitaran su ejemplo. Grandes disposiciones tiene el Sr. Asquerino para el teatro: por su desgracia es su deidad la política, aspira de continuo su atmósfera y forman el campo de sus ilusiones las utopías más pintorescas y encantadoras: a nosotros nos duele a fuer de amigos suyos que malgaste su talento de poeta en la política de ciertos hombres que como decía muy bien el malogrado autor del *Diablo mundo*, sólo puede darnos "Miseria y hambre y mezquindad y prosa."

([The author] has done a service to his party, not to dramatic literature, the absolute decadence of which will be inevitable if many authors follow his example. Mr. Asquerino is a talented dramatist, but unfortunately his God is the God of politics, he constantly tries to include it, and his illusions are formed by the most picturesque and enchanting utopias. As friends of his we are saddened to see him waste his poetic talent on the politics of certain men who can only bring us, as the tragic author of the *Diablo mundo* said so well, "Misery and hunger and meanness and prose.")

Another newspaper even accused Asquerino of dragging himself "por el cieno de las pasiones políticas" ("through the slime of political passions") (reported in *Revista de Teatros*, 2 September 1844).

Españoles sobre todo was immediately exported to the provinces, where it was received with similar acclamation and fear. In Valencia, it created a "furor" and ran for many performances (*Revista de Teatros*, 3 July 1844); in Sevilla, "El público aplaudió fuertemente las alusiones de que está sembrado el drama" ("The public loudly applauded the political allusions that are planted in the play") (*Revista de Teatros*, 27 July 1844). It played in Palma de Mallorca, Burgos, and other regional theatres. By mid-August, just a few months after its debut in Madrid, "está haciendo furor *en la mayor parte de los teatros de España*" ("it is causing a furor *in the majority of the theatres in Spain*") (*Revista de Teatros,* 17 August 1844, emphasis added). It was immediately published in the Galería Dramática collection and distributed widely. Eventually, though, the debate over the play and its reception became more interesting than the play itself. In Seville, the *Floresta andaluza* ingenuously denied any contemporary political overtones or allusions whatsoever to the play, which provoked a harsh response by the *Revista de Teatros* in Madrid. When the theatre in Málaga attempted to put it on in October, the civil governor stopped it:

Málaga: en esta ciudad nos vemos privados del gusto de solazarnos un rato con la famosa composición del señor Asquerino *Españoles sobre todo*. El señor jefe político ha prohibido la ejecución de esta pieza, y de cuantas se presenten que puedan en lo más mínimo criticar la situación actual: de modo que los cómicos se encuentran algunas veces desesperados para buscar piezas que no traten ni tengan una palabra alusiva a la libertad e independencia nacional. (*Revista de Teatros*, 27 October 1844)

(Málaga: In this city we have been deprived of the pleasure of spending some time with Mr. Asquerino's famous composition, *Españoles sobre todo*. The political chief has prohibited the performance of this piece and of any others which might however lightly criticize the current situation. This means that the actors sometimes are desperate to find plays which do not deal with or contain any allusions to freedom or national independence.)

Similar problems occurred in Valencia, due to the overenthusiastic response of the audience, which the authorities tried to squash by planting guards among the spectators:

Valencia: En una de las pasadas noches, se ha vuelto a poner en escena en el teatro de esta capital, el drama del Sr. Asquerino *Españoles sobre todo*. En algunas escenas llegó a tal punto el entusiasmo del pueblo que el alcalde Campo que presidía tomó serias disposiciones. Los alguaciles y los del ramo, se esparcieron entre las lunetas y corredores a fin de ahogar hasta la más pequeña muestra de una opinión tan general y pronunciada, en favor de las ideas liberales, de que abundan algunos episodios de aquel drama. Era de esperar que tan ridícula disposición produjera el efecto contrario que la autoridad se proponía y así fue que los espectadores no perdieron por ello ocasión de prodigar numerosos aplausos. (*Revista de Teatros*, 29 October 1844)

(Valencia: A couple of nights ago Mr. Aquerino's drama, *Españoles sobre todo* was put on again in this capital's theatre. The public's enthusiasm rose to such heights during certain scenes that Mayor Campo, who was presiding over the performance, took some serious measures: the constables and their helpers placed themselves in the boxes and the hallways in order to stifle even the slightest demonstration of approval on the part of the audience of the liberal ideas which abound in some of that play's episodes. One would hope that such a ridiculous measure would produce the opposite effect, which is exactly what happened: the audience lost no opportunity to applaud frequently.)

Even amateur acting companies out in the most remote villages tried to stage this bombastic play: in Valls, three hours outside of Tarragona, the local commandant stopped it out of fear of disorder (reported in *Revista de Teatros*, 7 February 1845). In spite of such arbitrary censorship, the play was performed all over the peninsula dozens of times throughout the

1840s. When Juan Lombía made a triumphal visit to Paris with his acting company in 1847, he took with him only Bretón's *El pelo de la dehesa* (1840) and Eusebio Asquerino's *Un verdadero hombre de bien* (A Real Man of Worth, 1845) and *Españoles sobre todo*, although *La Luneta* speculated that this latter play could probably not be performed in the French capital because "tiene ciertas alusiones a la Francia que aquella gente no toleraría" ("it contains certain allusions to France which they would not tolerate") (3 January 1847). It is interesting to compare these statistics with those for Zorrilla's *Don Juan Tenorio*, which had performances in March of 1844 and did not reappear until 25 October (the next season), when it was seen exactly one time; it never reached real popular status until late in the decade. As don Juan's universal message gained wide popular acceptance, Asquerino's limited, if stirring, political message slowly faded from the scene, although it was still remembered as late as 1859 in these terms:

Españoles sobre todo es una alusión viva, protestante, eficaz: la alusión de un ingenio claro y de un alma proba. Este drama no respira tanto la política de sentimiento, como el sentimiento de la política. El autor no tuvo que buscar su escuela. La llevaba en sí, y arrastrado por ella se fue al teatro. (*El Teatro Español*, 28 February 1859)

(*Españoles sobre todo* is a lively, protesting, efficient political statement, the statement of a clear genius and an upright soul. This drama does not so much breathe the politics of emotion as the emotion of politics. The author did not need to search out his school; he carried it within him, and he followed it into the theatre.)

It is not surprising that by 1844 (and even more so by 1845 with the appearance of Bretón's *Don Frutos en Belchite* and Vega's *El hombre de mundo*) Romanticism should have run its brief, if intense course. The death knell had been sounded as early as 1841, in fact, in the pages of the *Revista de Teatros*: "El exagerado drama romántico ha sido una llamarada que sólo ha brillado por un momento" ("Exaggerated Romantic drama has been a brief flame that lasted only for a moment"). Zorrilla and Asquerino proved that to be all too true.

In the margins of Romanticism

It would be a mistake to leave the impression that Romantic plays constituted the majority of the dramas seen and commented on during the 1830s and 1840s, although it is the Romantic plays which are most remembered today. In fact, they were a minority interest, both in terms of frequency of presentation in the repertories and of comment in social circles and in the newspapers. Still, they were shocking enough that parodies of them began to appear almost immediately. Parody, always the first step toward the dismantling of a paradigm, was recognized by many of the period's top writers as a mechanism through which they could pull in the reins of the wilder aspects of the new movement, which was, it must be confessed, attractive to many of them.

Romantic satire

The clearest example of the new mood – preceded, as we shall see, by other works in a similar vein – is Mesonero Romanos's prose satire of the exaggerations of the movement, "El romanticismo y los románticos" ("Romanticism and Romantic Authors"). We need not concern ourselves with all of the details of this brilliant and hilarious satire; rather, we should look briefly at its focus on the theatre of the day. Mesonero went right to the core of the problem, as he saw it, and regaled his readers with a synopsis of the play written by his Romantic "nephew." This putative play – "composición sublime, práctica explicación del sistema románti-co"[90] ("a sublime composition, a practical explanation of the Romantic system") as Mesonero describes it – brings together all of the tropes we have seen and fuses them into a twisted and grotesque compilation of what the anti-Romantics feared most in the movement, its loss (rejection) of order and rules. Subtitled, rather hysterically, but with acute awareness of many of the absurd subtitles attached to plays since the mid-1820s, "drama romántico natural, emblemático-sublime, anónimo, sinónimo, tétrico y espasmódico" ("a natural Romantic drama, emblematic and sublime, anonymous, synonymous, gloomy and convulsive") it was written – impossibly – in "diferentes prosas" ("in different proses"). Mesonero takes a swipe at the public's recently found obsession for calling for the author to present himself at the play's conclusion (begun, it is recorded, after a performance of García Gutiérrez's *El trovador*, and continued with such frequency that a mere year later it had become standard behavior for audiences to demand an appearance, whether the play was any good or not) by including a note on the title page which reads, "Cuando el público pida el nombre del autor ... " ("When the audience asks for the author's name ... "). The Romantic penchant for sweeping scenery and broad action becomes extended in *¡¡Ella!! ... y ¡¡El!!* (SHE!!! ... and HE!!!, the play's title) to an action which takes place over a one-hundred year period and "en toda Europa" ("everywhere in Europe"), and includes a recognizable cast of characters, which

---

[90] Mesonero Romanos, *Obras completas*. All quotes here from 200: 65.

Mesonero skews into a generic absurdity. The characters include a woman ("all women, all woman"), a lover, a Venetian duke (an obvious reference to Martínez de la Rosa), a tyrant, a page (a reference to Larra), a spy, a hangman, the Quadruple Alliance (!), a chorus of Carmelite nuns, and a chorus of "padres agonizantes" ("monks who assist the dying" – we are reminded of the ending of *Don Alvaro*), "un hombre del pueblo, un pueblo de hombres" ("a man of the town, a town of men"), one ghost who speaks and another who "grabs," and several *El trovador*-like witches and gypsies. Anyone familiar with the shared language of Romantic theatre – meaning everyone who went to the theatre in Madrid in the 1830s – saw at once the acuteness with which Mesonero pilloried the movement's obvious excesses.

Before Mesonero issued his *coup de grâce*, however, other authors had begun to satirize some of the more exaggerated characteristics of Romanticism. As early as 1833 Manuel Eduardo de Gorostiza "spoofed Romantic posturing"[91] in *Contigo pan y cebolla*, a play which has remained to this day popular throughout Spanish America (Gorostiza was Mexican-born, but his family returned to Spain when he was five years old). It premièred on 6 July at the Príncipe Theatre and was immediately hailed as a "buena comedia española" ("good Spanish comedy") by Bretón de los Herreros,[92] who pointed specifically to the role performed skillfully by Concepción Rodríguez (Latorre and Guzmán were also singled out for praise.) The play pokes fun at those idealistic young Romantics – like Mesonero's "nephew" would be later – who were convinced that love conquers all (as Grimaldi was still reminding audiences in *La pata de cabra*) and that the true path to a peaceful, loving existence was cut through a simple garden where a humble hut, a loaf of bread, and a lowly onion constituted the lovers' only basic needs. Unfortunately, Matilde's "caracter demasiado romántico"[93] ("overly Romantic character") blinds her to the realities of life and moves her to reject the hand of her sensible, ambitious, and rich suitor don Eduardo de Contreras. She possesses, as had numerous melodramatic, operatic and, soon, Romantic, heroes and heroines (in the opinion of their critics), a "cerebro destornillado" ("loose screw in her head" – Bretón's words), twisted by the over-enthusiastic

[91] See John C. Dowling, "Gorostiza's *Contigo pan y cebolla*: From Romantic Farce to Nostalgic Musical Comedy," *Theatre Survey* 28 (1987): 49. Dowling discusses the novels which turned Matilde's head. See also J. W. Banner, "The Dramatic Works of Manuel Eduardo de Gorostiza," dissertation (University of North Carolina, 1948) and Frank Dauster, "The Ritual Feast: A Study in Dramatic Forms," *Latin American Theatre Review* 9 (1975): 5–9.

[92] Bretón, "Primera representación de *Contigo pan y cebolla*, comedia original de D. Manuel Eduardo de Gorostiza," *Correo Literario y Mercantil* (8 July 1833).

[93] Bretón, "Análisis de la comedia en cuatro actos y en prosa de D. Manuel Eduardo de Gorostiza, titulada *Contigo pan y cebolla*," *Correo Literario y Mercantil* (10 July 1833).

reading of melodramatic novels and filled with wild ideas about life and love. Like don Quijote, Matilde's life is a product of literature, that is, her orientation and her behavior are patterned on literary tropes (a premise that Larra rejected, although he did confess that the subject matter was of "la mayor importancia"[94] ["the greatest importance"]). The work contains strong echoes of Sheridan's *The Rivals*, a play which Gorostiza probably knew from his years in exile in London (1824–1833).[95]

Bretón's fulsome praise, which fell just short of hyperbole, did not blind him to some of the play's weaker spots, although he missed the point somewhat when he criticized Matilde as too exaggerated, failing to see the farcical nature of her creation: "Lástima es que el carácter de Matilde sea tan exagerado, que puede llamársele falso ... es llevar a una altura inverosímil, increíble el entusiasmo del amatorio romanticismo" ("It is a shame that the character of Matilde is so exaggerated, in fact, it can even be called false...it is to take to new heights the unbelievable, incredible enthusiasm of amorous Romanticism"). This was precisely what Gorostiza was trying to achieve.[96] Larra, curiously, published two reviews, one which focused on the Molière/Moratín style of comedy as well as what he saw to be the main defect of the play – that Matilde, unlike don Quijote, was not really crazy, and therefore not as believable in the exaggerated postures of "estas niñas románticas"[97] ("these Romantic girls") – and the other, aimed at the female readers of *El Correo de las Damas*, questioning Gorostiza's premise that true love is a defeatist passion.[98] These criticisms stung the author, and a short time later there appeared a pamphlet written anonymously (by Pedro Angel de Gorostiza y Cepeda?) railing against Bretón's and Larra's "unfairness" and accusing them both of prejudice and ill will. The nonsense of the *Defensa de la comedia 'Contigo pan y cebolla', y contra las críticas que han hecho de ella los periódicos de Madrid* (Defense of the Play *Contigo pan y cebolla* and Against the Criticism that Madrid Newspapers Have Made of It) was answered both by Bretón in the *Correo Literario y Mercantil* and by Larra in *La Revista Española* on the same day, 13 August 1833. Larra, typically, was acerbic, mordant, and to-the-point: "En no diciéndoles el artículo que su obra es maravillosa, en hallándole defectos, hay en él mala fe, hay odio, hay malevolencia. Los elogios, sí, se aceptan; ésos nunca son

[94] Larra, "Primera representación de la comedia nueva de don Manuel Gorostiza titulada *Contigo pan y cebolla*," *La Revista Española* (9 July 1833).
[95] Richard B. O'Connell, "Gorostiza's *Contigo pan y cebolla* and Sheridan's *The Rivals*," *Hispania* 43 (1960): 384–387.
[96] Dowling sees this play also as more farce than traditional comedy. "Gorostiza's *Contigo*," p. 53.
[97] Larra, "Primera representación."
[98] Larra, "Teatros – Revista semanal," *El Correo de las Damas* (10 July 1833).

injustos" ("Since the article didn't tell them that the work was marvellous, since it found defects in it, there must be in it some sort of bad faith, hatred, malevolence. Praise, of course, is accepted because praise is never unfair").

Bretón, himself fast becoming the most consistently productive and interesting playwright of his day, tried his hand at Romantic satire in several plays, including possibly *Elena* (his longest work, 1834), *El plan de un drama* (The Outline of a Play, written with Ventura de la Vega, 1835), *Muérete ¡y verás!* (1837), and the one-act *La ponchada* (The Punch Seller, 1840). He had already mocked the woozy Romantic lover in his famous *Marcela, o ¿a cuál de los tres?* (1831), in the person of the aptly named don Amadeo Tristán del Valle. *Elena*, which premièred on 23 October 1834, just weeks after Larra's *Macías*, has been interpreted both as a parody of the Romantic movement and as Bretón's failed attempt to imitate the movement's "trivial manierismo"[99] ("trivial mannerisms"). He himself confessed in 1850 that "El moderno romanticismo estaba en su mayor auge, y era difícil que temprano o tarde dejase de llevar también alguna ofrenda a las aras del ídolo nuevo"[100] ("Modern Romanticism was on the rise and it was hard to resist taking an offering to the altar of this new idol"), but it is difficult to believe that as a comic writer he was not attracted to some of the more absurd devices creeping onto Madrid's stages. Bretón's friend and patron, Grimaldi, had returned to the stage as director of productions and it was he who staged the plays by Martínez de la Rosa, Larra, and Bretón. Grimaldi had read *Elena* a year earlier, but had been unable to bring it to the stage due to problems with the censors.[101]

Bretón sets up a love conflict similar at first to Moratín's *El sí de las niñas* – the elderly don Gerardo loves Elena (his niece in this case), but she loves the young soldier don Gabriel – but quickly moves the conflict from a mere difference of age to a melodramatic power struggle replete with hidden identities, fainting spells, passionate emotions, vengeance, bandits, and the final suicide of the uncle ("Al abrazarse Elena y el marqués suena un pistoletazo" ["When Elena and the marquis embrace a pistol shot is heard"] [V, 16]). Bretón's bluff exaggerations underscore the impossibility of the Gerardo-Elena match, and as the drama unfolds it becomes increasingly clear to the audience that Bretón has stacked the deck according to the theatrical conventions of the day but that he is using those conventions to work against expectations. The sudden

[99] Caldera and Calderone, "El teatro en el siglo XIX," p. 456.
[100] Reprinted in Bretón de los Herreros, *Obras*, I, p. 189.
[101] See José Escobar, "Un episodio biográfico de Larra, crítico teatral, en la temporada de 1834," *Nueva Revista de Filología Hispánica* 35 (1976): 53.

revelations (it is revealed in Act II that Victorina's fiancé, the "Marqués," is none other than Gabriel, who has thought himself to be rejected by Elena; upon discovering this fact she, like so many Romantic heroines, faints), changes in mood, and "unrealistic" situations which the critics have so harshly criticized as flaws in the play could very well be Bretón's clear-eyed view of the absurdities of Romantic drama, a view borne out by a look at his other attempts to satirize the movement. In 1834, though, the audience would have none of his wry look at dramatic literature, and the play disappeared from the stage after a scant three performances.

Somewhat more successful – partly because Romanticism's tropes were more deeply embedded in the mind of the public – were Bretón's later attempts at infusing laughter into the normally lugubrious Romantic paradigm. *El plan de un drama* played at the Cruz Theatre on 22 October 1835, to polite reception, but it was *Muérete ¡y verás!* (Bretón's declared favorite) which reconfirmed his place among the best dramatists of the day. It was also a significant personal success for him following its debut at the Príncipe on 27 April 1837, winning praise from the critics and a couple of dozen performances before the decade came to a close (it was revived nearly every decade during the author's long life, usually to enthusiastic response[102]). For the first time in his career Bretón was called to the stage by the audience following its initial performance. It was hardly a blockbuster hit, but this number of performances earned it a place among the documentable triumphs of the day.

Notwithstanding the *Eco del Comercio*'s labeling of the play as "romántica",[103] it is, as Caldera has detected, more than what Peers thought to be merely "semirromántica"; it is an outright parody which came close on the heels of Hartzenbusch's *Los amantes de Teruel*. Caldera's perceptive observation about the nature of parody in 1837 bears repeating:

Sin embargo, a diferencia de las demás piezas, ahora la parodia se realizaba en un registro diferente, en el que, si bien no faltaban rasgos cómicos, la comicidad no era lo esencial. Era más bien una clase de trascodificación a un nivel diferente de dramaticidad: Bretón acogía, a la par de Hartzenbusch, la antigua leyenda, quizá teniendo en cuenta alguna de las diversas realizaciones literarias, pero trasladándola a su época e interpretándola a través de personajes sacados del mundo de la burguesía.[104]

---

[102] See Simón Díaz, *Veinticuatro diarios. Madrid, 1830–1900* I (1968).

[103] Cited by Narciso Alonso Cortés in his edition of Bretón's *Teatro* (Madrid: Espasa Calpe, 1928), xxvii.

[104] Caldera and Calderone, "El teatro en el siglo XIX," pp. 479–480. Rupert Allen sees the play as fully Romantic – "The Romantic Element in Bretón's *Muérete ¡y verás!*," *Hispanic Review* 34 (1966): 218–227–while Silvia Novo Blankenship Chaskin recognizes it, particularly in Act III ("El entierro"), as "a clever parody of a Romantic drama": "Social Satire in the Works of Manuel Bretón de los Herreros," doctoral dissertation,

(Now, however, unlike other plays, parody was carried out in a different register, one in which, if not wholly without comic properties, comicality was not the essential ingredient. It was more akin to a kind of transcodification at a level different from that of "drama-ness": Bretón took, as did Hartzenbusch, the ancient legend, perhaps bearing in mind some of the various literary expressions of it, but moving it to his day and age, and interpreting it through personages taken from the middle class.)

In essence, Bretón weaves together both a contemporary plot line (trouble with the Carlist Wars) with a jokey view of the two major Romantic themes (love and death). The play "teaches" us what we can learn about ourselves, our friends and our lovers *after* death. At one moment (in Act IV, aptly titled "La resurrección" ["The Resurrection"]), Pablo, whom everyone thought to be killed in the wars (similar to Diego de Marsilla's supposed fate), makes a surprise appearance which stops the planned marriage of his ex-fiancée Jacinta to Matías, Pablo's friend. He appears like the Romantic ghosts – here, covered with a white sheet – and the effect on the audience is far from that of fright or horror; it is designed to provoke laughter. Froilán, upset because he will now not inherit any of Pablo's goods, witnesses what would be impossible in a "normal" Romantic play, a happy ending. Pablo allows Jacinta and Matías to proceed with the wedding, and announces that he will marry Isabel, Jacinta's sister, tomorrow. Presumably, they all live happily ever after.

Bretón uses masterfully the language of Romanticism to turn the movement on its head and pave the way, as Caldera has detected, for the high comedy of the 1840s and 1850s.[105] The use of middle class characters concerned with their economic wellbeing (Pablo discusses a loan he receives at 25 percent interest every four months [I, 6], which he honorably settles later on), their freedom to move about in society (Froilán, Jacinta's brother, initially opposes the proposed marriage of his sister to Pablo, but decides not to intervene because "las voluntades son libres; / las chicas tienen ya edad / para saber lo que se hacen. / Mi individuo y nada más" ["choices are free; the girls are of an age to know what they are doing. Myself and nothing more."] [I, 4]), and their dependence on information received from the newspapers (which they purchase on stage) are steps leading away from Romantic drama which Bretón will develop with even more skill in the next decade.

University of Virginia, 1968. Gerard Flynn resists calling it a full-blown parody: *Manuel Bretón de los Herreros*, pp. 81–89. For a look at his shorter plays, see Miguel Ángel Muro, *El teatro breve de Bretón de los Herreros* (Logroño: Instituto de Estudios Riojanos, 1991).

[105] Caldera and Calderone, "El teatro en el siglo XIX," p. 482.

Styles combined: Bretón, Rubí, and Vega

Bretón was gradually developing his own brand of comedy. From the beginning of his career, when Grimaldi orchestrated the staging of *A la vejez viruelas* (written in 1817, staged in 1824, published in 1825), through the final years of Fernando VII's repressive regime, when the very successful *Marcela, o ¿a cuál de los tres?* (1831) established him as the leading comic writer of his generation, and through the steady stream of alternatives to the Romantic ethos he produced in the 1830s, Bretón remained faithful to two things. On the one hand he always revered and, however obliquely at times, imitated the comedies of Moratín;[106] on the other, he consistently experimented with voice, point of view, and language in order to meet his own desire to entertain the audience. This is not to suggest that Bretón's comedies were in fact crass imitations of Moratín. On the contrary, he was already – as early as 1835–recognized as having developed his own brand of post-Moratinian comedy. *El Artista*, for example, wrote of "el género de Bretón" ("Bretón's genre") (II, p. 3) in order to differentiate his works from other types of comedy.

Bretón lived at the center of Madrid's theatrical activity throughout the 1830s and was unquestionably the most prolific playwright of his times (he wrote thirteen plays, both original and translations, in the 1832–1833 season alone). His plays were well attended, at times controversial (his harsh *Me voy de Madrid* [1835] irritated Larra so much that the two had a falling out which lasted for over a year), and always finely tuned to the concerns of the day. He produced, along with those works already cited, translations from the French (Racine, Scribe, La Touche, Ducange, and the immensely popular *Jocó o el orangután*, 1831), *refundiciones* (Lope, Calderón), and numerous original plays such as *Achaques a los vicios* (Pretexts for Vices, 1830), *La falsa ilustración* (False Enlightenment, 1831), *Un tercero en discordia* (A Go-Between for Discord, 1834), *Un novio para la niña* (A Boyfriend for the Girl, 1834), *Mérope* (tragedy, 1835), *Todo es farsa en este mundo* (The Whole World's a Farce, 1835), *La redacción de un periódico* (A Newspaper's Editorial Staff, 1836), *Flaquezas ministeriales* (Ministerial Weaknesses, 1838), *El ¡qué dirán!* (What People Will Say!, 1838), and so on and on. In addition, he had spent two years in the early part of the decade (1831–1833) as the main reviewer for *El Correo Literario y Mercantil*, from whose pages he educated his readers not only on the details of current drama but also on stage technique, acting styles, foreign theatre, translations, opera, and

---

106 See Chapter 1 ("Il magistero moratiniano") of Garelli, *Bretón de los Herreros*. Also, Ermanno Caldera, "L'età della ragione," *Quaderni di Filologia Romanza* 4 (1984): 7–22.

stage management.[107] As Alborg has noted, Bretón "dio realidad a la comedia española, prácticamente inexistente desde largo tiempo atrás, la hizo aplaudir y estimar, y salvó con plena dignidad la existencia del género"[108] ("brought the Spanish comedy, something for all intents and purposes non-existent for a very long time, into being. He made people applaud it and appreciate it, and he saved the very existence of the genre with full-fledged dignity"). His style was less bombastic than that of his Romantic cohorts, more attuned to the modified passions of the middle class, and more reflective of the moral concerns of that group. With satire, wit, subtly complicated situations, and musical language Bretón turned the Spanish stage into a mirror of contemporary society and enabled his audiences to see themselves, even with their numerous follies, reflected with humor and gentle kindness. Being a narcissistic crowd, it looked into that mirror night after night and for the most part, liked what it saw. Already by the end of the 1840s Bretón would be accused of repeating himself and falling into clichéd patterns of character and plot, but for now he was on top of the heap.[109]

El pelo de la dehesa (1840) turned out to be one of the author's most enduring and beloved productions. It premièred at the Príncipe theatre on 13 February with Juan Lombía and Teodora Lamadrid in the lead roles, and was immediately acclaimed as a hit. It appeared in the repertory every year (except 1847) for the next decade and even today it is remembered as "one of the best and liveliest of nineteenth-century Spanish plays."[110] Its initial success inspired Bretón to write a sequel, *Don Frutos en Belchite* (1845) which, while very diverting, failed to reach the same heights of public acceptance. *El pelo* follows a simple Moratinian pattern (five acts, verse, maintenance of the three unities) to tell a time-honored country

---

[107] Many of his articles have been collected in *Manuel Bretón de los Herreros: Obra dispersa. El Correo Literario y Mercantil* I, eds. J. M. Díez Taboada and J. M. Rozas (Logroño: Instituto de Estudios Riojanos, 1965). The promised second volume never appeared.

[108] Alborg, *Historia*, IV, p. 636.

[109] He tried to defend his choice of characters and plots in the "Prefacio del autor a la edición de 1850," reprinted in *Obras* I, pp. lviii–lxi. "Esto es verdad; pero ¿a qué escritor medianamente fecundo no le sucede algo o mucho de esto? ... En suma, no se me podrá reconvenir, puedo asegurarlo, de haberme calcado y reverdecido a mí propio tantas veces relativamente como Calderón con sus escondidos y sus tapadas, como Molière con sus médicos y sus cornudos, o como Moratín con sus viejos y sus niñas; y razón será que a mí se me perdonen culpas de que no libertó la humana flaqueza a un Calderón, a un Molière y a un Moratín" (lix – lx).

[110] Gareth A. Davies, "The Country Cousin at Court. A Study of Antonio de Mendoza's *Cada loco con su tema* and Manuel Bretón de los Herreros' *El pelo de la dehesa*," *Leeds Iberian Papers: Hispanic Drama* (Leeds: Trinity and All Saints College, 1991): 43. Davies suggests that Bretón's inspiration for *El pelo* came from Mendoza's Golden Age play. Ermanno Caldera, on the other hand, studies *El pelo* as Bretón's rewriting of his own *refundición* (*La fuerza del natural*, 1827) of Moreto's *El príncipe y el villano*. "Bretón o la negación del modelo," *Cuadernos de Teatro Clásico* 5 (1990): 141–153.

versus city tale. Don Frutos Calamocha (a homage to Moratín's similarly named servant in *El sí de las niñas?*), a rustic but well-off farmer from Belchite near Zaragoza, is set to arrive in Madrid in order sign a marriage contract with the noble but impoverished Elisa. This mismatch had been arranged between the parents of the two to settle some accrued debts. Even though they consider don Frutos to be an unsophisticated bumbler, they declare, "nosotras le puliremos" ("we'll polish him up") (I, 1). Elisa, however, is really still in love with her ex-fiancé Miguel, a soldier. When Frutos and Elisa first meet (I, 10), his mishandling of the situation is the cause of much mirth – and dismay – among the women (he says foolish things, confuses Elisa with her maid Juana, clumsily breaks a tea set); Bretón fills the scene with rich comic effects and creates the atmosphere of humor which will dominate the play. Elisa, naturally, is horrified by his behavior and refuses to marry such a crude man, but her scheming mother (who reminds us clearly of Moratín's doña Irene for her insistence that her daughter marry someone she does not love solely in order to claim an inheritance) insists. After a pile-up of scenes in which we see don Frutos's discomfort with the false ways of Madrid it becomes clear to us and to Elisa that he is a kind man and finally, as was to be expected, she realizes that innate goodness is more valuable than appearances, but ... too late. The wedding between don Frutos, who flees back to Aragón ("¡A Belchite! ¡A Belchite! / La corte no es para mí" ["To Belchite, to Belchite! The Court is not for me"] are his parting words [V, 7]), and Elisa is called off, but the play still ends happily with Elisa's marriage to her original suitor Miguel.

For Caldera, don Frutos is a Romantic comic hero: "la única diferencia entre el héroe romántico y el trágico consiste en que el primero logra hacer prevalecer lo real sobre lo ideal, mientras que el segundo sigue dando vueltas en su sueño imposible"[111] ("the only difference between the Romantic hero and the tragic one is that the first manages to make the real prevail over the ideal, while the second keeps insisting on his impossible dream"). In contrast, it might be argued that – other than the mere fact that the play was written during the Romantic period – Frutos displays few, if any, of the characteristics of the genuine Romantic hero. For one thing, the intense, burning love which was what sustained all the heroes we have previously seen is conspicuously absent from *El pelo de la dehesa*. Don Frutos does not love Elisa, nor she him, and in fact it is easy for both of them to walk away from their previously arranged marriage. His profession of love (II, 11) is notable for its blandness: his "dócil"

---

[111] See *La commedia romantica in Spagna*, especially pp. 144–151, and "El héroe cómico romántico: Don Frutos," in Caldera and Calderone, "El teatro en el siglo XIX," pp. 532–539.

heart wishes to "agradar" ("please") Elisa; she will marry him with "placer" ("pleasure") and gazes at him "con ternura" ("tenderly"). For another thing, there is a complete absence of any of the dark forces (fate, Satan, cruel "estrellas" ["stars"], etc.) which marked and gave impulse to previous plays. Finally, the happy ending moves the play out of the Romantic cosmos and into a comfortable, bourgeois world where solutions are found when men and women of good will act with reason instead of being forced by cruel fate into tragic postures. Pressing the case, it might be argued that the very term "Romantic comedy" is an oxymoron.

El pelo de la dehesa gives Bretón the opportunity to poke fun once again at many of the people and customs which had long been targets of his witty pen. He lambasts the stuffy nobility (Elisa's mother the Marquesa is subjected to particularly comic satire in her inability to reconcile don Frutos's money with his embarrassing lack of social graces), the false values of the downwardly mobile aristocracy, the gossipy and superficial nature of the daughters of this class, the silly social customs to which they attach such importance (don Frutos expresses his frustration that in Madrid they eat soup with a fork, melon with a spoon, and salad with "scissors"; Remigio, "entre dientes" ["under his breath"] explains to him that the "soup" was in fact ravioli [III, 1]), their corrupt and slothful entertainments (the women are just returning from a night of dancing when don Frutos is up and ready for work at 6:30 a.m.), and the supposed superiority of French ways and products over Spanish national goods. He even comments on the mania for opera, which leads Frutos to comment: "aquí se pasa la vida / en vestirse y desnudarse" ("here one spends one's entire life getting dressed and undressed") (III, 4), a custom which Nicolás Moratín had satirized eighty years earlier in *La petimetra* (1762). The play's hero, of course, is the charming, honest, generous, and kind don Frutos; only too late does Elisa realize that "Qué necia he sido / en no casarme con él" ("What a fool I was not to marry him") (V, 7). Bretón opts for the less materialistic side of Spanish life in *El pelo de la dehesa* in criticizing the Marquesa's decision to place her economic desires (not really needs since her money is spent in the most frivolous ways) over her daughter's happiness.

> ¿Qué papel hace en el mundo
> una marquesa sin coche?
> Tal boda no me hace gracia,
> pero el siglo es tan mercante ...
> También es aristocracia,
> la del dinero contante.   (I, 3)

(What role in the world would a marquesa without a carriage play? Such a marriage doesn't please me at all, but this century is so commercial ... Ready cash is also a type of aristocracy.)

Bretón's answer to the Marquesa's scrambling is obvious: marriage and love are not financial matters. In Caldera's words, the play focuses on "menosprecio de la corte y alabanza de aldea, pues, según una antigua tradición, pero con un fondo económico y ético-político adecuado a los tiempos nuevos"[112] ("condemnation of the capital and praise of the countryside according to an old tradition, but with a new economic foundation and a political ethic formed to meet the needs of these new times"). Similar concerns would be dramatized by other authors for the next thirty years in Spain as the Spanish middle classes nudged and grasped their way toward respectability, turning slowly away from the archaic structures of the *Ancien Régime* and emerging into a world where self worth and accomplishment competed with inherited titles and money as markers of social standing.

These were Bretón's best years. His plays dominated the repertory both in Madrid and in the provinces and he received nearly unanimous acclaim as a master of comedy and verse. His follow-up to *El pelo* coincided with the turning away from the Romantic cosmos already noted in *Don Juan Tenorio* and *Españoles sobre todo*. *Don Frutos en Belchite* (1845) shifted the focus of the action from Madrid to the provinces, and the play's hero, while the same wealthy farmer as before, is now more solid, weightier as a *bourgeois gentilhomme*. He is the dignified representative of an entire class (the respectable bourgeoisie) and Bretón steps forward toward the so-called *alta comedia* in finally joining the two individuals (and classes) in matrimony. He needs to kill off Elvira's husband and extricate Frutos from a previous commitment, but these potential obstacles are dispatched easily. Bretón is not in top form here, and the audience's cool reception of the play underscores this, but nonetheless there are several scenes which figure among his best insofar as craft and language are concerned. The confusions, faintings, discoveries and recognitions which end Act I are handled marvellously, and the creation of the weepy, anti-macho Mamerto is delightful. Love does triumph in the end, but it is a mild, comfortable, reasonable, *conjugal* love which will become increasingly the focus of high comedy.

El definitivo triunfo de la urbanidad que esta comedia confirma representa, quizá, el natural punto de llegada de un teatro que siempre se había movido en el marco de una mentalidad burguesa y en la burguesía había encontrado las formas más genuinas de una perspectiva existencial seria y rica de valores. Sin embargo, claro está que, alcanzada esta meta, la comedia romántica había terminado su tarea y tenía que dejar paso a nuevas formas teatrales.[113]

(The definitive triumph of urbanity that this comedy confirms represents, perhaps, the natural end point of a theatre which always had moved in the realm of the

112 Caldera and Calderone, "El teatro en el siglo XIX," p. 533.   113 *Ibid.* p. 539.

middle-class mentality and which had found in the middle class the most genuine way to express a serious and value-rich existential point of view. Nevertheless, it is clear that once this goal was met, Romantic comedy had completed its task and was forced to give way to new theatrical forms.)

Tomás Rodríguez Rubí (1817–1890), a southern poet and dramatist who started making a real name for himself in the early 1840s with the publication of his *Poesías andaluzas* (Andalusian Poems, 1841), had a different approach to theatre from that of Bretón initially, one more in keeping with the historical/political trend being developed by the Asquerino brothers as an outgrowth of Romantic interest in historical drama. While he wrote in a wide variety of theatrical genres, he contributed to nineteenth-century theatre in two distinct modes – the historical/political drama in the 1840s and, later, the *alta comedia*. Moved out of the mainstream of nineteenth-century theatre by later critics, Rodríguez Rubí was very much in the center of the action during the transitional period from Romanticism to the *alta comedia*. Peers dispenses with him as a "figura secundaria, pero no insignificante" ("a secondary, but not insignificant, figure") and, as have most later critics, failed to allot him any significant attention in his study.[114] In his own time, however, Rodríguez Rubí was considered to be an equal of Bretón, Gil y Zárate, Hartzenbusch, Rivas, García Gutiérrez, Zorrilla (he was an exact contemporary of Zorrilla), and Ventura de la Vega in productivity, interest, and originality. His fecundity, in fact, rivalled Bretón's, for he ultimately created nearly one hundred plays, fifty-nine of them in the seventeen-year period between 1840 and 1857 alone. For some, he was the logical heir to the bourgeois comedy developed by Bretón,[115] and in the eyes of the contemporary public, he eventually surpassed his acknowledged mentor in popular acceptance (Hartzenbusch in 1850 writes of him as "el más aplaudido de todos" ["the most applauded of them all"] among a group of dramatists which included Larra, Gil y Zárate, Bretón, and Vega[116]).

---

[114] Peers, *Historia* II, p. 206. Peers deals with him primarily as a minor Romantic poet; Alborg, following this lead, does not even mention his dramas in *Historia* IV. Only Caldera and Calderone have studied this interesting playwright in recent years; see "El teatro en el siglo XIX," pp. 517–519, 553–554.

[115] "Rubí sería en la segunda mitad del siglo XIX lo que Bretón había sido hasta ese período." Ana María Burgos, "Vida y obra de Tomás Rodríguez Rubí," *Revista de Literatura* 23 (1963): 83. This is the best study we have of Rubí to date, but it is marred by several factual errors. For example, Burgos claims incorrectly that Rubí was called to the stage to receive the audience's acclaim following the première of *Del mal el menos* (1840), "lo cual era raro entonces." (88). She also attributes *Españoles sobre todo* to Rubí (98), and dates *La bruja de Lanjarón* from 1855 (it was performed in Madrid in 1843) (93).

[116] Juan Eugenio Hartzenbusch, "Prólogo a la edición de 1850," *Obras de don Manuel Bretón de los Herreros* I, p. lvi.

For W. F. Smith, Rubí was merely a victim of the "uncertainty and indirection characteristic of that transitional period of the nineteenth century to which he belonged, during which the Spanish theatre was struggling out of the French entanglements of the Romantic era."[117] He produced a steady stream of well-received plays between the 1840s and the 1870s, works which were performed frequently in Madrid and in the provinces, and which were kept in print throughout his long life. He remained influential in literary circles, becoming director of the much-debated Teatro Español at mid-century, a member of the Spanish Royal Academy in 1860, and the Vice-President of the Consejo de Estado during the Restoration.

Following minor but encouraging successes with *Del mal el menos* (The Lesser Evil, 1840), *Toros y cañas* (Bulls and Sherry Glasses, 1840), *El diablo cojuelo* (The Crippled Devil, 1842), *Dos validos y castillos en el aire* (Two Court Favorites and Castles in the Air, 1842), *Isabel la Católica* (Isabella the Catholic, 1843), and *La bruja de Lanjarón* (The Witch from Lanjaron, 1843), Rodríguez Rubí turned his attention to more polemical writing. His first controversial play was *La rueda de la fortuna* (The Wheel of Fortune) published by Yenes in 1843 and dedicated to "don José Zorrilla, tributo de cariño y reconocimiento, de su apasionado amigo" ("José Zorrilla, as a tribute of endearment and recognition, from his enthusiastic friend") Rubí. (Zorrilla reciprocated by flinging a crown of flowers onto the stage following the play's debut in November). Like Asquerino's *Españoles sobre todo*, *La rueda de la fortuna* dealt with the themes of contemporary political posturing and maneuvering at Court, all within an historical setting. This new type of historical *comedia* drew together strands from Romantic drama, Golden Age *comedias de intriga* ("comedies of intrigue"), and the updated historical comedies popularized by Eugène Scribe in France (and, to the dismay of many Spanish critics, in Spain as well[118]). It was the most important play offered during the 1843 season, acted by the stars of the Príncipe, Julián and Florencio Romea, Matilde Díez, Antonio Guzmán, Teodora Lamadrid, and Jerónima Llorente.

---

[117] W. F. Smith, "The Historical Play in the Theatre of Tomás Rodríguez Rubí," *Bulletin of Hispanic Studies* 28 (1950): 221. A short biography of Rubí appeared in the *Revista de Teatros* (1–2 December 1844).

[118] Gassin, p. 307. French drama had secured a place on Spanish stages since the early 1820s, reaching its height in the 1830s and, to a slightly lesser degree, in the 1840s. Details are available in Gassin, Adelaide Parker and E. Allison Peers, "The Vogue of Victor Hugo in Spain," *Modern Language Review* 27 (1932): 36–57; "The Influence of Victor Hugo on Spanish Drama," *Modern Language Review* 28 (1933): 205–216; Thomas A. Gabbert, "Notes on the Popularity of the Dramas of Victor Hugo in Spain During the Years 1835–1845," *Hispanic Review* 4 (1936): 176–178; Piero Menarini, "La statistica

La rueda de la fortuna charts the rise to power of Fernando VI's minister, the Marqués de la Ensenada. Smith criticizes Rubí for "falsifying" history in his presentation of the Marqués, but in reading this play (and others like it) as historical documents he fails to realize that Rubí's goal was not the accurate depiction of a historical figure but rather the teaching of a contemporary lesson through the prism of history, however "falsified."[119] That lesson was simply that the Wheel of Fortune turns inexorably and the lowly can rise, but they can also fall (Clara's father, Diego, the Marqués de Santello, exemplifies the fall of a once-influential courtier; in Part 2 of *La rueda de la fortuna* [1845], Rubí will chart the fall of Ensenada himself). Rubí criticizes the false values of a society driven by power, contacts, snobbery, and the constant jockeying for position at Court through the shifting fortunes of Clara and her beloved Zenón (later, the Marqués de la Ensenada). Diego "sells" Clara to the Conde del Valle, since he sees his own fortunes rising by means of this arrangement.

Rubí places an odd but significant quote from the *Historia general de España* (General History of Spain) between Acts I and II of the printed version of the play. It will remind us of what Asquerino would center upon in *Españoles sobre todo* and clarify Rubí's allegorical intentions in *La rueda*:

así que, las relaciones entre España y Francia se hicieron severas, hasta que el monarca francés, conociendo que debía captarse la benevolencia de su antiguo aliado, mudó el embajador que tenía en Madrid; pero a pesar de esto no adelantó nada. Por otra parte la Inglaterra deseaba al mismo tiempo tener de su parte al gabinete español, y de esta suerte se movía una especie de lucha diplomática entre los agentes franceses e ingleses para ver cuál de las dos naciones conseguiría preponderancia en Madrid. Por entonces subió también al ministerio el marqués de la Ensenada.

(so relations between Spain and France became strained until the French monarch, knowing that he needed to win over the goodwill of his old ally, recalled the ambassador that he had in Madrid, but in spite of this things did not get better. On the other hand, England wanted at the same time to have the Spanish cabinet on its side, and that is why there developed a kind of diplomatic battle between the

commentata. Vent'anni di teatro in Spagna (1830–1850)," *Quaderni di Filologia Romanza* 4 (1984): 65–89.

[119] "The imposition of such on the Spanish scene necessarily falsified it. Thus Ensenada became an entirely different character from the character of history, for he was an able man, one of Spain's most enlightened ministers, but Rubí, in order to accommodate the Marquesa type, made him a spineless creature and a *camarista* ... These practices led inevitably to a false historical colour in the *comedias*, an effect that was offset somewhat by a choice of not-too-exalted characters and epochs for portrayal so that lapses in historical accuracy were not so obvious or objectionable as were the similar lapses in his Romantic dramas". (Smith, "The Historical Play," p. 225)

He does allow that "Rubí may not have been a student of history, but he knew court intrigues and court political types." (*Ibid.* p. 227)

French and the English agents to see which of the two nations would be able to hold sway in Madrid. That was when the marqués de la Ensenada became minister.)

Rubí creates, in the characters of the ambassadors to France and England, two meddling foreign conspirators, but he adds to them a Spanish woman, the Marquesa de Torrecuso, and charges her with undermining Ensenada's authority while rejecting the pressures of the two ambassadors.

> Los dos esconden fatales
> proyectos, y disimulan,
> y me obsequian, y me adulan
> y ... dejo a los dos iguales.   (II, 5)

(Both of them hide fatal plans, and they lie, and they flatter me, and they praise me, and ... they're both the same).

Ensenada, however, refuses to back either faction (in this, he anticipates Mendoza in *Españoles sobre todo*) and it is he who is rewarded with responsibility and power by the King. Soon thereafter, he clearly states: "Yo engañar quiero a todos / ... / quiero limpiar de traidores / y extranjeros la nación" ("I want to deceive all of them ... I want to rid the nation of traitors and foreigners") (III, 8). When it is proposed to him that he would benefit from throwing his lot in with France, he responds: "Yo no acepto tratados / que al honor de España insulten" ("I do not accept treaties which insult Spain's honor") (IV, 5). Rubí paints masterfully the shifting allegiances of the court hangers-on and foreigners, whose lies, posturing and self-interest impede Spain's progress. Ensenada's soliloquy in the final act (IV, 6) weighs the conspiracies of France and England against the interests of Spain; as he tells the Marquesa:

> Mi constante pensamiento,
> será que el nombre de España
> se pronuncie con respeto
> desde los ardientes climas
> hasta la región del hielo.   (IV, 7)

(My constant wish is for the name of Spain to be pronounced with respect everywhere from the hottest climates to the realm of ice.)

While *La rueda de la fortuna* packs a rousing political message, Rubí has not written a mere political tract. He keeps the play from slipping into tendentiousness by weaving into his story a string of interesting characters, both historical and fictional, who are clearly the sons and daughters of the Romantic heroes of recent years. Clara, pining away in love for

Ensenada, but threatened with marriage to the Conde del Valle and forced by her ambitious father to spy on the Marquesa, laments:

> Temblando estoy! ... ¿cuándo, cuándo,
> tu ambición se extinguirá?
> ¡Oh! ¿nunca se apagará
> tu sed de honores, de mando? ...
> ¿También a tu Clara obligas
> a entrar en tus planes ... ¡Oh! ...
> Y ... ¿qué es lo que entiendo yo
> de palaciegas intrigas?
> ¿Yo a la Marquesa espiar? ...
> ¡espiar! ... yo, que ... ¡ay de mí!
> solo para amar nací
> para sufrir y llorar! ...   (III, 7)

(I am trembling! When, when will your ambition be quelled? Oh, will your thirst for honors and power never be extinguished? Do you also demand that your Clara get involved in your schemes? Oh, and, what do I know about palace intrigues? I, spy on the Marquesa? Spy! I who... woe is me! I was born only to love, to suffer and to cry ...)

Clara, long-suffering because she understands (she thinks) that she is being used as a pawn in the larger political game, plays the Romantic heroine gracefully. She appears "cubierta" ("covered up") in a key scene in Act IV and struggles with the series of misunderstandings that Rubí has built into her character. The "Will Clara and Ensenada finally recognize their love and get together?" plot element is kept just below the surface of the political story, and injected into it at significant dramatic moments, most notably as the play reaches its climax in the final scenes of Act IV.

People liked this play and kept it on the boards for many nights, calling Rubí to the stage following each performance. It made it to eighteen straight performances and was only moved off the boards when Elías Noren, who played Clara's father, became sick. What is more, it made a lot of money:

No hacemos memoria de ninguna producción que se haya sostenido tantas noches y con tan pingues entradas, careciendo de aparato teatral hasta el punto de no haber tenido que gastar ni un solo real la empresa del Príncipe para ponerla en escena. Por un cálculo bastante exacto la última comedia del señor Tomás Rodríguez Rubí le ha producido al teatro no menos de cien mil reales libres. (*Revista de Teatros*, 11 October 1844)

(We cannot remember any other production which has stayed so many nights on the boards nor brought in such abundant profits, especially a play so lacking in stage machinery that the owners of the Príncipe did not have to spend a single *real* to put it on stage. We calculate that this latest comedy of Mr. Tomás Rodríguez Rubí has brought in no less than one hundred thousand *reales*.)

The papers praised the play as "una comedia sin rival en su género ... vivido y animado el diálogo, fluída la versificación, delicado el estilo" ("a comedy without rival in its genre ... it has lively and animated dialogue, fluid verses, a delicate style") (*Revista de Teatros*, 8 October 1843). Even the Queen was so impressed that she awarded Rubí with a Cross of the Order of Carlos III, which the management at the Príncipe, in apparent gratitude for the success of the play, encrusted with diamonds (*Revista de Teatros*, 1 December 1844); it was said that Rivas also gave him a special gift in recognition of this triumph. Part of its appeal, according to reports in the *Revista de Teatros*, was precisely Rubí's ability to move away from the "escuela terrorífica y extravagante" ("terrorific and extravagant school") of Romanticism and onto new territory.

Entre todos los dramas que vieron en el año pasado la luz pública, ninguno obtuvo una aceptación tan general como la obra el señor Rubí titulada *La rueda de la fortuna*. Para nosotros la principal causa del triunfo que alcanzó entonces el joven poeta, debe atribuirse al tacto delicado y al numen poético con que ha sabido dar un nuevo espíritu al teatro nacional, apartándose de la escuela terrorífica y extravagante que se había apoderado como por asalto del cetro de la escena española. (*Revista de Teatros*, 15 January 1845)

(Among all the plays that were seen in public last year none received as much wide-spread acceptance as the work of Mr. Rubí entitled *La rueda de la fortuna*. For us the main reason for the success that its young poet achieved was due to the delicate tact and poetic talent with which he managed to lend a new spirit to national theatre, moving away from the terrorific and extravagant school which had forcefully taken over the Spanish stage.)

La rueda stayed in the repertory of Madrid's minor theatres (it played often at the Instituto Español) and in the provinces for years. Rubí seemed to have stumbled upon a dramatic formula which enabled him to combine his real passion for politics with his undeniable dramatic talent; he returned to the formula several times in the next few years, most notably with *Bandera negra* (Black Flag, 1844), *La rueda de la fortuna, segunda parte* (1845), and *La corte de Carlos II* (1846).

Bandera negra proved to be even more provocative than *La rueda de la fortuna*, although – or perhaps because – it addressed similar historical and contemporary problems. Political ambition, conflict and hostility among the misdirected nobility, struggles for power, and machinations at Court filled Rubí's new play, set in 1661 in the house of don Luis de Haro, one of Felipe IV's key ministers, but situated conceptually in the Spain of 1844. Esperanza de Haro, a relative of the king's and widow of an important count, falls in love (reluctantly at first) with don Félix de Mendoza, the nephew of the Archbishop of Toledo. The dramatic conflict resides in the Luis de Haro/Archbishop struggle for influence over the

king, into which is inserted, in good Romantic fashion, the love story of
Esperanza and Félix. Félix is presented as a daring, noble young man, the
description of whom brings echoes of Espronceda's description of his own
don Félix in *El estudiante de Salamanca*. Rubí writes that his young man
is:

> Un valentón de Toledo
> y tan jugador de espada
> que da cada cuchillada,
> señora, que canta el credo.
> Un mes hará que más de mil
> son los duelos que ha tenido.
> Félix dicen que se nombra,
> y me aseguran también
> que cuando no halla con quien
> se acuchilla con su sombra:
> galanteador como él solo,
> airado, de vida inquieta,
> algo músico y poeta,
> mucho Adonis, mucho Apolo.
> Tan franco como valiente,
> pero a la vez tan perdido
> que nadie le ha conocido
> ni un amigo, ni un pariente   (I, 11)

(A valiant young man from Toledo and such a good swordsman that each thrust
hits home. He'll fight a thousand duels in one month's time. They say his name is
Félix, and they also assure me that when he can find no challenger, he duels with
his own shadow. He's a lover, angry, who lives an unsettled life, and he's also
something of a musician and poet – a lot of Adonis, a lot of Apollo in him. He's as
honest as he is daring, but at the same time so lost that no one, not even a friend or
relative, really knows him.)

The "bandera negra" of the title is a dual symbol, representing on the one
hand the "war" declared by Félix to win the hesitant Esperanza (I, 6) and
on the other the real political war brewing between the forces of Haro and
those of the Archbishop. Inés, Esperanza's friend and confidant, has a
"fatal y vago presentimiento" ("fatal and vague feeling") about the
"huracán / de la ambición" ("storm of ambition") she detects in her
elders (I, 8). When Haro suddenly falls ill and the king suggests that he
will replace him with Haro's son, one of the courtiers comments, "Os
juro, Guzmán, que son / fatales estos momentos: / eso de estar indecisos /
sin saber a qué atenernos" ("I swear to you, Guzman, that these are very
bad times: to be unsure without knowing where to turn") (II, 1), empha-
sizing the vacilating nature of court hangers-on.

Rubí piles up further complications, revealing in the process that he is still under the sway of Rivas, but with full-blown political implications taking the place of the more universal, cosmos-centered vision of don Alvaro. Rubí laces the play with Romantic images and language – talk of vengeance, "fatal estrella," "ciego frenesí," and "destino avaro", secret doors, masked men, compromising letters, and a highly charged political and emotional atmosphere – but turns away from the Romantic solution by writing a dénouement which stresses harmony, the nobility of the main character, and, more important, that "desde hoy entre los dos / no habrá más bandera negra" ("from today between the two of us there will no longer be a black flag") (IV, 9) as Félix and Esperanza embrace. The audience loved it: in the pages of *El Laberinto* (1 April 1844) Enrique Gil wrote:

Se pidió al autor por medio de las aclamaciones más estrepitosas, sinceras y unánimes que se han oído nunca en el teatro. No se puede decir de esta comedia que agradó, sino que encantó, hechizó a los espectadores de todas clases, sexos, opiniones y genios. Ni el éxito de *La rueda de la fortuna*, comedia del mismo autor, fue tan universalmente completo como éste ... *Bandera negra* es un espectáculo del que salen satisfechos por igual el corazón, la imaginación y el entendimiento de los espectadores: el primero por la elevación moral de los sentimientos y la viva simpatía que saben inspirar los personajes; la segunda por lo bien atado del nudo y la invención en el arreglo de los sucesos; el tercero por la verdad de los efectos y situaciones y la sencillez aparte noble naturalidad del desempeño ... *Bandera negra* descuella más que por lo raro de la trama y lo complicado y resuelto de los acontecimientos, por la verdad de los afectos, la originalidad del pensamiento y lo atrevido del dibujo.[120]

(The audience demanded, with the noisiest, most sincere and unanimous acclamations ever heard in the theatre, that the author come out on stage. One cannot really say that the people merely liked this play; they were enchanted by it, it bewitched spectators of all classes, sexes, opinions and inclinations. Not even *La rueda de la fortuna*, a play by this same author, was as universally successful as this one ... *Bandera negra* is the kind of performance from which one's heart, imagination and understanding leave equally satisfied: the first because of the moral level of the feelings and the lively sympathy that the characters inspire; the second because of the well-structured plot and the cleverness of the episodes; the third because of the truth of its effects and situations, and the simplicity and naturalness of the acting. *Bandera negra* excels not so much because of the unusual plot details or the play's incidents as because of the truth of its passions, the originality of its thought, and the daringness of its execution.)

Bandera negra played throughout March of 1844, then was reprised in April, June, and September of 1845, January, February, March, May, and November of 1846, February, April, September, and November of

---

[120] Cited by A. M. Burgos, "Vida y obra," p. 100. Smith's belief that "In *Bandera negra*, also, there is a political struggle but it is ill-defined, there is no villain-against-patriot motif, and no attempt is made at alignment of sympathies" ("The Historical Play," p. 227) seems unjustified.

1847, March, April, June, and November of 1848, and September of 1849, in addition to several times in the early 1860s (with Julián Romea playing the lead).

The mania for sequels of popular works reached a crescendo in the 1840s when Madrid's audiences got Zorrilla's *El zapatero y el rey, segunda parte* (1842), Bretón's *Don Frutos en Belchite* (1845), Zorrilla's *El puñal del godo* (continued as *La calentura* [The Fever] in 1847), and the Asquerino brothers' *Españoles sobre todo, segunda parte* (1847), among others. Rubí contributed to this trend with *La rueda de la fortuna, segunda parte* (1845), which addressed the fall from power of Ensenada. "Ha llegado la época de los beneficios" ("The period of theatre benefits has arrived"), writes the reviewer for the *Revista de Teatros* (15 January 1845),

y comoquiera que en el año cómico anterior algunas producciones merecieron buen éxito, sus autores se han apresurado a escribir la segunda parte de las obras que entonces agradaron, y los primeros actores a escogerlas para sus respectivos beneficios. La idea, si bien tiene mucho de interesada, no deja de ser por eso ingeniosa, porque al fin el complemento de una idea que ha gustado es el mejor cebo para atraer la concurrencia.

(and since during last year's season some plays deserved to be successful, their authors have hastened to write continuations of works that were hits then, and the best actors have moved to adopt them for their various benefits. The idea, if it smacks of self-interest, is nevertheless smart because in the long run the best guarantee of pulling in a full house is to use an idea that was successful before.)

The Royal Family was in attendance. Latorre, Lombía, and Matilde Díez performed the main roles (it was her benefit), but Lombía – inevitably compared with Antonio Guzmán's extremely popular performance in Part 1 – was criticized for not distinguishing this role (Ensenada's father) from others he had recently played, such as don Frutos (*El pelo de la dehesa*) and Diego Mendoza (*Españoles sobre todo*). Rubí, on the other hand, was praised in particular for having discovered a dramatic formula which integrated "razón" ("reason") and "buen gusto" ("good taste") with fluid, musical and natural versification and for having incorporated a political posture which could only please the audience, a group described in the same review as "una generación agitada por las pasiones políticas, y víctima de maquinaciones tenebrosas y de intrigas palaciegas" ("a generation stirred up by political passions, and victim of dark machinations and palace intrigues"). Clearly, to this reviewer, these plays carried not only a historical message, but also one which presents "los hechos de modo que puedan servir de ejemplo y de lección para los tiempos presentes" ("the facts in such a way that they can serve as an example and a lesson for modern times").

That "formula," however, caused Rubí problems when he overstepped the bounds of political correctness. Even though he insisted, disingenuously, that "yo en esta comedia no quiero decir más que lo que digo" ("in this play I don't mean to say more than I am saying") *La corte de Carlos II* (1846) was banned from the stage after a private reading which impelled one of the listeners to denounce it to the authorities. "¿Qué delito ha cometido esta comedia para ser prohibida?" ("What crime has this play committed to have been banned?") he whines, knowing full well that the play was inflammatory. It dealt with the themes of court power and influence, this time directly concerning the marriage of the King at a time when the international furor over the marriage of Isabel II had reached fever pitch. The various factions jockeying for position included the British-backed liberals, who favored one pretender, and the French-supported moderates, who favored another. The disputes were so bitter that Narváez, the Prime Minister, was forced out of office in April, 1846.[121] Carlos II's wedding in 1679 with either the daughter of the Emperor of Austria or with Luisa de Borbón had its exact parallel in modern-day Spain's gripping drama of the marriage of the Queen. Rubí got too close to the raw nerve of the situation – the Queen Mother (that is, María Cristina), conspiring unsubtly for the ascendency of the French faction, is seen as the villain in the play – and paid the price with the censorship, although the incident did nothing to diminish his immense popularity. When he rewrote it in 1852 as *Tres al saco* (Three in the Bag), the Queen Mother disappeared from it completely, effectively de-politicizing the play. In this form it encountered no obstacles for its performance. *Alberoni* (1846) contained a similar character (as in *Españoles sobre todo*, the Princesa of the Ursinos, another María Cristina figure in light disguise) and was similarly banned following a noisy and enthusiastic first-night reception.

Still, this patently political theatre was but one manifestation of the rich brew being mixed by playwrights of the 1840s, much of it a look toward the future as well as a response to the past. One further step in the dismantling of the Romantic outlook came on the heels of Zorrilla's *Don Juan Tenorio* in the form of an "anti-don Juan" play[122] which went even

---

121 See Carr, *Spain 1808–1975*, pp. 227–246, and Manuel Ciges Aparicio, *España bajo la dinastía de los Borbones* (Madrid: Aguilar, 1932): 267–292. The topic was commented on widely in the European press. Guizot's version of the events, published in his *Mémoires pour servir à l'histoire de mon temps* (Paris: M.-Lévy, 1858–1867) so angered Juan de Grimaldi that Grimaldi wrote a polemical, anonymous response to it in the pages of *Le Mémorial Diplomatique*. See Gies, *Theatre and Politics*, pp. 166–181.

122 The term is John Dowling's. See "El anti-don Juan de Ventura de la Vega," *Actas del VI Congreso Internacional de Hispanistas*, eds. Alan M. Gordon and Evelyn Rugg (University of Toronto Press, 1980): 215–218.

further than Zorrilla in rejecting the excesses of the don Juan type. Ventura de la Vega (1807–1865) placed himself in the center of the theatrical debates with the production of *El hombre de mundo* (Man of the World), first performed at the Príncipe Theatre on 2 October 1845.[123] It is a dual-edged comedy, one side containing a strong rejection of the Romantic ethos and the other a slice of "real life," and as such, a step toward the full development of the *alta comedia*. Vega would soon become the epicenter of the acrimonious debate over the creation and direction of the subsidized national theatre, the Teatro Español, in 1849, as we will see below, but for now he was on his way to becoming one of the most respected voices in Spanish playwriting in the 1840s. Previously, he was mostly known as a collaborator (he, Bretón, and Grimaldi wrote the now-lost *1835 y 1836, o lo que es y lo que será*, [1835 and 1836, or What Is and What Will Be]) and translator (in 1841 alone fourteen of his translations were performed at the Príncipe; twenty in 1842).

El hombre de mundo's immense and immediate popularity eclipsed that of *Don Juan Tenorio* (Zorrilla's play was performed thirty times between 1844 and 1849 [not at all, apparently, in 1845 or 1846]; Vega's had forty-four performances in a year's less time), *Españoles sobre todo, La rueda de la fortuna* and the other plays we have seen. It transformed Vega into one of the true stars of the theatrical scene and launched a career that included positions as Professor of Literature to the Queen and her younger sister, Comisario Regio of the Teatro Español, and finally, Director of the Conservatorio de Música de María Cristina. The play is a masterfully comic rejection of the kind of deeds perpetrated by the don Juan figure (Zorrilla had also rejected his excesses, as we have seen). Galdós unabashedly called it "una obra maestra" ("a masterpiece") twenty-two years after its première (*La Nación*, 4 March 1868). Vega's innovation was to place his don Juan figure into contemporary society and into a social stratum which accurately reflected the self-image of his audience. That is to say, he cleverly introduced the history of the don Juan type without the historical distancing, and forced his audience to see reflected on stage the confusions and chaos created when this figure reigns supreme. Julián Romea's performance in the title role coincided as well with the growing attachment among certain actors to a more natural style of acting, one which harmonized with what Madrid's middle class was

---

[123] It had been given a reading at Patricio de la Escosura's house (before an audience which included Rubí, Gil y Zárate, and Bretón, among others), then a private performance in the in-house theatre at the ranch of the Countess of Montijo in Carabanchel (in which Eugenia, the future Empress of France, played the role of Clara), before reaching the public stage. Antonio María Esquivel's painting entitled "Lectura de Ventura de la Vega en el Teatro del Príncipe" is believed to depict a reading of *El hombre de mundo*. See also Leslie, *Ventura de la Vega*.

slowly coming to expect on stage, that is, a moral mirror-image of itself. Zorrilla credited Romea with creating the "comedia de levita, que se ha dado en llamar de costumbres" ("comedy of the respectable gentleman, which has become known as the comedy of manners") even though he had acted in many of the core Romantic plays.[124] That Vega disputed the excesses of the Romantic movement was left without question following his speech to the Real Academia Española upon the occasion of his election to that body in 1845; it is this attitude he dramatized in *El hombre de mundo*.

La falange invasora logró por entonces su objeto: aun en aquellos que, fortaleci-dos con el estudio de los buenos modelos, profesaban los eternos principios del buen gusto, introdujo, por lo menos, la duda, deslumbrando a unos, imponiendo silencio a otros y arrancando a casi todos cobardes concesiones. En los que alcanzó a sorprender comenzando la tarea su triunfo fue completo. Estos, a la primera intimidación del apóstol del *romanticismo* (*palabra bárbara, que nada significa en castellano*), corrieron a alistarse bajo la enseña de la nueva secta.[125]

(The invading faction achieved its objective at that time: even in those who, having been fortified by the study of good models, professed the eternal principles of good taste, they introduced, at least, some doubts, confusing some of them, imposing silence on others and managing to wring cowardly concessions out of almost all of them. Its triumph was total among those whom it surprised at the beginning of their writing careers. At the very first intimidation by the apostle of *Romanticism* (*a barbaric word which means absolutely nothing in Spanish*), these new writers ran to enlist under the banner of the new sect.)

John Dowling has accurately captured the differences between Zorrilla's vision of the world and that of Vega in his description of Esquivel's painting, "Lectura de Zorrilla en el estudio de Esquivel" ("Zorrilla's Reading in Esquivel's Studio"), positing a subtle confrontation between Zorrilla's traditional, legendary vision and Vega's more bourgeois – "modern" if you will – look at the society in which he lived.[126] This modernity is amply on display in *El hombre de mundo*, "una

---

[124] Zorrilla, *Recuerdos del tiempo viejo*, in *Obras completas* II, p. 1819.

[125] Cited by José Montero Alonso, *Ventura de la Vega. Su vida y su tiempo* (Madrid: Editora Nacional, 1951): 127. Emphasis added.

[126] Dowling, "El anti-don Juan," p. 216. Dowling writes: "Así es que el grupo central se compone de Zorrilla, Ventura de la Vega, el pintor Esquivel, y el actor y poeta Romea. Falta Carlos Latorre, quien debía aparecer en la pintura de los actores. En este cuadro el confrontamiento simbólico parece ser entre Zorrilla – el poeta de la España católica, tradicional, legendaria, la España del machismo de Don Juan Tenorio, de Diego Martínez de la leyenda *A buen juez, mejor testigo*, y de Don Juan de Alarcón, joven seductor de *Margarita la Tornera* – y Ventura de la Vega y Julián Romea – representan-tes de la nueva España burguesa del XIX, la España que se viste de levita y chistera (Romea lleva la suya en la mano), la España que se enriquece con la desamortización de los bienes eclesiásticos, que establece la Bolsa de Madrid y construye el barrio madrileño de Salamanca."

comedia de las más bonitas que se han escrito en castellano" ("one of the loveliest comedies ever written in Spanish"), according to Juan Valera.[127] Vega has moved the play out of the salons, cemeteries, convents, and tempestuous natural surroundings of Romantic plays into the symbolic center of the high bourgeois world, the home, in this case the "gabinete elegante en casa de don Luis" ("elegant sitting room in don Luis's house"). As Dowling notes, this scenic space imitates the houses in which the audience lived, or wished to live.[128] The stage became a safe cultural haven which best reflected the aspirations of the Spanish middle class. Within this space audiences would now witness a return to harmony and comfort, in rejection of the shatteringly disharmonious *dénouements* served up in Romantic plays. Into and out of this elegant room stream representatives of the non-aristocratic, non-working upper class whose financial situation enables them to spend their time on frivolous (gossip and superficial intrigue are favorite pastimes) or artistic (the men go to the theatre every night) pursuits. Vega's cleverly plotted and fast-paced action swirls together a series of logical confusions, complex motives, and well-depicted individual psychologies in order to lead the audience to a pre-determined moral position.

Vega's innovation is to present not only a don Juan figure (here, an old friend of the hero don Luis, named appropriately enough don Juan) but also a *reformed* don Juan who is, in addition to repenting of his past, comfortably married to doña Clara and living a life of moral rectitude in Madrid. Don Juan married *and* reformed! This is a far cry from the Romantic heroes of the 1830s, and the logical next step away from Zorrilla's presentation of the type. It confirms the conservative shift we have noted in the social and literary world of 1844, and moves the audience into a new one. Luis, the ex-Tenorio, is the "man of the world," who as the play opens is voicing his opposition to the relationship between Emilia, Clara's sister, and the young Antoñito, in whom Luis sees vestiges of his own scandalous past. Luis and Clara love one another, but not with the wild Romantic passions reminiscent of past lovers, but with strong conjugal admiration and respect. Clara knows of Luis's past but believes that he is therefore a better husband, since he has got his youthful desires out of his system. "Dicen que los calaveras / son después buenos maridos" ("They say that carousers turn into good husbands"), she says, to which he answers, "No seré yo la excepción, / te lo ofrezco. Ya estoy fuera / de combate" ("I won't be an exception to the rule, I assure you. I am already out of combat") (I, 3). Luis expresses clearly his

---

[127] Juan Valera, *Ventura de la Vega, estudio biográfico-crítico* (Madrid: Pérez Dubrull, 1904): 41.
[128] Dowling, "The anti-don Juan," p. 218.

current (middle-class) values, radically different from the conquests and seductions of the typical don Juan:

> ¡La felicidad es ésta;
> ésta que ahora gozo! ¡Hallar
> una dulce compañera,
> una casa, una familia!
> ¡Esta vida me embelesa!
> Bien lo ves: yo casi nunca
> salgo. De noche una vuelta
> por el café, y al teatro;
> acabada la comedia,
> a casa.   (I, 3)

(This is happiness, this that I am now enjoying! To find a sweet companion, a house, a family! This lifestyle enchants me! You can see I hardly ever go out. At night I might go briefly to the café, then to the theatre; when the play is over, I come right home.)

Clara, too, rejects the Romantic model, viewing it as a mere passing fancy. What was previously considered the *sine qua non* of love – Romantic passion – is now seen as a threat to the stability of man-woman relationships. It is for her a mere "comedia," not real life. Referring to the possible marriage between her sister Emilia and Antoñito, she declares:

> ¿Casarlos? ¿Para exponerla
> a que al año se le antoje
> al niño ser calavera
> y la haga infeliz? No, no.
> Lo que quiero es que se vean
> a su sabor; que se juren
> amor y constancia eterna
> cada minuto; que agoten
> la cartilla de ternezas
> y requiebros; y verás,
> cuando sus amores pierdan
> el romántico barniz
> de carta, escondite y reja,
> cómo los dos se fastidian
> y se acaba la comedia.   (I, 4)

(Marry them? Expose her to the danger that in a year's time he reverts to his old ways and makes her unhappy? No, no. What I want is that they see one another as much as they want, that they swear love and eternal faithfulness every minute, that they express all sorts of endearments and flatteries, and you will see, when their love loses its romantic glow [when they're tired of the letters, secret meetings, and whisperings from behind ironwork grates], how they will get fed up with one another and the play will come to an end.)

Into this stable home comes don Juan, Luis's ex-buddy in escapades, whom he has not seen for over a year; he has a difficult time believing that Luis is *married*, in spite of Luis's protests about his previous life that "Aquello era una ilusión. / Sólo aquí la dicha existe" ("That was an illusion. True happiness exists only in here") (I, 7). Vega could not be more explicit about his rejection of the chaos and disharmony caused by those who follow the Romantic model. From the lips of don Luis spills forth Vega's core belief in marriage as the basis for social stability, in redemption via wedded bliss. The speech (I, 7) captures Vega's view of conjugal life while at the same time it brilliantly dismantles all the key assumptions of the Romantic cosmos by weaving into the speech the very images popularized by Romantic authors ("cautiva," "delirio," "fiebre," "fuego," "pena," "indiferencia fatal," "tedio," "demonio" ["capture," "delirium," "fever," "fire," "sorrow," "fatal indifference," "tedium," "devil"]), but turned toward a positive rendering of existence, not a negative one. The "fire" that warms lovers' hearts is no longer seen as the fire of passion, but rather as the fire of the hearth, fanned by friendship as well as by love. This long intervention is delivered to none other than don Juan. If part of the essence of Romanticism was the cult of the individual struggling against an injust society, here Vega presents a new model: the good citizen, the married man who wants "el público bien" ("the public good") rather than only his personal fulfillment. Don Luis even thinks about his (society's) children; Romantic heroes never had children. Since the speech encapsulates both the ideology of the play and the most important elements in the shift toward the *alta comedia*, it is worth reproducing in its entirety.

> Mira que es cosa
> de que no tienes idea,
> lo que cautiva y recrea
> el cariño de una esposa.
> Y no lo juzgues por ese
> con que te tiene embaucado
> la francesa: amor comprado,
> por mucho que te embelese . . .
> Ni es tampoco aquel delirio,
> aquella fiebre de amante,
> abrasadora, incesante,
> que más que gozo es martirio.
> Es fuego que da calor
> al alma, sin abrasar;
> es conjunto singular
> de la amistad y el amor.
> Huye de ti el egoísmo,
> porque hay a tu lado un ser

que tu pena y tu placer
los siente como tú mismo.
En vez de frivolidad
y de desprecio del mundo,
se despierta en ti un profundo
instinto de dignidad.
Quieres merecer del hombre
respeto, aprecio, interés,
porque refleje después
en la que lleva tu nombre.
Ese tu eterno viajar
por Francia, Italia, Inglaterra,
sin que haya un punto en la tierra
que alivie tu malestar,
¿qué es sino cansancio, di?
¿Qué es sino un vago deseo
de encontrar más digno empleo
a la vida que hay en ti?
¡Pues esa eterna vagancia,
ese vivir volandero
que te hace tan extranjero
en España como en Francia;
la indiferencia fatal,
o el tedio más bien que sientes
cuando ventilan las gentes
algún negocio formal;
todo eso, que yo he probado
cuando como tú vivía,
se borra, Juan, desde el día
en que te miras casado!
Ya por el público bien
te afanas, y en ti rebosa,
con el amor de tu esposa,
el de tu patria también.
Y el alma y los ojos fijos
en su porvenir tendrás,
porque esta patria, dirás,
es la patria de mis hijos.
En fin, Juan, el matrimonio
es origen, no lo dudes,
de las mayores virtudes
de la tierra. Y ... ¡qué demonio!
Mucho contra él se propala;
pero cuando todos dan
en casarse ... Vamos, Juan,
no será cosa tan mala.   (I, 7)

(Look, you have no idea what the love of a wife can do for you. And don't think
that the love that French woman says she has for you is the same thing: that is a

love you buy, no matter how bewitching it may seem ... Love isn't that delirium, that lover's fever, red-hot and uninterrupted, which is really more of a martyrdom than a joy. True love is a fire which warms the soul without scorching it. It is a unique conjoining of friendship and passion. You lose your selfishness because you have someone by your side who feels your sorrows and your pleasures the same as you do. Instead of frivolity and a disdain for the world, you find that a profound instinct for dignity is awakened in you. You want to deserve other men's respect, esteem, concern, because this will be reflected later in the woman who carries your name. Your constant wanderings through France, Italy, England, searching for some place which might bring you peace and comfort, what is that except a sort of exhaustion? What is it except a vague desire to find something worthwhile to do with your life? In your eternal travels, in the unsettled life that makes you as much a stranger in Spain as in France, in the fatal indifference or boredom you feel when people are conducting some formal business; all of that, which I also knew when I lived as you do, disappears, Juan, from the very day you marry! You begin to work for the public good, and you find that in addition to your wife's love, you also overflow with love of your country. And you will have your eyes and your soul fixed on its future, because this country is, you will say, also the country of my children. Finally, Juan, marriage is the origin, don't ever doubt it, of the greatest virtues on earth. And ... my word! So much seems to conspire against it, but when everyone gets married ... Come on, Juan, it won't be such a bad thing.)

Following many amusing plot complications in which Luis's past returns to haunt him ("Tu vida pasada / viene a envenenarlo todo" ["Your past life is coming back to poison everything"] [IV, 19]), the characters come back at the end to confirm Luis's vision of the world, one in which the stability of conjugal love forms the solid base upon which society can grow and prosper. Gabino Tejado reminded his readers in 1845 that the scandals of the Romantic heroes are a thing of the past: "Nadie está tan deseoso de silbidos que intente volver a presentar en nuestra escena las bacanales de Margarita de Borgoña, ni la repugnante perfidia de Lucrecia de Borgia, ni la osadía de Antony"[129] ("No one wants to be booed enough to bring back to our stage the orgies of Margarita de Borgoña, or the repugnant betrayal of Lucrecia de Borgia, or the audacity of Antony"). Don Juan loses; the married man and, interestingly, the woman, wins.[130] Romantic drama, as Navas Ruiz accurately depicts it,

viene a morir hacia 1845 tras haber transformado con un puñado de obras fundamentales el panorama del teatro español. Su muerte no es tanto el producto de los ataques contra él, sino de agotamiento interno. Ese agotamiento, esa crisis, es lo que se refleja en diversas opiniones de aquella hora. Para reemplazarlo, unos

---

[129] *El Laberinto* II (1845), p. 202.
[130] The triumphant woman, absent from the majority of the Romantic plays, will play a key role in the theatre in the second half of the century.

proponen un teatro histórico nacionalista, de escaso futuro; otros, con más visión, recurren a reflejar en la alta comedia los conflictos del momento.[131]

(dies around 1845 after having transformed, with a handful of fundamental works, the panorama of Spanish theatre. Its death is not so much a result of attacks against it as of internal exhaustion. That exhaustion, that crisis, is what one sees reflected in different solutions of the time. To replace it, some people propose a nationalistic historical theatre, but one with little future promise; others, who have more vision, move to reflect the period's conflicts in the *alta comedia*.)

The new paradigm has been established: Romanticism is out, the bourgeois *alta comedia* is in.

[131] Navas Ruiz, *El romanticismo español*, p. 133.

4 The theatre at mid-century

The year 1849 is another key year in the history of the theatre in Spain. The decade of the 1840s witnessed a significant shift in the power structure of the theatre. The monopoly of the Príncipe and the Cruz companies disappeared (although they remained the flagship theatres of the capital) as dozens of new theatres and theatrical companies were formed, merged, and eliminated in a move toward what would eventually approximate a free market. The repertory changed as more national, original plays were added which brought about – as much by accident as by design – the de-emphasis on translations and *refundiciones*. Censorship was less intense, while at the same time more conflict erupted inside and outside the theatres which performed political dramas. Significantly, inexpensive printed versions of the plays flooded the bookstores of the major cities. We have little information about actual print runs or consumers of these printed plays, but the rather astonishing quantity produced leads unequivocally to the suggestion that there existed a vastly expanded market for them. In fact, so active was the publishing industry that by February 1847 the newspaper *La Luneta* was complaining bitterly about the mass *pirating* of cheap editions. Beginning in the late thirties, but expanding rapidly in the forties and through the next several decades numerous collections of printed plays would appear, which evidently were widely distributed: the "Galería Dramática de Manuel Delgado" was the best known (it had more than 180 titles in print by 1846), but there also appeared collections like the "Biblioteca Dramática" (Casa Editorial de Medina, Madrid), the "Galería del Museo Literario," the "Colección de Obras Dramáticas y Líricas," and the "Biblioteca Lírico-Dramática." By the mid-1850s, as the title page (for example) of Rubí's *La hija de la providencia* (The Daughter of Providence) would demonstrate, the plays were distributed in eighty-three cities and towns across the country.[1] The publishing houses of Antonio Yenes, Repullés, José Rodríguez, and Cipriano López took the

---

[1] It is surprising to see distribution points which include not only large towns but also small ones such as Toro, Tuy, Ubeda, Motril, Chiclana, Ecija, Reus, etc. Who was buying these plays?

lead in making cheap editions available to the public, although plays were printed under the imprimatur of dozens of other individuals and corporations as well.

The year 1849 also marks an important passage in theatre ownership and administration since it brought with it the opening of the Teatro Español, the first true attempt at a subsidized, controlled national theatre in the country, something for which Grimaldi among others had argued forcefully in the twenties and thirties, but without success. The experiment was doomed to failure because of economic difficulties, political blockades, poor leadership and personal resentments, but it was nevertheless a noble one which raised the hopes of a generation of Spanish playwrights that the nation (that is, the government) would take an active interest in the intellectual welfare of the theatre. Michael Schinasi correctly notes that "among the unwritten chapters in the history of the nineteenth-century stage is one that provides a full account of the theatre reforms of 1849, and of the creation of a national theatre in the building that had formerly been the Teatro del Príncipe, on the site of the present day Teatro Español."[2] A full history of the reforms still remains to be written, but a closer look at the theatre in 1849 will prove instructive.

Enter, stage right: the National Theatre experiment

Hundreds of playwrights were producing for the stage by the end of the 1840s. The seemingly open policies of Isabel II had lowered the tensions fanned by censorship, and the public was more theatre-conscious than ever. In order to capitalize on these developments, in 1847, José Luis Sartorius, the powerful Conde de San Luis, initiated as Ministro de la Gobernación a series of reforms of the theatres in Madrid which would attempt to standardize the rights and responsibilities of the acting companies, the impresarios, the theatre owners, and – by extension – the repertory offerings of the theatres ("la escrupulosa elección del repertorio" ["the scrupulous selection of the repertory offerings"]). The most striking moves were the attempt to control all the theatres of the country and the metamorphosis of the Príncipe Theatre into the Teatro Español, a subsidized theatre of national scope which would henceforth be first among equals in the theatrical hierarchy. The stated goal of the dual document, entitled *Real decreto orgánico de los teatros del Reino, y Reglamento del Teatro Español* (Royal Organic Degree on the Kingdom's Theatres, and By-Law for the Teatro Español), promulgated on 30

2 Michael Schinasi, "The National Theater in Mid-Nineteenth Century Spain, and the Curious Project to Destroy a Block of Houses Facing the Teatro Español," *Resonancias románticas*, ed. John Rosenberg (Madrid: Porrúa, 1988): 195.

August 1847, was to "sacar los espectáculos teatrales de la postración en que por desgracia se hallan, regularizando convenientemente los del reino, y creando en Madrid un Teatro Español"[3] ("bring theatrical spectacles out of the depression which they unfortunately are suffering, organizing all of the theatres in the kingdom, and creating in Madrid a Spanish Theatre"). The project was approached with utmost seriousness, since it was confirmed in the founding papers that "este espectáculo es el termómetro de la cultura de los pueblos" ("theatre is the thermometer of a people's level of culture") and as such worthy of attention at the highest levels. One suspects that Sartorius, as a representative of the Queen's government, viewed with alarm the growing tendency of Spanish theatre to be contentious, mocking, and political, and wished to bring it back into the fold of respectability (as if it had ever been "respectable") through more strict controls. The abundance of theatres in the capital led naturally to the absence of centralized control: "Not only were there too many theatres but each theatre offered too many types of entertainment."[4] The printed version of the reform document was the result of eighteen months of revisions, and it was cleverly written, giving small benefits to the actors, praising the impresarios, and recognizing the importance of theatre within the national project while centralizing the whole endeavor.

It is the second document, the *Reglamento del Teatro Español*, which interests us for the moment, for it will transform a mere playwright/ businessman into a powerful dictator of the official stage, and reflect, through the two years of squabbling which took place inside and outside the Teatro Español, the state of the theatre at mid-century. The short history of the Teatro Español offers a microcosmic view of the strengths and weaknesses of the theatrical enterprise – and indirectly, of the national consciousness – at a time in which the middle classes were beginning to take hold of the reins of power in Spain. The *Reglamento*'s first act was the creation of a director, pompously called in the document and throughout his "reign" the "Comisario Regio" (this title would be the target of much mockery as the years unfolded), charged with important duties. The Comisario Regio was responsible for the selection of the plays to be performed (assisted by a "comisión de lectura" ["reader's committee"] to advise him); the hiring, firing and "classification" of the individuals contracted to act in the new theatre; the artistic direction of the enterprise; the development of the annual and monthly budgets (this along with the Secretary and the Treasurer); the writing of the rules for the administration, governance, and fiscal responsibility of the theatre;

---

[3] The *Decreto* was published by the Imprenta Nacional in February, 1849.
[4] W. F. Smith, "Rodríguez Rubí and the Dramatic Reforms of 1849," *Hispanic Review* 16 (1948): 311.

the adjudication of "todas las cuestiones que se susciten" ("all questions which might arise") concerning the rights and duties of the actors and other workers; the representation of the Teatro Español in all matters having to do with the courts and government offices; and the execution of the goals and wishes of the government. He was to become, in effect, the emperor of the official Spanish stage.

On paper this enterprise promised exciting new changes for the Spanish theatre, and an opening up of the artistic process. Authors were permitted to send copies of their plays to the Comisario Regio for consideration (they would be passed on to the reading committee) or to read the plays themselves before the committee. Decisions were to be made within thirty days, and once a play was accepted for performance, not more than one year was to pass before it was seen on the boards. Playwrights were to receive 10 percent of the gross intake for their plays when performed (3 percent if the play was one or two acts); half of that for a verse translation and one quarter of it for a prose translation, but original plays were to be encouraged above all others. As a bonus, a prize of 10,000 *reales* (something less than one third of the annual salary of the Comisario Regio) was to be given annually to the best original tragedy and the best original comedy, as determined by the Comisario Regio with advice from several commissions. Contracted actors were to receive steady salaries as well as retirement benefits when they were eligible, "a no ser que el Comisario Regio juzgue conveniente conservarlos en actividad" ("unless the Comisario Regio thinks it better to keep them on active status"). The Teatro Español also claimed exclusive rights to the performance of any plays admitted to its repertory, "no podrán ser ejecutadas en los demás [teatros] de Madrid" ("they cannot be performed in any other theatre in Madrid"). This strict government control, applauded ironically by many of the same authors, actors, and directors who had complained for twenty years about excessive government intervention in theatrical affairs, was a far cry from the *laissez-faire* policies demanded in the past.

Who was to become the head of this new venture? Who would be singled out as the leading player in the theatrical world at mid-century? Upon whom were to be placed the aspirations of a generation of playwrights and actors who had long clamored for significant reform? The Comisario Regio would be none other than "el hombre de mundo" ("the man of the world") himself, the distinguished playwright and translator Ventura de la Vega, with support, as we shall see, from some surprising quarters. Among the members of the board of consultants named by the Queen were Mesonero Romanos, Hartzenbusch, the comic actor Antonio Guzmán, and the distinguished composer Hilarión Eslava. Agustín Durán, the enormously respected member of the Real Academia Española de la Lengua, and Miguel Salvá, a member of the Real Academia de la Historia, were put in charge of the examination of works to be performed (that is, they were to be the official censors). Vega's acceptance of the appointment represented an about-face from positions he had voiced in the early forties, including one in which he praised the benefits of the open market and free competition: "En la competencia artística que de esto nacerá no pueden menos de ganar todos los artistas, los escritores y el público"[5] ("artists, writers, and the public can only gain from the artistic competition which will arise from this"). Such a position should hardly surprise us, however, for it paralleled the change in artistic mood from the noisily independent and conflictive Romantic dramatists to the more settled, security-seeking chroniclers of the Spanish middle class which dominated the theatres at mid-century. Still, it was an important moral shift which would be reflected in the repertory. The stated idea that the theatre was "el termómetro de la cultura de los pueblos" was reminiscent of the neoclassical ideal of theatre, and in fact, the *alta comedia* in some ways was a resurfacing of many of the techniques and beliefs of the neoclassical writers.

It is to this enlightened ideal that the theatre as a sociological institution turns as the mid-century approaches, just as there is a rekindling of interest in a literary neoclassicism that had never really died, and an attempt to achieve a *justo medio* between romanticism and neoclassicism, following the apogee of the romantic period in Spain.[6]

The Teatro Español was to "serve as a model in taste for the other theatres,"[7] but its actual creation caused friction in the months prior to its opening. Vega had appointed Juan del Peral, author of *Palo de ciegos* (Blind Man's Stick), a *zarzuela* which had been wickedly mocked in the press for its bad verses, as secretary of the new theatre commission, but the city's main actors, Julián Romea and his wife Matilde Díez, hated Peral for snide cracks he had inserted in *El Heraldo* earlier in the year, and consequently they threatened to boycott the theatre. Negotiations to secure their services were contentious and frequently cliff-hanging (*La Luneta* claimed that part of the final agreement to avoid "insurrection" was that Peral never again be permitted to write "más versos en toda su vida" ["any more verses in his whole life"] [25 February 1849]). Romea and Díez knew they held some powerful cards in the negotiations because a National Theatre without their participation was considered unthinkable by the public and the press. Sartorius himself, the Ministro de la

5 "Folletín. Teatros." *El Correo Nacional* (5 June 1841); cited by Schinasi, "The National Theater," p. 197.
6 Schinasi, "The National Theater," pp. 197–198.
7 Smith, "Rodríguez Rubí," p. 313.

Gobernación, met with Romea to try to convince him to join the company (*La Luneta*, 1 April 1849). At last, an acting company was pieced together which included Romea, Díez, José Valero, Antonio Guzmán, Jerónima Llorente, and Teodora and Bárbara Lamadrid, among others. Juan Lombía was scheduled to join the company, but he declined due to illness.[8]

When the Teatro Español finally got going, it fulfilled its mission only in part. Opened with fanfare on 8 April 1849, even Romea joined the festivities by reading some nondescript verses he had penned for the occasion.[9] The first performance was of a *refundición* of Calderón's *Casa con dos puertas mala es de guardar* (not an auspicious beginning for a theatre claiming to want to promote original productions) and the Teatro Español encountered so many conflicts during the first year that the government declared it a failure by the end of the first season. The offerings were odd – translations, silly comedies, every now and again an old play by Vega or Rubí or Tamayo – and few original plays were performed. The newspapers began whispering about Vega's resignation as early as mid-May of that first year. Even so, the government was willing – with a change in leadership – to steer it through a second season. Yet nothing could save it, and on 19 May 1851, a decree was issued which returned it to its old owner, the Madrid City Council. The causes of this noisy failure were many: playwrights were unable to produce a requisite number of quality plays for performance, the actors resented what they perceived to be the management's lack of appreciation for their skills (especially Julián Romea, the famous – and famously contentious – leading man[10]), competition from the other theatres, and harsh criticism from certain newspapers and envious contenders for the Comisario Regio's position. As Díaz de Escovar and Lasso de la Vega suggest:

Los buenos propósitos del Conde de San Luis se estrellaron contra la apatía del público, que dio en no ir al teatro el Príncipe, apatía que tiene su explicación en la falta de novedad que ofrecía el espectáculo; las comedias que ponía en escena se las sabía el público de memoria, y daban monotonía al espectáculo, precisamente en una época en que le hacían una competencia terrible los demás teatros.[11]

---

8   *La Luneta*, which hated Vega and the Teatro Español, greeted Lombía's return to Madrid in June with the following vicious comment: " . . . al paso que le damos el pésame, por la catástrofe de la muerte de un hijo con que se ha encontrado al llegar a Madrid, y por caer bajo el gobierno del Sr. Vega en el Teatro Español." (Summer 1849; number 29).

9   Julián Romea, *Prólogo escrito, y recitado en la inauguración de el Teatro Español* (n.p., n.d).

10 Romea left the Teatro Español after the first year; with him went his famous wife, Matilde Díez.

11 Narciso Díaz de Escovar and Francisco P. Lasso de la Vega, *Historia del teatro español* II (Barcelona: Montaner y Simón, 1924): 38.

(The good intentions of the Count of San Luis were shattered by the apathy of the public who did not go to the Príncipe Theatre, an apathy which has its explanation in the lack of new things offered by the theatre; the public knew by heart the comedies it put on stage, and this made things monotonous just at a time when other theatres were mounting a very serious competition against it.)

Smith states that the failure of the Teatro Español was more the fault of a public "out of sympathy with the movement" than of the failure to enforce the established rules or the hostility of artists and writers opposed to the theatre's leadership, but it is not at all true that "no one could question the sincere effort nor the tireless labor of these two men [Vega and Rubí]."[12] Groups sprang up immediately whose sole function was to mock the goings-on at the Teatro Español and Vega's leadership; the pages of one newspaper, *La Ortiga* overflow with invective, scorn, and satire against the new enterprise. As Smith recognizes, Rubí himself "contributed more than any other one person to the fiasco at the Teatro Español and the resultant fiasco of the whole program ... he virtually sabotaged the efforts of Ventura de la Vega during Ventura's brief period of directorship."[13] Rubí was one of the founders of *La Ortiga*, whose forty-four issues were published between 19 April and 4 November 1849.[14] It was ostensibly a paper of theatre reviews, commentary, and criticism, but it opened its pages to polemic, invective, and, as the first issue clearly stated, special scrutiny of the Teatro Español. Its tone was far from neutral.

Nosotros somos periodistas; vivimos de opiniones, y damos cuenta de las que a nosotros nos llegan. Se dice que el Sr. Comisario tiene un partido; se divulga que este partido se propone atacar a ciertos artistas y escritores, los cuales a su vez se afirma, que forman otro partido; se asegura que los agentes y críticos del partido, llamémoslo así, *comisarista*, son los primeros que han roto las hostilidades; se da por cierto que el partido del Comisario está inspirado por una capacidad traspirenáica, que en el lenguaje de los círculos literarios lleva el nombre poético de *ninfa Egeria.*

(We are journalists; we live off our opinions, and we take into account those which come to our attention. It is said that Mr. Manager has a band of his own; it is revealed that this band plans to attack certain actors and writers which, it is said, form a separate band. We hear that the agents and critics of the band which might be called *managerist* are the first to have broken out the hostilities. It is certain that

---

[12] Smith, "Rodríguez Rubí," p. 315.   [13] *Ibid.*

[14] *La Ortiga* is mentioned in both Hartzenbusch's and Sinclair's listings of Spanish newspapers, but not, surprisingly, in Simón Díaz, Seoane, or Gómez Rea. Eugenio Hartzenbusch e Hiriarte, *Periódicos de Madrid. Tabla cronológica* (Madrid: Sucesores de Rivadeneyra, 1876); Alison Sinclair, *Madrid Newspapers, 1661–1870* (Leeds: W. S. Maney, 1984); Simón Díaz, *Veinticuatro diarios*; María Cruz Seoane, *Historia del periodismo en España. 2. El siglo XIX* (Madrid: Alianza, 1983); Javier Gómez Rea, "Las revistas teatrales madrileñas (1790–1930)," *Cuadernos Bibliográficos* 31 (1974): 65–140.

the Manager's band is egged on by some sort of power from the other side of the Pyrenees, who in literary circles is referred to by the poetic name of *The Nymph Egeria*.)

The "ninfa Egeria" was none other than Vega's "trans-Pyrenean" friend Juan de Grimaldi.[15] Rubí's resentment was patent throughout the short life of *La Ortiga*, but his impact immense (he was, we remember, the most popular playwright of the time). He accused Vega – not without merit – of staging too many of his own translations, organizing a *claque* to applaud his efforts, distributing free tickets to his friends, and – almost – embezzlement (he accused Vega of not counting all the gate receipts in each day's gross take, something which would adversely affect the salaries paid to authors and actors, since their pay was based precisely on the gross receipts). He belittled him by calling him "un señor infinitamente pequeñito, caprichosito, rencorosito, principio y depósito de todas las pasioncillas pequeñillas" ("an infinitely tiny man, tinily whimsical, tinily rancorous, source and storehouse of all the tiny little passions of the day") (*La Ortiga*, p. 207).

Notwithstanding all the carping, some interesting things did occur at the Teatro Español during its short lifespan, although a quick glance at the repertory confirms Vega's critics' dismay at the lack of any real originality in the offerings.[16] These offerings included Moratín's classic *El sí de las niñas*, which played eight times in April and May, and *El viejo y la niña*; Rubí's 1843 *La rueda de la fortuna*, 1844 *Bandera negra*, and 1847 *Borrascas del corazón* (Tempests of the Heart); a number of comedies by Bretón (the 1831 *Marcela, o ¿a cuál de los tres?*, the 1832 translation of *La familia del boticario*, *Muérete ¡y verás* and *Una de tantas* [One of So Many], both from 1837, *Ella es él* [She is He] from 1838, *Pruebas de amor conyugal* [Proofs of Conjugal Love] from 1840 and, finally, an original

---

15 Details of this whole affair are given in David T. Gies, "Grimaldi, Vega y el Teatro Español (1849)," *Actas del X Congreso Internacional de Hispanistas* II (Barcelona: PPU, 1992): 1277–1283. Grimaldi is caricaturized in the issue of 2 July as a fat, fawning, pompous foreigner: "y en cuanto a la ninfa Egeria, el que hubiere encontrado un señor alto, tripón, feo, francés, algo viejo, que hace muchos cumplimientos, que se escucha mucho cuando habla, que se figura ser acá entre nosotros un oráculo, uno de estos hombres papelones y gesteros a lo grave, que de todo entienden, enciclopedias trashumantes y vividores examinadores, que se pase por la comisaría del Teatro Español, y le darán más señas y el hallazgo." *La Ortiga* could be hilarious and cruel: when commenting on Gertrudis Gómez de Avellaneda's *Saúl*, one of whose characters is Jonas (of the whale episode), the newspaper laments that Grimaldi has left the capital since he would be the perfect person to play the whale: "¡Lástima es que no se halle en Madrid la inolvidable Ninfa Egeria! ¡Qué ballena tan admirable! ¡Ni la que cuenta la Escritura!" (*ibid.* p. 216).

16 Michael Schinasi is preparing a study of all plays approved for performance in Spain's theatres in the year 1849, based on a censor's list of some 890 titles. In addition, see his "The Anarchy of Theatrical Genres in Mid-Nineteenth-Century Spain," *Romance Annual* 2 (1990): 534–538.

one-act comedy, *Una ensalada de pollos* [Chicken Salad]); José María Díaz's interesting *Juan sin tierra* (Juan the Landless, printed in 1848) and his *La reina Sara* (Queen Sarah); Gorostiza's old chestnuts, *Contigo pan y cebolla* and *Don Dieguito*; a few *refundiciones* (Lope's *Lo cierto por lo dudoso* and Calderón's *El médico de su honra* [The Physician of His Honour], for example); Vega's now standard *El hombre de mundo*; Hartzenbusch's *Los amantes de Teruel*, and numerous translations. In all, it was an undistinguished and disappointing year with few exceptions.

Rubí's own historical drama, *Isabel la Católica*, was the one resounding success of the season, since it appealed not only to the public taste for action and intrigue, but it also pleased the Queen herself, who heard Rubí read the play before a select audience at the Royal Palace prior to its opening on 24 January 1850, which she also attended. It earned Rubí the Carlos III medal for his contributions to the theatre, a special prize for the best dramatic production of the year, some additional income, and a run of twenty-seven performances, but Smith rightly characterizes it as less a true drama than a "series of striking pictures accompanied by gorgeous pageantry,"[17] that is, more spectacle than literature ("un libro de estampas" ["a book of prints"], in the words of Martínez Olmedilla[18]). It met the needs of a public hungry for confirmation of the glory of Spain and the stability of the monarchy (it was easy to project onto Matilde Díez's performance as Isabel I the aspirations of a nation now led by a second Isabel). Only the sudden illness of Matilde ("La perla de nuestros teatros" ["the pearl of our theatre"]) Díez took it off the stage. Rubí's only other offering was dug up from the year before, a drama called *La trenza de sus cabellos* (Her Braided Hair). Gómez de Avellaneda's original and important *Saúl* ran eight times in late October and early November, 1849, but the flap over the proposed production of her *Baltasar* and the favorable reading – but no production – given to her *Recaredo* underscored the lack of creative thinking on the part of the directors (more on her below).

The other original plays – part of what the Teatro Español had been reorganized to present – were a minor part of the repertory, and decidedly second-rate in quality. They included such titles as *Massaniello* by Gil y Zárate, a high Romantic five-act drama originally written in 1840 but not produced until now because of political difficulties ("incompatibilidad con el momento político"[19] ["incompatibility with the politics of the time"]). It was an interesting play, put on with much pomp and scenic style by the Teatro Español, and it had a respectable run from its debut on 22 February 1850 through the first week of March, but clearly public

[17] Smith, "Rodríguez Rubí," p. 317.
[18] Augusto Martínez Olmedilla, *Anecdotario del siglo XIX* (Madrid: Aguilar, 1957): 380.
[19] *Ibid.* p. 381.

sentiment had shifted between 1840 and 1850, and the intense feelings generated by earlier Romantic plays were attenuated ten years later. As Martínez Olmedilla states, "La obra es de contextura romántica, y el romanticismo pasó. Total: que *Massianelo* se fue al foso"[20] ("The work has a Romantic feel about it, and Romanticism had passed ... Conclusion: *Massianelo* went directly to the grave"). Other original plays included *La madre de San Fernando* (San Fernando's Mother), a four-act play by Cayetano Rosell, which played on 9 March 1850; Antonio Auset's *El lirio entre zarzas* (The Lily Among the Brambles), the three-act comedy which was chosen over Gómez de Avellaneda's *Baltasar* for the 30 April 1850 première; *El lunar de la marquesa* (The Marquesa's Beauty Mark), a four-act comedy by Ceferino Suárez Bravo which appeared on 18 May 1850; and a couple of one-act comedies by Bretón and Enrique Cisneros. None of these offerings produced much enthusiasm in the public, and by the end of the season the theatre's intake had plummeted to 2500–3000 *reales* per day, less than a quarter of what was needed to keep it on a firm financial footing. To trace briefly one of the plays from writing to production will give us a quick overview of the raised hopes generated by the Teatro Español. Cayetano Rosell, a well-known literary figure (author of poetry as well as the historical treatise, *Historia de las revoluciones de España desde la reacción de 1844* [A History of Spanish Revolutions From the Reaction of 1844]) finished writing *La madre de San Fernando*, specifically for presentation at the new theatre, in July, 1849. The following nine items, collected from newspaper accounts,[21] trace the project from its completion through acceptance by the Teatro Español's reading committee, selection of actors, rehearsals, and finally, première; hope and expectation ran high, but the deflating final entry says it all:

Don Cayetano Rosell, conocido escritor, acaba un drama titulado *La madre de San Fernando*, escrito para el teatro Español. (*La Epoca*, 6 July 1849)

Don Cayetano Rosell ha concluido el drama *La madre de San Fernando*, para el teatro Español, del que se hacen los mayores elogios. (*La Nación*, 7 July 1849)

Anteanoche fue leído y aprobado por la junta de lectura del Teatro Español el drama que con el título de *La madre de San Fernando* ha escrito el conocido literato don Cayetano Rosell. (*La España*, 23 September 1849)

La madre de San Fernando, de don Cayetano Rosell, aprobado por la junta de lectura; pronto se pondrá en escena. Los principales papeles: señora Lamadrid (doña Bárbara) y señor Valero. (*La España*, 4 November 1849)

---

[20] *Ibid.*   [21] Simón Díaz, *Veinticuatro diarios* IV, pp. 194–195.

Don Cayetano Rosell, que presentó a la junta de lectura el drama *La madre de San Fernando*, aprobado por ésta, lo verá puesto en escena lo más brevemente posible. Principales papeles: señora Lamadrid (doña Bárbara) y señor Valero. (*La Nación*, 6 November 1849)

La primera función que se pondrá en escena en el Teatro Español después de las de Navidad es el drama nuevo, original y en verso, titulado *La madre de San Fernando*, de cuyo éxito como obra literaria tenemos noticias muy ventajosas. (*La Nación*, 25 December 1849)

El lunes se pondrá por primera vez en escena en el Teatro Español el drama original en verso titulado: *La madre de San Fernando*, del señor don Cayetano Rosell. (*La Epoca*, 4 January 1850)

En el Teatro Español se está ensayando el drama nuevo, original del señor Rosell y en verso titulado *La madre de San Fernando*. (*La Epoca*, 17 February 1850)

Desastroso el drama *La madre de San Fernando*. (*La Nación*, 12 March 1850)

(Cayetano Rosell, a well-known writer, has just completed a drama called *San Fernando's Mother*, written for the Teatro Español. Cayetano Rosell has finished his play *San Fernando's Mother*, for the Teatro Español; they are praising it highly. Last night the Reading Commission of the Teatro Español read and approved the drama entitled *San Fernando's Mother*, written by the well-known author, Cayetano Rosell. *San Fernando's Mother*, by Cayetano Rosell, approved by the Reading Commission will be staged shortly. The principal parts will be played by Mrs. Lamadrid (Barbara) and Mr. Valero. Cayetano Rosell, who presented his play *San Fernando's Mother* to the Reading Commission, and had it approved, will see it on stage very shortly. The principal parts will be played by Mrs. Lamadrid (Barbara) and Mr. Valero. The first play to be performed at the Teatro Español following the Christmas season will be a new, original verse drama entitled *San Fernando's Mother*, which we have heard is quite successful as a literary work. On Monday the original verse drama entitled *San Fernando's Mother*, by Cayetano Rosell, will be performed at the Teatro Español. At the Teatro Español the new, original play in verse by Cayetano Rosell, *San Fernando's Mother*, is in rehearsals. *San Fernando's Mother* was a disaster.)

José María Díaz (1800–1888), a dramatist, journalist (he was an editor at *El Entreacto* with Gil y Zárate, García Gutiérrez, and Mariano Roca de Togores, as well as at the *Revista de Teatros*, *El Clamor Público*, *La Ortiga*, *La Iberia*, and *La Política* during his long career), poet and sometime bureaucrat (after 1868 he worked as secretary to the civil government in Cuba) about whom very little is known, deserves some attention. He had nearly three dozen plays printed and performed in Madrid between the years 1836 and 1877, plays which put forth his semi-Romantic, progressive social policies.[22] Caldera credits him with being the first Spanish dramatist to display concern for more immediacy in the historical drama, beginning with *Felipe II* in 1836: "Inauguraba un proceso de revisión de la historia, de su lectura en clave liberal y a menudo antimonárquica, lo que caracterizará tantas obras de 1837"[23] ("He began a process of historical revisionism, from his liberal and often antimonarchical readings, which would characterize so many works from 1837"). Several of his plays were criticized for their hyper-Romanticism ("abundan escenas de terror" ["scenes of terror abound"] in *Carlos IX y los Hugonotes* [Charles IX and the Huguenots], according to *La Nación*, 19 October 1856, and *La Garnoldi* was "recargada de situaciones fuertes, calcadas sobre la escuela romántica furiosa" ["overwrought with intense situations, based on the furious Romantic school"] in the opinion of *La Discusión*, 1 January 1858) and others were banned outright (*Catilina* in 1858, and *Luz en la sombra* [Light in the Shadow], 1860). Still, his plays, full of lyric moments and rich images, were a constant presence in Madrid for forty years. The play he presented for performance at the Teatro Español caused a controversy, not over technique or content, but rather over payments and author's rights. Since much of the play was inspired, as Díaz himself confessed, on previous versions of the history ("He escrito este drama teniendo muy presente la magnífica tragedia de Shecspeare [*sic*] y la no menos interesante de Ducis" ["I have written this drama with the magnificent tragedy of Shakespeare and the no less interesting tragedy of Ducis in mind"]), the question raised concerned whether he should be paid for an original work, as he demanded, or for a translation. It did echo Shakespeare's *King John* in J. F. Ducis's translation as *Jean sans Terre*,[24] but Díaz managed to add enough original touches in the fourth act to Hispanicize it – "Romanticize" it – and to turn it into a respectable hit. Díaz stuck close to his Romantic credo, particularly in the last act, in which the crazed Constanza, mother of the blinded then murdered royal

---

22 They include: *Elvira de Albornoz* (1836), *Baltasar Cozza* (1839), *Laura* (1839), *Julio César* (1841), *Una reina no conspira* (1844), *Lucio Junio Bruto* (1844), *Jefté* (1845), *Juan sin tierra* (1848), *La reina Sara* (1849), *Últimas horas de un rey* (1849), *Para vencer, querer* (1851), *Andrés Chenier* (1851), *¡Redención!* (1854), *Creo en Dios* (1854), *El justicia de Aragón* (1854), *Las cuatro estaciones* (1854), *Carlos IX y los Hugonotes* (1856), *Catilina* (1856), *La Garnoldi* (1857), *Luz en la sombra* (1860), *Misterios de carnaval* (1860), *La vuelta del presidio* (1860), *Gabriela de Vergy* (1862), *Beltrán* (1862), *Sin familia* (1863), *Virtud y libertinaje* (1863), *Mártir siempre, nunca rey* (1863), *Al año de estar casados* (1864), *El matrimonio de conciencia* (1864), *La muerta en el bosque* (1864), *Páginas de la vida* (1866), *La muérte de César* (1870), and *Trece de febrero* (1877).

23 Caldera and Calderone, "El teatro en el siglo XIX," p. 484.

24 See Alfonso Par, *Representaciones shakespearianas en España* (Madrid: Victoriano Suárez, 1936): 177–184. Par points out that some of Díaz's material also came from Delavigne's *Les enfants d'Edouard*, or Bretón's translation of it (*Los hijos de Eduardo*, 1835).

heir Arturo (played by a woman, Teodora Lamadrid) wanders through "arruinadas galerías" ("ravaged galleries") by moonlight. Lightning periodically underscores the tense atmosphere as Constanza delivers some moving lines about lost happiness, love, and death as Nevil and Hubert force the King to choose between death by dagger or suicide by poison. *Juan sin tierra* had already played at the Príncipe in December 1848 (a respectable eleven times) and several times in the spring of 1849 (as it had in Barcelona at the Teatro Liceo and – simultaneously – at the Teatro Principal), so it was hardly new to the Teatro Español's audience and hence it came and went without much public clamor during the 1849 season.

In all, the hopes generated by the Teatro Español were significantly higher than its accomplishments, but its failure was not just the failure of one theatre. Because of the way the 1847 *Reglamento* was written, the Teatro Español enjoyed more than mere moral superiority and government protection; it dictated the repertories of other theatres and received from them royalties on all plays performed in them. It also dictated name changes for several of the capital's other theatres: the Cruz became the Teatro del Drama and the Instituto became the Teatro de la Comedia. The net effect was that the Teatro Español was seen as a "tiburón que devora a los demás" ("a shark that devours all the other theatres") in the capital and even in the provinces (*El Correo de los Teatros*, 6 April 1851), impeding fair competition and exacting too high a price for its predominance. It forced several theatres into bankruptcy (the Circo and the Variedades both went under during the Teatro Español's period of supremacy). The rise and fall of the enterprise was summed up in *El Correo de los Teatros* (6 April 1851) as a "meteor of calamities":

El teatro de la calle del Príncipe, el Teatro Español, el célebre teatro modelo, ese teatro ergido hace poco para enaltecer nuestra civilización al nivel de las naciones más cultas, ese teatro en el que poetas y actores cifraban sus más bellas esperanzas, sus gratas ilusiones de un porvenir lleno de gloria ... ¡¡no existe ya!! Ha desaparecido después de haber brillado como un meteoro de calamidades.

(The theatre on Príncipe Street, the Teatro Español, the celebrated model theatre, that theatre put up a short time ago in order to bring our civilization up to the level of the most educated nations, that theatre in which poets and actors placed their loveliest hopes, their fond dreams of a glorious future ... no longer exists! It has disappeared after having shone like a meteor of calamities.)

The creation of the Teatro Español should have been the perfect opportunity to stimulate national talent, to put on original Spanish plays, to develop a well-trained acting company, and to claim an honorable place in European theatrical circles, but the ill-will, backbiting, jealousies, insistence on putting on French translations, and lack of vision of the people in charge ensured its collapse. The Teatro Español was doomed to failure from the beginning and its experiment finally came to nothing.

Zorrilla, *Traidor, inconfeso y mártir*

Hovering on the margins of the Teatro Español experiment were other playwrights and plays which for reasons of politics and personalities were never integrated into the new enterprise. By 1849 José Zorrilla was one of the country's most respected poets and dramatists. He had produced a steady stream of highly regarded plays (along with some bombs, it must be admitted) since early in the decade. Audiences particularly loved his two-part *El zapatero y el rey* (1840, 1842) and the short *El puñal del godo* (1843; the 1847 sequel to *El puñal*, entitled *La calentura*, flopped), as well as *Don Juan Tenorio*. The poet was scheduled to debut his new play, *Traidor, inconfeso y mártir* at the Príncipe Theatre in early 1849, but the remodeling being done there forced him to move it to the Cruz, where it opened on 3 March 1849. Zorrilla claims he wrote it at the behest of Julián Romea, who had helped cure him from a long illness and for whom he had never written a play, but conflicts over the performances left Zorrilla with a bitter taste in his mouth: "desde la representación de *Traidor, inconfeso y mártir*, dejé de escribir para el teatro"[25] ("after the debut of *Traidor, inconfeso y mártir*, I stopped writing for the theatre"). John Dowling sees this play as the last true hallmark of Romanticism in Spain, although he observes that "el punto de declinar del drama romántico empieza cinco años antes con la obra más conocida de todas, *Don Juan Tenorio*"[26] ("the point which initiated the decline of Romantic drama began five years previously with the best-known of all the works, *Don Juan Tenorio*"). For Ruiz Ramón it is also the final shot in the Romantic cannon; he calls the protagonist, Gabriel, "al lado de Don Juan y Don Alvaro, el más interesante prototipo del héroe romántico español"[27] ("besides don Juan and don Alvaro, he is the most interesting

---

25 José Zorrilla, *Recuerdos del tiempo viejo*, in *Obras completas* II, p. 1823. "no podía rehusar a Romea una obra que él y un nuevo editor me pedían a un tiempo. Pensé en un argumento, en el cual, sin salirme de mi terrorífico romanticismo, pudiera colocar un personaje característico adecuado a la escuela exclusiva al género personal de representación de Romea; y habiéndome procurado Salustiano Olózaga la causa original de *El pastelero de Madrigal*, amasé, amoldé y emprendí mi *Traidor, inconfeso y mártir*" (pp. 1817–1818).

26 Dowling, "The anti-don Juan," p. 218. Others credit García Gutiérrez's *Juan Lorenzo* (1865) with being one of the last plays in the Romantic canon, although José Escobar cleverly considers it to be "anti-Romantic." "Anti-romanticismo en García Gutiérrez," *Romanticismo* 1 (1982): 83–94.

27 Ruiz Ramón, *Historia del teatro español*, p. 332.

prototype of the Spanish Romantic hero"). Roberto Calvo Sanz, in his recent edition of the play, eschews the label "romantic," referring to it as "la obra paradigmática del drama histórico español en su etapa más tardía ... la obra quizá más perfecta de Zorrilla y la que tiene el mérito de cerrar, magníficamente, un ciclo dramático ya agotado"[28] ("the paradigmatic work of Spanish historical drama in its final stage ... it is perhaps Zorrilla's most perfect work and the one which has the virtue of closing, magnificently, a by-now exhausted dramatic cycle"). Whatever its label, it was Zorrilla's favorite play and one of his most dynamic creations.

Traidor, inconfeso y mártir is both an original work and a *refundición*, since Zorrilla based his play on Jerónimo de Cuéllar's well-known Golden Age comedy, *El pastelero de Madrigal*, which had been in the repertories for years (Dionisio Solís wrote an adaptation of it in 1812 which played frequently in the 1820s and early 1830s[29]), and perhaps on Patricio de la Escosura's novelization of the same theme, *Ni rey ni roque* (Neither the King Nor the Castle, 1835). Zorrilla made substantial changes in the concept and execution of the piece, and even received some significant assistance from his friend, José María Díaz.[30] Gabriel Espinosa displays the characteristics of the Zorrilla-type Romantic hero. He is kind, noble, fair, generous, firm, and mysterious – Zorrilla intended to write something "altamente dramático y profundamente misterioso"[31] ("eminently dramatic and profoundly mysterious") – yet also profoundly religious and serenely Catholic. His religious makeup is of a higher degree than that demanded by the external trappings of the Church, for he rejects the services of a confessor just before his death since a confession would force him to reveal his secret, which he is sworn to guard for both personal and political reasons. When, near the play's end, some of the mystery surrounding him seems on the verge of being cleared up, he responds to don Rodrigo's comment that "Es que a veces hallo en vos / un misterio que me espanta" ("I sometimes find in you a mystery that frightens me") (III, 2) with words which echo those of the repentant don Juan: "Es que tal vez se levanta / tras mí la sombra de Dios" ("Perhaps the shadow of God rises up behind me").

Zorrilla's success in this play comes from his subtle blending of mystery, love, and fear, all expressed in verses of luminous beauty and clarity. Is Gabriel Espinosa really don Sebastián de Portugal or is he merely a humble "pastelero de Madrigal" as he claims? At key moments

---

[28] José Zorrilla, *Traidor, inconfeso y mártir*, ed. Roberto Calvo Sanz (Madrid: Espasa-Calpe, 1990): 33 and 45.

[29] Gies, "Hacia un catálogo," p. 205; Shields, *The Madrid Stage*, p. 820.

[30] Zorrilla himself credited Díaz with "eficaz auxilio" with scenes 5–7 and 10–11 of Act II. See Calvo Sanz, *Traidor*, p. 79.

[31] Zorrilla, *Recuerdos*, p. 1818.

throughout the play Gabriel dangles before his friends and enemies the mysterious "truth" of his background, but he refuses to reveal the historical facts until after his inevitable death. The Romantic language (there is much talk of angels, fate, "sino fatal," Satan, prisons, and other images popularized in the previous fifteen or so years), the soaring musicality of the verses, the dramatic tension, the passionate yet tender love scenes between Gabriel and his "daughter" Aurora, and the final *Conjuración de Venecia/El trovador*-like revelation scene place the play squarely in the Romantic cosmos, but, as Dowling and Calvo Sanz suggest, too late to have any impact on the development of theatrical taste in the nineteenth century. The second half of the century belonged not to Zorrilla and company, but to the men and women who looked forward to contemporary society, not backward to an older, lamented Spain.

5 "This woman is quite a man!": women and the theatre (1838–1900)

It may surprise us to read "men **and women**" in the previous chapter, since we have not yet focused any attention on women.[1] Nor, of course, did the literary world of nineteenth-century Spain. As Simón Palmer has noted, "Un hecho evidente es que la sociedad española del siglo XIX e incluso de los primeros años del XX, no acepta a la mujer que escribe y lo más que llega es a perdonarla el que haga obras consagradas a temas insustanciales y dentro de la órbita familiar"[2] ("It is evident that Spanish society in the nineteenth century, and even in the first years of the twentieth century, does not accept women who write, and the closest it comes is to forgive her if she writes works on inane matters and within the family orbit"). Women were in general excluded from the theatre, except as actresses, although several did manage to break through the wall of silence which enclosed them to present translated works or, in the second half of the century, original plays to audiences in Madrid, Sevilla, Granada, Barcelona, and Palma de Mallorca.

From mid-century on, following in the footsteps of Gómez de Avellaneda, several women dramatists carved out small reputations for themselves in the capital or in the provinces. Among them we can count Rosario de Acuña, Julia de Asensi, Camila Calderón (pseudonym of Purificación Llobet), Emilia Calé, Isabel Cheix Martínez (who wrote under the masculine pseudonym of Martín Avila), Pastora Echegaray de González (known as Jorge Lacosta), Rosa de Eguílaz y Renart, Joaquina García Balmaseda, María Gertrudis Garecabe, Enriqueta Lozano de Vilchez, Elisa de Luxán de García Dana, Angela Martínez de Lafuente, Isabel María Morón, Adelaida Muñiz y Mas, Emilia Pardo Bazán, Rosa Pic de Aldawala, Natividad de Rojas, Josefa Rovirosa de Torrentes,

---

[1] Very little serious work on women dramatists has been done, although slowly this lack of attention is being remedied. While much has been published on Gómez de Avellaneda, she inexplicably receives only four slight references in the rich and important *Historia del teatro en España* II (ed. Díez Borque).

[2] María del Carmen Simón Palmer, "Mil escritoras españolas del siglo XIX," in *Crítica y ficción literaria: Mujeres españolas contemporáneas*, eds. Aurora López and María Angeles Pastor, (Granada: n.p., 1989): 44.

Faustina Sáez de Melgar, and Mercedes Velilla y Rodríguez. Many of these women wrote works which were published but never staged. They do not provide us with a unified voice, "feminine" or otherwise, nor were they writing as a group, drawing on one another for inspiration or support. Rather, they frequently wrote in isolation (with or without "a room of their own") and in a wide variety of styles with equally diverse concerns and levels of success. Often, their plays were in minor genres – one-act sainetes, zarzuelas, "juguetes cómicos," etc. – or performed/ published outside of the capital, limiting thereby their impact on the mainstream of theatre activity in Madrid. The political and social shift of the Restauración in the mid-1870s seemed to provide a climate more accepting of women playwrights than earlier decades; hence, the increase in activity in the last third of the century over that of the first two thirds. As Cristina Enríquez de Salamanca has stated, the "fiebre literaria" ("literary fever") of the second half of the century, when editorial houses discovered the business potential of the novel, swept women into its realm as well.[3] Withal, women as playwrights were numerous and active (although less so than in other genres), and deserve our attention if for no other reason than their having been so completely excommunicated from standard literary and theatrical histories.[4]

Many of these women published their work in the provinces. While little information is available about performances of some of their plays (if indeed they were ever performed), we do know that editions of them were printed with some regularity. The following listing will give us a rapid overview of this activity. Manuela Cambronero enjoyed substantial success in Valladolid in 1842 with her play *Safira* ("el éxito ha sido brillante" ["it was a brilliant success"] according to the *Revista de Teatros*, which reviewed it on 1 February 1842). Trinidad Aceves published *El novio de la niña* (The Girl's Boyfriend), a one-act "juguete cómico" in Sevilla in 1871. Isabel Cheix Martínez published *La adoración de los reyes* (The Adoration of the Magi) and *Magdalena*, both one-act religious plays for children, in Sevilla in 1896. Enriqueta Lozano de Vilchez was active in her native Granada, where she published at least a half dozen one-, three-, and four-act plays, including *Una actriz por amor* (An Actress for the Love of It) in 1847, *Dios es el Rey de los Reyes* (God is

---

3 Cristina Enríquez de Salamanca, "¿Quién era la escritora del siglo XIX?" *Letras Peninsulares* 2 (1989): 81.
4 Gómez de Avellaneda is the only woman dramatist mentioned in Díez Borque, *Historia del teatro en España*, II. Surprisingly, only Acuña, García Balmaseda, Echegaray, and Silva are included in Caroline Galerstein, ed., *Women Writers of Spain: An Annotated Bibliography* (New York: Greenwood Press, 1986). María del Carmen Simón Palmer has provided much solid bibliographical information in her recent *Escritoras españolas del siglo XIX: Manual bio-bibliográfico* (Madrid: Castalia, 1991).

the King of Kings) in 1852, *Don Juan de Austria* and *María o la abnega-ción* (María, or Self-Denial) in 1854, *La ruina del hogar* (The Downfall of Hearth and Home) in 1873, and *La primera duda* (The First Doubt, date unknown). In Barcelona and Palma de Mallorca Angelina Martínez de Lafuente published *Misterios del corazón* (Mysteries of the Heart, 1865) and *El cura de Son Rapiña* (The Priest from Son Rapiña, 1868), the first a five-act drama which had its première in February 1865 and the second a one-act comedy performed in February 1868. Rosa Pic de Aldawala also published (and premièred) her one-act "joguina" in Catalán in Barcelona on 12 March 1877; it was called *Com sucsuheix moltas vegadas* (As It Often Happens). Josefa Rovirosa de Torrentes published *Lorenza* in Barcelona as early as 1845, while Mercedes Velilla y Rodríguez published her short *El vencedor de sí mismo* (Defeated by Himself) in Sevilla in 1876 and another short piece, *¡Noche buena!* (Good Night!) in Barcelona in 1895. All of the others published – and sometimes staged – their works in Madrid.

Gertrudis Gómez de Avellaneda – referred to by Hartzenbusch, appar-ently in an admiring way (!), as "mucho hombre"[5] ("quite a man") – made a brief appearance during our discussion of the rise and fall of the Teatro Español, and we shall begin a quick look at women dramatists with her.

Gertrudis Gómez de Avellaneda

Gómez de Avellaneda (1814–1873), clearly the best-known woman dramatist of the Spanish nineteenth century, came to the attention of the Madrid theatre-going public when her *Munio Alfonso* was staged in 1844 (*Leoncia*, her first play, was staged in Seville in 1840 before she moved to the capital).[6] She was already appreciated as a poet (*Poesías*, 1841) and novelist (*Sab*, 1841, and *Dos mujeres* [Two Women], 1842), but her incursions onto the stage were to have a more immediate impact. Hugh A. Harter has even suggested that "while Tula's reputation has subsisted through her lyrical poetry, it might well be argued that her renown should rest instead on her dramatic creativity."[7] Between 1840 and 1858 she wrote sixteen full-length plays (plus several shorter pieces), matching in productivity and creativity many of her male counterparts, and frequently surpassing them in popular reception. Zorrilla remembered her as "una

---

[5] Cited by Martínez Olmedilla, *Anecdotario*, p. 380. Typically, Martínez Olmedilla gives most of the credit for Gómez de Avellaneda's talent and success to Juan Nicasio Gallego, the extraordinary man "detrás de esta mujer excepcional."

[6] See Félix Menchacatorre, "Una tragedia del romanticismo ecléctico: *Munio Alfonso*, de la Avellaneda," *Revista Iberoamericana* 51 (1985): 823–830.

[7] Hugh A. Harter, *Gertrudis Gómez de Avellaneda* (Boston: Twayne, 1981): 78.

de estas lumíneas, poéticas y celestes apariciones" ("one of these luminous, poetical, and heavenly visions") who nevertheless challenged the
theatrical *status quo* with works of a determined and original nature, yet
even he, typical of his era and his orientation, could not resist couching
his description of her in masculine terms: her poems contained "pensamientos varoniles" ("manly thoughts") which revealed "algo viril y fuerte
en el espíritu encerrado dentro de aquella voluptuosa encarnación mujer-
il"[8] ("something manly and strong in a spirit locked inside that volup-
tuous womanly flesh").

Gómez de Avellaneda developed a genre of plays which might be
characterized as religious Romanticism. These were dramas which drew
heavily upon the Romantic motifs dominant in the plays of the mid-
thirties and early forties, but embedded in a construct which highlighted
not angst but religious sentiment. Such plays would naturally have been
inconceivable without the example of Zorrilla, particularly in his *Don
Juan Tenorio*. No fewer than five of her original plays were staged in
Madrid in 1852 alone, just three years following the debut of her biblical
tragedy *Saúl* on 29 October 1849. This was one of the few undeniable
triumphs of the problem-ridden Teatro Español, which she understood to
be a potentially important focus for theatrical renovation at mid-century.
In 1849 she wrote to Vega expressing her views on the need to guard
against inept censorship and to defend the dignity of the writer.

¿Conque andan VV. en arreglo de Teatros? ¡Ay Vega!, en nombre del cielo que no
establezcan VV. junta de censura en que figuren Cazurros y otros entes semejan-
tes. No permita V. que se humille tanto a los pobres poetas que para darles el
derecho de ser juzgados por el público hayan de someterse antes a ser juzgados
por malos poetastros y ruines folletinistas. Aquí donde estoy, apartada de las
intrigas que se agitarán en todo momento cerca de VV.; aquí en mi retiro modesto,
donde trabajo sin ambición, y donde pido al cielo por nuestra pobre literatura,
levanto mi voz para encargar a V., para suplicarle mire por ella y por su decoro.
Para mí nada pido, pero pido altamente por la dignidad del poeta. Si se estableise
una junta censora como la que hubo últimamente en la que al lado de nombres
respetables se permitieron colocar los de Cazurro y no sé cuántos aún más
oscuros, por mi parte quedaré excluída del teatro; quedaré condenada a quemar
mis dramas, porque jamás los sujetaré a la censura de un comité semejante. No me
desdeño de ser poeta ni de confesar que necesito del producto de mis trabajos;
pero no me desdeño, porque antes moriría de hambre que degradar lo más
mínimo la dignidad en que mi concepto alcanza la poesía; porque antes inutiliza-
ría mi talento que rebajar mi carácter.[9]

---

[8] Zorrilla, *Recuerdos*, p. 2051. He continued: " ... era una mujer; pero lo era sin duda por
un error de la naturaleza, que había metido por distracción una alma de hombre en
aquella envoltura de carne femenina"; *ibid.* p. 2052.

[9] Pilar Lozano Guirao, "El archivo epistolar de don Ventura de la Vega," *Revista de
Literatura* 13 (1958): 136.

(So, you're working on organizing the theatres? Oh, Vega! In the name of Heaven do not create a Censorship Board on which people like Cazurro might serve. Do not humiliate poor poets who, in order to be given the right to put their works up for public scrutiny, must first submit them to be judged by rotten versifiers and decrepit scribblers. From where I am, far from the intrigues that are always going on near you, here in my modest retirement, where I work without ambition, and where I pray to Heaven for our poor literature, I raise my voice to charge you, to beg you to look out for it and for its honor. I ask nothing for myself, but I ask a lot for the dignity of the poet. If a censorship board is created like the last one on which, alongside respectable names, there appeared others like Cazurro and I don't know how many other lesser-known ones, I shall stay away from the theatre. I will be condemned to burn my plays, because I will never subject them to the censorship of such a panel. I am not loathe to call myself a poet nor to confess that I need the money that my works produce; but I would die of hunger before debasing in the slightest the dignity which poetry has for me, and I would stop using my talent before I would bring down my reputation.)

The strength of these words is indicative of the intelligence and power of the author. She defended without compromise the rights of authors (and of women authors in particular) and the right to freedom of expression. She would be sorely disappointed with the Teatro Español a year later when the reader's committee passed over her *Recaredo*, but for now the enterprise seemed promising and she delivered *Saúl* to Vega. Other disappointments and snubs came later, including the bitter controversy initiated by her request to be admitted to the all-male Real Academia Española, which, notwithstanding the views of writers like Zorrilla that she was some type of male artist trapped in a female body, was turned down solely because of her sex. She was therefore doubly marginalized (she was an "outsider" from the colonies in Cuba as well as a woman), struggling for intellectual independence in a society run by white men: a "pioneering literary woman [who] boldly entered a territory hostile to women," in Susan Kirkpatrick's phrase.[10]

The original version of *Saúl* was penned in 1844 but not performed at the time, despite plans for its opening in Paris. It was read before an appreciative audience at the recently-formed Liceo Artístico y Científico, but it was not until 1849 that it received the deluxe production desired by the author. And a deluxe production it was: the Teatro Español commissioned four impressive new decorations for it (all so spectacular that they were given an ovation the night of the *estreno*), populated it with all the characters written in by Gertrudis – which included some 150 people in

[10] Susan Kirkpatrick, *Las románticas*, p. 133. Kirkpatrick focuses her attention on Gómez de Avellaneda's novels and poetry, where autobiography intersects with her writing more than in the dramas. See also Nelly E. Santos, "Las ideas feministas de Gertrudis Gómez de Avellaneda," in *Homenaje a Gertrudis Gómez de Avellaneda*, eds. Gladys Zaldívar and Rosa Martínez de Cabrera (Miami: Ediciones Universal, 1981): 132–141.

the first scene alone – and spent, according to the carping review published by Vega's enemies in *La Ortiga* (4 November 1849), some 40,000 *reales* on the production. Advanced notice claimed it to be "infinitamente superior a cuanto hasta ahora se ha representado en el Teatro Español" ("infinitely superior to everything that has been performed at the Teatro Español up to this time") (*La España*, 26 October 1849). Yet its success did not come solely from the external trappings. On the contrary, Gómez de Avellaneda, drawing from previous treatments of the biblical theme (Alfieri and Soumet, according to Cotarelo[11]), created a series of believable characters who inhabited, as she saw them, a "drama real" rather than "una creación."[12] It is a rich play, crammed with ideas and conflicts over pride, free will, spiritual independence, envy, temporal versus ecclesiastical power, arrogance, love, filial obedience, and friendship, all sustained by a consistent use of heroic *romance* verse (eleven syllables with assonantal rhyme). Romantic images and themes abound in all four acts. She populates the play with types and images from Romantic theatre – the tyrant, the use of predictions, the talk of fate, the belief in the strength of love, the use of supernatural shadows and raptures, the father who mistakenly kills his own son, the suicide of the main character) – yet uses them solely as a scrim on which to paint a strong religious and moral message. Saul is a tragic figure, a supremely proud man whose belief in his own strength and knowledge proves to be his undoing. His conflicting allegiances and impassioned emotions underscore his betrayal of God's divine justice, and he is reduced to nothing when he discovers that in haste he has mistakenly killed his own son Jonathan. Crushed, he takes his own life, yet the audience is left with both the catharsis of tragedy and the hope of a bright future for David who will now inherit the throne of Israel (as predicted from the beginning).

While searching for an original voice, Tula (as Gertrudis was known among her friends) did not neglect theatrical history. She drew upon the Romantic playwrights' experiments with historical drama and emotional brinksmanship ("¡Al borde estoy de una profunda sima! / ¡Es el sepulcro de una estirpe entera!" ["I am on the edge of a deep abyss! It is the grave of an entire race!"] wails Saul [IV, 10]), as well as from the popular *comedias de magia* ("La roca se derrumba a pedazos, y aparece la sombra del profeta. Saúl cae de rodillas y su interlocutora desaparece por entre los riscos" ["The cliff comes crashing down in pieces, and the shadow of the prophet appears. Saul falls to his knees and his interlocutor disappears among the rocks"] [IV, 7]). The musical interludes, standard in most Spanish plays of the time, were well integrated in order to advance

---

[11] Emilio Cotarelo y Mori, *La Avellaneda y sus obras* (Madrid: Olózaga, 1930): 176.
[12] *Ibid.* p. 177.

the plot as well as entertain the audience.[13] Still, as a woman who refused "to conform to the restrictive norms of middle-class femininity,"[14] she wrote into this play (and others) interesting female characters who also refused to be neutralized by the powerful men around them. In *Saúl*, it is Micol who is given the role of running interference between a father careening toward tragic destruction, and a lover charged with defending his people. She sides with David, even when the prophecy reveals that it is this humble shepherd who will unseat the great king Saul. When forced to choose between love and filial obedience, she chooses the former, which ironically becomes one of the causes of the tragic dénouement. Yet her choice is not just an emotional one since she sees that justice will be served by her support of David against her father.[15] The result of this mixture of dramatized history, biblical story, feminism, the religious strain in Romanticism, and tragedy is a powerful and well-crafted play, of which the author was justifiably proud:

Mi última tragedia ha hecho mucho ruido; se ha dicho mucho bien y mucho mal de ella, que es lo bastante para darle celebridad. Se han gastado gruesas sumas en ponerla en escena; augustas distinciones la han favorecido; severos críticos la han encomiado; un público ávido y curioso ha llenado el teatro largo tiempo. En fin, ha sido un suceso teatral que me ha puesto más en evidencia que lo estaba ya. He sido colmada de lisonjas en bailes de altas regiones, en saraos particulares; en todas partes.[16]

(My last tragedy made a lot of noise; a lot of good and bad things have been said about it, which is enough to give it some celebrity. Considerable sums of money have been spent in putting it on stage, some notable honors have been accorded it, harsh critics have praised it, and a curious and enthusiastic public has filled the theatre for quite a while. In sum, it has been a theatrical success which has made me more noticeable than I was before. I have been showered with praise at very tony dances and at private soirées; everywhere.)

On 21 October 1852 Tula staged another hit ("estrepitosamente aplau-dida" ["wildly applauded"] according to the next day's *La Esperanza*) at the Príncipe Theatre, this time a three-act verse comedy called *La hija de*

---

[13] It was not always easy to find actors equipped to act and sing. Recognizing this, the author appended the following note to the end of Act I: "En la ejecución puede cantarse sólo la primera cuarteta, bajando el telón mientras tanto. El arpa deberá colocarse de modo que pueda parecer que es David quien canta, aunque lo haga otro, oculto cerca de él, toda vez que no es fácil que el actor encargado del papel del rey profeta posea también el talento musical." *Obras de Gertrudis Gómez de Avellaneda* II, ed. José María Castro y Calvo (Madrid: Atlas, 1978) (BAE 278): 234.

[14] Kirkpatrick, *Las románticas*, pp. 206–207.

[15] This leads Enrique Laguerra, in a rather superficial article on "La mujer en las tragedias de Gertrudis Gómez de Avellaneda," to conclude that "la Avellaneda parece defender los derechos de la mujer en las circunstancias de Micol." Zaldívar and Martínez de Cabrera, *Homenaje a Gertrudis Gómez de Avellaneda*, p. 195. A more coherent appreciation of Avellaneda's work is to be found in Beth Miller, "Gertrudis the Great."

[16] Cotarelo, *La Avellaneda*, p. 183.

las flores (The Daughter of the Flowers). As she had done with the Romantic ethos in *Saúl* (and which will become even more evident in *Baltasar*), in this play she once again inverts an accepted pattern and plays against her audiences' expectations. The play which she turns on its head in *La hija de las flores* is none other than Moratín's venerable *El sí de las niñas*, which had been a constant in the repertory for years, but now recast with Tula's "feminist" twist. The old man-young girl marriage arranged by an ambitious mother has been converted into an old woman-young man situation arranged by a father and uncle. The marriage between 23–year-old Luis, the nephew of the Count of Mondragón, and 36–year-old Inés, the daughter of the Baron of X, has been arranged by the men for their convenience (the Baron wants grandchildren, the Count wants to ensure that his nephew finds a companion). The problem is that the engaged couple has never met and that neither wants the wedding to proceed; they do wed only out of a sense of filial obedience. Gómez de Avellaneda's ingenuity comes from her "hermosa creación fantástica" ("lovely fanciful creation") (*La Epoca*, 22 October 1852) – appropriately named Flora – who so strongly identifies with the flowers in the garden where she lives that she "becomes" a flower. Flora *is* a flower, not only in her own mind (she uses the first person plural when speaking of the flowers) and in name but also by virtue of a birthmark in the shape of a *fleur de lis* which she bears on her shoulder. She is thought to be an orphan taken in by Tomasa and Juan, the Baron's housemaid and gardener, but she lives among the flowers of their garden and finds solace and companionship among them. In the end she is revealed of course to be the daughter of Inés, who was raped years ago and abandoned by her violator (revealed to be the Count). The baby was thought to have died, but instead was rescued by Inés's companion Beatriz and raised in secret.

The play is not so much anti-Romantic as non-Romantic; that is, middle-class values dominate instead of unstructured emotion. Tula creates moments in the play which might have led a decade earlier to a Romantic tragedy (Luis complains, "¡Mi ventura! ... ¡Oh Dios! ... ¡paciencia! / ¿Hay bien, hay dicha en el mundo? / ¡Todo es amargo e inmundo / en esta infausta existencia!" ["My happiness! Oh, God! Patience! Is there any luck, and joy in the world? Everything is bitter and rotten in this accursed existence!"] [I, 5]) but diverts the moment instead down a pleasantly bourgeois path. Luis and Inés are concerned with the force exerted by society's view of them (as are their elders), and neither wants to risk condemnation or disapproval by breaking the pre-arranged marriage promise. Even more tellingly, when Flora suggests that she and Luis run away and get married, he responds with words unimaginable in the mouth of a Romantic hero,

Mas ¿cómo vivir los dos
solos, pobres, desvalidos,
por ese mundo perdidos?

...

    mas deberes
tienen los hombres honrados
y hay compromisos sagrados
que hoy impiden lo que quieres.   (II, 5)

(But how can the two of us live alone, poor, destitute, lost in the world? ... but honorable men have duties and there are sacred obligations that prohibit us from doing what you want today.)

In the manner of Golden Age comedies, harmony is restored in the end by dual marriages (Flora and Luis, the Count and Inés). Tula, aided by the strong acting of stars like Julián Romea (who played the Count), at the height of his fame during these years, and the ever-popular Antonio Guzmán (as Inés's father), proved that she could achieve success with comedy as well as with tragedy. Appropriately, hundreds of flowers ("una lluvia de flores" ["a shower of flowers"] *La España*, 24 October 1852) rained down on the stage following the first performance. For Cotarelo, echoing nearly all of the critics of the play, this charming – and today unfortunately forgotten – comedy places the author squarely "entre nuestros primeros poetas"[17] ("among the our first-rank poets").

Religious concerns and tragic outcomes are striking notes in many of her dramatic works. *Baltasar*, perhaps her most successful play, draws upon both elements to tell a grand story of the fall of a corrupt empire. It was staged by the actor/impresario José Valero at the Novedades Theatre on 9 April 1858, although she had begun writing it in 1852 and had read it to a group of intellectuals and writers four years later. It replayed at the Circo Theatre at the beginning of the 1859–1860 season, before moving to the Teatro Principal in Barcelona. In the figure of a woman, Elda, Gómez de Avellaneda captures "la primera revelación de la dignidad humana"[18] ("the first glimmer of human dignity") through whom a vain and egotistical tyrant will learn – too late – the power of virtuous conduct. Baltasar, the despotic central character, discovers faith and love in his final moments and only at his death is he granted divine clemency (this note reminds us of the death of Zorrilla's don Juan). As the author explains in her impassioned prologue,

Joaquín extiende sus manos sobre la cabeza del sacrílego moribundo, perdonándole en nombre del Dios de Abraham, del Dios único, universal ... y resonando todavía aquellos ecos de misericordia sobre la tumba del escéptico – que proclama

---

[17] *Ibid.* p. 234.   [18] Prologue to *Baltasar*, in *Obras* II, p. 193.

en su último suspiro la justicia de Dios y la dignidad del hombre – se alza el inspirado acento del profeta, anunciando entre las ruinas de la civilización arrollada por el soplo divino, la libertad del pueblo escogido y la reedificación del templo en que será promulgada la nueva ley de gracia, que, rompiendo las cadenas de los pueblos y disipando las sombras de la idolotría, hará santa la potestad y gloriosa la obediencia.[19]

(Joaquín places his hands over the head of the dying man, pardoning him in the name of the God of Abraham, the only, universal God ... and with the sounds of mercy still echoing over the tomb of the non-believer – who proclaims in his last breath God's justice and man's dignity – the animated voice of the prophet rises up, announcing among the ruins of a civilization brought down by a divine condemnation, the freedom of the chosen people and the rebuilding of the temple in which the new law of grace will be put forth, which, breaking the chains of the people and scattering the shadows of idolatry, will make his jurisdiction holy and obedience a glorious thing.)

This is not really a biblical play, nor a strictly historical one since only three of the characters in it come from history. The majority of the work is fiction, imagined action, and artistic creation, and therein lies its strength.

Baltasar, king of Babylonia, has lost all interest in life and glory since everything comes too easy to him. "¿Qué sufres?" ("What's the matter with you?") asks his mother Nitocris. "¡La existencia!" ("Existence!") is Baltasar's significant answer (II, 4). He has it all, and is consequently unmotivated to seek more success or riches. He uses the Romantic term "fastidio"[20] ("fatigue") to characterize his dismay.

> Si quieres vencer
> este infecundo fastidio,
> contra el cual en balde lidio,
> porque se encarna en mi ser,
> ¡muéstrame un bien soberano,
> que el alma deba admirar! ...
> que yo no pueda alcanzar
> con sólo extender la mano.
> ¡Dame – no importa a qué precio –
> alguna grande pasión,
> que llene un gran corazón,
> que sólo abriga desprecio!   (II, 4)

[19] *Ibid.* pp. 193–194.
[20] Russell P. Sebold has shown how "fastidio universal" was Meléndez Valdés's way of characterizing Romantic angst. "Sobre el nombre español del dolor romántico," in *El rapto de la mente. Poética y poesía dieciochescas*, 2nd. edn. (Barcelona: Anthropos, 1989): 157–169.

(If you want me to overcome this sterile fatigue, against which is it useless for me to fight because it is deeply rooted in my very being, show me something truly good, something worthy of admiration! ... Something that I cannot have by just reaching out for it. Give me, at whatever price, a grand passion that might fill up the heart which now is filled only with disdain!)

Tula repeatedly draws on such Romantic moments to build the tension in her play. She places her characters in physical and metaphysical prisons and chains, likens them to angels or tyrants, uses prophecies to move the plot forward, and sets up love and vengeance as the two dominant emotions in conflict. What moves the play out of the Romantic cosmos, however, is her insistence on salvation. Baltasar, like don Juan, is saved by the love of a woman. In the former's case, he discovers that the feelings Elda has stirred in him save him from his own spiritual obliteration (even though the love is not requited) and enable him finally to understand the words spoken to him by Elda's father Joaquín (words which echo those of don Juan in II, iii, 2):

> ¡Hay ese Dios, que tú niegas,
> de los señores Señor,
> ante el cual el rey y el siervo
> iguales, hermanos son,
> y a su justicia suprema
> contra ti se alza mi voz!   (IV, 8)

(There exists that God, which you deny, the Lord of Lords, before whom the king and the servant become equals, become brothers, and my voice rises up against you to his supreme justice!)

As befits the tragic conception of the play, Baltasar dies at the hands of the people in order to pave the way for a more benevolent reign of believers, but not before being pardoned for his sins by Joaquín ("nuestra santa religión / hace un deber del perdón" ["Our holy religion makes forgiveness a duty"] [IV, 12]) and seeking his own spiritual salvation by recognizing the one true God:

> Ese Dios ... ¡Madre! ... yo muero ...
> ¡Mas la verdad resplandece! ...
> El Dios que al hombre engrandece ...
> ese ... ese es el verdadero!   (IV, 12)

(That God ... Mother! ... I am dying ... But the truth is shining through! ... The God who exalts man ... that one ... that one is the true God!)

One of the most striking innovations in Gómez de Avellaneda's theatre is the powerful role she frequently writes for her principal female character. Unlike the often-retiring heroines of Romantic plays,[21] who live in the shadows of their male counterparts and are as often as not instruments of his (or God's) wishes, Gómez de Avellaneda creates determined, stubborn, opinionated women who, until overwhelmed by forces beyond their purview, are manifestly in control of their lives. Nowhere is this more evident than in *Baltasar*, where Elda's audacity not only lends her dimension but also precipitates the king's reawakening to emotion (in a delicious inversion of the standard response, it is the man Rubén, Elda's beloved, who cries [I, 7] and it is Joaquín, her father, who faints [I, 8]). Few women, threatened as Elda is by the vengeance of a king set on destroying her people, have talked with such force in a Spanish play to date:

ELDA.	¡Que en la infausta soledad es el llanto nuestro acento ... y alas no halla el pensamiento en donde no hay libertad! ...
NIT.	El rey te escucha.
BALT.	Y te manda cantar.
ELDA.	¡No! ¡No puedo obedecer! ... ¡Mi pueblo gime, señora, bajo atroz yugo! ... ¡No hay en el mundo cadenas que rindan la voluntad! ...
BALT.	Y su padre, que está preso, ¿qué crimen ha cometido?
ELDA.	El defender su corona, que el tuyo abatió tirano. (II, 4)
(ELDA.	Our voice in the accursed solitude becomes a flood of tears ... and thought cannot take wing where freedom does not exist!
NIT.	The king is listening to you.
BALT.	And he orders you to sing.
ELDA.	No! I cannot obey! ... My countrymen moan, ma'am, beneath a cruel yoke! ... There are

---

[21] There are exceptions, of course, but none of the Romantic heroines reaches the level of independence and aggression accorded them by Tula. Even Leonor, in *El trovador*, who proclaims her independence by poisoning herself rather than submitting to an unwanted marriage, faints as Manrique takes her out of the convent (III, 5).

	no chains in the world that can subdue one's will-power! ...
BALT.	And your father, who is imprisoned, What crime has he committed?
ELDA.	The crime of defending the throne which yours took from him despotically.)

Finally, however, Elda reverts to type and joins her sisters in the typical Romantic fate: delirium or death (she goes crazy in a scene judged excessive by the actress scheduled to play it and consequently shortened in the performances[22]). What this means, of course, is a return to a fully providentialist world view which rejects the radical rebelliousness of Romanticism yet again.

The play's popularity is understandable and well-deserved. It ran for more than fifty performances and received nearly unanimous praise from the critics, an unheard-of triumph for a serious play. Within ten years it was achieving similar success in Mexico. Gómez de Avellaneda handles the characterizations, dramatic tension, entrances and exits, verse and meter, and crescendos of interest with superb skill, and provides a stirring religious message in which good triumphs over evil. In addition, she weaves elements from Spain's theatrical past (Romanticism, historical drama, magical plays) into her work while inverting the standard Romantic paradigms.

Gertrudis Gómez de Avellaneda was the first in a short but distinguished line of female dramatists in nineteenth-century Spain. The male-dominated theatre world was a closed shop into which women were admitted with real reluctance. Many of the authors we will discuss below made entry into the theatre only with the help of husbands (often collaborators) or, in some cases, only under the guise of masculine pseudonyms. Little scholarly work has been carried out on these women, who await a full study of their achievements.

One of the few woman writers active in the theatre before the arrival of Gómez de Avellaneda was Joaquina Vera, a minor actress (she performed in Bretón's *Una vieja* [An Old Lady] in 1844) who produced a steady stream of plays "arregladas" ("arranged") or translated "libremente" from the French which were published in Madrid from the late

---

[22] In notes placed in the printed versions, Gómez de Avellaneda defended Elda's behavior as not just "un simple delirio, sino una intuición misteriosa de la grande y próxima catástrofe," but recognized that "Todos los versos señalados con comillas al margen se suprimieron en la representación por parecer largo el delirio de Elda a la actriz que desempeñaba el papel de ésta " (IV, 6). The actress in question was a young woman named Rodríguez, no relation as far as we know, to Grimaldi's wife Concepción Rodríguez, who was now living in Paris.

1830s on. Few, however, were produced. The only production notice we have is of a translated *sainete* called *El disfraz* (The Disguise), which appeared just once at the Teatro Variedades on 24 October 1847.[23] Her earliest and most extensive translation was *Elisa, o el precipicio de Bessac* (Elisa, or the Destruction of Bessac), a five-act drama published in Madrid in 1839 and again in 1844, but most of her works were one-act comedies (*Toma y daca, o que se queje aquel que pierda* [Give and Take, or Let He Who Loses Complain], 1840; *Dos amos para un criado* [Two Masters for a Servant], 1844; *Cuando se acaba el amor* [When Love Ends], 1844; *De España a Francia o una noche en Vitoria* [From Spain to France or a Night in Vitoria], 1858; *En todas partes hay de todo* [Everything Everywhere], 1858; *¿Quién es su madre?* [Who is Her Mother?], 1873). Notwithstanding her early presence in the theatrical world, little notice was taken of her (she is mentioned just twice in the newspapers of the day[24]) and little is known of her today, although the *Revista de Teatros* did condescend to praise her talents, uncommon in "muchas personas de su sexo":

Hemos tenido el gusto de leer la piececita en un acto *Dos amos para un criado*, traducida libremente del francés por la señorita doña Joaquina Vera, y que habrá de representarse un día de estos en el teatro del Circo: la corrección del lenguaje, la ligereza y gracia del diálogo, la sencillez del plan, y lo bien arreglada que está a nuestro teatro son clara muestra de las buenas dotes que adornan a esta señorita, dotes que la colocan en una línea adonde no llegarán muchas personas de su sexo. (28 August 1844)

(We have had the pleasure of reading the little one-act piece *Dos amos para un criado*, translated freely from the French by Miss Joaquina Vera, and which will be performed at the Circo Theatre one of these days soon. The correctness of the language, the lightness and grace of the dialogue, the simplicity of the plot, and the excellence of the adaptation to our theatre are clear signs that this young woman is blessed with good skills, skills which place her in a class to which not many people of her sex belong.)

Carolina Coronado (1823–1911), who began to make a name for herself as a poet in the early 1840s,[25] tried her hand at drama during the 1840s as well, producing *Alfonso el León* in Badajoz in late 1844 (reported

---

[23] Herrero Salgado, *Cartelera*, p. 51. *Dos amos para un criado* may have been performed at the Teatro del Circo in late 1844.

[24] The *Diario de Avisos* gave notice of her *Dos amos para un criado*, *Toma y daca*, and *Elisa o el precipicio de Bressac*, "comedias traducidas del francés por la señorita Joaquina Vera" (30 August 1844).

[25] See "Waterflower: Carolina Coronado's Lyrical Self-Representation," in Kirkpatrick, *Las románticas*, pp. 208–243.

in the *Revista de Teatros*, 19 December 1844). She had hoped to move it to Madrid, but it never received a production there. Instead, *El cuadro de la esperanza* (The Picture of Hope) was performed at the Liceo Artístico in 1848, with little success, and of another play, *El divino Figueroa* (The Divine Figueroa), all that remains is the title. She was unable to transfer into theatrical form the gracious and delicate poetry she had become famous for creating, and wisely concentrated her energies on the latter.[26]

Rosario de Acuña

We shall focus here only on the most prolific or interesting of the group, although a deeper study of the productions of women dramatists in nineteenth-century Spain is essential if we are to grasp the full complexity of theatrical activity during that time. It would be attractive to posit a unified "feminist" voice in their writings, discover embryonic impulses of modern-day feminism or rejection of stifled aspirations, but the reality of their writing is more diverse than such a scheme suggests and consequently more interesting. One of the most successful of the women dramatists was Rosario de Acuña y Villanueva de la Iglesia (1851–1923), recently rescued from oblivion by María del Carmen Simón Palmer's new edition of *Rienzi el tribuno* (Rienzi the Political Orator, 1876) and *El padre Juan* (Father John, 1891).[27] Acuña did take a strong stance for freedom, which, combined with her obvious talent for provocation and plain-speaking, has earned her the description as "la pionera de la literatura femenina del librepensamiento español"[28] ("the pioneer of Spanish free-thinking feminine literature"). She supported civil marriage, for example, which had only been legalized in Spain in 1870, and by the mid-1880s was equating the status of women in her society with that of slaves ("mujer, es decir, esclava" ["a woman, that is to say, a slave"]). Her "freethinking" views are amply in evidence in her dynamic plays, which produced as much hostility as acclaim among her audiences (Nancy Membrez reports that an article in the *Revista de Madrid* in 1884 claimed that she was

---

[26] This information is second-hand; I have been unable to locate copies of the plays mentioned. Her nephew, Ramón Gómez de la Serna, maintained a discreet silence about her playwriting in his *Mi tía Carolina Coronado* (Buenos Aires: Emecé, 1942). All three are listed in Simón Palmer, *Escritoras españolas*, but with no bibliographical or performance information.

[27] Rosario de Acuña. *Rienzi el tribuno. El padre Juan (teatro)*, ed. María del Carmen Simón Palmer (Madrid: Castalia/Instituto de la Mujer, 1990). See the entry on her by Nancy Membrez, in Galerstein, *Women Writers*, pp. 4–6.

[28] Simón Palmer, "Introducción," *Rienzi el tribuno*, p. 7.

"para los hombres una literata, y para las mujeres una librepensadora, y no inspira entre unos y otras simpatías"[29] ["for men she was a woman of letters, and for women she was a freethinker, which does not inspire much sympathy in either group"]). Even more, later in life she was threatened with jail and forced to flee into exile for her political stance in support of workers' rights.

Acuña had the good fortune to have her very first play, *Rienzi el tribuno*, put on stage at the Teatro del Circo on 12 February 1876, and received with general acclaim (she was praised as "varonil" ["masculine"] of course[30]). The reviews were favorable, and many of the capital's most distinguished authors – among them Rivas (junior), Hartzenbusch, Serra, Echegaray, and Alarcón – presented her with a gift-book of poems several days after the debut. It is a historical play on the same theme elaborated by Carlos Rubio in his tragedy, *Nicolás Rienzi*, put on at the Teatro Español in 1872 (the same lead actors, Elisa Boldún and Rafael Calvo, even starred in both productions), itself loosely based on a novel, Sir E. Bulwer-Lytton's *Rienzi o el último Tribuno*, which had been serialized in the *Revista de Teatros* in late 1844. Wagner's opera on the same subject had played in Madrid on 5 February 1876, just days before Acuña's play was first performed. The controversial theme, the class conflict in fourteenth-century Rome between the aristocracy and the commoners, had resonance during the turbulent years of Spain's First Republic. As we shall see below, the mid-1870s brought a brief resurgence of Romantic emotion and tropes to the Spanish theatre (the struggle against tyranny, the force of love, the role of destiny, mysterious relationships, masked characters, suicide) and Acuña's drama contains elements of such neo-Romantic sensibility. The noble and generous hero, Nicolás Rienzi, is pitted against the oppressive Pedro Colonna, who succeeds in crushing him. What makes Rienzi different is that he is put forth as the voice of the people, and throughout most of the play a strong socialist note is struck. When María's friend Juana criticizes the "pueblo" as "niño grande y consentido / que se olvida de ayer viendo el mañana" ("a large spoiled child who forgets yesterday when it thinks about tomorrow") (I, 1), María responds:

> no puedo consentir que en mi presencia
> a los hechos de Rienzi pongas tacha;
> y el que escarnece al pueblo a Rienzi ofende,
> que es amigo del pueblo que lo aclama.
>
> . . .
> ¡Y sin embargo, Juana, soy del pueblo!
> Tú lo sabes, mi padre trabajaba.   (I, 1)

---

[29] Galerstein, *Women Writers*, p. 4.   [30] Simón Palmer, *Rienzi el tribuno*, p. 26.

(I cannot allow you to criticize Rienzi's accomplishments in my presence. Whoever mocks the people offends Rienzi, a friend of the common men who support him... And withal, Juana, I am of common stock! You know this; my father worked for a living.)

A significant exchange between María and Rienzi underscores the author's commitment to the common man and her suspicion of the privileged noble class (to which she belonged, although she always refused to use the title of Countess of Acuña which she inherited):

RIENZI   quiero que el sol de la justicia brille
                 como en tiempos mejores
                 haciéndonos iguales,
                 que todos somos hombres y mortales.
                 ...

MARIA   Pero no sin luchar llegará el día en
                 que el pueblo romano
                 se apellide liberto y soberano.

RIENZI   Lo sé muy bien, la raza de los nobles
                 a ese plan gigantesco no se aviene,
                 ella vive gozando como reina
                 y de vida cambiar no le conviene.
                 ...

                 donde el pueblo llegando al heroísmo
                 derrumbe las postreras atalayas
                 que sirven de guardia al feudalismo.   (I, 5)

(RIENZI: I want the light of justice to shine as it did in better
                 times, making us all equals, since we are all men and
                 mortal ones at that. ...

MARIA: But the day when the Roman people can call them-
                 selves free and sovereign will not come without a
                 fight.

RIENZI: I know that all too well. Nobles will not acquiesce to
                 this important change, since they live like kings and
                 will not easily change their lifestyles ... It will take
                 heroic efforts to bring down the watchtowers that
                 protect the feudal system.)

This defense of the working class was not new on the Spanish stage, but it was unprecedented in a woman. In the late 1840s and 1850s writers such as Fernando Garrido, Pablo Avecilla, and Sixto Cámara wrote stirring plays in support of the rising working class. In Acuña, Rienzi is the eponymous character, but the story really belongs to his wife María. Colonna's sexual blackmail of María (similar to Tarquino's blackmail of Lucrecia in Moratín senior's play of 1762) enables her to discover strength of character ("me siento valiente en el peligro" ["I feel courageous when danger is present"] [I, 1]). In a different exchange, Colonna tells Juana, "Me asombra que te escuche con paciencia, / que eres sierva y a todos los desprecio" ("I am surprised that I am listening to you patiently, since you are just a servant and I despise them all"), to which she responds, "Desprécianos y acaso llegue el día / que te mires esclavo de los siervos" ("Go ahead and despise us. One day you might find yourself enslaved by your servants") (I, 6). When speaking of the aristocracy, Rienzi himself states:

> esa gente fiada en sus blasones
> no atiende ni discursos ni razones,
> y obedece a dudosa jerarquía.   (I, 6)

(Those people who hide behind their noble coats of arms do not listen to speeches nor reasoned arguments, and they obey a dubious authority.)

The protest against the oppression of the masses comes across in *Rienzi el tribuno* clearly and with conviction, but as we shall see, Acuña finally seems rather divided about the role of the common man in the country's governance.

Aside from the strong support of the working class, Acuña delivers another message in her play, one warning against the civil conflict in the Spain of her day.[31] Above all, Rienzi and María struggle to avoid civil war in Rome between the supporters of Rienzi and those of his enemies among the noble classes, a conflict which echoes the ideology of the recently fought second Carlist War of 1873–1874. As Juana fears, Rome is a nation of laws but not everyone has agreed to uphold them:

> Además esa ley no está jurada,
> y aunque al pueblo le agrade, la nobleza
> puede muy bien negarse a recibirla
> y entonces, claro está, viene la guerra.   (II, 4)

(Besides, that law has not gone into effect and although the people might support it, the nobility might very well refuse to accept it and then, of course, war will result.)

Acuña, however, produces an interesting switch in the "Epílogo" (really, Act III) which takes place seven years later. The audience has been led, through its identification with the plight of María, to support Rienzi who

---

[31] Clarín recognized (if somewhat patronizingly) her liberal ideas in his satirical poem, "Revista del año cómico (1875 a 1876)," reproduced by Noël M. Valis, "Dos poesías de almanaque, por Leopoldo Alas," *Anales de Literatura Española de la Universidad de Alicante* 7 (1991): 195–205. Alas writes: "sólo juzgo oportuno / reservar un aplauso cariñoso / para *Rienzi el Tribuno*, / brillante ensayo de una señorita / liberal, inspirada y muy bonita."

seemed to have the interests of the people at heart. However, we learn that Rienzi has imposed severe and very unwelcome taxes on the commoners, and they have reacted with displeasure. Rebellion is brewing in the streets, secret anti-Rienzi posters are being stuck up around Rome, and even murmurs of "Death to Rienzi" are being heard in the public squares. Rienzi imputes this to his enemies Colonna and Orsini, but even he is caught in a passionate conflict, expressed in a stirring sonnet which soon became repeated throughout Madrid:

> ¡Oh! libertad, fantasma de la vida,
> astro de amor a la ambición humana
> el hombre en su delirio te engalana,
> pero nunca te encuentra agradecida.
> Despierta alguna vez, siempre dormida
> cruzas la tierra, como sombra vana;
> se te busca en el hoy para el mañana,
> viene el mañana y se te ve perdida.
> Cámbiase el niño en el mancebo fuerte
> y piensa que te ve ¡triste quimera!
> Con la esperanza de llegar a verte
> ruedan los años sobre la ancha esfera
> y en el último trance de la muerte,
> aún nos dice tu voz, ¡espera, espera!   (III, 2)

(Oh, freedom, you phantom of life, star of love for human ambition, man in his delirium dresses you up, but he never finds you grateful. Wake up for once, you always cross the land asleep, like a useless shadow; if one looks for you today thinking about tomorrow, tomorrow comes and one finds you lost. The little boy grows into a strong young man and thinks he sees you [what a sad illusion!]. With the hope of one day seeing you, the years go by, and in the throes of death, your voice still whispers, "Wait, wait!").

Rienzi sees the people tricked by Colonna and unwilling to be reasoned with; they turn on him and behead him in the square in front of the Capitolio. He dies a victim of the people's violence, but he himself is not blameless. Acuña draws from Romantic melodrama for the final scenes in which María, forgetting momentarily about the future of their young son, plunges a dagger into her breast as the palace goes up in flames.

In the final analysis the playwright is not quite sure what the real message of this early play should be. She produces a well-structured plot, interesting conflicts, passionate characters, and lively dialogue full of striking interjections, but the message seems somewhat muddled. Is the "pueblo" a dignified and oppressed group which deserves – and demands – freedom, or is it merely an uncontrollable mass incapable of defending itself against manipulation by self-serving leaders? She seems unable to decide and the play, while stirring and very well constructed, loses ideological force precisely because of, ironically, its balanced nature. Colonna, Rienzi, and the "pueblo" itself are all implicated in the final tragedy. Perhaps it is this very ambiguity which makes it so interesting. Nevertheless, it was received with enthusiasm by the critics and the audience, and years later, when the problematic *El padre Juan* was shut down by the authorities, *Rienzi el tribuno* was deemed safe enough to be put on in its place (*La Independencia*, 4 April 1891).

El padre Juan created a *succès de scandale* when it was first staged at the Teatro de la Alhambra on 3 April 1891. As Simón Palmer notes, it is a "compendio de sus ideas sobre la sociedad de su tiempo"[32] ("a compendium of her ideas on the society of her time"), ideas now strongly grounded in the freethinking anticlericalism which had come to typify Acuña's thinking as well as that of much of the liberal sector of *fin de siècle* Spain. It is territory which Galdós had worked over in several novels and plays (Acuña's hero is an atheistic Madrid-based engineer, reminiscent of *Doña Perfecta*'s Pepe Rey), and it expresses a deep strain of antagonism against the oppressive, obscurantist attitudes which inhibited, for the author and others, Spain's moral and industrial progress. Acuña is even more daring than Galdós, as she creates two young people who not only plan a civil marriage but also the transformation of a local religious shrine into a health spa. The spa, a small community designed to help the sick and the poor, would be built in front of the convent and provide real charity, not the pious and hypocritical charity of the church. As Isabel explains,

Nuestros pueblos son un semillero de rencillas, cuentos, calumnias, pequeñas maldades, e ínterin los bienes conventuales aumentan, desde los púlpitos se toma carácter de apóstol, y una enemistad sorda, mezcla de rencor y cobardía, late con rumores de culebra en torno de todos nosotros, cambiando la fe de las almas en repugnante esperanza de recompensas. (I, 10).

(Our villages are a breeding ground for resentments, gossip, calumny, and small corruptions, and in the meantime the convent's riches grow, words from the pulpits take on apostolic importance, and a quiet hatred, a mixture of animosity and cowardliness, howls all around us like serpents' whispers, changing the faith that people have into a repugnant hope of material reward.)

Ramón is a "buen republicano" ("good republican") in his beliefs. The play posits the "useless" work of the religious establishment against the new socialism's desire to reform and transform society through social engineering. The elements are set for a series of conflicts of power, ideology, and religious beliefs, and Acuña does not disappoint, grafting onto her play the surprising (neo-Romantic) revelation that the priest

[32] Simón Palmer, *Rienzi el tribuno*, p. 30.

who has so strongly opposed Ramón, and therefore has been indirectly responsible for his death, is really his father. The last several scenes are intensely Romantic in construction, tone, and language, indistinguishable at moments from the hyper-emotional plays of the 1830s except for the pointedness of their accusations:

[Isabel, holding the body of Ramón.] ¡Oh! ¡Sola! ... Sin él ... para siempre ... No ... ¿Qué misterio ha encerrado su vida? [...] ¿Qué sombra es aquella? ¡Providencia bendita! ¡El Padre Juan! ¡Aquí la víctima y el verdugo! ... ¡Oh! ¡Baja, sombrío fantasma de un mundo de tinieblas y dolores! ... Ven a posarte como ave fatídica sobre los despojos de tu rencor. No serás salvo, ¡no! Pensaste ofrecer a Dios en rescate de tus culpas la muerte de un hereje, y Dios te contesta con el cadáver de ¡tu hijo!! (III, 10)

(Oh! I am alone! Without him ... forever ... No ... What mystery has been locked up in his life? What shadow is that? Blessed providence! Father Juan! Here the victim and the executioner! ... Oh! Get down, gloomy ghost from a world of darkness and pain! Come and roost like a buzzard on the spoils of your hatred. You will not be saved, no! You thought you could offer God the death of a heretic in exchange for your sins, and God answers you with the body of ... your son!)

Acuña paces the drama so as to make it build gradually in intensity, letting loose in the third act a torrent of emotion (underscored by an overabundance of ellipses and exclamations) without losing sight of her fiercely anticlerical message. Echoes of Jovellanos and the reformers of the eighteenth century resound in Ramón's thesis-speech at the center of the play:

Nuestra población rural está sumida en la ignorancia más espantosa, en un atraso moral repugnante. Creo de necesidad que la *Escuela*, la *Granja modelo*, el *Instituto industrial* con el *Hospital* y el *Asilo*, se levanten en nuestros campos como templos benditos, donde el pueblo español empiece a comulgar en la religión del racionalismo ... Soy rico, joven, feliz: ¿será bien que vaya a aumentar la hueste del vicio y de la vanidad? ... Mi sitio es éste, debo ser útil a mis compatriotas: mi inteligencia y mis riquezas deben sembrar de beneficios el solar de mis mayores. (II, 4)

(Our rural population is kept in the most horrifying ignorance, in a disgusting moral backwardness. I believe that the School, the Model Farm, the Industrial Institute with the Hospital and the Asylum, must be erected on our lands like sacred temples where the Spanish people can begin to take communion in the religion of rationalism ... I am rich, young, happy: would it be proper for me to increase the vice and vanity that reign? ... My place is here, I need to be useful to my countrymen. My intelligence and my wealth should sow benefits in the ancestral dwelling of my elders.)

There is some rough stuff here, strong language which not surprisingly upset a lot of people. "¡Oh! ¡Fraile impío! ¡Desde este momento comienza nuestra lucha! ¡Apresta las fuerzas del pasado para defenderte, que yo invocaré las energías del porvenir para derribarte!" ("Oh, you godless friar! Our struggle has just begun! Gather up the forces of the past to defend yourself with, because I will invoke the energies of the future to bring you down!"), shouts Ramón as the closing words of Act II. The final Romantic elements are subsumed into a contemporary setting and the prose lends an immediacy to the play that verse would not. It is no surprise that it was banned after just one performance, but the subject matter was so controversial that the printed version of the play sold out in two editions of two thousand copies each within days of appearing in Madrid.[33]

Acuña's strong feminism is also boldly in evidence in the play. She states that the play's most important character is not Ramón or even the titular Padre Juan (who interestingly has no speaking role even though he represents the entire rural population's beliefs in superstition, devils, possessions, and other religious-associated phenomena). In the "Apuntes de estudio para los tres papeles más importantes del drama" ("Notes for Preparing the Three Most Important Roles") appended to the printed version of the play, Acuña writes that Isabel is the "personificación de la mujer del porvenir; de la mujer ideal, de la mujer que ha de surgir en la gran familia humana como producto acumulado de todas las herencias de nuestras heroicas antepasadas y de nuestras ilustradas presentes" ("the personification of the woman of the future; of the ideal woman, of the woman who shall rise up out of the great human family like a synthesis of all the qualities of our heroic sisters from the past and of our enlightened sisters from the present"). It is she on whom the play's moral force pivots since she will be the embodiment of freethinking ("panteista sin saberlo" ["pantheist without knowing it"]) and the representative of "la razón emancipada de todo dogma, de toda doctrina" ("reason freed from all dogma and doctrine"). She should be, as Acuña underlines in her notes, the type of woman about whom is said, "*mujeres como ésa no las hay, pero así debrían ser todas*"[34] ("women like her don't exist, but all women should be like her").

Acuña wrote three other plays, all of them staged either in Madrid or, in the case of her second effort, *Amor a la patria* (For Love of Country), in Zaragoza. This one-act tragedy, written under the pseudonym Remigio Andrés Delafón for performance on 27 November 1876 in Zaragoza, recounts that city's heroic defense of itself against French troops on 2 July 1808. It is a story Rosario claims to have heard numerous times from her grandmother and "más de una vez he llorado conmovida"[35] ("more than

33 Simón Palmer, *Escritoras españolas*, p. 6.
34 Simón Palmer, *Rienzi el tribuno*, pp. 233–234.
35 Rosario de Acuña, *Amor a la patria* (Madrid: José Rodríguez, 1877): 5.

once I cried, affected by it") but she also draws from Modesto Lafuente's *Historia de España* (vol. 23, 1869) for additional details. It is the type of play which harks back to the short patriotic works used for propaganda purposes during the War of Independence and the first Carlist War. It is equally bombastic ("¡¡Aún vienen más franceses!! / ¡¡Sí; el infierno / sin duda de sus antros los vomita!!" ["The French are still coming!! Yes, no doubt Hell vomits them up from its caverns!!"]) and predictable, but it has a voice that marks it specifically as Acuña's. In response to María's lament that she and her mother can do nothing to stop the onslaught, her mother Inés declaims, "¡¡Por la patria mía, / *aunque mujer*, la sangre de mis venas / late con entusiasmo!!" ("*Although I am a woman* the blood in my veins beats with enthusiasm for my country!!") (I, 1; emphasis added). Inés is a strong woman, the daughter of a wealthy noble family who abandoned her background to marry a mere artisan. Widowed now, she has struggled to keep her family together, but misses her son Pedro, who disappeared nine years before when he was fifteen years old. Inés would normally inspire her son to defend his country against the invaders, but María reminds her, "Si no puedes decírselo a tu hijo, / con entusiasmo lo escuchó tu hija" ("If you can't tell your son, your daughter will listen enthusiastically") (I, 1). When the men arrive to barricade the house, María insists to herself, "No han de verme llorar" ("They shall not see me cry") (I, 2), but it is Inés who must choose between her country and her son, who returns secretly as a French soldier. Naturally, she chooses the former in Acuña's tableaux which presents the woman as the hero and the man as the traitor who sold his honor for wealth and prestige. The progressive newspaper *La Iberia* judged it to be "una de las más brillantes escenas de nuestra epopeya de principios del presente siglo" ("one of the most stirring scenes of our national epic from the beginning of this century") (24 January 1879).

In *Tribunales de venganza* (Courts of Vengeance), performed in Madrid at the Teatro Español on 6 April 1880 by members of the famous Calvo family,[36] Acuña presents another tragic drama with a historical theme. She draws heavily upon the Romantic tropes once again popularized in the theatre, creating a perfectly tuned "neo-Romantic" play infused with all of the standard motifs and images. *El Imparcial* liked its "imágenes etéreas, sublimidades heroicas, conceptos brillantes" ("ethereal images, heroic grandeur, brilliant conceits") (7 April 1880), but Julio Nombela alludes to other critics who held less generous opinions: "La crítica elogió la versificación del drama, pero encontró la acción sin interés, sin

---

[36] Performing in this play were the well-known Rafael and Ricardo Calvo, plus Alfredo, Fernando, and José. For more on this famous family of actors, see Luis Calvo Revilla, *Actores célebres del Teatro del Príncipe o Español* (Madrid: Impr. Municipal, 1920).

caracteres y sin resortes verdaderamente dramáticos"[37] ("The critics praised the play's versification, but found the rest to be without interest, characters, or really dramatic moments"). In addition to the vengeance, last-minute discoveries, prisons, and so on, Acuña manages to turn the central theme slightly away from one of love and existential anguish toward a class conflict. Don Luis Cavanillas, representative of the local titled class (he is the governor of Valencia), fights Guillén Sorolla, a "comunero" dedicated to resisting what he and his people view to be the oppressive policies of their rulers. As threats of rebellion rise, it is Cavanillas who uses lowly means (he kidnaps Guillén's beloved Andrea and bribes Guillén's traitorous servant Asil) to achieve his goals. According to Asil, Guillén and his defenders "aborrece[n] de muerte a los señores" ("have a mortal hatred for their masters") (II, 5) and, to Acuña's mind at least, with good reason. Still, in this early stage of her writing career Acuña attenuates the socialist message by subsuming it into the Christianized ethic which marks neo-Romantic Spanish drama. She follows the lead of Gómez de Avellaneda by creating a strong heroine – "sabes que no soy hembra asustadiza" ("you know that I am not a woman who frightens easily") Andrea tells Guillén (III, 6) – but the real impact of the play comes from the intersection of vengeance and politics with a Christian acceptance of death. Asil, the moorish traitor (who orchestrates Guillén's death and only too late finds out that he is really his own brother), notices that the condemned man awaits death with resignation:

> ¡Qué sereno camina! El cristianismo,
> le da a la muerte un cetro soberano.
> ¡Qué poder tiene sobre el ser humano
> ese bello ideal del heroismo!   (III, 10)

(How calmly he carries himself! Christianity gives death a pre-eminent sceptre. What power that beautiful heroic ideal has over mankind!)

She is still years away from the rabid anticlericalism of *El padre Juan*.

La voz de la patria (The Country's Voice), a one-act "cuadro dramático" ("dramatic scene") performed at the Teatro Español on 20 December 1893, is Acuña's last known incursion into drama. Like *El padre Juan*, it takes place not in a distant, Christianized, neo-Romantic past, but in "la época actual y días de la fecha" ("the present day and age"). In a moving dedication to her recently deceased father, the author confesses that this play is not "obra de lucha, de controversia; es el eco de una realidad del presente"[38] ("work of conflict and controversy; it is a

---

[37] Julio Nombela, *El Teatro* (25 April 1880): 53–54.
[38] Rosario de Acuña, *La voz de la patria* (Madrid: R. Velazco, 1893): 6.

reflection of a current reality"). However, she does insist that the keys to
"la realidad de la vida" ("the reality of life") come from this triple
command: "Anda, Trabaja, Ama" ("Move Forward, Work, Love").
Such musings give voice in the play to a conflict over the meaning of
patriotism. María is concerned that her son Pedro has been called up
again to serve in the army and will be shipped off to fight Moors in Africa;
Juan, the boy's father, thinks that his mother is over protective and not
sensitive to the boy's patriotic duty:

> ¡Olvida el *amor-instinto*:
> ese hijo que tanto vale
> para ti, vino a la tierra
> con deber incuestionable
> de prestarla sus virtudes,
> su inteligencia, su sangre,
> sin retroceder un punto
> en su camino de avance;
> tu misión de madre humana
> consiste en no desviarle
> de esa ruta ...   (I, 1)

(Forget about your instinct for love: that boy, who you think is worth so much,
came to this earth with the unquestionable duty of using his goodness, his
intelligence, his blood for it. He must not turn back; your mission as a mother is to
insure that he not be detoured from that journey ...)

María wants Pedro to desert over the mountains to France in order to
protect himself against what she characterizes to be "el orgullo de los
hombres" ("men's pride") (I, 2). Honor and country to her are merely
words, "ese ilusorio fantasma" ("that illusive spectre") (I, 2). The play
itself threatens to be merely words, an academic exercise in the form of a
dialogue, until Acuña springs on us her trump card: Isabel, Pedro's
fiancée (they are to be married within a month), in pleading with her
boyfriend to save himself from possible death, reveals (with the conni-
vance of Pedro's mother) that she is pregnant. Pregnant, unmarried
heroines are few in number in Spanish drama, but Acuña's decision to
stay focused on the theme of patriotism rather than a potentially more
interesting theme of free will and women's rights keeps the play from
having much dramatic interest. The outcome is predictable as Juan pins
one of his own medals on his son's chest in anticipation of the glory he
will find in war.

> Y si la muerte con su férrea mano
> lograse ahogar tu juvenil aliento,
> tu padre le dirá que fuiste un héroe
> y vivirá tu nombre bendiciendo.

Y así de España los gloriosos días
en las edades servirán de ejemplo,
vigor prestando a la familia humana
al ser contados por extraños pueblos.   (I, 8)

(And if war's iron hand manages to snuff out your youthful breath, your father
will say that you were a hero and he will keep your name blessedly alive. In that
way the glorious days of Spain will serve as an example for future generations,
giving strength to the family of man when recounted by foreign peoples.)

The woman's voice is silenced once more.

Adelaida Muñiz y Mas

More prolific than Rosario de Acuña was Adelaida Muñiz y Mas (d.
1906), author of at least fourteen one- to four-act plays,[39] published and
performed in Madrid between 1892 and 1898, and contributor to the
Cádiz-based newspaper, *Revista Teatral* (1898).[40] Muñiz was a versatile
dramatist, equally at home writing biblical dramas as she was creating
satirical sainetes. Her first long play was the three-act drama, *Mancha
heredada* (Inherited Dishonour), first performed at the Teatro de la
Zarzuela on 27 April 1892. Although the title page brags that it was
"estrenado con gran aplauso" ("put on to great applause") no notice of it
appears in Simón Díaz's important (if uneven) *Veinticuatro Diarios* so it is
difficult to trace its performance history. The play itself is set in the last
decade of the century, that is, "época actual" ("nowadays") and as the
title suggests, it is heavily influenced by the dramatic theory and practice
of Henrik Ibsen, although the voice of Zorrilla also echoes throughout the
verses (in particular, in the lovely *décimas* of I, 5).[41] We are in the world of
the professional middle class as the play opens in don Julián's law office.
Julián became famous when he defended a lowly criminal accused (correctly) of a hideous crime. Following the trial and imprisonment of the
man, Julián took charge of his orphaned daughter Margarita, who knows
nothing of her ignominious origins until Julián, after confessing his love
for her and being rejected, swears vengeance and reveals the truth. She is
in love with Rafael, the Count of Puente Real, but, shamed by the

---

[39] These works include *La herencia del Tenorio* (1892), *Mancha heredada* (1892), *La huida a
Egipto* (1893), *Ilusión y desengaño* (1893), *El nacimiento del Hijo de Dios* (1893), *El pilluelo
de Madrid* (1894), *Nada* (1895), *Pajaritos de papel* (1895), *Maruja Carmela* (1896), *Roja y
gualda* (1898), and the following, whose exact dates have not been found: *Cambio de
cartas* (before 1894), *Por el nombre* (before 1895; published in 1899), *El secreto del
sumario* (before 1895), and *El bergantín Fantasma* (before 1895).
[40] Simón Palmer, *Escritoras españolas*, p. 457.
[41] Halfdan Gregersen, in his important study of *Ibsen and Spain* (Cambridge, MA: Harvard
University Press, 1936), takes no notice of Muñiz.

revelation of her status as the daughter of a criminal, perceives that she lacks honor – as one of the characters states, "¡Ya no tiene un nombre honrado!" ("She no longer has an honorable name!") (III, 2) – and decides to dedicate her life to God rather than marry Rafael or accede to the disgusting proposition of her adoptive father. The old-fashioned theme of lost honor was difficult for modern audiences to identify with, but the plight of the young heroine's victimization by rules established by men had special resonance in a decade of protest, rising anarchy, and the questioning of women's "traditional" roles. Still, her "mancha heredada" haunts her, becomes a stumbling block for those around her (Rafael's titled mother will never permit a situation in which "nuestra sangre preclara / se unirá a la de un bandido" ["our illustrious blood mixes with that of an outlaw"] [III, 5]) and threatens to pull her down into a life of repressed desire and denial. It is only Rafael who stands firm against his society's unjust condemnation of an individual for the sins of her father. "Busca honor en tus acciones, / no en tus pasados abuelos" ("Look for honor in your actions, not in your ancestors") (III, 5) he counsels his mother. Even she is a victim of rigid hierarchy, for when forced to choose between "nuestro blasón" ("our coat of arms") and her son's love, she chooses the former and does not come around until it is too late: Rafael has already shot Julián in a duel. It then becomes clear that the "mancha heredada" is not necessarily only Margarita's blemish, but also that of Rafael, Julián, the Condesa, and even Padre Gabriel, all of whom are trapped within a rigid social structure which creates witting and unwitting victims. As a delirious Rafael states:

> ¡Madre, calla!
> El mundo todo, según decías,
> *por ser quien era* la despreciaba,
> y en cambio estaba de mí orgulloso
> por ser mi estirpe noble y preclara;
> pues bien, desde ahora somos iguales;
> nuestra corona está manchada,
> toma más sangre, riega tu lodo;
> ¡sociedad necia, tu orgullo sacia!   (III, 8)

(Mother, be quiet! The whole world despised her, as you said, *for who she was*, but on the other hand, it was proud of me because of my noble and illustrious pedigree; well then, from now on we are equals; our crown is stained. Here, take more blood and sprinkle it on your muck; foolish society, satiate your pride!)

Margarita becomes the double victim of the men's stubborn attachment to false love and honor. In the final scenes she has sacrificed her love and freedom to become a Sister of Charity, but returns to Julián's death bed to comfort him. Rafael enters the room in an attempt to persuade her to run away with him, abandoning both Julián and her religious vows, but Julián, thinking their presence a prearranged plot (reminiscent of Alfonso's interpretation of seeing don Alvaro and doña Leonor together on the same mountainside), pulls out a pistol and shoots at Rafael. The double victimization occurs when Margarita places herself between Julián and Rafael and is fatally wounded. The metaphor is clear: woman is sacrificed between the foolish whims of false honor and false love.

This same year, 1892, Muñiz wrote another of the dozens of parodies of Zorrilla's *Don Juan Tenorio* which had sprung up in Spanish theatres since Mariano Pina's amusing *Juan el Perdío* first appeared in Madrid in 1848.[42] Her contribution to what became a kind of cottage industry was entitled *La herencia del Tenorio* (Tenorio's Inheritance), and it drove yet another nail into the coffin of the 'serious' don Juan, for what is being played with here is not don Juan's immortal soul but rather his inheritance. It is the ultimate "middle-classization" of Zorrilla's Romantic hero. Performed at the Teatro del Príncipe Alfonso on 12 November 1892 (with "extraordinario éxito" ["extraordinary success"] according to the title page), it lampoons several key scenes in the *Tenorio* through exaggeration and melodrama. Brígida does not hand Inés a small missal but rather "un libro enorme, envuelto en un periódico" ("a huge book, wrapped up in a newspaper") (I, 1) from which falls "una enorme carta" ("a huge letter"). The comic dimension of the two props signals to the audience that an inflation of the paradigm is at hand (and, naturally, a deflation of it will be forthcoming), underscored by Inés's question-and-answer, "¿Pero, es que sabe escribir? / ¡Jesús, qué ilustrado está!" ("You mean he knows how to write? My, how learned he is!") (I, 1). Money, not love, is what motivates Inés:

BRÍG.	Eso es amor sin lecciones.
INÉS.	¿Amor has dicho?
BRÍG.	Pasión.
INÉS.	(*Transición*)
	No, Brígida, es afición
	a sus benditos millones. (I, 1)

(BRIG.	That's love, not learning.
INES.	Did you say love?
BRIG.	Passion.
INES.	(*Changing*)
	No, Brigida, it's an attachment to his blessed millions.)

---

42 *Juan el Perdío* was performed at the Cruz Theatre on 26 December 1848; it was revived at the Teatro Martín in 1879, when it was seen in conjunction with Zorrilla's *Don Juan Tenorio*. By 1880 it was in its fifth published edition (Salamanca: Francisco Núñez, 1880).

Muñiz lampoons the Spanish middle class's equating of money with love, or rather, the substitution of the latter by the former. In her conception of the play's plot, don Juan's aunt has threatened to disinherit him if he does not marry Inés, but Juan would rather lose his inheritance than his freedom. The comedy is broad and on target, inverting the *Tenorio*'s most famous lines for comic effect: "¡Inés, angel *planchador*!" ("Ines, ironing angel!") (I, 2), don Juan begins his talk with Inés, followed by Brígida's "Pobre garza aquí nacida, / ¿qué sabe ella si en la vida / hay más medios de engañar?" ("Poor heron born here, what does she know if in life there are other ways to deceive?") (I, 2). By the time the famous divan scene appears (the divan, however, is transformed into a basket of clothes to be ironed), the author, with perfect comic pitch, maneuvers the scene from one of tender love in the original to one of physical slapstick and jokes in the parody. The audience, which knows the original by heart, could not help but laugh at the not-so-subtle undermining of the Romantic lovers. In order further to bring the audience into the parody, Muñiz establishes several "metatheatrical" moments when the actors speak directly (in a kind of conspiracy) with the audience or, more clearly, when don Juan makes his first appearance after Brígida identifies him in the audience:

BRÍG.	¿No ves que está el teatro lleno y puede estar él también?
INÉS.	¿Habrá empleado, oh espanto! algún poder infernal?
BRÍG.	No le habrá costado tanto una entrada general.
INÉS.	¿Y podrá? (*Con acento cómico*)
BRÍG.	Sin gran trabajo.

   . . .

(*El actor se acerca lentamente y sube por la silla del director de orquesta . . .*
[Brígida] dándole la mano para que pueda subir.)

                (I, 1)

(BRÍG.	Can't you see that the theatre is full, and he might be here too?
INÉS.	What fear! Do you think he might have used some infernal power?
BRÍG.	No, a general admission ticket wouldn't have cost him so much.
INÉS.	Do you think he could?
BRÍG.	Yes, easily.

[*The actor slowly rises and climbs onto the stage using the orchestra director's chair. Brigida gives him a hand to help him up.*])

Even the scene where the ghost of Gonzalo enters without opening the doors is played for broad "metatheatrical" effect: "Es que llaman en el foro, / y antes era entre telones / ... / y aquí va a llevarse un susto / hasta el mismo apuntador" ("Someone is knocking from backstage – it used to be from between the curtains – ... and watch! Even the prompter is going to be startled when he comes out"). Both Muñiz and her audience knew Zorrilla inside out.

A Christmas play, *El nacimiento del Hijo de Dios o La adoración de los Santos Reyes* (The Birth of the Son of God or The Adoration of the Three Kings), was staged at the Teatro del Príncipe Alfonso on Christmas Eve, 1892, and was printed early in the new year. Muñiz wrote it in collaboration with José de la Cuesta. As befitted the season, the work had a huge cast, luxurious costumes (described in detail by the author[43]), and special music contributed by T. F. Grajal. In it, she brings together many strands of the type of theatre which had never gone out of public favor during the previous seven decades: scabrous humor and infighting among the servants (here, shepherds, one of whom is a typical *gracioso* type) which is found both in the numerous *refundiciones* of Golden Age plays and in the *alta comedia*; elements of the still-popular, if by now completely drained of meaning, *comedia de magia* ("Cuadro III" takes place with a "decoración infernal o fantástica" ["infernal or fantastic set"] populated by singing devils who reappear periodically throughout the play); sacred drama of the type dignified by Gómez de Avellaneda before it became standard fare for Christmas entertainments; and short set-pieces reminiscent of the *teatro por horas* genre which, as Nancy Membrez has demonstrated, held a central place in the theatrical enterprise of the last thirty years of the century.[44] For a Christmas play Muñiz has buried in her work some rather daring images, one of which refers to Bato, the rich but obnoxious shepherd who wonders if María is in love with him, whose friend Jusepe comments, "Ya verás tú cómo cambia / cuando tu vara florezca" ("You'll see how she changes when your staff blooms") (I, iv, 1). The structure of the play is awkward, if lively – it contains three acts and sixteen "cuadros" composed of fifty-three rapidly changing scenes – but it is an undeniably spirited retelling of the Christmas story.

Adelaida Muñiz's versatility is demonstrated in her next long play, *El pilluelo de Madrid o Los hijos del pueblo* (The Little Rogue from Madrid, or The Sons of the People), performed at the Teatro del Príncipe Alfonso on 12 November 1893. It draws on the theatre of social consciousness which would become, as will be seen below, one of the hallmarks of the

43 For example, the Archangel Gabriel was to wear "Mallas de carne. Calzadillo blanco, de lujo. Peto y faldetas blancos, con adornos dorados. Alas blancas. Cintillo dorado. Cinturón blanco y dorado." *El nacimiento del Hijo de Dios* (Madrid: Viuda de J. Ducazcal, 1893): 8.
44 Membrez, "The 'teatro por horas'."

theatre of the last decade of the century. The dominant note is one of class conflict. From the first scene, Gabriel, the fifteen-year-old "pilluelo," establishes his role as a commentator on the class divisions which mark Madrid.

GAB.	Cuando de un pobre se trata, lo malo se cree mucho antes.
	. . .
	Los pobres por triste gracia vamos, aunque esto la asombre, a la misma escuela.
LUISA.	¿El nombre? . . .
GAB.	¡Escuela de la desgracia! Lo que el rico en largos años no llega a ver en su vida, lo aprende el pobre en seguida a fuerza de desengaños . . . (I, 1)

(GAB.	When one is dealing with a poor person, they tend to believe the bad about him before believing anything else. . . . Although this might surprise you, all us poor people go to the same school.
LUISA.	What's it called?
GAB.	The School of Hard Knocks! What a rich man never manages to learn, the poor man learns right away, forced to by bitter experience . . .)

Money, riches, the lack of riches, coins, and gold become the linguistic currency of the play, creating a series of images which continually underscores the chasm separating the rich from the poor. Even though poor himself, Gabriel provides aid and succor to his orphaned girlfriend Juanilla; in fact, "soy ¡su único amparo!" ("I am her only protection!") (I, 1) he proclaims, much to his employer's amusement. "Se burlan, mas sin razón" ("They mock us, but they have no reason to do so") (I, 2) he mutters bitterly. Juanilla, a simple dressmaker, is seen by Miguel, the rich son of the family, as much more honest and desirable than the frivolous women whose company he usually keeps. Once again, Muñiz establishes the rich versus poor dichotomy, this time in the words of Miguel, although it is clear by his attitude that he is merely "slumming":

> Cansado de enamorar
> a esas damas que su hechizo,
> fundan tan sólo en un rizo,
> en un lazo, o un collar;
> hastiado de los salones
> y su ficticio oropel,

> mi amor descendió, Gabriel,
> a otras más bajas regiones.
> Al fin es justo que fíe
> de una niña encantadora,
> que ni miente cuando llora,
> ni me engaña cuando ríe.   (I, 4)

(Tired of falling in love with those women whose charms are to be found only in a curl, a bow, or a necklace; fed up with the salons and their phony glitter, my love descended, Gabriel, to lower regions. It's only fair that I can trust a charming girl who neither lies when she cries nor deceives me when she laughs.)

She is merely another commodity for him to bet on and "robar" ("rob") if necessary. He and his friend the Viscount kidnap Juanilla, enlisting Gabriel and Blas, the chauffeur, to help. His desire for her is purely as a possession linked with his ego: "En que seas siempre mía / está mi orgullo empeñado" ("My pride is pledged to making you mine forever") (II, 7), and his harsh words to Gabriel aptly sum up the nobility's general disdain for the lower classes:

> Con nacer tan sólo
> fuiste deshonrado,
> que eres por herencia
> ladrón y gitano.
> De plebeya sangre,
> de raza de esclavos,
> a la servidumbre
> fuiste destinado.
> Ignorante y necio
> me cortas el paso,
> y a mí, águila noble
> que cruza el espacio,
> se atreve el mezquino
> y pobre gusano.
> Tu instinto te arrastra,
> te guía a lo malo,
> tu vida es indigna,
> tu cuerpo un harapo.
> ¡Vives de limosna,
> y en fin, no te mato,
> porque no mereces
> morir a mis manos!   (II, 8)

(You were dishonored at your very birth because you are by nature a thief and a gypsy. Of plebeian blood, a race of slaves, you were destined to be a servant. Ignorant and foolish, you get in my way. I, a noble eagle who soars through space, blocked by a miserable and poor worm. Your nature drags you along, impels you toward evil; your life is unworthy, your body a sack of rags. You live off of charity. I shall not kill you because you are not worthy of dying by my hand.)

Gabriel's response is equally harsh.

From an unexpected source – the judge's wife doña Luisa – comes a condemnation of the penal system, where a man "aprende el mal y sale / maestro en una semana ... / Creo que la cárcel es / mal lazareto del alma" ("learns about wickedness and comes out a master criminal within a week ... I believe that jail is a bad hospital for the soul") (III, 1). This comment provides the author with an opportunity to launch into a short debate on social justice, the efficacy of punishment, and the inequalities of the justice meted out between the rich and the poor:

> ¡Cuando un infeliz se pierde,
> si la miseria le arrastra,
> la sociedad grita «¡crimen!»
> y de su lado lo aparta;
> y si un hombre noble y rico
> de lodo su nombre mancha,
> con indulgencia culpable
> exclamáis «¡calaverada!»
> y ni el mundo le desprecia,
> ni le retira su gracia!   (III, 1)

(When a poor soul gets lost, dragged down by misery, then society shouts, "Criminal!" and removes him from its midst; but if a rich and noble man stains his name with mud, society merely shouts indulgently "Foolish action!" and neither scorns him nor withholds its pardon from him.)

Gabriel, the accused but innocent boy, must find a way out of his predicament while those around him display greed (Blas), corruption (the Viscount is a bad influence on Miguel; the police are easily bribed with a little wine), blindness (the judge), or lust (Miguel). Muñiz has drawn on some old melodramatic techniques to tell her story (Juanilla turns out to be the daughter who long ago was stolen from Luisa and the judge), but she does so with flair and a keen ear for believable dialogue, and, more daringly, she avoids a facile, sappy ending. Gabriel, released from jail after the truth is revealed, instead of accepting the hand of Juana (now of elevated lineage), insists that he will go out into the world, make a name for himself, and return when he is worthy of her love. It is not a conventional happy ending, only one with the promise of a future happiness.

Dramatic monologues (*Ilusión y desengaño* [Illusion and Deceit]), comic parodies (*La herencia del Tenorio, Maruja Carmela*), biblical dramas (*La huída a Egipto* [The Flight into Egypt], *El nacimiento del Hijo de Dios*), and patriotic harangues (*Roja y gualda* [Red and Yellow]) characterize the versatility of Adelaida Muñiz, the dominant woman dramatist of the 1890s.

Enriqueta Lozano de Vilchez

In Granada there appeared, as early as 1847, a one-act original comedy written by Enriqueta Lozano de Vilchez (1829 or 1830–?). This very prolific writer was known more for her poetry and novels than for her dramas.[45] The majority of her prose and poetic works contain a decidedly religious tone and content, similar to that which is easily detected in many of her plays (her friend Josefa Bueno dedicated a poem to "mi querida amiga la escritora católica" ["my dear friend the Catholic writer"] in 1879). However, her first drama, *Una actriz por amor* [An Actress for the Love of It], performed at the Literary and Artistic Society in Granada on 3 July 1847, deals with other matters. Written predominantly in *cuartetas* and *quintillas*, it is a play about playing, acting, and the life of the theatre, in which Anselmo's nephew has given up a boring business career in Madrid in order to take over the reins of the theatre in Sevilla, convinced that along that path lies glory and fulfillment. His visit to his aunt and uncle in Granada provokes a crisis. Anselmo's wife María recognizes, as did Larra years earlier, than the actor's lot is a tough one and that skill, talent, and knowledge are essential to the profession.

> Para hacerse aplaudir
> es menester reservar
> un don para hacer reir,
> otro para hacer llorar.
> ¿O juzgas que es fácil cosa
> conmover el corazón
> de una muchedumbre ansiosa
> de ruido y de agitación?
> ¿O al que tiene el alma llena
> de una tristeza sombría,
> hacerle olvidar su pena
> y trocarla en alegría?
> No; lo dije, y lo sostengo;
> esa es difícil carrera,
> y por imposible tengo
> su acogida lisonjera.   (I, 1)

(To be applauded in the theatre one must have the capacity to make people laugh and cry. Or do you think that it is easy to stir the hearts of a public seeking noise and excitement? Or to get someone whose soul is filled with sadness to forget his

[45] See Simón Palmer, *Escritoras*, pp. 396–404 for a complete bibliography of her works.

sorrows for a while and laugh a little? No, I have said it before and I will say it again: that is a difficult profession, impossible to be a success in.)

Lozano herself acted the part of Anselmo's daughter, Emilia, childhood companion of Enrique, who in fact proves the play's thesis from a feminine perspective: drawing solely upon her talents as an actress, Emilia avenges herself for Enrique's past affront (he left her to go off to Madrid) and tricks him into falling in love with her all over again. She plays the role of "Julia García," an abandoned young woman set upon joining his acting company and leaving for Sevilla, as well as the role of "Doña Sabina Olmedo," "Julia's" enraged mother, who accuses Enrique of being her daughter's seducer. In a third ruse, Emilia presents herself as a common peasant woman set on marrying him and joining his company, but he finds her manners "groseros" ("disgusting"): "no podría present-arla / en tertulias ni paseos" ("you'll never be able to take her to tertulias or out for a stroll") (I, 15). Lozano neatly captures several of the clichéd images men have of women (the beauty, the shrewish mother-in-law, the common hausfrau) and undermines the stereotypes by combining them all in one person, a woman first and last revealed to be gracious, intelligent, and talented. Naturally, as was demanded by the genre, they will marry and live, presumably, happily ever after – with Emilia having the upper hand.

Lozano's next known effort, a short sacred play called *Dios es el Rey de los Reyes* (God is the King of Kings) was printed in Granada in 1852, but we have no information about performances it received, if any.[46] Its interest lies more in the fact of its authorship – an original play written in a variety of metrical styles by a woman in the early 1850s – than in its content or execution. It was probably written as a Christmas entertainment, typical of the plays created during holiday seasons, but Lozano turns it into a type of suspense mystery. (Religious dramas would become a staple in the theatre in the second half of the century; one of their most popular purveyors was her contemporary and compatriot Enrique Zumel.) The shepherds and Joseph believe that the three "grandes señorones" ("great lords") who have been spotted on the road to Bethlehem have been dispatched by Herod to hurt the child. They take measures to protect Mary and the baby Jesus, and are only calmed when an angel

---

46 The back page of the printed version of *Dios es el Rey* (Granada: José María Zamora, 1852) lists the titles of two other short plays by Lozano published by Zamora in the "Repertorio Dramático" series before 1852: *Un doble sacrificio* (2 acts) and *Una noche menos y un desengaño más* (1 act). The series, according to a list of book dealers handling the printed volumes – provided with *Don Juan de Austria* (1854) – was widely distributed. Some ninety cities and towns were in the distribution network. Zamora declares unequivocally that he will prosecute "con arreglo a las leyes vigentes" anyone who puts on the plays in the "Repertorio Dramático" without receiving his permission.

appears to assure them that "aun no es llegado el día de que muera / el hijo que llevaste en tus entrañas" ("the day has not yet arrived when the fruit of your womb will die") (I, 7). The play ends with the expected *tableau vivant*.

The first sustained efforts of which we have notice are two longer plays published in Granada in 1854, *Don Juan de Austria* and *María o la abnegación. Don Juan de Austria*, a historical drama as the title reveals, is much more ambitious than anything Lozano had written to this date. It was an attempt to imitate the historico-political dramas of the 1840s – popularized above all by Rodríguez Rubí, Zorrilla, and the Asquerinos – but it added little to the predictable good-guy-vs-bad-guy scenario. Although Lozano demonstrates good use of poetic meter and an interesting play on the religious angle (the Catholic Spaniards against the Flemish/French Protestants) she fails to present consistent or logical characters, and most notably to create dramatically convincing entrances and exits for them. One hears echoes from previous plays, including don Juan Tenorio's famous "Por dondequiera que fui" ("Everywhere I went") speech in Alejandro Farnesio's comment,

> Ya lo veis, doquiera vamos
> la victoria conseguimos,
> y aunque muy pocos seamos
> siempre venciendo salimos
> cuando la lid empeñamos.   (III, 9)

(So you see, wherever we went victory was ours, and even though there were only a few of us, we always came out winners when we got into battles.)

In fact, the heroine María's function in the play parallels that of Zorrilla's Inés in that she is there to "save" the title character. Even though she rather coquettishly tells her father, "que hablar de patria y valor / no está bien a una mujer" ("a woman shouldn't really speak of things like country and bravery") (I, 3) she has every intention of intervening in the affairs of Juan de Austria if need be, even if this means blocking her father's involvement in an as yet undefined conspiracy against the prince. As Inés had saved Tenorio, so María changed her father following her mother's death (he even uses images which Zorrilla employed):

> Tú sabes que lo he cumplido;
> yo era altivo y atrevido,
> mas de tu aliento el aroma
> de tigre me ha convertido
> en una humilde paloma.   (I, 3)

(You know that I have changed; I was arrogant and bold, but your fragrant words have changed me from a tiger into a humble dove.)

Later, María asks the prince, in a clear reprise of don Juan's famous question to the Comendador,

> Dime, don Juan, ¿es verdad
> que nuestras almas no mueren,
> y que hay una eternidad
> que les otorga que esperen
> hallar la felicidad? (IV, 5)

(Tell me, don Juan, is it true that our souls do not die, and that there is an eternal life for those who want to find happiness?)

While this provides yet another example of how deeply embedded Zorrilla's play became in the dramatic mentality of the nineteenth century, it does not add up to an interesting or new interpretation of the theme.

The other play produced that year, *María o la abnegación* is also a historical drama, but it harkens back more to the psychological impulses of *Una actriz por amor* in that it presents two cousins who grow up "in love" but who get separated when the man becomes distracted by someone else. (One is tempted to wonder if this situation had any resonance in the early life of the author.) Here, Lozano has absorbed the classical lessons of her predecessors by maintaining the unities of time, place, and action. (The neoclassical unities were still very much alive in the theatre of the nineteenth century, not only in revivals of Moratín's plays, but also in comedies written by Bretón and others.) One interesting element in this play is the heroine's emotional disintegration in Act II, when she is forced to sacrifice her honor to save her cousin Raúl; she takes refuge in hysteria, convulsive laughter, and temporary insanity – a frequent recourse of the heroines of French and Spanish melodramas. We hear a brief echo of Espronceda's bitter lament in "Canto a Teresa" (the second canto of his extended Romantic poem, *El diablo mundo*) in María's cry,

> ¡Ay! ¿Quién me llama, di? ¡Qué voz he oido,
> que hace brotar así del alma mía
> dulces memorias de placer perdido?
> Di mi nombre otra vez con ese acento
> que el corazón de dicha me estremece:
> habla, dentro del alma tu voz siento
> y un recuerdo de amores me parece. (III, 7)

(Oh, who calls me, who? What voice have I heard that stirs in my soul sweet memories of lost pleasure? Say my name again with that voice that makes my heart tremble with happiness: speak, deep in my soul I feel your voice and it seems like a memory of bygone loves.)

In III, 10 she repeats her conviction, as did Espronceda, that life and happiness are mere illusions. None of this is sustained enough to give real dramatic strength to what is a competent and interesting, but hardly transcendental, work.

Of more interest, perhaps because it is a product of the author's maturity, is the last play produced by Lozano, *La ruina del hogar* (1873).[47] Here we detect two concerns, not only of hers, but of the Spanish middle classes in general: the role of women in contemporary society, and the central place occupied by money in the middle-class world. At the play's opening, we suspect we will be following an independent heroine, one who complains to her brother of the restrictions placed on her solely because of her sex. Adela states:

> tú puedes salir de casa,
> ver el mundo, mientras yo,
> ¡siempre sola, siempre aquí!
> esto aburre y desconsuela ...   (I, 1)

(you can leave the house, see the world, while I – always alone, always here! – am bored and saddened by this ...)

Lozano quickly turns the tables on this embryonic feminist by revealing her to be not an independent, educated woman but a silly person overly concerned with glitz, frills and the acquisitive power of money. Lozano disapproves strongly of her frivolous desire to imitate the elegant and rich María's style of dress and, in fact, it is her whining that puts into motion a series of events which nearly result in catastrophe for the family. Money is the root of this play's action: Carlos needs money to pay for medicine and for a month's stay in the country to regain his failing health; Adela needs money to buy elegant finery; Miguel needs money to repay the funds he illegally spent on a dress and jewels for Adela (he had found a sum of money and was waiting for someone to claim it); Mr. Lara needs money to maintain his business interests; the venerable parents of Carlos, Adela, and Miguel need money to support themselves in their old age. Lara, María's father, is a perfect representative of the new, money-driven society. He neglects his daughter ("más piensas en los números que en mí" ["you think more about your numbers than you do about me"] she says [II, 2]), but has done so not out of greed but out of his perceived need to provide for her following her mother's death. However, "¿No eres ya bastante rico?" ("Aren't you already rich enough?") she asks (II, 2). He reveals himself to be a long way away from the relaxed, pleasure-seeking

---

[47] *La primera duda* appeared in Granada (Viuda e Hijos de Zamora) with no date attached. Caldera calls it "su postrer drama," but makes no reference to *La ruina del hogar* of 1873. See Ermanno Caldera, "La perspectiva femenina en el teatro de Joaquina García Balmaseda y Enriqueta Lozano," *Escritoras románticas españolas*, ed. Marina Mayoral (Madrid: Fundación Banco Exterior, 1990): 211.

society of a mere century ago when he states, in an ironic updating of the
typical eighteenth-century Anacreontic ode:

> Goza del vivir,
> y déjame trabajar:
> tu edad es de disfrutar,
> la mía la de adquirir.   (II, 2)

(Enjoy your life and let me work: at your age you should be enjoying things, at
mine, I should be acquiring them.)

This is the ultimate post-Romantic world, the result of what Vega's *El
hombre de mundo* revealed, that is, the man who no longer identifies with
love, but merely with work and the importance of money. The money
problem weaves itself throughout the play, cropping up at significant
moments, discussed by everyone in various forms, and always propelling
the action forward. Carlos observes that the poor suffer society's disdain:
"Yo pobre nací / y al pobre desdeña el mundo" ("I was born poor, and
the world hates poor people") (II, 10). Still, it always comes back to a
criticism of Adela, who "ama el lujo con extremo, / y que gasta más que
debe / en adornos" ("loves luxuries too much and spends more than she
should on finery") (II, 3). Lozano's play captures the Spanish middle-
class obsession with money, and comments on its negative consequences
for the peace and tranquility of family relations. By the time she wraps it
all up in the final scene, sorting out each character's place in this grand
money scheme, the audience is pummeled with a heavy-handed and
reactionary moral lesson issued by Fernando, the patriarch, in words
which undermine completely Adela's opening lament about her lack of
freedom:

> Que sólo de la mujer
> la dulce misión serena,
> consiste en ser hija buena
> y ejemplo de madres ser;
> y que en su santa quietud
> feliz y bella se siente,
> si escritas lleva en la frente
> la bondad y la virtud.
> Mas ese afán de brillar
> que hoy a la mujer domina,
> es, hija mía, la ruina
> de la dicha y del hogar.   (III, 13)

(The woman's solemn mission in life is to be a good daughter and an exemplary
mother; to feel happy and beautiful in her sainted silence, if she carries the words
"goodness" and "virtue" written on her forehead. But the insistence on showing

off that has taken over women today is, my daughter, the end of happiness and of the home.)

Adela acquiesces.

As we have seen from these few examples, women dramatists of the nineteenth century approached their craft from a variety of social, thematic, and structural angles. Caldera has discerned in García Balmaseda and Lozano what he claims to be "una sensibilidad típicamente femenina"[48] ("a typically feminine sensibility"), but this strikes me as unconvincing and facile. These women did not speak in a unified, "feminine" voice, but rather in a multiplicity of voices tuned to their personal and social situations. Later in the century we do find women coming out of isolation by working together on group projects such as newspapers and journals for women:

En 1870 la prensa femenina se halla en su apogeo y gran número de mujeres se consagran a la literatura. La mayor parte de toda esta producción proviene de Madrid, donde radican las clases sociales a quienes puede interesar este tipo de publicaciones: la aristocracia, los funcionarios, los políticos y la burguesía instruida. Pero también otras ciudades, particularmente Barcelona, Valencia y Cádiz se ven presas de esa fiebre de publicaciones.[49]

(In 1870 the feminine press is in its heyday and a large number of women decide to become writers. The majority of their production comes out of Madrid, where the social classes interested in this kind of publication are most numerous: the aristocracy, government workers, politicians, and the educated middle class. But also in other cities, particularly in Barcelona, Valencia and Cadiz, one sees women taken over by that publication fever.)

On the staff of *La Ilustración de la Mujer* (Barcelona, 1883–1887), for example, we find Rosario de Acuña, Julia Asensi, Emilia Calé, and Faustina Sáez de Melgar. Voices we have left unheard (Martínez de Lafuente, García Balmaseda, Calderón, Cheix Martínez, Saéz de Melgar, and others) speak in the same rich and varied way. The real question is: what else was written and produced by women during the last century which has fallen through the cracks of literary history? The history of women in Spanish theatre is as much a history of absence as it is of presence, and the absence can speak very eloquently.

[48] Caldera, "Perspectiva feminina," pp. 207–208.
[49] Adolfo Perinat and Isabel Marrades, *Mujer, prensa y sociedad en España, 1830–1939* (Madrid: Centro de Investigaciones Sociológicas, 1980): 28–29.

6   High comedy, and low

The theatre of the second half of the century, following the indecorous failure of the Teatro Español, builds upon the growing middle class's insecurity about its political and economic situation. Issues which might previously have been discussed at home were now being debated in the public forum of the theatre, and the public discussion helped to raise the consciousness (and the demands) of this segment of Spanish society. Middle-class tastes were eclectic, which will account for the multiplicity of themes, genres, styles, and language which rush breathlessly onto the stage.[1] In fact, the *alta comedia* comprises one of the best series of documents we possess about the Spanish middle class, that is, the *upper* middle class, since the plays capture not only the anxieties but also the manners, customs, look, frailties, and strengths of this newly privileged segment of society. For that reason they are frequently referred to as *comedias de costumbres* (*costumbrismo burgués*) as well as *altas comedias*. The plays were considered documents by the dramatists who consciously set out to reflect that class – their class – in their plays. Tomás Rodríguez Rubí insisted that the scholars of the twenty-first century will have to turn to the plays of his contemporaries if they wish to understand in depth what Spanish nineteenth-century society was all about, and he was right:

a ellos será preciso que acudan los eruditos del siglo XXI, cuando deseen conocer y avalorar la manera de sentir en nuestros días: nuestra conciencia, cuando hacemos uso de la historia; nuestra cultura, nuestro lenguaje, ora escogido, ora apasionado, ora vulgar, y basta los grados de la moral pública en la severidad o benevolencia con que se censuren, toleren o disculpen los vicios, las deformidades y la corrupción de la sociedad en que vivimos.[2]

---

[1] María Pilar Espín Templado points out how the one-act *sainete* takes on an independent life of its own after 1870, no longer strictly connected to the longer play being offered. "El sainete en el último tercio del siglo XIX, culminación de un género dramático en el teatro español," *Epos* 3 (1987): 102. For this reason, as I did in the previous chapter, I will discuss all revelant plays regardless of generic distinction or length.

[2] Rodríguez Rubí, "Excelencia," p. 12.

(Scholars from the twenty-first century will have to turn to these plays if they want to understand and appreciate the way we feel today: our conscience, when we make use of history; our culture, our language [at times carefully modulated, at times impassioned, at times common], and public morality and how severely or benevolently the vices, deformities, and corruption of the society we live in are censured, tolerated, or pardoned.)

In his presentation of the high comedy Ruiz Ramón makes a similar observation:

Tratemos de describir este mundo dramático que conquistó a la burguesía madrileña a lo largo de casi veinticinco años. Nos encontramos en el corazón mismo de la mejor sociedad, dos de cuyos más conspicuos representantes son el libertino, azote de la institución del matrimonio y de la familia, y el hombre de negocios, adorador del interés y del tanto por ciento. El dramaturgo, defensor del matrimonio y de la familia frente al poder destructor del libertino, y de los valores espirituales (nobleza del alma, generosidad y desinterés, idealismo moral) frente al positivismo materialista (egoísmo, cálculo, pasión del dinero) se convierte en portavoz de los principios éticos que deben regir toda sociedad cristiana y hace papel de director de conciencia que, denunciando el mal que gangrena la sociedad, sermonea a su público.[3]

(Let's try to describe this dramatic world that took over the middle class of Madrid for a period of almost twenty-five years. We find ourselves at the very heart of the best of society, two of whose most conspicuous representatives are the libertine, the scourge of the institution of marriage and of the family, and the businessman, worshipper of banking interest and percentages. The playwright, a defender of marriage and the family against the destructive power of the libertine, and of spiritual values [nobility of the soul, generosity and disinterestedness, moral idealism] against materialist positivism [egoism, accounts, passion for money] becomes the spokesman for the ethical principles which should dominate any Christian society, and he plays the role of the director of conscience who, denouncing the evil that rots society, preaches to his public.)

We already discerned this shift in Vega, and now it will move to center stage, so to speak. If Romantic plays and historical dramas questioned the contemporary political scene, the *alta comedia* will present a paradigm of virtue by unmasking vice, greed, ambition, and infidelity on a personal level. The grand gesture of the Romantic stage becomes toned down to a familiar scale; characters begin to whisper and sit rather than shout and faint. The broad brush strokes with which many Romantic dramatists painted are transformed, by more careful attention to psychological realities and personal motives, into subtle canvases on which are detailed the lives and loves of the bourgeoisie. As Jesús Rubio Jiménez has written, by mid-century, "la burguesía, ya no agitadora y revolucionaria, sino instalada en el poder, fue el grupo social que controló en aquellos

---

[3] Ruiz Ramón, *Historia*, (1983), pp. 345–346.

años la sociedad española"[4] ("the middle class, no longer agitated and revolutionary, but rather now installed in power, was the social group which controlled Spanish society during those years"). With the *alta comedia* we begin to see what has been called the modern comedy in Spain. Audiences which previously were asked to identify with the symbolic space of the characters are now asked to witness their own lives on stage, and to contemplate the actions and reactions of characters which mirrored their more immediate concerns. That space changes from the ruined mansions, cemeteries, caves, and jails of Romanticism into comfortable drawing rooms and offices which reflect the values and attitudes of the nascent bourgeoisie. What was happening, of course, was a dismantling of mainly symbolic theatre and the creation of a more "realistic" school of writing which nonetheless conceptualized dramatic space in symbolic terms.

The term *alta comedia* was in use as the second half of the century dawned. Eugenio de Ochoa, in his diatribe against the plethora of theatres in Madrid in 1853, writes of the dramatic genres being cultivated by his contemporaries, among which he included the "alta comedia."[5] More pointedly, Rodríguez Rubí, credited with being an initiator of the *alta comedia* in Spain, spoke of the "interrumpida magnética corriente" ("interrupted magnetic current") which tied what was going on on stage to the audience without forgetting the "orden económico" ("economic order") which the theatre demands.[6] That is to say, the theatre is capable of (and responsible for) fomenting not only of spiritual values (virtue) but also material benefits. This is an entirely new focus for theatre, never before defended with such eloquence in such an august forum as the Real Academia Española. Rubí maintained:

Se ve, pues, que el teatro, además del respeto que merece, como todo aquello que resiste sin gastarse a la rueda voladora de los años, lleva también en su fecundo seno un manantial inagotable de ideas para solaz del espíritu, y de bienes positivos *para el sustento y atenciones de la vida material.*[7]

(So one sees that the theatre, besides the respect which it earns, as does everything that resists the toll of the years without getting older, also carries within its fertile bosom an inextinguishable source of ideas to console the spirit as well as positive benefits *for the support and maintenance of material life.*)

This is precisely what we will see in the *altas comedias* written by playwrights as diverse as Rubí himself, Manuel Tamayo y Baús, Adelardo López de Ayala, Luis de Eguílaz, Narciso Serra, and Enrique Zumel,

---

[4] Rubio Jiménez, "El teatro en el siglo XIX," p. 627.
[5] Eugenio de Ochoa, "Sobre el estado actual de los teatros en España," *Revista Española de Ambos Mundos* I (1853): 66.
[6] Rodríguez Rubí, "Excelencia," p. 13.   [7] *Ibid.* p. 14. Emphasis added.

among others, and it is one of the elements which plants itself firmly in the dramaturgy of the last third of the century (as we saw in Lozano's *La ruina del hogar*, for example). These authors privileged "pensamientos trascendentales" ("transcendental thoughts," from a review of Eguílaz's *La cruz del matrimonio* [The Cross of Matrimony] in the newspaper *El Contemporáneo*, 22 December 1861) over plot or character.

This is not to imply that the playwrights of this period foresaw some glorious new golden age of dramaturgy on the horizon. On the contrary – and well in keeping with their predecessors and contemporaries – both Ochoa and Rubí filled their articles with the usual laments concerning the decline of the Spanish theatre, and both offered suggestions on how to bring it out, as Rubí put it, of "la situación en que yace hoy el de España: ... es constitucional el padecimiento, aguda la dolencia, común la infección, universales el conflicto y las angustias"[8] ("the condition which Spain lies in today: ... the suffering is constitutional, the pain sharp, the infection generalized, and the conflict and anguish wide-spread"). Such protestations, by now *de rigueur* among playwrights and critics, allowed Rubí to posit a solution, in keeping with the new trend in playwriting. What was wrong with the theatre today, declared Rubí, was its dependence on "tipsy, dishonest" boulevard comedies which displayed an overabundance of "chistes inspirados por la fiebre del sensualismo"[9] ("jokes inspired in the fever of sensualism"). Implied in his statements was the need to rediscover the moral compass of Spanish theatre, although he finally concludes that what is really needed is another series of government regulations similar to those enacted in 1849, a new "proyecto de reforma teatral"[10] ("plan for theatrical reform"). A similar analysis of the moral impact of drama was elaborated by José Fernández Espino in his 1862 article, "De la moral en el drama"[11] ("On Morality in Drama"). The obsession with morality in the theatre was hardly surprising given the high level of corruption in public life. Bankers, businessmen, and politicians dominated public discourse, all too frequently putting personal interest before the public good, while the man in the street became progressively more disillusioned with the country's political and spiritual leadership. The resulting pressure exploded finally in 1868.

Theatrical reform would not be brought about by legislation but by example. As Antonio Ferrer del Río stated in his reply to Rubí's inaugural address to the Royal Academy, the theatre should teach men to be free, strong, generous, ennobled by true virtue, upright, and magnanimous, which is precisely what the *alta comedia* tried to do. This moraliz-

---

[8] *Ibid.* pp. 20–21.   [9] *Ibid.* p. 21.   [10] *Ibid.* p. 28.
[11] José Fernández Espino, "De la moral en el drama," *Estudios de literatura y de crítica* (Madrid: Imprenta de la Andalucía, 1862).

ing attitude showed itself clearly in the comic works of the new wave of Spanish dramatists, although the *alta comedia* cannot be easily defined with one or two simple adjectives. The instability of the middle class at mid-century (notwithstanding its ascendency), combined with the divergent political and social pressures weighing upon it, created a climate in the theatre which was at once mixed and unsettled. One thing was clear, however: the new dramatists wanted both to reflect their class and to guide it toward a more stable future. As Rubio Jiménez notes, "Los dramaturgos españoles no trataban de mostrar cómo era la realidad, sino que acababan siempre insistiendo en cómo debía ser"[12] ("Spanish dramatists did not try to show reality as it was, but always ended up insisting on how it should be"). What this meant for the theatre was not only a shift in the themes being presented, but also a profound change in the conception of dialogue and psychology (as far as the characters were concerned) and in the structure of the plays. As the *alta comedia* moved toward a more realistic mode of expression, playwrights abandoned the high emotionalism of Romantic drama, the exaggerated language of the characters, the intense symbolism of the scenery, and the artificial dénouements so prevalent in the plays of the 1830s and 1840s. Ambiguity rather than declamation, couched in a more realistic ambience (although still written in verse for the most part), became the dominant language of these plays.

The high comedy was hardly the only form of theatre in the period from mid-century to the Glorious Revolution of 1868 and beyond. Many other dramatists made decent livings, and attracted wide-spread attention, with their comedies, dramas, zarzuelas, and short parodies. Aside from the names we have already seen, the most active of these writers are Enrique Pérez Escrich (whose first work was performed in 1850), A. Francisco Camprodón (1851), Luis Mariano de Larra (1851), Luis de Eguílaz (1853), Miguel Pastorfido (1854), Carlos Frontaura y Vázquez (1856), Manuel Ortiz de Pinedo (1857), Rafael del Castillo (1859), Enrique Gaspar (1860), Eusebio Blasco (1862), Mariano Pina (1864), Miguel Ramos Carrión (1866) and Francisco Javier de Burgos (1866). However, since the *alta comedia* most clearly typified the dramaturgy of this period, we shall take a look at it first.

Prelude to the *alta comedia*

Although the *alta comedia* enjoyed its apogee in the twenty years following the collapse of the Teatro Español, several playwrights of the 1840s had already discerned the new impulses which would define the *alta*

---

[12] Rubio Jiménez, "El teatro en el siglo XIX," p. 638.

comedia post-1850. We saw how Vega's *El hombre de mundo* turned the Romantic paradigm on its head by transforming the don Juan character into a middle-class husband. Likewise, Rodríguez Rubí, whom W. F. Smith has called the "originator" of the *alta comedia* in Spain, wrote several plays which display the characteristics of this type of comedy.[13] As early as 1844, nearly a full year before Vega's *El hombre de mundo* was performed in Madrid, the newspaper *Revista de Teatros* (2 December 1844) hailed Rubí as a master of the *alta comedia*: "Aun se halla en la flor de su juventud: la fecundidad de su ingenio es prodigiosa: tan excelso brilla en el género lírico, como en el de costumbre, como en la *alta comedia*" ("He is still very young; the fertility of his talent is impressive: he shines equally in the lyric theatre, in the theatre of manners, and in the *alta comedia*," emphasis added). Praise for Rubí's theatre exceeded that issued during the 1840s for the theatre of Bretón, Vega, Gil y Zárate, Hartzenbusch, and the majority of those dramatists best remembered today. Smith guesses that about half of his plays can be considered to be *altas comedias* (a somewhat exaggerated figure), and he detects early signs of this type of playwriting in *Toros y cañas* (1840), *Rivera* (1841), *Dos validos y castillos en el aire* (1842), and *Detrás de la cruz el diablo* (The Devil Lurks Behind the Cross, 1842), while claiming that Rubí developed the *alta comedia* more fully in five plays published between 1843 and 1845 (two of which, *La rueda de la fortuna* and *Bandera negra*, we have already seen in a different light).[14]

Contemporary political and financial corruption was the theme of *El arte de hacer fortuna* (The Art of Getting Rich), which played at the Príncipe Theatre on 9 December 1845 to solid acclaim and moved to Barcelona and Granada in January, 1846 (it reappeared in 1868, 1874, and 1883, during conflictive moments in Spanish nineteenth-century history). It railed against corruption and greed by presenting a bright but unscrupulous wheeler-dealer (a stand-in for José de Salamanca?) who manipulates and wheedles his way into a substantial fortune, and, hence, into access to the government at the highest levels. *El hombre feliz* (The Happy Man, 1848) is a sequel to this play, and the much-later *¡El gran filón!* (A Vein of Gold!, 1874) takes up its theme of economic corruption and exploitation once again. Still, it was not until after the plays of Tamayo and López de Ayala became popular in the mid-1850s that Rubí

---

13 W. F. Smith, "Contributions of Rodríguez Rubí to the Development of the *alta comedia*," *Hispanic Review* 10 (1942): 53.

14 Smith, "Contributions of Rodríguez Rubí," p. 56. Smith makes a case for including the historical plays in the *alta comedia* type of drama since Rubí focuses more on the didactic social note than on historical fact. He is certainly correct in asserting "Rubí was little interested in the historical scene *per se* but employed it only as a convenient medium for the portrayal of the contemporary scene," p. 57.

focused on the non-historical contemporary society in which he lived. *La familia* (The Family) opened at the Circo Theatre on 11 April 1866 (Narciso Serra, in his capacity as Censor de Teatros, approved it for performance on 10 April), with Matilde Díez in the lead role, and the newspapers immediately claimed for it a "señaladísimo éxito" ("very notable success") (*La Epoca*, 12 April 1866), but it was never one of Rubí's most highly regarded works. It was rather a good (bad?) example of the hundreds of morality plays written in the second half of the century. It is of little literary interest, weakened by preachiness (the aptly named Santos declaims *ad nauseam* things like "¡He aquí los amargos frutos / del desorden en las casas!" ["Here you see the bitter result of disorder in the home!"] [II, 9], "¡Qué olvido de la virtud!" ["What neglect of virtue!"] [II, 10], and "En el exceso está el quid" ["The main point is in the excess"] [II, 11]) and shopworn images, but it was what the public found comforting. Santos delivers several long speeches in Act II in which he implores Narcisa to be a better mother, not to indulge her son Sabino so much in order that he should grow up to be a strong, family-oriented man. Her love is misguided, "infecundo, ciego" ("barren, blind") since she does not know how to discipline him. Such messages addressed post-Romantic concerns for the wellbeing of society and the proper methods of child-rearing, education, family harmony, and interpersonal relationships – a kind of nineteenth-century primer by theatrical Dr. Spocks. The play lacks dramatic focus although it abounds in moral messages as Santos preaches his lesson of stability and harmony to each of the major characters one by one. The frequency of this type of play reveals the anxiety of a society in transition. Jacinto Octavio Picón praised *La familia*, among others, for reflecting "el medio social en que se produce"[15] ("the social ambience in which it is produced").

With *¡El gran filón!* (1874) Rubí once again demonstrated that the *alta comedia* abandoned past history to focus almost exclusively on modern-day society (it was a "fotografía de la sociedad actual" ["a photograph of today's society"] according to the reviewer for *La Epoca* on 17 December 1874). This play's main interest stems from its concentration on the political world of post-Isabeline Madrid when individuals and interest groups often succeeded in manipulating governments through vote-stuffing in congress and rabble-rousing in the press. Rubí draws on many literary traditions for certain elements in the play, including the pica-resque, *costumbrismo*, and Romanticism, but his main concern is the capacity of modern hucksters to organize conspiracies for political power, no longer in the halls of the royal palace, but now in the halls of congress.

---

15 Jacinto Octavio Picón, "Don Tomás Rodríguez Rubí," in *Autores dramáticos contempo-ráneos* II (1882): 77.

What the audience sees is the effect of *amiguismo* on the political structure as well as the paralyzing effect of the constant rise and fall of political power brokers. Several ne'er-do-wells rise to positions of prominence – Minister of War, Chancellor of the Exchequer, Minister of Public Works – in governments manipulated by the clever, blackmailing Jacinto, who also manages to manipulate the Stock Market for his personal gain and that of his party. We see the effects of unemployment brought on by the whims of politics and the instability of such governments, problems which also form much of the social fabric woven by Galdós into his novels. Jacinto believes that "En política, señores, / no hay enemigo ni amigo. / No hay más que conveniencia" ("In politics, my friends, there are neither enemies nor friends; there is only expediency") (III, 2). Such cynical "realism" accurately reflected the dominant public mood of the early 1870s, when business and personal interests (Jacinto reminds his friends that they belong to his "fracción personal" ["personal faction"] [III, 2]) dominated public life in Spain. Rubí's stated objective, written in the dedication of the play to his friend of twenty years, Ramón de Campoamor, was to "contribuir a sofocar el incendio de la patria" ("help douse the fire that consumes the country"). He wrote this "anatomía de nuestro desvencijado cuerpo social" ("dissection of our divided social body") in order to "exponer con la debida mesura algunos de los vicios sociales más arraigados ya en nuestras costumbres"[16] ("calmly expose some of the most firmly rooted social ills that plague our habits"). ¡*El gran filón!* played at the Teatro Español in December, 1874, and immediately went into a second printing; it was revived in 1883. The very types depicted in the play attended the première and applauded "los intencionados chistes, los gracejos, los epigramas de que el diálogo está lleno" ("the barbed jokes, the witticisms, the epigrams that fill the dialogue") (*La Epoca*, 4 December 1874); this select public, which understood perfectly well the aims of Rubí's criticism, clamored for tickets for weeks thereafter. "Desde las primeras escenas el público supo apreciar aquella crítica despiadada y cruel, pero exacta, tanto de los vicios de la sociedad actual como de las miserias de la política moderna" ("From the very first scenes the public knew how to appreciate that wicked and cruel – but exact – criticism of the vices of today's society and of the evils of modern politics") (*La Epoca*, 4 December 1874).

Manuel Tamayo y Baús

Manuel Tamayo y Baús (1829–1898) sought to paint "el retrato moral del hombre" ("a moral portrait of man") in his plays, eschewing the depiction of "real" life since "ni todo lo que es verdad en el mundo cabe en el

---

16 Tomás Rodríguez Rubí, ¡*El gran filón!* 2nd. edn. (Madrid: José Rodríguez, 1874), no page number.

teatro"[17] ("not everything that is true in this world has a place in the theatre"). This tendency to moralize and to force the dénouements of his plays leads Gerard Flynn to call him "Tamayo of the Happy Ending,"[18] and Rubio Jiménez to note that such moralization became a hallmark of the entire period.[19] This "morality" was of course the conservative, Catholic, middle-class set of values which was not to become seriously challenged until the end of the century when anticlericalism and support for workers found their voices on Spanish stages. Spanish theatre under Isabel II (whose three-time prime minister Ramón de Narváez set the tone of the political debate), the Restauración, and the Regencia – even taking into account the years of the first Republic and the influence of novelistic realism and naturalism – was predominantly a conservative, middle-class affair.

Tamayo's first staged play, *Juana de Arcos* (Joan of Arc, performed in Madrid in 1847), had evident Romantic overtones, as did several of his next efforts. It was not until the debut, on 7 December 1853, of his tragedy *Virginia* that he was fully accepted as a star in the Madrid literary firmament.[20] This eagerly awaited play met the expectations of the audience and of the critics, who commented on it widely in the capital's newspapers. Tamayo had invested much labor in the work, managing to write a tragedy that was at once deeply felt and cleverly executed. Other hits followed, among them *La ricahembra* (The Rich Woman, 1854; written in collaboration with Aureliano Fernández Guerra) and especially *La locura de amor* (The Foolishness of Love, 1855), both historical dramas which examined with impressive subtlety the complex psychological motivations of female characters. *La locura*, which concerns the trials of the unfortunate Juana la Loca, achieved a "triunfo ... apoteósico"[21] ("exalted triumph") even more impressive than that of *Virginia* two years previously.

It was not until later that year, however, with the appearance of *Hija y madre* (Daughter and Mother), and, in 1856, with *La bola de nieve* (The Snowball), that Tamayo began to discern – and subsequently to lead – the shift occurring in the theatre toward a more contemporary, "realistic," drama. Tamayo felt proud of *Hija y madre* and considered it to be among his best creations. The public of his day agreed (*La Epoca* rated it "una de las mejores de este joven autor" ["one of this young author's best plays"]

---

[17] Tamayo y Baús, "Discurso leído ante la Real Academia Española (1858)," in *Obras completas de Manuel Tamayo y Baús* (Madrid: Ediciones FAX, 1947), p. 1136.
[18] Gerard Flynn, *Manuel Tamayo y Baús* (New York: Twayne Publishers, 1973): 30.
[19] Rubio Jiménez, "El teatro en el siglo XIX," p. 632.
[20] Ramón Esquer Torres provides a thorough study of *Virginia* in his book, *El teatro de Tamayo y Baús* (Madrid: CSIC, 1965): 29–66.
[21] *Ibid.* p. 88.

on 25 May 1855), but later critics have relegated it to a place of secondary importance among his works, most likely because of the touches of the old *comedia lacrimosa* and the strong Romantic overtones of the last-minute revelation which brings the plot to a close. (Contemporary audiences loved such melodramatic touches; modern critics tend to sneer in despair at their artificiality.)[22] It is a play which deals with the importance of strong family ties (a subject Rubí picked up on later, as we have seen) and the role of marriage as a vehicle for upward mobility. It is the play in which, according to Neale H. Tayler, Tamayo discovered the importance of moral values in his theatre, revealing a social consciousness which is one of the characteristics of the *alta comedia*.[23]

Tamayo's control of dramatic technique is amply evident in *Hija y madre*'s three acts. Ostensibly, the play tells the tale of María, the lost orphan who turns out to be, in the best Romantic tradition, the daughter of the Countess of Valmarín, but it is really about class pretentions and social mobility. Any viewer who had suffered the travails of Rugiero or Manrique (el trovador) would figure out as early as Act 1, Scene 1 that the Countess's long-lost daughter Elena would appear in disguise and be recognized as hers by the play's end. However, that was clearly not Tamayo's main concern. What he wanted to do was look into contemporary social structures and how money, business dealings, and social pretentions help to maintain them. The Countess is being blackmailed by the jealous marquesa over an unpaid debt, for example, while it is also revealed that the Countess's daughter was kidnapped by bandits set on extracting money from her in return. Still, Tamayo is not entirely critical of "la gente de calidad" ("people of quality"), for he sees in them the hope for Spain's recovery, but only if they return to the values which in his judgment create unity and harmony in society rather than fragmentation and chaos. The play's whole structure pivots on the revelation that the Countess, who ran away from home at the age of sixteen, is in reality the lost daughter of Andrés (Elena's "father"). She denies her suspicion that she is indeed his daughter since her ambition to marry the prestigious Duque de Campo Real and fear of ridicule by the "gente de calidad" – "el mundo me acobarda, espántame el escándalo" ("the world frightens me; I am afraid of scandal") (III, 3) she says – keep her from admitting that she is of humble origin. She has traded external trappings for internal harmony and love. But "Tamayo of the Happy Ending" assures that she

---

22 Ironically, Esquer Torres reports that *Hija y madre* was in the 1950s Tamayo's most frequently performed play in Spanish provincial theatres. *Ibid.* p. 112.
23 Neale H. Tayler, *Las fuentes del teatro de Tamayo y Baús: Originalidad e influencias* (Madrid: Gráficas Uguina, 1959): 89. For Esquer Torres, it is not until *La bola de nieve* that such concerns manifest themselves.

comes to her senses, recognizes her father and daughter, and they all live happily ever after.

Similar impulses control *La bola de nieve*, performed for the first time in Madrid on 12 May 1856, to a large and boisterous audience who judged it to be an "éxito completísimo" ("complete success") (*La Nación*, 17 May 1856). In short order it became one of the standard repertory offerings of the next few decades, appearing in different theatres – the Circo, the Lope de Rueda, the Español, the Eslava, the Apolo – in 1863, 1864, 1869, 1870, 1872, 1876, 1877, 1879, 1882, and so on. Performances on its twentieth anniversary garnered it the following praise in the pages of *El Imparcial*: "la obra es extraordinaria. Parece escrita para demostrar que en los actos ordinarios de la vida, en la prosa de un hogar pacífico, pueden hallarse resortes dramáticos, hondas emociones para el público, vivo interés y creciente anhelo en los que siguen el desenvolvimiento de la trama" ("it is an extraordinary work. It seems to have been written to demonstrate that in life's ordinary acts, in the common situations of the peaceful home, one can find dramatic material, deep emotions for the public, lively interest, and a growing eagerness among those who are following the plot's twists and turns") (14 November 1886).

By the debut of *La bola de nieve* Tamayo felt even more confident in his new-found morality and the result of this confidence was a brilliant play on the theme of Spanish envy. Tamayo identified envy as one of the great social ills of his society, grounded in the Spanish temperament and expressed on both an individual and a collective plane. Such destructive emotions can "snowball" into poisoned relationships and family chaos. Clara, consumed with jealousy and suspicion over the behavior of her innocent fiancé Fernando, manages not only to lose him but also her best friend María as well. Her obsession threatens the friendship between Fernando and Luis, Clara's brother, and also spills over onto Luis's treatment of the household servants, creating a microcosmic look at society as a whole. Tamayo once again insists that virtue is more valuable than money. As Fernando says,

¿Y te llamas noble? Necio,
¿valen más que su beldad
tus riquezas? ¿Más tu nombre
que su virtud? ¿Lo que da
mérito y fama tan sólo
en esta vida fugaz,
que lo que Dios en el cielo
premia con lauro inmortal?
Bien dices; razón te sobra;
la unión era desigual:
no mereces tú una dicha
que ni aun sabes apreciar.   (II, 13).

(You call yourself noble? You idiot, is your wealth worth more than her beauty? Your name more than her virtue? Fame and celebrity in this brief life more than the things that God rewards with immortal distinction? But you are right, I concede: this match was uneven. You don't deserve a treasure that you don't even know how to appreciate.)

These lessons, which strike us today as obvious and conventional, became nevertheless part of the conservative mantra of mid-nineteenth-century theatre, constantly put forth by playwright after playwright as a "solution" to society's decline into immorality and false values. Tamayo was a master at such moral posturing, and he knew how to write quick-paced dialogue, how to draw out a scene, and how to capture in short strokes the quirks and foibles of his characters. His lessons were welcomed and applauded by the wide theatre-going audience of the 1850s, 1860s, and 1870s, who looked around in increasing despair at the immorality of their governments (and of the royal family above all) and at the corruption of the burgeoning shopkeepers, businessmen, and nouveau riche landowners who seemed to rule Spain.

Tamayo revealed that the "good" spaces of his society were the comfortable, middle-class interiors of his contemporaries rather than the rustic outside spaces which the Romantics had used to such stunning effect. Twenty years previously the contrast between outside spaces and inside spaces favored the former. In *Don Alvaro*, *El trovador*, or even *Don Frutos en Belchite* (Tamayo quotes from this play in *Lances de honor*[24] [Duels of Honor]), for example, the drawing-rooms and palace interiors were places where the hero ran into conflict with the representatives of an oppressive, closed or frivolous society, but in the *alta comedia* it is the other way around. Natural settings are frequently places where the hero feels out of sorts, out of control, in fact, out of his "natural" element. Identity becomes associated with the constructs of society – of the upper middle class society which is Tamayo's milieu – rather than with man's wilder nature, even though the dramatists of the time insisted on criticizing the corruption of that society. Issues become resolved in the interiors of bourgeois homes, inside the *hogar* which symbolized family unity and values, rather than in the interiors of rich people's residences or in parks, gardens, or other outside places.

Lances de honor (1863) demonstrates this observation. The villain of the piece, Pedro de Villena, is a liberal politician who has surrounded himself with the trappings of wealth and power associated (in Tamayo's mind) with the representatives of his class and ideological persuasion. The play opens in Villena's "gabinete lujosamente amueblado" ("luxuriously fur-

---

[24] "Belchite, Belchite quiero / la corte no es para mí" says Fabián García's wife in II, 1.

nished sitting-room") and it soon becomes evident that Villena is a corrupt, overbearing character who thrives on the fractiousness of the political arena. He attacks his conservative opponents for the sport of it, creating instability in the government and seeking to further his own agenda. His rival, the modest representative, Fabián García, cannot wait until the end of his term so he can return to "normal" life, which for him is a life surrounded by his friends and family. Tamayo sets up the political division in a neat dialogue between Miguel, Fabián's son, and his friend Paulino, Villena's son.

MIGUEL. — Acabarás por hacerme reír. ¿Qué tacha puede ponérsele a mi buen padre, que es casi un santo?

PAULINO. — Bien parecen los santos en el almanaque, pero muy mal en unas Cortes del siglo diecinueve. Todo el mundo se rió el otro día del buen señor.

MIGUEL. — ¿Por qué?

PAULINO. — Porque empezó su discurso invocando el auxilio de Dios.

MIGUEL. — ¿Y qué tiene de risible que un hombre implore el auxilio de Dios cuando va a influir con su conducta en la suerte de todo un pueblo?

PAULINO. — Anda, simplón. Tu reloj atrasa por lo menos un siglo.

MIGUEL. — Pues a mí me parece que el tuyo señala una hora funesta. (I, 3)

(MIGUEL. — You'll make me laugh. What can they criticize my father for, who is almost a saint?

PAULINO. — Saints are fine for a holy calendar, but hardly for a nineteenth-century Parliament. Everyone laughed at him the other day.

MIGUEL. — Why?

PAULINO. — Because he began his speech by invoking God's help.

MIGUEL. — What is so funny about a man invoking God's help when what he is about to do will affect the lives of a whole nation?

PAULINO. — Come on, you fool. Your watch is at least a century behind the times.

MIGUEL. — Well it seems to me that yours is marking a very sad time.)

This captures perfectly Tamayo's reaction against the growing anti-clericalism of Spanish society. The entire debate takes place in Villena's elegant drawing-room. Villena despises Fabián, among other reasons because his wife does her own shopping (she is seen buying tomatoes in the local market) and the couple have a carved *ecce homo* in their home, which represent of course the family- and church-oriented values which Tamayo so eloquently defends. The "lance" promised in the title is threatened in the first act, but Fabián's brother, a conservative provincial governor, refuses to participate in it solely because it would destroy the family of one or the other of the combatants ("Si él muriese en duelo, sería viuda su mujer y huérfano su hijo" ["If he were to die in the duel, his wife would be left a widow and his son an orphan"] [I, 3]). The others laugh at him when he quotes the Fifth Commandment against killing.

When the author gives voice to Fabián, the real hero of the play, the scene shifts to the latter's "despacho modestamente amueblado" ("modestly furnished office") where he expounds his theories of life and politics. Act II opens with Fabián and his wife engaged in symbolic activities: he reads (the thoughtful man) while she sews (the traditional, homebound woman). Tamayo criticizes those who think that dueling will solve personal problems and presents the core of his thinking on the issue in II, 5, but even though the adults manage to avoid the threatened duel, the younger generation – Paulino and Miguel – challenge one another and end up by the third act in physical conflict. "¡Oh, qué trabajo cuesta ser hombre de bien" ("being an upright man is a lot of work") laments Fabián (II, 11). Fabián sees Villena as the source of the trouble: "Es usted uno de esos audaces que por los méritos de intrigar a todas horas, de traficar villanamente con su conciencia, de enriquecerse por arte de magia, adquieren el derecho de llamarse hombres importantes, y son vivo testimonio de lo que en el mundo pueden el descaro y la procacidad" ("You are one of those daring types who, by conspiring at all hours of the day and night, by villainously forgetting your conscience, by getting rich through trickery, acquire the right to call themselves important men, and who are living proof of how far having no scruples can get you in this world") (II, 13).

Act III takes place, significantly, in "el campo" ("the country") where the two sons of the political opponents have decided to settle their grievance with pistols. Tamayo ends the play with a sappy religious message similar to don Juan's last-minute conversion: Villena, says, "Dios verdadero, creo en Ti" ("The one true God, I believe in you") (III, 6) amongst mutual pardons and prayers. Candelaria, mother of the dead Miguel, comforts the family's old antagonist by reassuring him, "Murió mi hijo para que usted resucitara" ("My son died so that you might be reborn") (III, 6). This ending, which strikes us as hackneyed today, was just what Tamayo's public demanded in the mid-1860s, and he was only too happy to oblige since his moral stance was a defense against what was in fact a growing corruption and inconsistency in his society, one which would lead inevitably to the explosion of September, 1868. Plays such as this one did little to change society's behavior, but they did at least reflect both the author's and the audience's anxieties.[25] In a way, Tamayo's intense religiosity is a logical extension of Gómez de Avellaneda's religious plays, updated from biblical times to encompass contemporary society.

Tamayo's acknowledged masterpiece is *Un drama nuevo*, a complex and entertaining play written on the same theme as *La bola de nieve*, but placed within a series of shifting perspectives which play on reality and fantasy in the theatre world. In *La bola* Fernando had referred to the jealous Clara as "mi Otela" ("my female Othello") (I, 9) and it is this aspect that Tamayo picks up in *Un drama nuevo*, first performed at the Teatro de la Zarzuela on 4 March 1867. It has received much critical attention, not only because of its intimate connection to Shakespearian drama, but also because of its subtle interweaving of theme and form.[26] The themes include jealousy, life in the theatre, love, vengeance, and artistic ambition. The close parallel between the play-within-the-play and the "real" life of the actors enables Tamayo to play out a series of misunderstandings, tensions, and emotions which he merges together into a beautiful prose work. The actors mouth words from the drama they are performing which accurately capture their own emotional states, and the audience therefore participates in the delicious ambiguity created as scenic fiction and "real" life merge. As Tamayo posits it, in real life the actors are acting; it is on stage where they live out their real emotions. The fusion at the end is so complete that the three levels of play – the play we are watching, the play being performed by the actors, and the play of emotions in each character – merge into one and become indistinguishable.

Tamayo's concept of reality did not yet encompass the broader social view which would be developed by the novelists and dramatists of the last third of the century. His was a purely artistic reality, an aesthetic reality in which art shaped each character's thoughts and actions. He rejected imitation of common speech as "absurdo." As he explained in his inaugural address to the Spanish Royal Academy in 1859,

Pero entiéndase bien que al hablar de realidad considero comprendidos juntamente en ella la materia y el espíritu, lo visible y lo invisible ... Y no se olvide tampoco que el mundo y la esfera de la dramática son cosas del todo diferentes. A

---

[25] See Ramón Esquer Torres, "Tamayo y Baús y la política del siglo XIX," *Segismundo* 1 (1965): 71–91.

[26] See Lester G. Crocker, "Techniques of Ambiguity in *Un drama nuevo*," *Hispania* 39 (1956): 412–418; José Alberich, "El papel de Shakespeare en *Un drama nuevo* de Tamayo," *Filología Moderna* 10 (1970): 301–322; Roberto Sánchez, "Los comediantes

no poder representarse en la ficción escénica más que sucesos positivamente acaecidos, sin alterarlos de manera ninguna; si un personaje cualquiera no hubiese de poder hacer ni decir sino lo que hubiese hecho y dicho en la vida, ni hablar más que en prosa incorrecta como habla la gente, ni siquiera usar otro idioma que el suyo natural, el arte y la realidad serían lo mismo, o, antes bien, el primero no existiría. Nadie, al sustentar que debe ser verdadero, ha querido nunca dar a entender semejante absurdo.[27]

(But understand this clearly: when I speak of reality I include in it both material and spiritual matters, the visible and the invisible . . . Do not forget that the world and the theatre are totally different things. If one were not able to put into a fictitious work anything that did not actually happen in real life, if a character were not able to do or say anything that was not done or said in real life, nor speak in anything other than the incorrect prose that people normally speak in, nor even use any language other than his own natural language, then art and reality would be the same thing, or, rather, art would not even exist. No one who suggests that art should be realistic has ever implied anything so absurd.)

Audiences and critics reacted favorably to *Un drama nuevo*, both in Spain and abroad (an English translation was performed in Canada and New York in 1879 to "ruidoso triunfo" ["a noisy triumph"] according to *La Epoca* [20 September 1879], a Portuguese version was performed in Lisbon in 1881, and an Italian version was played – of all places – at Teatro Lírico in Barcelona in 1889 before moving to Rome in 1891) and it remains unquestionably Tamayo's best-remembered work. The author remains faithful to his concept of scenic "reality," but this time does not pull out a happy ending, comforting himself and his audience instead with a plea by Shakespeare for us to pray for the dead and for their killers. The moral message of the *alta comedia* remains intact, but the happy ending is sacrificed to a deeper and darker tragedy, which is why this play has been remembered above all the others.

When Fabián lamented "Oh, qué trabajo cuesta ser hombre de bien" in *Lances* in 1863 he was foreshadowing the theme and title of Tamayo's last play, *Los hombres de bien* (The Upright Men), performed in the Lope de Rueda Theatre in Madrid on 17 December 1870. With it, Tamayo laid down his pen and, according to Manuel de la Revilla, "tuvo el malísimo gusto de descender a la arena política bajo el negro pendón del absolutismo neo-católico"[28] ("had the very bad taste to descend into the poli-

del XIX: *Un drama nuevo*," *Hispanic Review* 48 (1980): 435–447. Oddly, however, it is excluded from Díez Borque's generally complete *Historia del teatro en España* II.

27 Tamayo y Baús, "Discurso leído ante la Real Academia Española," p. 1136. William Elwood has recognized Schiller as one of Tamayo's sources for this "Discurso." "Schiller and Tamayo: The Influential Essay," *Text and Presentation: The University of Florida Department of Classics Comparative Drama Conference Papers* IX, ed. Karelisa Hartigan (Lanham: University Press of America, 1989): 35–45.

28 Revilla, "Manuel Tamayo y Baús," *Obras*, p. 74.

tical arena beneath the black standard of neo-Catholic absolutism"). Criticized as overly moralistic and old-fashioned, he turned his attention to politics. In part his exit from the theatre was caused by the lack of enthusiasm generated by *Los hombres de bien*. Post-1868 audiences had little tolerance for the preachy, sermonish (if diverting) reactionary stance of Tamayo. The title of the play is ironic, for in it Tamayo severely criticizes the "hombres de bien" who rule Spanish society, accusing them of cowardice, hypocrisy and immorality.

Tamayo creates the same symbolic spaces in *Hombres* as before: Acts I and II take place in the interior of don Lorenzo de Velasco's country home, while Act III, in which the atheist Leandro Quiroga goes mad, takes place outside in the garden of the house. The final scenes capture the disorder created by the lack of faith in God. The heroine, like so many of the melodramatic heroines of the past forty years, likewise becomes a symbol of that internal and external disorder. She appears with her hair disheveled and loose, and her "traje en desorden"[29] ("dress all messed up"). Tamayo's parting shot to Madrid's theatrical world has the heroine on her knees, "juntando las manos en actitud de súplica" ("joining her hands in supplication"). The values he had defended so vigorously in his theatre and in his Royal Academy speech – "el cumplimiento del deber, la práctica de la virtud, el heroísmo, la abnegación, el dominio del espíritu sobre la materia"[30] ("the fulfillment of duty, the practice of virtue, heroism, self-denial, the domination of the spirit over the flesh") – held less fascination in the form he was providing them for contemporary audiences. He wrote no more plays.

More high comedy: López de Ayala and Núñez de Arce

Three other practitioners of the *alta comedia* deserve some attention. Two of these dramatists – López de Ayala and Núñez de Arce – have clung, however tenuously, to the literary canon, and reappear at times in histories of literature. The other, Narciso Serra (1830–1877), has been completely, if unjustifiably, forgotten (see below). These men write of "ordinary" people. Their heroes and villains are not the passionate, unruly Romantic heroes, nor grand mythological gods, nor exaggerated comic types. They are our neighbors, who are not killed, nor banished to Hell,

---

[29] These disheveled women (usually dressed in white), symbols of social disorder or emotional chaos, are frequent in Spanish drama from the 1820s through the 1850s. They appear in Grimaldi's *La huérfana de Bruselas* (1825), García Gutiérrez's *El rey monje* (1837), Gil y Zárate's *Carlos II el hechizado* (1839), and Lozano de Vilchez's *María o la abnegación* (1854), among others, and even appear as late as 1894 in Muñiz's *El pilluelo de Madrid* (1894).

[30] Tamayo y Baús, "Discurso leído ante la Real Academia Española," p. 1139.

nor saved at the last minute by supernatural forces; rather, the villains slink off, chastened, at the end and the heroes return to their comfortable, ordered lives.

Todos los días tropezamos con alguno de esos hombres cuyo egoismo les lleva a concebir y pregonar un sistema moral para la vida, donde se disculpen y hasta se ennoblezcan los vicios y los crímenes de la suya; con uno de esos distinguidos infames que aspiran por medio de modales elegantes y correctos a difundir entre los pueblos un nuevo evangelio, donde la perfidia y la bajeza sean consideradas de buen tono, y las más nobles virtudes patrimonio sólo de los cursis.[31]

(Every day we trip across one of those men whose egotism leads them to conceive and defend a moral system which forgives and at times ennobles vices and crime; or one of those distinguished but infamous types who aspire, through the use of elegant and impeccable manners, to spread among us a new gospel in which treachery and evil are considered to be good form, and where noble virtues are thought to belong only to fools.)

In that way they are more realistic, more believable than the purely symbolic characters of earlier dramas. Still, it would be dangerous to view these plays as "realistic," since they capture broad symbolic truths of the society in which and for which they were written.[32] They are, however, natural and truthful, as we shall see. One near-contemporary critic of Ayala called him one of the "good" realists, whatever that could mean.[33]

Poet, playwright, and politician, Adelardo López de Ayala is best remembered today – when he is remembered at all[34] – for two or three of the plays he wrote between 1851 and 1878. In those plays, as José María Castro y Calvo underscores, is to be found "el reflejo de una sociedad; una sociedad que él mismo calificó de mala, y que en nombre de los viejos

---

31 Carlos Guaza y Gómez Talavera, *Músicos, poetas y actores* (Madrid: F. Maroto, 1884): 167.

32 Robert Lott in particular misses the point of *Consuelo* and other *altas comedias* by demanding that they be "realistic" and then criticizing them when they are not. Yet like the earlier Romantic dramas, the *alta comedia* often captured a symbolic reality rather than a mimetic one. What Lott sees as "mannered approaches to realism" were not that at all but rather attempts to highlight in broad terms the concerns, successes, and failures of upper-middle-class society. See Robert E. Lott, "On Mannerism and Mannered Approaches to Realism in *Un drama nuevo*, *Consuelo*, and Earlier Nineteenth-Century Spanish Plays," *Hispania* 54 (1971): 844–855. Even Coughlin criticizes Ayala for his "failure to create a truly realistic theater." See Edward V. Coughlin, *Adelardo López de Ayala* (Boston: G. K. Hall, 1977): 101.

33 "... lejos de ser un poeta romántico y melenudo, como su faz indicaba, era realista, pero realista en el buen sentido de la palabra ... es la personificación del realismo, pero no del realismo asqueroso y descarnado que se quiere importar ahora del extranjero, sino el bello y artístico realismo que tuvo su orígen en nuestros escritores del siglo de oro," Guaza y Gómez Talavera, *Músicos, poetas y actores*, p. 166.

34 Diego Marín writes, "Pocas reputaciones literarias del siglo pasado habrán sufrido un eclipse comparable al de Adelardo López de Ayala." "El valor de época de Adelardo López de Ayala," *Bulletin of Hispanic Studies* 29 (1952): 131.

principios del teatro español clásico quiere rectificar"[35] ("the reflection of a society; a society which he himself judged to be bad, and which he wants to improve in the name of the old principles of Spanish classical theatre"), that is, the very concerns which typify the *alta comedia*. His theatre is somewhat more bombastic than Tamayo's, slightly less convincing on a human scale, but it nonetheless serves as an important point of transition between the emotional posturing of late Romantic works and the more subtle, psychological drawing-room comedies of the early twentieth century. At the beginning of his writing career Ayala proclaimed his desire to lay out a moral, profound, and consoling plan of drama to which he remained faithful all his life. The society he lived in was a society swept up in money-making and go-go chic (similar to the 1980s in the United States, perhaps). Middle-class matrons cared intensely about fashion and fashionable things while their husbands envied José de Salamanca's seemingly endless capacity to generate capital – and to spend it on dazzling parties for the upper crust. Businesses expanded, railroads cut across the barren landscape, fortunes were won and lost, and banks and the stock exchange came to dominate polite conversation. In Castro y Calvo's words, "La fiebre de oro lo consumía todo"[36] ("Gold fever consumed everything"). In fact, where previously dramatic tension hinged on problems of honor and the appearance of honor (as in the plays of the Golden Age, for example) or on issues of power and love (as in Romantic plays), by the second half of the nineteenth century it came to pivot around money and financial gain. Shares in companies, business dealings, stock prices, and moneymaking became the motivating forces in many of the dramas written by these authors. That is, ethics and morals no longer are the exclusive domain of the personal; now they are also played out on a more public stage, that of people's economic status. This excess is precisely what Tamayo, López de Ayala, and the others exposed in their moralistic plays.

El tejado de vidrio (The Glass Roof) is the first of López de Ayala's most interesting high comedies (the others are *El tanto por ciento* [The Percentage], 1861; *El nuevo don Juan* [The New Don Juan], 1863; and *Consuelo*, 1878), and it opens on a social note. Mariano, sitting in his "sala lujosamente amueblada" ("richly appointed room") scolds Julia for retreating from her "duties" in society:

> mas antes
> honraba usted con frecuencia
> mis salones: iba al Prado

---

[35] "Estudio preliminar," *Obras completas de don Adelardo López de Ayala. Teatro*, ed. José María Castro y Calvo (Madrid: Atlas, 1965) (BAE 180): xi.
[36] *Ibid.* p. cxxxii.

en su linda carretela;
turnaba en el Teatro Real
con mi esposa o la marquesa;
vivía como se vive
en Madrid. Ya usted desdeña
la sociedad; ya se pasan
meses enteros sin verla ...   (I, i; emphasis added)

(but you used to come by here with some frequency; you took rides in the Prado in your beautiful coach; you went with my wife or the marchioness to the Royal Theatre; *you lived as one lives in Madrid.* Now you scorn society, months go by when we don't see you ...)

Mariano, a businessman, is married to Dolores, who is never satisfied with what she has, and the play soon begins to revolve around the equation love = commerce = money. Julia, it turns out, is secretly married to the Conde del Laurel, who cannot reveal the marriage because his rich uncle will disinherit him if he finds out he has wed. As the plot develops it seems to be about fidelity, jealousy, gossip, and betrayal, but the motivation of the characters is purely economic, since most of them – Dolores and the Count above all – are frantic to preserve their standing in society, something which can only be done with wealth. Mariano tolerates the presence of the Count in his house, even after it becomes clear that he represents a potential threat to the stability of his household, only because he hopes to realize financial gain from business dealings with him and his rich uncle. Mariano himself brags throughout the play of the expensive things he has bought Dolores; he has bought her love, something of which she appears to be aware: "¿Para qué vayas / a todo el mundo diciendo / los ochavos que te cuestan / mis caprichos?" ("Why do you tell everyone how much the things I buy cost you?") she asks (III, 1). Ayala develops an amusing plot line of intrigue and confusion, but lurking just below the surface is a corrosive view of these frivolous people who get too easily side-tracked by visions of economic grandeur. Naturally he settles it all amicably by the end when Mariano declares, "No más vida turbulenta" ("I don't want any more of this disorderly life") (IV, 11), but the point has been well made.

Several years later Ayala premièred *El nuevo don Juan* in Madrid (13 May 1863) at the Teatro del Circo, to generally favorable reviews. Most of the newspapers praised it – "el autor ha conquistado una hoja más para su corona de autor dramático" ("the author has put another feather in his dramatist's cap") (*La España*, 14 May 1863), "entusiastas elogios y felicitaciones" ("enthusiastic praise and congratulations") (*La Esperanza*, 15 May 1863) – although *La Esperanza* complained of its "false" characters (23 May 1863). Nonetheless, it became one of the hits of the

1862–1863 theatrical season, along with Tamayo's *Lo positivo* (The Right Track), Núñez de Arce's *Deudas de la honra* (Debts of Honor), and Rafael María Liern y Cerach's magical comedy, *La almoneda del diablo* (The Devil's Auction). Ayala originally wrote this as a zarzuela but decided instead to turn it into a full-length comedy. The plot line, an entertaining satire of the don Juan character, continues in the vein of the numerous parodies of this figure which became so frequent on Spanish stages following the appearance of Zorrilla's *Don Juan Tenorio* in 1844, but Ayala adds several twists to his presentation of the hyper-sexed seducer. Here, the don Juan type is dangerous not because he kills his rivals or deflowers his lovers, but because he represents a threat to domestic and conjugal tranquility, along the lines we saw in Vega's *El hombre de mundo*. As in Vega's play, the husband, Diego, was once a *calavera* himself, and his past comes back to haunt him in the person of don Juan, who threatens Diego's middle-class values, but who becomes, *mutatis mutandis*, the deceiver deceived. (Similarities to Cervantes's *El curioso impertinente* are hardly accidental, since Ayala wrote a version of this work in 1853.) Juan's intended victim, Elena, is married to Diego, a businessman (what else?), who is obsessed with a matter of family finances. There is much talk of "vender" ("selling") and "ventas" ("sales") in the play, underscoring the capitalist consciousness of the upper middle class. Ayala once again pulls out a happy ending and don Juan goes off, if not repentant, at least humbled by his failures. In fact, Ayala takes the wind out of the sails of this charming seducer by having him cower beneath a table, then spend the entire third act of the play locked up in an on-stage closet!

The conflict between honor and money is intensified in Ayala's next really successful play, *El tanto por ciento*, a three-act verse drama staged at the Teatro del Príncipe for the first time on 18 May 1861. It was recognized from its debut as a "comedia de primer orden" ("first-rank play") (*La Epoca*, 20 May 1861), and in truth there had been few plays in recent memory which stimulated such nearly unanimous and enthusiastic praise in the newspapers.[37] Later in the decade Galdós declared it to be "la obra más trascendental de nuestro teatro moderno" ("the most far-reaching work of our modern theatre") (*La Nación*, 9 February 1868). It was certainly Ayala's most widely reviewed, seen, and read play ("a estas horas todo Madrid ha visto la comedia, y dentro de poco la conocerá por la representacíon y por la lectura el resto de España" ["by now everyone in Madrid has seen the play, and shortly everyone in the rest of Spain will have either read it or seen it performed"] *El*

---

[37] It had its detractors: Vicente Rodríguez Varo, writing in *El Contemporáneo* (4 December 1861) listed the numerous defects – improbabilities in the action – he found in the play.

Contemporáneo, 4 June 1861), and it clinched his election to the Spanish Royal Academy. Within two weeks performances were begun in Valencia and Bilbao, and the author was still receiving praise and attention for it months after the première; it did not close until the summer season shut the doors of the theatre in the end of June, and its reappearance in November of the same year filled the theatre for weeks. By May, 1862, it was being performed in French in Paris, and its Spanish versions made yearly appearances on Madrid's stages for years to come (1863, 1864, 1868, 1872, 1876, 1879, 1880, 1883, 1886 [in Sevilla], 1889 [with Antonio Vico], and 1897).

The whole play revolves around who has money and who does not, and who will do what to whom to get more of it. It is the earliest example on the Spanish stage of what we now call "white-collar crime": Roberto plots ways to swindle his childhood friend Pablo out of land he owns near Zamora which is in the line of a government canal being planned. If the canal project is approved by Congress the land will increase substantially in value and whoever owns it will "ganar fortunas inmensas" ("make a huge amount of money") (I, 1). The issue of canal building was a controversial one when Ayala was penning the play; in fact, a canal project at the Ebro river produced a steady stream of commentary in the press and it even stimulated Gaspar Núñez de Arce to write a work entitled "Inauguración del canal del Ebro" (Inauguration of the Ebro Canal) in 1857, a series of letters originally written to the newspaper *La Iberia*. In Ayala's play, Pablo takes a promissory note on it from Roberto (the audience gets a brief lesson on just what a "carta de gracia" is) in order to pay off a parcel of land he has bought for his intended wife, the widowed countess Irene. Everyone gets into the economic act: the servants, who have saved some money over the years, decide to buy shares in the proposed transaction from Roberto, as do Pablo's "friends" Gaspar and Petra. The servants represent an odd mix of money and love: even among them there exists a financial hierarchy (Sabino has 12,000 *reales* saved up while Ramona has only 8,000, prompting Sabino to observe, "Que paran en mal / matrimonios desiguales" ["Unequal marriages come to grief"] [I, 4]). Even the news from the daily papers, which Petra reads with gleeful fascination, are hideous crimes committed because of business deals gone bad (in I, 8, for example). Such problems were not merely literary, as Guaza y Gómez's question suggests: "¿Quién no ha presenciado y aún intervenido en algunas de las contiendas que el interés del dinero riñe a cada instante con los sentimientos generosos y los afectos dulces del corazón?"[38] ("Who has not at one time or another seen or been

---

[38] Guaza y Gómez Talavera, *Músicos, poetas y actores*, p. 167.

involved in the conflicts that money can provoke in even the most generous and tender of hearts?'").

If Pablo cannot come up with 15,000 *reales* to pay off the note, he will lose the property in Zamora, but this is precisely what Roberto hopes will happen. He sells shares to the others in the hopes of increasing his earnings *thirty times*, even though he knows that this will ruin his old friend. "Una cosa es la amistad, / y el negocio es otra cosa" ("Friendship is one thing, business quite another") he states coldly (I, 13), a thought echoed somewhat later by Pablo's servant Sabino, who insists, "Y una es lealtad, / señor, y el negocio es otra" ("Loyalty is one thing, sir, and business another") (I, 15). All Roberto cares about is the bottom line, his profits: "¡El negocio es lo primero!" ("The business deal is the first thing!") (I, 16). When Gaspar questions the ethics of putting such pressure on a friend, Roberto retorts, "¿Qué te asombra? / Parece que tú no vives / en este siglo" ("What are you so surprised about? It seems as though you aren't living in this century") (I, 14), a clear indication of Ayala's attitude toward his century's loss of moral rectitude. Roberto even justifies his actions by asserting that it is better that a "friend" take over the farm land than an unknown.

Ayala includes in the play a love plot and some mechanical business with letters and flowers, but the true focus of the play is the gross materialism in mid-nineteenth-century Spanish society. The canal itself becomes a political football, and while the manipulations in Congress take place off stage, it is clear that economic interests have come to dominate not only the intimate lives of "friends" but also public discourse and action. Ayala, being himself an elected official, knew very well the political world he was criticizing. By Act III the conspiracies expand to include those of Roberto and Sabino against the other three investors, confirming Sabino's dictum that "los negocios empiezan / por muchos, y poco a poco / entre poquitos se quedan" ("business deals begin involving a lot of people, but little by little very few of them remain") (III, 2), a slap at the nouveau riche businessmen who were beginning to dominate Ayala's Spain – "los dorados momentos de Salamanca llevando en su alma el pecado de la ambición" ("the golden moments of Salamanca carrying in their soul the sin of ambition") in Castro y Calvo's words.[39] Perhaps the harshest statement is Isabel's observation of the irony of a society which punishes only poor criminals, not rich ones: "No hay diferencia en los dos / delitos, y en la sentencia / a uno muerte, a otro opulencia ..." ("There is no difference in the two crimes, yet one is sentenced to death and the other to vast wealth ...") (III, 7). Yet Ayala

---

[39] Castro y Calvo, "Estudio preliminar," p. xxviii.

resolves it all peacefully and comically. Roberto manages to cheat his fellow investors out of their shares, dreaming of enormous returns for himself, only to see Pablo meet the deadline for the return of the promissory note. So not only does he not realize a financial gain, but by having purchased the shares of his co-conspirators, he has lost some 36,000 *reales* of his own money. Isabel delivers the final moral lesson:

> que ese afán de enriquecer
> el cuerpo a costa del alma,
> es universal veneno
> de la conciencia del hombre,
> que nos tapa, con el nombre
> de negocio, tanto cieno ...   (III, 14)

(that desire to enrich the body at the cost of the soul is a wide-spread poison that affects man's conscience, that covers us, in the name of business, with so much slime ...)

The villains of the past suffered death or banishment or humiliation; in the *altas comedias* which revolve around money, the villain suffers a worse fate than those – he suffers economic loss. Revilla was correct when he judged *El tanto por ciento* "la mejor de todas las obras del eminente poeta"[40] ("the best of this eminent poet's plays") and it clearly was Ayala's most widely reviewed and widely performed play.

Consuelo obliquely deals with similar issues. Revilla properly credits the author with the desire to "retratar la sociedad presente, planteando los problemas del orden moral que le preocupan, y atendiendo tanto o más al estudio psicológico de los caracteres que al desarrollo de la intriga"[41] ("portray present-day society, analyzing the problems of moral order that preoccupy it, and paying as much attention to the psychological study of the characters as to the plot"), an observation which defines the *alta comedia* and which applies fully to *Consuelo*. Here he brings together all the things which have characterized his dramaturgy – smooth dialogue, lyrical pauses, interesting characters, convincing situations, "exquisito gusto"[42] ("exquisite taste"), and clear moral vision of individual and social behavior. Ayala turned the play in to the Teatro Español's administration in September of 1876, and even read the play to the impresario Ducacal in December of that year, but it was not performed until 30 March 1878, a delay which is difficult to understand. When it finally did appear, it received general – but not uncritical – acclaim. As the critic of *El Siglo Futuro* (9 April 1878) wrote:

---

[40] Revilla, "Don Adelardo López de Ayala," *Obras*, p. 26.   [41] *Ibid.* p. 25.
[42] *Ibid.* p. 28.

Es obra de mucho aliento; es un episodio de la lucha entre el bien y el mal, entre la conciencia y el deber, entre el hombre y el ángel. Es una comedia humana, llena de verdad. Es un cuadro informe y borroso de pasiones sin freno, en el que todo marcha ciega y violentamente al fin que se propone el autor.

(It's an inspired work; it's an episode in the battle between good and evil, between conscience and duty, between man and angel. It's a human comedy, full of truth. It's a shapeless and blurred depiction of no-holds passion, in which everything moves blindly and violently toward the ending that the author proposes.)

Critics generally see *Consuelo* simply as a drama of "ambition," that is, of a woman whose ruthless climb up society's ladder sets her up for the fall she suffers at the end. This is true enough, but behind the play's exterior one finds the same social criticism evident in Ayala's other plays, criticism directed at the economic structure of Spanish society. Consuelo's ambition has everything to do with her need to live the good life, to compete with her peers (similar to what we saw in *El tejado de vidrio*) and to participate in the money culture of the 1870s. She rejects the man who really loves her, the modest engineer Fernando, for Ricardo, the rich and flashy businessman whom she eventually marries. Consuelo does not merely want to participate in the "have" culture, she wants to own the things she sees. It is not enough for her to stroll through the museums or to enjoy the fresh air of public parks: she needs to *own* them. In a revealing dialogue with her mother she asks,

> Di, mamá: ¿no te agradara
> que fuese tuya una quinta
> espaciosa e inmediata
> a Madrid, con pabellones
> de buen gusto, rodeada
> de soberbios eucaliptus
> que la atmósfera embalsaman ...   (I, 11)

(Tell me, Mother, wouldn't you like to have a spacious estate near Madrid, with pretty pavilions surrounded by huge Eucalyptus trees that perfume the air ...)

Consuelo does not long for vague riches. As an acute observer of the wealthy, she is perfectly specific about what she wants, which type of house, garden, music, paintings. When her mother asks her if certain paintings that can be seen in the Prado Museum (Murillo's "Santa Isabel," for example) don't inspire in her spiritual longings and noble feelings of humility and elegance, Consuelo answers that, well, yes, they do, but her strongest desire is to possess them: "Sí, mamá: porque me agradan / los buenos cuadros, quisiera / meterlos dentro de casa" ("Yes, Mother: it's because I like good pictures that I want to place them in my house") (I, ii). She must own them and make them part of her economic armament against a continually upwardly mobile society. Marrying Fernando is therefore out of the question; she will marry Ricardo whose "inmensa / fortuna pone a mis plantas" ("immense wealth he's placing at my feet") (I, 11).

By the second act Consuelo has married Ricardo, although she confesses to her mother that she did so for money, not love.

> Es verdad: le di mi mano
> sin amarle. Su soberbia
> posición, su tren, su lujo
> resucitaron las muertas
> memorias de mi colegio:
> recordé mis opulentas
> amigas ...   (II, 3)

(It's true: I gave him my hand without being in love with him. His important position, his ostentation, his finery all brought back to me those lost memories from my school days: I thought of my wealthy friends ...)

The implication here, that Consuelo is not entirely alone or responsible for her materialism, underscores Ayala's criticism of his entire society, not just of certain individuals. Consuelo is a type, a representative of her class. As Coughlin observes, "Ayala is not so much condemning the individual but rather the materialistic society with its false values which has formed her."[43] It is also suggested in the play that her father shared similar values in his striving to climb the ladder of military success.

Ricardo in the meantime is flirting with an opera singer and is making arrangements with Fernando, the director of an export-import business, to be named to a post in Paris in order to be with her in the French capital. The complications of this act could have been resolved by Ayala had he wanted *Consuelo* to be another middle-class farce in which, following a series of misunderstandings, petty jealousies, and mistaken identities, the participants return to a world of order restored, safely ensconced within the walls of their comfortable bourgeois rooms. Yet he chose instead to use the play to send his parting message to Restoration Spain: focus on true love and virtue, not on money, power, and social esteem. By the play's end, Consuelo has lost her one true love, her mother, her honor, her husband, and her self-respect, all because of her preening ambition to compete in a superficial, valueless society. Fernando tells her,

> ¿De qué lloras y te espantas?
> ¿Qué te importa que jamás
> logres amor? Vivirás
> como tantas, como tantas,

43 Coughlin, *Adelardo López de Ayala*, p. 99.

cercada de ostentación,
alma muerta, vida loca,
con la sonrisa en la boca
y el hielo en el corazón.   (III, 10)

(Why are you crying? What are you afraid of? Why do you care that you don't find love? You'll live like so many other women, so many others, surrounded by appearances, with a dead soul, a crazy life, a smile on your lips, and ice in your heart.)

Money is no substitute for love and harmony. Consuelo is left alone and bitter, "como tantas, como tantas" in the Madrid of the 1870s.

Less interesting, perhaps, but nonetheless worthy of mention are the plays of Gaspar Núñez de Arce (1832–1903). Núñez de Arce was more applauded for his poetry than for his dramas, something which baffles modern readers of those rather pedestrian verses. In his day, individual poems, which he began to publish when he was twenty years old, and poetry collections reached truly astonishing numbers of editions: "Gritos del combate" (Battle Cries), "Poemas cortos" (Short Verses), and "¡Sursum corda!" were all published more than a dozen times; "La selva oscura" (The Dark Jungle), "La visión de fray Martín" (Friar Martin's Vision), "Maruja," and "Ultima lamentación de Lord Byron" (Lord Byron's Last Lament) reached more than thirty editions each; and "El vértigo" (Vertigo) had more than fifty separate editions at the last count. His dramatic production was scant, and today it is all but forgotten with the exception of *El haz de leña* (Kindling): between 1859 and 1875 he published some two dozen plays of varying lengths and genres (comedy, drama, zarzuela). He was a frequent contributor of political commentary to the newspapers of the capital during the 1850s, signalling perhaps his deep interest in the ideological movements of the day, an interest which clearly (some would say excessively) manifested itself in his literary production. His name does not appear in the recent *Historia del teatro en España*, volume II.

In 1860 Núñez de Arce staged his first two one-act comedies at the Príncipe Theatre in Madrid (29 October 1860). *Un lobo y una raposa* (A Wolf and a Vixen) stimulated little enthusiasm but *¡Cómo se empeñe un marido!* (How Hard a Husband Tries!) received decent comments in the press, along with *La España*'s suggestion that he try his hand at serious theatre ("El señor Núñez de Arce debía dedicarse a escribir una obra seria donde luciera con más espacio sus dotes de escritor dramático" ["Mr. Núñez de Arce should have written a serious work where his dramatic skills would be better displayed"] 31 October 1860). When he finally got around to producing that longer drama, *Deudas de la honra*, which appeared at the Lope de Vega Theatre on 17 January, 1863, it was received in some quarters with modest applause ("lisonjero" ["pleasing"] and "discreto" ["prudent"] were the adjectives used by several critics to describe its success), although two newspapers claimed for it "un gran éxito" ("a huge success") (*El Contemporáneo*, 18 January 1863) and "extraordinario éxito" ("an extraordinary success") (*El Pensamiento Español*, 19 January 1863). The fact is it had quite a good run: it was still on a few days later when *El Pensamiento Español* claimed that the author "puede colocarse entre los mejores dramáticos" ("can be placed among the best playwrights") and within weeks it had been shown in two other theatres in the capital (the Teatro de la Zarzuela and the Teatro Jovellanos); shortly thereafter it moved on to Barcelona and Zaragoza.

The author's next concerted effort at playwriting came in 1867 with *Quien debe paga* (He Who Owes Pays) a three-act verse comedy first performed at the Príncipe on 18 October of that year. This led him to begin writing what was to become his best-remembered play, *El haz de leña*, begun in 1867, finished in 1870, but, due to his heavy involvement in the political scene during these turbulent years, not performed in Madrid until 14 November 1872. Now at the height of his literary and political career, Núñez was flattered to have one of his plays, *Justicia providencial* (Providencial Justice), accepted for performance in the leading theatre of Paris, an interesting reversal of the usual one-way flow of plays from Paris to Madrid. Within two years he was voted into the Spanish Royal Academy, which he joined formally in May, 1876.

Strictly speaking, only *Deudas de la honra*, *Quien debe paga*, and *Justicia providencial*, all written in the conflictive years preceding the fall of Isabel II, can be considered high comedies. They deal with moral issues and social customs in a society which Núñez thought severely lacking in faith and ethical standards. He, too, along with Tamayo and Ayala, condemned the heightened materialism of his times. *El haz de leña* is not an *alta comedia* but rather a Romantic historical drama, similar in scope to those written in collaboration with Antonio Hurtado (1825–1878) during the previous decade: *El laurel de la Zubia* (Zubia's Reward, 1865), *La jota aragonesa* (The Aragonese Dance, 1866), performed in the Teatro Español on 10 March 1869, and *Herir en la sombra* (Collide in the Dark, 1866). Still, since it has been called by some critics the "finest historical drama of the century,"[44] it deserves our attention here. Also, if we agree with Hayden White's dictum that "Every representation of the past has specifiable ideological implications," the play comments on more than the Spanish sixteenth century.[45]

---

[44] Lewis E. Brett, "Núñez de Arce," in *Nineteenth-Century Spanish Plays* (New York: Appleton-Century-Crofts, 1935): 571.
[45] White, *The Tropics of Discourse*, p. 69.

El haz de leña treats a subject previously dealt with by Schiller, Alfieri and others: the mysterious circumstances surrounding the death of Felipe II's first-born son don Carlos in 1568. While Núñez has generally been considered a dramatist who reacted against Romanticism, this play is full of Romantic tropes and postures – it is a kind of *Don Alvaro* redux – and as such it serves as a bridge between the historical dramas of earlier times and the teeth-gnashing honor plays of Echegaray's "neo-Romantic" period. The ostensible theme is unbridled ambition, but it is of a very different sort from what audiences saw in Tamayo's *Consuelo* a few years later. Here, Prince Carlos is accused by his father of encouraging the Protestant rebellions in the Low Countries in order to inherit a throne more quickly. Felipe is concerned with the disquiet in his kingdoms. Núñez skilfully weaves together a political drama on a historical theme with a social comedy on the theme of families in crisis, since not only is the royal family in profound conflict, but so is that of the heroine Catalina and her brother Cisneros, who take different sides in the schism. Cisneros is out to ruin Felipe II for the part he played in the execution of their father in an *autodafé* some years back, and Carlos will be the means to achieve that end; Catalina, in turn, has fallen in love with Prince Carlos. Where Cisneros's duplicitous thirst for vengeance provides fuel for the split between Felipe and his son, Catalina tries, unsuccessfully, to save the prince from the fate that awaits him.

Romanticism abounds, and threatens to overwhelm whatever more modern dramatic concerns Núñez hoped to weave into the play (if indeed he had any such intention). Carlos casts himself in the role of the suffering Romantic hero, complaining that he suffers under the yoke of "un tirano en vez de un padre" ("a tyrant rather than a father") (I, 9). He views the palace as a "cárcel" ("jail"):

> por cárcel tengo el palacio
> donde vegeto cautivo.
> Ved si con razón me quejo,
> pues vuestra mano me cierra
> el camino de la guerra
> y la entrada en el Consejo. (I, 9)

(the palace is for me a jail in which I languish captive. My complaints are justified, since it is your hand which closes off the road to war and a place on the Counsel).

Phrases such as "el gozo de Satanás" ("Satan's joy") (I, 11), "risa sardónica" ("sardonic grin") (I, 11), and "mi pecho es un calabozo" ("my heart is a dungeon") (II, 3) haunt the play and form a network of images strongly associated with Romantic theatre. The audience had absorbed such images through years of exposure to them, and consequently later dramatists, such as Núñez, could exploit them easily. The mere presence of "embozados" ("men in disguise") conjured up images from the past, and not unintentionally. In a soliloquy reminiscent of Rivas's don Alvaro, Cisneros laments,

> ¡Desgraciado, desgraciado
> de mí! Cuando considero
> que he nacido caballero
> ilustre, rico y honrado,
> y me miro en este estado
> tan lejos de lo que fui,
> y mido en mi frenesí
> todo el fondo del abismo,
> ¡oh! me horrorizo yo mismo
> del odio que hierve en mí ...   (III, 3)

(I am so unfortunate! When I think that I was born an illustrious, rich, and honored gentleman, and that I now find myself in this state, so far from what I once was, and I see in my frenzy the depths of the abyss, oh!, even I am frightened by the hatred that boils in me ...)

He then tells don Carlos, "Mala estrella os acompaña, / señor" ("you are followed by an evil sign, my lord") (III, 4), prompting him later on to comment,

> ¿Y cómo, si llevo en mí
> todo el fuego del infierno?
> Si en este insondable abismo
> llevo mi ambición inquieta
> que aprisionada y sujeta
> se ha vuelto contra mí mismo.   (IV, 3)

(How can this be, if I carry within me all the fires of Hell? In this deep abyss I carry my impatient ambition that, now imprisoned and tied up, has turned against me.)

"Mi vida es pesado yugo" ("My life is a heavy yoke") (IV, 4) he tells his father, reminding the audience of don Alvaro's moving "¡Qué cargo tan insufrible / es el ambiente vital" ("What an insufferable burden this life is") (III, 4), words which re-echo several scenes later in his confession to his father: "Casi desde que nací / viene siendo para mí / dura carga aborrecida" ("Almost since birth life has been for me a hated and difficult burden") (IV, 6). Soon thereafter, don Carlos cries, "Ay, qué abismo tan profundo / de maldad!" ("What a deep abyss of evil!") (IV, 11). Catalina, in her love for don Carlos, is the "única luz que ilumina / mi profunda oscuridad" ("only light that illuminates my profound darkness") (IV, 5); she is charged with his salvation, even if, like Tenorio's Inés, it may cost her her own: "Os lo juro / por mi eterna salvación" ("I swear to you on my eternal salvation") (IV, 5). When at last Catalina and don Carlos find one another and confess their mutual love, it is too late ("¡Oh, suerte aciaga!" ["Oh, terrible fate!"][IV, 12]) since politics and fate have intervened to crush any potential happiness they might have wished for (as happens in Romantic plays from *La conjuración de Venecia* onward). They find one another and, similar to don Alvaro and Leonor, but in reverse, he dies.

Following *El haz de leña* Núñez de Arce's career developed along poetic and political lines. He remained a celebrated figure in Madrid's social circles, but, excepting a three-act zarzuela written with Arrieta in 1875 (*Entre el alçalde y el rey* [Between the Mayor and the King]) he wrote nothing more for the theatre. His plays were produced from time to time (*El haz de leña* in 1887, *¡Quien debe paga!* in 1888, *Deudas de la honra* in 1894, etc.), although his real fame came from the widely read and circulated poems which he produced until his death in 1903.

The Generation of 1850: Narciso Serra, Luis de Eguílaz, and Luis Mariano de Larra

At mid-century a new generation of playwrights began to stage works in Madrid. Born in or near 1830, this generation includes Narciso Serra (1830–1877), Luis de Eguílaz y Eguílaz (1830–1874), and Luis Mariano de Larra (1830–1901). Their work shares the goals and accomplishments of the *alta comedia* and is characterized by an interest in the economic realities of their day, strong moral posturing, a concentration on middle- and upper-middle-class characters, a predominately urban environment, and an attempt to convey refined emotion and sentimentality to their audiences as opposed to the intense emotionalism which characterized Romantic drama.

In 1881 the distinguished orator, politician, and intellectual Antonio Cánovas del Castillo organized the publication of a two-volume set of plays titled simply, *Autores dramáticos contemporáneos y joyas del teatro español del siglo XIX* (Contemporary Dramatists and Jewels of Nineteenth-Century Spanish Theatre).[46] Cánovas introduced the volume with a competent general history of the Spanish theatre, and each play was preceded by an introduction written by a distinguished author or scholar, among them Cayetano Rosell, Juan Valera, Aureliano Fernández Guerra, Marcelino Menéndez y Pelayo, and Jacinto Octavio Picón. Included among the "jewels" of nineteenth-century playwriting are authors who had naturally been consecrated as "canonical," that is,

---

[46] Madrid: Impr. Fortanet, 1881–1882.

playwrights and plays which had received the approbation of decades of critical and popular acclaim (sometimes much less, as in the case of Ayala). These included, as might be expected, Rivas's *Don Alvaro*, Zorrilla's *Traidor, inconfeso y mártir*, Hartzenbusch's *Los amantes de Teruel*, Vega's *El hombre de mundo*, Núnez de Arce's *El haz de leña*, López de Ayala's *Consuelo*, and Tamayo's *Un drama nuevo*. Also among these masterworks of the Spanish stage is to be found a play called *¡Don Tomás!* by Narciso Serra.

Serra, one of his period's most talked-about authors, remains practically unknown today. The only thing written about him is Narciso Alonso Cortés's little-known 1930 study[47] (most of which came from Fernández Bremón's introduction to *¡Don Tomás!* in the Cánovas volume) yet he was a constant presence in the theatres and newspapers from 1848 (when he penned his first poems) to the end of the century, well beyond his premature death in 1877. Revilla considered him to be the equal in comic genius of Bretón, Vega, and Ayala,[48] and his colorful personality, combined with the rather tragic physical problems which plagued him, made him an endless subject of gossip and commentary in the capital. Reputed to be the "natural" son of the soldier-poet Ros de Olano (who had written, among other things, the panegyric introduction to Espronceda's *El diablo mundo* in 1842), Serra earned a reputation as a wild-living ("gran trasnochador" ["a real partier"] according to Alonso Cortés[49]), humorous, womanizing, and brave soldier-writer whose facility with poetic meter provoked envy and awe among his friends and acquaintances. He depicted this life in a military *cuadro de costumbres* called *El amor y la Gaceta* (Love and the Gazette, 1863), a play which dealt with a matter of serious concern to soldiers – Leopoldo O'Donnell's recent decree that any soldier wishing to marry must prove he has the substantial sum of 80,000 *reales* (presumably, so the individual and his family would not become wards of the state).[50] Its daring questioning of the fairness of the decree got it into some difficulties with the censors, but it was allowed to be staged and became a modest hit for the author.

47 Alonso Cortés, "Narciso Serra," in *Quevedo en el teatro y otras cosas* (Valladolid: Colegio Santiago, 1930).
48 Revilla, "Don Adelardo López de Ayala," p. 26.
49 Alonso Cortés, "Narciso Serra," p. 140.
50 Alonso Cortés elabora: "Escribióla Serra con motivo de un Real decreto dictado por O'Donnell – a quien, por cierto, dedicó la obra a su impresión – , transcendentalísimo para los militares, pues les prohibía solicitar licencia para contraer matrimonio sin depositar antes la cantidad de 4.000 duros. Es aquí donde figuran la capitana Canela, el teniente Zapata, el cura castrense Murillo y otros personajes, que acaso den a conocer las costumbres, nada aristocráticas, a lo que se ve, de aquellos militares, pero que originan una acción vulgar y deslavazada." *Ibid.* p. 178.

> Don Leopoldo, don Leopoldo,
> usted hace mi desgracia:
> que venga la democracia,
> que venga pronto a mandar,
> a ver si empieza por dar
> algún decreto oportuno
> para que se case uno
> cuando se quiera casar. (III, 6)

(Don Leopoldo, don Leopoldo, you are the cause of my misfortune: I hope democracy comes soon, let it hurry so it might issue forth some timely decree that will let a person marry when she wants to.)

His own ironic commentary on his well-known lifestyle ("Yo no comprendo esa vida / de jugar y de beber / y trasnochar, no señora" ["I don't understand that life of gambling and drinking and staying out until all hours, no ma'am"] [I, 5]) amused a public suitably versed in his escapades. Anecdotes abound about his ability to produce impromptu comic verses – even in the most unlikely situations (once, when he lay wounded on a battlefield) – and satirical *redondillas*, which he whipped off in cafés for the amusement of his friends. The final speech of *El amor y la Gaceta* amply demonstrates his witty, if silly, accumulation of untranslatable rhyme and alliteration:

> Pepa, para que se sepa,
> aquí mi amor se destapa
> y dejara de ser Papa
> por ser tu marido, Pepa.
> Ay, Pepa, que no me quepa,
> que yo me quepa en la tripa
> ni aun el humo de la pipa,
> como yo te engaña, Pepa.
> Mi amor, que por todo trepa,
> por todas partes de Europa
> navegará viento popa
> como tú me quieras Pepa.
> Sé tú hoja de esta cepa,
> que mi amor no vuelve grupa;
> no me hagas al alma pupa,
> y quiérame mucho, Pepa. (III, 9)

The popularity of the play was enhanced by Matilde Díez, who played the lead role, and Mariano Fernández, a young comic actor of great promise (he went on to fame as Grimaldi's don Simplicio) in the role of the Potrero.

Serra, who began his career in the theatre as an actor in a company of traveling artists, wrote and produced dozens of plays during his short lifetime, although his first real job was as a soldier. Just prior to the outbreak of the Revolution of 1854 he settled in Madrid, where he staged his first successful play, *La boda de Quevedo* (Quevedo's Wedding), on 27 January 1854, at the Lope de Vega Theatre. His theatrical career and his political career seemed to be on the upswing when he was given a post in the offices of the Ministerio de la Gobernación and finally named Censor de Teatros in 1864, a job he carried out with surprising harshness (surprising, according to the newspaper *La Discusión*, because some of his own plays had been criticized for precisely the "moral laxity" which he protested in some of the works he banned). Even so, he tended to be more thoughtful of the plays under consideration than his predecessor Ferrer del Río. Much of the business of censorship was arbitrary and whimsical, and Ferrer banned or cut plays for a number of reasons: if he did not like the list of characters (*La casa de doña España* [Miss Spain's House]), if he discovered "inmoralidad de sus argumentos" ("immorality in the plot") (*Los delirios de un poeta* [A Poet's Fantasies]; the author of this play, Pedro María Pardo, tried to pull a fast one on Ferrer by turning it in a second time under a different title), or if it dealt with anything controversial (*Infamia por intereses* [Dishonor by Business Affairs] turned on a matter "pendiente del fallo de los tribunales de justicia" ["pending the decision of a court of law"]). Serra's job was to read all plays presented for performance in Madrid and in the provinces, and sign a pre-printed government form which either banned the play altogether, allowed it to be performed "con las supresiones hechas" ("with the cuts made"), or permitted its immediate staging.[51] He banned plays he found offensive to "la Religión cristiana" (*Los dos renegados* [The Two Renegades] of 1864), too daring politically, or too "immoral." Jesús Rubio Jiménez states that he held "actitudes políticas intransigentes" ("intransigent political beliefs") which provoked "airadas protestas contra sus prohibiciones"[52] ("noisy protests against his bans"). He attempted to ban García Gutiérrez's *Juan Lorenzo* because of its "tendencia política" ("political inclination") but public outcry forced him to back down. As reported in *La Iberia*, a panel named to investigate the case found his position to be "violenta y ridícula" ("misconstrued and ridiculous") (19 November 1865). He also attempted to prohibit the staging of J. M. Gutiérrez de

---

[51] The form read: "Ministerio de la Gobernación. / Subsecretaria. / Al Gobernador de la provincia de [province name], Madrid [day] de [month] de 186[year]. / De Real orden, comunicada por el Sr. Ministro de la Gobernación devuelvo a V. E. para los efectos consiguientes, la obra dramática titulada: [title] / la cual ha sido examinada por el Censor especial de Teatros, con cuyo dictamen, puesto en la misma, ha tenido a bien S. M. conformarse. / Dios, etc. El Subsecretario / Munuta. [signature]."

[52] Jesús Rubio Jiménez, *Ideología y teatro en España: 1890–1900* (Universidad de Zaragoza, 1982): 205.

Alba's *Revista de 1865* (Review of 1865).[53] The squabble which erupted over his banning of the one-act review, *Un golpe de estado* (A Coup d'Etat) in May of 1867, reveals his concern that plays with too many "tendencias políticas" could subvert public confidence in the government. Several of the play's longer speeches needed to be toned down by the author, José María Nogués, before Serra would permit its performance. His concern – justifiable, given the political instability which would erupt within a year in Madrid – was that the theatre would become a place for "desaguado de pasiones que no deben tener asiento en él, o a demostraciones en cierto modo subversivas" ("a discharge of passions that should not take place in it, or a place of subversive demonstrations"). "Subversive demonstrations" in the theatre were of course the real fear. The play, even with the cuts demanded by the censor, was never performed. Serra left the job, and lost his 26,000 *reales* annual salary, when censorship was abolished following the Revolution of 1868.[54] He died in poverty in 1877, but his recognition was such that Zorrilla served as one of the pallbearers at his funeral.

Was Serra as good as his public seemed to think? Juan Valera frequently praised his achievements, noting that his work was invariably "salpicada de chistes y fácilmente versificada"[55] ("filled with jokes and good verses") and claiming for him the mantle of the great dramatists of the previous generation.

Cada cual dirá lo que mejor le pareciere, pero yo diré siempre, o casi siempre, que el Teatro español no está en completa decadencia; que todavía viven Hartzenbusch, Vega, Bretón y el duque de Rivas; y que entre los jóvenes hay algunos que heredarán dignamente a estos maestros, descollando sobre todos don Narciso Serra, al menos en la comedia.[56]

(Everyone is entitled to his opinion, but I will always, or almost always, say that Spanish theatre is not in complete decline. Hartzenbusch, Vega, Bretón, and the

---

[53] Archivo Histórico Nacional, Consejos, Legajo 11.391, no. 1. Cited by Rubio Jiménez, *Ideología*, p. 205. Rubio Jiménez continues: "provocó la reacción del dramaturgo, que solicitó al Ministerio de Gobernación la creación de un jurado, que revisara el dictamen. Formado éste por Hartzenbusch, López de Ayala, Ferrer del Río y Martínez Villergas, emitieron un informe 'favorabilísimo' de que el drama fuera representado. El contencioso tuvo gran eco en la prensa. En la revista *Gil Blas* apareció una escena en que dialogan Serra y Juan Lorenzo criticándose" (205). See Carlos Cambronero, "Cosas de antaño: Apuntes para la historia de la censura dramática," *Revista Contemporánea* DLXXVIII (December 1899): 594–609.

[54] Archivo Histórico Nacional. Legajo 11.391. He had suffered a previous period of unemployment from the job in November 1866, but was reappointed in January 1867. Eguílaz was named as the interim censor, but he never took over; instead, Luis Fernández Guerra served until Serra's reappointment.

[55] Juan Valera, "Revista de Teatros," in *Obras completas* II (Madrid: Aguilar, 1961): 163.

[56] *Ibid.* p. 172. In 1861, Valera included Serra among the great poets Vega, García Gutiérrez, and Ayala, "que son poetas de buena ley y saben escribir dramas y comedias," 245.

Duke of Rivas are still alive, and among the younger generation there are a few who will inherit their masters' skills, Narciso Serra outdoing them all, at least in the comedy.)

Alonso Cortés takes a decidedly different stance: "Al leer una y otra comedia de Narciso Serra hasta el total conocimiento de su labor dramática, el desencanto no puede ser mayor. Espera uno ver confirmadas alguna vez las apreciaciones de la crítica, que le pone entre los mejores autores de la época, y la comprobación no llega nunca"[57] ("After reading all of Narciso Serra's plays and arriving at a full understanding of his dramatic production, one's disappointment cannot be greater. One hopes to find confirmation of some of the critical appreciation, something that will place him among the best playwrights of his time, but that confirmation never arrives"). He wrote too much and too quickly, which resulted in plays which rarely rose above mediocrity and disorder. Still, the testimony of his age claimed for him a key spot on Parnassus. His first play, *La boda de Quevedo* (1854), figures among his best productions. Not only did it skillfully recreate the ambience of the Golden Age (although it stretches historical accuracy, as was frequent in historical comedies of the nineteenth century), but it also cleverly imitated Quevedo's style and language. The presence of the notable actors Julián Romea and Antonio Guzmán in the cast added to the play's favorable reception, and the audience had become used to seeing figures from its literary past portrayed on stage. In fact, Quevedo had been somewhat of a growth industry since Patricio de la Escosura made him a lead character in *La corte del Buen Retiro* (The Court at the Buen Retiro Palace, 1837); following him, Quevedo appeared in numerous plays, among them Escosura's own sequel, *También los muertos se vengan* (Dead Men Also Avenge Themselves, 1844), Eulogio Florentino Sanz's excellent *Don Francisco de Quevedo* (1848), Bretón's *¿Quién es ella?* (Who is she?, 1849), Eguílaz's *Una broma de Quevedo* (A Joke by Quevedo, 1853) and his three-act zarzuela, *Cuando ahorcaron a Quevedo* (When They Hung Quevedo, 1857), and Francisco Botella y Andrés's *Una noche y una aurora* (A Night and A Dawn, 1856).[58] Serra was a master at light poetry, a facile improviser of *romances* and *redondillas*, talents amply on display in a one-act zarzuela about Cervantes called *El loco de la guardilla* (A Crazy Man in the Attic, 1861), whose historical inaccuracies (there is a poeticized version of a meeting between Cervantes and Lope) offended Alonso Cortés but delighted contemporary audiences (it received a "ruidosa ovación" ["noisy ovation"] according to *La Epoca* of 10 October). A

---

[57] Alonso Cortés, "Narciso Serra," p. 152.
[58] Alonso Cortés, "Quevedo en el teatro," in *Quevedo en el teatro*, pp. 5–43.

sequel, *El bien tardío* (Too Late to Help), failed when it was performed in 1867.

¡Don Tomás! was written off as a "comedia cuyo argumento carece de interés, pues desde el comienzo se descubre el desenlace" ("a play without any interest whatsoever since from the very first moment one knows what the outcome will be") by the always-cranky *La Discusión* (6 May 1858), but in reality it was popular enough to be played in July of 1859 (and "muy aplaudida" ["very well applauded"] *La Discusión* had to confess) and again in 1860, 1864, 1865, 1870, and beyond. By the early sixties it was considered a "graciosísima comedia" ("delightful comedy") (*La Iberia*, 28 August 1860) and would be so remembered throughout the author's lifetime. *El Imparcial* (27 September 1877) called it "la más acabada obra de nuestro tiempo" ("the most perfect play of our time"). Serra set the play in Madrid in 1858, so there could be no question as to whom it was directed – the upper-middle-class snobs, climbers, and liars whose presence in contemporary society was becoming more and more noticeable. Doña Tomasa, the demanding, scheming wife of don Jesús (Serra cracks many jokes at the expense of don Jesús, whose name is a frequently used Spanish exclamation of surprise or blessing) puts on airs and runs her household like a military barracks. Her husband complains (in a play on words) that she is a "mujer de gobierno, / mas de gobierno absoluto" ("a housekeeper, but an absolutist housekeeper") while he prefers "algo de Constitución" ("something more constitutional") (I, 3). Their daughter, the ironically named Inocencia, prepares to marry her cousin don Tomás, whom she has not seen for nearly seven years. She insists that he will need to get down on his knees to ask her hand in marriage, and until he does, she will not consider their old contract as valid. He, on the other hand, has changed his mind in the interim, and arrives in Madrid from Andalucía determined not to marry ("no he encontrado una mujer / que lo merezca" ["I haven't found a woman who deserves me"] [I, 13]). Inocencia swears revenge with the same tool – frankness – employed by her cousin, who, upon feeling her rejection, decides to win her over (which was precisely her goal). *La Discusión* was right in noting that one can determine the dénouement from the beginning (the weight of theatre tradition demanded the happy reconciliation of the lovers by the play's end), but nevertheless Inocencia and Tomás are a delightful pair of squabbling lovers, whom Serra surrounds with comic types who blend into the action of the play seamlessly. Serra spices up the plot by having one of Tomás's former girlfriends arrive in Madrid and by leaving the question of a sizeable inheritance for him open to question, but as the final act comes to a close, don Tomás sinks to his knees and asks her to marry him. They all live, presumably, happily ever after. Once

again, the audience learns the value of consistency, modesty, and the importance of maintaining the status quo.

1861 was a year of triumph and tragedy for Serra. He had successfully presented a number of plays to Madrid audiences, but in early November he suffered a serious stroke which brought him so close to death that last rites were administered on 8 November 1861. While he was sufficiently recovered by the end of the year to be declared out of danger, the stroke had left him paralyzed on the left side, and periodic relapses weakened his body – if not his spirit or his productivity – over the years. He became commonly referred to as "el desgraciado poeta Narciso Serra" ("the unfortunate poet Narciso Serra") confined to a wheelchair and, frequently, his bed. The illness did terminate plans he had for the publication of a theatre review to be titled *El Mochuelo* (The Owl), the prospectus of which he wrote, characteristically, in comic verses.[59] He enjoyed success with his *refundición* of Hartzenbusch's classic magical comedy, *Los polvos de la madre Celestina* in 1863, as well as with the amusing *El amor y la Gaceta* the same year and the zarzuela *Luz y sombra* (Light and Shadow) in 1867 (parodied as *El testamento de un brujo* [A Warlock's Testament] by Ricardo Puente y Braña within months of its debut). By 1870 he was enjoying a mini-revival and the theatres were crowded with his works: *¡Don Tomás!* played at the Circo Theatre, *El loco de la guardilla* at the Lope de Rueda, *Luz y sombra* also at the Circo, and *Perdonar nos manda Dios* (God Demands That We Pardon One Another) and *Dos napoleones* (Two Napoleons) at the Teatro Español. "El señor Serra ha probado una vez más que todos los géneros son iguales" ("Mr. Serra has proved once again that all genres are the same") (*Correspondencia de España*, 30 November 1870). One of his last works, a zarzuela entitled *Entre bastidores* (Behind the Scenes) returned to the ever-popular theme of what we would call today "metatheatre," that is, theatrical works about the theatre. (Ventura de la Vega, in a nod to Larra, had staged *Yo quiero ser cómico* [I Want to be an Actor] in 1857.) Serra's work was a slight effort, but it captured perfectly the still-precarious situation of actors and impresarios in Spain's theatres. The petty jealousies, backbiting, jockeying for position, ego-driven conflicts of the actors and directors are all intensified by the lack of sufficient funding or support on the part of the theatre owners. As the Autor explains:

> Que en vista de todo; en vista
> de sus muchas exigencias,
> de que por desavenencias
> no se puede formar *lista*;

[59] Ana María Freire López, "Un proyecto desconocido del dramaturgo Narciso Serra," *Anales del Instituto de Estudios Madrileños* 28 (1990): 661–664.

que las cosas van mal dadas,
que todo se viene abajo,
y que donde no hay *trabajo*
menos puede haber *entradas*;
que se ha perdido la hebra
y se deshace el tejido,
la empresa lo ha conocido
y se ha declarado en quiebra.   (I, 9)

(When one considers all the demands of this profession, that because of misunderstandings one cannot get an *acting company* together, that everything is screwed
up, that the whole enterprise is collapsing, and that where there is no *work* there
can hardly be any *gate receipts*; that the thread is lost and the cloth is unravelling,
the owners have owned up to it and have declared bankruptcy.)

By 1876, the year before his death, Serra's fame had declined, and he
seemed to be on the verge of being relegated to posterity, called "pobre,
enfermo, paralítico, olvidado" ("poor, ill, paralyzed, forgotten") by *La
Epoca* on the eve of a benefit to raise money for him. He died a poor and
broken man ("reducido a extrema pobreza, aliviado tan sólo alguna vez
por la generosidad de sus admiradores" ["reduced to extreme poverty,
helped only every now and again by the generosity of his admirers"] *El
Imparcial*, 27 September 1877), but his death restimulated interest in his
works, which remained in repertory for decades after his demise. Zorrilla,
Ramón de Campoamor, and José Echegaray were among the pallbearers
at his funeral, and Zorrilla wrote a touching cycle of poems to his fallen
friend, confessing with some shame that "viéndole agonizar le abandona-
mos"[60] ("seeing him suffer we abandoned him"). Fernández Bremón
summed him up in these words:

Narciso Serra fue un poeta malogrado, un improvisador de comedias, un pobre
que enriquecía a las empresas teatrales, un autor adorado por el vulgo, del cual se
reía a carcajadas, y por los literatos graves como Hartzenbusch, que le toleraban
sus descuidos en gracia de la frescura y donaire de sus versos; aplaudido hasta por
las gentes meticulosas, a quienes escandalizaba, como Tirso, con la libertad de sus
epigramas, pero nunca con la intención de sus comedias. Idolo de la juventud
atolondrada, versificador de café y gran trasnochador, nadie le buscaba en los
salones, bibliotecas ni ateneos, sino en las casas de juego, en los cuerpos de
guardia, fondas y bastidores de teatros. Fue autor, militar y censor de comedias.
Vivió en el aturdimiento y murió como un cristiano.[61]

(Narciso Serra was an unfortunate poet, an improviser of plays, a poor soul who
enriched theatre companies, an author adored by the common man, who laughed
riotously at plays, and by serious literary types like Hartzenbusch, who tolerated

---

[60] Zorrilla, "A Narciso Serra," *Obras completas* II, p. 627.
[61] Fernández Bremón, Introduction to *¡Don Tomás!*, in Cánovas, *Autores dramáticos*, p.
363.

his mistakes for the sake of the freshness and wit of his verses. He was applauded even by the most demanding people, whom he scandalized, as did Tirso, with the daring of his epigrams, but never intentionally in his plays. He was an idol of the giddy young, a café-scribbler and a real partier, no one ever went to look for him in high-toned salons, libraries, or literary clubs, but rather in gambling houses, military barracks, inns, and theatre back-rooms. He was an author, a military man, a censor of plays. He lived wildly and died like a Christian.)

For Valera, Serra was "el primer poeta cómico de España, después de Bretón"[62] ("Spain's greatest comic poet, after Bretón"). However, because of his interest in thesis and philosophy, his plots tended to be weak, a fact recognized by the theatre critic of *El Teatro Español*, who reviewed his popular *La calle de la Montera* (Montera Street) on 1 February 1859, in these terms: "El Sr. Serra es un verdadero poeta, conoce el lenguaje y versifica con mucha facilidad; hemos de convenir, no obstante en que no son suficientes tan excelentes dotes para escribir una buena comedia. Es menester estudiar, ante todo, la acción del drama y ver si es bastante a mantener el interés creciente en toda la obra" ("Mr. Serra is a true poet, he knows the language and writes verses with great facility; we must agree, however, that these qualities are not sufficient to write a good play. One must also study, above all, the play's action and see if it is enough to maintain growing interest throughout the entire work"). Still, the lively energy of his plays, the warm characterizations of his creations ("Serra sentía sus personajes, no los ideaba fríamente"[63] ["Serra felt his characters, he didn't think them out coldly"]), and the naturalness of his dialogue should rescue him from oblivion.

Another member of the Generation of 1850 and one of the most prolific dramatists of his day is Luis de Eguílaz, whose thesis plays are less than earth-shaking in their originality but who nevertheless managed to produce a steady stream of solid, well-received entertainments which were perfectly pitched to his audiences. Eguílaz's traditionalist bent and easy erudition (his plays are sprinkled with intertextual references and homages to Góngora, Fray Luis de León, his friend Hartzenbusch, the painter Federico de Madrazo, the Scottish philosopher David Hume, etc.) made him a favorite with Spain's conservative intellectual elite (Durán, Hartzenbusch, and others constantly supported his work), but he was capable of barbed criticism of the establishment which often provoked harsh reaction from his detractors. For example, when he restaged one of his earliest plays, *Las prohibiciones* (Prohibitions), at the Teatro del Príncipe on 20 October 1853 (it opened first in January of that year),

---

[62] Valera, "Revista de Teatros," in *Obras completas* II, p. 246.
[63] Fernández Bremón, Introduction to *¡Don Tomás!*, p. 356.

Eugenio de Ochoa penned a scathing attack of the play for its criticism of establishment figures. As Donald Allen Randolph reports,

Al comentar la comedia, Ochoa se acalora condenando la presentación cínica de un ministro que es un tunante o de un diputado que es un canalla. Dice que la mofa del individuo es la mofa de la institución, y si hacemos perder el respeto a ellos por defectos personales, haremos perder el respeto también por los que sancionan la ley: el Gobierno y la Iglesia. Siendo diputado él mismo es más comprensible su actitud un poco de *noli me tangere*.[64]

(When commenting on the play, Ochoa gets all worked up condemning the cynical depiction of a minister who is a rake and an elected representative who is a scoundrel. He says that if one mocks the individual one also mocks the institution, and if we lose respect for individuals because of their personal defects, we will also end up losing respect for those who sanction such conduct: the Government and the Church. One can understand his "don't touch me" attitude, seeing as he himself was an elected representative.)

The play itself hardly merited a major literary squabble. It was a rather dull comedy based on the idea that prohibiting something makes it all the more desirable (a covert acknowledgment of the nature of censorship?). One notes the presence of Moratín in the play's concern for the education of young women, of Larra in its presentation of the venal newspaper owner who pays poorly but turns a tidy profit from the efforts of his journalists, and of Larra and Mesonero Romanos in the young heroine who, according to her tutor don Fernando, gets so heated up after reading certain books that he fears that she will give "el corazón / al primero con quien hable" ("her heart to the first person who speaks with her") (I, 3). Even stronger is the influence of the late eighteenth-century lachrymose comedy. Don Gabriel, the play's most balanced character, cries copious tears at the slightest thought of virtue and goodness. Generosity and virtue stimulate his tear ducts in a way unseen since Jovellanos and Cienfuegos[65] and he is presented as a noble, loving character. When things work out well in the end (Gonzalo and Catalina can marry, and don Fernando resolves to treat them as his own children), don Gabriel is left on the stage, "llorando de placer" ("weeping with pleasure") III, 19).

The contrasts of rich and poor are starkly presented in the play's settings: Act I takes place in the attic flat of the poor poet Gonzalo (exactly ninety-seven steps up from the street, a statement on Madrid's

[64] Donald Allen Randolph, *Eugenio de Ochoa y el romanticismo español* (Berkeley: University of California Publications in Modern Philology, 1966): 150.
[65] See D. T. Gies, "Cienfuegos y las lágrimas de virtud," *Coloquio Internacional sobre el teatro español del siglo XVIII*, eds. Mario Di Pinto, Maurizio Fabbri, and Rinaldo Froldi (Albano Terme: Piovan Editore, 1988): 213–226. Also, Joan L. Pataky Kosove, *The*

middle class's well-known hatred of climbing steps) while Act II is set in the richly appointed house of the wealthy and odious banker don Fernando. The presence of this millionaire banker signals some of the concern for the evil of unbridled wealth (or at least, of the accumulation of wealth untempered by moral considerations) which will become so evident in later plays. Fernando is much more interested in the potential success of one of his enemies in securing a government position – which will compromise his banking business and cause him to lose money – than he is in the wellbeing and wedding plans of his orphaned ward Carolina. The moral key to *Las prohibiciones* is revealed by don Gabriel in the exact center of the play. As he tells his brother Fernando:

> Pronto oirás tu hora fatal;
> tu vida pende de un hilo ...
> y no morirás tranquilo,
> porque has hecho mucho mal.
> Vivir de placeres lleno,
> con laureles, con amor,
> con riquezas ... Sí señor!
> Mas cuando la senectud
> viene con sus desengaños;
> cuando terribles los años
> nos llevan al ataúd;
> entonces, adiós honores ...
> adiós falsos oropeles,
> adiós mentidos laureles,
> adiós riquezas y amores.
> El alma sufre batida
> por desengaño profundo,
> y todo el oro del mundo
> no da un minuto de vida.   (II, 10)

(You will soon hear the trumpet call; your life is dangling by a thread ... and you will not die peacefully because you have done a lot of evil in your life. To live full of pleasure, crowned with laurels, with love, with wealth ... Yes, sir! But when old age comes along with its disappointments, when the awful years drag us toward the grave, then, goodbye honors, goodbye false glitter, goodbye phony laurels, goodbye wealth and love. The soul is vanquished by profound deception and all the gold in the world cannot add one minute to life.)

Just in case we – or his audience – did not get the message, Eguílaz repeats it in the next act (III, 9).

Such excessive moralizing prompted the newspaper *La Epoca* to com-

'Comedia lacrimosa' and Spanish Romantic Drama (1773–1865) (London: Tamesis, 1977) and María Jesús García Garrosa, *La retórica de las lágrimas. La comedia sentimental española, 1751–1802* (Valladolid: Caja de Ahorros y Monte de Piedad de Salamanca, 1990).

plain that "El señor Eguílaz lleva su punto de moralizar y sermonear al público hasta un extremo de exageración y casi degenera en monomanía" ("Mr. Eguílaz takes his moralizing and sermonizing the public to an exaggerated extreme which almost degenerates into monotony") (21 January 1853), although the writer's real complaint might have been of the author's stern criticism of journalists and the press ("su pintura carece de verdad y exactitud" ["his view lacks truth and accuracy"]). If hackneyed speeches such as Eguílaz's sound hollow today, they nonetheless underscored one of the great concerns of the playwrights of the time and became an oft-repeated warning issued from the *cátedra* of the theatre. Eguílaz hoped that the new generation would steer Spain on a new course: "Gastada generación, / haz plaza a la juventud" ("Let the old generation make way for the new") (III, 10). Alas, it was not to be.

Eguílaz quickly became one of the most applauded dramatists working in Madrid. He staged numerous productions there during the 1850s – *Alarcón*, 1853; *Una tarde de Quevedo* (An Afternoon of Quevedo, 1853); *El caballero del milagro* (The Knight of the Miracles, 1854); *La espada de san Fernando* (San Fernando's Sword, 1854); *Una virgen de Murillo* (One of Murillo's Virgins, 1854), and *Entre todas las mujeres* (Among All Women, 1854), both in collaboration with Luis Mariano de Larra; *La vergonzosa en palacio* (The Shy Woman at Court, 1855, a play on Tirso's famous work); *Una aventura de Tirso* (Tirso's Adventure, 1855); *La vida de Juan, soldado* (The Life of Juan the Soldier, 1856); *La llave de oro* (The Golden Key, 1856); *La vaquera de la Finojosa* (The Cowherder from Finojosa, 1857); *Grazalema*, 1857; *El patriarca del Turia* (The Patriarch of the Turia, 1858), *Las querellas del rey sabio* (The Wise King's Complaints, 1858, written in "fabla antigua," a modish imitation of medieval language championed by Durán), etc. By the time he wrote *Mentiras dulces* (Sweet Lies) in 1859, he was a recognized star of Madrid's stage.

Mentiras dulces was a sequel to his very popular early play, *Verdades amargas* (Bitter Truths) which had first been performed in January, 1853, was later selected to inaugurate the 1853–1854 season at the Príncipe, and had reached seven published editions by 1867. *Verdades amargas* captured "las necesidades de su siglo" ("the needs and wants of his century") (Roque Barcia, writing in *El Teatro Español*, 28 February 1859), but if the first play was marked by its cynicism, this one was the reverse: as Eguílaz stated in the dedication, "esta comedia concluye diciendo que hay venturas que gozar, que hay verdades que creer" ("in the final analysis this comedy says that there are good things to enjoy, that there are truths to believe"). The mood of the public was darker than he was willing to concede in 1859, and this story of a reformed *calavera* (which reminds us in several ways of Vega's *El hombre de mundo*) failed to ignite any sparks

of interest. *La Discusión* reported that it was "escuchada con más benevolencia de la que se merece" ("heard with more kindness than it
deserves") (3 April 1859) while *La Iberia* accurately judged it "falsa de
plan y pensamiento, pero con bellos trozos de poesía" ("phony in plot
and design, but with lovely bits of poetry in it") (3 April 1859).

His next play, *El padre de los pobres* (The Father of the Poor), was a
"fiasco" (*La Discusión*, 6 January 1860), and was justifiably received "con
marcada frialdad" ("with notable coldness") (*La Iberia*, 6 January 1860).
Still, Eguílaz kept churning out plays, the majority of them received more
favorably than these two failures. *La vaquera de la Finojosa* (1861) was a
frequently revived hit, as was *La cruz del matrimonio*, a "comedia de
costumbres" which stimulated wide acclaim when it appeared at the
Teatro Variedades on 28 November 1861.[66] Advanced word-of-mouth for
this work was extremely favorable, prompting the Queen herself to show
up for the play's debut. By mid-December it was the capital's most hotly
sought theatre ticket, and the first edition of its printed version sold out
within a few weeks. Within months it had appeared in theatres in La
Coruña, Valencia, and Murcia. Julián Romea, the most popular and
best-trained actor in Spain, successfully revived it in 1864, and by 1870 it
was playing in Italy as *La croce del matrimonio* (*El Entreacto*, 10
December 1870).

La cruz del matrimonio is a sappy, arch-conservative play which propa-
gates the belief that not only is a woman's place in the home, but that the
accepting and long-suffering wife is the authentic moral center of that
home.[67] Perhaps because of this fact, it was a huge hit.

La primera calidad del éxito de *La cruz del matrimonio* es de tener un fin moral
muy marcado; ser la prueba en acción de una tesis, lo cual es muy del gusto del
día, en que, confundidos el arte, la poesía y la ciencia, piensan los autores en
enseñar algo, y antes de buscar argumentos o enredos para sus dramas, buscan
pensamientos trascendentales. (*El Contemporáneo*, 22 December 1861)

(The main reason for the success of *La cruz del matrimonio* is that it has an
obvious moral purpose; it is the acting out of a thesis, which is very much to
today's taste, in which art, poetry and science blend together. Authors think about
teaching something, and before they look for a plot or plot twists, they look for
transcendental thoughts.)

---

[66] One of the few studies to include any mention of Eguílaz's work is Oreida Chú-Pond, *La
figura del Mesías en el teatro romántico español* (San José, Costa Rica: Fundación San
Judás Tadeo, 1988), in which she studies *Grazalema* (1857), *La payesa de Sarriá* (1860),
and *El padre de los pobres* (1860).

[67] Brigit Aldaraca discusses these issues in relation to the novels of the last third of the
century. See *El angel del hogar: Galdós y la ideología de la domesticidad en España*
(Madrid: Visor, 1992).

Here, as in other dramas of the *alta comedia* type, character and action are subordinated to theme and thesis. Mercedes and Enriqueta adopt very different strategies to deal with their gad-about husbands ("calaveras") who lie and finagle in order to gamble, enjoy a lively night life, and run around with assorted girlfriends (who frequently in these kinds of plays are Italian actresses or singers; in fact, *La Traviata* is woven through this play in theme and music). They become the thesis and antithesis of the play's philosophical stance. Enriqueta's approach, encouraged by her frivolous and ultra-Frenchified aunt Clara (a revival of the hilarious *petimetra* type so ably satirized a century before by Nicolás Fernández de Moratín), is to fight Manuel on every front, making herself disagreeable, argumentative, and combative in order to get him to stop his immoral behavior. Mercedes, on the other hand, remains loving, supportive, quiet, and dignified, even as her husband Félix betrays her in countless ways. Eguílaz signals the contrast between the two women from the play's outset. Enriqueta appears in Act I, scene 1, dressed elegantly, while Mercedes's percale dress is "mucho más sencillo" ("much simpler"). To heighten the difference between the two women, Eguílaz reveals that Enriqueta's son has remained in Paris (where she used to live) with a nursemaid, while Mercedes and Félix's son is the center of his mother's attentions. Mercedes, the good wife and good mother who spends her days sewing, praying, and taking care of her husband and child, wins out (naturally) in the end: Félix tearfully accepts the disharmony his behavior has caused:

> la mujer
> que ama a un hijo con tibieza,
> que no cose y que no reza ...
> ¡honrada no puede ser!   (III, 9)

(the woman who loves her child tepidly, who does not sew nor pray ... cannot be an honorable woman!)

Mercedes confirms his judgment: "es de la mujer el centro / su casa" ("the woman is the center of the home") (III, 12) and proclaims that they will carry the "cruz del matrimonio" together. While such saccharine moralizations strike us as bland and cliché-ridden today, Eguílaz's audience received them with open applause, for it saw in them a necessary corrective of what seemed to be a dissolving social order.[68]

---

[68] Eguílaz linked the play's *desenlace* to a well-known Madrid insurance company, *La Tutelar*, the mention of which prompted its director to make the author an honorary member of the society. As Eguílaz wrote in a newspaper article, "Desde hace mucho tiempo admiro esas sociedades de seguros sobre la vida, por medio de las cuales una madre buena y cariñosa puede, despojándose de algo de lo superfluo, asegurar lo necesario a sus hijos. ¿Y habiendo de nombrar una, como no preferir La Tutelar, que por

One of Eguílaz's best plays was the now completely forgotten *Quiero y no puedo* (I Want To But I Can't), which had its debut at the Teatro de la Zarzuela on 10 March 1867. Similar in theme and focus to Ayala's magistral *El tanto por ciento*, it deals with government contracts, business arrangements, and the tight relationship which existed between official policies and individual fortunes in the financial world. If anything, it is even more powerful than *El tanto por ciento* because Spain had just lived through one of the most corrupt periods in its history and was about to blow apart with a force unexpected by any of the contending sides. Ayala's warning has now become a reality. Eguílaz confessed that this play was his favorite, since it had cost him the most time and effort to write, and it shows. Set in Madrid, in "186–," it was contemporary in the extreme. Using a rather awkward anatomical image, the author wrote in the foreword:

Pertenece esta comedia a un género en el cual, como he dicho en la sétima edición de *Verdades amargas*, el pensamiento lo es todo: los caracteres, el argumento y el diálogo, le están completamente subordinados: el poeta no inventa, deduce dentro de las prescripciones más severas de la lógica; todo es, en fin, forma, menos el pensamiento mismo, que debe dominarlo todo, que debe estar en todos los personajes, desarrollarse en todas las escenas, palpitar debajo de todas las frases; que debe ser, para acabar, la sangre de la comedia, que partiendo del corazón , vaya a dar vida hasta a las más insignificantes moléculas de los miembros.

(This comedy belongs to a genre in which, as I have said in the seventh edition of my play *Verdades amargas*, the main idea is everything: characters, plot, and dialogue are completely subordinated to it. The poet does not invent things, rather he deduces them from strict logic. Everything, in the end, boils down to form, except the main idea itself, which should dominate everything, which should be seen in every character, developed in every scene, beat beneath every sentence; it should be the lifeblood of the play, which moving out from the heart should give life even to the smallest molecules of the extremities.)

The "sangre" of this play was the utter corruption of political and business interests in Spain on the eve of Revolution. Don Fernando, an opulent banker, is surrounded by Sofía, his superficial and social-climbing wife; Emilia, his shop-aholic daughter; Eugenio, a phony noble who aspires to marry well (that is, to marry Emilia); don Pedro, a once-wealthy speculator who lost his fortune (and his wife and children) playing the market, and who now does Fernando's books; and two scheming Jewish investors. These characters typify for Eguílaz the frivolous, class-conscious, money-grubbing society which dominates his country. Only Consuelo, Fernando's daughter raised by an aunt in the

ser la más antigua es la que más deja sentir su benéfico influjo en el seno de las familias?"
El Contemporáneo (10 December 1861).

countryside (where she had been sent because of her health) and Luis, the gentle, hard-working bureaucrat who aspires to Consuelo's hand, rise above the muck of self-interest and petty greed. Luis prefers to make his way up in the world "paso a paso" ("step by step") (I, 7), an attitude scorned by Eugenio, who believes that one must spend, advance, and marry well to "make it" in society. That Eguílaz viewed this on a broad social level becomes crystal clear when Fernando says to Eugenio, "gastas más de lo que tienes . . . / Y no eres tú solo, no. / Todo el mundo está en un tris / desde hace más de un decenio. / El mismo país, Eugenio . . . / ¿Qué no gasta este país?" ("You spend more than you have . . . and you are not alone, no. Everyone is in the same boat for more than a decade. The country itself, Eugenio . . . What money does this country not spend?") (II, 12).

Complications occur when it is discovered that Fernando, a seemingly prosperous banker, is in deep financial trouble because of some bad investments and a shady past. The audience is tipped off at the outset when the scene opens in the "gabinete de la casa de don Fernando suntuosamente decorado [con] extraordinario lujo en el mueblaje" ("don Fernando's sitting room, sumptuously decorated with impressive furnishings"); it has learned to be suspicious of excessive luxury and ostentation. Emilia, just returned from a shopping expedition with her sister and mother, criticizes Consuelo for asking the price of things, fearful that "¿Te es a ti igual que te tengan / por persona de alta clase, / o así . . . por una cualquiera?" ("Is it all the same to you whether people take you for a high-class person or . . . just anybody?") (I, 1). While Consuelo pays close attention to the financial news reported in the newspapers (because she has noted that her father's moods frequently parallel the rise or fall of the stock market, dismissed as "siempre negocios" ["business as usual"] by Sofía), Emilia wants nothing to do with such matters, which she sees as beneath her dignity (an attitude clearly reflective of the Spanish nobility's disdain for work of any kind). As long as she has enough cash to spend she is happy. For her, there is little difference between selling stocks and selling bolts of cloth.

> ¿No somos bastante ricos?
> ¿Por qué no compra dehesas
> y grandes bosques y cotos
> y vive así de sus rentas
> como viven las personas
> decentes?
> . . .
> Vender títulos y acciones
> o vender paños y telas,
> todo es vender, todo es uno.   (I, 1)

(Aren't we rich enough already? Why don't you buy some pastures and forests and hunting preserves, and live off your rental income like decent people do? ... Selling patents and stocks or selling cloths and fabrics, it's still all selling, it's all the same thing.)

Sofía, in the meantime, aspires to a ministerial position for her husband, since it is clear that those in government positions make money with their investments.

Quiero y no puedo is a deliciously complicated comedy which reflects perfectly the concerns and shortcomings of upper-middle-class Spanish society in the mid-1860s. One need only read the opening chapters of Galdós's *Fortunata y Jacinta*, in which he recounts the background of the wealthy shopkeeping family of Juanito Santa Cruz, to appreciate the importance of money and appearance for this generation of Spaniards. It is a world based on false appearances, phantom money (Fernando gives a brilliant ball even when he is on the verge of ruin in order to trick people into believing that he still has access to funds), and false credit. Don Pedro is aware of the consequences of such manipulations. As he tells Fernando, there is a short step between manipulation and criminal behavior:

> pueden conducirle al crimen.
> Hoy con un cuento inventado
> algún pago aplazará.
> Mañana mano echará
> de un depósito sagrado,
> y si esto no toma en cuenta
> hará al fin de la jornada
> una vez de una quiebra honrada,
> una quiebra fraudulenta.   (III, 4)

(these things can lead him to crime. Today with a white lie he delays a payment. Tomorrow he takes a little from a client's fund, and if he isn't careful he'll end up turning an honorable difficulty into a fraudulent bankruptcy.)

Equílaz captured a real truth: his message seemed equally valid in the 1980s as it was in the 1860s.

Equílaz strikes a note of social consciousness, similar to those later developed so compassionately by Dicenta and his contemporaries, when he demonstrates concern over the chasm that exists between the rich and the poor in Madrid.

> Hay contrastes
> en el mundo a los que nunca
> he podido acostumbrarme.
> Al entrar en esta casa
> deslumbradora y brillante;
> al contemplar la riqueza

de esos salones de baile,
siento oprimida mi alma,
porque hace solo un instante
que salí de una bohardilla
donde he encontrado una madre
con tres niños que lloraban:
– yo sospecho que de hambre.   (II, 5)

(There are differences in the world which I've never been able to get used to. When I come into this dazzling house, when I contemplate the wealth of those ballrooms, I feel as though my soul is suffocating because just a moment ago I left a garret where I found a mother with three little children who were crying – I suspect from hunger.)

There is much poverty in Madrid, "mas los ricos ... no lo saben" ("but the rich ... are not aware of it") (II, 5). It is Consuelo who gives her last ounce of gold to a needy family, and the moral victory brings her own family, now poor itself due to Fernando's forced bankruptcy, to the recognition that they should accept Luis's offer to support them from his new job as governor of Huelva, since "de la riqueza el trabajo / la puerta nos abrirá" ("work will open the door to wealth for us") (III, 10). Too bad Spain refused to heed the warning, according to Eguílaz, who was named archivist in the Academia de la Historia four years before his death in 1874. Many of his plays and zarzuelas stayed in the repertory for the rest of the century, and his daughter Rosa briefly achieved attention in the capital when she staged *Después de Dios* (After God) in 1889.

Another second-generation dramatist enjoyed notable success at midcentury. Luis Mariano de Larra (1830–1901), the son of Mariano José de Larra and Pepa Wetoret, was one of the country's most active authors.[69] Born in the same year as Narciso Serra and Luis de Eguílaz (1830), he wrote more than fifty plays and zarzuelas, some in collaboration with playwrights such as José María Larrea (*Las tres noblezas* [The Three Nobilities, 1853]), Eguílaz (*Una virgen de Murillo*, 1854), Ventura de la Vega (*Barómetro conyugal* [Conjugal Barometer]), and Serra (*Los infieles* [The Unfaithful, 1860]), and enjoyed the public's acclaim for more than fifty years (*as a dramatist*, he was much more popular in his time than his famous father). Like his father, Luis Mariano wrote newspaper commentaries (for *La Epoca*), translations and "adaptations" of French plays, original dramas, poetry, and a novel, but it was as a playwright and librettist for the zarzuela that he captured the public's attention. His zarzuelas were frequently written in collaboration with other authors such as Ramón de Navarrete (*Cadenas de oro* [Gold Chains, 1864]) or

---

[69] Eguílaz is mentioned once in Díez Borque's *Historia del teatro en España*, II; Larra is not mentioned at all.

García Gutiérrez (*El conde y el condenado*[70] [The Count and the Condemned Man]) and were produced with music by the three best musicians
of the day, Cristóbal Oudrid, Gaztambide, and Francisco Asenjo Barbieri. He was a kind of pen-for-hire, working with a wide range of writers
and musicians over a period of more than four decades. The newspapers
provided continuous coverage of his productions, from his first attempt at
historical drama, *Juicios de Dios* (God's Judgments, 1848), through his
last comedies and musicals at the century's close. In 1872 he was awarded
the Gran Cruz de Isabel la Católica in recognition of his years of service
to the theatre.

Larra's plays never reached beyond mere pleasantness. While tech-
nically proficient, and a skilful rhymester (his verse was praised as "fácil,
elevada y armoniosa" ["light, elevated, and harmonious"] by *La Epoca* in
1853), he loaded his comedies up with derivative ideas and middle-of-the-
road ideological postures. Newspaper criticisms reveal the frequent use of
words like "floja" ("weak"), "trivial," "no del todo original" ("not
completely original"), "no es muy buena" ("not very good"), "reg-
ularcilla" ("mediocre"), "éxito satisfactorio" ("satisfactory success"), or
(rarely) "agradable" ("pleasant") to describe his works (naturally, *La
Epoca*, for which he wrote, was softer on him than its competitors). *La
Iberia* even criticized "la precipitación con que el autor escribe sus obras"
("the haste with which the author writes his plays") (3 January 1858). The
audience could guess the dénouement of most of Larra's plays by the first
act, which might in fact have been part of their attraction. He was a
comfortable dramatist, one who could be counted on to deliver anodine
messages in easy doses. He offered "moralidad y elevación" ("moral
uplift") as *La España* noted in 1863. He counseled his audience to be
loyal, consistent, faithful, not overly ambitious, and steadfast. Surprisingly, *La primera piedra* (The First Stone), which he wrote in early 1861,
was prohibited by the censors and was not ready for performance until
December, 1862; the nature of the censor's objections remains unknown.

Even the collaboration with Serra, *Los infieles* (1860), was a slight work
devoid of coherent thinking, which nonetheless hinges on the ever-present
preoccupation of Spain's middle class, money. (Most of Larra's plays
take place in Madrid during the year of their performance, adding a note
of contemporaneity to them). It achieved modest success at the Príncipe
Theatre when it opened on 19 January 1860, in spite of *La España*'s
warning that "tiene muchos fallos y defectos y no es una obra original"
("it is weak and has a lot of defects, and it is not an original play") (21

---

[70] I have not seen this work. It is not listed in Adams, *The Romantic Dramas of García
Gutiérrez*, nor in any other sources I have been able to check. This reference is from the
title page of Larra's *Los corazones de oro* (Madrid: Alonso Gullón, 1875).

January 1860). Another case in point is the play he wrote at the actor Emilio Mario's request for the inauguration of the new Teatro de la Comedia in 1875. Mario was the theatre's new impresario and stage director, and he needed a play in a hurry for the opening. Larra obliged with *Los corazones de oro* (Hearts of Gold), admittedly taken from a French melodrama but transformed, in the author's words, from a "dramón" into a "comedia sencilla y tierna." "Simple and gentle" were effects that Larra not only strove to achieve but also what he accomplished: the play tells the tale of a pair of lovers who are tested to see if their relationship will be affected by the presence of great wealth or not. Does Federico love Consuelo – a poor seamstress who is really the heiress to an immense fortune left by her mother, a marquesa – for herself alone? Will his intentions change if he comes into money? Such questions test the fantasies of a rising middle class, one which dreams of great wealth (they looked around themselves and saw that it was possible) but whose dreams are never satisfactorily realized. Luis Arratia is yet another venal banker: Andrés wonders how it is that he was fired before from a job paying him 4,000 *reales* a year, but now that he has money there will be a job for him at 30,000:

> Me dijeron
> que sólo lo hacían para
> nivelar los presupuestos,
> y pues hoy a los de cuatro
> les dan treinta o más, yo pienso
> que ya estarán nivelados
> y con sobras ...   (II, 1)

(They told me that they only did it to balance the budget, but now they give 30,000 or more where they used to give 4 and I suspect that the budget is already balanced, and even that there are surplusses ...)

The same preoccupation with economic wellbeing that infused the other plays we have seen is evident here, but Larra seems to provide a counter message to the one we have described thus far. Whereas in many of the other plays of this period the audience is warned against the dangers of excessive ambition and wealth (because it corrupts), Larra seems to be concerned to warn his audience to stay in its place, that is, not to get any ideas about rising up in society. He does warn, however, of the dangers of playing the stock market and of living on excessive credit, two *leitmotifs* heard consistently in the plays of this period. The newspapers praised *Los corazones de oro* as one of Larra's best works ("una de sus mejores creaciones" ["one of his best creations"]); indeed, it ran for nearly three months at the end of 1875 and was brought back for short runs in 1880 and 1899.

Once in a while Larra rose above mediocrity and achieved more than modest success with his plays (*Flores y perlas* [Flowers and Pearls, 1860]; *Estudio del natural* [The Genius's Study, 1863]; *En brazos de la muerte* [In the Arms of Death, 1865]; *Bienaventurados los que lloran* [Blessed Are Those Who Weep, 1866]), but gradually he turned to the more popular zarzuela as a source of income and fame. One of his plays created such a scandal when it was first put on that it was withdrawn from the stage after a couple of performances: journalists objected to the "calumny" of *Los misterios del Parnaso* (The Mysteries of Parnassus, which premièred on 7 September 1868, during volatile times) because it satirized their profession. The newspapers refused to advertise it. The zarzuela *Sueños de oro* (Dreams of Gold), staged with an expensive set in 1872, was such a big hit that the public "rompió las puertas y ventanillas del despacho a fin de obtener localidades" ("broke down the doors and windows of the ticket booth in order to get a ticket") (*La Iberia*, 3 January 1873) and *El barberillo de Lavapiés* (The Little Barber of Lavapies, 1874), written with music by Barbieri, became a staple in the zarzuela repertories and even played in Paris in 1892.

While the dramatists of the *alta comedia* succeeded in articulating the problems of their class, what they failed to do was to move theatre into new areas of structure and staging. That is, they refused to experiment with techniques such as split stages, non-mimetic visual spaces, mixed chronology, and fluid temporal sequences which might have advanced the theatrical idiom of the day. They offered no radical new solutions to staging difficulties or significant new inventions in backdrops or lighting. The authors of the *alta comedia* criticized social mores but in fact did not challenge seriously the assumptions of middle-class and upper-middle-class Spanish society. They viewed from a distance what was happening, and complained about it, but did not seem really to be deeply troubled by what they saw, on an existential level, as were their predecessors the Romantic dramatists. None of the authors studied expresses any serious disquiet about the society in which he/she lives in ideological or spiritual terms. Their focus on theme ultimately did not challenge the public to do anything or to think any radical new thoughts, and their concern for marriage rather than love presents a remarkable (and significant) contrast with Romantic drama. They wrote, after all, plays with happy endings rather than tragedies. While in most cases the dramatists mentioned here did their work with skill and conviction, thematic concerns are not enough and the *alta comedia*, while essential for our understanding of the society of mid-nineteenth-century Spain, remains more a curiosity than a significant force for today's readers.

Spoofs, parodies, zarzuelas, and other scenic diversions

Theatre in Spain in the nineteeth century, as now, was not only Art (when it was that); it was also spectacle and commerce. Seats needed to be filled, actors paid, and playwrights fed, and few dramatists from last century – if any – were able to exempt themselves from the pressures of commerce. By the mid-1850s, parodies and musical entertainments had become standard fare in the theatres of the court (we have already seen the enormous staying power of the magical comedies). As José Fernández Bremón wrote in 1881,

No basta el arte para satisfacer las exigencias de estrenos y novedades, y la necesidad ha creado un oficio, que sustituye a aquel, y que es a la literatura lo que la pintura de muestras a la de exposiciones y museos. Hábiles y sagaces industriales se codean con los autores de conciencia, y sólo muy tarde comprende el público el engaño.[71]

(Art alone cannot meet the demands of opening nights and new plays, and this need has created a new type of job which relates to art the way the painting of shop signs relates to museums and art galleries. Clever and sagacious businessmen have moved into the domain of serious playwrights, and only too late does the public realize the deception.)

Certainly, from the time of Grimaldi, this was a fact of life in Madrid's theatrical world, and a riotous jumble of genres crowded onto the stages in order to win the public's acclaim (and pesetas).

The major hit of the 1851 season was Ventura de la Vega's *Jugar con fuego* (Playing With Fire), a work which reached four editions by 1854.[72] Written as a zarzuela (billed as a "comic opera" because of its length), with bright, lilting music by Francisco Asenjo Barbieri (1823–1894), the three-act play delighted audiences for months following its première at the Teatro del Circo on 6 October 1851. Vega's friends expressed doubts about whether a serious playwright – and one currently at the height of his influence – should bother with minor genres, but generic distinctions were beginning to blur during this period and Vega felt intrigued enough by a collaboration with Barbieri to plunge ahead with the project;[73] besides, Vega's wife was the prima donna of the Teatro Real in the Plaza de Oriente, so he was not far removed from the world of music. There were other precedents: Rodríguez Rubí and Joaquín Gaztambide had

[71] Fernández Bremón, "Don Narciso Serra," p. 359.
[72] In 1992 this zarzuela was chosen by "Cultural Capital of Europe" Madrid to kick off the musical comedy season. It opened at the Teatro de Madrid (Vaguada) on 7 June 1992.
[73] "Sus amigos querían disuadirle de aquel cambio de género, que parecía implicar cierto desprestigio para él. Sensatamente, Ventura se encogió de hombros ante tal hipótesis: tal teatro es un género como otro." Martínez Olmedilla, *Anecdotario*, p. 387.

written *Tribulaciones* (Afflictions), which failed to spark any interest at the Circo Theatre in mid-September. Vega also seemed committed to elevating the generally low tone of musical theatre by attempting to write a high-quality script. It paid off: the Circo remained sold-out for weeks following the play's première and *Jugar con fuego* became the most popular zarzuela written to date in Spain. It produced substantial royalties for Vega as well as for the group of investors who had taken over the recently bankrupt Circo in an attempt to restimulate interest in Spanish, rather than Italian, music. *La comtesse d'Egmont* (The Countess of Egmont), the original French comedy by Lancelot which had inspired the plot of *Jugar con fuego*, was successfully staged at the Teatro Variedades in January 1852, and Vega began writing a sequel within weeks (*El marqués de Caravaca* [The Marquis of Caravaca], eventually mounted in April, 1853). *Jugar con fuego* caused a sensation ("haciendo verdadero furor" ["exciting a real furor"], *La Epoca*, 22 April 1853) in Santander before settling into the repertories of companies in Madrid and the provinces.

The text alone, while clever enough and written in smooth verse, would not rescue *Jugar con fuego* from oblivion, but the combination of agreeable characters, several very funny scenes (notably in the madhouse in Act III where Félix has been dispatched by the Marqués de Caravaca), and the three interesting scenic spaces (a riverbank during a celebration of the Night of Saint John in Act I, the Palacio del Buen Retiro in Act II, and the asylum in Act III) with Barbieri's lively and lyrical music insured the zarzuela's success. The balance between text and music distinguished the comic opera from grand opera, in the opinion of one of the reviewers of Vega's work in *El Correo de los Teatros* (12 October 1851): "En el drama lírico de grandes proporciones o de espectáculo, como suele decirse, se admite o se tolera el predominio de la música sobre las palabras; pero en la ópera cómica, que no es otra cosa sino la comedia con música, esta no es sino un simple auxiliar de aquella obligado a realzar sus bellezas, no a eclipsarlas" ("In large-scale, or spectacular – as it's often called – lyric drama one accepts the dominance of music over word; but in comic opera, which is really only a comedy set to music, music is just a simple aid to help the words come through in all their beauty, not overshadow them"). Days later (9 November) the newspaper claimed that this work marked a watershed moment in the musical stage in Spain: "ha cerrado las puertas del teatro lírico español a las trivialidades de mal género indebidamente conocidas con el nombre de zarzuelas, y ha dicho: «De aquí nadie pasa»" ("Spanish lyrical theatre has closed its doors to those trivial little plays unfairly called zarzuelas, and it has proclaimed: 'You can't come in' "). Vega's play stimulated a resurgence of the zarzuela at mid-century.

The growing popularity of the zarzuela was accompanied by an intensified interest in theatrical parodies. The proliferation of comedies and dramas brought about a similar proliferation of spoofs of the best-known plays. One of the first playwrights to mine the lode of parody in the nineteenth century was, not surprisingly, Bretón de los Herreros, who frequently integrated into his plays scenes which parodied the exaggerated Romantic emotionalism of the mid-1830s. *Todo es farsa en este mundo* (1835) and *Muérete ¡y verás!* (1837) both contain scenes which poke fun at Romantic drama. Whereas Mesonero Romano's article "El romanticismo y los románticos" is not a play, it does make hilarious mockery of the lugubrious silliness of his "nephew's" play *¡El! y ¡Ella!*. One of the most active early parodists was Agustín Azcona, whose talent for skewering grand opera was evident in his "parodia discretísima"[74] ("very ingenious parody") of *Lucrecia Borgia*, which he titled *La venganza de Alifonso* (Alifonso's Revenge, 1847), his zarzuela *El sacristán de San Lorenzo* (The Sexton of San Lorenzo, 1847), based on Donizetti's *Lucía de Lammermoor*, and his montage parody of scenes from several Bellini operas, *El suicidio de la Rosa* (La Rosa's Suicide, 1847). Antonio García Gutiérrez took the unusual (and perhaps unique) step of publishing a parody of his own Romantic play *El trovador*, which he called *Los hijos del tío Tronera* (Uncle Tronera's Children, 1846). Another parody of *El trovador* appeared in 1864 as *El cantador* (The Singer) by Frederic Soler. Later, *Venganza catalana* (1864) was barely on the stage before it received two separate send-ups, one by one of the most prolific of the parodists of his day, Juan de Alba, as *La venganza de Catana* (Catana's Revenge, 1864) and the other by Soler as *La venganza de la Tana* (La Tana's Revenge, 1864). Gil y Zárate's *Guzmán el Bueno* (Guzman the Good, 1842) was pilloried at least twice during the last century, first as *El tío Zaratán* (Uncle Zaratán, 1857), by José María Gutiérrez de Alba, and later as *Guzmán el Malo* (Guzman the Bad, 1885) by Francisco Flores García. Other examples abound, including Mariano Pina Domínguez's *Los amantes de Churiana* (The Lovers of Churiana, 1845) and Eusebio Blasco's *Los novios de Teruel* (The Fiancés of Teruel, 1867), both parodies of Hartzenbusch's well-known drama, and *La borracha de profesión* (A Drunk by Profession, 1868), an anonymous parody of Rodríguez Rubí's *Borrascas del corazón* (Storms of the Heart).[75]

[74] Hartzenbusch's words, cited by Cotarelo, "Ensayo histórico sobre la zarzuela, o sea el drama lírico español desde su origen a fines del siglo XIX," *Boletín de la Real Academia Española* 20 (1933): 302.

[75] See Salvador Crespo Matellán, *La parodia dramática en la literatura española* (Universidad de Salamanca, 1979), and the excellent thesis by Nancy Membrez, *The 'teatro por horas,'* for additional details. Membrez comments that these theatrical parodies were a "vital, if parasitic, component of one-act play production" (379). Also, Valentina

The most frequently parodied play in the nineteenth-century canon was unquestionably Zorrilla's *Don Juan Tenorio*. As this work gradually took its place as one of the key plays – if not *the* key play – of the nineteenth century, imitations and parodies of it sprang up in such profusion that they became a cottage industry for authors and impresarios for nearly a century following its debut in 1844.[76] *Don Juan Tenorio* lent itself as few plays did to the process of parody because of its deep spirituality, its heightened theatricality, and the fact that its audiences knew whole scenes by heart because it was repeated so frequently on the stage. Clarín had a difficult time convincing his readers that Ana Ozores, "la regenta" ("the magistrate's wife") had never seen nor read the *Tenorio*, although apparently she did know some "versos sueltos de él como todos los españoles"[77] ("assorted verses from it, like all Spaniards"). (Her ignorance of the *Tenorio* struck don Alvaro as "imperdonable" ["unforgiveable"].) Alonso Cortés perhaps exaggerated somewhat when he referred to "mil parodias, muy graciosas algunas"[78] ("a thousand parodies, some of them very funny") but he pointed to an important literary phenomenon. The fact is there were more than two dozen imitations, continuations, and parodies of *Don Juan Tenorio* written, performed, and published during the nineteenth century alone (many more appear in the twentieth century). An incomplete list of those titles published during the nineteenth century would include *Juan el perdío* (Juan the Lost Soul), by Mariano Pina y Bohigas (1848), *L'agüello pollastre*, by Chusep Baldoví (1859), *Don Giovanni Tenorio*, by Ramón Domínguez Herbella (1864), *Un Tenorio moderno* (A Modern Tenorio), by José María Nogués (1864), *Juan el perdío, segunda parte*, by "Luis Mejías y Escassy" (1866), *Don Juan Tenorio, burdel en cinco actos y 2.000 escándalos* (Don Juan Tenorio, a Brothel in Five Acts and 2,000 Scandals), an anonymous pornographic parody (1874), *El convidado de piedra* (The Stone Guest), by Rafael del Castillo (1875), *Doña Juana Tenorio* (Miss Juana Tenorio), by Rafael María Liern y Cerach (1876), *Las mocedades de don Juan Tenorio* (Don Juan Tenorio's Youth), by Juan de Alba (1877), *Tenorio y Mejía* (Tenorio and Mejia), by Leandro Torromé Ros (1877), *Un Tenorio de broma* (A Tenorio in Jest), by Bonifacio Pérez Rioja (1879), *El novio de doña Inés*

Valverde Rodao, " 'Lo que son trigedias' o la parodia dramática de 1830 a 1850," *Quaderni di Filologia Romanza* 4 (1984): 135–161.

76 See Gies, "La subversión de don Juan: Parodias decimonónicas del *Tenorio*, con una nota pornográfica," *España Contemporánea*, in press. Martin Nozick mentions just four nineteenth-century parodies of the *Tenorio* in his article, "Some Parodies of *Don Juan Tenorio*," *Hispania* 33 (1950): 242–250; George Mansour identifies more in "Algunos don Juanes olvidados del siglo XIX," *Revista de Estudios Hispánicos* 2.2 (1968): 251–264.

77 Leopoldo Alas, (Clarín), *La regenta* II, ed. Gonzalo Sobejano (Madrid: Castalia, 1981): 29.

78 Alonso Cortés, *Zorrilla, su vida y sus obras*, pp. 352–353.

(Inés's Boyfriend), by Javier de Burgos (1884), *El nuevo Tenorio* (The New Tenorio), by Joaquín María Bartrina (1886), *Juanito Tenorio* (Little Juan Tenorio), by Salvador María Granés (1886), *Doña Inés de mi alma* (Inés of My Soul), by Felipe Pérez y González (1890), *Don Juanito* (Little Juan), by Ramiro Blanco (1891), *La herencia del Tenorio* (Tenorio's Inheritance), by Adelaida Muñiz y Mas (1892), *Don Mateo Tenorio* (Matthew Tenorio), by Angel de la Guardia (1895), *Don Juanico* (Don Johnny), by Jaime Llopart Munné (1896), *Juaneca*, by Juan Tavarés (1896), *La noche del Tenorio* (Tenorio's Night), by Felipe Pérez Capo (1897), *¡Tenorios!*, by A. Ferrer y Codina (1897), *El audaz don Juan Tenorio* (The Daring don Juan Tenorio), by Antonio Careta y Vidal (1898), and *Un Tenorio y un Mejía*, by Salvador Bonavía (1898). The cannibalization of this text responded to deep impulses stemming as much from its marvellous theatricality as from its religious message. As Jesús Rubio Jiménez writes, "La extraordinaria popularidad alcanzada hizo que cada uno lo utilizara según su gusto. Produjo infinitas anécdotas y abundante literatura de consumo como pliegos y parodias teatrales por no hablar de las numerosas versiones teatrales, novelescas y ensayísticas"[79] ("The play's extraordinary popularity meant that everyone could use it however he wanted. It produced an infinite number of stories and a great deal of popular literature such as handbills and theatrical parodies, to say nothing of the numerous versions in theatre, novels and essays"). Gradually, every Spaniard came to know Zorrilla's text – or, more likely, certain moments of it – and the familiarity engendered an intimacy between the spoken/written word and the hearer/reader. *Tenorio* settled into the "collective consciousness" of Spain[80] and reappeared in a startling number of literary forms throughout the century. Literature began not only to imitate and reflect life, but also to influence it, and *Tenorio* entered into a dialogue with playwrights and audiences which on the one hand stretched the parameters of Zorrilla's text while on the other enriched each successive reading of the original.

The first parody of *Don Juan Tenorio* appeared barely four years after the debut of the original. Mariano Pina y Bohigas's *Juan el perdío* (1848) consciously played with Zorrilla's text, as the cover page of the printed version attests: "es una parodia de la primera parte de *Don Juan Tenorio*" ("it is a parody of the first part of *Don Juan Tenorio*"). Pina's characters make fun of the most extravagant moments in Zorrilla's text, and the parody's comic value resides in its double literary game, that is, the jokes

[79] Jesús Rubio Jiménez, "*Don Juan Tenorio*, drama de espectáculo: plasticidad y fantasía," *Cuadernos de Investigación Filológica* 15 (1989): 11.
[80] Timothy Mitchell, *Violence and Piety in Spanish Folklore* (Philadelphia: University of Pennsylvania Press, 1988): 169.

in Pina's text which are funny in themselves but which become doubly funny when heard or read in relation to the text to which they allude. Linda Hutcheon points out that the language of parodic texts is subversive in the sense that it refers as much to itself as to the text which it is parodying.[81] Still, the comic authority of Pina's work never manages to gain total independence since it is always and inextricably linked to the original work. This ironically enriches Zorrilla's text since the audience hears two texts at the same time, that is, it hears Pina's jokes and poetry while at the same time it hears Zorrilla's original words, which it knows by heart. In 1848 the audience hears, for example, Pina's don Juan ask Inés, "¿No es cierto, Chatiya mía, / que esto es mejó quer comé?" ("Isn't it true, darling, that this is better than eatin'?") but it also hears Zorrilla's famous verse, "¿No es cierto, paloma mía, / que están respirando amor?" ("Isn't it true, my dove, that they are exhaling love?"). The three scenes which attract the most attention by the parodists are the famous bet between don Juan and don Luis (I, i, 12), don Juan's letter to doña Inés (I, iii, 3), and the sofa scene (I, iv, 3). For this reason, between Pina's words cited above, José María Nogués's "Y más se aumenta este ardor / que en mi pecho se ha encerrado, / porque todo a vuestro lado / está respirando amor" ("And this passion which is encased in my heart increases, because everything around you is exhaling love") (*Un Tenorio moderno*, 1864), and Adelaida Muñiz y Más's "¿No es cierto, lechuza mía, / que no respiran amor?" ("Isn't it certain, my hag, that they're not exhaling love?") (*La herencia del Tenorio*, 1892) there is little psychic distance. Such deformations, rather than compromising the original work, serve to enrich both it and the new work.[82]

Rafael Liern y Cerach's parody in *Doña Juana Tenorio* (1876) goes even further in subverting the supposed seriousness of Zorrilla's main character. The title page already proclaims its allegiance to Zorrilla: it is an "imitación burlesca de escenas de *Don Juan Tenorio*" ("burlesque imitation of scenes from *Don Juan Tenorio*"). Liern lifts moments, characters, scenes, and words from his model and then inverts the gender tension by converting the libidinous don Juan into doña Juana and the innocent Inés into a young religious student appropriately named Serafín. Doña Juana's exploits hardly pale when compared to don Juan's. As she brags, she has seduced

---

[81] Linda Hutcheon, *A Theory of Parody* (New York: Methuen, 1985): 69.

[82] "It is also often possible to infer from a parodic text a certain vitalizing, competitive response on the part of the encoder to the past of his art. Doing consciously what time does more slowly, parody can work to distort the shapes of art, synthesizing from them and from the present of the encoder a new form – not one burdened, but enriched, by the past." *Ibid.* p. 97. Jeffrey T. Bersett has elaborated this idea in a graduate paper on Pina's

seis títulos de Castilla
tres matadores de toros,
el que da las banderillas,
un alquilador de coches,
un flauta, dos organistas,
el director general
de una sociedad vinícola,
un capitán de Farnesio,
dos tenientes de Pavía,
cien cabos, catorce quintos,
un furriel de la milicia,
toda la Guardia Civil
inclusa la infantería,
y los alumnos de leyes,
con más los de medicina
de Madrid, de Barcelona,
de Valencia y de Sevilla.   (I, 6)

(six nobles from Castilla, three bullfighters, the banderillero, a guy who rents carriages, a flute player, two organists, a general director of a wine growing society, a captain from Farnesio, two lieutenants from Pavia, one hundred corporals, fourteen conscripts, a militia quartermaster, the entire Civil Guard including the infantry, and all the law and medicine students from Madrid, Barcelona, Valencia and Sevilla.)

This inversion of the sexual stereotype is repeated throughout the work. Serafín gives himself over to the sexual power of Juana, repeating Inés's famous words, "Mira, Juana, yo lo imploro / de tu hidalga compasión, / o arráncame el corazón / o ámame, porque te adoro" ("Look, Juana, I beg for your illustrious compassion; either tear out my heart, or love me, because I adore you"). The middle-class obsession with itself and its possessions, which we have seen in detail in other works, is reflected here as Juana details everything she will buy for Serafín in exchange for his favors: ties, shirt collars, cuff links, socks, underwear, hats, handkerchiefs, and much, much more in a listing of consumer goods unthinkable in the eighteenth century or even in the first half of the nineteenth.

The submerged codes and intertextual references which kept these parodies in the popular eye also reveal in microcosm other characteristics we have been tracking in nineteenth-century Spanish theatre. From the preoccupation with money and middle-class morality (*Un Tenorio moderno*) to the first notes of feminist consciousness (*Juanita Tenorio, Un Tenorio feminista* [A Feminist Tenorio]), from the purely literary parody (*Un Tenorio modernista* [A Modernist Tenorio]) to the pornographic

Juan el perdío, which I hope will be published some day. I am grateful to him for several perceptive suggestions he made on this matter.

spoof (*Don Juan Tenorio, burdel en cinco actos*), these works comment on and rewrite Zorrilla's masterful text, underscoring the unquestionable authority of Zorrilla's *Don Juan Tenorio* and enriching each subsequent reading of it.

Romantic dramas, while clearly lending themselves to parody because of their already exaggerated natures, were not the only plays to be parodied. In fact, almost nothing was considered sacred, and any play which achieved even modest public support soon appeared in twisted form on the streets or stages of the capital. Leopoldo Cano y Masas staged his *La opinión pública* (Public Opinion) on 18 October 1878; by 4 November José María Fuentes and Conrado Solsona had put on their parody of it, *La voz del pueblo* (The Public's Voice). *Consuelo*, López de Ayala's extremely well-received comedy of 1878, was not immune from a burlesque rendering by Salvador María Granés, who played on the heroine's name by calling his work *Consuelo ... de tontos* (Comfort ... of Fools, 1878). *Mancha que limpia* (A Stain that Cleanses, 1894), José Echegaray's emulation of Ibsen, was immediately spoofed as *Mancha, limpia ... y da esplendor* (It Stains, It Cleans...and It Shines) by Gabriel Merino at the Teatro Romea on 12 March 1895. Merino was also the author of two funny put-downs of Galdós's dramas, one of *La de San Quintín* (The Woman from San Quentin), which he called *La del Capotín* (The Woman With the Little Cloak, 1894) and the other of the infamous *Electra*, dubbed *Electroterapia* (Electrotherapy, Teatro Apolo, 11 April 1901). José Feliu y Codina's immensely popular three-act comedy, *María del Carmen*, which premièred at the Teatro Español on 14 February 1896, was parodied by Adelaida Muñiz y Mas as *Maruja Carmela*, staged at the Nuevo Teatro de Maravillas in September of that year. Other examples abound.

We might conclude with the following observation: "Los acontecimientos literarios han tenido siempre, pero sobre todo en la época contemporánea, un valor inmenso y una trascendencia gigantesca"[83] ("Literary happenings have always had – but even more so in modern times – immense worth and important consequences"). A society in turmoil seethed beneath the surface of hundreds of plays written and performed in Spain between 1850 and 1870 and beyond.[84] That many of them had

---

[83] Guaza y Gómez Talavera, *Músicos, poetas y actores*, p. 170.

[84] My own analysis of these plays leads me to wonder if Yxart actually read them, for he writes them off in the following terms:

Un lloriqueo y gimoteo continuo en las damas [it's the men who frequently do the crying]; verdaderos lugares comunes en boca de los barbas evangelizadores, vicarios saboyanos de venerables canas, persuasivos y tiernos; tibias emociones de padres, hijos y novios, a la vista de las reliquias domésticas ... ; una continua exitación al perdón de las injurias, a la resignación cristiana, a preferir "las tiernas

money and morality at their center was indicative of the larger social reality, and these plays became not only morality lessons, but also lessons in economics for the public at large. Whereas in Romantic drama nobody worked, in the drama of mid-century everybody worked, speculating, earning money, and lusting after riches. Such a focus is not surprising in a post-Hugo world (Spanish authors knew *Les misérables* well). With this new focus on the middle class, historical dramas moved from center stage to the periphery. Historical dramas were still written, of course – García Gutiérrez had two late hits with *Venganza catalana* (1864) and *Juan Lorenzo* (1865); Núñez de Arce's *El haz de leña* was popular, as we have seen; Vega attempted a revival of the historical tragedy in 1865 with *La muerte de César* (The Death of Cesar) – but Madrid's audiences preferred to see themselves on stage rather than their ancestors. The *alta comedia* lost steam by the mid-1870s, but not before leaving a residue of social commentary which would lead, however indirectly, to Galdós's incisive dissection of the middle class, Echegaray's problematic analysis of middle-class morals, the criticism of Dicenta and his group of the division between rich and poor, and the measured drawing-room comedies of Benavente.

afecciones, la felicidad tranquila y sosegada que se encuentra en la práctica de la virtud y en las modestas pretensiones del que permanece ajeno a la ambición."

El arte escénico en España I, p. 53.

7   Conflicting visions: neo-Romanticism, ridicule, and realism

By 1870, notwithstanding the chaos which dominated the political panorama, Spain's theatres seemed to be healthy and thriving. According to *El Entreacto* of 4 March 1871, "Hay en España 335 teatros con 169.376 localidades, donde se celebra por término medio de cada año 8.000 funciones dramáticas, 1.000 de ópera y 3.000 de zarzuela" ("Spain has 335 theatres with 169,376 seats, where on average some 8,000 dramatic works, 1,000 operas, and 3,000 zarzuelas are put on each year"). Fifteen of these theatres were in Barcelona, eleven in Madrid (although Madrid had more total seats than Barcelona), four each in Cádiz and Zaragoza, three each in the Balearic Islands, Córdoba, Sevilla, and Valladolid, two each in Alicante, La Coruña, Granada, Lérida, Málaga, Salamanca, and Valencia, and one in every other provincial capital except Castellón, Logroño, and Toledo. There existed some 45 dramatic societies which promoted theatre in the provincial capitals. These statistics, if accurate, are extraordinary, for they reveal a lively interest in theatre and a significant rise in the number of playhouses from just a decade previously – 91 in capital cities (up from 74) and 244 in small towns (up from 219). Printed texts were also readily available and thereby increased public knowledge of and attention to the theatre. Several publishers dominated the industry of printing inexpensive editions of recent plays. The publishing houses of José Rodríguez, Vicente Lalama, J. M. Ducazcal, and R. Velasco (there were others) published thousands upon thousands of texts which the public apparently scooped up with relish. Unquestionably, the availability of the texts, which became wide-spread shortly after mid-century, increased the general popularity of theatre.[1] The periodical press played an ever-increasing role in informing and educating the public as theatre criticism became a minor, more respected genre in the hands of

---

[1] Literary publishing was active before mid-century, of course. *El Heraldo* of 1847 (10 July) claimed that in one year the Imprenta de Mellado had published 155,000 volumes; *La Epoca* wrote in 1852 (29 March) that there were 400 book publishers and sellers in Madrid alone. See Zavala, "La literatura: romanticismo y costumbrismo," p. 115. Of particular interest is Jean-François Botrel, *La diffusion du livre en Espagne (1868–1914)* (Madrid: Casa de Velázquez, 1988).

Clarín, Manuel de la Revilla (1846–1881), José Yxart (1852–1895), Galdós, Julio Nombela, and others.

Such riches did not stop critics from issuing their constant laments about the nature of the works written or their dire predictions about the institution's imminent demise, of course. When one grapples with the issue of "quality" theatre, as Clarín did in his newspaper criticisms in the 1880s and 1890s, the panorama is somewhat less encouraging. The reigning generic "anarchy" (García Lorenzo's word) caused much wringing of hands among more sophisticated literary types, but it did not stop authors from writing copious amounts nor the public from refusing to give up their nightly theatre habit. If it is true that Restoration drama was dominated by a few great names (Echegaray, Galdós, Dicenta, Sellés, Gaspar), it is likewise true, as we have come to expect, that dozens of other playwrights penned thousands of titles, all of which competed in the most energetic ways for space and the public's attention.

The conservative ideology which dominated politics also appeared to dominate the theatre, although a healthy tension was building between the conservatives and the progressive thinkers known as "regeneracionistas" or "krausistas." The conservatives always saw theatre as prescriptive rather than descriptive, and hence, responsible for directing public morality, so, even though the intensity of the thesis dramas diminished somewhat during the last third of the century, such dramas never really disappeared. New voices and new patterns emerged with the (even attenuated) arrival of realism and naturalism to Madrid's theatres, but the dominant paradigm was still the "comedia de costumbres." The difference lay, of course, in the subtly shifting customs being depicted on stage. For Jesús Rubio Jiménez, the two authors most deserving of credit for "modernizing" the stage in the last third of the century are Enrique Gaspar (1842–1902) and Benito Pérez Galdós (1843–1921), but before turning to these figures we need to take a look at several other names and trends operating at that time.

The playwright as magician: Echegaray

Serious critics since the first third of the century had attempted to steer the public away from melodramatic plays which they considered to be forced, unnecessarily complicated, falsely emotional, and simplistic. Such efforts were doomed to failure because of the powerful emotional sweep of melodrama and because of the satisfying insistence on Manichean conflict and tension followed by a frequently shocking ending. Stimulated in part by Romantic drama and in part by the astonishing popularity of Hugo and Eugene Sue, a genre which Rubio Jiménez aptly labels "melodrama social" became a staple in the theatre following the two-part translation of Sue's *Les mystères de Paris* (The Mysteries of Paris) in 1844 and 1847.[2] Other "mysteries" appeared with frequency, including Juan Rico y Amat's *Misterios de Palacio* (Mysteries of the Palace, 1852), the younger Larra's *Los misterios del Parnaso* (The Mysteries of Parnassus, 1868), and Jesús López Gómez's *Los misterios de Madrid* (The Mysteries of Madrid, 1878).[3]

One of the most powerful presences in late nineteenth-century theatre was the re-configured Romanticism of José Echegaray (1832–1916). Until recently, Echegaray received the scorn of critics, less for the literary value of his work, which is considerable, than for the unpardonable sin of winning the Nobel Prize in 1904 which, in the minds of many, should have gone to Galdós. In spite of being disparaged by the likes of Azorín and Valle Inclán (who called Echegaray "el viejo idiota"[4] ["the old idiot"]), his concept of theatre, one which freely mixed the old tropes of Romanticism with the new morality of the *alta comedia* and of theatrical realism, occupied a central place in Madrid's theatrical life for over two decades, beginning with the huge success of *El libro talonario* (The Cheque Book, starring Antonio Vico and Matilde Díaz) and *La esposa del vengador* (The Avenger's Wife, again with Vico) in 1874. Author of sixty-six plays, Echegaray drew upon his country's literary history in his attempt to write for his public, the Spanish upper middle class by now fully in control of the social, economic, and political reins of power. He aimed to please not his critics, but those bourgeois men and women who became his staunch defenders. "Lo difícil es escribir dramas que gusten en época de transición," he said, "cuando todo anda revuelto, cuando una sociedad entera vacila y no sabe lo que quiere ni dónde va"[5] ("The difficult thing is to write plays which please the public during times of transition, when everything is all topsy-turvy, when an entire society is wavering and does not know what it wants nor where it is going"). Such vacilation indeed characterized the complexity of the Restoration period, which two critics have summed up accurately in this manner:

La salida de los traumatismos sociopolíticos del Sexenio Liberal conforma un tipo de sociedad cuyo conocimiento es imprescindible para entender su compleja

---

[2] See Menarini et al., *El teatro romántico español (1830–1850)*.
[3] Rubio Jiménez also lists *Misterios de honra y venganza* (1843), by Gregorio Romero Larrañaga, *Misterios de bastidores* (1849), by Francisco Montemar, *Misterios de la calle de Toledo* (1866), by R. Morales de Castro, and the anonymous *Misterios de San Petersburgo* (1864), *Misterios del corazón* (1864), *Misterios de la calle del gato* (1866), *Misterios del Rastro* (1874), *Misterios de la familia* (1877), *Misterios de la noche* (1893), and *Misterios de Barcelona*. "El teatro en el siglo XIX," p. 673.
[4] Javier Fornieles Alcaraz, *Trayectoria de un intelectual de la Restauración: José Echegaray* (Almería: Confederación Española de Cajas de Ahorro, 1989): 9.
[5] Antón del Olmet and García Carrafa, *Echegaray*, p. 179.

calidad artístico-literaria. El primer fenómeno significativo es el hecho de que hayan sido necesarios dos golpes militares para estabilizar definitivamente una situación que tiene dos componentes fundamentales, los intereses socio-económicos de la burguesía isabelina que protagonizó la Restauración y el prestigio ideológico tradicionalista de la oligarquía aristocrática que renace efímeramente vencedora y agresiva después de aquella derrota de 1868.[6]

(The end of the socio-political traumas of the six-year period brings into being a type of society which we must comprehend if we are to understand its complex artistico-literary quality. The first important phenomenon is the fact that two military coups have been necessary to stabilize completely a situation that has two fundamental components, the socio-economic interests of the Isabeline bourgeoisie that initiated the Restoration and the traditionalist ideological prestige of the aristocratic oligarchy which was briefly reborn, triumphant and aggressive, following the defeat of 1868.)

Echegaray's dramatic power is unquestionable, and if at times it threatens to overwhelm the reader or viewer with high-pitched emotionalism, it nonetheless manages to reach deep into the emotional center of the audience in order to extract a nugget of truth or reveal a deeply hidden human secret. The author was a man of his times, the cultured combination of business and scientific acumen (he was an engineer by profession, similar to Galdós's Pepe Rey), professorial gifts, political experience, and literary talent whose articles on scientific matters in newspapers such as *Los Conocimientos Útiles* (Useful Knowledge) and *El Economista* had an impact on his society well beyond the proscenium arch. Rather than being a retrograde throwback to an older time, Echegaray, by virtue of his close association with workers' rights, his defense of individual freedom, his openness to new currents (he was an active supporter of Ibsen and Dicenta), and his progressive social ideas, should be seen as a harbinger of the new age, as he was by many of his contemporary followers. In 1905, newspapers commented on his "anticatholicism" and his "modern, revolutionary" theatre.[7]

As both an appointed and an elected politician Echegaray was fully immersed in the social realities of his time, something which his theatre, which strikes many modern readers as escapist and superficial (Ruiz Ramón writes his work off as "drama-ripio"[8] ["verbiage drama"]),

---

[6] Carmen Menéndez Onrubia and J. Avila Arrellano, *El neorromanticismo español y su época. Epistolario de José Echegaray a María Guerrero* (Madrid: CSIC, 1987): 30.

[7] Fornieles, *Trayectoria*, p. 10.

[8] "Al tratar de definir el teatro de Echegaray, mejor que las denominaciones de drama neorromántico o de melodrama social que utilizan los críticos, me parece la de drama-ripio, pues esta denominación capta, sin más, su esencia. Su teatro, no importa cuál sea su asunto, es, radicalmente, ripio. En cualquiera de sus niveles: vocabulario, sentimiento, pensamiento, acción." Ruiz Ramón, *Historia*, p. 350. For a different view, see José Manuel Cabrales Arteaga, "El teatro neorromántico de Echegaray," *Revista de Literatura* 101 (1989): pp. 77–94.

addresses deeply. How is it that a collection of works which seemingly reached back into one of the most troubled and conflictive moments of Spanish history and literature held the interest of a society which viewed itself as modern, developing, and pan-European? The recent rejection of the tired conservatism of Isabel II and her acolytes opened Spain to a period of intense self-scrutiny and instability. The combination of businessmen, nouveau aristocrats and industrialists who seized power never quite figured out what to do with the power they had achieved, nor what to do with the growing discontent among the lower classes, primarily the proletariat (whose voice, as we shall see, was beginning to be heard on the boards). For six years neither the monarchy, nor the Republic, nor the more radical alternatives (a Carlist dictatorship) seemed to offer stability to a country boiling over with new-found energy and old frustrations. With the restoration of the Bourbon monarchy in 1875, the upper and middle classes breathed a collective sigh of relief, not realizing right away that the problems which had fostered the insecurities of the previous six or seven years had not gone away. Indeed, the new "solutions" would be presented from the same traditionalist view as that which had dominated Spain for so many years. Gradually, the "failure" of Spanish history began to be analyzed by numerous intellectuals, from Galdós, Castelar, and Cánovas del Castillo to, later, the "krausistas" and the young socialists who would become the Generation of 1898. Echegaray too joined in the analysis and critique.

Muchos como Castelar y Echegaray, sin dejar de ser liberales demócratas en sus principios y de propiciar el republicanismo como forma de gobierno, consideran que la regeneración moral sólo puede lograrse a través del idealismo tradicionalista. Otros como Galdós, después de un análisis de los hechos – *Episodios Nacionales, Doña Perfecta, Gloria*, y *La familia de León Roch* – , llegan a una especie de empate culpable del fanatismo tradicionalista y la exaltación liberal, destrozándose ambos mutuamente y sin posibilidad de solución.[9]

(Many people such as Castelar and Echegaray, without ceasing to be liberal democrats in their principles and supporting republicanism as a form of government, think that moral regeneration can only be achieved through a kind of traditionalist idealism. Others such as Galdós, after an analysis of the facts – *Episodios Nacionales, Doña Perfecta, Gloria*, and *La familia de León Roch* – arrive at a kind of guilty stand-off between traditionalist fanatism and liberal excess, destroying themselves mutually and with no possibility of finding a solution.)

He signed, along with Galdós, Nicolás Salmerón, and other progressives, the manifesto of the Partido Republicano y Progresista in 1880.

　　Echegaray became a dramatist almost by accident. His first professions – engineer, mathematician, founder of the Banco de España, politician –

9 Menéndez Onrubia and Avila Arrellano, *El neorromanticismo*, p. 27.

hardly suggested the arena of his greatest successes, the theatre. Still, by the time he decided to write and produce his first plays he had become curious about the process of theatre and how it could both reflect and guide public opinion. His dramas evolve from the *alta comedia* rather than breaking with it in any radical ways. He treats themes of egotism, financial corruption, blind ambition, and family relationships, as did the playwrights of the *alta comedia,* but he does so always keeping in mind the language of Romanticism and the social ambience of realism. This seemingly odd mix gives his dramas real power, since the intensified language and emotion, juxtaposed with a scenic space with which the audience could readily identify, created a dual impact: on the one hand the spectator felt comfortable with his creations while on the other he or she reacted with shock or disgust at the emotional or physical carnage seen on stage. It is as though don Alvaro or the troubadour had exchanged their rather quaint finery for business suits and moved in next door. In the words of one of his contemporaries, Echegaray "set the Spanish stage on fire" with his powerful creations.[10] People loved and hated his plays, but no one remained indifferent to them.

The Nobel Committee specifically praised the fact that Echegaray drew from "las grandes tradiciones del teatro español" ("the great traditions of Spanish theatre") in his "genial y copiosa" ("brilliant and abundant") work.[11] Such attention to the past is clearly evident in *En el puño de la espada* (At The Hilt of the Sword), first performed in Madrid at the Apolo Theater on 12 October 1875. In this play the author revives the type of historical tragedy first perfected by Calderón and later popularized during the early Romantic period (and which, to be sure, never disappeared from the boards, as García Gutiérrez's two late Romantic plays, *Venganza catalana* in 1864 and *Juan Lorenzo* in 1865 demonstrate). It is his first play to reveal completely his attraction to that "romanticismo de volcán o de ciclón"[12] ("volcanic or cyclonic Romanticism") that so

---

[10] Luis Alonso, *Autores dramáticos contemporáneos* II (Madrid: n.p., 1881): 535.

[11] Cited by Amando Lázaro Ros in his edition of Echegaray's *Teatro escogido* (Madrid: Aguilar, 1964): 11. Lázaro quotes additional praise from the Nobel Committee's citation: Como sus antecesores, sabe presentar colisiones en extremo emocionantes y de palpitante interés entre temperamentos e ideales diferentes, y, como ellos, se complace en estudiar los más complicados casos de conciencia. Domina magistralmente el arte de producir en el público el terror y la piedad, notorios elementos fundamentales de la tragedia. Igual que en los maestros de la antigua dramática española, verifícase en él una notable unión de la más viva imaginación con el más depurado sentimiento artístico. Con este motivo, se puede decir que él – como lo afirmó un crítico ciertamente poco simpático hacia él – *que es de pura casta española.* Sin embargo, su concepción del mundo es vasta ... tiene rasgos de una humanidad universal.

[12] *Ibid.* p. 31. See also Librada Hernández, "Clarín, Galdós y Pardo Bazán frente al teatro de Echegaray," *Anales de Literatura Española de la Universidad de Alicante* 8 (1992): 95–108.

irritated his critics. What is notable about the play is the author's deep attachment to the accoutrements of Romantic drama, that is, to the complex relationships, the intensity of emotions, the play of light and shadow, the stage props (daggers, masks), and the lugubrious settings which characterized some of the most memorable plays of the nineteenth century. The problem with *En el puño de la espada* is that Echegaray forgot that his audience was also well versed in these tricks, so that the key psychological crisis, as explained in Act I, scene 1 by Violante (note the name) – she had been attacked and wounded twenty years before by a masked stranger – holds little mystery for the viewers. The audience can hardly be immune to the obvious symbolism of the first scene, which finds Nuño cleaning an old blood-stained dagger as he explains the details of a long-ago tragedy to Brígida. The title signals the presence of the dagger, which makes an appearance at significant moments in the text. As in *El trovador*, the details of that tragedy will come back to haunt the family. Still, it is fun to see how Echegaray works it out, how he weaves the "negro destino" ("black destiny") (I, 9), "fatal estrella" ("fatal star") (I, 9), and "mal presagio" ("evil omen") (III, 1), the theme of vengeance and honor, and the convoluted tensions into the play's structure. One brilliant *coup de théâtre* left the audience aghast: Fernando, presumed son of don Rodrigo, the marqués de Moncada, and doña Violante, is in truth the son of Juan de Albornoz, the powerful conde de Orgaz, who had dishonored Violante years earlier. In the count's castle hangs a portrait of the count as a twenty-year-old youth (the same age as Fernando today), placed near a large open window. In Act III, scene 8, Fernando enters through the window, framed by it in juxtaposition to the portrait; the similarity between Fernando and the portrait of Orgaz is so striking that there remains no doubt in the audience's mind that Fernando is his natural son. The resulting conflict between the supposed antagonists, Fernando and the count, becomes then a struggle between father and son, which Echegaray works out with tropes from *Don Alvaro*:

> JUAN (A FERNANDO).   ¿Quién te trajo?
> FERNANDO.   ¡Belcebú,
>   que él también te trajo a ti!
> JUAN.   ¿Y cómo llegaste aquí?
> FERNANDO.   ¡Por asalto, como tú!   (III, 13)
>
> (JUAN [TO FERNANDO]. Who brought you here?
> FERNANDO.   Beelzebub, who also brought you!
> JUAN.   And how did you get here?
> FERNANDO.   By storm, same as you!)

At another crucial juncture in the same scene, Violante shouts, "¡Lo quiere el cielo divino! ... / ¡Cúmplase su voluntad!" ("What the divine Heaven wants! ... Let its will be done!").

Echegaray pushes the Romantic paradigm further two years later in *O locura o santidad* (Insanity or Saintliness, 1877), a play dedicated to Antonio Vico, the great actor who had starred in many of the author's earlier productions (*El libro talonario, La esposa del vengador, La última noche* [The Last Evening], *En el puño de la espada*, and *Cómo empieza y cómo acaba* [How It Begins and How It Ends]). In this play he seems to be struggling with Romantic language in order to uncover some basic truths about human nature. Vicente García Valero tells of the powerful impact made on Echegaray by Alexander Dumas's *Ricardo Darlington*, which he saw in Madrid in 1853: many of his "asuntos terroríficos" ("terrifying effects") stemmed as much from this French source as from the Spanish Romantic theatre.[13] The question Echegaray poses is, "Can honesty ever cross the borders of rationality and become irrational?" Echegaray posits this question in the context of literature, specifically *Don Quijote*, whose eponymous hero became crazy after reading too many chivalresque novels. In *O locura o santidad* Lorenzo reads not only Cervantes's great novel (the play opens on Lorenzo quoting from the book) but too many scientific tracts, and when his attachment to scientific rationalism interferes with the conduct of his daily behavior, his family and friends declare him insane and call the local psychiatric ward. As his wife Angela tells a friend, "¿Lo ve usted? Como siempre: leyendo y pensando" ("You see? As always: reading and thinking") (I, 2) and she tells Lorenzo that "te embrutece la ciencia" ("science is making you irrational") (I, 3). His supposed insanity consists of his stubborn desire to confess the truth of his existence, a truth recently learned from his long-lost wet nurse Juana who, it is revealed, is really his mother. The chain of events let loose by this discovery threatens to disinherit his wife and daughter, and to dishonor his family's good name. Lorenzo lives on the margin of sanity, and in a delicious piece of stage ambiguity, Echegaray structures the ending of the second act in such a way as to leave doubt as to whether Lorenzo's impassioned and anguished embrace of his weak, infirm mother has contributed to her death. Does she die in his arms or has he crushed her to death? The dramatic tension returns at the play's conclusion when we witness a similar embrace of his daughter Inés.

The Romantic connection is made through Lorenzo and Angela's daughter Inés, a young woman whose character had been seen on the Spanish stage for decades. The audience understood the type of heroine

---

[13] Vicente García Valero, *Crónicas retrospectivas del teatro por un cómico viejo* (Madrid: Librería Gutenberg de José Ruiz, 1910): 287.

she would be, even more so when described by Tomás, the family doctor/ friend in these terms:

¿Cual es su enfermedad? Una de las que causan más estragos entre los vivientes. ¿Qué nombre tiene? Amor le llaman los poetas; nosotros, los médicos, le damos otro nombre. . . . Ello es que, hablando seriamente, y dadas las condiciones de esa niña, su temperamento nervioso, su sensibilidad extrema y ese su romántico amor, la dolencia es grave . . . Creo que Inés ha heredado la imaginación exaltada y fantástica de su padre, que hoy la fiebre del amor circula por todas sus venas en olas de fuego. Y si no la casan ustedes, y muy pronto, con Eduardo; si ella llega a comprender que sus esperanzas no han de realizarse, los delirios de su fantasía y las violencias de su pasión, aunque no sé en qué forma, sé por desdicha que han de herirla de muerte. (I, 2)

(What is ailing her? One of those illnesses that wreak havoc among the living. What's it called? Poets call it love; we doctors give it another name . . . All kidding aside, given that girl's state, her nervous temperament, her extreme sensitivity and her romantic love, the illness is serious . . . I think that Inés has inherited the exalted and fantastic imagination of her father, that today the fever of love is running through her veins in waves of fire. And if you do not marry her, and very quickly, to Eduardo, if she comes to realize that her hopes will not be met, I know that unfortunately the delirium of her fantasy and the violence of her passion will kill her, although I am not sure exactly how.)

Indeed, Echegaray does not seem yet able to mock such characteristics (he will do so years later in *Mancha que limpia* [1895], for example) and we are presented with a flighty, infantile, high-strung young woman whose character is in part inherited from her father and in part determined by her environment.

The central conflict of the play, however, is not so much the Romantic love story as it is the issue of social standing and honor, so common in Restoration dramas. Lorenzo is wealthy and respected (as was Calderón's Pedro Crespo) but social barriers might prohibit the marriage of his daughter to the noble son of the Duquesa de Almonte. Lorenzo refuses to beg the Duquesa to "allow" her son to marry his daughter; on the contrary, he demands that she come to him:

¡Yo suplicar! ¡Yo rogar! ¡Humillarme yo! No soy yo ciertamente quien ha de ir a pedirle su hijo; ella es la que debe venir a mi casa a pedirme la mano de Inés. Las conveniencias sociales, el respeto a la mujer, mi propio decoro, así lo exigen. (I, 2)

(Me, beg! Me, plead! Humiliate myself! It is clearly not I who should go to ask for her son's hand; she is the one who should come to my house to ask for the hand of Inés. Social convention, respect for women, and my own integrity demand it.)

It is this tension that Echegaray works out in the powerful *O locura o santidad*, and the tension becomes a microcosm of Echegaray's view of Spanish society. Lorenzo insists that he does not want to be "honrado a medias" ("half-way honorable") (II, 4). The action takes place in the upper-middle-class drawing room of Lorenzo and moves from a confused reality (a dull winter morning in Act I) through depths of frustration (night in Act II) to a possible solution (daybreak in Act III). The play does not offer a happy ending (Echegaray moves away from the fixed happiness of the *altas comedias*); instead, it offers the possibility of hope: even though Lorenzo is hauled away to a mental hospital at the end, his daughter Inés, with her inheritance intact and her marriage assured, promises, "¡Yo iré a salvarte!" ("I will come to save you!") (III, 14).

Echegaray's attachment to Romantic language and theme ushered in a rediscovery of earlier Romantic plays (*Don Alvaro* and *El trovador* were both seen at the Teatro Español in early 1880). In his plays Echegaray remained true to his own *ars poetica*, which he stated in a sonnet reminiscent of Lope's "Arte nuevo de hacer comedias" ("New Art of Writing Comedies"). In it, he compared his dramatic *modus operandi* to the lighting of sticks of dynamite:

> Escojo una pasión, tomo una idea,
> un problema, un carácter, y lo infundo,
> cual densa dinamita, en lo profundo
> de un personaje que mi mente crea.
> La trama al personaje le rodea
> de unos cuantos muñecos, que en el mundo
> o se revuelcan por el cieno inmundo,
> o resplandecen a la luz febea.
> La mecha enciendo. El fuego se propaga,
> el cartucho revienta sin remedio
> y el astro principal es quien lo paga.
> Aunque a veces también en este asedio
> que al Arte pongo y que el instinto halaga ...,
> ¡me coge la explosión de medio a medio!

(I pick a passion, take an idea, a problem, a characteristic, and I bury it, just like dynamite, in the depths of a character that my mind creates. The plot surrounds that character with some puppets who are either trampled into the filthy mud or who shine in the sun's bright light. I light the fuse. The fire spreads, the shell explodes without fail and the main star is the one who pays for it. Although sometimes I throw some Art into this siege and am rather proud of what my instinct has done ... the explosion catches even me off guard!)

Such explosive dramaturgy – theatre of high emotion and high conflict (dialogue, in the clever words of Ruiz Ramón, "superadmirativo y superpuntisuspensivo y superentrecortado"[14] ["super-marvellous and super-suspensepointy and super-intermittent"]) – captured in some ways the high tension of the times. This was a period of debate and polemic,

[14] Ruiz Ramón, *Historia*, p. 356.

conflictive politics and social tensions, and uncertainty and doubt. Echegaray's charged language enabled him (and perhaps his audience) to grapple with seemingly irreconcilable social and political differences. The Manicheanism of his plays was a way of processing and interpreting the Manicheanism of Spain in the last decades of the nineteenth century. Echegaray managed to cast a spell over his audiences, to bewitch them with the power of his words. As Alonso Cortés has perceptively noted:

¿Qué era este cúmulo de infortunios, de delitos, de casualidades, de portentosos sucesos? ¿Era el romanticismo redivivo? Así lo entendieron muchos entonces y así ha seguido interpretándose después. Admitamos que fuera el romanticismo; pero corregido y aumentado. Más aún: alterado en forma tal, que en nada se parecía al del duque de Rivas, al de García Gutiérrez, al de Hartzenbusch. Aquél respetaba la lógica de la pasión y despertaba emociones más o menos fuertes; el de Echegaray, saltando por todas las verosimilitudes, producía una exitación nerviosa. Con la inextricable urdimbre de acontecimientos estupendos, de lances terroríficos, de transiciones inesperadas, Echegaray lograba fascinar, más bien marear, a sus públicos y se apoderaba de su voluntad.[15]

(What was this accumulation of disgraces, crimes, chance occurrences, prodigious events? Was it Romanticism revived? That's the way a lot of people at the time understood it and have continued to understand it ever since. We must admit that it was Romanticism, but a corrected and augmented kind. What's more, it was so changed that it did not resemble at all the Romanticism of the Duke of Rivas, of García Gutiérrez, of Hartzenbusch. That Romanticism followed the logic of passion and awoke more or less strong emotions; Echegaray's Romanticism, doing away with all vestiges of verisimilitude, produced a nervous excitation in the viewer. With the inextricable warp of wondrous incidents, terrifying deeds, unexpected transitions, Echegaray managed to hypnotize his audiences, or rather make them dizzy, and thereby take over their will.)

This was the dramatist as magician, but they were magic tricks angrily rejected by a new generation of artists and intellectuals. In 1903 Azorín posed the question, "¿En qué país fantástico, quimérico, vive toda esta gente?"[16] ("In what fantastic, unreal country do all these people live?").

Echegaray's recognized masterpiece is *El gran galeoto*. This 1881 play followed the basic outline of plays such as Tamayo's *Un drama nuevo* which dealt with suspicions of amorous misconduct and jealousy fed by a society obsessed with gossip and the "¿qué dirán?" ("What will people say?"). Galeoto, the individual who served as intermediary between Lancelot and his lover in European legend, came to signify in Spain a person who sows doubt and suspicion through gossip and innuendo; for

---

[15] Narciso Alonso Cortés, "El teatro español en el siglo XIX," in *Historia general de las literaturas hispánicas* IV, ed. Guillermo Díaz-Plaja, 2nd. part (Barcelona: Editorial Vergara, 1953, 1968), 309.
[16] José Martínez Ruiz (Azorín), *Obras completas* VII (Madrid: Aguilar, 1947): 1082.

Echegaray, "el gran galeoto" was the whole of Spanish society. Ernesto, while discussing his proposed drama with his friend Julián, claims:

Figúrese usted que el principal personaje, el que crea el drama, el que lo desarrolla, el que lo anima, el que provoca la catástrofe, el que la devora y la goza, no puede salir a escena ... ese personaje es ... *todo el mundo* ... ("Diálogo," Scene 2)

(Imagine that the main character, the one who creates the drama, the one who develops it, the one who infuses it with life, the one who provokes the tragic ending, the one who relishes it and enjoys it, cannot ever be onstage ... that character is ... *everyone* ...)

He sets the play, not surprisingly, in "Epoca moderna; año 18 ... ; la escena, en Madrid" ("Modern times; the year 18 ... ; the place, Madrid") and in a thoroughly middle-class environment. This reminds us, uncannily, of Galdós's discovery of the middle class as apt material for novels. Gastón Fernández has written: "Aware of the public's receptivity to highly emotional plays, he set as his goal a theatre based on 'weeping, grief, and death.' Although the tone of his dramas can be considered anachronistic, he achieved a degree of modernity and originality in his works through the introduction of contemporary settings and social problems and by gradually discarding legendary settings and the use of verse."[17] This echoes Luis Calvo's complaint that Echegaray "no conmueve las almas, sino los nervios"[18] ("does not stir people's souls, but rather their nerves").

Echegaray's breakthrough here was not in the arena of theme or language, but in the play's structure. It is true that the play is replete with the hyper-emotionalism of Romanticism and neo-Romanticism – the first scene amply testifies to the charged linguistic register that Echegaray had always exploited so well – but he was able finally to move beyond the traditional structures he had created in his early plays to a pre-Pirandellan author-within-the-text mode. The setting up of a frame into which the real author of the play injects a fictional author who then presents the play he has "written" is of course reminiscent of Rivas's understudied *El desengaño en un sueño*, but in *El gran galeoto* he creates a prologue in prose dialogue (the rest of the play is in verse) which serves to present both the case study of the play and his (Echegaray's) *ars poetica dramatica*. The work we see, then, is supposedly the play written by Ernesto. The "Diálogo" is an important meditation on the act of writing and it provides the viewer/reader with Echegaray's thoughts on the creative

[17] Gastón Fernández, "José Echegaray y Eizaguirre," in *Critical Survey of Drama* II, ed. Frank N. Magill (Englewood Cliffs, NJ: Salem Press, 1986): 528.
[18] Calvo Revilla, *Actores célebres*, p. 37. See also Caldera, "Echegaray, tra la parola e il silenzio," in *Symbolae Pisanae. Studi in onore di Guido Mancini* I, eds. Blanca Perñán and Francesco Guazzelli (Pisa: Giardini, 1989): 85–98.

process, thoughts he will then work out in the body of the play itself. As the "Diálogo" opens, Ernesto is blocked, unable to fill "esta hoja en blanco" ("this blank page"). It is the arrival of his friend Julián from a performance at the Teatro Real which sparks the interchange of ideas between the two men. Ernesto's main frustration is the realization that between the idea and the written work lies an abyss which is difficult, if not impossible, to fill.

Consiste en que al imaginarlo, yo creí que la idea del drama era fecunda, y al darle forma, y al vestirla con el ropaje propio de la escena, resulta una cosa extraña, difícil, antidramática, imposible.[19] ("Diálogo," 2)

(The problem is that when I thought it up, I believed that the idea for the play was ripe with possibilities, but when I gave it form, when I dressed it up with the clothing appropriate to the stage, it turned out to be something strange, difficult, undramatic, impossible.)

In this introduction Echegaray also answers his critics who accused him of throwing anything into his dramas in order to provoke a reaction, without thinking of the dramatic consequences of those words and deeds. Ernesto protests,

cuando yo sólo pretendo demostrar que ni aun las acciones más insignificantes son insignificantes ni perdidas para el bien o para el mal, porque sumadas por misteriosas influencias de la vida moderna pueden llegar a producir inmensos efectos ... todo ha de ser sencillo, corriente, casi vulgar .... El drama va por dentro de los personajes: avanza lentamente ... ("Diálogo," 2)

(when I only try to demonstrate that not even the most seemingly insignificant actions are really insignificant nor useless for better or for worse, because brought together by the mysterious influences of modern life they can produce huge effects ... everything must be simple, commonplace, almost vulgar ... The drama develops inside the characters: it advances slowly ...)

Julián, echoing Echegaray's critics, scoffs at his new concept of drama:

Un drama en que el principal personaje no sale; en que casi no hay amores; en que no sucede nada que no suceda todos los días; que empieza al caer el telón en el último acto, y que no tiene título, yo no sé cómo puede escribirse, ni cómo puede representarse, ni cómo ha de haber quien lo oiga, ni cómo es drama. ("Diálogo," 2).

(A play in which the main character does not come out on stage, in which there are practically no love affairs, in which nothing happens that doesn't happen every day, that begins when the curtain comes down in the final act, and that has no title; I don't know how someone could write something like this, nor how it could

---

[19] It is curious that Ernesto uses the same clothing metaphors used years later by Juan Ramón Jiménez in a similar attempt to explain the evolution of his writing in his poem, "Vino, primero, pura".

be staged, nor how anyone would go to hear it, nor how it could even be called a drama.)

The debate inspires Ernesto, and, just as Lope had done in his sonnet on the writing of a sonnet, Ernesto declares, "¡El drama empieza! Primera hoja: ya no está en blanco" ("The play begins! First page: it's no longer blank") and we then see the play he is writing, which he decides to call *El gran galeoto.*

The play itself is a turn on Cervantes's "El curioso impertinente," in which the obsessive desire to test a woman's innocence leads inexorably to the suspicion of her guilt. Ernesto's obsessions, similar to Lorenzo's in *O locura o santidad* (which anticipate Ibsen's 1866 play *Brand*, not translated into Spanish until 1903[20]), mark a clear line between good and evil, right and wrong. In the play he is a guest in the house of don Julián and his younger wife Teodora, an innocent living arrangement which town gossip has turned into something questionable; in fact, the gossipers suggest that the play Ernesto is writing is really about his relationship with Teodora. Since the play we are seeing is indeed the play Ernesto has told his friend about in the "Diálogo"-prologue, the ironic truth is that they are right – it *is* about Ernesto and Teodora, but not in the way the people suspect. Through a series of lies, confusions, and coincidences, don Julián becomes convinced of the validity of the gossip and what he had feared most – that Ernesto and Teodora were lovers – inexorably becomes true by the play's end. The dénouement is tragic, powerful, and unforgettable since the play's only villain – malicious, unfocused gossip – has no tangible form so the punishment, which must of course be visited on "real" characters, is that much more frustrating and unfair, although perfectly logical within the play itself.[21]

After additional successes with *El hijo de don Juan* (1892, inspired by Ibsen's *Ghosts*) and *Mariana* (a wonderful psychological profile of a woman trapped in an honor conflict – "the play is a masterly one," wrote

---

[20] Gregersen, *Ibsen and Spain*, p. 183. Direct knowledge of Ibsen in Spain was limited, however. As Rubio Jiménez points out:

Aunque abundan las referencias críticas [a Ibsen] no había representaciones ya que faltaba en Madrid una tradición cultural que las propiciase y por otro lado, no existía una tradición cultural obrera notable. El conocimiento de Ibsen fue sobre todo libresco. Pese al ingente número de teatros en funcionamiento, tantos que a más de un crítico preocupaba tal diversidad y lo fácilmente que quedaban vacíos, el sistema de producción era siempre el mismo, interesando más llenar el teatro y obtener buenas recaudaciones que cualquier otro fin. *Ideología*, p. 67.

[21] Not everyone agrees. Angel López García asserts, "Claro que un lector con un mínimo de sensibilidad estética no puede menos que soliviantarse ante la acumulación de tópicos, sensiblerías y efectismos lacrimógenos que esmaltan el texto dramático de Echegaray." "Echegaray y la cultura de masas," *Homenatge a José Belloch Zimmerman*, eds. Emili Casanova and Joaquín Espinosa (Università de Valencia, 1988): 255.

George Bernard Shaw[22] – also from 1892), Echegaray produced *Mancha que limpia* in 1895. This prose work also echoes Ibsen. Justo, played by Ricardo Calvo, tells Matilde, played by Echegaray's prime actress, María Guerrero, that children inherit not only the facial features of their parents, but also their "instintos y pasiones" ("instincts and passions") (I, 6). Less interesting than *El hijo de don Juan* or *Mariana* because of its excessive preachiness (little moral lessons are frequently delivered by the aptly named don Justo), *Mancha que limpia* does present the interesting novelty of a woman (Matilde) who plunges a knife into the neck of her rival, Enriqueta, on stage.

José Echegaray, the most successful playwright in the second half of the nineteenth century in Spain, moved theatrical discourse forward. Notwithstanding the generations of scorn heaped upon him (again, the attitude of Ruiz Ramón is symptomatic of much of the criticism he has received: "el teatro de Echegaray es, por excelencia, teatro fantasmagórico, puro *flatus voci*, en el que cada personaje, sin distinción de sexo, es, en sustancia y en sus accidentes, una pasión inútil, hueca de toda verdad"[23] ["Echegaray's theatre is, above all, a phantasmagorical theatre, pure *flatus voci*, in which each character, of whatever sex, is, in his essence and in his actions, a frivolous passion, empty of any truth"]), his genius was to capture the new social spirit (the same one captured in other parts of Europe by Ibsen, Strindberg, and, later, Pirandello[24]) with a language which his audiences recognized. He aspired to create "el sublime horror trágico" ("sublime tragic horror") as he confessed in the dedicatory he wrote to the actor Rafael Calvo in *En el seno de la muerte* (In Death's Bosom). Some of his contemporaries, among them Manuel de la Revilla – while still claiming him to be "una de las figuras más originales y notables que registra nuestra historia literaria en el presente siglo"[25] ("one of the most original and noteworthy figures in the literary history of our century") – nevertheless opposed such aspirations as false and disturbing:

---

[22] George Bernard Shaw, *Dramatic Opinions and Essays* II (New York: Brentano's, 1916): 190. Wadda C. Ríos-Font provides an interesting interpretation of female roles in *Mariana* in "The Impersonation on the Feminine," *Hispanófila* 107 (September 1992): 21–30.

[23] Ruiz Ramón, *Historia*, pp. 350–351.

[24] " . . . perhaps now a few clearings may be found which will reveal him as a playwright who shows kinship not only with his literary ancestors, but one who is also a link from the past to the twentieth century, so ably represented by Luigi Pirandello." Wilma Newberry, "Echegaray and Pirandello," *PMLA* 81 (1966): 129. It must be noted, however, that Ibsen's revolutionary message found a more hospitable reception in the theatres of Cataluña than in more conservative Madrid. The influence of Ibsen's *A Doll's House* on the female characters of Gaspar and Dicenta has been traced by Maryellen Bieder, "The Modern Woman on the Spanish Stage: The Contributions of Gaspar and Dicenta," *Estreno* 7 (1981): 25–28.

[25] Revilla, "D. José Echegaray," *Obras*, p. 117.

El movimiento neo-romántico y pseudo-realista, iniciado a deshora por la escuela del señor Echegaray, ha sido obstáculo no pequeño para que nuestra literatura dramática siga por estos bien encaminados senderos, y ha traído hondas perturbaciones a la española escena.[26]

(The neo-Romantic and pseudo-realistic movement, begun at an untimely moment by Mr. Echegaray's school, has been a sizeable obstacle to allowing our dramatic literature to proceed down the right road, and it has brought deep confusion to Spanish theatre.)

More measured voices have found in Echegaray's melodramas a movement from liberal Romanticism to the social dramas of the 1890s, a movement which passed from the *misterio* plays through Galdós (*Doña Perfecta*, for example) and Benavente.[27] Perhaps this accounts for the absence of humor in his plays.

Angel Guimerà (1845–1924), a talented poet – in his time he was hailed as one of the best poets in the country – and one of the leaders of the Catalán *Renaixença* in the second half of the century, wrote dozens of enormously successful dramas in his native language which drew on the metaphors and themes of the neo-Romantics.[28] His rich use of color imagery, superb understanding of dramatic space, and ability to capture with sensitivity complex human emotions made him a favorite of the Catalán theatre-going public. Outside of Spain he was considered to be "one of the most forceful, most resourceful, and most masterful of the dramatists of our time."[29] His first play, *Gala Placidia* (1879), captured the attention of a public hungry for lyrical emotion and Romantic passion and was called "la primera tragedia que figura en la literatura genuinamente catalana" ("the first tragedy of what can be called genuinely Catalán literature") (*El Heraldo de Madrid*, 18 November 1891) transforming the author into one of the founding fathers of modern Catalán literature (along, perhaps, with Victor Balaguer [1824–1902] and Frederic Soler [1839–1895]). Other hits followed – *Judith de Welp* (1883) and *El fill del rey* (The King's Son, 1886) – but it was with *Mar i cel* (Sea and Sky, 1888) that Guimerà sealed his reputation as a respected dramatist. *Mar i cel* was widely acclaimed as one of the best plays produced for the stage in Spain[30] and was immediately translated into Spanish by another well-

[26] Revilla, "Adelardo López de Ayala," *Obras*, pp. 28–29.

[27] See Gonzalo Sobejano, "Echegaray, Galdós y el melodrama," *Anales Galdosianos* (supplement 1978): 91–115; and Wadda C. Ríos-Font, "The Melodramatic Paradigm: José Echegaray and the Modern Spanish Theater," doctoral dissertation (Harvard, 1991).

[28] See Curet, *El arte dramático en el resurgir de Cataluña*, pp. 27–32.

[29] John Garrett Underhill, "Introduction" to *Martha of the Lowlands*, translation by Wallace Gillpatrick of *Tierra baja* (New York: Doubleday, 1902): v.

[30] Juan Sardá, writing in *La España Moderna* (1888), claimed it to be "una de las mejores producciones de nuestro teatro regional, y una de las mejores que por estos años ha producido el teatro en España." Cited in *Enciclopedia Universal Ilustrada* XXVII

known playwright, Enrique Gaspar. It is pure Romanticism, crammed with heightened emotionalism, exalted love, tense conflict, sparkling lyricism, individual sacrifice, rhapsodic and melodic moments, and inevitable tragedy.

Slowly, Guimerà moved away from neo-Romanticism toward religious dramas (*Jesús de Nazareth*, 1894; *Les monges de Sant Aymant* [The Monks of Saint Aymant], 1895) and rural/social tragedies,[31] a move signaled by a gradual shift from verse to prose dramas. Following *En Pólvora* (1893), Guimerà became more interested in the sociology of his environment than its costumbrista or Romantic elements. His main characters tended to be the working man and the peasant rather than the *bourgeois gentilhomme* or the noble bandit. Two plays which reflect this later trend, *María Rosa* (1894), a penetrating study of the situation of the poor, and *Terra baixa* (Lowlands, 1897), contain some of the author's best writing and most complex psychological insights.

Terra baixa was translated into Spanish by none other than José Echegaray, and performed at the Teatro Español in 1898 by the María Guerrero company, unquestionably Spain's leading theatre company of the time. In fact, it was premièred in Madrid before being shown in its native Barcelona because several directors in that city had rejected it as "inmoral" and "pecaminosa"[32] ("sinful"). Soon thereafter the Madrid company took the play to Paris for its European première. In its original language it subsequently received hundreds, if not thousands, of performances; translations of it appeared in Portuguese, Italian, French, English (as early as 1902), German, Swedish, Russian, Czech, Serbian, Dutch, and Yiddish.[33] Full of realistic detail and compelling action, the play builds in power to its shattering (if not wholly unexpected) conclusion. Manelich, the simple shepherd, has been forced down from his *locus amoenus* in the mountain to marry Marta, the ward of the evil landowner Sebastián, in order to provide Sebastián with a seemingly respectable cover for his abuse of Marta. Everything in the vicinity – the land, the mill, the huts, the people – "belong" to Sebastián, who represents the oppressive oligarchy of the Catalán uppercrust pitted against the simple

(Madrid: Espasa, 1925): 274. In 1990 the Dagoll Dagom Company turned it into a musical drama, and performed it with great success in Barcelona and Madrid.

31 Xavier Fabregas divides Guimerà's production into five stages; the second stage moves from neo-Romanticism to realist concerns. *Angel Guimerà: les deimensions d'un mite* (Barcelona: Ediciones 62, 1971): 41–42.

32 Lily Litvak, "Naturalismo y teatro social en Cataluña," *Comparative Literature Studies* 5 (1968): 291.

33 A complete listing of Guimerà's plays is provided by Fabregas, pp. 36–41. See also his *Història del teatre català*, pp. 131–142. Fabregas's earlier study, *Aproximació a la historia del teatre català* (Barcelona: Curial, 1972), contains much useful information about the development of Catalán theatre in Spain.

laborers. Sebastián wields his power arbitrarily, and Guimerà from the beginning equates Sebastián with the "wolf", the same animal which has terrified Manelich's sheep for years up on the mountain. When we hear that Manelich has succeeded in strangling a wolf with his bare hands in order to save what he most loves and prizes (his flock, his "family") we know that the same fate will befall Sebastián; it does in the play's violent climax (III, 16). The most interesting character, however, is Marta, whose self-identity is intimately connected to her social class, her mysterious and faintly dishonorable background, and her relation to the men in her life. She feels worthless, "owned", lacking any real identity of her own or power outside of the male sphere. The play in many ways is a fairy tale, ripe for a Freudian/Lacanian reading to uncover its deep symbolic structure. It is as a symbolic, psychological drama that audiences identified with it so strongly, not as a realist one as is sometimes claimed.[34]

Social/socialist drama

By the end of the century three distinct phenomena were vying for the public's attention in the theatre. The first two were the arrival of Galdós as a dramatist and the avalanche of satires, vaudeville reviews, and short parodies which hit Spanish stages (these will be treated below); the third was the explosion of social – "realist" as it was often called – drama. The critics of the period often confused their terminology, mixing concepts such as "social," "socialista," "realista," and "naturalista" into a stew of inexact descriptive adjectives. Workers' movements and socialism as a coherent political ideology emerged slowly and sporadically from the late 1830s and early 1840s on, and gained real political force by the last decades of the century. As Gonzalo Menéndez-Pidal reminds us, "todo lo que concierne a la historia de la organización proletaria hispana en la primera mitad del siglo XIX es más bien inconexo e inseguro, contando, eso sí, con la casi constante hostilidad de los gobiernos, incluso en sus etapas liberales"[35] ("everything that deals with the history of worker organization in Spain in the first half of the nineteenth century is generally incoherent and uncertain, considering, of course, the almost constant hostility of the various governments, even liberal ones"). Social dramas, or dramas which focused on the plight of the working class in an attempt to reform the living conditions of the dispossessed, did not suddenly appear on Spanish stages in the 1890s with Joaquín Dicenta's provocative

---

[34] Fabregas calls it simply a "drama romàntic amb elements realistes." *Angel Guimerà*, p. 38.

[35] Gonzalo Menéndez-Pidal, *La España del siglo XIX vista por sus contemporáneos* I (Madrid: Centro de Estudios Constitucionales, 1988): 448.

Juan José (1895) or Guimerà's moving *Terra baixa* (1897), in spite of García Pavón's exaggerated claim to the contrary.[36] The reformist and moralizing intent of such late dramas needed to be defended against those who saw in them merely scabrous or shocking things.[37] As Sellés stated in the prologue to *Las vengadoras* (The Avenging Women, 1892), "El arte realista es, pues, tan moralizador como el idealista, con una diferencia de procedimientos: Uno enseña lo que debe hacerse; otro enseña lo que debe evitarse"[38] ("Realist art is just as moralizing as idealist art, with a difference of approach: One teaches what ought to be done; the other teaches what ought to be avoided"). From mid-century on some Spanish playwrights had demonstrated sensitivity to certain social issues, as had their French counterparts. (Translated versions of some of the French plays – Sue's *Los misterios de París, Nuestra Señora de París*, and others – had been performed more than 1,000 times by the century's end.[39]) Surprisingly, even Echegaray was credited with a sort of "ruptura ideológica" ("ideological break") with the bourgeois establishment by one critic and with being a "naturalista" by another. The anarchist press of the early 1880s praised Echegaray (and even Ayala), along with Eugenio Sellés (*El nudo gordiano* [The Gordian Knot], 1878), Leopoldo Cano (*La pasionaria* [The Passion-Flower], 1883), and Francisco Pleguezuelo (*Mártires o delincuentes* [Martyrs or Delinquents], 1884), for criticizing the falseness and complacency of the middle-class family.[40]

Theatre which concerned itself with the situation of the workers, the lower classes, and the downtrodden divided itself into two distinct periods in the nineteenth century. The first period was the 1850s when political turmoil and the arrival of foreign theory sparked a small but significant appearance of "socialist" themes. Iris Zavala has demonstrated that "literatura obrerista" ("workers' literature") had been known in Spain since mid-century.

El socialismo democrático se conoció en España a partir de la primera mitad del ochocientos a través de unos cuantos difusores en Cádiz, Madrid y Barcelona. En 1841 apareció un denso resumen de las ideas fourieristas, *Fourier, o sea explana-*

---

36 "El drama social comenzó en España exactamente la noche el 29 de octubre de 1895, en el Teatro de la Comedia, con el estreno de *Juan José.*" Francisco García Pavón, *Teatro social en España* (Madrid: Taurus, 1962): 36. Carlos Serrano sensibly judges this claim to be "excesiva." "Notas sobre teatro obrero a finales del siglo XIX," *El teatro menor en España a partir del siglo XVI* (Madrid: CSIC, 1983): 263.

37 Alfonso Sastre has defined "social drama" based on the nature of the subject matter covered and the intention of the dramatist. See *Drama y sociedad* (Madrid: Taurus, 1958).

38 Rubio Jiménez, *Ideología*, p. 38. See Peter Bly, "Galdós, Sellés y el tratamiento literario del adulterio." In *Actas del X Congreso Internacional de Hispanistas*, II, ed. Antonio Vilanova (Barcelona: PPU, 1992): 1213–1220.

39 Albert Soubies, *Le théâtre en France de 1871 à 1892* (Paris: E. Flammarion, 1893). Cited by Rubio Jiménez, *Ideología*, p. 15.

40 See the anonymous article, "La cuestión social en el teatro," *Revista Social (Eco del Proletariado)* 141 (14 February 1884). José Alcázar Hernández described *O locura o*

ción del sistema societario (Barcelona, 1841) ... Los sansimonianos eran conocidos y aparecieron artículos expositivos en *La Revista Europea* y *La Revista Peninsular*, que dirigía Andrés Borrego, con quien colaboraba Larra ... El socialismo más militante surge a partir de 1846 – Sixto Cámara, Fernando Garrido, Francisco Javier Moya, Federico Beltrán, figuran entre los más conocidos – . Ellos encabezaron revoluciones, firmaron manifiestos, crearon grupos y partidos, escuelas para obreros; además fundaron periódicos, escribieron novela, poesía y teatro con finalidad aleccionadora y propagandística.[41]

(Democratic socialism was known in Spain since the first half of the 1800s through a handful of activists in Cadiz, Madrid and Barcelona. In 1841 there appeared a dense synopsis of Fourierist ideas, *Fourier, o sea explanación del sistema societario* [Fourier, or An Explanation of the Societal System, Barcelona 1841] ... The Sansimonistas were known, and there appeared explanatory articles in *La Revista Europea* and *La Revista Peninsular*, directed by Andrés Borrego, with whom Larra had worked ... The most militant socialism grew after 1846 – Sixto Cámara, Fernando Garrido, Francisco Javier Moya, Federico Beltrán are among the best known. They spearheaded revolutions, signed manifestos, created groups and political parties, schools for workers; in addition they founded newspapers, wrote novels, poetry, and plays with an eye toward instruction and propaganda.)

We have already seen how the *alta comedia* questioned and criticized the money-obsessed upper middle class in Spain. The early proponents of socialist theatre pushed that criticism further and provided a background for the later works of Sellés, Cano, Guimerà, Dicenta, and, it could be safely argued, Galdós. Often they took the characters and time frames of Romantic theatre – bandits, beggars, and thieves from a distant past – and placed them in new morality plays in which the plight of such characters evoked pity and indignation rather than fear or scorn.

Early socialist plays frequently used historical drama, a genre into which new life had been breathed by the Romantics, as the platform for their investigation of the problems of "los de abajo" ("the underdogs"). Félix Mejía, for example, published what Zavala calls his "ardorosa defensa de la democracia y el federalismo" ("fiery defense of democracy and federalism") (*La Suiza libre*, A Free Switzerland) in 1846,[42] while José María Díaz staged his version of *Juan sin tierra* (via Shakespeare and Ducis) at the Príncipe Theatre in 1848. However, it was Sixto Sáenz de la Cámara (1826–1862, known as Sixto Cámara) who presented the issues in the clearest and most tendentious way in *Jaime el Barbudo* (Juan the Bearded), first put on at the Cruz Theatre on the national holiday, 2 May 1853. The play begins as a relatively simple historical drama crammed with Romantic language and images; the first three acts develop straight-

santidad as "naturalista" (!) in his article "Del naturalismo en nuestro teatro moderno," *Revista de España* 84 (January – February 1882): 371–379.
[41] Zavala, "La literatura," pp. 133–134.   [42] *Ibid.* p. 136.

forwardly themes of honor, defense against oppression, bravery, and love. Echoes of Rivas's *Don Alvaro* and Espronceda's "Canción del pirata" resound at key moments in the play (II, 14 and Epilogue, 1, for example).[43] It is hardly a full-blown "workers' drama" but slowly Cámara lards his language with allusions to the oppressed masses and to the injustices meted out by social inequity. Clara's father, don Ciriaco, hints at one of the play's points of tension when he reveals why he wants Clara to marry the marqués de Cuestas-Altas, reasons which have nothing to do with love or happiness: such a union will help them "olvidar así nuestro modesto linaje" ("forget our modest background") (I, 1), that is, he will buy, with her as the coin of the realm, "una noble ejecutoria" ("a noble patent of nobility"). Clara is painfully aware of his eagerness to sacrifice her: "Según eso, padre mío, / ¿que venda queréis a un hombre / mi corazón por su nombre, / por sus rentas mi albedrío?" ("According to that, my father, you want to sell my heart to a man for his name, my freedom for his income?") (I, 1). The author then puts into the mouth of don Ciriaco the following statement about the society he lives in: "¿No comprende tu razón / que, para ser hoy felices, / no basta, no, lo que dices, / sino plata y posición?" ("Don't you understand that to be happy these days it is not enough to have what you say, no, one must also have money and a good position?") (I, 1). That is the crux of the matter: "plata y posición" are the only real coins in Spanish society, and don Ciriaco is willing, even eager, to trade his daughter (another possession) for them. By Act III he is delighted with the thought that his daughter, who has made it very clear that she loves Captain Gonzalo, not the marqués, will be a titled woman (III, 14). The marqués suggests that being poor is as bad as being evil.

[43] In the Epilogue the chorus of bandits sings,

Hijo soy de la aventura,
y mi patria las montañas,
que en sus lóbregas entrañas
seguro asilo me dan.
Pasajero
ten la brida,
o a tu vida
pongo fin:
que es mi gloria
la venganza,
la matanza
y el botín.
Puesta a precio mi cabeza
por el mundo se pregona;
pero si el rey me perdona
desprecio el perdón del rey.
Que es mi dicha mi caballo
y la presa el bien que adoro,
la libertad mi tesoro,
la independencia mi ley ...

También ese mundo necio,
si me sorprende arruinado,
me mirará con deprecio:
que tiene en tan poco aprecio
al pobre como al malvado.
Y aun si es rico el malhechor,
sus crímenes la perdona;
quien en este mundo, ¡oh dolor!
es el oro el que mejor
a los hombre nos abona.				(I, 14)

(The world, if it suddenly finds me poor, will look at me with contempt. It has as little regard for the poor person as for the evil one. But if the evil person is rich, his crimes are pardoned. Truth is, in this world – what a pity! – money is the best security a man can have.)

Cámara's defense of the poor and downtrodden works its way into the first three acts of the play in stages. Act II takes place in a "casa de campo, pobre," ("a poor country home") yet even though "poor," it contains a writing box, signaling to the audience that the inhabitants are literate and intelligent. His clearest statements on the social inequities and money-grubbing status of those in power (social as well as political) comes in the epilogue (the play is structured into three acts and an epilogue). The drama evolves into a political tract in which Jaime, the noble bandit, delivers lessons on man's inhumanity to man, the brotherhood of man, and man's innate goodness, ideas culled as much from Rousseau and Cienfuegos as from the more hotly debated Fourier (we remember that a synopsis of his ideas had appeared in Barcelona as early as 1841). Jaime tells his cohorts:

Desengañaos;
por un error oprimimos
a nuestros propios hermanos,
víctimas como nosotros
de leyes que no formaron;
el mundo pesa sobre ellos
como también ha pesado
sobre nosotros un día ...			(Epílogo, 8)

(Wise up. Unfortunately we oppress our brothers, who are victims as we are of laws they do not make; the world causes them sorrow just as it has caused us sorrow ...)

The bandits reveal how each in turn was forced into a life of crime by injustice or hunger ("mi pobre madre anciana / muriendo sin amparo, / pedí pan, no me lo dieron" ["my poor old mother, dying without any help, I asked for bread for her, but they would not give me any"]), to which Jaime asks with anguish, "¿Quién al oir tales cosas / dirá que el hombre es malo?" ("Who can hear such things and still say that man is evil?") (Epílogo, 8). Iris Zavala reminds us that "como política práctica, el socialismo democrático llegó a influir en algunos grupos e individuos; campeones del progreso, que intentaron proporcionarle la felicidad y el bienestar a los más pobres guiados por la nueva «ciencia social», a la que alude Larra"[44] ("as practical politics, democratic socialism managed to influence some groups and individuals; champions of progress who tried to bring happiness and wellbeing to the poorest members of society, guided by the new 'social science' to which Larra alluded"). Jaime continues his harangue against the "¡Sabia ley la que separa / a los pueblos que son hermanos!" ("Wise law that divides people who are in fact brothers!") (Epílogo, 8). There is much more: the nobility of the workers, the inherent honor of work ("ni hay tampoco tan dulce / como el pan de su trabajo" ["there is nothing as sweet as the bread earned by working"]), and so on. *Jaime el Barbudo* is a forceful early defense in Spain of the working class and the injustices visited upon them by the money-obsessed, social-climbing individuals who rule the country, ideas brought into Spain as early as 1839 with the publication of Alvaro Flórez Estrada's *La cuestión social*[45] (The Social Question). Although set during the War of Independence in 1811–1812, Cámara's play is clearly meant to be an allegory of how he viewed Spain. Jesús Rubio studies briefly this "melodrama de bandidos"[46] ("melodrama with bandits") which contains some trenchant observations on the conflict of classes which would become a dominant theme of playwriting at the end of the century. This play, along with several radical political pamphlets Cámara wrote and published during these years, landed him in hot water with the government, which jailed him in 1854. He died in exile after fleeing Spain following a new attempt at a radical overthrow of the government.

More influential than Sixto Cámara was his friend and biographer Fernando Garrido (1821–1883), a firebrand defender of socialism who wrote numerous pamphlets and studies of progressive issues. He was a follower of Charles Fourier (1772–1837), whose ideas he introduced into Spain.[47] His newspapers, among them the short-lived *La Atracción* (The Attraction, 1846) and the censored *La Organización del Trabajo*

---

44 Zavala, "La literatura," p. 135.
45 See Menéndez-Pidal, *La España del siglo XIX*, p. 445.
46 Jesús Rubio Jiménez, "Melodrama y teatro político en el siglo XIX. El escenario como tribuna política," *Castilla* 14 (1989): 141.
47 For a selection of the ideas of Fourier and their reception in Spain, see Antonio Elorza, *El fourierismo en España* (Madrid: Ediciones de la Revista de Trabajo, 1975).

(The Organization of Work, 1848)[48], propagated republican political ideas and declaimed the corruption of the Bourbon monarchy. An early pamphlet, *Propaganda democrática: Defensa del socialismo* (Democratic Propaganda: A Defense of Socialism), earned him a year-long jail sentence in Madrid followed by a period of exile until 1854. 1854 was a difficult year for workers, many of whom were fired from their government posts in an attempted cut-back and subsequently faced starvation as the result of a poor harvest and a foolhardy policy of grain exports which left local cupboards bare. The political situation was volatile.[49] In 1855 Garrido penned a play, *Un día de revolución* (A Day of Revolution), a lightly veiled look at social issues of his day which so provoked the government that censorship, which had been lax as an official policy during the Bienio (1854–1856), was reinstated and intensified between 1855 and 1857.[50]

Un día de revolución is an incendiary paean of praise to the "pueblo," a no-holds-barred defense of republicanism against what Garrido had long thought to be the abuses of monarchism. While Martínez Pastor exaggerates the case by claiming Garrido to be "el primer español en darse cuenta que el teatro ... era un vehículo muy adecuado para la expresión fácil de un mensaje aunque este mensaje fuera revolucionario"[51] (the first Spaniard to realize that the theatre ... was a very apt vehicle for the easy declaration of a message, even though that message might be revolutionary") (dramatists during the War of Independence had discovered this fact), Garrido does play a central role in the creation of revolutionary theatre. The piece in question takes place in Paris during the Revolution of 1848, but refers quite directly to the uprisings in Madrid in 1854, uprisings which Garrido wholeheartedly endorsed. Subtlety was not one of Garrido's strong suits as a dramatist, nor was it meant to be. Blondel, a loving, reasonable, and kind socialist/republican – far from the rabble-rousing anarchist often depicted by conservatives – fights a double battle for the hand of his beloved Laura, whom her tutor wishes to marry off as a "brillante ornate de la corte" ("brilliant court decoration") (I, 1) to a rich Baron, and for the freedom of his people against the "despotismo inmundo" ("evil despotism") (I, 23) of the government. Laura's tutor, Mr. Bareste, dreams of "contrato, títulos y millones" ("contracts, titles,

---

48 This newspaper, "debió tener una gran importancia entre las filas de los demócratas socialistas." Iris M. Zavala, *Románticos y socialistas* (Madrid: Siglo Veintiuno, 1972): 154.
49 See E. V. G. Kiernan, *The Revolution of 1854 in Spanish History* (Oxford: Clarendon Press, 1966).
50 Rubio Jiménez, "La censura," p. 203.
51 Eugenio Martínez Pastor, *Fernando Garrido: Su obra y su tiempo* (Cartagena: Instituto de Estudios Cartaginenses, 1976): 164.

and millions") (I, 2) if he manages to marry her to Baron Fremoit; Laura becomes a commodity, a simple means of exchange between him and the Baron. As the characters debate the collapsing economy and their threatened social situation, the playwright clearly positions himself on the side of violent revolution: "pero creo que todos tus discursos pesan menos que las bayonetas en la balance del orden" ("but I think that all of your speeches carry less weight than the bayonets in keeping order") (I, 3) as Bareste tells the Baron. Such ideas corresponded to what Garrido had been writing in pamphlets and newspaper articles previously; in 1854 he had called for workers to arm themselves against a repressive monarchy and in 1855 he penned his important *La república democrática federal universal* (The Universal Federal Democratic Republic) in which he elaborated his ideas on social class and republicanism.[52] Blondel, however, is the true revolutionary in the play. He confirms to Laura that "la revolución ha abierto hoy sus puertas para todos: el día que va a concluir decidirá de la suerte del pueblo; tal vez de la del mundo" ("the revolution has opened up its doors to everyone today: by the day's end the fate of the people will be decided, perhaps that of the whole world") (I, 5). When the baron attempts to discredit Blondel by accusing him of being "un republicano ... un socialista," the play's hero responds proudly, "En efecto lo soy, y me glorío de ello" ("In fact I am, and I'm proud of it") (I, 10). Blondel represents not only the united workers but also, for Garrido, women's rights. As Laura tells him, he is:

el revelador que, encarnando en mi inteligencia el ideal de un mundo de justicia, de amor y libertad, me elevas a mis propios ojos sacándome del estrecho círculo en que giran las ideas de las mujeres, gracias a su mezquina educación. Me has enseñado a comprender, a llorar las desgracias del miserable mundo en que vivimos, y esperar en su regeneración. (I, 5)

(the one who opened my eyes to the ideal of a world of justice, love, and freedom, who brought me out of the narrow circle of ideas where women tend to stay because of their terrible educations. You have taught me how to understand, how to weep for the misfortunes of the miserable world we live in, and hope for its regeneration.)

Blondel connects this idea to the larger revolution when he proclaims, "Es el pueblo que reclama, con las armas en la mano, sus derechos, su asiento en el banquete de la vida" ("It is the people who, armed, reclaim their rights, their seat at the banquet table of life") (I, 5). At the play's conclusion Blondel delivers sentiments reminiscent of Cienfuegos's or Quintana's more stirring denouncements of tyranny and oppression:

---

[52] Eliseo Aja, *Democracia y socialismo en el siglo XIX español. El pensamiento político de Fernando Garrido* (Madrid: Edicusa, 1976): 22.

Pueblo heroíco: los viles, los traidores,
los que envidian tu arrojo y tu nobleza,
los que quieren hacerse tus señores,
esos calumnian tu inmortal grandeza.
Mas ya ha llegado de triunfar el día;
porque a pesar del despotismo inmundo
vencerás a la infame tiranía.
Libre serás mientras exista el mundo.   (I, 23)

(Heroic people: the vile ones, the traitors, those who envy your fearlessness and your nobility, those who want to become your masters, they are the ones who slander your immortal greatness. But our time has come; because in spite of the vile despotism you will triumph over evil tyranny. You will be free as long as the world exists.)

Un día de revolución was apparently performed once in early May, 1855 (according to the progressive newspaper *La Iberia*) but it was pulled from the boards immediately. It was certainly more effective political propaganda than theatre.

Un día de revolución was not Garrido's only attempt to use theatre as a platform for his anti-monarchical ideas, although he had little success at having them staged. As early as 1847 he wrote *Don Bravito Cantarrana*, a one-act piece which on the surface plays with themes made familiar to audiences by such works as Moratín's classic *El sí de las niñas* and Breton's *El pelo de la dehesa* and *Don Frutos en Belchite*, that is, the ability of a girl to choose her husband and the conflict between "sophisticated" city dwellers and their more rustic country cousins. Yet Garrido's political stance and rabid hatred of the social status quo quickly turned the comedy into a political tract with feminist overtones. As early as the first scene, Bravito tells his girlfriend Teodorita, "No temáis, no, los rigores / de paternal tiranía; / ya la igualdad en amores / impera en la monarquía. / ... / Completan cuadros bellos / como te cito en mi abono, / ver cien veces los plebeyos / subir por amor a su trono" ("Don't be afraid of the harshness of paternal tyranny, because equality now reigns in the monarchy ... It's a pretty thing to see common people rise up through love to reach the throne") (I, 1). This cutting allusion to María Cristina's infamous relationship with her lover, a shopkeeper's son named Muñoz who had served in her army and whom she subsequently named Duke of Riansares, sets the tone of the piece. The coup, however, is the incendiary statement in scene 10 which insured its absence from the stages in Madrid. Bravito, a journalist whom Hipólito opposes as a suitable match for his daughter, shouts hysterically at his rival (this, on the eve of the Revolution of 1848):

Mañana el mundo sabrá
quién es usted, y arderá
Troya ...
...
        La Nación
por feota le tendrá.
Cuando el feroz comunismo
blandiendo la tea incendiaria,
enaltezca el pauperismo,
la horda patibularia
le arrastrará a usted al abismo.
...
¿A ser déspota se atreve
hombre atroz, en este siglo?
En este siglo diez y nueve ...
¡no cuela ya el despotismo!

(Tomorrow the world will see who you really are, and Troy will burn ... The
Nation will see your ugliness. When ferocious communism, blandishing the
burning torch, exhalts poverty, the harrowing tribe will drag you into the abyss.
Do you dare to be a despot, you heinous man, in this century? In the ninetenth
century ... there is no room for despotism!)

Strangely, Garrido seemed to give up on the theatre as a platform for
his radical ideas, although he continued to write plays. *La más ilustre
nobleza* (The Most Illustrious Nobility), first performed at the Princesa
Theatre on 6 March 1856 (it was seen again on 18 May 1860, at the Circo
Theatre), is a disappointing and hackneyed rehash of tired Romantic
themes with nary a revolutionary idea in it. (It is almost as if it were
written by someone else). After a confusing series of who-is-related-to-
whom episodes, the author reaches the same conclusion reached by
Calderón's Pedro Crespo 200 years earlier, "que es la nobleza del alma, /
la más ilustre nobleza" ("the nobility of the soul is the most illustrious
nobility") (III, 20). Garrido turned his attention to writing his superb
Historia de las clases trabajadores (History of the Working Classes) and
La república, both of which appeared in 1870.

The republican propaganda plays of Garrido and Cámara did not go
unchallenged by other playwrights in the capital during the 1850s. Francisco Botella y Andrés (1832–1903) posed a counter argument to what he
perceived (correctly) to be the subversive plays of the republican anti-
monarchists. *El rico y el pobre* (The Rich Man and the Poor Man),
performed at the Instituto Español on 18 February 1855, was an intensely
partisan work which defended the Bourbon monarchy of Isabel II against
her most virulent attackers. Yet defending the monarchy in 1855 was
neither a particularly easy stance nor a particularly popular one, given the

high unemployment, hunger, and economic instability plaguing the country. Botella seemed at first glance to be writing a textbook accumulation of grievances of the poor and downtrodden against their oppressors. Adela's poor-but-honorable boyfriend tells her, for example, "no está lejos el momento en que el pueblo oprimido recobre sus derechos y selle con su sangre el nombre de la santa causa" ("the time is not far off when the oppressed people will reclaim their rights and will seal with blood the name of their sainted cause") (I, 2) or later,

Me contemplo un gigante capaz de hacer desaparecer de un soplo esos palacios que insultan nuestra pobreza y esos banquetes que ultrajan nuestra miseria. Oh, porque el pueblo, Adela, cuando ese pueblo levante su tremenda espada y caiga como un torrente sobre sus opresores, entonces ... (I, 2)

(I see myself as a giant capable of blowing away those palaces that insult our poverty and those banquets that offend our misery. Oh, because the people, Adela, when the people lift up their huge sword and let it fall like a torrent on their oppressors, then ...)

Shortly thereafter, Pedro, Adela's poor-but-honorable father, tells her,

¡Trabajo! ¿Sabéis lo que me han contestado cuando he ido a buscarlo? "Andad, buen hombre, no os queremos, sois demasiado viejo". ¡Caridad! ¿Sabéis lo que me han dicho al implorarla? "Trabajad, buen hombre, sois demasiado joven para pedir limosna." Maldita sociedad. (I, 4)

(Work! Do you know what they said to me when I went looking for a job? "Come on, man, we don't want you because you are too old." Charity! Do you know what they told me when I asked for it? "Get a job man, you are too young to be begging." Damned society.)

In reality, however, such words just set up the real ideological underpinning of the drama, which is the ennoblement of the poor in order to keep them quiescent. Pedro is idealized in his poverty, made to be pure, strong, honest, and unsullied – not the noble savage but the noble pauper. In Act II he returns a wallet containing 100,000 *reales* he found in the street, further confirming his selflessness and strength of character. On the other hand, Botella makes the evil Count the leader of a group of individuals who conspire against the Queen, "entre los que titulándose republicanos pretenden destruirle" ("among those who calling themselves republicans are trying to destroy her") (I, 12); Pedro naturally is the faithful monarchist. The Queen is not responsible for their poverty, he insists; rather, it is her advisors who corrupt and protect her. Pedro is set up to be admired for being "duro como una piedra; un hombre montado a la antigua" ("hard as a rock; a man of staunch old values") (I, 6), that is, a representative of the "old" values which, for Botella and his conservative supporters, made Spain strong and noble. (These ideas are clearly vestiges of the Böhl and Durán line of traditionalist thinking which remained very strong in Spanish literary and philosophical circles throughout the course of the century.[53]) The "popular uprising" that ends the play is not that hoped for by the Count but rather one which confirms the validity of Isabel: "la libertad ha triunfado de la tiranía" ("freedom has triumphed over tyranny") (IV, 8).

A similar idealization of the poor occurs in *Los pobres de Madrid* (The Poor People of Madrid), a "drama en seis actos y un prólogo" ("play in six acts and a prologue") by the prolific journalist Manuel Ortiz de Pinedo, which follows closely the plot structure of many *novelas de folletines* (in fact, the collection which published this play, the Museo Dramático Ilustrado, put out one or two plays per week at the cost of one *real* per fascicle, a kind of *teatro por entregas*[54]). There is no record that this adaptation of a French melodrama was performed at the time of its publication (1858), suggesting that it was written to be read rather than performed, although it does show up at the Teatro Novedades in 1872; however, the *Enciclopedia Universal Ilustrada* claims that it was so "perfectamente adaptada a los gustos del público español, que durante más de cuarenta años se mantuvo en los carteles" ("perfectly suited to the tastes of the Spanish public that it remained in the repertory for more than forty years") (vol. XL, 735).

Botella could even joke with such volatile and topical matters. The "juguete cómico" performed at the Instituto Theatre on 31 December 1854 (published in 1855) called *Furor parlamentario* (Parliamentary Furor) is as anti-revolutionary and pro-monarchy as his other plays. In it he refers clearly to the destinies of men like Cámara and Garrido ("¡Cielos! Si será algún demócrata perseguido por la justicia" ["Good Heavens! Could it be some democrat pursued by justice!"] [scene 3]), but sides with D. Félix, who declaims, "Pero en fin, todos hemos errado, y la revolución echó un velo sobre nuestras deplorables equivocaciones" ("In the end we were all wrong, and the revolution drew a veil over our

---

[53] See Flitter, *Spanish Romantic Literary Theory and Criticism*, pp. 5–49.
[54] The line between drama and the "folletines" was becoming less well-defined. Enrique Pérez Escrich (1829–1897), the master "folletinista" of mid-century Spain, was at this time also writing plays. His first play was performed in 1850 (*El rey de bastos*). In 1856 alone he wrote *Sálvese el que pueda*, *No hay vida más que en Paris*, *Retratos originales*, *El maestro de baile*, *El ángel malo*, and *La pasión y muerte de Cristo*. An exceedingly prolific writer, he produced between 1857 and 1861 numerous other stage works: *Juan Diente*, *Herencia de lágrimas*, *La dicha del bien ajeno*, *Amor y resignación*, *La mosquita muerta*, *Géneros ultramarinos*, *El cura de aldea*, *La mala semilla*, *Los moros del Riff*, *El movimiento continuo*, *Caricaturas*, *Gil Blas*, *El que siembra, recoge*, *La corte del rey poeta*, *La hija de Fernán Gil*, *Ver y no ver*, *Las garras del diablo*, and *El vértigo de Rosa*. He turned the play *El cura de aldea* (which Luis Mariano de Larra accused him of plagiarizing from his own *La oración de la tarde* [1860]) into one of his most successful novels.

deplorable mistakes") (scene 3). Botella opposes the mere existence of a parliamentary system, since in his view the parliament's inefficiency inhibits the progress of the monarchy: "Otra costumbre parlamentaria; discutir y perder el tiempo es todo una misma cosa" ("Another parliamentary habit: to discuss things and to waste time is the same thing") (I, 7). Nor does he display much confidence in the Cortes's ability to produce a workable constitution:

LUISA:	La Constitución de usted no me parece muy buena, al menos yo no la acepto.
FÉLIX:	¡Ay, señora! Dios quiera que sea mejor la que se redacte en otra parte. (I, 7)
(LUISA:	Your Constitution does not seem to me to be very good, at least I cannot accept it.
FÉLIX:	Oh, ma'am! I hope to God that it is better than the one the others are drawing up.)

Similar jaundiced sentiments are expressed in *La unión liberal* (The Liberal Union), a one-act comedy performed at the Teatro de Variedades on 24 February 1855. The title refers not to the well-known political party formed in 1858, but to the manifesto issued by the revolutionaries in July, 1854,[55] and against which Botella rails in this short work. He plays with a hotly debated political concept and applies it to a domestic farce, making fun along the way of the supposed "progresistas."

JUAN:	¿Tú también eres político?
EDUARDO:	¿Quién no lo es? ... ¿Quién es moderado en el día? Ese partido se ha fundido en el crisol de la libertad, y vuelve a presentarse al mundo vestido de miliciano; hoy todos somos progresistas. (I, 4)
(JUAN:	Are you a politician too?
EDUARDO:	Who isn't? ... Who is a moderate these days? That party was founded in the crucible of freedom, and now it's presenting itself to the world dressed in militia uniforms; today we are all progressives.)

When Eduardo, the slimy politician who tries to seduce the wife of his friend Juan, says to Luisa,

Señora, usted es una mujer encantadora; yo la adoro a usted; vamos a formar entre los dos un sistema de gobierno constitucional. Usted será la reina, yo seré el pueblo. (I, 7)

(Madame, you are a delightful woman; I adore you. Let's form a kind of constitutional government between us. You will be the queen, I will be the people.)

---

[55] See Miguel Artola, *Partidos y programas políticos 1808–1936* (Madrid: Aguilar, 1974–1975): 49–51.

she responds, "No; yo quiero ser absoluta. No me gustan los términos medios" ("No; I want to be absolute. I don't like these half-way measures"). Luisa finally opts for her "monarchical" husband over the "democratic" suitor: "Es un sistema que tiene grandes defectos [the monarchy], pero al cabo es el mejor" ("It is a system with a lot of flaws, but in the final analysis it's the best there is") (scene 14).

It does not take a large stretch of the imagination to figure out the ideological posture of his play *La expulsión de los jesuitas* (The Expulsion of the Jesuits, 1855). Botella became so involved in the political world that he abandoned the theatre after penning some fifty plays and devoted his life exclusively to the political arena: he became a staunch supporter of Narváez's Partido Moderado in Sevilla, a deputy in the Cortes until its change in 1868, and a defender of the politics of González Bravo. During the Restoration, for which he lobbied incessantly, he reentered the Cortes first as a deputy from Valencia and later from Alicante.

Hence, the political crises and social ills of the day made their way into the theatre in different forms. If Cámara, Garrido and others set the early groundwork for socialist theatre in Spain (always mindful of their minority roles) it was not until the 1880s and 1890s that their ideas flourished on Spanish stages – transformed and adapted to new circumstances – in the works of Eugenio Sellés, Enrique Gaspar,[56] Angel Guimerà, and Joaquín Dicenta. We have seen as well how Rosario de Acuña touched upon these volatile matters in her two major plays.

Eugenio Sellés (1842–1926) bridges the *alta comedia* and the drama of social reform in his first real hit, *El nudo gordiano* (performed at the Teatro Apolo on 28 November 1878, several months after the appearance of López de Ayala's *Consuelo*), which reached three printed editions before the end of the year of its debut. His progressive politics became evident in the work he did for the newspapers *La Iberia*, *La Revolución*, and *El Universal*, but it was his life in the theatre that interested him most of all. His first drama, *La torre de Talavera* (The Talavera Tower), which Sellés claimed was written when he was eighteen years old, was supported by José Echegaray for production at the Teatro Español in 1877 in time for the retirement of the noted actress Elisa Boldún. In *El nudo gordiano*, he touches on the time-worn theme of honor, placed in contemporary Madrid as a kind of homage to his "master" Echegaray, but in it he adds a shocking twist: when her honor is questioned, the main character demands a divorce. Its daring presentation and reportedly superb acting (principally by Antonio Vico in the role of Carlos, the suspicious and

---

[56] On Gaspar, see in particular Leo Kirschenbaum, *Enrique Gaspar and the Social Drama* (Berkeley: University of California Press, 1941) and Daniel Poyán Díaz, *Enrique Gaspar. Medio siglo de teatro español* (Madrid: Gredos, 1957).

vengeful husband), earned it notoriety as well as productions in Huesca, Zaragoza, Béjar, Jaén, and other provincial theatres. The "Gordian Knot" of the title is of course the marriage bond, which is severed only with difficulty and not without pain. In fact, while Sellés courageously raises the issue in a dramatic context (civil divorce had been legalized in Spain during the previous decade) he does not support it, even when domestic violence is involved (Carlos strikes his wife Julia in the face). Carlos reacts to Severo's suggestion that he "sepárate legalmente" ("get a legal separation") with immediate passion:

CARLOS.   ¡Un divorcio! ¡Un patente
                 de corso! ¡Torpe licencia
                 para que el vil, sin cerrojos
                 riesgos, viva a su anchura,
                 paseando la infame hartura
                 de su dicha a nuestros ojos!
SEVERO.   Esa es la ley ...
CARLOS.   Justas son
                 las leyes que de esto tratan
                 al robado maniatan
                 ¡y desatan al ladrón!   (II, 8)

(CARLOS: A divorce! Some permission! It's just a stupid license
                 which allows the worthless scoundrel to live however
                 he wants, parading his salacious life before our eyes!
SEVERO: It's the law ...
CARLOS: And what laws! Laws that handcuff the victim and
                 let the thief go free!)

He ends the play in a kind of "el médico de su honra" manner in which Carlos shoots his wife then "nobly" burns a letter which might exculpate him by blaming her death on suicide. He calmly goes off to jail. The play's immense popularity suggests the public's thirst for controversial subjects as well as Sellés's willingness to tackle such themes. *El Imparcial* reported that divorce was "la solución de un problema con sobrada frecuencia planteado en el hogar doméstico" ("the solution to a problem which is all too frequently seen in the home") (29 November 1878). By 1880 the play was in its fifteenth printing, the first fourteen having been sold out in less than two years.

Sellés continued his look into social issues in *Las esculturas de carne* (Statues of Flesh) (Teatro Apolo, 1 February 1883), which appeared, as Jesús Rubio Jiménez reminds us, "en pleno debate sobre el naturalismo"[57] ("right in the midst of the debate over naturalism"). Considered to be one of the first theatrical texts which focused on naturalism, *Las esculturas de carne* presents Clemente and Benigno, two rich old men

[57] Rubio Jiménez, "El teatro en el siglo XIX," p. 681.

whose self-centeredness becomes a metaphor for their class. They remain wilfully ignorant of and unconcerned with the world outside their drawing rooms, and float in a moral stupor of laziness and inertia for which they eventually pay a stiff price. They are nothing more than "esculturas de carne" with no moral fibre. Sellés molds the concept into a domestic drama which turns on the hatred engendered by the scoundrel Juan between Emilia, Clemente's daughter, and Carmen, Benigno's young second wife, a seething hatred which erupts in a tense scene in Act III (when Emilia bites Carmen we are reminded of the shocking fight between the women in Zola's *Germinal*). The melodramatic (neo-Romantic) ending underscores naturalism's idea (so skillfully exploited by Ibsen) that the sins of the fathers are visited upon the sons. The public was "sorprendida y como asustada" ("surprised and almost frightened") at the play's première, and comments on it centered on its "crudezas realistas" ("realistic crudeness") (*El Imparcial*, 2 February 1883). According to this newspaper *Las esculturas de carne* provoked the same type of intense reaction engendered by "las contiendas entre clásicos y románticos sobre los dramas de Victor Hugo" ("the battles between the classicists and the Romantics over the dramas of Victor Hugo") that is, passionate debate over the nature and role of drama in a modern society.

Sellés pushed the bounds of respectability too far for Madrid society in *Las vengadoras* (Teatro de la Comedia 10 March 1884), "objeto de grandes debates" ("subject of extensive debates") according to the *Correspondencia de España* (11 March 1884). It was booed and denounced as "naturalista y escandalosa" ("naturalist and scandalous") (*La Iberia*, 11 March 1884) because it told the story of a prostitute, Teresa, who has an affair with an aristocrat, Luis, and drives him to suicide. "Escándalo inaudito"[58] ("An unprecedented scandal") was how José Yxart described it. The theme of the gentleman and the hooker was used over and over again in French drama but never broached before on the Spanish stage. Sellés defended his rather scabrous moral lesson in the prologue he wrote to the work: "El arte realista es tan moralizador como el idealista, con una diferencia de procedimientos: Uno enseña lo que debe hacerse; otro, lo que debe evitarse"[59] ("Realist art is just as moralizing as idealist art, with a difference of approach: One teaches what ought to be done; the other, what ought to be avoided"). Yet he backed away from the play's strong realism in a second version he wrote in 1891; in this reincarnation Luis escapes to America rather than committing suicide.

More willing than Sellés or Guimerà (whose theatre Ruiz Ramón has characterized merely as "más o menos social"[60] ["more or less social"]) to

---

[58] Yxart, *El arte escénico en España*, I, p. 155.   [59] Cited by Yxart, *ibid.* p. 156.
[60] Ruiz Ramón, *Historia del teatro español (Desde sus orígenes)*, p. 359.

confront real social issues was Joaquín Dicenta (1863–1917). Theatre had been moving away from the exclusivity and high-mindedness of the *alta comedia* and neo-Romanticism for several years, becoming more comfortable with focusing on the lower classes and the working man than before. Not only the authors already mentioned, but also voices like Josep Felíu i Codina (*La Dolores*, 1892), Galdós (*La de San Quintín*, 1893) and Leopoldo Cano (*La pasionaria*, 1893), whose heroes were members of the working class, made their mark on the Spanish stage. We might even look to Ricardo de la Vega, whose enormously popular *La verbena de la paloma* (The Festival of the Dove, 1894) focused on the working class, or Clarín, whose drama *Teresa* (1895) takes place near the opening of a mine, for indications of the growing sensitivity to social issues. Félix González Llana and J. Francos Rodríguez, taking inspiration from Hauptmann's *Die Weber* (The Weavers), which was played in Barcelona in 1894, wrote about "El estado infeliz de las clases trabajadoras" ("The unhappy lot of the working classes") in *El pan del pobre* (The Poor Man's Bread, first performed at the Teatro Novedades, 14 December 1894), a kind of Romantic play in which capitalist society takes the place of an evil or uncaring God.[61] It was immediately parodied as *El pan de picos* (The Bird's Beak's Bread) by Eduardo Montesinos and Angel Vergara. However, it was Dicenta, a powerful dramatist as well as a committed champion of the downtrodden, who succeeded best in fusing theatre with social concerns; that is, Dicenta was first and foremost a man of letters who wove into his writing a well-defined social posture rather than a pamphleteer with aspirations to the stage.

Early in his career Dicenta followed the path opened by Echegaray. *El suicidio de Werther* (Werther's Suicide, 1888), *La mejor ley* (The Finest Law, 1889), and *Los irresponsables* (The Irresponsible People, 1890) drew upon neo-Romantic tropes to delve into themes such as self-worth, love between individuals of different social classes, and family relationships. In *El suicidio de Werther* Fernando, a young painter, discovers himself to be the son of a courtesan, Carlota, a discovery which convinces him that her lowly station will squash his ambition to be a successful painter. When in fact his girlfriend marries someone else, Fernando grabs a dagger and rips up the one painting that has brought him fame and perhaps immortality, "El suicidio de Werther," and in a life-imitates-art action, plunges the same dagger into his heart and dies. Ricardo and Rafael Calvo, the famous father and son team, played the main roles in this, Dicenta's first play. Later on, interspersed between the triumphs of his social trilogy,

---

[61] *El pan del pobre* provoked a lively polemic in the newspapers of Barcelona. The Count of Argüelles accused the authors of supporting anarchy, and political and ideological battles ensued. See Rubio Jiménez, *Ideología*, pp. 152–158.

Juan José (1895), *Aurora* (Dawn, 1902), and *Daniel* (1907), he produced plays which suggest the drawing-room comedies of Benavente (who was quickly becoming the dominant playwright of the new century).

Somehow, the adjective "varonil" ("manly") entered Spanish critical discourse last century as one of the highest forms of praise for a dramatist. Hartzenbusch applied it, unwisely, to the work of Gertrudis Gómez de Avellaneda, and it reappears with some frequency in newspaper reviews of male dramatists. Dicenta himself is credited with possessing "renombre de escritor varonil" ("fame as a manly writer") in the review of *Luciano* (1894) which appeared in *La Correspondencia de España* (26 February 1894), although the term is never defined and it rarely depicts with any accuracy a quality of prose. It seems to have more to do with theme and conviction than with artistic integrity or aesthetics. *Luciano* treats divorce, as had Sellés's *El nudo gordiano*, but in a much more crass way since Dicenta's depiction of the wife in this play leaves no room for sympathy for her. She is arrogant, hostile to her husband, critical of his art (he is a sculptor), mean to his mother, and vulgar. Such a creation not only justifies divorce, it demands it, so the shock value of the play is severely compromised by Dicenta's lack of balance.

Juan José reflects, directly and indirectly, an awareness of the injustices perpetrated on the lower classes by those "in charge" of society. This is not a new discovery, even in Spain, where Garrido and his supporters had actively sought to raise public consciousness in this area.[62] Yet the founding of the socialist party in 1874 and the rise of the anarchist movement in the mid-1880s did more than radical theoreticians and journalists to make the public acutely aware of the growing separation between the classes in late nineteenth-century Spain. Workers became more and more vociferous – and violent – in demanding their rights. In 1890 Dicenta clearly articulated the need for theatre to "recoger la realidad palpitante de aquellos vicios, aquellas injusticias, aquellos problemas sobrios, que agitan y corroen a las modernas sociedades y presentarlos a los ojos del público solicitando, con el poderoso lenguaje del arte, resolución y su remedio"[63] ("reform those vices, injustices, serious problems that affect and rot modern societies, and put them before the public,

---

62 Rubio Jiménez reminds us: "Se ha mitificado la significación de *Juan José*, olvidando lo propicio del ambiente en que se estrenó y que, lejos de iniciar, como tantas veces se ha dicho, el *drama social*, no hace sino continuar la tradición de melodramas sociales a lo que ya he aludido." "El teatro en el siglo XIX," p. 686. In fact, Jaime Mas Ferrer overstates the case when he claims that Dicenta and *Juan José* "inauguraban en la historia de nuestro teatro lo que después se llamaría 'drama social'." *Vida, teatro y mito de Joaquín Dicenta* (Alicante: Instituto de Estudios Alicantinos, 1978): 109.

63 "La verja cerrada," *El Resumen* (24 June 1890), cited in Rubio Jiménez, "El teatro en el siglo XIX," p. 686.

asking, in the powerful language of art, for resolution and remedy"). This is precisely what he attempts to do in *Juan José*: find "resolución y su remedio" to several pressing problems identified by him and his socialist/ republican friends as sources of conflict in modern Spain. It is an angry play. Dicenta lived his dramas, that is, his world was that of the Bohemian lower classes. The same concerns echoed in the realist and naturalist novels of the last third of the century – the crisis of the petit bourgeoisie and the working class, the life of the artist, marital problems, the stabilization of the economy, crime, doubts about Christianity, rejection of class differences – all appeared in his plays with growing intensity. "He detests the bourgeoisie for their exploitation of the worker, but even more for their self-righteous condemnation of those who sin through weakness," as H. B. Hall has written.[64] Juan José, the simple man who merely struggles to work and make a living, finds himself in conflict with a society which deprives him of those basic needs. As a child – "huérfano" ("an orphan") like so many of his Romantic predecessors – he was forced to beg, something which he refuses to do as an adult. For him, work is a right, not an "alm" granted by those in power:

¿Qué me miras? ... Ya puedes suponértelo; no hay trabajo; no lo encuentro en ninguna parte, ¡en ninguna! ... ¿De qué sirve tener buena *voluntá* y buenos brazos y saber su oficio ... ¿De qué? ... ¡Ni que el trabajo fuese una limosna *pa* que a uno se lo nieguen! ... Pues qué, ¿no hay más que condenar a un hombre a morirse de hambre o a pedir por Dios? ... ¿Hay en esto justicia? ... Y si no la hay, ¿por qué sucede? ¡Luego dicen que si los hombres matan y roban! ... ¡Qué van a hacer! (II, 6)

(What are you looking at? You can guess what my problem is; there is no work, I can't find a job anywhere, anywhere! ... What good is it to have the *desire* to work and good strong arms and a skill? ... What good is it? ... It's not as though work is a favour that can be denied a person! ... So, are the only choices that a man either die of hunger or become a beggar? ... Is that fair? ... And if it isn't, why does this happen? Then they complain when men kill and steal! ... What else can they do?)

Juan José so captured the public's attention following its debut at the Teatro de la Comedia on 25 October 1895, that it quickly became a kind of socialist *Don Juan Tenorio* which, instead of being shown on All Soul's Day, was performed on 1 May each year in honor of International Workers' Day as a symbol of social protest. Numerous local politicians tried (sometimes successfully) to have it banned, and the Church vigorously protested the fact that Juan José and Rosa lived together without the benefit of marriage, but such injunctions could not stop it from being performed. Azorín, indignant that María Guerrero was taking "modern"

---

[64] "Joaquín Dicenta and the Drama of Social Criticism," *Hispanic Review* 20 (1952): 46.

plays like Echegaray's *Mariana* to the audiences in Paris, suggested that she take *Juan José* instead: "Si hay algo nuevo y vigoroso en nuestra dramaturgia, ciertamente no es *Mariana*, ni *El estigma*; es *Juan José*, aplaudido por todos los públicos de España, ensalzado por la crítica, postergado por la Academia" ("If there is something new and lively in our playwriting, it certainly is not *Mariana* nor *El estigma*; it is *Juan José*, applauded by everyone in Spain, praised by the critics, ignored by the Academy") (*El Progreso*, 15 February 1898). After Zorrilla's play it was the most frequently performed play in the Spanish repertory between 1895 and 1939 (some 100,000 performances have been documented by the Sociedad de Autores de Madrid[65]).

Dicenta reveals his ideological position early in the play, which opens on a tavern scene in which Perico reads haltingly from the newspaper the following declaration: "No es posible soportar en silencio la conducta de un gobierno que así viola los sacratísimos derechos del ciudadano. Hora es ya de que el noble pueblo español proteste de tan inicuos atentados y salga a la defensa de la libertad y de la patria escarnecidas por los secuaces de la reacción" ("It is impossible to accept in silence the conduct of a government that violates in this way the sacred rights of its citizens. It is time for the noble Spanish people to protest such wicked deeds and to come out in defense of freedom and the nation which have been mocked by the followers of the reactionary right") (I, 1). Dicenta's dramatic conflict posits the "señorito burgués" ("middle-class master") Paco against the downtrodden bricklayer Juan José for "ownership" of Rosa, Juan José's girlfriend. It is class war in microcosm, played out against the petty tyrannies of economic inequality and desperation, and cemented together by a Romantic love story of sacrifice and passion. The author arrives at a "solution" previously unmentioned by dramatists: whereas the heroes of previous plays simply bemoan their inferior status and complain, however bitterly and articulately, about social injustice, Juan José, when blocked from getting the food he needs to feed himself and Rosa, resorts not to begging (as had the "noble" family in Ortiz de Pinedo's *Los pobres de Madrid*, to cite just one example) but to outright theft. He simply steals what he needs, forcing those around him to reject charity for real social justice. The revolutionary nature of the play was not lost on contemporary critics, whose descriptions of the playwright as a "revolucionario" filled the pages of the newspapers. C. Fernández Shaw, in the pages of *La Epoca*, praised the "tendencia revolucionaria que desde el principio al fin de la obra la anima por completo" ("revolutionary bent which completely dominates the play from beginning to end") (30

65 See Mas Ferrer, *Vida, teatro y mito*, p. 138.

October 1895). Even the young socialists of the Generation of 1898 saw clearly the implications of Dicenta's play. For Unamuno,

El drama del señor Dicenta es bueno artísticamente por revelar la esencia de la vida social de hoy en uno de sus aspectos; por ser resplandor de la verdad, por revelarnos la bondad significativa de un mundo. No es bueno por tener tesis socialista, sino que tiene tesis socialista por ser bueno.[66]

(Mr. Dicenta's play is good artistically because it uncovers the essence of social life today, because it shines with truth, because it reveals to us a world's expressive goodness. It is not a good play because it has a socialist thesis, but rather it has a socialist thesis because it is a good play.)

José Martínez Ruíz, "Azorín," also discerned clearly the author's revolutionary message: "*Juan José* es un drama atrevido, audaz, bárbaro ... Hay en la obra la energía de un filósofo, el empuje de un revolucionario ... Sí, *Juan José* no es drama, *Juan José* es el drama de nuestros días. Es la encarnación, el símbolo de esta sociedad *fin de siglo*, que se apresta a una lucha terrible"[67] ("*Juan José* is a daring, bold, fierce play ... There is in it the energy of a philosopher and the impulse of a revolutionary ... Yes, *Juan José* is not a drama, *Juan José* is *the* drama of our times. It is the embodiment, the symbol of this *end-of-century* society, ready for a terrible struggle"). Later critics have missed the point of Dicenta's revolutionary stance (Ruiz Ramón writes it off as a "drama de pasiones individuales"[68] ["drama of individual passions"] while Rubio Jiménez claims that "la dimensión de crítica social de la obra es simplista y maniquea"[69] ("the social criticism of the play is simplistic and Manichean").

In these ways Dicenta advanced the theatrical idiom on to new planes, places where many critics, to be sure, did not want to be. Zamacois complained from Paris, while comparing Dicenta's play with Mirbeau's *Les mauvais bergers*, "La ola socialista crece," recognizing at least how he has "expresado la creciente inquietud de esta sociedad desquiciada que busca a tientas nuevos cimientos para el edificio político del porvenir, y respondiendo a las necesidades de la época en que vive"[70] ("The socialist wave is growing ... [he has] expressed the growing unease of this confused society which searches randomly for new foundations on which to construct the political buildings of the future, and which responds to the needs of the times in which they live"). Dicenta forced at least a segment of his society to wake up to the social realities which, for him and many others, created untenable inequalities. In the pages of *La Epoca* (30

---

[66] Miguel de Unamuno, "Juan José," *La Lucha de Clases* (7 December 1895).
[67] José Martínez Ruíz, "Crónica," *El Progreso* (15 February 1898).
[68] Ruiz Ramón, *Historia del teatro español (Desde sus orígenes)*, p. 363.
[69] Rubio Jiménez, "El teatro español en el siglo XIX," p. 686.
[70] Eduardo Zamacois, "El socialismo en el teatro," *España Artística* 55 (1 February 1898).

October 1895) he was hailed as a dramatist for "la nueva generación" ("the new generation") a man capable of "pensando alto, sintiendo hondo y hablando claro" ("thinking deeply, feeling passionately, and speaking clearly"). As González Llana had insisted, "el arte debe siempre inspirarse en *las agitaciones* del medio en el cual vive"[71] ("art should always find inspiration in *the disturbances* of its surroundings"). The theatre, in its eternal dual role as mirror and pulpit, enabled Dicenta to enter into the debate and encourage his public to do the same.[72]

It might surprise us to see the name of Leopoldo Alas ("Clarín") among the list of socialist dramatists, but he felt deeply the connection between theatre and society. His play *Teresa* (1895) created such a scandal that it lasted for just two days in Madrid following its debut on 20 March at the recently renovated Teatro Español, and only one day in Barcelona, where, following its showing on 15 July, the public judged it to be "cruda, repugnante y de malísimo efecto" ("crude, revolting, and producing an awful effect") because of its "manifiestas tendencias socialistas"[73] ("obvious socialist tendencies"). García Pavón claims for it status as the first Spanish socialist play because of Alas's incorporation of the lower classes as the play's real protagonist.[74] Alas himself wrote that for the first twenty years of his life he thought he would be an actor or a dramatist, and he claimed to have written more than forty plays, which he often acted out loud in the privacy of his study.[75] His dedication to theatre criticism is well known.[76] The poor reception in Madrid (with Galdós,

---

71 González Llana and Francos Rodríguez, *El pan del pobre* (México: Tip. 'El Fénix' Aguila, 1896): 1. Emphasis added.

72 Maryellen Bieder has pointed out Dicenta's unconventional views on marriage and women, as well, noting how "the transformation of Spanish drama in the last decade of the century carried with it the reshaping of the female role and the emergence of the modern woman on the Spanish stage." "The Modern Woman," p. 25.

73 *Almanaque del Diario de Barcelona para 1895* (Barcelona, 1986): 84, cited by Lily Litvak, "Naturalismo y teatro social," p. 286.

74 Francisco García Pavón, "Clarín y su teatro social," in *Textos y escenarios* (Barcelona: Plaza y Janés, 1971): 63–66. By the same author, "Inicios del teatro social en España (1895)," in a collection of essays, *El teatro y su crítica* (Málaga: Instituto de Cultura de la Diputación Provincial, 1975): 203–207. A more balanced view is provided by J. Carlos Mainer, "Notas sobre la lectura obrera en España (1890–1930)," in his *Literatura popular y proletaria* (Universidad de Sevilla, 1986): 53–123.

75 Si supiera usted que *acaso* esa era mi *verdadera vocación*. En mi vida he representado en teatros caseros ni públicos después de los doce o catorce años, pero a los diez años decían cuantos me veían *representar* que yo era una maravilla, y por lo que recuerdo, y lo que más tarde he hecho a mis solas (sobre todo cuando escribía dramas – más de 40, todos perdidos – y me los declamaba a mí mismo), tenía sin duda gran disposición y un poder de apasionarme y exponer la pasión figurada con gran energía y verdad ... Actor y autor de dramas, esto creí que iba a ser de fijo hasta los dieciocho o veinte años. Cited by Rubio Jiménez, *Ideología*, p. 158.

76 See the amusing satirical poems he wrote against Pina y Domínguez, Echegaray, Pérez Escrich, and other dramatists in 1876. Valis, "Dos poesías," pp. 195–205. Clarín got very

Menéndez Pelayo, Palacio Valdés, and other dignitaries in the audience) wounded Clarín: "¿No había en mis veinte años de literatura nada que respetar? ¿No había en *Teresa* nada que aplaudir?" ("Wasn't there anything in my twenty-year literary career deserving of respect? Wasn't there anything in *Teresa* to applaud?") he asked.[77] He always called it "Mi Teresa."[78]

Teresa is a one-act work of concentrated power. Clarín had been encouraged to return to the theatre by his friends Galdós and Echegaray (Echegaray read the manuscript version of the play and proclaimed it "hermosísimo" ["very beautiful"]) as well as by the distinguished actress María Guerrero, who eventually played the title role. The play's socialist intentions were hardly hidden by the author, whose main character – in spite of the brutality, hunger and humiliation which she suffers at the hands of her lover Roque – sides with the "pueblo" (Roque) against the corruption of the upper middle class (represented by the "señorito" Fernando). Fernando "studies" the poor, as though they were archeological artifacts or botanical specimens, a distant curiosity. Teresa and Roque reject his patronizing posture. Roque states, "Los míos son mis compañeros; los explotados, los miserables ... El obrero no quiere limosa" ("My friends are my companions; people who are exploited, miserable ... The working man does not want charity") (I, 3), and at the play's end (I, 11) Teresa mixes her blood not with that of Fernando but with the "people," Roque.

Comic flight: ridicule and parody

Not all dramatists confronted social inequity or political chicanery with the same serious approach as the neo-Romantics or the socialist dramatists. One of the predominant modes of theatrical discourse in the second half of the nineteenth century in Spain was the short satirical playlet – referred to as a whole as the "género chico" – called, as we have seen, by a bewildering array of generic names, including "humorada," "juguete," "juguete cómico," "sainete," "apropósito," "bufonada cómica,"

interested in theatre criticism and developed a plan to publish commentary in *Faro Moderno* in Barcelona; he did produce two articles for this newspaper. Adolfo Sotelo, "Clarín y la crítica de teatros (dos artículos desconocidos en *Faro Moderno*, 1899)," *Segismundo* 20 (1986): 223–256.

[77] Clarín, "Palique. Correspondencia particular," *Madrid Cómico* (13 April 1895); reproduced by Sotelo, "Clarín y la crítica de teatros," p. 242. See Leonardo Romero Tobar's introduction of the play for an examination of the play's reception. Leopoldo Alas, *Teresa. Avecilla. El hombre de los estrenos*, ed. Romero Tobar (Madrid: Castalia, 1975): 41–54.

[78] Roberto Sánchez, "Clarín, su *Teresa* y los cómicos," *Hispanic Review* 55 (1987): 463.

"disparate," and the like.[79] Short plays developed into a wildly popular (and wildly remunerative) phenomenon known as the "teatro por horas" which Nancy Membrez has studied with exhaustive patience and valuable results.[80] She claims for them the "complete domination of the Madrid theatre scene" by the end of the century, adding further that they form the "common denominator of virtually all theatre activity from 1867 to 1922."[81] Juan García López, like many of his fellow commentators, got it all wrong when he dismissed these short plays as having "escasa trascendencia literaria"[82] ("scant literary value") for, as we shall see, they were indeed central to the theatrical enterprise of the second half of the century.

It would be unrealistic here to attempt a complete study of this rich vein of theatre in nineteenth-century Spain, so we shall focus instead on a few representative moments, some of which reach back to the first half of the century for their inspiration.[83] We shall also take a look at longer parodies and satires, which often formed a tightly woven dialogue of theatrical discourse throughout the century.

For example, we have seen how Zorrilla's *Don Juan Tenorio* created an entire sub-genre of plays written exclusively to make fun of it. The submerging and mixing of codes became frequent on Spanish stages in the latter half of the century and produced a constant give-and-take of literature which enriched the theatre immeasurably. It is not surprising that Juan de Grimaldi's immensely popular *comedia de magia, La pata de cabra*, became the target of a musical satire entitled *Don Simplicio Bobadilla Majaderano y Cabeza de Buey*, the name of Grimaldi's macarronic main character. Perhaps the success of Vega's *Jugar con fuego* led Tamayo to try his hand at composing a *zarzuela*, but his effort was not well received at its debut on 7 May 1853 (the same year as his serious tragedy *Virginia*). One newspaper reviewer thought it "disparatada" ("foolish") (*El Mensajero*, 8 May 1853) while another called it "un conjunto de despropósitos" ("a collection of nonsense") (*Clamor del Público*, 10 May 1853).[84] Indeed, it was: Tamayo got lost in a series of magical tricks which had little

---

[79] Luciano García Lorenzo, "La denominación de los géneros teatrales en España durante el siglo XIX y el primer tercio del siglo XX," *Segismundo* 5–6 (1967): 191–199. According to García Lorenzo's listing, 234 works were called "sainetes," 304 were called "juguete" or "juguete cómico," and dozens more were called by other names. See also Schinasi, "The Anarchy of Theatrical Genres."

[80] Membrez, "The 'teatro por horas'."   [81] *Ibid.* p. 3.

[82] Juan García López, *Historia de la literatura española*, 14th. edn. (Barcelona: Editorial Vicens-Vives, 1969): 483; cited by Membrez, p. 4.

[83] Membrez provides an excellent, if still incomplete, listing of parodies since the early 1700s. "The 'teatro por horas'," pp. 899–938. See also Alonso Zamora Vicente, "Literatura paródica," in his *La realidad esperpéntica* (Madrid: Gredos, 1969): 25–53.

[84] Both cited by Pilar Quel Barastegui, "*Don Simplicio Bobadilla* de Manuel Tamayo y Baus, o la segunda parte de *La pata de cabra*," in *Teatro di magia*, ed. Ermanno Caldera (Rome: Bulzoni, 1991): 35–36.

to do with the play's structure or argument, but the play lasted through a series of performances thanks mostly to the attractive new sets and the music composed by four musicians: Francisco Asenjo Barbieri, José Inzenga, Hernando Pecha, and Joaquín Gaztambide. Still, Tamayo wove Grimaldi's text into his own "continuation," building on the original and on the audience's intimate knowledge of it. He even includes direct textual references to *La pata de cabra* (at one point Tamayo writes, "Sale del mismo modo y con el mismo traje que en *La pata de cabra* ["He comes out the same way and dressed the same as in *La pata de cabra*"][II, 4]), leading Quel Barastegui correctly to conclude, "Tamayo no sólo aprovechó el tema de *Todo lo vence amor*, sino que además, de forma consciente, repitió en algunos puntos detalles, expresiones, efectos escénicos"[85] ("Tamayo not only took over the plot of *Todo lo vence amor*, but he also consciously repeated some of its details, expressions and scenic effects"). Grimaldi's play was performed in Madrid the day after the debut of Tamayo's *zarzuela*. Bobadilla makes another appearance in a "juguete cómico" some years later, but in name only. *El señor de Bobadilla* (Mr. Bobadilla), by Juan Redondo y Menduiña, was performed at the Teatro de Varie-dades on 13 February 1886. Redondo had achieved some small fame as the author of comic one-acters (*El gabán de Ruperto* [Rupert's Overcoat, 1878]; *La copa de la amargura* [The Cup of Bitterness, 1882]; *Los bolistas* [The Billiard Players, 1883]; *La pantalla* [The Screen, 1885]; and others), most of them performed in the theatres in Madrid in the late 1870s and 1880s. This farce is a domestic comedy of confused identities in which don Homobono Bobadilla is mistaken for a baker, a tailor, a doctor, and a clergyman; it is only the title, which appeals vaguely to the audience's memory of Grimaldi's main character, which refers in a general way to the earlier play.

The rise in the popularity of foreign operas in Madrid in the 1820s and 1830s gave rise to a parallel phenomenon in the 1830s and 1840s: the comic *zarzuela* inspired by such works as *Lucrecia Borgia*, *Lucía de Lammermoor*, *El pirata*, and *La Straniera*. One of the most active paro-dists of opera was the actor-turned-stage-director-turned-parodist Agustín Azcona.[86] Romantic dramas were similarly a facile target for satire and parody. Their exaggerated emotionalism and melodramatic plot twists left them open to the satirist's pen. We have seen how early on Bretón spoofed the style of Romantic plays (*Muérete ¡y verás!*, 1837) and how García Gutiérrez produced a self-parody of *El trovador* in *Los hijos de la tía Tronera* (1846). Others followed at mid-century: *Los amantes de Chinchón* (Juan Martínez Villergas and others, 1848), *Los novios de Teruel*

---

[85] *Ibid.* p. 44.   [86] See Crespo Matellán, *La parodia dramática*.

(Eusebio Blasco, 1867), *El amor de un boticario* (The Pharmacist's Love, Angel María Segovia, 1872), and *Isabel y Marcilla* (Angel María Segovia, 1887) all spoofed Hartzenbusch's *Los amantes de Teruel*; *Matías* (Ramón Franquelo y Martínez, 1863) parodied Larra's *Macías*; *El cantador* (Federic Soler and Conrado Roure, 1864) was a catalán parody of García Gutiérrez and Verdi. García Gutiérrez's *Venganza catalana* (1864) inspired four parodies within months of its debut: *La venganza de Catana* (Juan de Alba), *La venganza de la Tana* (Federic Soler), *La venganza de un gitano* (A Gypsy's Revenge, Francisco de Paula Sinquemani), and *Venganza murciana* (Murcian Vengeance, Manuel Juan Diana).

Political spoofs and satires also became staples in theatres – whenever the authors could get them past the censors. The case of the *Revista de 1864 y 1865* is instructive in what it reveals about the nervousness of authorities when it came to putting on plays with obvious political allusions. *Revista* was a comic *zarzuela* written by José María Gutiérrez de Alba which passed the censors and was performed up to twenty-nine times at the Teatro del Circo ("ruidoso éxito que ha sacado al público de sus casillas" ["a noisy success that has forced the people out of their houses"] *La Iberia*, 5 February 1865). Yet all of a sudden, when a move was planned to the Teatro Jovellanos, the Civil Governor of Madrid banned it, leading Gutiérrez to issue strenuous protests to the Ministro de la Gobernación.[87] Someone, unknown to the author, had gone around "infiriendo considerables prejuicios a tercera persona" ("suggesting that the play would do considerable damage to a third party") and got the play banned. Worse yet, the provincial impresarios, who had planned to run it in their theatres, also got cold feet and began to inundate the central offices of Gobernación with telegrams requesting clarification on its permissibility ("¿Puede representarse en este teatro la zarzuela *Revista de 1864 y 1865*?" ["Can the zarzuela *Revista de 1864 y 1865* be put on in this theatre?"] asks the governor of Zamora). Gutiérrez was angry, but got nowhere, and the play disappeared from the boards.

One of the most vitriolic and active of the political satirists was Eduardo Navarro Gonzalvo (1846–1902), whose angry and pointed attack on the new king Amadeo of Savoy was brutally disrupted when first performed at the Teatro Calderón in December, 1870. *Macarronini I* – "el estreno más sensacional y emocionando de aquella época"[88] ("the most sensational and emotion-filled debut of that time") – so irritated the right-wing supporters of a group called the "Partida de la Porra" ("The Bludgeon Party"), that they swooped into the theatre with clubs and knives, cut up the scenery and the curtains, and wounded some of the

[87] Archivo Histórico Nacional: Consejos: 11.391, n. 11.
[88] Flores García, *Memorias íntimas*, p. 55.

spectators. The incident caused a real political scandal, commented on in the newspapers for days.[89] The ex-representative Fermín Gonzalo Morón published a widely circulated pamphlet called *El pueblo, el Gobierno y la Partida de la Porra* (The People, the Government, and the Bludgeon Party) in which he condemned not only the attack itself but the city authorities for refusing to take adequate measures against the perpetrators (the play had been approved, after all, by Martos, the interim governor of Madrid); sections of the pamphlet were read in Parliament. The printed version of the play did frighten the authorities, who saw to it that the printed edition, which the author had paid for himself, was confiscated.[90]

Navarro wrote several hundred political *revistas* in the last thirty years of the century (he staged one every other month in 1874 alone), but none reached the popularity of *Los bandos de Villafrita* (The Proclamations of Friedville), which became the first Spanish play to be performed 300 consecutive times (!) following its opening in Madrid in 1884.[91] It was another work destined to offend the authorities, specifically the Conservative Civil Governor of Madrid, Raimundo Fernández Villaverde (whose name is parodied in this title and several others – "Villa-anémica," "Villaplácida" ["Anemicville," "Placidville"] – written by Navarro in subsequent years). Navarro's satires had a serious purpose: as Nancy Membrez tells us, his tactic was "to persuade and educate the masses to the election fraud of the *turno pacífico* [and to mold] the opinions of a generation of Spaniards,"[92] a goal at which he succeeded admirably.

Sellés's *El nudo gordiano* (1878) was parodied as *El nudo corredizo* (The Easily Untied Knot, Enrique González Bedma, 1878) and *El nudo morrocotudo* (The Strong Knot, Luis Cuenca, 1878), and Lopez de Ayala's *Consuelo* (1878) became the hilarious *Consuelo ... de tontos* at the hands of Salvador María Granés. After the early Romantic dramas, the most frequently parodied works in the nineteenth century were the neo-Romantic dramas of Echegaray and his school. *O locura o santidad* became *Música celestial* (Heavenly Music, Ricardo de la Vega, 1877), while *La muerte en los labios* (Death on the Lips) was pilloried as *Con la miel en los labios* (With Honey on Her Lips, Enrique Sánchez Seña, 1880). *El gran galeoto* received its spoofing as *Galeotito* (Francisco Flores

---

[89] A hair-raising account of the attack was printed in *La Igualdad* and reprinted in *El Pensamiento Español* (1 December 1870).

[90] Nancy Membrez, "Eduardo Navarro Gonzalvo and the *revista política*," *Letras Peninsulares* 1.3 (1988): 322.

[91] Statistic provided by García Valero, *Crónicas retrospectivas*, p. 47.

[92] Membrez, "Eduardo Navarro Gonzalvo," p. 326. The *turno pacífico* was the phrase used to describe the peaceful alternating of governments between the liberals and the conservatives.

García, 1881),[93] while *Mancha que limpia* got a triple dose of parody in *Mancha, limpia* ... *y da esplendor* (Gabriel Merino, 1895), *Mancha que mancha* (A Stain that Stains, Pedro Gómez Candela, 1895), and *Mancho, piso y quemo* (I Stain, I Trample and I Burn, Castillo, 1895). *La adelfa* (The Oleander, Francisco Pérez Collantes, 1884) and *La sanguinaria* (The Blood-wort, Salvador María Granés, 1884) were take-offs of Leopoldo Cano's *La pasionaria* (1883). Even the masters of serious social drama, Dicenta and Galdós, received their share of mockery: *La de San Quintín* (1894) inspired Granés's *La de don sin don* (The Woman With the Knack for Having no Knack), Felipe Pérez y González's *La de vámonos* (The Woman from Let's Get Out of Here), and Gabriel Merino's *La del capotín*; *Electra* (1901) generated *¡Alerta!* (Vigilant!, Rafael Muñoz Esteban, 1901), *La Electra galdosa* (Jaime Molgosa Valls, 1901), and *Electroterapia* (1901), while *Juan José* (1895) turned into *Pepito* (Celso Lucio, 1895). Ricardo de la Vega's immensely popular *zarzuela*, *La verbena de la paloma* (1894) received at least two parodic treatments: *Los gelos de la Coloma* (Miss Coloma's Jealousies, Angel Guasch y Tombas, 1894) and *La romería del halcón* (The Excursion of the Falcon, Enrique López Marín and others, 1894). There are dozens more examples worth studying, but we shall focus briefly on just two representative examples from the second half of the century.

Galdós and the new aesthetic

Benito Pérez Galdós (1847–1920), the greatest novelist of nineteenth-century Spain, began and ended his writing career as a dramatist. *Quien mal hace, bien no espere* (Whoever Does Wrong Should Expect Nothing Good,1861), *El hombre fuerte* (The Strongman, 1863–1865), *La expulsión de los moriscos* (The Expulsion of the Moors, 1865) and *Un joven de provecho* (A Useful Kid, 1867) were all written before the publication of his first novel, *La Fontana de Oro* (The Golden Fountain) in 1870. He was as concerned with theatre throughout his long writing career as he was with novels. As early as 1865 he had complained that "la crítica dramática está en un estado deplorable: redúcese a una disertación de gacetilla, sin más criterio que el que da cuatro o cinco noches de asistencia al teatro"[94] ("dramatic criticism is in a deplorable state: it is reduced to being a few lines in the newspaper written by someone whose only credential is that he's gone to the theatre four or five nights in a row"), a situation he rectified as soon as he got the opportunity. Under his guidance, *La*

---

[93] See Alberto Castilla, "Una parodia de *El gran Galeoto*," *Hispanófila* 26 (1983): 33–40.
[94] *Revista de Movimiento Intelectual de Europa* (1865), cited by Leo Hoar, *Benito Pérez Galdós y la Revista del Movimiento Intelectual de Europa* (Madrid: Insula, 1968): 108.

Revista de España initiated a serious section of theatre criticism – the "Crítica estadística teatral" – as early as 1872, which was published regularly for the duration of the journal's history.[95] As he himself wrote in *Memorias de un desmemoriado* (Memoirs of a Forgetful Man):

Mi vocación literaria se iniciaba con el prurito dramático . . . . Invertía parte de las noches en emborronar dramas y comedias . . . . Respirando la densa atmósfera revolucionaria de aquellos turbados tiempos, creía yo que mis ensayos dramáticos traerían otra revolución más honda en la esfera literaria.[96]

(My literary vocation began with a strong dramatic itching . . . I spent part of my evenings scribbling dramas and comedies . . . Breathing in the dense revolutionary atmosphere of those turbulent times, I thought that my dramatic pieces would bring on another, deeper revolution in literary circles.)

His plays were frequently original, often polemical, and in general received with alternate doses of praise and scorn, and his reputation as a dramatist declined in inverse proportion to his well-deserved fame as a first-rate novelist. Even though he was considered to be one of the best and most serious Spanish dramatists of his day, it was not until the 1970s and 1980s that serious attention to his dramas began to rise again. Not only did he write more than two dozen plays, but he wrote vast quantities of theatre criticism, and his novels themselves often reveal his interest in the life of the stage.

Galdós's theatre rejected the emotionalistic Romanticism of Echegaray and his followers as inappropriate to contemporary middle-class concerns, although his own library contained more works of Echegaray than any other contemporary playwright.[97] His characters tend to talk and think, react and contemplate, plan and absorb ideas rather than scream and shout, faint and gesture. In this regard he is more in tune with the new wave of European dramatists – Ibsen, Chekov, Hauptmann, Maeterlinck – making a mark in Spain at the end of the century than he is with the great Spanish playwrights of his own century.[98] Still, he knew his own country's theatrical tradition and drew on it. He took on the *alta comedia* as the grounding for his plays, but attached to it a personal and socio-

---

[95] See Margaret A. Ballantyne, "Indice de la *Revista de España* bajo la dirección de Galdós," *Hispania* 73 (May, 1990): 332–344.

[96] Benito Pérez Galdós, *Memorias de un desmemoriado*, in *Obras completas*, ed. Federico Carlos Sainz de Robles (Madrid: Aguilar, 1975): 1430–1431. Cited by Menéndez Onrubia, *Introducción al teatro de Galdós* (Madrid: CSIC, 1983): 50.

[97] Chanon Berkowitz, *La biblioteca de Benito Pérez Galdós* (Las Palmas: El Museo Canario, 1951): 157 ff.

[98] "Maeterlinck acabó convirtiéndose en el autor más representativo del teatro simbolista. La recepción que se hizo de sus obras en España, por ello, es la mejor prueba del interés y reacciones que suscitó el simbolismo en su vertiente teatral." Rubio Jiménez, *Ideología*, p. 43.

logical element not present in the works of López de Ayala, Tamayo y Baús, Serra, Larra, or the others. As Stanley Finkenthal has noted, if Romantic dramas demand a symbolic reading, Galdós's dramas demand a sociological, ideological, and historical reading; that is, Galdós never abandoned ideas for technique, content for form.[99] Early in his career, writing against *Rabagas*, a play by Sardou, Galdós condemned the work's content, privileging politics over aesthetics:

> Es imposible negar que la obra está escrita con ingenio y enérgico sarcasmo; pero es profundamente escéptica, y de ella se deduce que no hay más forma de gobierno que el absolutismo. Esta teoría, ya bastante desacreditada en las regiones de aquende el telón, lo está también bastante en el escenario, y por este error sin duda *Rabagas* no es otra cosa que una mala comedia.[100]

> (It is impossible to deny that the play is written with wit and sarcastic energy; but it is profoundly skeptical, and from that one can deduce that there is no form of government other than absolutism. This theory, now sufficiently discredited in the world beyond the theatre curtain, is also discredited within the theatre, and because of this mistake *Rabagas* is really nothing except a bad comedy.)

Galdós goes after large social issues in his plays rather than individual concerns. His themes tend toward the conception of Reality, the search for Truth, deep-rooted corruption, the regeneration of Spain, the failure of religious education, the power of the clergy, or the problems of *caciquismo* (a type of political leadership) rather than the evils of gossip, petty jealousies, moral corruption, or ambition (the thematic mainstays of the *alta comedia*). It is almost as though he fused the *alta comedia* with socialist or realist theatre to create something new and unsettling. Several of his best plays – *Electra* (1901), *Mariucha* (1903) and *Casandra* (1905), for example – prove his unquestionable commitment to social reform and even suggest an attachment to the type of play written by Cámara, Garrido, and Dicenta. As Menéndez Onrubia reminds us, Galdós was "un escritor eminentemente político" ("an eminently political writer") and these plays were written during his "etapa de suave anarquismo"[101] ("mildly anarchistic period").

One of the most articulate early defenses of Galdós as a dramatist was published in 1970 by Gonzalo Sobejano, who analyzed Galdós's theatre within a continuum which led from "novela narrada" ("narrated novel") to "novela hablada" ("spoken novel") to drama.[102] Sobejano divides

---

99 See Stanley Finkenthal, *El teatro de Galdós* (Madrid: Fundamentos, 1980).
100 Galdós, "Crónica de la quincena," *La Ilustración de Madrid* (15 March 1872); cited by Finkenthal, *El teatro*, p. 29.
101 Carmen Menéndez Onrubia, *Introducción al teatro de Galdós* (Madrid: CSIC, 1983): 29, 77.
102 Gonzalo Sobejano, "Razón y suceso de la dramática galdosiana," *Anales Galdosianos* 5 (1970): 39–54. The whole issue of the relationship between novel and drama is an

Galdós's theatre into two broad types, "dramas de la separación" ("plays of separation") and "dramas de la conciliación" ("plays of reconciliation") which encompass four broad thematic concerns: the will to resist false honor, deceit, and hypocrisy; freedom from fanatism; power; and charity. These are placed within a broad definition which combines realism, naturalism, social drama, and contemporary drama into what he perceptively labels "transcendental realism" (following Eduardo Gómez de Baquero's 1905 term, "dramática trascendente").

Suelen los críticos definir la dramática galdosiana con títulos como "realismo," "naturalismo," "drama social" o "drama contemporáneo." De poner un título, el más adecuado sería "realismo trascendental." Es una dramática realista porque, salvo algún caso, los sucesos y personajes que ofrece pertenecen virtualmente a la sociedad española conocida por el autor ... Pero este realismo es siempre trascendental: está animado y dirigido por una intención de trascender del tablado a la vida social. El teatro de Galdós no es puro espectáculo artístico ni costumbrismo descriptivo, sino la ilustración dramática de unas ideas que, obrando en las conciencias, deben llegar a todos y levantar su nivel moral.[103]

(Critics tend to define Galdós's dramatic writing with labels such as "realism," "naturalism," "social drama" or "contemporary drama." If we have to put a label on it, a more adequate one would be "transcendental realism." It is realist playwriting because, except in a few cases, the incidents and characters that he creates belong to the society which he knew best ... But this realism is always transcendental: it is enlivened and directed by a desire to transcend the picture of social life. The theatre of Galdós is not pure artistic spectacle nor descriptive *costumbrismo* [local customs], but the dramatic illustration of ideas which, working on the public's conscience, should reach them all and elevate their moral level.)

Menéndez Onrubia adds to this mix a psychological ingredient which, for her, explains many of Galdós's dramas.

Galdós's plays are dense, intellectual, and thoughtful. "No entusiasman" ("They don't excite you") proclaims Menéndez Onrubia,[104] but they did provoke unusual comment and reaction in their day. Between his youthful attempts at playwriting from the 1860s and his real arrival as a dramatist in the 1890s lies a world of success as a narrator. When he turned back to the theatre it was to produce *Realidad* in 1892, a deconstruction of the reality/illusion theme that had been a constant in Spanish theatre since the time of Calderón. Galdós's five-act drama was performed at the Teatro de la Comedia on 15 March, remaining there for

interesting one which becomes particularly polemicized during the last twenty years of the century. See Rubio Jiménez, *Ideología*, pp. 75 ff., and Roberto G. Sánchez, "Clarín y el romanticismo teatral: examen de una afición," *Hispanic Review* 31 (1963): 216–228, among others.

[103] Sobejano, "Razón y suceso," p. 46.   [104] Menéndez Onrubia, *Introducción*, p. 22.

twenty-two consecutive nights. The Comedia, as managed by actor-director Emilio Mario, became the home for Spain's more experimental dramas, that is, it aspired to be "el albergue de la comedia española contemporánea"[105] ("the asylum for the contemporary Spanish comedy"). In this theatre Mario staged such works as Enrique Gaspar's *Las personas decentes* (Decent People, 1890), Echegaray's *Mariana* (1892), Josep Felíu y Codina's *La Dolores* (1892), Jacinto Benavente's *El nido ajeno* (Someone Else's Nest, 1894) and *Gente conocida* (People We Know, 1896), and Dicenta's *Juan José* (1895), as well as Galdós's *La loca de la casa* (The Madwoman of the House, 1893).

What distinguishes *Realidad* from the dozens of truth-and-honor plays which even in Galdós's own days seemed to dominate Madrid's theatres (Echegaray, who was in the audience the night of the play's première, was the major playwright of the 1880s and 1890s) is Galdós's refusal to resolve the conflict by traditional means, that is, his distaste for blood vengeance to "wash" clean a man's stained honor. The theatre-going public was trained to expect and demand action – drama! – but Galdós perceived accurately the subtle shift into a modern sensibility and created a play whose action is interior rather than exterior. The audience was used to Echegaray's high passion, but Galdós gave them instead a drama of man's marrow and soul rather than of his hormones and blood. By doing so he changed the definition of drama in the 1890s and placed, as Rubio Jiménez has put it, "en entredicho el 'ethos' de la Restauración"[106] ("the 'ethos' of the Restoration on notice"). It was a risky enterprise, and he paid for it in the criticism of spectators and reviewers who for the most part did not understand what he was trying to do. Although the immediate audience reception was enthusiastic, commentators complained about the lack of "action," particularly in Act III, about the "stilted" monologues, about the author's "inability" to free himself from narrative (the memory of the novel *Realidad* from 1889 was still fresh), and about the unsuitability of the anti-climactic last act. Some were quick to declare the play a "fracaso" ("failure") which "no tiene nada de dramático" ("has nothing dramatic about it") (*El País,* 16 March 1892).[107] They failed to discern that the conflict Galdós develops in the play is a deep psychological conflict rather than the usual superficial blood-and-guts confrontation that frequented Spanish stages. Emilio Bobadilla wrote that "en el drama

---

105 Sobejano, "Efectos de *Realidad*," p. 55.   106 Rubio Jiménez, *Ideología*, p. 96.
107 This and other critical comments, unless otherwise indicated, come from William H. Shoemaker, "La acogida pública y crítica de *Realidad* en su estreno," *Estudios Escénicos* 8 (1974): 25–40. See also Theodore A. Sackett, *Galdós y las máscaras. Historia teatral y bibliografía anotada* (Verona: Università degli Studi di Padova, 1982) and Angel Berenguer, *Los estrenos teatrales de Galdós en la crítica de su tiempo* (Comunidad de Madrid, 1988).

de Galdós no hay lucha, y, por consiguiente, no hay conflicto dramático" ("in Galdós's play there is no struggle, and, consequently, no dramatic conflict"). Melchor de Palau even declared that "no es en rigor un drama" ("it's not really a drama"). Others, notably Emilia Pardo Bazán (who attended the first night performance with the Duchess of Osuna) and Clarín, did recognize the novelty and importance of Galdós's theatrical experiment (the *Correspondencia de España* [16 March 1892] called it "el acontecimiento literario de la temporada" ["the literary happening of the season"]). The critic for *La Libertad* (16 March 1892) even recognized in Galdós's play "un drama que no cabe en los moldes antiguos y que está en pugna con la institución secular del teatro tal y como lo entendieron los que hasta ahora dieron vida a las producciones escénicas" ("a play which does not fit into the old patterns and which is in conflict with the secular institution of the theatre as it was understood by those who up until now have written for it"), but critical analysis of the play remained under-developed until the appearance of Gonzalo Sobejano's 1974 article, "Efectos de *Realidad*," in which he declares the play to be "la más valiosa de las obras dramáticas de Galdós ... Ninguna novela, ningún drama de aquel tiempo pueden considerarse superiores a estos de Galdós en exploración de la verdad psíquica, complejidad y entrecruce de conflictos personales, moralidad liberadora y atrevimiento experimental"[108] ("Galdós's best dramatic work ... No novel, no play from that time can be considered better than this play in the exploration of psychic truth, in complexity, and in the interweaving of personal conflicts, free-thinking morality, and experimental daring").

Realidad is a complex and problematic play which on the surface deals with questions of adultery, honesty, love, and family relationships but which, just under those surface themes, confronts the uneasy and shifting nature of truth and "reality" in late nineteenth-century Spain. In five acts which took some five hours to perform, Galdós investigates the ability of the human psyche to absorb double realities, to appear to be one thing while being "in reality" something else. He does more than trot out the age-worn theme of hypocrisy, so dear to the dramatists of the *alta comedia*, by allowing his characters to be self-consciously aware of their positions, to confront the dissonance created between their external actions and their internal beliefs and feelings. Each of the three protagonists – Augusta, Tomás, and Federico – must develop a moral posture consonant not with the social "qué dirán" ("what people will say") that

---

[108] Sobejano, "Efectos de *Realidad*," p. 41. Sobejano reproduces a similar comment written by Azorín in 1895: "*Realidad*, lo creo firmemente, y por eso no dudo en consignarlo ante el lector extranjero, es para mí una de las mejores obras de nuestro teatro contemporáneo. Orozco, el protagonista, es un tipo digno de Shakespeare ... ".

so preoccupied Echegaray in, for example, *El gran galeoto*, but rather with their own internal code. The trouble is, they become irreconcilable and the individuals are condemned to a tragic end. Federico Viera commits suicide in Act IV not because his adultery has been discovered and punished by the cuckolded husband Tomás Orozco but because of just the opposite: Orozco's moral strength (rigidity?) forgives him, a burden Federico cannot bear. Orozco does not hate his wife or her lover; on the contrary, he loves them, which puts on both of them a crushing weight. The "drama" is generated by their growing awareness of the disparity between what appears to be happening and what is really going on. Such awareness becomes, rather than a unifying factor in their complex relationship, a divisive one: "La verdad de cada uno le escinde en sí mismo y le separa de los otros dos"[109] ("Each man's truth divides him within himself and separates him from the other two"). These are good people brought down not by the inexorable fate of Romanticism, but by the reality of human nature. Their tragedy is unnerving because it cuts close to the bone of the spectator. The title of the play, it soon becomes clear, is sadly ironic.

Sobejano highlights three technical innovations in *Realidad*: Galdós's courage to develop his exposition slowly, building carefully toward the final tragedy; the anticlimactic fifth act; and the use of paired monologues in place of traditional dialogue. The dramatist gives space to his characters to reveal their inner selves by refusing to short-cut the dramatic process with high emotion. Each of the first three acts functions as exposition (normally, exposition is taken care of in the first act alone), in part because the play contains three protagonists instead of the usual one. Galdós lets each character unveil his or her "reality" by tracing their thoughts and deeds. The core external conflict – the whispered adultery of Orozco's wife Augusta with his friend Federico – is set out in layers, carefully, and in a language which creates subtle tensions through pauses, revelations, oblique suggestions, and silences. By the time Federico puts his hands on the pistol laid out by Manuel Infante in Act IV, the external conflict, which would have ended here had the play been written by Rivas, García Gutiérrez, Zorrilla, Sellés or Echegaray, dissolves into a brilliant Act V in which those left to pick up the pieces (Augusta, Orozco) must come to terms with their lives together and apart. It is the daring final act which confirms Galdós's desire to challenge the *status quo ante* of Spanish dramaturgy. He creates a memorable and highly charged scene between Augusta and Orozco (V, 4) without once raising his voice or those of his characters (something inconceivable in Romantic drama). The scene is

109 *Ibid.* p. 46.

unsettling, although it should not be since Augusta, at the very beginning of the play, stated clearly her rejection of the Romantic paradigm:

Pero yo, ¿qué culpa tengo de que usted se haya vuelto tonto? ... ¡Muerte, locura, suicidio! ¡Eso sí que es de mal gusto! No, el hombre de la discreción y de las buenas formas no incurrirá en tales extravagancias. (I, 3)

(But what fault is it of mine that you have gone crazy? ... Death, madness, suicide! Those things are in truly bad taste. No, the discreet and serious man will not fall into such follies.)

When Orozco embraces the "image" of Federico in the final scene – a spectral reappearance with whom Orozco needs to make amends and explain his cool reserve – the play's themes fuse together in a moment which has Romantic undertones but whose psychological reality removes it from the external emotionalism of Romantic theatre.

Tú y yo nos elevamos sobre esta miseria de las pasiones, del odio y del vano juicio del vulgo. No sé aborrecer. Me has dado la verdad: yo te doy el perdón. Abrázame. (Dirígese hacia la imagen, que se desvanece cuando Orozco le tiende los brazos.) (V, 5)

(You and I rise above these trifling passions, hatred, and the people's shallow judgment. I do not know how to hate. You have shown me the truth: I forgive you. Embrace me. [He moves toward the shadow, which disappears as Orozco opens his arms.])

Realidad, Galdós's drama of double realities, challenged its audience to accept new paradigms, ones which forced them toward a new theatrical construct, a "nuevo teatro, del teatro actual" ("a new theatre, a theatre for today") as Enrique Díez Canedo wrote in 1931 at the play's revival.[110]

Notwithstanding the decidedly mixed reception of Galdós as dramatist, more plays made their way to the boards in the next few years. *La loca de la casa*, a comedy first shown at the Teatro de la Comedia on 16 January 1893, was followed by the failed *Gerona* (3 February 1893), and then by *La de San Quintín* (27 January 1894) within a year's time. This last comedy enjoyed wide popular success, reaching more than fifty performances in Madrid alone and being "honored" with two parodies within three weeks of its debut in the capital. *La del capotín, o Con las manos en la masa* (the title plays off Galdós's dominant metaphor, the making – kneading, molding – of bread), by Gabriel Merino, pilloried Galdós's attempt to fuse the moribund Spanish aristocracy with a new socialist vision of the future. *La de vámonos*, by F. Pérez y González, mocked the couple's escape to greener pastures. In Galdós's play, the impoverished duchess marries a young socialist of ignoble birth and runs off to Western

---

[110] Cited by Sobejano, *ibid.* p. 54.

Pennsylvania with him, America being a golden land of opportunity and new beginnings for the author.

Casándose con Víctor, no sólo rechaza al rico Don César, que aspiraba a casarse con ella, sino que rechaza también Ficóbriga y todo lo que representa. América, como escenario, tiene un significado especial para Galdós ... América es el hogar del hombre hecho a sí mismo, del hombre que se hizo rico y ganó su independencia y su dignidad personal por medio del trabajo.[111]

(Having wed Victor, she not only rejects the rich don Cesar, who had hoped to marry her, but she also rejects Ficóbriga and everything it stands for. America, as a setting, holds a special meaning for Galdós ... America is the place of the self-made man, of the man who became rich by his own means and who gained his independence and his personal dignity through work.)

Galdós's don César proclaims the marriage "¡Inaudita fusión, amasijo repugnante en que veo la mano de Lucifer! ... Es un mundo que muere" ("This is an unheard of union, a repellant plot in which I see the hand of Lucifer ... It is a world that is dying") to which don José counters, "No, hijos míos: es un mundo que nace" ("No, my children: it is a world being born") (III, 7). One looks to the past; the other to the future: the author's ideological position could not have been more clearly stated. Other plays – *Los condenados* (The Condemned, 1894), *Voluntad* (Willpower, 1895), *Doña Perfecta* (1896), and *La fiera* (The Shrew, 1896) moved him toward his most polemical drama.

The public and critical reception of *Electra* (1901) astonished even those who knew Galdós to be a provocative writer. The vehemence of his attack on Spain's "blind" clergy – the "bacillus mística" ("mystical germ") as he called it in *La loca de la casa* – surprised nearly everyone and produced riots in the streets of Madrid following its première at the Teatro Español on 30 January 1901.[112] Part of the public outcry was related to the fact that the play reflected a real case currently making headlines in the country – the famous Ubao case, about which Galdós,

---

[111] Finkenthal, *El teatro*, p. 43. See also Sebastián de la Nuez, "El tema de América en el teatro de Galdós," *Homenaje a Pedro Sainz Rodríguez* II (Madrid: Fundación Universitaria Española, 1986): 461–472.

[112] Ignacio Elizalde, "Azorín y el estreno de *Electra* de Pérez Galdós," *Letras de Deusto* 3 (1973): 67–79; Elena Catena, "Circunstancias temporales de la *Electra* de Galdós," *Estudios Escénicos* 18 (1974): 79–112; Ramón Lapesquera, "1901. *Electra*, de Galdós, en Iruñea," *Navarra insólita* (Pamplona: Pamiela, 1984): 35–45; Benito Madariaga de la Campa, "La crítica de *Electra* en la prensa de Cantabria," in *Galdós. Centenario de Fortunata y Jacinta*, ed. Julián Avila Arellano (Madrid: Universidad Complutense, 1987): 325–335; E. Inman Fox, "*Electra*, de Pérez Galdós (Historia, literatura y la polémica entre Martínez Ruiz y Maeztu)," *Ideología y política en las letras de fin de siglo (1898)* (Madrid: Espasa Calpe, 1988): 65–93; Theodore A. Sackett, "*Electra* desde la perspectiva de la crítica semiológica y arquetípica," *Revista de Literatura* 102 (1989): 462–482.

like everyone else, was well-versed – but the play's lasting value has little to do with such topicality. Galdós has created a play with dynamic characters, dramatic motion toward a surprising climax, and tension among various social and familial forces. It ran for over eighty consecutive nights in the Spanish capital, then moved on to Sevilla (where the Church hierarchy officially prohibited parishioners from seeing it),[113] Paris, where it ran for nearly one hundred and eighty nights, followed by another thirty-two in Rome, Buenos Aires (where it played in four theatres consecutively), Chile, Peru, Venezuela, and Russia. The published version – eight editions in Spain plus another nine in foreign countries – sold some 30,000 copies during its first month in print, and the title itself was immediately taken over by commercial interests; there began to appear in Spain Electra chocolates, Electra cigarettes, Electra hats, and the famous restaurant Lhardy named a special dish Electra. In a more serious vein, several intellectuals, among them Ramón María del Valle-Inclán, Ramiro de Maeztu, Pío Baroja, and Antonio Machado, gathered together to publish a new literary journal called *Electra*. Galdós had become the spiritual father of a new generation of liberal writers and thinkers. The reviewer for *El Globo* (31 January 1901) put it succinctly:

Electra no es solamente una obra dramática de singularísimo mérito, sino un hermoso, brillante, magnífico manifiesto de las aspiraciones de la juventud intelectual española, que al aprestarse en estos días a dar batalla al clericalismo, ha encontrado en Pérez Gáldós su indiscutible jefe.

(*Electra* is not merely a dramatic piece of unusual merit, but also a beautiful, brilliant, magnificent statement of the hopes of Spain's intellectual youth who, having decided lately to do battle against clericalism, have found in Pérez Galdós their unquestionable leader.)

It is a simple tale simply told, but in a rich, deep, and complex psychological and social context. Don Salvador de Pantoja, the family priest, reveals to the infantile Electra the long-buried secret that her fiancé Máximo, a young scientist, is in truth her brother which naturally ends the proposed marriage. Electra, poised to enter a convent, is visited by the ghost of her dead mother (here Galdós draws again on a recourse used at the end of *Realidad*) who reveals to her disturbed daughter that Pantoja's statement is a lie. Electra is "saved" by Máximo. The play is Galdós's masterwork, according to the author himself:

En *Electra* puede decirse que *he condensado la obra de toda mi vida*, mi amor a la verdad, mi lucha constante contra la superstición y el fanatismo y la necesidad de que olvidando nuestro desgraciado país las rutinas, convencionalismo y mentiras,

---

[113] See Fernando Hidalgo Fernández's well-documented study, *El estreno de "Electra," de Pérez Galdós, en Sevilla* (Ayuntamiento de Sevilla, 1985). Hidalgo provides an interesting synopsis of the Ubao case, 45–49.

que nos deshonran y envilecen ante el mundo civilizado, pueda realizarse la transformación de una España nueva que, apoyada en la ciencia y en la justicia, pueda resistir las violencias de la fuerza bruta y las sugestiones insidiosas y malvadas sobre las conciencias.[114]

(You could say that *I have condensed my entire life* into *Electra*, my love for the truth, my constant fight against superstition and fanaticism and the need for our country to forget its past habits, conventionality, and lies which dishonor us and which shame us in the eyes of the civilized world. We need to bring into being a new Spain, one supported by science and justice, one capable of resisting the forces of brutishness and the insidious and evil undermining of our conscience.)

Electra is a symbol of the Spain – undereducated, immature, exposed to dark forces, and in need of scientific liberation – that Galdós wishes to carry into the twentieth century, out of the realm of religious fanaticism and into the realm of truth, personal freedom, and scientific objectivity. She represents progress, change, and resistance against the power of the clergy. Azorín recognized this immediately, and wrote: "Yo contemplo en esta divina Electra el símbolo de la España revidida y moderna"[115] ("I think about this divine Electra as the symbol of a revived and modern Spain"). She is a strong character, one who, while made infantile by a poor (Jesuit) education, nevertheless resists the advances of suitors who "quieren anularme, esclavizarme, reducirme a una cosa ... angelical. No lo entiendo" ("want to turn me into a nothing, enslave me, reduce me to some sort of ... angelical thing. I don't understand") (I, 13).[116] Ruiz Ramón criticizes Galdós for the depiction of an "infantile" Electra: "¿Quién no se ha sorprendido viendo el infantilismo de Electra, que juega con muñecas ... de que tenga dieciocho años?"[117] ("Who hasn't been surprised, after seeing the infantilism of Electra, who plays with dolls ... to discover that she is eighteen years old?"). Yet such a comment misses the point of the psychological nature of the drama where the doll clearly symbolizes the interior emotional conflicts of Electra/Spain. Electra displaces the emotions onto the doll, which is strongly associated with memories of her mother (II, 5).

Galdós develops two dominant metaphors in the play: electricity and the fusion of metals. Electra, like electricity itself according to don Urbano, "destruye, trastorna, ilumina" ("destroys, disturbs, illuminates") (I, 2). (This metaphor captured the attention of Galdós's parodic

---

114 From an interview, "En casa de Galdós," *Diario de Las Palmas* (7 February 1901); reproduced in Finkenthal, *El teatro*, p. 112. Emphasis added.
115 Cited in Fox, "*Electra*," p. 83.
116 Strong women had always been a part of Galdós's theatre. See Lisa P. Condé, *Women in the Theatre of Galdós. From Realidad (1892) to Voluntad (1895)* (Lewiston, NY: Edwin Mellen Press, 1990).
117 Ruiz Ramón, *Historia*, p. 368.

nemesis Gabriel Merino, who staged an uproarious one-act "humorada" called *Electroterapia* on 11 April 1901 at the Teatro de Apolo.) Galdós, however, was after more serious ends. Máximo's scientific laboratory – the symbol of modernity and rationality – contains "aparatos para producir energía eléctrica" ("equipment to produce electrical energy") (III, stage note). Using electrical conduction, Máximo attempts to fuse metals, as Galdós will ultimately fuse the rational scientist Máximo himself with Electra/Spain. At the crucial moment when Máximo's scientific experiment succeeds (III, 11) he states: "Voy a decir a nuestros tíos que te reclamo, que te hago mía, que serás mi compañera y la madrecita de mis hijos" ("I am going to tell our aunt and uncle that I claim you, that I am making you mine, that you will be my companion and the mother of my children"). Electra sees her soul as a "laboratorio" (V, 6). The future of Spain appears secured, which it is only after Electra projects the ghost of her mother into her life and hears her reject Pantoja's lies: "Lo que oiste fue una ficción ... Si el amor conyugal y los goces de la familia solicitan tu alma, déjate llevar de esa dulce atracción ... Dios está en todas partes" ("What you heard was a lie ... If conjugal love and the joys of a family entreat your soul, give in to that sweet attraction ... God is everywhere") (V, 9). The battle over Electra's soul is won finally by Máximo: Galdós reveals his optimism in 1901 that the goal to reform society is not only a noble one, but one which can be achieved.

More dramas followed *Electra*, some of them quite astonishing in tone and subject matter. In *Casandra* (1910), for example, Galdós posits physical violence as a possible solution to the pernicious influence of the clergy and the Church, a position which provoked the most violent response since *Electra*.[118] In this play he combines several of the themes he had developed earlier – the villainy of the clergy, the evil of money, the corruption of political power – and writes a dénouement which horrified a large segment of his audience: Casandra, caught up in a web of money, deceit, and frustration, stabs to death doña Juana (associated throughout the play with the Church), then cries as the curtain falls, "He matado a la hidra que asolaba la tierra ... Respirad, Humanidad" ("I have killed the poisonous serpent that laid waste to the land ... Humanity, you may now breathe freely") (IV, 4).

Yet it is appropriate to end our discussion of nineteenth-century Spanish theatre with *Electra*. Galdós, an acute observer of middle-class Spanish society, knew that society's strengths and weaknesses like no other writer of his time. His theatre provided "una renovación de la temática teatral y una subida de nivel del contenido del drama

---

[118] One disenchanted reactionary wrote to the author: "Su obra *Casandra* es falsa, estúpida, abominable. Váyase a la mierda señor." Reproduced in Finkenthal, *El teatro*, p. 160.

español"[119] ("a renewal of the subject matter of theatre and a rise in the level of the content of Spanish drama"). His refusal to repeat the paradigms of the past enabled him to create not only a dialogue with that past but also a new model for the future. The society in his theatre was a modern society, battling against the weight of the past in order to forge a new beginning. Playwriting would never again slip back into purely thematic concerns or the rhetorical devices all too evident in the plays of his predecessors. More than most of his contemporaries, Galdós wanted to fuse theatre and society, that is, to write into the theatre his society's deepest needs and aspirations, and to force his audience out of its bourgeois complacency. "The greatest single impulse towards a realistic middle-class drama of social criticism was provided by the incursion of Galdós into the theatre."[120] He grappled with large themes and important social issues in an attempt to steer Spain toward an enlightened future rather than allowing her to flounder in the outdated concerns of days gone by. His determination to experiment with theatrical form and language, and thereby encourage his audiences to confront new "realities" earned him both the praise of his contemporaries and their scorn. As Finkenthal writes,

Galdós escondía tras sus dramas un propósito serio, no eran un simple medio de entretenimiento. Descubrió una condición patológica en la sociedad: los responsables de la dirección no utilizaban su poder para el bien común. El remedio que escogió Galdós fue la obra problemática: la presentación de un problema serio al público para que éste llegara a un cierto punto de vista.[121]

(Galdós hid a serious purpose behind his plays, which were not merely a simple pastime. He uncovered a pathological condition in society: those responsible for the direction of society did not use their power for the common good. The solution which Galdós chose was to write problematical works: putting before the public a serious problem in order to get them to see it from a certain point of view.)

His "teatro problemático" never shied away from its main mission of enlightenment, change, and challenge. The awarding of the Nobel Prize to Echegaray in 1904 seemed to signal that neither Spain nor the international community was ready to hear Galdós's message. But hear it they would, even if it took years for them to do so.

---

[119] Ruiz Ramón, *Historia*, p. 365.   [120] Hall, "Joaquín Dicenta," p. 53.
[121] Finkenthal, *El teatro*, p. 203.

Conclusion

Canon formation and the writing of literary history are tricky and unreliable matters. As we have seen, what we typically think of as the "history" of nineteenth-century Spanish theatre is nothing of the sort. Rather, it is a far more complex and varied phenomenon than we are generally led to believe, and to chart it with any degree of accuracy forces us into a series of decisions – choices – which may indeed be the "ideological acts" that Hayden White warned us about. This is precisely what happened as literary history, specifically theatrical history, began to be written in and for the nineteenth century. Cánovas del Castillo, the enormously influential Conservative politician and intellectual, set the tone and the parameters of the debate in the mid-1880s in two works. The first, *Autores dramáticos contemporáneos y joyas del teatro español del siglo XIX* republished the texts of what he considered to be those "joyas" ("jewels"): *Don Alvaro, Juan Lorenzo, Traidor, inconfeso y mártir, El hombre de mundo, ¡Don Tomás!, Los amantes de Teruel, ¡El gran Filón!, Muérete ¡y verás!, Guzmán el bueno, El haz de leña, Consuelo, Un drama nuevo*, and *O locura o santidad*. He followed up on these "jewels" with a study of *El teatro español* (The Spanish Theatre) where he made his ideological claims most forcefully:

Llenad hoy mismo en Madrid cualquier teatro, no de críticos, no de señoras y caballeros de los que visitan actualmente a París, no de filósofos o publicistas informados por el reinante espíritu cosmopolita, sino de genuino y *castizo pueblo español* y, con mejor o peor ejecución, haced que ante él se representen, por ejemplo, el *Don Alvaro* del duque de Rivas, la generalidad de las obras de García Gutiérrez, y sobre todo, *El trovador, Los amantes de Teruel*, de Hartzenbusch, *Don Juan Tenorio*, o la primera parte de *El zapatero y el rey*, los dramas históricos nacionales como *Guzmán el bueno*, de Gil y Zárate, o *El haz de leña*, de Nuñez de Arce, los que algo tienen de caballeros de López de Ayala, o de Echegaray, y mal pecado si no veis producirse las mayores emociones de que sea la escena capaz. Pues no hay que vacilar; lo que se aplaude es la poesía, *la poesía nacional* .... No busquéis en las obras citadas profundos, ni menos áridos análisis del alma humana; no exacta observación psicológica, buscad *poesía nacional*.[1]

---

[1] Antonio Cánovas del Castillo, *El teatro español* (Madrid: Editorial Ibero-Americana, 1885): 100–101. Emphasis added.

(Fill any of Madrid's theatres today not with critics, not with the kind of gentlemen and women who go to Paris frequently, not with philosophers or publicists informed by the reigning cosmopolitan spirit, but with genuine and *pure Spanish people* and put on, more or less adequately, for example, the Duke of Rivas's *Don Alvaro*, any of García Gutiérrez's plays but above all *El trovador*, Hartzenbusch's *Los amantes de Teruel*, *Don Juan Tenorio* or the first part of *El zapatero y el rey*, national historical dramas like Gil y Zárate's *Guzmán el bueno*, or Núñez de Arce's *El haz de leña*, any of those that have gentlemen in them by López de Ayala, or by Echegaray, and you'll be surprised if you don't see the greatest emotional response you can imagine in the audience. Do not be tricked; what people applaud is poetry, *national poetry* ... Don't look for deep or dry analyses of the human soul in these plays, don't look for precise psychological observation, look for *national poetry*.)

This, of course, merely sums up with little subtlety the dominant trend of theatre criticism throughout the century, but it is intensified in the last twenty years as the country agonized, in its pre-1898 mode, about the role it was to have in the world. Cánovas, the Conservative politician, established a suitably conservative structure for theatre history. Yet while Cánovas looked back, playwrights like Galdós looked ahead.

It becomes impossible then to "conclude" any one thing about the dramatic literature of nineteenth-century Spain, but as the corpus of plays we know about grows, the entire panorama of theatre changes and tells a much more dynamic story than the one we have heard before, one more acutely engaged in the dialectic of the time and more attuned to the social and ideological discourse of the nineteenth century. Julio Caro Baroja once asked, "¿Qué queda del [teatro] del siglo XIX español, italiano o francés en conjunto? Una proporción exigua de títulos. Aún los que se conocen sirven más para leídos que para representados. Hay que estar metido en los problemas de la época para encontrar la enjundia"[2] ("What remains of Spanish, Italian or French nineteenth-century theatre as a whole? A small number of titles. Even the ones we know are better read than performed. One must be half-immersed in the problems of that period in order to find its substance"). Julio Nombela had suggested something similar in 1880 when he refused to accept the generally held belief that the theatre was "tan enfermo, tan moribundo" ("sick and dying") as other critics would have their readers believe. Nombela, embarking on a moral crusade, saw the theatre as an apt reflection of the society in which it was written and performed:

No está en decadencia el Teatro español, no lo están ni siquiera los que a su vida contribuyen como poetas y como intérpretes: lo que está en decadencia, lo mismo en la esfera del arte que en las demás esferas sociales, es la abnegación, el sentimiento del deber, el deseo de cultura.[3]

[2] Caro Baroja, *Teatro popular y de magia*, p. 240.   [3] *El Teatro*, 25 May 1880.

(Spanish theatre is not in decline, nor are those who write for it or act in it: what is in decline, the same in the realm of art as in all other social realms, is self-denial, the sense of duty, the desire to be more cultured.)

This echoed what we have already seen from the "Decreto" (1849) which had already called theatre "el termómetro de la cultura de los pueblos" ("the thermometer of a people's level of culture") an idea repeated frequently throughout the century. It is heard yet again in 1872 in Juan Sureda's claim that "el teatro es el espejo de la sociedad; en él se contempla toda entera ... En el teatro se ve el pasado y el presente, y se sueña el porvenir"[4] ("the theatre is the mirror of a society; in it one sees everything whole ... In the theatre one sees the past and the present, and one dreams about the future"). In many ways, theatre was politics not only in the broadest sense but also in that it echoed the polemics, fears, positions, ideologies, and desires of nineteenth-century Spain.[5]

The theatre, and the public's perception of it, changed radically in the nineteenth century. "Official" theatres were followed by commercial theatres, "teatros caseros" ("theatres at home") (Lombía comments on their "pernicious" nature in 1845[6]), institute and school theatres, provincial theatres, and the "teatros por horas." As the periodical press gained in readership and importance, it tracked the whereabouts of dramatists, actors, and singers, discussed their travel plans, their contract negotiations, their battles with their putative bosses, their states of health. This was the beginning of modern-day celebrity, and the attention accorded them in the press gave them legitimacy, a place in society previously denied them (we remember that it was only in the first half of the nineteenth century that actors were permitted to use "don" or "doña" before their given names; this soon became standard procedure). People cared about the theatre, argued about it, and even when their motives were suspect frequented it. Two theatres at the century's beginning expanded to dozens at the century's end. In many ways it not only reflected society but guided it, persuaded it, cajoled it into new areas of thought. All of the plays, even the worst among them, tell us something about the audience, the playwright, and the society of the time. Publishing empires grew up nourished by the production of printed plays: in 1844 alone Manuel Delgado published editions of Gil y Zárate's *El fanático por las comedias* (Crazy for Comedies), Zorrilla's *La copa de marfil* (The Ivory Chalice) and *Don Juan Tenorio*, Rodríguez Rubí's *Bandera negra,* Hartzenbusch's *Floresinda*, García Gutiérrez's *Gabriel* and *Empeños de una venganza* (Vows of Vengeance), Rivas's *El desengaño en un sueño,* and

---

[4] Juan Sureda, "El teatro en nuestros días," *Revista de España* 25 (13 April 1872): 426.
[5] Rubio Jiménez, "Melodrama y teatro político."   [6] Lombía, *El teatro*, p. 113.

Miguel Agustín Príncipe's *Periquito entre ellos* (A Parrot Among Them). Later, V. de Lalama, José Repullés, J. M. Ducazcal, Cipriano López, and, especially, José Rodríguez published thousands of additional titles. Only when studied in context do they reveal a true picture of the "history" of nineteenth-century theatre.

The sheer volume and complexity of the works we have studied threaten to overwhelm any coherent or simplistic argument about what they "mean," and any attempt at a totally inclusive, synoptic view of those works would be unreliable and ultimately useless. Perhaps that is as it should be. "Literary history" is seen by some as an oxymoron. Can it be done? Should it be done? Perhaps not, but it invariably is done.[7] What we are left with, rather than a list of titles, is a series of sign posts and, I hope, an awareness of the need to study the theatre of the Spanish nineteenth century more closely, to revisit those works and authors – Grimaldi, Serra, Asquerino, Rodríguez Rubí, Muñiz y Más, Alba, Botella, Calderón (Camila), Cheix Martínez, Eguílaz, Granés, Guimerà, Larra (Luis Mariano de), Lozano, Merino, Núñez de Arce, Zumel, and dozens of others – too long buried beneath multiple modern editions of the same "masterworks" as always. Only then can we accurately chart the richness of the theatre in nineteenth-century Spain.

[7] See Robert Johnstone, "The Impossible Genre: Reading Comprehensive Literary History," *Publications of the Modern Language Association* 107 (January, 1992): 26–37.

Bibliography

Acuña, Rosario de. *Rienzi el tribuno. El padre Juan (teatro)*, ed. María del Carmen Simón Palmer. Madrid: Castalia, 1990.

Adams, N. B. "French Influence on the Madrid Theatre in 1837." *Estudios dedicados a D. Ramón Menéndez Pidal* VII. 7 vols. Madrid: CSIC, 1950–1962, 135–151.

"Notes on Spanish Plays at the Beginning of the Romantic Period." *Romanic Review* 27 (1926), 128–142.

"Sidelights on the Spanish Theaters of the Eighteen-Thirties." *Hispania* 9 (1926), 1–12.

"Siglo de Oro Plays in Madrid." *Hispanic Review* 4 (1936), 342–357.

"Spanish Plays at the Beginning of the Romantic Period." *Romanic Review* 17 (1926), 128–142.

The Romantic Dramas of Antonio García Gutiérrez. New York: Instituto de las Españas, 1922.

Aguilar Piñal, Francisco. *Bibliografía de autores españoles del siglo XVIII*. 7 vols. to date. Madrid: CSIC, 1981–.

Cartelera prerromántica sevillana, 1800–1836. Madrid: CSIC, 1968.

Sevilla y el teatro en el siglo XVIII. Oviedo: Cátedra Feijoo, 1974.

Aja, Eliseo. *Democracia y socialismo en el siglo XIX español. El pensamiento político de Fernando Garrido*. Madrid: Edicusa, 1976.

Alas, Leopoldo (Clarín). "Contrapunto." *El Solfeo* 7 March 1875.

"La decadencia del teatro y la protección del gobierno." *El Solfeo* 11 April 1876.

La regenta, ed. Gonzalo Sobejano. 2. vols. Madrid: Castalia, 1981.

Teresa. Avecilla. El hombre de los estrenos, ed. Leonardo Romero Tobar. Madrid: Castalia, 1975.

Alberich, José. "El papel de Shakespeare en *Un drama nuevo* de Tamayo." *Filología Moderna* 10 (1970), 301–322.

Alborg, Juan Luis. *Historia de la literatura española, IV. El romanticismo*. Madrid: Gredos, 1980.

Alcalá Galiano, José. "¿Se halla en decadencia el teatro español?" *Revista Contemporánea* II, 1876.

Aldaraca, Brigit. *El ángel del hogar: Galdós y la ideología de la domesticidad en España*. Madrid: Visor, 1992.

Allen, John J. *The Reconstruction of a Spanish Golden Age Playhouse. El Corral del Príncipe, 1583–1744*. Gainesville: University of Florida Press, 1983.

Allen, Rupert. "The Romantic Element in Bretón's *Muérete ¡y verás!*" *Hispanic Review* 34 (1966), 218–227.

Alonso, Luis. *Autores dramáticos contemporáneos.* Madrid: n. p., 1881.

Alonso Cortés, Narciso. "El teatro español en el siglo XIX," in *Historia general de las literaturas hispánicas* IV, ed. Guillermo Díaz-Plaja, 2nd. part (Barcelona: Editorial Vergara, 1953, 1968), 261–337.

José Zorrilla. Su vida y sus obras. 2nd. edn. Valladolid: Santarén, 1943.

"Narciso Serra." *Quevedo en el teatro y otras cosas* (Valladolid: Colegio Santiago, 1930), 129–202.

Álvarez Barrientos, Joaquín. "Acercamiento a Félix Enciso Castrillón." *II Seminario de Historia de la Real Sociedad Bascongada de los Amigos del País* (San Sebastián: n.p., 1989), 59–84.

"Aproximación a la incidencia de los cambios estéticos y sociales de finales del siglo XVIII y comienzos del XIX en el teatro de la época: comedias de magia y dramas románticos." *Castilla* 13 (1988), 17–33.

"La comedia de magia. Estudio de su estructura y recepción popular." Unpublished doctoral dissertation, Universidad Complutense, Madrid, 1987.

"Problemas del género en la comedia de magia," in *El teatro español a fines del siglo XVII. Historia, cultura y teatro en la España de Carlos II*, eds. Javier Huerta Calvo, et. al. (Amsterdam: Rodopi, 1989), 301–310.

Andioc, René. "Sobre el estreno de *Don Alvaro*," in *Homenaje a Juan López-Morillas*, ed. José Amor y Vázquez (Madrid: Castalia, 1982), 63–86.

Teatro y sociedad en el Madrid del siglo XVIII. Madrid: Castalia, 1976.

Anne, Théodore. *Madrid ou Observations sur les moeurs et usages des espagnols au commencement du XIX siècle.* Paris: Pillet Aîné, 1825.

Antón del Olmet, Luis, and Arturo García Carrafa. *Echegaray.* Madrid: Impr. "Alrededor del Mundo," 1912.

Araujo, Demetrio. "El teatro español y su decadencia." *Revista Contemporánea* IX, 1877.

Artola, Miguel. *Partidos y programas políticos 1808–1936.* Madrid: Aguilar, 1974–1975.

Avrett, Robert. "A Brief Examination into the Historical Background of Martínez de la Rosa's *La conjuración de Venecia.*" *Romanic Review* 21 (1930), 132–137.

Ballantyne, Margaret A. "Indice de la *Revista de España* bajo la dirección de Galdós." *Hispania* 73 (May, 1990), 332–344.

Ballew, H. L. "The Life and Work of Dionisio Solís." Unpublished doctoral dissertation, University of North Carolina, 1957.

Banner, J. W. "The Dramatic Works of Manuel Eduardo de Gorostiza." Unpublished doctoral dissertation, University of North Carolina, 1948.

Barceló Jiménez, Juan. *Historia del teatro en Murcia*, 2nd. edn. Murcia: Academia de Alfonso X el Sabio, 1980.

Bentivegna, Patricia. "Parody in the Género Chico." Unpublished doctoral dissertation, University of Pittsburgh, 1974.

Berenguer, Angel. *Los estrenos teatrales de Galdós en la crítica de su tiempo.* Comunidad de Madrid, 1988.

Berkowitz, Chanon. *La biblioteca de Benito Pérez Galdós.* Las Palmas: El Museo Canario, 1951.

Bieder, Maryellen. "The Modern Woman on the Spanish Stage: The Contributions of Gaspar and Dicenta." *Estreno* 7 (1981), 25–28.

Bly, Peter. "Galdós, Sellés y el tratamiento literario del adulterio." in *Actas del X Congreso Internacional de Hispanistas*, II, ed. Antonio Vilanova (Barcelona: PPU, 1992), 1213–1220.

Botrel, Jean-François. *La diffusion du livre en Espagne (1868–1914)*. Madrid: Casa de Velázquez, 1988.

Boussagol, Gabriel. *Angel de Saavedra, duc de Rivas. Sa vie, son oeuvre poétique.* Toulouse: Privat, 1926.

Brent, Albert. "Larra's Dramatic Works." *Romance Notes* 8 (1967), 207-212.

Bretón de los Herreros, Manuel. *Manuel Bretón de los Herreros. Obra dispersa. El Correo Literario y Mercantil*, eds. J. M. Díez Taboada and J. M. Rozas. Logroño: Instituto de Estudios Riojanos, 1965.

Obras de D. Manuel Bretón de los Herreros. 5 vols. Madrid: Ginesta, 1883.

Teatro, ed. Narciso Alonso Cortés. Madrid: Espasa Calpe, 1928.

Brett, Lewis E., ed. *Nineteenth-Century Spanish Plays*. New York: Appleton-Century- Crofts, 1935.

Brown, Jonathan. *The Golden Age of Painting in Spain*. New Haven: Yale University Press, 1991.

Burgos, Ana María. "Vida y obra de Tomás Rodríguez Rubí." *Revista de Literatura* 23 (1963), 65–102.

Burgos, Carmen de. *Fígaro. Revelaciones*. Madrid: Impr. "Alrededor del Mundo", 1919.

Cabrales Arteaga, José Manuel. "El teatro neorromántico de Echegaray." *Revista de Literatura* 101 (1989), 77–94.

Cacho Blecua, Juan Manuel. "*Ataúlfo*, tragedia inédita del duque de Rivas." *El Crotalón* 1 (1984), 393–465.

Caldera, Ermanno. "Bretón o la negación del modelo." *Cuadernos de Teatro Clásico* 5 (1990), 141–153.

"De *Aliatar* a *Don Alvaro*: Sobre el aprendizaje clasicista del duque de Rivas." *Romanticismo* 1 (1982), 109–126.

"Echegaray, tra la parola e il silenzio," in *Symbolae Pisanae. Studi in onore di Guido Mancini*, eds. Blanca Perñán and Francesco Guazzelli, 2 vols. (Pisa: Giardini, 1989), I: 85–98.

La commedia romantica in Spagna. Pisa: Giardini, 1978.

"La magia nel teatro romantico," in *Teatro di magia*, ed. Ermanno Caldera (Rome: Bulzoni, 1983), 185–205.

"*La pata de cabra* y *Le pied du mouton*." *Studia Historica et Philologica in honorem M. Batllori* (Rome: Instituto Español de Cultura, 1984), 567–575.

"La perspectiva femenina en el teatro de Joaquina García Balmaseda y Enriqueta Lozano," in *Escritoras románticas españolas*, ed. Marina Mayoral (Madrid: Fundación Banco Exterior, 1990), 207–217.

"L'età della ragione." *Quaderni di Filologia Romanza* 4 (1984), 7–22.

"Sulla 'spettacolarità' delle commedie di magia," in *Teatro di magia*, ed. Ermanno Caldera (Rome: Bulzoni, 1983), 11–32.

Caldera, Ermanno, and Antonietta Calderone. "El teatro en el siglo XIX (1808–1844)," in *Historia del teatro en España. II. Siglos XVIII y XIX*, ed. José María Díez Borque (Madrid: Taurus, 1988), 377–624.

Calderone, Antonietta. "Catalogo delle commedie di magia rappresentate a Madrid nel Secolo XVIII," in *Teatro di magia*, ed. Ermanno Caldera (Rome: Bulzoni, 1983), 236–268.

Calvo Revilla, Luis. *Actores célebres del Teatro del Príncipe o Español*. Madrid: Impr. Municipal, 1920.

Cambronero, Carlos. "Comella." *Revista Contemporánea* CXII–CXIV (1896).

"Cosas de antaño: Apuntes para la historia de la censura dramática." *Revista Contemporánea* MLXXVIII (December 1899), 594–609.

Campos, Jorge. *Teatro y sociedad en España (1780–1820)*. Madrid: Moneda y Crédito, 1969.

Cañada Solaz, Rosa Julia. "El col.loqui valenciano en los siglos XVIII y XIX," in *Actas de las jornadas sobre teatro popular en España*, eds. Joaquín Álvarez Barrientos and Antonio Cea Gutiérrez (Madrid: CSIC, 1987), 85–107.

Cánovas del Castillo, Antonio. *El teatro español*. Madrid: Editorial Ibero-Americana, 1885.

Cánovas del Castillo, Antonio, ed. *Autores dramáticos contemporáneos y joyas del teatro español del siglo XIX*, 2 vols. Madrid: Imprenta Fortanet, 1881–1882.

Cardwell, Richard. "*Don Alvaro* or the Force of Cosmic Injustice." *Studies in Romanticism* 12 (1973), 559–579.

Carmena y Millán, Luis. *Crónica de la ópera italiana en Madrid*. Madrid: Manuel Minuesa de los Ríos, 1878.

Carner, Sebastián. *Tratado de arte escénico*. Barcelona: La Hormiga de Oro, 1890.

Carnero, Guillermo. *Los orígenes del romanticismo reaccionario español*. Universidad de Valencia, 1978.

"Recursos y efectos escénicos en el teatro de Gaspar Zavala y Zamora." *Bulletin Hispanique* 91 (1989), 21–36.

"Temas políticos contemporáneos en el teatro de Gaspar Zavala y Zamora," in *Teatro politico spagnolo del primo ottocento*, ed. Ermanno Caldera (Rome: Bulzoni, 1991), 19–41.

"Un ejemplo del teatro revolucionario en la España revolucionaria." *España Contemporánea* 1 (1988), 49–66.

Caro Baroja, Julio. *Teatro popular y de magia*. Madrid: Revista de Occidente, 1974.

Carr, Raymond. *Spain 1808–1975*. Oxford: Clarendon Press, 1982.

Casalduero, Joaquín. "La sensualidad en el romanticismo: sobre el *Macías*." *Estudios sobre el teatro español*, 2nd. edn. (Madrid: Gredos, 1967), 219–231.

Castilla, Alberto. "Una parodia de *El gran Galeoto*." *Hispanófila* 26 (1983), 33–40.

Catalina, Manuel. *Los actores*. Madrid: Víctor Saiz, 1877.

Catena, Elena. "Circunstancias temporales de la *Electra* de Galdós." *Estudios Escénicos* 18 (1974), 79–112.

Chaskin, Silvia Novo Blankenship. "Social Satire in the Works of Manuel Bretón de los Herreros." Unpublished doctoral dissertation, University of Virginia, 1968.

Chaulié, Dionisio. *Cosas de Madrid*. 2 vols. Madrid: Correspondencia de España, 1886.

Chicote, Enrique. *Cuando Fernando VII gastaba paletó...Recuerdos y anécdotas del año de la nanita*. Madrid: Instituto Editorial Reus, 1952.

Chú-Pond, Oreida. *La figura del Mesías en el teatro romántico español*. San José, Costa Rica: Fundación San Judás Tadeo, 1988.

Ciges Aparicio, Manuel. *España bajo la dinastía de los Borbones*. Madrid: Aguilar, 1932.

Coe, A. M. *Catálogo bibliográfico y crítico de las comedias anunciadas en los periódicos de Madrid desde 1661 hasta 1819*. Baltimore: Johns Hopkins, 1935.

Colao, Alberto. *Máiquez, discípulo de Talma*. Cartagena: F. Gómez, 1980.

Condé, Lisa P. *Women in the Theatre of Galdós. From Realidad (1892) to Voluntad (1895)*. Lewiston, NY: Edwin Mellen Press, 1990.

Corbière, Anthony S. *Juan Eugenio Hartzenbusch and the French Theater*. Philadelphia: University of Pennsylvania Press, 1927.

Cortázar, Eduardo de. "Crítica estadística-teatral (La temporada de 1871–1872)." *Revista de España* 26 (28 June 1872), 624–635.

"Crítica estadística-teatral (La temporada de 1872–1873)." *Revista de España* 32 (28 June 1873), 557–572, and 33 (25 July 1873), 129–142; 275–283.

Cotarelo y Mori, Emilio. *Bibliografía de las controversias sobre la licitud del teatro en España*. Madrid: Archivos, Bibliotecas y Museos, 1904.

"Ensayo histórico sobre la zarzuela, o sea el drama lírico español desde su origen a fines del siglo XIX." *Boletín de la Real Academia Española* 19 (1932), 625–671, 753–817; 20 (1933), 97–147, 271–315, 469–506, 601–642, 735–787; 21 (1934), 113–161, 273–317, 463–505, 629–671, 858–910.

Isidoro Máiquez y el teatro de su tiempo. Madrid: José Perales, 1902.

La Avellaneda y sus obras. Madrid: Olózaga, 1930.

Coughlin, Edward V. *Adelardo López de Ayala*. Boston: G. K. Hall, 1977.

"Neoclassical *refundiciones* of Golden Age *comedias* (1772-1831)." Unpublished doctoral dissertation, University of Michigan, 1965.

Crespo Matellán, Salvador. *La parodia dramática en la literatura española*. Universidad de Salamanca, 1979.

Crocker, Lester G. "Techniques of Ambiguity in *Un drama nuevo*." *Hispania* 39 (1956), 412–418.

Curet, Francisco. *El arte dramático en el resurgir de Cataluña*. Barcelona: Editorial Minerva, 1917.

Curry, Richard. "Dramatic Tension and Emotional Control in *Los amantes de Teruel*." *West Virginia University Philological Papers* 21 (1974), 36–47.

Custine, Adolphe. *L'Espagne sous Ferdinand VII*. 2 vols. Paris: Ladvocat, 1838.

Dauster, Frank. "The Ritual Feast: A Study in Dramatic Forms." *Latin American Theatre Review* 9 (1975), 5–9.

Davies, Gareth. "The Country Cousin at Court. A Study of Antonio de Mendoza's *Cada loco con su tema* and Manuel Bretón de los Herreros's *El pelo de la dehesa*." *Leeds Iberian Papers: Hispanic Drama* (Leeds: Trinity and All Saints College, 1991), 43–60.

Deleito y Piñuela, José. *Estampas del Madrid teatral fin de siglo*. Madrid: Saturnino Calleja, [1946].

Dérozier, Claudette. *La Guerre d'Independance espagnole à travers l'estampe (1808–1814)*. 2 vols. Université de Lille III, 1976.

Di Pinto, Mario. "En defensa de Comella." *Insula* 504 (1988), 16–17.

Díaz de Escovar, Narciso, and Francisco P. Lasso de la Vega. *Historia del teatro español.* 2 vols. Barcelona: Montaner y Simón, 1924.

Dicenta, Joaquín. *Juan José*, ed. Jaime Mas. Madrid: Cátedra, 1982.

Díez Borque, José María, ed. *Historia del teatro en España.* 2 vols. Madrid: Taurus, 1988.

Donoso Cortés, Juan. *Obras de D. Juan Donoso Cortés*, ed. Manuel Donoso Cortés. 4 vols. Madrid: San Francisco de Sales, 1904.

Dowling, John C. "El anti-don Juan de Ventura de la Vega," in *Actas del VI Congreso Internacional de Hispanistas*, eds. Alan M. Gordon and Evelyn Rugg (University of Toronto Press, 1980), 215–218.

"Gorostiza's *Contigo pan y cebolla*: From Romantic Farce to Nostalgic Musical Comedy." *Theatre Survey* 28 (1987), 49–58.

"Moratín's Creation of the Comic Role for the Older Actress." *Theatre Survey* 24 (1983), 55–63.

"The Inquisition Appraises *El sí de las niñas*, 1815–1819." *Hispania* 44 (1961), 237–244.

"The Madrid Theatre Public in the Eighteenth Century: Transition from the Popular Audience to the Bourgeois." *Transactions of the Seventh International Congress on the Enlightenment: Studies on Voltaire and the Eighteenth Century* (Oxford: The Voltaire Foundation, 1989), 1358–1362.

Durnerin, James. "Larra, traducteur de Scribe et de Ducange." *Ecriture des marges et mutations historiques* (Université de Besançon, 1983), 41–52.

Ebersole, Alba. *La obra teatral de Luciano Francisco Comella.* Valencia: Albatros, 1985.

Echegaray, José. *Teatro escogido*, ed. Amando Lázaro Ros. Madrid: Aguilar, 1964.

Elizalde, Ignacio. "Azorín y el estreno de *Electra* de Pérez Galdós." *Letras de Deusto* 3 (1973), 67–79.

Elorza, Antonio. *El fourierismo en España.* Madrid: Ediciones de la Revista de Trabajo, 1975.

Elwood, William. "Schiller and Tamayo: The Influential Essay," in *Text and Presentation. The University of Florida Department of Classics Comparative Drama Conference Papers* IX, ed. Karelisa Hartigan (Lanham: University Press of America, 1989), 35–45.

Enciso Castrillón, Félix. *Principios de literatura, acomodados a la declamación, estractados de varios autores españoles y extrangeros para el uso de los alumnos del Real Conservatorio de Música de María Cristina.* Madrid: Repullés, 1832.

Engler, Kay. "Amor, muerte y destino: la psicología de Eros en *Los amantes de Teruel*." *Hispánofila* 70 (1980), 1–15.

Enríquez de Salamanca, Cristina. "¿Quién era la escritora del siglo XIX?" *Letras Peninsulares* 2 (1989), 81–107.

Escobar, José. "Anti-romanticismo en García Gutiérrez." *Romanticismo* 1 (1982), 83–94.

Los orígenes de la obra de Larra. Madrid: Editorial Prensa Española, 1973.

"Un episodio biográfico de Larra, crítico teatral, en la temporada de 1834." *Nueva Revista de Filología Hispánica* 35 (1976), 44–72.

Espín Templado, María Pilar. "El sainete en el último tercio del siglo XIX, culminación de un género dramático en el teatro español." *Epos* 3 (1987), 97–122.

Esquer Torres, Ramón. *El teatro de Tamayo y Baús.* Madrid: CSIC, 1965.
"Tamayo y Baús y la política del siglo XIX." *Segismundo* 1 (1965), 71–91.
Fábregas, Xavier. *Angel Guimerà: les deimensions d'un mite.* Barcelona: Ediciones 62, 1971.
Aproximació a la historia del teatre català. Barcelona: Curial, 1972.
Historia del teatre català. Barcelona: Millà, 1978.
Fernández, Gastón. "José Echegaray y Eizaguirre," in *Critical Survey of Drama* II, ed. Frank N. Magill (Englewood Cliffs, NJ: Salem Press, 1986), 526–534.
Fernández Bremón, José. "Don Narciso Serra," in Cánovas del Castillo, *Autores dramáticos contemporáneos* I: 347–363.
Fernández Cabezón, Rosalía. "Ataúlfo visto por dos trágicos: D. Agustín de Montiano y el duque de Rivas." *Castilla* 8 (1984), 95–100.
"Los sainetes de Gaspar Zavala y Zamora." *Castilla* 12 (1987), 59–72.
"Pervivencia de Calderón de la Barca en los albores del siglo XIX: *El soldado exorcista* de Gaspar Zavala y Zamora," in *El teatro español a fines del siglo XVII,* ed. Javier Huerta Calvo (Rodopi: Amsterdam, 1989), 623–635.
Fernández de Córdoba, Fernando. *Mis memorias íntimas.* 2 vols. Madrid: Atlas, 1966.
Fernández Espino, José. "De la moral en el drama." *Estudios de literatura y de crítica.* Madrid: Impr. de la Andalucía, 1862.
Fernández Muñoz, Angel Luis. *Arquitectura teatral en Madrid.* Madrid, Editorial El Avapiés, 1988.
Ferrer del Río, Antonio. *Galería de la literatura española.* Madrid: Mellado, 1846.
Finkenthal, Stanley. *El teatro de Galdós.* Madrid: Fundamentos, 1980.
Flitter, Derek. *Spanish Romantic Literary Theory and Criticism.* Cambridge University Press, 1992.
Flores García, Francisco. *Memorias íntimas del teatro.* Valencia: F. Sempere, 1909.
Flynn, Gerard. *Manuel Bretón de los Herreros.* Boston: G. K. Hall, 1978.
Manuel Tamayo y Baús. New York: Twayne Publishers, 1973.
Fornieles Alcaraz, Javier. *Trayectoria de un intelectual de la Restauración: José Echegaray.* Almería: Confederación Española de Cajas de Ahorro, 1989.
Fox, E. Inman. "*Electra,* de Pérez Galdós (Historia, literatura y la polémica entre Martínez Ruiz y Maeztu)." *Ideología y política en las letras de fin de siglo (1898)* (Madrid: Espasa Calpe, 1988), 65–93.
Francos Rodríguez, José. *Contar vejeces. De las memorias de un gacetillero (1893–1897).* Madrid: Compañía Ibero-Americana de Publicaciones, 1928.
Freire López, Ana María. "Un proyecto desconocido del dramaturgo Narciso Serra." *Anales del Instituto de Estudios Madrileños* 28 (1990), 661–664.
Funes, Enrique. *La declamación española.* Seville: Díaz y Carballo, 1894.
Gabbert, Thomas A. "Notes on the Popularity of the Dramas of Victor Hugo in Spain During the Years 1835–1845." *Hispanic Review* 4 (1936), 176–178.
Galerstein, Caroline, ed. *Women Writers of Spain: An Annotated Bibliography.* New York: Greenwood Press, 1986.
García Castañeda, Salvador. "El marqués de Casa-Cagigal (1756–1824), escritor militar." *La Guerra de la Independencia (1808–1814) y su momento histórico* II (Santander: Centro de Estudios Montañeses, 1979), 743–756.
"Los hermanos Asquerino o el uso y mal uso del drama histórico." *Quaderni di Filologia Romanza* 4 (1984), 23–42.

"Moralidad y reformismo en las comedias del marqués de Casa-Cagigal." *Romanticismo* 1 (1982), 25–34.

García Garrosa, María Jesús. *La retórica de las lágrimas. La comedia sentimental española, 1751–1802.* Valladolid: Caja de Ahorros y Monte de Piedad de Salamanca, 1990.

García López, Juan. *Historia de la literatura española,* 14th. edn. Barcelona: Editorial Vicens-Vives, 1969.

García Lorenzo, Luciano. "La denominación de los géneros teatrales en España durante el siglo XIX y el primer tercio del siglo XX." *Segismundo* 5–6 (1967), 191–199.

García Pavón, Francisco. " 'Clarín' y su teatro social." *Textos y escenarios* (Barcelona: Plaza y Janés, 1971), 63–66.

"Inicios del teatro social en España (1895)," in *El teatro y su crítica,* a collection of essays (Málaga: Instituto de Cultura de la Diputación Provincial, 1975).

Teatro social en España. Madrid: Taurus, 1962.

García Valero, Vicente. *Crónicas retrospectivas del teatro por un cómico viejo.* Madrid: Librería Gutenberg de José Ruiz, 1910.

Garelli, Patrizia. *Bretón de los Herreros e la sua 'formula comica'.* Imola: Galeati, 1983.

Gassin, Roberto Dengler. "El drama romántico francés en Madrid (1830–1850)," in *Imágenes de Francia en las letras hispánicas,* ed. Francisco Lafarga (Barcelona: PPU, 1989), 307–315.

Gies, David T. *Agustín Durán: A Biography and Literary Appreciation.* London: Tamesis Books, Ltd., 1975.

"Cienfuegos y las lágrimas de virtud," in *Coloquio Internacional sobre el teatro español del siglo XVIII,* eds. Mario Di Pinto, Maurizio Fabbri, and Rinaldo Froldi (Albano Terme: Piovan Editore, 1988), 213–226.

"Dionisio Solís, entre dos/tres siglos." *Entre Siglos* 2 (1993), 163–170.

"Don Juan contra don Juan: Apoteosis del romanticismo español," in *Actas del VII Congreso Internacional de Hispanistas* II, ed. G. Bellini . 2 vols. (Rome: Bulzoni, 1982), 545–551.

"*Don Juan Tenorio* y la tradición de la comedia de magia." *Hispanic Review* 58 (1990), 1–17.

"Entre drama y ópera: la lucha por el público teatral en la época de Fernando VII." *Bulletin Hispanique* 91 (1989), 37–60.

"Glorious Invalid: Spanish Theater in the Nineteenth-Century." *Hispanic Review* 61 (1993), 28–51.

"Grimaldi, Vega y el Teatro Español (1849)," in *Actas del X Congreso Internacional de Hispanistas* II, ed. Antonio Vilanova (Barcelona: PPU, 1992), 1277–1283.

"Hacia un catálogo de los dramas de Dionisio Solís (1774–1834)." *Bulletin of Hispanic Studies* 68 (1991), 197–210.

"Hacia un mito anti-napoleónico en el teatro español de los primeros años del siglo XIX," in *Teatro politico spagnolo del primo ottocento,* ed. Ermanno Caldera (Rome: Bulzoni, 1991), 43–62.

"Imágenes y la imaginación románticas." *Romanticismo* 1 (1982), 49–59.

" 'Inocente estupidez': *La pata de cabra* (1829), Grimaldi and the Regeneration of the Spanish Stage." *Hispanic Review* 54 (1986), 375–396.

"*In re magica veritas*: Enrique Zumel y la comedia de magia en la segunda mitad del siglo XIX," in *La comedia de magia y de santos*, eds. F.J. Blasco, E. Caldera, J. Álvarez Barrientos, and R. de la Fuente (Madrid: Júcar, 1992), 433–461.

"José Zorrilla and the Betrayal of Spanish Romanticism." *Romanistiches Jahrbuch* 31 (1980), 339–346.

"Juan de Grimaldi y el año teatral madrileño, 1823-1824," in *Actas del VIII Congreso Internacional de Hispanistas* I, eds. A. David Kossoff, José Amor y Vázquez, Ruth H. Kossoff, and Geoffrey W. Ribbans, 2 vols. (Madrid: ISTMO, 1986), 607–613.

"Larra, Grimaldi and the Actors of Madrid," in *Studies in Eighteenth-Century Literature and Romanticism in Honor of John C. Dowling*, eds. Linda and Douglass Barnette (Newark, Delaware: Juan de la Cuesta, 1985), 113–122.

"Larra, *La galería fúnebre* y el gusto por lo gótico." *Romanticismo* 3–4 (1988), 60–68.

"La subversión de don Juan: Parodias decimonónicas del *Tenorio*, con una nota pornográfica." *España Contemporánea*, in press.

"Notas sobre Grimaldi y el 'furor de refundir' en Madrid (1820–1833)." *Cuadernos de Teatro Clásico* 5 (1990), 111–124.

"Rebeldía y drama en 1844: *Españoles sobre todo*, de Eusebio Asquerino." *Homenaje a Ermanno Caldera*. Rome: Bulzoni, in press.

Theatre and Politics in Nineteenth-Century Spain: Juan de Grimaldi as Impresario and Government Agent. Cambridge University Press, 1988.

"Visión, ilusión y el sueño romántico en la poesía de Espronceda." *Cuadernos de Filología* 3 (1983), 61–84.

Gil, Bernardo, and Antonio González. *Manifiesto que dan los autores de los teatros de la Cruz y Príncipe*. Madrid: Repullés, 1820.

Gil y Carrasco, Enrique. *Obras completas de D. Enrique Gil y Carrasco*, ed. Jorge Campos. BAE 74. Madrid: Atlas, 1964.

Gómez de la Serna, Ramón. *Mi tía Carolina Coronado*. Buenos Aires: Emecé, 1942.

Gómez Rea, Javier. "Las revistas teatrales madrileñas (1790–1930)." *Cuadernos Bibliográficos* 31 (1974), 65–140.

Gorostiza, Manuel Eduardo de. *Contigo pan y cebolla*, ed. John C. Dowling. Valencia: Albatros, 1992.

Gregersen, Halfdan. *Ibsen and Spain*. Cambridge, MA: Harvard University Press, 1936.

Grimaldi, Juan de. *La pata de cabra*, ed. David T. Gies. Rome: Bulzoni, 1986.

Guaza y Gómez Talavera, Carlos. *Músicos, poetas y actores*. Madrid: F. Maroto, 1884.

Guizot, François Pierre Guillaume. *Mémoires pour servir à l'histoire de mon temps*. 8 vols. Paris: Michel-Lévy, 1858–1867.

Hall, H. B. "Joaquín Dicenta and the Drama of Social Criticism." *Hispanic Review* 20 (1952), 44–66.

Harter, Hugh A. *Gertrudis Gómez de Avellaneda*. Boston: Twayne, 1981.

Hartzenbusch, Juan Eugenio. *Los amantes de Teruel*, ed. Salvador García Castañeda. Madrid: Castalia, 1971.

Los amantes de Teruel, ed. Jean Louis Picoche. Paris: Centre de recherches hispaniques, 1970.

Los amantes de Teruel, ed. Jean Louis Picoche. Madrid: Alhambra, 1980.
"Noticias sobre la vida y escritos de D. Dionisio Solís. 1839." *Ensayos poéticos y artículos en prosa, literarios y de costumbres* (Madrid: Yenes, 1843), 173–214.

Hartzenbusch e Hiriarte, Eugenio. *Periódicos de Madrid. Tabla cronológica.* Madrid: Sucesores de Rivadeneyra, 1876.

Hernández, Librada. "Clarín, Galdós y Pardo Bazán frente al teatro de José Echegaray." *Anales de Literatura Española de la Universidad de Alicante* 8 (1992), 95–108.

Herrero, Javier. "Terror y literatura: Ilustración, revolución y los orígenes del movimiento romántico," in *La literatura española de la Ilustración: Homenaje a Carlos III*, ed. José Luis Varela (Madrid: Universidad Complutense, 1988), 131–153.

Herrero Salgado, Félix. *Cartelera teatral madrileña (1840–1849).* Madrid: CSIC, 1963.

Hespelt, Herman. "The Translated Dramas of Mariano José de Larra and their French Originals." *Hispania* 15 (1932), 117–134.

Hidalgo Fernández, Fernando. *El estreno de "Electra," de Pérez Galdós, en Sevilla.* Sevilla: Ayuntamiento de Sevilla, 1985.

Hoar, Leo. *Benito Pérez Galdós y la Revista del Movimiento Intelectual de Europa.* Madrid: Insula, 1968.

Hutcheon, Linda. *A Theory of Parody.* New York: Methuen, 1985.

Izquierdo, Lucio. "El teatro en Valencia (1800–1832)." *Boletín de la Real Academia Española* 69 (1989): 257–305.

Johnson, Jerry. "Azucena, Sinister or Pathetic?" *Romance Notes* 12 (1970), 114–118.

Johnstone, Robert. "The Impossible Genre: Reading Comprehensive Literary History." *Publications of the Modern Language Association* 107 (January, 1992), 26–37.

Jovellanos, Gaspar Melchor. *Memoria para el arreglo de la policía de los espectáculos y diversiones públicas y sobre su origen en España.* Madrid: Sancha, 1812.

Kiernan, E. V. G. *The Revolution of 1854 in Spanish History.* Oxford: Clarendon Press, 1966.

Kirkpatrick, Susan. *Larra: El laberinto inextricable de un romántico liberal.* Madrid: Gredos, 1977.

'*Las románticas': Women Writers and Subjectivity in Spain, 1835–1850.* Berkeley: University of California Press, 1989.

"Liberal Romanticism and the Female Protagonist in *Macías.*" *Romance Quarterly* 35 (1988), 51-58.

Kirschenbaum, Leo. *Enrique Gaspar and the Social Drama.* Berkeley: University of California Press, 1941.

Kosove, Joan L. Pataky. *The 'Comedia lacrimosa' and Spanish Romantic Drama (1773–1865).* London: Tamesis Books, Ltd., 1977.

Krupat, Arnold. "Native American Literature and the Canon," in *Canons*, ed. Robert von Hallberg (University of Chicago Press, 1983), 309–335.

Lafarga, Francisco. *Las traducciones españolas del teatro francés (1700–1835).* 2 vols. Universidad de Barcelona, 1983–1988.

Laguerra, Enrique. "La mujer en las tragedias de Gertrudis Gómez de Avellaneda," in *Homenaje a Gertrudis Gómez de Avellaneda*, eds. Gladys Zaldívar and Rosa Martínez de Cabrera (Miami: Ediciones Universal, 1981), 183–199.

Lapesquera, Ramón. "1901. *Electra*, de Galdós, en Iruñea." *Navarra insólita* (Pamplona: Pamiela, 1984), 35–45.

Larra, Mariano José de. *Macías*, eds. Luis Lorenzo-Rivero and George Mansour. Madrid: Espasa-Calpe, 1990.

Obras de Mariano José de Larra, ed. Carlos Seco Serrano. 4 vols. Madrid: Atlas, 1960.

Larraz, Emmanuel. "La satire de Napoléon Bonaparte et de Joseph dans le théâtre espagnol: 1808–1814," *Hommage à André Joucla-Ruau* (Aix-en-Provence, Université de Provence, 1974), 125–137.

Théâtre et politique pendant la Guerre d'Independance espagnole: 1808–1814. Aix-en-Provence: Université de Provence, 1988.

Larraz, Emmanuel, ed. *La guerre d'indépendance espagnole au théâtre: 1808–1814*. *Antologie*. Aix-en-Provence: Université de Provence, 1987.

Latorre, Carlos. *Noticias sobre el arte de la declamación*. Madrid: Yenes, 1839.

Leslie, John Kenneth. *Ventura de la Vega and the Spanish Theatre, 1820–1865*. Princeton University Press, 1940.

Litvak, Lily. "Naturalismo y teatro social en Cataluña." *Comparative Literature Studies* 5 (1968), 279–302.

Llorens Castillo, Vicente. *El romanticismo español*. Madrid: Castalia, 1979.

Lombía, Juan. *El teatro: origen, índole e importancia de esta institución*. Madrid: Sánchez, 1845.

Lope, Hans-Joachim. "La imagen de los franceses en el teatro español de propaganda durante la Guerra de la Independencia (1808–1813)." *Bulletin of Hispanic Studies* 68 (1991), 219–229.

López de Ayala, Adelardo. *Obras completas de don Adelardo López de Ayala*. *Teatro*, ed. José María Castro y Calvo. 3 vols. BAE 180–182. Madrid: Atlas, 1965.

López García, Angel. "Echegaray y la cultura de masas," in *Homenatge a José Belloch Zimmerman*, eds. Emili Casanova and Joaquín Espinosa (Universidad de Valencia, 1988), 251–258.

Lorenz, Charlotte M. "Seventeenth Century Plays in Madrid From 1801–1818." *Hispanic Review* 6 (1938), 324–331.

Lott, Robert E. "On Mannerism and Mannered Approaches to Realism in *Un drama nuevo*, *Consuelo*, and Earlier Nineteenth-Century Spanish Plays." *Hispania* 54 (1971), 844–855.

Lovett, Gabriel. *The Duke of Rivas*. Boston: Twayne, 1977.

Lozano Guirao, Pilar. "El archivo epistolar de don Ventura de la Vega." *Revista de Literatura* 13 (1958), 121–172; and 14 (1959), 170–197.

Madariaga de la Campa, Benito. "La crítica de *Electra* en la prensa de Cantabria," in *Galdós. Centenario de Fortunata y Jacinta*, ed. Julián Avila Arellano (Madrid: Universidad Complutense, 1987), 325–335.

Mainer, J. Carlos. "Notas sobre la lectura obrera en España (1890–1930)." *Literatura popular y proletaria* (Universidad de Sevilla, 1986), 53–123.

Mansour, George. "Algunos don Juanes olvidados del siglo XIX." *Revista de Estudios Hispánicos* 2.2 (1968), 251–264.

María y Campos, Armando de. *Manuel Eduardo de Gorostiza y su tiempo*. Mexico: La Nación, 1959.

Marín, Diego. "El valor de época de Adelardo López de Ayala." *Bulletin of Hispanic Studies* 29 (1952), 131–138.

Martínez de la Rosa, Francisco. *La conjuración de Venecia*, ed. María José Alonso Seoane. Madrid: Cátedra, 1993.

Obras completas de Francisco Martínez de la Rosa, ed. Carlos Seco Serrano. 8 vols. BAE 148–155. Madrid: Atlas, 1962.

Francisco Martínez de la Rosa. Obras dramáticas, ed. Jean Sarrailh. Madrid: Espasa-Calpe, 1933, 1972.

Martínez Espada, M. *Teatro contemporáneo. Apuntes para un libro de crítica*. Madrid: Ducazcal, 1900.

Martínez Olmedilla, Augusto. *Anecdotario del siglo XIX*. Madrid: Aguilar, 1957.

Martínez Pastor, Eugenio. *Fernando Garrido: Su obra y su tiempo*. Cartagena: Instituto de Estudios Cartigenenses, 1976.

Martínez Ruiz, José (Azorín). *Obras completas*. 9 vols. Madrid: Aguilar, 1947.

Mas Ferrer, Jaime. *Vida, teatro y mito de Joaquín Dicenta*. Alicante: Instituto de Estudios Alicantinos, 1978.

Mas i Vives, Joan. *El teatre a Mallorca a l'època romàntic*. Barcelona: Ediciones Catalanes, 1986.

Mayberry, Nancy and Robert. *Francisco Martínez de la Rosa*. Boston: Twayne, 1988.

McClelland, I. L. *Spanish Drama of Pathos, 1750–1808*. 2 vols. University of Toronto Press, 1970.

The Origins of the Romantic Movement in Spain. Liverpool University Press, 1937.

McGaha, Michael. "The 'Romanticism' of *La conjuración de Venecia*." *Kentucky Romance Quarterly* 20 (1973), 235–242.

McKendrick, Melveena. *Theatre in Spain, 1490–1700*. Cambridge University Press, 1989.

Membrez, Nancy. "Eduardo Navarro Gonzalvo and the *revista política*." *Letras Peninsulares* 1.3 (1988), 320–330.

"The Mass Production of Theater in Nineteenth-Century Spain." *Hispanic Issues* 3 (1988), 309–356.

"The 'teatro por horas': History, Dynamics and Comprehensive Bibliography of a Madrid Industry, 1867–1922 ('género chico,' 'género ínfimo' and Early Cinema)." Unpublished doctoral dissertation, University of California, Santa Barbara, 1987.

Menarini, Piero. "Hacia *El trovador*." *Romanticismo* 1 (1982), 95–108.

"La statistica commentata. Vent'anni di teatro in Spagna (1830–1850)." *Quaderni di Filologia Romanza* 4 (1984), 65–89.

Menarini, Piero, Patrizia Garelli, and Félix San Vicente, eds. *El teatro romántico español (1830–1850). Autores, obras, bibliografía*. Bologna: Atesa, 1982.

Menchacatorre, Félix. "Una tragedia del romanticismo ecléctico: *Munio Alfonso*, de la Avellaneda." *Revista Iberoamericana* 51 (1985), 823–830.

Menéndez Onrubia, Carmen. *Introducción al teatro de Galdós*. Madrid: CSIC, 1983.

"Las 'despedidas' de Antonio Vico y la crisis teatral de 1888–1892." *Segismundo* 19 (1985), 217–241.

Menéndez Onrubia, Carmen, and J. Avila Arellano. *El neorromanticismo español y su época. Epistolario de José Echegaray a María Guerrero.* Madrid: CSIC, 1987.

Menéndez Pidal, Gonzalo. *La España del siglo XIX vista por sus contemporáneos.* 2 vols. Madrid: Centro de Estudios Constitucionales, 1988.

Mesonero Romanos, Ramón de. *Obras completas de D. Ramón de Mesonero Romanos,* ed. Carlos Seco Serrano. 5 vols. Madrid: Atlas, 1967.

Miller, Beth. "Gertrude the Great," in *Women in Hispanic Literature: Icons and Fallen Idols,* ed. Beth Miller. Berkeley: University of California Press, 1983, 201–214.

Mitchell, Timothy. *Violence and Piety in Spanish Folklore.* Philadelphia: University of Pennsylvania Press, 1988.

Montero Alonso, José. *Ventura de la Vega. Su vida y su tiempo.* Madrid: Editora Nacional, 1951.

Moratín, Leandro Fernández de. *El sí de las niñas,* ed. René Andioc. Madrid: Castalia, 1969.

Epistolario, ed. René Andioc. Madrid: Castalia, 1973.

Obras de D. Leandro Fernández de Moratín. 3 vols. Madrid: Real Academia Española, 1830.

Muñoz Morillejo, Joaquín. *Escenografía española.* Madrid: Real Academia de Bellas Artes de San Fernando, 1923.

Muro, Miguel Ángel. *El teatro breve de Bretón de los Herreros.* Logroño: Instituto de Estudios Riojanos, 1991.

Navas Ruiz, Ricardo. *El romanticismo español.* 4th. edn. Madrid: Cátedra, 1990.

Newberry, Wilma. "Echegaray and Pirandello." *Publications of the Modern Language Association* 81 (1966), 123–129.

Nombela, Julio. *Proyecto de bases para la fundación de una escuela especial del arte teatral.* Madrid: Imprenta del Hospicio, 1886.

Nozick, Martin. "Some Parodies of *Don Juan Tenorio.*" *Hispania* 33 (1950), 242–250.

Nuez, Sebastián de la. "El tema de América en el teatro de Galdós." *Homenaje a Pedro Sainz Rodríguez* II (Madrid: Fundación Universitaria Española, 1986), 461–472.

Nuñez Ruiz, Gabriel. "El teatro en la Almería de Fernando VII." *Cuadernos Hispano-americanos* 407 (1984), 102–107.

Ochoa, Eugenio de. "Sobre el estado actual de los teatros en España." *Revista Española de Ambos Mundos* I (1853), 61–73.

O'Connell, Richard B. "Gorostiza's *Contigo pan y cebolla* and Sheridan's *The Rivals.*" *Hispania* 43 (1960), 384–387.

Oliva, César. "Espacio y espectáculo en la comedia de magia de mediados del siglo XIX," in *La comedia de magia y de santos,* eds. F. J. Blasco, E. Caldera, J. Álvarez Barrientos, and R. de la Fuente (Madrid: Júcar, 1992), 421–431.

Par, Alfonso. *Representaciones shakespearianas en España.* Madrid: Victoriano Suárez, 1936.

Parker, Adelaide, and Edgar Allison Peers. "The Influence of Victor Hugo on Spanish Drama." *Modern Language Review* 28 (1933), 205–216.

"The Vogue of Victor Hugo in Spain." *Modern Language Review* 27 (1932), 36–57.

Pattison, Walter T. "The Secret of Don Alvaro." *Symposium* 21 (1967), 67–81.

Peers, Edgar Allison. *Historia del movimiento romántico español.* 2 vols. Madrid: Gredos, 1967.

"Some Observations on *El desengaño en un sueño.*" *Homenaje ofrecido a Menéndez Pidal* (Madrid: Hernando, 1925), 583–587.

Peña y Goñi, Antonio. *España, desde la ópera a la zarzuela.* Madrid: Alianza, 1967.

Peñaranda, C. "Algunas observaciones sobre la decadencia del teatro español contemporáneo." *Revista Contemporánea* XIII, 1878.

Peñas Varela, Ermita. *Macías y Larra. Tratamiento de un tema en el drama y en la novela.* Universidad de Santiago de Compostela, 1992.

Pereira, Aureliano J. "La decadencia del Teatro Español." *Revista Europea,* 1 April 1877.

Pérez Galdós, Benito. *Obras completas,* ed. Federico Carlos Sainz de Robles. 8 vols. Madrid: Aguilar, 1975.

Perinat, Adolfo, and Isabel Marrades. *Mujer, prensa y sociedad en España, 1830–1939.* Madrid: Centro de Investigaciones Sociológicas, 1980.

Picoche, Jean Louis, ed. *Los amantes de Teruel. Introduction, édition critique et sinoptique précedeés d'une étude sur le monde du théâtre à Madrid entre 1833 et 1850.* Paris: Centre de Recherche Hispanique, 1970.

Picón, Jacinto Octavio. "Don Tomás Rodríguez Rubí." *Autores dramáticos contemporáneos* 2 vols. (Madrid: n.p., 1882), 65–81.

Pino, Enrique del. *Historia del teatro en Málaga durante el siglo XIX.* 2 vols. Málaga: Arguval, 1985.

Tres siglos de teatro malagüeño (xvi–xviii). Málaga: Sección de Publicaciones, 1974.

Porset, Fernando. *De telón adentro.* Madrid: R. Alvarez, 1912.

Poyán Díaz, Daniel. *Enrique Gaspar. Medio siglo de teatro español.* Madrid: Gredos, 1957.

Quel Barastegui, Pilar. "*Don Simplicio Bobadilla* de Manuel Tamayo y Baús, o la segunda parte de *La pata de cabra,*" in *Teatro di magia,* ed. Ermanno Caldera (Rome: Bulzoni, 1991), 33–53.

Quel Barastegui, Pilar, ed. *El diablo verde.* Rome: Bulzoni, 1989.

Randolph, Donald Allen. *Eugenio de Ochoa y el romanticismo español.* Berkeley: University of California Publications in Modern Philology, 1966.

Revilla, Manuel de la. *Obras de D. Manuel de la Revilla.* Madrid: Víctor Saiz, 1883.

Reyes Peña, Mercedes de los. "El Teatro de Vista Alegre: Un coliseo de segundo orden en la Sevilla de la primera mitad del siglo XIX." *Archivo Hispalense* 70 (1987), 93–114.

Ríos Carratalá, Juan Antonio. *Románticos y provincianos (La literatura en Alicante, 1839– 1866).* Universidad de Alicante, 1986.

Ríos-Font, Wadda C. "The Impersonation on the Feminine: Gender and Melodramatic Discourse in the Theatre of José Echegaray." *Hispánofila* 107 (September, 1992), 21–30.

"The Melodramatic Paradigm: José Echegaray and the Modern Spanish Theater." Unpublished doctoral dissertation, Harvard University, 1991.

Rodríguez Rubí, Tomás. "Excelencia, importancia y estado presente del teatro."

Discursos leídos ante la Real Academia Española (Madrid: Matute, 1860), 1–39.

Rogers, P. P. "Dramatic Copyright in Spain Before 1850." *Romanic Review* 25 (1934), 35– 39.

"The Peninsular War as a Source of Inspiration in the Spanish Drama of 1808–1814." *Philological Quarterly* 8 (1929), 264–269.

Romea, Julián. *Manual de declamación para uso de los alumnos del Real Conservatorio de Madrid*. Madrid: F. Abienzo, 1859.

Prólogo escrito, y recitado en la inauguración de el Teatro Español. N.p., n.d.

Romero Tobar, Leonardo. "La *Colección general de comedias* de Ortega (Madrid, 1826– 1834)." *Varia Bibliographica. Homenaje a José Simón Díaz* (Kassell: Editions Reichenberger, 1988), 599–609.

Mariano José de Larra. Textos teatrales inéditos. Madrid: CSIC, 1991.

"Noticias sobre empresas teatrales en periódicos del siglo XIX." *Segismundo* 8 (1972), 235–279.

Roura i Aulinas, Lluis. "Napoleón: ¿Un punto de acuerdo entre la reacción y el liberalismo en España?" in *Les espagnoles et Napoleon*, ed. Gerard Dufour (Aix-en-Provence: Université de Provence, 1984), 35–50.

Rubio Jiménez, Jesús. "El realismo escénico a la luz de los tratados de declamación de la época," in *Realismo y naturalismo en España en la segunda mitad del siglo XIX*, ed. Yvan Lissorgues (Barcelona: Anthropos, 1988), 257–286.

"El teatro en el siglo XIX (1845–1900)," in *Historia del teatro en España* II, ed. José María Díez Borque (Madrid: Taurus, 1988), 627–762.

Ideología y teatro en España: 1890–1900. Universidad de Zaragoza, 1982.

"La censura teatral en la época moderada: 1840–1868. Ensayo de aproximación," *Segismundo* 18 (1984), 193–231.

"La recepción crítica del naturalismo teatral en España." *Boletín de la Biblioteca Menéndez Pelayo* 62 (1986), 345–357.

"Melodrama y teatro político en el siglo XIX. El escenario como tribuna política." *Castilla* 14 (1989), 129-149.

Ruiz Ramón, Francisco. *Historia del teatro español*. Madrid: Alianza, 1967.

Historia del teatro español (Desde sus orígenes hasta 1900), 5th. edn. Madrid: Cátedra, 1983.

Ruiz Silva, Carlos. "El teatro de Antonio García Gutiérrez." *Segismundo* 19 (1985), 151–216.

Saavedra, Angel de, Duke of Rivas. *Don Alvaro o la fuerza del sino*, ed. Ermanno Caldera. Madrid: Taurus, 1986.

Don Alvaro o la fuerza del sino, ed. D. L. Shaw. Madrid: Castalia, 1986.

Obras completas. 5. vols. Madrid: Real Academia Española, 1854.

Sackett, Theodore A. "*Electra* desde la perspectiva de la crítica semiológica y arquetípica." *Revista de Literatura* 102 (1989), 462–482.

Galdós y las máscaras. Historia teatral y bibliografía anotada. Verona: Università degli Studi di Padova, 1982.

Salcedo, Emilio. *Teatro y sociedad en el Valladolid del siglo XIX*. Valladolid: Ayuntamiento, 1978.

Sánchez, Roberto. "Between Macías and Don Juan." *Hispanic Review* 44 (1976), 27–44.

"Clarín, su *Teresa* y los cómicos." *Hispanic Review* 55 (1987), 463–474.

"Clarín y el romanticismo teatral: examen de una afición." *Hispanic Review* 31 (1963), 216–228.

"Los comediantes del XIX: *Un drama nuevo*." *Hispanic Review* 48 (1980), 435–447.

Sanchis Guarner, Manuel. *Els inicis del teatre valencià modern, 1845–1874*. Valencia: Università de Valencia, 1980.

Santos, Nelly E. "Las ideas feministas de Gertrudis Gómez de Avellaneda," in *Homenaje a Gertrudis Gómez de Avellaneda*, eds. Gladys Zaldívar and Rosa Martínez de Cabrera (Miami: Ediciones Universal, 1981), 132–141.

Sastre, Alfonso. *Drama y sociedad*. Madrid: Taurus, 1958.

Scarano, Laura Rosana. "El modelo paródico como forma de enlace intertextual. (De Echegaray a Valle-Inclán)" *Letras de Deusto*, 21 (1991), 183–189.

Schinasi, Michael. "The Anarchy of Theatrical Genres in Mid-Nineteenth-Century Spain." *Romance Annual* 2 (1990), 534–538.

"The National Theater in Mid-Nineteenth Century Spain, and the Curious Project to Destroy a Block of Houses Facing the Teatro Español," in *Resonancias románticas,* ed. John Rosenberg (Madrid: José Porrúa, 1988), 195–205.

Sebold, Russell P. "Sobre el nombre español del dolor romántico." *El rapto de la mente. Poética y poesía dieciochescas,* 2nd. edn. (Barcelona: Anthropos, 1989), 157–169.

Seoane, María Cruz. *Historia del periodismo en España. 2. El siglo XIX*. Madrid: Alianza, 1983.

Serrà Campins, Antoni. *El teatre burlesc mallorquí, 1701–1850*. Barcelona: Curiel, 1987.

Serrano, Carlos. "Notas sobre teatro obrero a finales del siglo XIX." *El teatro menor en España a partir del siglo XVI*. Madrid: CSIC, 1983.

Shaw, Donald L. "Acerca de *Aliatar* del duque de Rivas" *Entre Siglos*, 2 (1993): 237–245.

"*Ataúlfo*: Rivas's First Drama." *Hispanic Review* 56 (1988), 231–242.

"Towards the Understanding of Spanish Romanticism." *Modern Language Review* 58 (1963), 190–195.

Shaw, George Bernard. *Dramatic Opinions and Essays*. 2 vols. New York: Brentano's, 1916.

Sherman, Alvin F., Jr. "*Jocó o El orangután*: Another Step Toward the Understanding of the Romantic Hero," *Ojáncano* 5 (1991): 24–38.

Shields, Archibald K. "The Madrid Stage, 1820–1833." Unpublished doctoral dissertation, University of North Carolina, 1933.

Shoemaker, William H. "La acogida pública y crítica de *Realidad* en su estreno." *Estudios Escénicos* 8 (1974), 25–40.

Siciliano, Ernest A. "La verdadera Azucena de *El trovador*." *Nueva Revista de Filología Hispánica* 20 (1970), 107–114.

Simón Díaz, José, ed. *Veinticuatro diarios. Madrid 1830-1900*. 4 vols. Madrid: CSIC, 1968–1975.

Simón Palmer, María del Carmen. "Construcción y apertura de teatros madrileños en el siglo XIX." *Segismundo* 11 (1975), 85–137.

El gas y los madrileños. Gas Madrid y Espasa Calpe, 1989.

Escritoras españolas del siglo XIX. Manual bio-bibliográfico. Madrid: Castalia, 1991.

"Mil escritoras españolas del siglo XIX," in *Crítica y ficción literaria: Mujeres españolas contemporáneas*, eds. Aurora López and María Angeles Pastor. Granada: n.p., 1989, 39–59.

Sinclair, Alison. *Madrid Newspapers 1661–1870. Computerized Handbook Based on Hartzenbusch*. Leeds: W. S. Maney, 1984.

Sirera, Josep Lluís. *El teatre Principal de Valencia*. Valencia: Institució Alfons el Magnàmim, 1986.

Smith, W. F. "Contributions of Rodríguez Rubí to the Development of the *alta comedia*." *Hispanic Review* 10 (1942), 53–63.

"Rodríguez Rubí and the Dramatic Reforms of 1849." *Hispanic Review* 16 (1948), 311–320.

"The Historical Play in the Theatre of Tomás Rodríguez Rubí." *Bulletin of Hispanic Studies* 28 (1950), 221–228.

Sobejano, Gonzalo. "Echegaray, Galdós y el melodrama." *Anales Galdosianos* (supplement 1978), 91–115.

"Efectos de *Realidad*." *Estudios Escénicos* 8 (1974), 41–61.

"Razón y suceso de la dramática galdosiana." *Anales Galdosianos* 5 (1970), 39–54.

Sotelo, Adolfo. "Clarín y la crítica de teatros (dos artículos desconocidos en *Faro Moderno*, 1899)." *Segismundo* 20 (1986), 223–256.

Soubies, Albert. *Le théâtre en France de 1871 à 1892*. Paris: E. Flammarion, 1893.

Stoudemire, Sterling A. "A Spanish Play on the Fair Rosamond Legend." *Studies in Philology* 28 (1931), 325–329.

"Dionisio Solís's 'refundiciones' of Plays (1800–1834)." *Hispanic Review* 8 (1940), 305–310.

"Don Antonio Gil y Zárate's Birth Date." *Modern Language Notes* 46 (1931), 171–172.

"Gil y Zárate's Translations of French Plays." *Modern Language Notes* 48 (1933), 321–325.

"The Dramatic Works of Gil y Zárate." Unpublished doctoral dissertation, University of North Carolina, 1930.

Subirá, José. *Historia y anecdotario del Teatro Real*. Madrid: Plus Ultra, 1949.

Un vate filarmónico: Don Luciano Comella. Madrid: Real Academia Española, 1932.

Suero Roca, María Teresa. *El teatre representat a Barcelona de 1800 a 1830*. 2 vols. Barcelona: Institut del Teatre, 1987.

Tamayo y Baús, Manuel. *Obras completas de Manuel Tamayo y Baús*. Madrid: Ediciones FAX, 1947.

Tayler, Neale H. *Las fuentes del teatro de Tamayo y Baús: Originalidad e influencias*. Madrid: Gráficas Uguina, 1959.

Thomason, Phillip Brian. "The *Coliseo de la Cruz*: Madrid's First Enclosed Municipal Playhouse (1737–1859)." Unpublished doctoral dissertation, University of Kentucky, 1987.

Underhill, John Garrett. "Introduction" to *Martha of the Lowlands*, translation by Wallace Gillpatrick of *Tierra baja* (New York: Doubleday, 1902), v–xx.

Valera, Juan. *Obras completas*, ed. Luis Araujo Costa. 3 vols. Madrid: Aguilar, 1958–1961.

Ventura de la Vega, estudio biográfico-crítico. Madrid: Pérez Dubrull, 1904.

Valis, Noël M. "Dos poesías de almanaque, por Leopoldo Alas." *Anales de Literatura Española de la Universidad de Alicante* 7 (1991), 195–205.

Valladares y Saavedra, Ramón de. *Nociones acerca de la historia del teatro, desde su nacimiento hasta nuestros días.* Madrid: Imprenta de la Publicidad, 1848.

Valverde Rodao, Valentina. " 'Lo que son trigedias' o la parodia dramática de 1830 a 1850." *Quaderni di Filologia Romanza* 4 (1984), 135–161.

Varey, J. E., N. D. Shergold, and Charles Davis, eds. *Los arriendos de los corrales de comedias de Madrid: 1587–1719*, London: Tamesis Books, Ltd., 1987.

Ventura Crespo, Concha María. *Historia del teatro en Zamora.* Zamora: n.p., 1988.

Vico, Antonio. "Isidoro Máiquez, Carlos Latorre y Julián Romea. La escena española desde comienzos del siglo. La declamación en la tragedia, en el drama y en la comedia de costumbres." *La España del siglo XIX.* Madrid: Ateneo, 1886.

White, Hayden. *The Tropics of Discourse.* Baltimore: Johns Hopkins, 1978.

Yxart, José. *El arte escénico en España.* 2 vols. Barcelona: La Vanguardia, 1894–1896. Reprinted Barcelona: Alta Fulla, 1987.

Zamacois, Eduardo. "El socialismo en el teatro." *España Artística* 55 (1 February 1898).

Zamora Vicente, Alonso. "Literatura paródica." *La realidad esperpéntica* (Madrid: Gredos, 1969), 25–53.

Zavala, Iris M. "La literatura: romanticismo y costumbrismo," in *Historia de España, XXXV, 2. La época del romanticismo*, ed. José María Jover Zamora (Madrid: Espasa Calpe, 1988), 5–183.

Románticos y socialistas. Madrid: Siglo Veintiuno, 1972.

Zorrilla, José. *Obras completas*, ed. Narciso Alonso Cortés. 2 vols. Valladolid: Santarén, 1943.

Traidor, inconfeso y mártir, ed. Roberto Calvo Sanz. Madrid: Espasa-Calpe, 1990.

Index of names

Index of plays